Opinions Throughout History

National Security
vs.
Civil & Privacy Rights

Opinions Throughout History

National Security
vs.
Civil & Privacy Rights

Micah L. Issitt

Grey House
Publishing

PUBLISHER:	Leslie Mackenzie
EDITORIAL DIRECTOR:	Laura Mars
PROJECT EDITOR:	Betsy Maury
MARKETING DIRECTOR:	Jessica Moody
PRODUCTION MANAGER:	Kristen Hayes

Grey House Publishing, Inc.
4919 Route 22
Amenia, NY 12501
518.789.8700
Fax 518.789.0545
www.greyhouse.com
e-mail: books@greyhouse.com

Publisher's Cataloging-In-Publication Data
(Prepared by The Donohue Group, Inc.)

Names: Issitt, Micah L.
Title: National security vs. civil & privacy rights / Micah L. Issitt.
Other Titles: National security versus civil and privacy rights
Description: [First edition]. | [Amenia, New York] : Grey House Publishing, [2018] |
Series: Opinions throughout history | Includes bibliographical references and index.
Identifiers: ISBN 9781682177204 (hardcover)
Subjects: LCSH: Privacy, Right of–United States–Public opinion–Sources. | National security–United States–Public opinion–Sources. | Civil rights–United States–Public opinion–Sources. | Privacy, Right of–History.
Classification: LCC JC596.2.U5 I87 2018 | DDC 323.4480973–dc23

Table of Contents

Permanent Imbalance

Publisher's Note

Grey House Publishing is pleased to offer the first volume in a new series–*Opinions Throughout History*. Each single, in-depth volume is designed to follow the evolution of public opinion on a current, controversial topic as it changed throughout history. Each volume will discuss a range of primary and secondary source documents, including newspaper and magazine articles, speeches, court decisions and other legislation. These documents will be accompanied by expert commentary and analysis to guide the reader through the process of how each document contributed to, or is a reflection of, changing attitudes on important issues of public interest.

This first volume–*Opinions Throughout History: National Security vs. Civil & Privacy Rights*–starts with a detailed *Introduction* that defines privacy from 1750 BCE, why it's important, and the controversy surrounding it. This is followed by a *Timeline* of significant events related to national security and challenges to privacy rights, and then 28 documents, arranged in chronological order, that relate to the topic. Most of them are reprinted in their entirety, and clearly distinguished by a shaded title bar. Often, the document is broken up into sections to better demonstrate the points discussed in the 1,500 words of analysis and commentary that accompany it, detailing the significance of the document and how it reflects the ongoing tension between opposing priorities of national security and privacy rights.

The time period of the content covered is sweeping. The volume begins with the landmark 1890 *Harvard Law Review* article by Boston attorney Samuel Warren and future Supreme Court Justice Louis Brandeis, "The Right to Privacy," which sets the legal framework for understanding privacy and civil rights, and ends with *Recoding*

Privacy Law: Reflections on the Future Relationship Among Law, Technology, and Privacy by Urs Gasser of the Berkman Klein Center for Internet & Society at Harvard from 2016. Each chapter is enhanced by a valuable *Introduction*, list of *Topics Covered*, *Conclusion*, *Discussion Questions*, and *Works Used*. Also included are photos and other images, quotations, and sidebars. All footnote references to the text start on page 511.

Back matter includes *Historical Snapshots* that provide broad overviews of political, social and cultural developments that give the reader an understanding of the political and social climate of the time. Also included is a list of *Primary and Secondary Sources* that appear in this volume, and a *Glossary* of frequently used terms related to national security and civil and privacy rights. A *Bibliography* and detailed *Index* complete the volume.

The next *Opinions Throughout History* volume is *Immigration* and is scheduled for the Spring.

Introduction

PRIVACY vs. SECURITY: AN ANCIENT BALANCE

What is more important: privacy or security? This is a question that has perplexed and intrigued philosophers, theologians, legal scholars, politicians, and the public alike for untold millennia. Human societies, wherever they occur and whatever form they take, require both: a system to protect against the dangers of the world and the ability for citizens to find refuge, to develop and keep private rituals and practices, and to have room away from the public gaze and the pressures of social life. Part of this debate necessarily involves trying to define what privacy is and why it is important.

REGULATION OF THE ENVIRONMENT

All people need both privacy and social interaction to function as human beings and as members of a society. But what is this desire for private space or private time? Is it a function of social pressure or cultural development? Research in animal behavior indicates that the need for privacy is a complex concept but one that has been considered since the beginning of time, when animals first began to organize in groups for survival.

In the 1967 book *Privacy and Freedom*, Columbia University law professor Alan Westin argues:

> *Man likes to think that his desire for privacy is distinctively human, a function of his unique ethical, intellectual, and artistic needs. Yet studies of animal behavior and social organization suggest that a man's need for privacy may well be rooted in his animal origins, and that men and animals share several basic mechanisms for claiming privacy among their fellows.*

One basic finding of animal studies is that virtually all animals seek periods of individual seclusion or small-group intimacy. This is usually described as the tendency towards territoriality, in which an organism lays private claim to an area of land, water, or air and defends it against intrusion by members of its own species….Studies of territoriality have even shattered the romantic notion that when robins sing or monkeys shriek, it is solely for the "animal joy of life." Actually, it is often a defiant cry for privacy…[i]

Even the most solitary creature must engage in some level of social interaction when it comes time to mate, and, for many species, social interaction is a part of daily life. Animals that live in groups derive a plethora of benefits, including increased safety from predators and other threats, and the opportunity to cooperate to find food or care for young. Social interaction is so essential to the lives of some animals that, without it, they may develop severe behavioral, emotional, and cognitive problems. Psychological research has routinely demonstrated that humans in complete isolation, like other species, also develop cognitive and emotional issues and it is no accident that forced isolation (such as solitary confinement in prison) is used as a form of torture.

Behavioral studies have also shown that even the most social animals need space, the ability to isolate themselves from others. In a study of rats forced to live in close quarters, for instance, researchers found that the rats became aggressive and violent towards one another, displaying increased stress and an inability to effectively care for themselves or their children, with many dying early deaths from cardiac failure or other health problems seeming related to the increased stress of constant social interaction and pressure.[ii] The negative effects of unwanted attention on animals has been so well documented in scientific research that some scientists have raised the issue of whether nonhuman animals also deserve some fundamental right to privacy.[iii]

If the need for privacy is an animal, rather than only a human, need, a basic definition of privacy might be one derived from the function that privacy plays on a more basic biological level. In a 1977 article in the *Journal of Social Issues*, Duke University scholars Peter Klopfer and Daniel Rubenstein define privacy in relation to animal behavior:

> *...a regulatory process that serves to selectively control access of external stimulation on one's self or the flow of information to others. It has been appropriately likened to the processes that produce changes in the permeability of a cell's membrane...*

From this perspective, the development of social and private behavior might be an outgrowth of the same basic biological need accomplished by the membrane of a single cell; the need to control the input and output of information, or stimuli. However, a cell or a rat, a chimpanzee or a human, need to engage in behaviors that facilitate this process, seeking out others when social interaction is needed and isolating themselves to avoid overstimulation. The need to balance privacy and interaction is therefore a process, rather than a state of being.

Klopfer and Rubenstein offer this parable as a metaphor for this process:

> *The degree and character of the privacy an organism attains must represent a compromise between competing forces. A German parable (cited in Wilson, 1975, and attributed to Leyhausen) recounts the dilemma of two hedgehogs that sought*

to keep warm by huddling closely together. Warming was thus achieved, but their prickly spines produced another problem. This resolved when they drew apart. Courtesy (the compromise between competing forces) represented that distance at which heat exchange and tactile discomfort were perfectly balanced. This distance, not incidentally, would be expected to change with ambient temperature.[iv]

CODIFYING PRIVACY RIGHTS

When humans were mostly nomadic, wandering in groups across wide areas, there may have been little need to establish privacy rights beyond basic norms of courtesy. It was when humans started settling in permanent villages (accompanying the development of agriculture in Western Syria about 12,000 years ago) that the need for privacy laws became more evident. When living in settlements, in relatively close quarters, the pressure of the social sphere became more pronounced and the ownership of property more important to human life. This evolution therefore required societies to begin to codify the rules regarding personal and private space.

The Code of Hammurabi, written about 1750 BCE, is the earliest complete law and record and demonstrates that, in the ancient warrior kingdoms, violating the social order often involved severe penalties. For instance, while murder was punishable by death, so was accusing someone of murder if the person turned out to be innocent. Article 21 of the code is the earliest known privacy law, and makes it a crime to purposefully spy on one's neighbor. Specifically, the law states, "If a man makes a breach into a house, one shall kill him in front of the breach and bury him in it."[v]

The idea that eavesdropping or spying on others is a crime appears in many ancient texts, including the Bible, the Quran, and ancient Jewish spiritual writings. These prohibitions served as the basis for later laws, like the Justices of the Peace Act, enacted by King Edward III of England in 1361, which prohibited both eavesdropping and "peeping toms." This represents the first and most basic level of privacy rights, the right to isolation from one's neighbors.

Basic privacy rights can therefore be found in the foundational spiritual systems that influenced European and later American thought on the issue.

While privacy from other citizens is an essential element, it is also necessary to determine the rights of individuals with regard to the state and institutions of society. For instance, many societies believe that an individual's medical information should be protected and this too is an ancient facet of privacy rights. Ancient Greek physician Hippocrates originated the code of medical ethics that is, in altered form, still practiced in the cultures descended from ancient Greece and often called the Hippocratic Oath:

> *Whatever, in connection with my professional service, or not in connection with it, I see or hear, in the life of men, which ought not to be spoken of abroad, I will not divulge, as reckoning that all such should be kept secret.*[vi]

The treasured wisdom of ancient Greek and Roman philosophers exerted a heavy influence on European thinkers over the centuries, but the early laws of the European world were also highly influenced by religious morality. The Bible, the Quran, and ancient Jewish texts all contain references to the moral value of privacy, typically in relation to one's neighbors and with regard to the ownership of property and inviolate institutions of society (like marriage and professional contracts). How a society defines privacy rights is therefore also a function of how the society's moral values develop. Defining privacy rights according to moral values becomes more difficult as the range of norms expressed within a culture expands. This occurs more rapidly in cultures with high levels of immigration and in cultures that embrace freedom of religion and belief and so privacy rights needed to evolve beyond the moral philosophy of religious scripture.

A combination of Greek and Roman philosophy with elements of Christian thought can be seen in the British "common law," laws established through court cases or precedent, rather than through legislation. British common law, which began to be developed just after the Norman Conquest of 1066, was the basis of most law in the United Kingdom (and therefore also in the United States) until the 19th century. The strength of common law lies in the fact that the law is generalized so that the courts can use it to justify enforcing rules not included in official statutes.

By the 1700s, British common law recognized the right to privacy as an outgrowth of the right to property. Charles Pratt, the 1st Earl of Camden (an English lawyer who lived from 1714 to 1794) was a pioneer in privacy rights and it was Lord Camden who helped to establish the legal basis of privacy rights in regard to the relationship between citizens and the needs of the state to protect national security.

In the 1765 case of *Entick v. Carrington*, three officers of the King entered the house of a local man, Entick, without permission. They searched the house and removed papers containing written criticisms of the royal government but, in the trial, Camden denied the legality of the search, saying in his decision:

> *...our law holds the property of every man so sacred, that no man can set foot upon his neighbour's close without leave; if*

he does he is a trespasser, though he does no damage at all; if he will tread upon his neighbour's ground he must justify it by law…we can safely say there is no law in this country to justify the defendants in what they have done; if there was, it would destroy all the comforts of society; for papers are often the dearest property a man can have.[vii]

THE NEEDS OF THE STATE

In the *Entick* case, the needs of the state conflicted with the right to property (and privacy of property) as established in common law. Therefore, while the state had an interest in preventing the dissemination of anti-monarchy literature, such as that found in Entick's house, Camden's ruling prioritized the individual's right to privacy over the needs of the state and established a precedent that the government must prove justification before being allowed to invade a person's home or claim his or her property.

It is easy to understand how the right to privacy interferes with the goals of the state. In principal, law enforcement would be most effective if agents had the capability to conduct complete and total surveillance of all people at all times, to enter any home, or to seize any property at will. The problem is, individuals do not always trust the state or the agents of the state and, indeed, provisional distrust of the government has been justified again and again by the many instances in history in which governments have abused or oppressed citizens using the organs of security in the interest of public safety. In an authoritarian society, security is more straightforward. The state may conduct any investigation deemed necessary and may dole out punishments not only to those who commit crimes but also to those who display the tendency to express ideas that might threaten the state's power. Those seeking to escape the abuses of authoritarianism formed societies like the United States, with constitutional guarantees designed to limit state power and protect against abuse.

In the legal language of privacy law in the United States, there is a "balancing test," in which judges and legal experts are asked to determine when the needs of the state, or the potential threat to public safety and security, outweigh the right to privacy. This balance is reflected in the need to obtain court orders and judicial warrants before violating a person's privacy or property. There are many situations in which agents of the state can legitimately argue for the need to violate a person's privacy. For instance, in the case of a public health outbreak, it can be argued that the state needs to conduct health examinations and citizens do not have the right to refuse such examinations, even though they involve a violation of personal freedoms. There is little debate over whether or not the state has the right to invade privacy when the need arises, but rather, the debate focuses on how to decide when the state's justification is sufficient and to make sure that there are oversight measures in place to prevent the state from abusing its power.

Historians studying the early United States have found that, in the early 1700s, American colonists were regularly subject to searches by British authorities, often based on little evidence or reason for suspicion. Some historians believe that this abuse of power was part of the motivation that led to the American Revolution. The right to property and the freedom from unjustified invasions of the home were foundational civil liberties included in the 1791 Bill of Rights, the first ten amendments to the United States constitution. However, the framers did not see fit to codify a right to privacy specifically, and this led to more than a century of debate about how to establish a legal right to privacy and define the limits of this right with regard to the interests of the state and the goal of facilitating productive commerce.

OPINION AND POLICY

This volume covers aspects of the privacy vs security debate from the nineteenth century through the twenty-first century. In 2000, all Americans were entitled to a basic right to privacy established through constitutional law, common law, and statutory law. However, due to the ongoing threat of radical militant groups, U.S. laws changed between 2001 and 2017, providing government agents with broad powers to invade the privacy of American citizens for the purposes of combating this threat. Furthermore, Americans in 2018 face a rapidly changing privacy landscape due to the fact that the transmission, collection, and use of personal data had developed into a massive, global industry. Because of the traditional American skepticism of corporate regulation, out of the debatable belief that regulation reduces productivity and innovation, Americans have also been forced to sacrifice their personal privacy in favor of using modern technological services and products.

The state of the privacy/security debate in the 21st century is therefore one of broad dissatisfaction and confusion, with the public, in general, feeling that the state and commercial entities have too much leeway to invade their privacy, but uncertain about how to fix this situation while still permitting the state to effectively cope with threats and without discouraging corporations from producing products and services that help people to advance their personal and professional goals.

The relationship between policy and public opinion is complex and indirect. In some situations, a relatively small number of people promote their view of a certain issue so passionately and effectively, that laws are stalled or prevented, even if a majority of the public supports an alternative standpoint on the issue. For instance, while the majority of Americans support stronger gun-control regulations, including universal background checks, the small but vociferous gun-rights lobby has been successful in preventing legislation on the issue. Similarly, while there is disapproval across partisan lines of the freedoms given to corporations to collect and use data from users, a small but powerful lobby of anti-regulation advocates and corporate lawyers has prevented regulation. If and when such laws are created, therefore, they will already lag well behind the weight of public opinion or interest.

Politicians do not represent the public directly, but do so through a complex filter of interest groups, fund raising organizations, and political coalitions and this complicates the relationship between public will and public policy. The history of privacy rights is one of negotiation, controversy, debate, disagreement, and occasional reconciliation. Governmental agencies, interest groups, and corporations that benefit from personal information, regularly resist new privacy laws and find ways to circumvent those already in place. Civil liberties advocates, meanwhile, continue in the tradition of the constitutional framers, making it their goal to ensure that every piece of legislation, policy, executive order, and judicial decision is subject to scrutiny against the civil rights guarantees of the constitution.

Americans want both privacy and security. They want to live in a world free from crime, foreign threats, outbreaks of disease and the many other dangers that governments help to combat. They also want to live in a world where they can reliably escape the gaze of the public, companies looking to use private citizens' personal information for profit, and even from the watchful eyes of the state. There is no answer to the question of which is more important, as both privacy and security are necessary to human life and essential to happiness. Finding the balance is therefore not so much a goal as a process, a continual balancing and rebalancing to achieve equilibrium between the individual and his or her society and between altruism and selfishness. The public view of privacy and security continues to change and laws, gradually and eventually, reflect the broader push of cultural evolution within society.

In the United States, a nation that has embraced a challenging matrix of advanced citizenship and multiculturalism, this effort is ongoing and contentious but reveals, through the ebb and flow, the great variety of hopes, dreams, and fears that fueled the foundation of the nation and continue to define its evolution.

Micah L. Issitt

Works Used

Keenan, Kevin M. *Invasion of Privacy: A Reference Handbook*. Santa Barbara, CA: ABC-Clio, 2005.

Keim, Brandon. "Should Animals Have A Right To Privacy?" *Wired*. Conde Nast. Jan 25 2016. Web. 16 Nov 2017.

Klopfer, Peter H. and Daniel I. Rubenstein. "The Concept *Privacy* and Its Biological Basis." *Journal of Social Issues*. Vol 33, No 3, 1977. Pdf.

McFarlane, Ben, Hopkins, Nicholas, and Sarah Nield. *Land Law: Text, Cases, and Materials*. New York: Oxford University Press, 2015.

Moore, Adam D. *Privacy Rights: Moral and Legal Foundations*. University Park, PA: Pennsylvania State University Press, 2010.

Rengel, Alexandra. *Privacy in the 21st Century*. Boston: Martinus Nijhoff Publishers, 2013.

Soma, John, Rynerson, Stephen, and Erica Kitaev. *Privacy Law in a Nutshell, 2d*. St. Paul, MN: Thomson/West, 2008.

Westin, Alan. *Privacy and Freedom*. New York: Athenum, 1967.

Notes

i. Westin, *Privacy and Freedom*, pg 8.
ii. Moore, *Privacy Rights: Moral and Legal Foundations,* pg 49.
iii. Keim, "Should Animals Have A Right To Privacy?"

iv. Klopfer and Rubenstein, "The Concept *Privacy* and Its Biological Basis."
v. Rengel, *Privacy in the 21st Century*.
vi. Keenan, *Invasion of Privacy: A Reference Handbook*.
vii. McFarlane, Hopkins, and Nield, Land Law: Text, Cases, and Materials.

Historical Timeline

1788: State legislatures ratify the U.S. Constitution, establishing the basic precedent for all future constitutional law

1791: The U.S. Congress ratifies the Bill of Rights, creating the first 10 amendments to the United States Constitution

1868: The Fourteenth Amendment to the U.S. Constitution guarantees all citizens the right to due process under the law

1890: Warren and Brandeis publish "The Right to Privacy" in the *Harvard Law Review*.

1923: Supreme Court case of *Meyer v. Nebraska* establishes that the liberties protected under the Fourteenth Amendment guarantees the right to enjoy the privileges of citizenship, both tangible and intangible

1928: *Olmstead v. United States*

1934: The Federal Communications Commission (FCC) is established under the Federal Communications Act (FCA)

1942: *Goldman v. United States*

1945: The NSA secretly creates Project SHAMROCK

1950: Senator Joseph McCarthy delivers a shocking speech claiming that more than 200 communist spies have infiltrated the U.S. government

1951:	*Dennis v. United States*
1959:	*Barenblatt v. United States*
1961:	*Mapp v. Ohio*
1965:	*Griswold v. Connecticut*
1967:	*Katz v. United States*
	Willis Ware of RAND Corporation writes *Security and Privacy in Computer Systems*
1968:	The Omnibus Crime Control Act holds that police needed to obtain a warrant before engaging in wiretapping operations
1969:	Joseph Licklider creates the Advanced Research Projects Agency Network (ARPANET), which was the forerunner of the Internet
1971:	The Pentagon Papers leaks from the press raise the issue of the Freedom of the Press versus the privacy of the government to conceal information about national security operations
1972:	*Eisenstadt v. Baird*
1974:	The Watergate Scandal results in the revelation that the CIA had been conducting widespread surveillance of American dissidents and foreign leaders without judicial oversight
	The Privacy Act is established
1975:	Senator Frank Church leads of series of hearings about the secret NSA SHAMROCK operation in place since

1945 that involved intercepting communications from American citizens

1978: Congress passes the 1978 FISA Act

1980: The Intelligence Oversight Act (IOA) updates legal standards regarding federal agencies utilizing digital data

1981: President Reagan issues Executive Order 12333

1986: The Electronic Communications Privacy Act is established

1994: Netscape creates the "cookie"

2001: The September 11 terrorist attacks result in congress authorizing the Bush Administration to utilize military methods to combat terrorism

The Bush administration secretly authorizes the President's Surveillance Program (PSP), utilizing E.O. 12333

The U.S. PATRIOT Act alters existing laws to facilitate better communication between the state's intelligence branches in the effort to combat terrorism

The Transportation Security Administration (TSA) is established, creating the "No Fly" and "Selectee" lists that limit the right to travel on airplanes in the United States

2005: The PATRIOT Act was reauthorized without substantial changes as congress favors security concerns over warnings that the law creates the potential for civil liberties violations

The *New York Times* publishes articles resulting from leaks revealing the secret President's Surveillance Program (PSP) established by the Bush administration

2007:   The Bush Administration plans to make data taken from spy satellites available to law enforcement and thus to enable spy satellite equipment to be used to conduct domestic surveillance

2008:   Congress passes Section 702, or the FISA Amendment Act, which is used to permit a massive NSA and CIA domestic surveillance program gathering telephone and Internet data from millions of American citizens

2012:   The Obama Administration proposes a Consumer Privacy Bill of Rights guaranteeing individuals the right to greater control over the use of their digital data, forming the basis of a general governmental philosophy

2013:   The *Guardian* and the *Washington Post* publish the first series of articles derived from leaked NSA and CIA documents delivered by Edward Snowden

The Senate Judiciary committee holds hearings to determine if the executive surveillance operations carried out under the PATRIOT Act were a violation of constitutional law

Snowden leaks reveal that the NSA and CIA had been attempting to force corporations to provide a backdoor to encryption systems that would allow federal agents to bypass consumer encryption

2015:   Terrorist attacks in France reignite fears of domestic terrorist violence

The PATRIOT Act is replaced by the USA Freedom Act

Federal Courts order Apple, Inc. to create a new operation system that would enable federal investigators to bypass security on an iPhone. Apple refuses on the basis of security concerns

The FCC publishes official rules of "neutrality"

2016:   The EU establishes the General Data Protection Regulation (GDPR), described as the strongest digital data privacy law in the world

2017:   The "Vault 7" secrets, a leak of 9,000 CIA documents, reveal details of the CIA's attempts to break through encryption used by Internet companies to secure consumer data

President Trump appoints Ajit Pai to head the FCC, who abolishes the FCC neutrality protections

Congress debates whether or not to renew the controversial Section 702 FISA Amendment used to authorize NSA domestic intelligence operations since 2008

Introduction

A citizen's legal right to privacy has been on the minds of citizens and legal officials for more than 120 years. One of the first important articles to discuss the origins of right-to-privacy law was written in 1890 by Boston lawyer Samuel Warren and future Supreme Court justice Louis Brandeis. In their article, Warren and Brandeis conduct a detailed review of historic British and U.S. "common law,"—laws based on court decisions rather than legislation—and conclude that it was time to create a new right-to-privacy law in the United States. They felt that American citizens deserve to be legally protected from commercial and corporate privacy invasions—in which a company or individual violates the privacy of another individual for profit or personal gain. With this, they advocated for "the right to be let alone."

Because this 1890 "The Right to Privacy" article was the legal start to the conversation about privacy rights in this country, it was chosen as the first document to analyze in this new work—*Opinions Throughout History: National Security vs. Civil and Privacy Rights*. The further you move through this volume, the more you will understand why Brandeis and Warren's article is one of the most often-cited law review articles in history and the arguments made by the authors in favor of privacy protections are still cited by jurists, scholars, and politicians debating the issue in the 2010s. It makes a clear, compelling argument about the right to privacy and, indeed, covers privacy from many angles—from health conditions to personal relationships to "processes of the mind." Most interesting, too, is that many of the issues written about in 1890 are still unresolved in 2018.

Topics covered in this chapter include:
- Journalism ethics and "fake news"
- Common law and statutory law
- Philosophy of privacy rights
- Commercial invasion of privacy

This Chapter Discusses the Following Source Document:
Warren, Samuel D. and Louis D. Brandeis. "The Right to Privacy." *Harvard Law Review*, Vol. 4, No. 5. (Dec. 15, 1890), pp. 193-220.

1788 State legislatures ratify the U.S. Constitution, establishing the basic precedent for all future constitutional law

1791 The U.S. Congress ratifies the Bill of Rights, creating the first 10 amendments to the United States Constitution

The Right to Privacy
Foundations of a Constitutional Debate (1890)

In 1890, Boston attorney Samuel Warren and future Supreme Court justice Louis Brandeis published a now-famous review article, "The Right to Privacy," in an issue of *Harvard Law Review*. The article partially reprinted here, and the discussion about privacy rights that it ignited, would inform more than a century of debate and legislation. In later years government and state surveillance, and the need to balance privacy and national security, would sit at the center of the debate. When Warren and Brandeis wrote their seminal article, however, their main concern was to combat what they saw as the pervasive and invasive spread of tabloid journalism:

> *To satisfy a prurient taste the details of sexual relations are spread broadcast in the columns of the daily papers. To occupy the indolent, column upon column is filled with idle gossip, which can only be procured by intrusion upon the domestic circle.*

In the years leading up to Brandeis and Warren's article, several prominent court cases dealt with issues surrounding the publication of photos, personal details, and rumors about the lives of public figures. The problem was, in many ways, similar to the debate about "fake news" in the 2010s, in that (at least in Brandeis and Warren's opinion) the popular press of the era was guilty of publishing unsubstantiated rumor and gossip. Further, the two legal experts argued that, in pursuit of rumor and information for their articles, journalists were violating the privacy of the individuals and families targeted for exposés and articles.

In their article, Brandeis and Warren advocated for an approach to privacy defined first in an 1880 paper by jurist Thomas Cooley on tort law, in which Cooley defined privacy as a "right to be let alone."

1868 | The 14th Amendment to the U.S. Constitution guarantees all citizens the right to due process under the law

1890 | Warren and Brandeis publish "The Right to Privacy" in the *Harvard Law Review*

Guided by this somewhat folksy definition, Brandeis and Warren explored precedent laid out in "common law," a body of British legal principles derived from common custom and precedent, rather than established statutes. In the late nineteenth century, British common law was the basis for an extensive list of laws adopted by U.S. states covering a variety of issues, and so legal discussions in the nineteenth century tended to draw on common law arguments, especially where insufficient recent court decisions existed to justify arguments on an issue. They noted, in their discussion, that common law principles had already been used, in England, to generate a right to privacy without legislation or statute:

THE RIGHT TO PRIVACY
Samuel Warren and Louis Brandeis
Harvard Law Review, **1890**
Source Document Excerpt

Lord Cottenham stated that a man "is that which is exclusively his," and cited with approval the opinion of Lord Eldon, as reported in a manuscript note of the case of *Wyatt v. Wilson*, in 1820, respecting an engraving of George the Third during his illness, to the effect that "if one of the late king's physicians had kept a diary of what he heard and saw, the court would not, in the king's lifetime, have permitted him to print and publish it;" and Lord Cottenham declared, in respect to the acts of the defendants in the case before him, that "privacy is the right invaded."

Building on precedent from common law, Brandeis and Warren utilized a concept of legal evolution to justify the argument that there should be a distinct legal framework for protecting privacy.

1923   *Meyer v. Nebraska* establishes that the 14th Amendment guarantees privileges of citizenship

1928   *Olmstead v. United States* rules that wiretapping is not a form of search and seizure defined by the 14th Amendment

"The Right to Privacy"
continued

Gradually the scope of these legal rights broadened; and now the right to life has come to mean the right to enjoy life,—the right to be let alone; the right to liberty secures the exercise of extensive civil privileges; and the term "property" has grown to comprise every form of possession—intangible, as well as tangible.

Thus, with the recognition of the legal value of sensations, the protection against actual bodily injury was extended to prohibit mere attempts to do such injury; that is, the putting another in fear of such injury. From the action of battery grew that of assault. Much later there came a qualified protection of the individual against offensive noises and odors, against dust and smoke, and excessive vibration. The law of nuisance was developed. So, regard for human emotions soon extended the scope of personal immunity beyond the body of the individual. His reputation, the standing among his fellow-men, was considered, and the law of slander and libel arose. Man's family relations became a part of the legal conception of his life, and the alienation of a wife's affections was held remediable. Occasionally the law halted, as in its refusal to recognize the intrusion by seduction upon the honor of the family. But even here the demands of society were met. A mean fiction, the action per quod servitium amisit, was resorted to, and by allowing damages for injury to the parents' feelings, an adequate remedy was ordinarily afforded. Similar to the expansion of the right to life was the growth of the legal conception of property. From corporeal property arose the incorporeal rights issuing out of it; and then there opened the wide realm of intangible property, in the products and processes of the mind, as works of literature and art, goodwill, trade secrets, and trademarks.

This development of the law was inevitable. The intense intellectual and emotional life, and the heightening of sensations that came with the advancement of civilization, made it clear to men that only a part of the pain, pleasure, and profit of life lay in physical things. Thoughts, emotions, and sensations demanded legal recognition, and the beautiful capacity for growth that characterizes the common law enabled the judges to afford the requisite protection, without the interposition of the legislature.

1934
The Federal Communications Commission (FCC) is established under the Federal Communications Act (FCA)

1942
Goldman v. United States rules that using electronic listening devices does not violate the 14th Amendment

Essentially, Brandeis and Warren argued that the interpretation of other rights, such as the right to property and the freedom from injury, had demonstrated a gradual shift from literal, physical interpretation, to broader interpretations needed to protect the intangible assets of personhood. Property rights, which once referred specifically to physical property, had thus been expanded to cover, also, the ownership of ideas and what became known as "intellectual property." Similarly, the right to live free from injury was gradually expanded to include emotional injury and injuries to a person's professional or personal reputation, in the form of libel or slander.

"The Right to Privacy"
continued

These considerations lead to the conclusion that the protection afforded to thoughts, sentiments, and emotions, expressed through the medium of writing or of the arts, so far as it consists in preventing publication, is merely an instance of the enforcement of the more general right of the individual to be let alone. It is like the right not be assaulted or beaten, the right not be imprisoned, the right not to be maliciously prosecuted, the right not to be defamed. In each of these rights, as indeed in all other rights recognized by the law, there inheres the quality of being owned or possessed— and (as that is the distinguishing attribute of property) there may some propriety in speaking of those rights as property. But, obviously, they bear little resemblance to what is ordinarily comprehended under that term. The principle which protects personal writings and all other personal productions, not against theft and physical appropriation, but against publication in any form, is in reality not the principle of private property, but that of an inviolate personality.

If we are correct in this conclusion, the existing law affords a principle from which may be invoked to protect the privacy of the individual from invasion either by the too enterprising press, the photographer, or the possessor of any other modern device for rewording or reproducing scenes or sounds. For the protection afforded is not confined by the authorities to those cases where any particular medium or form of expression has been adopted, not to products of the intellect. The same protection is afforded to

1945 The National Security Agency secretly creates Project SHAMROCK

1950 Senator Joseph McCarthy delivers a shocking speech claiming that more than 200 communist spies have infiltrated the U.S. government

continued

emotions and sensations expressed in a musical composition or other work of art as to a literary composition; and words spoken, a pantomime acted, a sonata performed, is no less entitled to protection than if each had been reduced to writing. The circumstance that a thought or emotion has been recorded in a permanent form renders its identification easier, and hence may be important from the point of view of evidence, but it has no significance as a matter of substantive right. If, then, the decisions indicate a general right to privacy for thoughts, emotions, and sensations, these should receive the same protection, whether expressed in writing, or in conduct, in conversation, in attitudes, or in facial expression.

Brandeis and Warren also recognized that there were certain conditions in which an individual could be seen as having forfeited his or her privacy rights. They recognized, for instance, that an individual who is a public figure must necessarily forfeit some of his or her rights against the publication of information, whether such information might be seen as private in other instances, when such information is in the public interest.

"The Right to Privacy"
continued

There are persons who may reasonably claim as a right, protection from the notoriety entailed by being made the victims of journalistic enterprise. There are others who, in varying degrees, have renounced the right to live their lives screened from public observation. Matters which men of the first class may justly contend, concern themselves alone, may in those of the second be the subject of legitimate interest to their fellow-citizens. Peculiarities of manner and person, which in the ordinary individual should be free from comment, may acquire a public importance, if found in a candidate for public office. Some further discrimination is necessary, therefore, than to class facts or deeds as public or private according to a

1951 *Dennis v. United States* rules that government limits to speech is legal only to prevent a threat to public safety or security

1959 *Barenblatt v. United States* rules that it's legal to order people to reveal personal details if national threat is perceived

"The Right to Privacy"
continued

standard to be applied to the fact or deed per se. To publish of a modest and retiring individual that he suffers from an impediment in his speech or that he cannot spell correctly, is an unwarranted, if not an unexampled, infringement of his rights, while to state and comment on the same characteristics found in a would-be congressman could not be regarded as beyond the pale of propriety.

Although Brandeis and Warren's assertion that the right to privacy could be derived from common law, the authors argued that, "It would doubt-less be desirable that the privacy of the individual should receive the added protection of the criminal law, but for this, legislation would be required." Essentially then, while Brandeis and Warren supported statutes to protect privacy, their argument, based on the facility of using available principles, was meant to argue for preexisting grounds to protect privacy in the courts.

On a more philosophical level, the definition of privacy as the "right to be let alone" or as a matter of "inviolate personality," speaks to a fundamen-tal challenge in the effort to create and amend laws protecting privacy, and the difficulty in defining and elucidating the concept so as to render it vulnerable to legal protection. Brandeis and Warren's 1890 article also initiated a new branch of legal philosophy, dedicated to studying privacy as a right, claim, or value and to determining when and how legal protec-tions were needed to protect the privacy of individuals in various situa-tions. This effort evolved and expanded over time, with many different proposals on how to view privacy and its importance in human life.

In a 2002 analysis of the various legal conceptualizations of privacy, for instance, George Washington University Law School expert on privacy

1965   *Griswold v. CT* rules in favor of married couples' right to privacy   **1967**   *Katz v. United States* rules wiretaps a form of search and seizure   Willis Ware of RAND Corporation writes *Security and Privacy in Computer*

law Daniel Solove cites one argument regarding the nature of privacy and the link between personal privacy and social/personal dignity:

> ────────── *...social practices have developed to conceal aspects of life that we find animal-like or disgusting as well as activities in which we feel particularly vulnerable and weak. We scrub, dress, and groom our- selves in order to present ourselves to the public in a dignified manner. We seek to cover up smells, discharge, and excretion because we are socialized into viewing them with disgust. We cloak the nude body in public based on norms of decorum. These social practices, which relegate these aspects of life to the private sphere, are deeply connected to human dignity. Dignity is, in part, the ability to transcend one's animal nature, to be civilized, to feel worthy of respect. Indeed, one form of torture is to dehumanize and degrade people by making them dirty, stripping them, forcing them to eliminate waste in public, and so on. When social practices relating to dignity are disrupted, the result can be a severe and sometimes debilitating humiliation and loss of self-esteem.* [1]
>
> ──────────

In the years leading up to Brandeis and Warren's article, several prominent court cases dealt with issues surrounding the publication of photos, personal details, and rumors about the lives of public figures. The problem was, in many ways, similar to the debate about "fake news" in the 2010s, in that (at least in Brandeis and Warren's opinion) the popular press of the era was guilty of publishing unsubstantiated rumor and gossip. Further, the two legal experts argued that, in pursuit of rumor and information for their articles, journalists were violating the privacy of the individuals and families targeted for exposés and articles.

1968   The Omnibus Crime Control Act holds that police needed to obtain a warrant before engaging in wire-

1969   Joseph Licklider creates the Advanced Research Projects Agency Network (ARPANET), which was

Philosophical critics, commenting on this ongoing debate, have even suggested that the concept of privacy itself might be largely illusory, and that there is, therefore, no legal way of defining the concept that satisfies the simultaneous needs of government and individuals. In Ancient Greece, for instance, there was no guaranteed right to privacy because the government itself was conceived of as existing in the "public interest" and, therefore, the right of the government to know all that was available about citizens was, too, seen as appropriate for the greater good.[2]

For many Americans, empowering the state to gather unfettered information on the lives of individuals, as the law allowed in ancient Greek democracy, might be seen as a violation of deeply held, if poorly defined, freedoms. Further, some privacy rights advocates have argued that a fundamental right to privacy should be considered part of a fundamental American creed. Touching on this common value and common inter- est concept of privacy, Brandeis and Warren argued that violations of privacy, however subjective the injury resulting from such violations, might be seen a violation of an individual's right to enjoy life and thus protected as an extension of the most basic and unalienable right to life and liberty promised by the U.S. Constitution.

Between 1890 and 2017, U.S. courts developed a framework for privacy rights by using sections of other rights granted in the Constitution and the Bill of Rights. Aspects of laws prohibiting unreasonable search and seizure, or governmental invasion of property, as well as protections of free speech, free expression, and free association, have been used, in concert, to justify and develop privacy laws. According to a 2012 study, Warren and Brandeis' article had been cited more than 3,600 times, making it the second-most-cited law review article of all time, and this demonstrates the scope of interest in the issue over the ensuing century.

As a Supreme Court Justice, between 1916 and 1939, Brandeis had the opportunity to apply his legal arguments to the evolving debate over

1971 The Pentagon Papers leaks from the press raise the issue of the Freedom of the Press versus the privacy of the government to conceal information about national security operations

1972 *Eisenstadt v. Baird* rules that the right to privacy applies to individuals

privacy law in the courts. Over the years, the debate evolved beyond (though still including) the allegations of corporate privacy violations (like the tabloids reviled by Brandeis and Warren or the debate over Facebook and other Internet companies selling customer data in the 2010s), to include a debate over violations by the state when attempting to combat crime or ensure public safety. This goal, balancing national security and civil rights, is a fundamental strain in legal and public policy debate throughout the twentieth and twenty-first centuries, resulting in landmark court cases, contentious and even violent public debate, and years of congressional compromise and conflict, reflecting the broader, underlying evolution of American values.

1974

The Watergate Scandal results in the revelation that the CIA had been conducting widespread surveillance of American dissidents and foreign leaders without judicial oversight

The Privacy Act is established

CONCLUSION

Warren and Brandeis' article was influential in early 1900s court cases regarding privacy rights and played a major role in later debates (in the 1960s) over whether or not there was a constitutional right to privacy inherent in the Bill of Rights. The primary issue for the authors was to protect citizens from commercial or corporate privacy invasions—in which a company or individual violates the privacy of another individual for profit or personal gain. Commercial violations of privacy became a major issue in the 2000s and 2010s as part of the national debate over the "data economy" in which companies like Facebook, Google, and Twitter collect data on users and sell data to advertisers and other entities for profit. It is important to note that, though the Warren and Brandeis article was published in 1890, many of the issues raised by the authors have yet to be resolved in US culture or law.

1975   Senator Frank Church leads a series of hearings about the secret NSA SHAMROCK operation involved intercepting communications from American citizens

1978   Congress passes the 1978 FISA Act

DISCUSSION QUESTIONS

- Do modern journalists invade the privacy of their subjects?
- What is the difference between tabloid journalism and other kinds of journalism?
- Do social media companies, like Facebook and Twitter, violate the privacy of consumers?
- Are Brandeis and Warren's arguments still relevant in the 21st century?

Works Used

Hardwick, Daniel W. "Defining Privacy." *Notre Dame Journal of Law, Ethics & Public Policy*. Vol. 14, Iss 2. Jan. 1, 2012.

Shapiro, Fred, and Pearse, Michelle. "The Most-Cited Law Review Articles of All Time." *Michigan Law Review*. Vol. 110, Iss 8. 2012.

Solove, Daniel. "Conceptualizing Privacy." *California Law Review*. Vol. 90, Iss 4. July 2002.

1980 The Intelligence Oversight Act (IOA) updates legal standards

1981 President Reagan's E.O. authorized wiretapping

1986 The Electronic Communications Privacy Act is established

"Open Administration"

1970 © The Herb Block Foundation

1994 Netscape creates the "cookie" allowing computers to monitor Internet users

2001 The September 11 terrorist attacks result in Congress authorizing the Bush Administration to utilize military methods to combat terrorism

Introduction

This chapter discusses the Fourth Amendment of the Bill of Rights, which protects U.S. citizens from unreasonable search and seizure. The basis of this discussion is the 1928 Supreme Court case *Olmstead v. United States*, in which Justice Louis Brandeis, co-author of the "Right to Privacy" document discussed in Chapter 1 was a presiding justice. In this case, a man accused of creating and running an illegal liquor smuggling operation was arrested by government agents based on information obtained through a wiretap on a private telephone. The Supreme Court was then asked to determine if the wiretap violated the individual's Fourth Amendment freedoms from unreasonable search and seizure. The majority decided that it did not, with only Justice Brandeis disagreeing.

The *Olmstead* case was the first time that the Supreme Court was asked to determine the legality of wiretapping and the first time that the court weighed the relevance of the Fourth Amendment to a more general right to privacy. Fast forward 89 years to the primary source document reprinted in this chapter, an article from journalist Karen Abbott in a July 2017 issue of *The New Yorker*. Here, the author explores the history of the Olmstead Case and its relevance to the early 20th century debate over privacy, telephone technology, and the Fourth Amendment—issues still being debated.

Topics covered in this chapter include:
- Wiretapping
- Commercial/corporate privacy rights
- The Fourth Amendment of the Bill of Rights
- Commercial invasion of privacy
- Technology and privacy rights
- Supreme Court cases on Privacy Rights

This Chapter Discusses the Following Source Document:
Abbott, Karen. "The Bootlegger, The Wiretap, and the Beginning of Privacy." *The New Yorker.* July 5, 2017.

2005

The PATRIOT Act was reauthorized without substantial changes as Congress favors security concerns over warnings that the law creates the potential for civil liberties violations

The *New York Times* publishes articles resulting from leaks revealing the secret President's Surveillance Program (PSP) established by the Bush administration

Defining Search and Seizure
The Olmstead Case and the Legality of Wiretapping (1928)

Louis Brandeis, co-author of the influential *The Right to Privacy* law review of 1890, became an Associate Justice of the Supreme Court in 1916. In the 1928 case of *Olmstead v. United States*, Brandeis and the court, for the first time, debated the constitutional nature of the right to privacy in relation to the Fourth Amendment protections against unreasonable searches and seizures. The case was one of the most controversial and debated court decisions of the decade and aspects of the case informed further judicial precedent for decades after the court's ruling.

The 1928 Supreme Court case began with the prohibition of alcohol, a legislative initiative fought for by a powerful, conservative minority concerned about the well-documented effects of alcohol addiction and abuse. Prohibition reduced the supply of alcohol, but did nothing to reduce demand and so the nation plunged into a chaotic era marked by the emergence of a powerful, violent criminal underworld organized around the trade in illegal alcohol.

Roy Olmstead, a 33-year-old father of two and a former lieutenant in the Seattle, Washington police before being fired from the police for illegally smuggling whiskey, was a major figure in the Seattle criminal underground of the 1920s. Olmstead transitioned from law

Police officers look over distilling equipment and guns confiscated during a Prohibition raid, Chicago, ca.1920s. (Photo by Chicago History Museum/Getty Images)

2007 The Bush Administration plans to make data taken from spy satellites available to law enforcement to be used to conduct domestic surveillance

2008 Congress passes Section 702, or the FISA Amendment Act, which is used to permit a massive NSA and CIA domestic surveillance program

officer to professional bootlegger, using his political and personal connections to build a vast network of allies who helped him smuggle large quantities of liquor into Seattle. By accounts of the era, Olmstead was something of a public hero and had received the local appellation "King of the Puget Sound Bootleggers." His reputation was based, in part, on the fact that Olmstead preferred bribery to violence, and thus that his smuggling enterprise was peaceful in comparison to the violent mobs that emerged in the illegal industry in other cities. With such a large enterprise to manage, Olmstead conducted much of his business over the telephone, and this habit proved to be the key to his downfall.

In 1924, the state prohibition authority enlisted the help of New York wiretapping expert Richard Fryant to investigate Olmstead's operation. Over months, Fryant collected enough information to implicate Olmstead and dozens of members of his organization, including police and public officials, in a conspiracy to violate prohibition law. When the prohibition authority finally seized one of Olmstead's shipments, the case came to trial, and the courts found Olmstead guilty, sentencing him to $8,000 in fines and four years hard labor.[5]

Olmstead had been confident that the information obtained by Fryant would be inadmissible in court, because wiretapping, at the time, was illegal in Washington (a misdemeanor crime). Such state laws were established using "common law" provisions and were, essentially, the only existing privacy protections involving

BOOTS AND BOOZE

Individuals who violated prohibition laws, importing and distributing liquor were sometimes known as "bootleggers," a term first used in newspaper articles discussing the emergence of the anti-prohibition underworld. The origin of the term is uncertain, though it has been suggested that the term came from the Civil War, referring to soldiers who would smuggle bottles of alcohol into dry camps, concealed within their boots.[4]

2012 The Obama Administration proposes a Consumer Privacy Bill of Rights guaranteeing individuals the right to greater control over the use of their digital data

2013 The *Guardian* and the *Washington Post* publish the first series of articles derived from leaked NSA and CIA documents delivered by Edward Snowden

the use of emerging wiretapping technology. After his conviction, Olmstead challenged the ruling on constitutional grounds, arguing that the use of a wiretap to gain evidence against him (which was illegal according to Washington state law) violated his Fourth and Fifth Amendment rights.

The Fifth Amendment guarantees all Americans the right to due process under the law and, among other things, guarantees that:

> *No person...shall be compelled in any criminal case to be a witness against himself.*[6]

Olmstead's attorneys argued that Olmstead's wiretap essentially meant that he had been forced, against his will, to testify against himself, and they argued that this was a violation of Fifth Amendment guarantees. The Fourth Amendment argument in the case refers to the section of the Bill of Rights designed to curtail tyranny and authoritarian application of police and military powers:

> *The right of the people to be secure in their persons, houses, papers, and effects, against unreasonable searches and seizures, shall not be violated, and no warrants shall issue, but upon probable cause, supported by oath or affirmation, and particularly describing the place to be searched, and the persons or things to be seized.*

In the 1928 ruling, the Supreme Court ruled 5–4 to uphold Olmstead's conviction. Writing the majority opinion on the case, Chief Justice and former President William Howard Taft wrote that Olmstead's claim that the search violated his Fifth Amendment rights was invalid on the basis that Olmstead had not been "compelled" to give evidence and that, in the conversations recorded over the telephone, Olmstead had spoken freely and without governmental manipulation.

The Senate Judiciary committee holds hearings to determine if the executive surveillance operations carried out under the PATRIOT Act were a violation of constitutional law

Snowden leaks reveal that the NSA and CIA had been attempting to force corporations to provide a backdoor to encryption systems that would allow federal agents to bypass consumer encryption

In addressing the issue of whether the wiretap constituted an illegal search or seizure, the court's majority opinion established a legal precedent that became the crux of the debate over privacy rights for nearly half a century. Taft noted that the majority surveyed common law and statutory precedent and determined that verbal communication was not a form of property as described in the Constitution and thus that a wiretap was essentially a method of "overhearing" a conversation and not a search or seizure.

As Chief Justice and former President William Howard Taft argued, in the majority opinion of the court:

> *By the invention of the telephone fifty years ago and its application for the purpose of extending communications, one can talk with another at a far distant place. The language of the Amendment cannot be extended and expanded to include telephone wires reaching to the whole world from the defendant's house or office. The intervening wires are not part of his house or office any more than are the highways along which they are stretched. And further:*
>
> *The United States takes no such care of telegraph or telephone messages as of mailed sealed letters. The Amendment does not forbid what was done here. There was no searching. There was no seizure. The evidence was secured by the use of the sense of hearing, and that only. There was no entry of the houses or offices of the defendants.*

In the Olmstead case, the government agents responsible for eliciting the wiretap and collecting evidence did not argue that the methods used in their investigation were legal or followed due process. In fact, the inves-

2015

| Terrorist attacks in France reignite fears of domestic terrorist violence | The PATRIOT Act is replaced by the USA Freedom Act | Federal Courts order Apple, Inc. to create a new operation system that would enable federal investigators to bypass security on an iPhone. |

tigators conceded that, if wiretapping were defined as a type of search and seizure, then the evidence would necessarily be inadmissible. Taft and a majority of the justices reviewing the case likewise agreed that the government had not adhered to the rules governing searches, but argued that wiretapping was not a form of search, and thus not protected.

Taft and the majority further argued for an interpretation that favored the government's aims over civil liberties, by arguing, effectively, that the ends could be seen as justification of the means. In a sentiment echoed repeatedly for decades by defenders of government surveillance programs, Taft explained this position:

> *A standard which would forbid the reception of evidence if obtained by other than nice ethical conduct by government officials would make society suffer and give criminals greater immunity than has been known heretofore.*

Louis Brandeis, already a pioneer in the legal protection of privacy since he co-authored the seminal 1890 law review article "The Right to Privacy," wrote the dissenting opinion on the case. Brandeis argued that the interception of personal communications, whether by the government, or by private individuals, must constitute a variety of search and seizure and, therefore, must be protected by Fourth Amendment guarantees. In the ensuing decades, Brandeis' dissenting opinion became the most famous and lasting aspect of the Olmstead case and some of the arguments made by Brandeis regarding the right to privacy and the dangers of government surveillance provided a prescient view of the future:

> *Moreover, "in the application of a constitution, our contemplation cannot be only of what has been, but of what may be." The progress of science in furnishing the Government with means of espionage is not*

The FCC publishes official rules of "neutrality"

2016

The EU establishes the General Data Protection Regulation (GDPR), described as the strongest digital data privacy law in the world

likely to stop with wiretapping. Ways may someday be developed by which the Government, without removing papers from secret drawers, can reproduce them in court, and by which it will be enabled to expose to a jury the most intimate occurrences of the home. Advances in the psychic and related sciences may bring means of exploring unexpressed beliefs, thoughts, and emotions. "That places the liberty of every man in the hands of every petty officer" was said by James Otis of much lesser intrusions than these. To Lord Camden, a far slighter intrusion seemed "subversive of all the comforts of society." Can it be that the Constitution affords no protection against such invasions of individual security?

Brandeis delved further into the issue, questioning not only the legal standing of the court's ruling, but also the philosophical underpinnings of the court's basic approach to protecting the spirit, as well as the text of the Constitution:

The protection guaranteed by the Amendments is much broader in scope. The makers of our Constitution undertook to secure conditions favorable to the pursuit of happiness. They recognized the significance of man's spiritual nature, of his feelings, and of his intellect. They knew that only a part of the pain, pleasure, and satisfactions of life are to be found in material things. They sought to protect Americans in their beliefs, their thoughts, their emotions, and their sensations. They conferred, as against the Government, the right to be let alone— the most comprehensive of rights, and the right most

2017

The "Vault 7" secrets, a leak of 9,000 CIA documents, reveal details of the CIA's attempts to break through encryption used by Internet

President Trump appoints Ajit Pai to head the FCC, who abolishes the FCC neutrality protections

valued by civilized men. To protect that right, every unjustifiable intrusion by the Government upon the privacy of the individual, whatever the means employed, must be deemed a violation of the Fourth Amendment.

In this article, from the July 5, 2017 edition of *The New Yorker*, Karen Abbott, historian and best-selling author of *Sin in the Second City* and *American Rose*, revisits the Olmstead case and examines the roots of the Supreme Court debate over privacy rights in light of the twenty-first century's emerging challenges to privacy laws.

THE BOOTLEGGER, THE WIRETAP, AND THE BEGINNING OF PRIVACY
by Karen Abbott
The New Yorker, July 5, 2017
Source Document

Nearly a century before a U.S. President accused his predecessor of ordering a "tapp" on his private telephone line, and before he tweeted a warning to the head of the F.B.I. that he had "better hope that there are no 'tapes' of our conversations," a professional spy, armed with a pack of cigarettes and an earpiece, hid in the basement of the Henry Building, in downtown Seattle, catching crackling bits of words being spoken miles away. Richard Fryant had worked as a wiretapper for the New York Telephone Company, tasked with eavesdropping on his own colleagues, and now took freelance assignments in the Queen City. On this occasion, he was seeking dirt on Seattle's corrupt mayor—who was suspected of having ties to Roy Olmstead, a local bootlegger—for a political rival. At the behest of his client, Fryant rigged micro-wires to a certain exchange, ELliott-6785, and began to listen.

"They got that load," one man said, breathing heavily.

"The hell they did—who?" asked another.

Congress debates whether or not to renew the controversial Section 702 FISA Amendment used to authorize NSA domestic intelligence operations since 2008

"The Bootlegger, the Wiretap, and the Beginning of Privacy" continued

"The federals."

The men speaking on ELliott-6785 hung up, but the conversation had only just begun.

Criminals and Prohibition officials alike called Olmstead "the good bootlegger," a moniker that reflected his singular business philosophy. He never diluted his whiskey with water or corrupted it with poison; he declined to dabble in the seedier offshoots of his profession, such as drugs or prostitution; and he abhorred violence, forbidding members of his organization from carrying weapons ("No amount of money is worth a human life," he cautioned). If apprehended, his men were instructed to rely on bribes instead of violence.

Olmstead had a particular respect for policemen, having been a member of the Seattle force for thirteen years, reaching the rank of lieutenant. In 1920, with the onset of Prohibition, the thirty-three-year-old married father of two ventured to the other side of the law, making midnight runs to retrieve imported Canadian liquor from tugboats in the Puget Sound. This practice earned his dismissal from the force and made him a local celebrity. With his old police colleagues on his payroll, he was free to conduct business brazenly and with impunity, often unloading his booze at high noon from trucks marked "Fresh Fish." Seattle citizens were thrilled to glimpse Olmstead on the street, wearing a fine suit and carrying a wallet fat with money, always ready with a joke. As one acquaintance noted, "It made a man feel important to casually remark, 'As Roy Olmstead was telling me today.'"

Olmstead's organization, composed of an ever-growing staff of attorneys, dispatchers, clerks, skippers, navigators, bottlers, loaders, drivers, deliverymen, collectors, and salesmen, dominated the bootlegging scene in the Pacific Northwest. They relied heavily upon the telephone for day-to-day operations, using it to take orders, communicate updates on deliveries, and warn of impending raids, their words coursing across a web of wires connecting the city's fifty-two thousand devices (approximately one for every six citizens). Olmstead set up his communication headquarters in the Henry Building, just a block from the Federal Building, and established three exchanges: ELliott 6785, 6786, and 6787. One of his men, a former taxi dispatcher, sat during business hours at a roll-top desk, taking and making calls, keeping meticulous records of each transaction. If a serious matter arose, such as an employee's arrest, Olmstead himself called a friend on the Seattle police force to have it quashed.

1788 State legislatures ratify the U.S. Constitution, establishing the basic precedent for all future constitutional law

1791 The U.S. Congress ratifies the Bill of Rights, creating the first 10 amendments to the United States Constitution

continued

At the end of each day, the dispatcher unplugged the three telephones, to stop their ceaseless ringing, and the routine began anew in the morning.

In early 1924, Olmstead was approached by Richard Fryant, the freelance wiretapper who had been hunkered down in the basement of the Henry Building, listening to Olmstead's lines. As the bootlegger would soon learn, Seattle's Prohibition Director, William Whitney, had heard of Fryant's surveillance and recruited him as a federal agent.

In Olmstead's version of events, Fryant presented him with a heavy stack of paper, explaining that the pages contained verbatim transcripts of conversations that had been conducted on the bootlegger's office phone. For ten thousand dollars, Fryant said, the transcripts could be his. A quick perusal of the pages confirmed their authenticity.

A call from a cop to a worker at Olmstead's headquarters:

"Down under the Fourth Avenue Bridge is a car with seven gallons of moonshine in it, and I was wondering if it is yours."

"No . . . I don't think it is ours because we don't handle moonshine."

A call from Olmstead to the police station:

"Hello, Roy, what is on your mind?"

"One of your fellows picked up one of my boys. . . . I don't give a damn what they do but I want to know before he is booked."

"I'll take care of it for you, Roy."

A joking exchange between Olmstead and a dispatcher:

"The federals will get you one of these days."

"No, those sons of bitches are too slow to catch cold," Olmstead quipped.

Reading the pages, Olmstead maintained his composure. As a former police officer, he said, when he'd finished reading, he knew a thing or two about the "rules of evidence." Wiretapping was illegal in the state of Washington, so the pile of paper would be useless in a courtroom. Furthermore, Fryant could go straight to hell.

Olmstead's bravado did not prevent him from hiring a telephone repairman to search the Henry Building first thing in the morning. Together, they found and removed three temporary taps (affixed with coil wire rather than soldered)—two in the basement and one in the women's restroom. Still unsettled, Olmstead returned the

1868 The 14th Amendment to the U.S. Constitution guarantees all citizens the right to due process under the law

1890 Warren and Brandeis publish "The Right to Privacy" in the *Harvard Law Review*

"The Bootlegger, the Wiretap, and the Beginning of Privacy"
continued

following day and discovered that all three taps were back.

Fryant and Whitney's wife, Clara, a skilled stenographer, continued to monitor ELliott-6785 from an office one floor below. At each day's end, Clara gathered up the handwritten notes and typed them with fastidious precision. The pile of paper continued to grow.

For the first time in his bootlegger career, Olmstead started exercising some discretion about his words—but only some, because he still trusted that Fryant's wiretapping evidence would never withstand legal scrutiny. When managing the arrival of his whiskey boats in Puget Sound, he used a public pay phone to issue instructions and directions. For less sensitive issues, he continued to use his office line, and even had fun at the wiretapper's expense, calling Whitney profane names and giving false orders about the timing and location of deliveries. It amused him to imagine the Prohibition chief sitting alone in the freezing rain, grasping his gun and waiting for boats that would never come.

Whitney's patience paid off in October, 1924, when Canadian officials seized one of Olmstead's boats. Three months later, a federal grand jury returned an indictment against Olmstead and ninety co-defendants

for conspiracy to violate the National Prohibition Act. The "Whispering Wires" case, as it came to be called, concluded with a guilty verdict, a fine of eight thousand dollars, and a sentence of four years' hard labor. Convinced that his Fourth and Fifth Amendment rights had been violated (the right against unreasonable searches and seizures and against self-incrimination, respectively), Olmstead put his lawyers to work on *Olmstead v. The United States*. The Circuit Court of Appeals upheld his conviction, maintaining that, because the federal agents' wiretapping pursuits did not require them to trespass on Olmstead's property or confiscate physical possessions, there had been no breach of rights.

The Supreme Court heard *Olmstead v. The United States* in February 1928, and, in a 5–4 decision, upheld Olmstead's conviction. Chief Justice William Howard Taft, speaking for the majority, recognized the murky morality of wiretapping. Nevertheless, he argued that the practice served a greater good. "A standard which would forbid the reception of evidence if obtained by other than nice ethical conduct by government officials would make society suffer and give criminals greater immunity than has been known heretofore," he wrote.

1923   *Meyer v. Nebraska* establishes that the 14th Amendment guarantees privileges of citizenship

1928   *Olmstead v. United States* rules that wiretapping is not a form of search and seizure defined by the 14th Amendment

continued

He rejected the heart of Olmstead's case, insisting that "the Amendment does not forbid what was done here. There was no searching. There was no seizure. . . . The reasonable view is that one who installs in his house a telephone instrument with connecting wires intends to project his voice to those quite outside."

The dissenting opinion was penned by Justice Louis Brandeis, for whom the issue of privacy was both ancient and increasingly, inescapably modern. In 1890, while practicing law in Boston, he had co-authored an article published by the *Harvard Law Review* titled "The Right to Privacy"—a manifesto, as Jill Lepore has written in this magazine, that argues for the existence of "a legal right to be let alone—a right that had never been defined before." Although the telephone was still decades away from being a familiar and necessary aspect of our lives, nearly every line of "The Right to Privacy" reveals prophetic insight into current concerns about how best to shield our innermost selves. "The intensity and complexity of life have rendered necessary some retreat from the world," Brandeis wrote.

"The Right to Privacy" became a seminal work, and one that clearly influenced Brandeis himself as he considered Olmstead's case. When the Founding Fathers crafted the Constitution, he wrote in his dissent, the right to be let alone was inherent in the notion of pursuing happiness. To protect that right, "every unjustifiable intrusion by the government upon the privacy of the individual, whatever the means employed, must be considered a violation of the Fourth Amendment. . . . If the government becomes a lawbreaker, it breeds contempt for the law."

The media, although invested in a world where sensitive information might be easily and readily obtained, largely favored Brandeis's view. The *Times* declared that the Olmstead decision allowed "universal snooping." The *New Haven journal-courier* predicted that "every Tom, Dick and Harry" would hereafter practice wiretapping without fear of reprisal. The editors of the weekly magazine *Outlook* were even more blunt, likening the verdict to a "new Dred Scott" and predicting dire consequences: "We must weather the devastating effects of a decision that outrages a people's sense of a security which they thought they had."

Forty years later, the Supreme Court finally caught up with Justice Brandeis, refining the Olmstead decision in two separate cases. In June 1967, *Berger v. New York* considered

1934 The Federal Communications Commission (FCC) is established under the Federal Communications Act (FCA)

1942 *Goldman v. United States* rules that using electronic listening devices does not violate the 14th Amendment

"The Bootlegger, the Wiretap, and the Beginning of Privacy" continued

the appeal of Ralph Berger, a public-relations consultant who had been convicted of conspiracy to bribe the chairman of the New York State Liquor Authority. Under the authority of a New York statute, police wiretapped Berger's phone for two months, and played excerpts of their recordings during the trial. In a 6–3 decision, the Supreme Court ruled that the New York law was "too broad in its sweep"—specifically too long, as the two-month surveillance amounted to "a series of intrusions, searches, and seizures" that violated the defendant's Fourth Amendment rights.

Six months later, the Supreme Court directly addressed the legacy of the Olmstead decision, in the case of Charles Katz, a California man convicted of placing illegal gambling wagers across state lines. Without a warrant, F.B.I. agents wiretapped public pay phones along Sunset Boulevard, hiding the device atop the bank of booths and listening in as Katz placed bets in Miami and Boston. The Court of Appeals upheld Katz' conviction, concluding that, since there had been "no physical entrance," his privacy had not been compromised.

In a 7–1 ruling, the Supreme Court reversed this decision, arguing that the Fourth Amendment protects people, not places, and that its reach cannot depend on "the presence or absence of a physical intrusion" into any given space. Citing Justice Brandeis's manifesto, the Court established the protection of a person's "general right to privacy" (emphasis the Court's) and "his right to be let alone."

Olmstead served his four-year sentence. Yet, in a way, he managed to win his case. Victory came in the form of a Presidential pardon, granted by Franklin D. Roosevelt, on Christmas Eve of 1935, which restored all of his rights as a citizen and cancelled the fine. Roosevelt was influenced, in part, by Olmstead's nascent transformation: he'd quit drinking, converted to Christian Science, and started teaching the Bible to prisoners, who frequently asked if he was really *that* Roy Olmstead, the "good bootlegger," the rum-running king of Puget Sound. His standard reply—"No, not any more. The old Olmstead is dead"—amounted to fewer than a hundred and forty characters, and were the words he wished the whole world to hear.

1945 The National Security Agency secretly creates Project SHAMROCK

1950 Senator Joseph McCarthy delivers a shocking speech claiming that more than 200 communist spies have infiltrated the U.S. government

There is little data suggesting how the American public felt about the issues being debated in the nation's highest court, and whether a majority of people would have supported Brandeis or Taft at the time that the case was initially decided. What is clear is that the *Olmstead* case, as one of the most high-profile cases of the era, helped to shape and reflect an evolving public consciousness regarding the legal right to privacy and also forced the American public, for the first time, to consider how the technological innovations of their time might impact their civil liberties in the future.

1951

Dennis v. United States rules that government limits to speech is legal only to prevent a threat to public safety or security

1959

Barenblatt v. United States rules that it's legal to order people to reveal personal details if national threat is perceived

CONCLUSION

In 1928, most of the Supreme Court justices argued that wiretapping was not a form of search and/or seizure, and so held that the investigation did not violate Olmstead's Fourth Amendment protections. The dissenting opinion in the case (delivered by Justice Louis Brandeis) held that the right to privacy must apply to telephone communications and not only to written communications or private property. This opinion was widely cited in later cases regarding privacy laws and Fourth Amendment protections. Over subsequent decades, the public and the courts came to recognize that the telephone had become a "public utility," which is a technological system protected and managed in the public's interest, rather than only for corporate profit and benefit. As this change occurred, the courts began extending privacy protections that applied to written and private correspondence, to telephone communications. The evolution of legal thought regarding the telephone system as a public utility is relevant to twenty-first century debates over the right to privacy in digital communication, including email, instant messaging, cellular and text messages, and social media.

1965 Griswold v. CT rules in favor of married couples' right to privacy

1967 Katz v. United States rules wiretaps a form of search and seizure

Willis Ware of RAND Corporation writes *Security and Privacy in Computer*

DISCUSSION QUESTIONS

- Should consumers have a right to privacy regarding digital data (information sent through cellular or Internet networks)?
- Should the Internet and cellular networks be considered a public utility like the telephone system and U.S. Postal Service?
- Do you agree with the court's ruling in Olmstead or with the dissenting opinion? Explain why.
- How is the idiom, "the ends justify the means," relevant to the *Olmstead* case?

Works Used

Howell, Bill. *Alaska Beer: Liquid Gold in the Land of the Midnight Sun*. Charleston, SC: American Palate, 2015.

Metcalfe, Philip. *Whispering Wires: The Tragic Tale of an American Bootlegger*. Portland, OR: Inkwater Press, 2007.

"*Olmstead v. United States* 277 U.S. 438 (1928)." *Justia*. Justia. 2017. Web. 31 Oct. 2017.

1968 The Omnibus Crime Control Act holds that police needed to obtain a warrant before engaging in wire-

1969 Joseph Licklider creates the Advanced Research Projects Agency Network (ARPANET), which was

1971 The Pentagon Papers leaks from the press raise the issue of the Freedom of the Press versus the privacy of the government to conceal information about national security operations

1972 *Eisenstadt v. Baird* rules that the right to privacy applies to individuals

Introduction

This chapter explores changes in privacy law brought about by Section 605 of the Federal Communications Act of 1934. The Federal Communications Act did not prohibit wiretapping by federal agents, but Section 605 of the law made it illegal for any person (other than the sender or receiver) to repeat any information obtained from a private communication. This meant that, although federal agents were legally allowed to listen in, they could not repeat the information they learned in public. In 1937, and again in 1939, the Supreme Court interpreted Section 605 to mean that federal agents could not testify in court using information taken from a wiretap.

The primary source in this chapter, the Supreme Court transcript from the 1942 case of *Goldman v. United States*, demonstrates how federal agents used a loophole to circumvent the privacy protections issuing from the 1934 law. In an investigation of a suspected conspiracy to commit fraud by a lawyer named Martin Goldman, federal agents used a "detectophone" to listen to Goldman's telephone conversations through a wall, rather than through the phone lines. Because the agents did not tap Goldman's phone and did not hear both sides of the conversation, the prosecution argued that no actual "interception" had taken place and that the interception, therefore, did not violate Section 605 of the 1934 statute. The Supreme Court was, therefore, asked whether or not listening to one side of a telephone conversation was also covered by the 1934 law.

Topics covered in this chapter include:
- Wiretapping
- The Fourth Amendment of the Bill of Rights
- Commercial invasion of privacy
- Technology and privacy rights
- Supreme Court cases on privacy rights

This Chapter Discusses the Following Source Document:
Goldman v. United States, 316 U.S. 129 (1942).

1975 Senator Frank Church leads a series of hearings about the secret NSA SHAMROCK operation involved intercepting communications from American citizens

1978 Congress passes the 1978 FISA Act

Retro Wireless Surveillance
The Federal Communications Act of 1934 and *Goldman v. United States* (1942)

THE FEDERAL COMMUNICATIONS ACT (1934)

The 1934 Federal Communications Act (FCA) was the first set of federal laws governing telephone communication. The FCA created the Federal Communications Commission (FCC) and accomplished a number of key economic controls on the industry. Section 605 of the act was an attempt to use the newly established legislation to place limits on surveillance through the telephone system.

Section 605 of the FCA pertained to wiretapping, but did not make the process illegal or require that federal agents obtain a warrant before engaging in the practice. The Supreme Court had ruled, in the 1928 case of *Olmstead v. United States,* that wiretapping was *not* a form of search and seizure (covered by the Fourth Amendment) because it did not involve physical searching or the seizure of physical property. This ruling left wiretapping, as a tool for investigation, on uncertain ground. State laws had already been enacted to prohibit wiretapping in many cases, but no similar federal laws existed. Federal and state law enforcement agencies had, therefore, regularly engaged in the process, without obtaining warrants through the courts.

The statutory language of Section 605 was summarized by Supreme Court Justice Owen Roberts:

> ————— *Section 605 of the Federal Communications Act provides that no person who, as an employee, has to do with the sending or receiving of any interstate communication [302 U.S. 379, 381] by wire shall divulge or publish it or its substance to anyone other*

1980 | The Intelligence Oversight Act (IOA) updates legal standards

1981 | President Reagan's E.O. authorized wiretapping

1986 | The Electronic Communications Privacy Act is established

> *than the addressee or his authorized representative or to authorized fellow employees, save in response to a subpoena issued by a court of competent jurisdiction or on demand of other lawful authority; and 'no person not being authorized by the sender shall intercept any communication and divulge or publish the existence, contents, substance, purport, effect, or meaning of such intercepted communication to any person.'*

The Supreme Court was asked to interpret the meaning of Section 605 with regard to the legality of federal wiretapping in the cases of *Nardone v. United States* (1937) and *Nardone v. United States* (1939). The cases involved a group of alcohol smugglers who had been arrested after federal agents had wiretapped phone lines used by the suspects. The legal issue came when federal agents testified, in court, about information obtained through their wiretap. In 1937, and again in 1939, the Supreme Court ruled that, although the intentions and goals of the federal agents might be just, and the end result might serve the public interest, the actions of federal agents clearly constituted a violation of the 1934 law.

Writing the majority court opinion, Justice Owen Roberts explained in 1937:

> *We nevertheless face the fact that the plain words of Section 605 forbid anyone, unless authorized by the sender, to intercept a telephone message, and direct in equally clear language that 'no person' shall divulge or publish the message or its substance to 'any person.' To recite the contents of the message in testimony before a court is to divulge the message. The conclusion that the act forbids such testimony seems to us unshaken by the government's arguments.*

1994 Netscape creates the "cookie" allowing computers to monitor Internet users

2001 The September 11 terrorist attacks result in Congress authorizing the Bush Administration to utilize military methods to combat terrorism

The decision in the *Nardone v. United States* cases thus provided additional precedent on the legality of wiretapping, and this was sufficient for U.S. Attorney General Robert Jackson to order all federal agents to discontinue wiretapping in 1940. However, the federal wiretapping rules did not apply to the states, and state agents, therefore, continued to regularly use wiretaps without court approval after Attorney General Jackson's order.[7]

GOLDMAN v. UNITED STATES (1942)

The Supreme Court revisited the issues of wiretapping, surveillance, and privacy in the 1942 case of *Goldman v. United States* involving a pair of attorneys involved in a case of bankruptcy fraud. Attorney Martin Goldman, his brother Theodore Goldman, and partner Jacob P. Schulman, all lawyers, were involved in a conspiracy to obtain money illegally during a bankruptcy proceeding. Goldman and Schulman attempted to enlist the aid of the attorney for the creditors involved in the case, Robert Hoffman, who refused to take part in the scheme, but later apparently agreed to go along with the fraud when coerced. Unbeknownst to Goldman and Schulman, Hoffman explained the scheme to federal agents, who began an investigation. The agents attempted to install a wiretap in Goldman's office, but the wiretap would not work and, frustrated, the investigators resulted to using a "detectophone," to listen in on conversations occurring in Goldman's office through Schulman's office wall.

Because Section 605 of the Federal Communications Act prohibited federal agents from introducing information obtained through a wiretap in court, had the wiretap installed by the agents worked as planned, the information so obtained would have been inadmissible. However, there were no specific laws prohibiting federal agents from listening in with another type of device that did not specifically utilize telephone wires.

Goldman contended that the use of information obtained through the detectophone, without judicial oversight, constituted a violation of his Fourth

The Bush administration secretly authorizes the President's Surveillance Program (PSP), utilizing E.O. 12333

The U.S. PATRIOT Act alters existing laws to facilitate better communication between the state's intelligence branches in the effort to combat terrorism

The Transportation Security Administration (TSA) is established, creating the "No Fly" and "Selectee" lists that limit the right to travel on airplanes in the United States

Amendment freedom from unreasonable search and seizure, and violated Section 605 of the Federal Communications Act. The court ruled against Goldman's claims, and upheld his conviction, with Justice Owen Roberts delivering the majority opinion.

On the issue of whether the court's use of detectophone data violated Section 605, Roberts explained:

GOLDMAN V. UNITED STATES
Source Document Excerpt

The petitioners contend that a communication falls within the protection of the statute once a speaker has uttered words with the intent that they constitute a transmission of a telephone conversation. The validity of the contention must be tested by the terms of the Act fairly construed.

So considered, there was neither a "communication" nor an "interception" within the meaning of the Act. The protection intended and afforded by the statute is of the means of communication, and not of the secrecy of the conversation.

Essentially, then, though Goldman may have intended to engage in a telephone conversation, because federal agents were not intercepting Goldman's communication through the telephone lines, the court favored a narrow interpretation of the law and ruled that the conversation, as overheard through the detectophone, was not protected by the Federal Communications Act.

As to the issue of whether the investigators violated Goldman's Fourth Amendment protections, Roberts and the majority found no justification to distinguish the *Goldman* case from the *Olmstead* case and ruled, therefore, that the court would adhere to earlier precedent.[8]

2005

The PATRIOT Act was reauthorized without substantial changes as Congress favors security concerns over warnings that the law creates the potential for civil liberties violations

The *New York Times* publishes articles resulting from leaks revealing the secret President's Surveillance Program (PSP) established by the Bush administration

Goldman v. United States
continued

In asking us to hold that the information obtained was obtained in violation of the Fourth Amendment, and that its use at the trial was, therefore, banned by the Amendment, the petitioners recognize that they must reckon with our decision in *Olmstead v. United States*. They argue that the case may be distinguished. The suggested ground of distinction is that the Olmstead case dealt with the tapping of telephone wires, and the court adverted to the fact that, in using a telephone, the speaker projects his voice beyond the confines of his home or office and, therefore, assumes the risk that his message may be intercepted. It is urged that where, as in the present case, one talks in his own office, and intends his conversation to be confined within the four walls of the room, he does not intend his voice shall go beyond those walls and it is not to be assumed he takes the risk of someone's use of a delicate detector in the next room. We think, however, the distinction is too nice for practical application of the Constitutional guarantee and no reasonable or logical distinction can be drawn between what federal agents did in the present case and state officers did in the Olmstead case.

The petitioners ask us, if we are unable to distinguish *Olmstead v. United States*, to overrule it. This we are unwilling to do. That case was the subject of prolonged consideration by this court. The views of the court, and of the dissenting justices, were expressed clearly and at length. To rehearse and reappraise the arguments pro and con, and the conflicting views exhibited in the opinions, would serve no good purpose. Nothing now can be profitably added to what was there said. It suffices to say that we adhere to the opinion there expressed.

As in the *Olmstead* case, the court was divided in its opinion. In delivering the minority opinion, Justice Frank Murphy reiterated and expanded on the arguments made by Justice Brandeis in the 1928 case.

2007

The Bush Administration plans to make data taken from spy satellites available to law enforcement to be used to conduct domestic surveillance

2008

Congress passes Section 702, or the FISA Amendment Act, which is used to permit a massive NSA and CIA domestic surveillance program

Goldman v. United States
continued

One of the great boons secured to the inhabitants of this country by the Bill of Rights is the right of personal privacy guaranteed by the Fourth Amendment. In numerous ways, the law protects the individual against unwarranted intrusions by others into his private affair. It compensates him for trespass on his property or against his person. It prohibits the publication against his will of his thoughts, sentiments, and emotions regardless of whether those are expressed in words, painting, sculpture, music, or in other modes. It may prohibit the use of his photograph for commercial purposes without his consent. These are restrictions on the activities of private persons. But the Fourth Amendment puts a restraint on the arm of the Government itself, and prevents it from invading the sanctity of a man's home or his private quarters in a chase for a suspect except under safeguards calculated to prevent oppression and abuse of authority.

It will be conceded that, if the language of the Amendment were given only a literal construction, it might not fit the case now presented for review. The petitioners were not physically searched. Their homes were not entered. Their files were not ransacked. Their papers and effects were not disturbed. But it has not been the rule or practice of this Court to permit the scope and operation of broad principles ordained by the Constitution to be restricted, by a literal reading of its provisions, to those evils and phenomena that were contemporary with its framing.

The conditions of modern life have greatly expanded the range and character of those activities which require protection from intrusive action by Government officials if men and women are to enjoy the full benefit of that privacy which the Fourth Amendment was intended to provide. It is our duty to see that this historic provision receives a construction sufficiently liberal and elastic to make it serve the needs and manners of each succeeding generation. Otherwise, it may become obsolete, incapable of providing the people of this land adequate protection. To this end, we must give mind not merely to the exact words of the Amendment, but also to its historic purpose, its high political character, and its modern social and legal implications.

With the passing of the years since 1787, marked changes have ensued in the ways of conducting business and personal affairs. Many transactions of a business or personal character that, in the eighteenth century, were conducted at home are now carried on

2012 The Obama Administration proposes a Consumer Privacy Bill of Rights guaranteeing individuals the right to greater control over the use of their digital data

2013 The *Guardian* and the *Washington Post* publish the first series of articles derived from leaked NSA and CIA documents delivered by Edward Snowden

continued

in business offices away from the home. If the method and habits of the people in 1787 with respect to the conduct of their private business had been what they are today, is it possible to think that the framers of the Bill of Rights would have been any less solicitous of the privacy of transactions conducted in the office of a lawyer, a doctor, or a man of business than they were of a person's papers and effects?

For privacy advocates like Justice Brandeis and Justice Murphy, the *Goldman v. United States* decision was based on too narrow a reading of constitutional guarantees, resulting in the determination that only a person's possessions and property need be protected by privacy laws. As the privacy rights issue proceeded, the struggle to balance national security and personal privacy was becoming clearer both legally and philosophically. In the 1940s, the Supreme Court's approach was to grant leeway to the state, at least in cases where the ends (conviction of a criminal or addressing a national security threat) might be seen as justifying the means.[9]

In the years after *Goldman*, America entered the Cold War, a transformative phase in American culture marked by a national panic about the perceived threat of communism. As the anti-communist ideologues of the era purposefully stoked fantastic fears in the populace, utilizing the resulting panic to enhance their power and prestige, the perception of a broad, largely inchoate, and nevertheless menacingly imminent threat motivated lawmakers and voters to favor national security concerns over civil liberties, and this resulted in one of the most oppressive periods in American history.

The Senate Judiciary committee holds hearings to determine if the executive surveillance operations carried out under the PATRIOT Act were a violation of constitutional law

Snowden leaks reveal that the NSA and CIA had been attempting to force corporations to provide a backdoor to encryption systems that would allow federal agents to bypass consumer encryption

CONCLUSION

In their ruling on the 1942 case, a majority of the court found that listening to one side of a conversation, without directly tapping the phone lines, was not a violation of the 1934 statute. Therefore, in determining whether or not the use of a detectophone violated Goldman's Fourth Amendment rights, the court relied on the 1928 *Olmstead* case, in which the majority ruled that the Fourth Amendment protections applied only to physical searches and seizures. Justice Frank Murphy delivered the dissenting opinion, arguing that such a narrow interpretation of the Fourth Amendment failed to reflect the way that telephone communication had evolved to become an important form of private communication. In the twenty-first century, courts and legislators debating privacy rights would use similar arguments, on both sides, to debate whether or not new methods of virtual communication, such as email, cellular data, and social media posts, should be protected by the Fourth Amendment.

2015

Terrorist attacks in France reignite fears of domestic terrorist violence

The PATRIOT Act is replaced by the USA Freedom Act

Federal Courts order Apple, Inc. to create a new operation system that would enable federal investigators to bypass security on an iPhone.

DISCUSSION QUESTIONS

- Do you agree with the court's ruling in the 1942 *Goldman* case or with the dissenting opinion? Explain why.
- Did the loophole used by federal agents to obtain data on Goldman violate the intentions of the 1934 law? Why or why not?
- Did Justice Murphy's dissenting opinion anticipate challenges to privacy that technology brought in the twenty-first century?

Works Used

Gray, David. *The Fourth Amendment in an Age of Surveillance*. New York: Cambridge UP, 2017.

Nardone v. United States (1937). *Findlaw*. Thomson Reuters. 2017. Web. 27 Oct. 2017.

Solove, Daniel J., Rotenberg, Marc, and Paul M. Schwartz. *Privacy, Information, and Technology*. New York: Aspen Publishers, 2006.

Stephens, Otis H. and Richard A. Glen. *Unreasonable Searches and Seizures: Rights and Liberties Under the Law*. Santa Barbara: ABC-CLIO, 2006.

The FCC publishes official rules of "neutrality"

2016

The EU establishes the General Data Protection Regulation (GDPR), described as the strongest digital data privacy law in the world

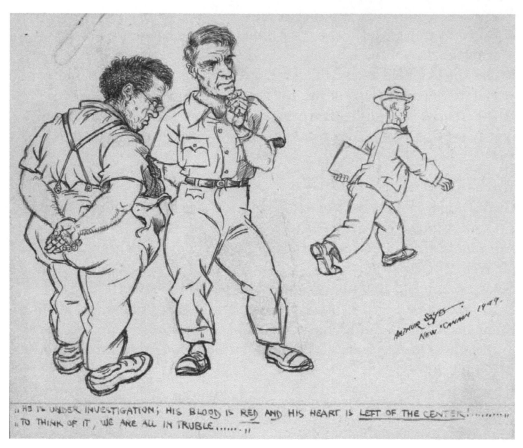

Artist Arthur Szyk spoke out against McCarthyism, noting that the rationale for suspicion—"red blood" and a "heart left of center"—was so broad as to implicate nearly every American of Communist sympathies.

2017

The "Vault 7" secrets, a leak of 9,000 CIA documents, reveal details of the CIA's attempts to break through encryption used by Internet

President Trump appoints Ajit Pai to head the FCC, who abolishes the FCC neutrality protections

Introduction

In the 1940s and 50s, the United States and the former Soviet Union were competing to become the world's leading military and economic power. Both nations used espionage to accomplish this goal, with American spies operating in Russia and attempting to steal military secrets, and Russian spies doing the same in the United States. High profile arrests involving Russian spy rings operating in the United States helped create a national panic centered around the fear that hidden communist spies could infiltrate and overthrow the American government. This fear, stoked by politicians for professional gain, by newspapers for profit, and by the military to justify spending, resulted in a national panic. The House Un-American Activities Committee (HUAC) was empowered to determine if new legislation was needed to address the threat of communist "subversion," but the committee exceeded this mandate and functioned as an independent court, investigating thousands of academics, political activists, and artists with suspected ties (often tenuous) to communism or socialism and doling out punishments in the form of loss of livelihood and public humiliation.

This chapter includes experts from the Supreme Court 1959 case of *Barenblatt v. United States*, in which the court was asked to interpret the legality of some of the committees' more controversial activities. The case involved a former academic, Lloyd Barenblatt, who had been called before the HUAC, and refused to divulge whether or not he belonged to the American Communist Party. Barenblatt had, thus, been charged with contempt for refusing to provide information, and argued that such a demand violated his First Amendment protections of free speech and free association. While, under normal circumstances, an American citizen cannot be forcibly made to reveal personal details

Congress debates whether or not to renew the controversial Section 702 FISA Amendment used to authorize NSA domestic intelligence operations since 2008

about his or her beliefs or associations, prosecutors argued that America was in a state of emergency and that communist subversion was an imminent threat to national security. The Supreme Court was, thus, tasked with determining whether the threat to national security posed by communist spies was sufficient to justify violating First Amendment protections.

Topics covered in this chapter include:
- The House Un-American Activities Committee
- U.S.–Russian relations
- The U.S. Bill of Rights
- First Amendment protections
- Freedom of Speech
- Freedom of Association
- Separation of Powers

This Chapter Discusses the Following Source Document:
Barenblatt v. United States, 360 U.S. 109 (1959)

Privacy and the Red Menace
Barenblatt v. United States (1959)

*When public men indulge themselves in abuse, when they
deny others a fair trial, when they resort to innuendo and
insinuation, to libel, scandal, and suspicion, then our
democratic society is outraged, and democracy is baffled.
It has no apparatus to deal with the boor, the liar, the lout,
and the antidemocrat in general*

—*Senator William Fulbright.*[10]

The Red Scare

From the 1940s to the mid-1960s, American society plunged into the
depths of a hysterical panic concerning the perceived threat of communism, both as a growing military, political force abroad and as a potentially insidious force growing *within* American society. The reasons for
this are complex and include the rapid growth of communist powers (the
Soviet Union and China) and the real, though greatly exaggerated, threat
of foreign espionage. The postwar communist panic is sometimes called
"McCarthyism," in recognition of the role of Senator Joseph McCarthy
of Wisconsin, a previously little-known junior senator who transformed
himself into the champion of America's anti-Communist movement, and
led a massive, state-sponsored investigation of the American people that
brought about one of the most oppressive periods in American history.

McCarthy was a relatively minor figure until, as news that the Soviet
Union had developed atomic weapons sent ripples of fear through the
American public, and as McCarthy faced a tough reelection campaign
with little in the way of public support, he seized the opportunity to pro-
pel himself to prominence. On February 9, 1950, McCarthy, delivering a
speech in Wheeling, West Virginia, made one of the most famous claims
of his controversial career:

1868 The 14th Amendment to the
U.S. Constitution guarantees all
citizens the right to due
process under the law

1890 Warren and Brandeis publish
"The Right to Privacy" in the
Harvard Law Review

———————   *While I cannot take the time to name all the men in the State Department who have been named as members of the Communist Party and members of a spy ring, I have here in my hand a list of 205.*[12]

Although McCarthy is widely viewed as a lone paranoid responsible for the widespread civil rights abuses of the red menace era, this is not the case. McCarthy didn't create the national panic, rather he was an opportunist who used the prevailing fear to his advantage. In the 1940s and 50s, the U.S. government knew, factually, that the Soviet Union had spies in the United States. Some high-profile spies had also been found hiding within the U.S. Communist Party. For instance, Elizabeth Bentley, a member of the U.S. Communist Party, was later revealed to have been the leader of a spy ring that delivered information to the Soviets before the war. Bentley turned herself in to the FBI in 1945 and gave the names of spies to the government.[13]

For those in the U.S. intelligence community, the existence of spies was no revelation. The United States had spies in Russia, as well as in many other parts of Europe. The espionage war had long existed as a secret, quiet battleground underlying the more public machinations of military powers and politicians. However, when the existence of communist spies and spy rings was revealed to the public, the American people sensed a frightening new threat, the idea that one of their own neighbors, workmates, or even old friends might secretly be a spy working for the Soviets. This had the effect of turning the American people against themselves. Fear and paranoia spread and many were culpable. Journalists fanned the flames to sell newspapers, while politicians stoked fears to promote military spending.

The situation might be familiar to those living in the twenty-first century, as the fear that seized the American people was not dissimilar from the

1923   *Meyer v. Nebraska* establishes that the 14th Amendment guarantees privileges of citizenship

1928   *Olmstead v. United States* rules that wiretapping is not a form of search and seizure defined by the 14th Amendment

twenty-first century terrorism panic in the United States. Then, as now, the American people were willing to tolerate or even embrace civil rights violations if they believed that such measures were needed to prevent an imminent threat to their safety and security. McCarthy was a propagandist who used the prevailing fears of the moment to advance his career and he did this by issuing inflammatory and captivating claims. He characterized the situation as an "all-out battle between communistic atheism and Christianity," and claimed that the goal was the overthrow of America. This "fake news" campaign seized on American patriotism, nationalism, and the motivation to defend religious convictions and McCarthy transformed himself from a largely ignored junior senator with few accomplishments who was almost certainly going to lose his reelection bid, to a minor celebrity with powers beyond that of any other legislator of the era.

Congress and the courts authorized McCarthy and a group of like-minded politicians to hold hearings to investigate the issue. The Constitution permits the legislature to hold hearings towards the purpose of deciding whether to create legislation to deal with a specific

AMERICAN PROPAGANDIST
Joseph Raymond McCarthy, born in Grand Chute, Wisconsin, earned a law degree and served as a circuit court judge in Wisconsin before attempting to win election as district attorney. Hoping that military service would enhance his career, McCarthy enlisted in the Marines, where he served as an intelligence officer advising pilots flying missions over Japan. McCarthy, in his later political career exaggerated his role in the military, calling himself "tail-gunner Joe" and claiming to have "fired more bullets than any marine in history" during his engagements with the enemy. Utilizing his war record, McCarthy was elected to the Senate in 1946 by a narrow margin, claiming, during the campaign (and without evidence), that his opponent had been supported by communists.[11]

1934

The Federal Communications Commission (FCC) is established under the Federal Communications Act (FCA)

1942

Goldman v. United States rules that using electronic listening devices does not violate the 14th Amendment

"Don't Fall for Enemy Propaganda" poster by Jack Betts.
(Photo by Swim Ink 2, LLC/CORBIS/Corbis via Getty Images)

1945   The National Security Agency secretly creates Project SHAMROCK

1950   Senator Joseph McCarthy delivers a shocking speech claiming that more than 200 communist spies have infiltrated the U.S. government

issue. McCarthy thus used the House Un-American Activities Committee (HUAC), established in 1938 to investigate the German-American Bund, which was believed to have ties to Hitler's Nazi Party. The committee called hundreds of Americans to testify in a series of controversial hearings, including academics, intellectuals, actors, writers, artists, and government employees, accused of having ties to Communist organizations, governments, or of being connected to alleged spy rings. Individuals called before the committee were given the opportunity to cooperate, which meant identifying other individuals for the committee to investigate, or were threatened with a "blacklist," which meant that the committee would use its influence to prevent the individual from holding a job or participating in other rights of citizenship.[14]

Arguably, the HUAC violated constitutional law by essentially functioning as a branch of the justice department, rather than a tool for legislative deliberation. By punishing individuals through public exposure and loss of livelihood, the HUAC also violated the Due Process clause of the Constitution guaranteeing American citizens the right to judicial protections. Furthermore, by essentially making membership in the U.S. Communist Party a crime, the HUAC violated constitutional freedoms of speech, religion, and assembly.

Such methods were believed to be necessary, in McCarthy's view, because the communist party was not a legitimate political party, but rather, a tool for the clandestine takeover of America. This was not true, nor was it even remotely true that most members of the U.S. Communist Party sought to overthrow the government, nor was it true that most Americans who were interested in communism had been involved, in any way, with any espionage activity. None of these claims were accurate and none of these claims could be corroborated and yet McCarthy and allies made all of these claims and set about identifying and punishing not only those who were members of the communist party, but any who had even the

1951   *Dennis v. United States* rules that government limits to speech is legal only to prevent a threat to public safety or security

1959   *Barenblatt v. United States* rules that it's legal to order people to reveal personal details if national threat is perceived

most remote ties to communism and socialism. This included academics and intellectuals who studied communist philosophy, individuals who had relatives in the Soviet Union or whose families had migrated from communist countries.

In 1950, the same year that McCarthy delivered his fiery West Virginia speech, Senator Margaret Chase Smith of Maine stood up on the Senate floor to speak out about the abuses committed by McCarthy and the HUAC:[15]

Those of us who shout the loudest about Americanism in making character assassinations are all too frequently those who, by our own words and acts, ignore some of the basic principles of Americanism:

- *The right to criticize.*
- *The right to hold unpopular beliefs.*
- *The right to protest.*
- *The right of independent thought.*

The exercise of these rights should not cost one single American citizen his reputation or his right to a livelihood nor should he be in danger of losing his reputation or livelihood merely because he happens to know someone who holds unpopular beliefs. Who of us does not? Otherwise none of us could call our souls our own. Otherwise thought control would have set in.[16]

1965   *Griswold v. CT* rules in favor of married couples' right to privacy

1967   *Katz v. United States* rules wiretaps a form of search and seizure

Willis Ware of RAND Corporation writes *Security and Privacy in Computer*

AMERICANS......
DON'T PATRONIZE REDS !!!!

——•——

YOU CAN DRIVE THE REDS OUT OF TELEVISION, RADIO AND HOLLYWOOD.....

THIS TRACT WILL TELL YOU HOW.

WHY WE MUST DRIVE THEM OUT:

1) The REDS have made our Screen, Radio and TV Moscow's most effective Fifth Column in America . . . 2) The REDS of Hollywood and Broadway have always been the chief financial support of Communist propaganda in America . . . 3) OUR OWN FILMS, made by RED Producers, Directors, Writers and STARS, are being used by Moscow in ASIA, Africa, the Balkans and throughout Europe to create hatred of America . . . 4) RIGHT NOW films are being made to craftily glorify MARXISM, UNESCO and ONE-WORLDISM . . . and via your **TV Set** they are being piped into your Living Room—and are poisoning the minds of your children under your very eyes ! ! !

So REMEMBER — If you patronize a Film made by RED Producers, Writers, Stars and STUDIOS you are aiding and abetting COMMUNISM ... . . . every time you permit REDS to come into your Living Room VIA YOUR TV SET you are helping MOSCOW and the INTERNATIONALISTS to destroy America ! ! !

Typical U.S. anticommunist literature of the 1950s, specifically addressing the entertainment industry.

1968   The Omnibus Crime Control Act holds that police needed to obtain a warrant before engaging in wire-

1969   Joseph Licklider creates the Advanced Research Projects Agency Network (ARPANET), which was

Senator Smith was lauded for her bravery and conviction in the papers and by those senators and representatives who, like her, felt the effort to uncover Communist subversion had gone too far.[17] Gradually, more and more public figures spoke out against the HUAC and the mindset behind the public panic. McCarthy was discredited as investigations found that he did not have, and never had, a list of "card-carrying" communists working for the government and that many of his other claims had been equally fabricated. Recognizing that the threat emerged from within their own party, a group of Republican senators, including Smith, were responsible for bringing McCarthy's reign to an end. Smith and her colleagues recommended, and eventually succeeded in having McCarthy censured within the Senate. McCarthy accused his critics of subversion and cowardice in the face of the communist threat, but these accusations did little. McCarthy was censured in 1954, largely stripped of his power and prominence.

BARENBLATT v. UNITED STATES

In the 1959 case of *Barenblatt v. United States*, the Warren Court was asked to review the constitutional legality of the investigations conducted by the HUAC under McCarthy. Specifically, former graduate student Lloyd Barenblatt had been convicted of contempt after Barenblatt refused to divulge information to the committee regarding his alleged membership in the Communist Party. Barenblatt's attorneys attempted to overturn the conviction and argued that the committee's actions violated Barenblatt's First Amendment rights to study, discuss, and associate with individuals interested in Communist philosophy or history.

A majority of the court ruled to uphold Barenblatt's contempt conviction, arguing, in general, that the need to protect national security outweighed Barenblatt's right to free speech and expression and his right to privacy in belief and association. In writing the court's majority opinion, Justice Marshall Harlan II explained that, within the scope of the powers granted

1971   The Pentagon Papers leaks from the press raise the issue of the Freedom of the Press versus the privacy of the government to conceal information about national security operations

1972   *Eisenstadt v. Baird* rules that the right to privacy applies to individuals

to the HUAC, the committee's actions did not violate constitutional guarantees and thus Barenblatt's conviction was lawful and constitutional.

BARENBLATT V. UNITED STATES
Source Document Excerpt

The power of inquiry has been employed by Congress throughout our history, over the whole range of the national interests concerning which Congress might legislate or decide upon due investigation not to legislate; it has similarly been utilized in determining what to appropriate from the national purse, or whether to appropriate. The scope of the power of inquiry, in short, is as penetrating and far-reaching as the potential power to enact and appropriate under the Constitution.

The decision of the court hinged on the fact that members of the court had embraced the widespread belief that Communists were seeking to overthrow the American government. Although potentially true of some radical Communist organizations and groups, such a goal could not be attributed to the ideology of communism as a whole, nor to the majority of those who studied the philosophical roots of Communist, Marxist, and Socialist philosophy. Nevertheless, for a majority of the Supreme Court in 1959, such claims had been established as fact in the ideological war of the era:

Barenblatt v. United States
continued

The first question is whether this investigation was related to a valid legislative purpose, for Congress may not constitutionally require an individual to disclose his political relationships or other private affairs except in relation to such a purpose.

That Congress has wide power to legislate in the field of Communist activity in this Country, and to conduct appropriate investigations

1974

The Watergate Scandal results in the revelation that the CIA had been conducting widespread surveillance of American dissidents and foreign leaders without judicial oversight

The Privacy Act is established

Barenblatt v. United States
continued

in aid thereof, is hardly debatable. The existence of such power has never been questioned by this Court, and it is sufficient to say, without particularization, that Congress has enacted or considered in this field a wide range of legislative measures, not a few of which have stemmed from recommendations of the very Committee whose actions have been drawn in question here. In the last analysis this power rests on the right of self-preservation, "the ultimate value of any society." Justification for its exercise in turn rests on the long and widely accepted view that the tenets of the Communist Party include the ultimate overthrow of the Government of the United States by force and violence, a view which has been given formal expression by the Congress.

On these premises, this Court in its constitutional adjudications has consistently refused to view the Communist Party as an ordinary political party, and has upheld federal legislation aimed at the Communist problem which in a different context would certainly have raised constitutional issues of the gravest character. On the same premises this Court has upheld under the Fourteenth Amendment state legislation requiring those occupying or seeking public office to disclaim knowing membership in any organization advocating overthrow of the Government by force and violence, which legislation none can avoid seeing was aimed at membership in the Communist Party. Similarly, in other areas, this Court has recognized the close nexus between the Communist Party and violent overthrow of government. To suggest that because the Communist Party may also sponsor peaceable political reforms the constitutional issues before us should now be judged as if that Party were just an ordinary political party from the standpoint of national security, is to ask this Court to blind itself to world affairs which have determined the whole course of our national policy since the close of World War II...

The dissenting opinion in the case was written by Justice Hugo Black, who concurred with Chief Justice Warren and Justice William O. Douglas. Black objected to the concept that the First Amendment protections afforded to American citizens should be judged on a case-by-case basis against the needs or desires of the state and argued that such an approach, subordinating civil liberties to state goals, was itself a threat to the fundamental values of the nation:

1975 Senator Frank Church leads a series of hearings about the secret NSA SHAMROCK operation involved intercepting communications from American citizens

1978 Congress passes the 1978 FISA Act

continued

The First Amendment says in no equivocal language that Congress shall pass no law abridging freedom of speech, press, assembly or petition. The activities of this Committee, authorized by Congress, do precisely that, through exposure, obloquy and public scorn. The Court does not really deny this fact but relies on a combination of three reasons for permitting the infringement: (A) The notion that despite the First Amendment's command Congress can abridge speech and association if this Court decides that the governmental interest in abridging speech is greater than an individual's interest in exercising that freedom, (B) the Government's right to "preserve itself," (C) the fact that the Committee is only after Communists or suspected Communists in this investigation.

I do not agree that laws directly abridging First Amendment freedoms can be justified by a congressional or judicial balancing process. There are, of course, cases suggesting that a law which primarily regulates conduct but which might also indirectly affect speech can be upheld if the effect on speech is minor in relation to the need for control of the conduct. With these cases I agree. Typical of them are *Cantwell v. Connecticut*, and *Schneider v. Irvington*. Both of these involved the right of a city to control its streets. In *Cantwell*, a man had been convicted of breach of the peace for playing a phonograph on the street. He defended on the ground that he was disseminating religious views and could not, therefore, be stopped. We upheld his defense, but in so doing we pointed out that the city did have substantial power over conduct on the streets even where this power might to some extent affect speech. A State, we said, might "by general and non-discriminatory legislation regulate the times, the places, and the manner of soliciting upon its streets and holding meetings thereon." But even such laws governing conduct, we emphasized, must be tested, though only by a balancing process, if they indirectly affect ideas. On one side of the balance, we pointed out, is the interest of the United States in seeing that its fundamental law protecting freedom of communication is not abridged; on the other the obvious interest of the State to regulate conduct within its boundaries. In *Cantwell* we held that the need to control the streets could not justify the restriction made on speech. We stressed the fact that where a man had a right to be on a street, "he had a right peacefully to impart his views to others." Similar views were expressed in Schneider, which concerned ordinances prohibiting the distribution of handbills to prevent littering. We forbade application of such ordinances when they affected literature designed to spread ideas. There were other ways, we said, to protect the city from

Barenblatt v. United States
continued

littering which would not sacrifice the right of the people to be informed. In so holding, we, of course, found it necessary to "weigh the circumstances." But we did not in Schneider, any more than in *Cantwell*, even remotely suggest that a law directly aimed at curtailing speech and political persuasion could be saved through a balancing process. Neither these cases, nor any others, can be read as allowing legislative bodies to pass laws abridging freedom of speech, press and association merely because of hostility to views peacefully expressed in a place where the speaker had a right to be. Rule XI, on its face and as here applied, since it attempts inquiry into beliefs, not action—ideas and associations, not conduct—does just that.

To apply the Court's balancing test under such circumstances is to read the First Amendment to say "Congress shall pass no law abridging freedom of speech, press, assembly and petition, unless Congress and the Supreme Court reach the joint conclusion that on balance the interest of the Government in stifling these freedoms is greater than the interest of the people in having them exercised." This is closely akin to the notion that neither the First Amendment nor any other provision of the Bill of Rights should be enforced unless the Court believes it is reasonable to do so. Not only does this violate the genius of our written Constitution, but it runs expressly counter to the injunction to Court and Congress made by Madison when he introduced the Bill of Rights. "If they [the first ten amendments] are incorporated into the Constitution, independent tribunals of justice will consider themselves in a peculiar manner the guardians of those rights; they will be an impenetrable bulwark against every assumption of power in the Legislative or Executive; they will be naturally led to resist every encroachment upon rights expressly stipulated for in the Constitution by the declaration of rights." Unless we return to this view of our judicial function, unless we once again accept the notion that the Bill of Rights means what it says and that this Court must enforce that meaning, I am of the opinion that our great charter of liberty will be more honored in the breach than in the observance.

But even assuming what I cannot assume, that some balancing is proper in this case, I feel that the Court after stating the test ignores it completely. At most it balances the right of the Government to preserve itself, against Barenblatt's right to refrain from revealing Communist affiliations. Such a balance, however, mistakes the

1994 Netscape creates the "cookie" allowing computers to monitor Internet users

2001 The September 11 terrorist attacks result in Congress authorizing the Bush Administration to utilize military methods to combat terrorism

continued

factors to be weighed. In the first place, it completely leaves out the real interest in Barenblatt's silence, the interest of the people as a whole in being able to join organizations, advocate causes and make political "mistakes" without later being subjected to governmental penalties for having dared to think for themselves. It is this right, the right to err politically, which keeps us strong as a Nation. For no number of laws against communism can have as much effect as the personal conviction which comes from having heard its arguments and rejected them, or from having once accepted its tenets and later recognized their worthlessness. Instead, the obloquy which results from investigations such as this not only stifles "mistakes" but prevents all but the most courageous from hazarding any views which might at some later time become disfavored. This result, whose importance cannot be overestimated, is doubly crucial when it affects the universities, on which we must largely rely for the experimentation and development of new ideas essential to our country's welfare. It is these interests of society, rather than Barenblatt's own right to silence, which I think the Court should put on the balance against the demands of the Government, if any balancing process is to be tolerated. Instead they are not mentioned, while on the other side the demands of the Government are vastly overstated and called "self preservation." It is admitted that this Committee can only seek information for the purpose of suggesting laws, and that Congress' power to make laws in the realm of speech and association is quite limited, even on the Court's test. Its interest in making such laws in the field of education, primarily a state function, is clearly narrower still. Yet the Court styles this attenuated interest self-preservation and allows it to overcome the need our country has to let us all think, speak, and associate politically as we like and without fear of reprisal. Such a result reduces "balancing" to a mere play on words and is completely inconsistent with the rules this Court has previously given for applying a "balancing test," where it is proper: "[T]he courts should be astute to examine the effect of the challenged legislation. Mere legislative preferences or beliefs . . . may well support regulation directed at other personal activities, but be insufficient to justify such as diminishes the exercise of rights so vital to the maintenance of democratic institutions."

(B) Moreover, I cannot agree with the Court's notion that First Amendment freedoms must be abridged in order to "preserve" our country. That notion rests on the unarticulated premise that this Nation's security hangs upon its power to punish people because of what they think, speak or write about, or because of those with whom they

The Bush administration secretly authorizes the President's Surveillance Program (PSP), utilizing E.O. 12333

The U.S. PATRIOT Act alters existing laws to facilitate better communication between the state's intelligence branches in the effort to combat terrorism

The Transportation Security Administration (TSA) is established, creating the "No Fly" and "Selectee" lists that limit the right to travel on airplanes in the United States

Cover to the propaganda comic book, "Is This Tomorrow," 1947.

2005

The PATRIOT Act was reauthorized without substantial changes as Congress favors security concerns over warnings that the law creates the potential for civil liberties violations

The *New York Times* publishes articles resulting from leaks revealing the secret President's Surveillance Program (PSP) established by the Bush administration

Barenblatt v. United States
continued

associate for political purposes. The Government, in its brief, virtually admits this position when it speaks of the "communication of unlawful ideas." I challenge this premise, and deny that ideas can be proscribed under our Constitution. I agree that despotic governments cannot exist without stifling the voice of opposition to their oppressive practices. The First Amendment means to me, however, that the only constitutional way our Government can preserve itself is to leave its people the fullest possible freedom to praise, criticize or discuss, as they see fit, all governmental policies and to suggest, if they desire, that even its most fundamental postulates are bad and should be changed; "Therein lies the security of the Republic, the very foundation of constitutional government." On that premise this land was created, and on that premise it has grown to greatness. Our Constitution assumes that the common sense of the people and their attachment to our country will enable them, after free discussion, to withstand ideas that are wrong. To say that our patriotism must be protected against false ideas by means other than these is, I think, to make a baseless charge. Unless we can rely on these qualities—if, in short, we begin to punish speech—we cannot honestly proclaim ourselves to be a free Nation and we have lost what the

Founders of this land risked their lives and their sacred honor to defend.

(C) The Court implies, however, that the ordinary rules and requirements of the Constitution do not apply because the Committee is merely after Communists and they do not constitute a political party but only a criminal gang. "[T]he long and widely accepted view," the Court says, is "that the tenets of the Communist Party include the ultimate overthrow of the Government of the United States by force and violence." This justifies the investigation undertaken. By accepting this charge and allowing it to support treatment of the Communist Party and its members which would violate the Constitution if applied to other groups, the Court, in effect, declares that Party outlawed. It has been only a few years since there was a practically unanimous feeling throughout the country and in our courts that this could not be done in our free land. Of course it has always been recognized that members of the Party who, either individually or in combination, commit acts in violation of valid laws can be prosecuted. But the Party as a whole and innocent members of it could not be attainted merely because it had some illegal aims and because some of its members were lawbreakers. Thus in *De Jonge v. Oregon* (1937), on stipulated facts

2007 The Bush Administration plans to make data taken from spy satellites available to law enforcement to be used to conduct domestic surveillance

2008 Congress passes Section 702, or the FISA Amendment Act, which is used to permit a massive NSA and CIA domestic surveillance program

Barenblatt v. United States
continued

that the Communist Party advocated criminal syndicalism—"crime, physical violence, sabotage or any unlawful acts or methods as a means of accomplishing or effecting industrial or political change or revolution"—a unanimous Court, speaking through Chief Justice Hughes, held that a Communist addressing a Communist rally could be found guilty of no offense so long as no violence or crime was urged at the meeting. The Court absolutely refused to concede that either De Jonge or the Communist Party forfeited the protections of the First and Fourteenth Amendments because one of the Party's purposes was to effect a violent change of government.

Later, in 1948, when various bills were proposed in the House and Senate to handicap or outlaw the Communist Party, leaders of the Bar who had been asked to give their views rose up to contest the constitutionality of the measures. The late Charles Evans Hughes, Jr., questioned the validity under both the First and Fifth Amendments of one of these bills, which in effect outlawed the Party. The late John W. Davis attacked it as lacking an ascertainable standard of guilt under many of this Court's cases. And the Attorney General of the United States not only indicated that such a measure would be unconstitutional but

declared it to be unwise even if valid. He buttressed his position by citing a statement by J. Edgar Hoover, Director of the Federal Bureau of Investigation, and the declaration of this Court in *West Virginia Board of Education v. Barnette*, that:

Even the proponent of the bill disclaimed any aim to outlaw the Communist Party and pointed out the "disadvantages" of such a move by stating that "the Communist Party was illegal and outlawed in Russia when it took over control of the Soviet Union." Again, when the Attorney General testified on a proposal to bar the Communist Party from the ballot he said, "an organized group, whether you call it political or not, could hardly be barred from the ballot without jeopardizing the constitutional guarantees of all other political groups and parties."

All these statements indicate quite clearly that no matter how often or how quickly we repeat the claim that the Communist Party is not a political party, we cannot outlaw it, as a group, without endangering the liberty of all of us. The reason is not hard to find, for mixed among those aims of communism which are illegal are perfectly normal political and social goals. And muddled with its revolutionary tenets is a drive to achieve power through the ballot, if

2012 The Obama Administration proposes a Consumer Privacy Bill of Rights guaranteeing individuals the right to greater control over the use of their digital data

2013 The *Guardian* and the *Washington Post* publish the first series of articles derived from leaked NSA and CIA documents delivered by Edward Snowden

continued

it can be done. These things necessarily make it a political party whatever other, illegal, aims it may have. Significantly until recently the Communist Party was on the ballot in many States. When that was so, many Communists undoubtedly hoped to accomplish its lawful goals through support of Communist candidates. Even now some such may still remain. To attribute to them, and to those who have left the Party, the taint of the group is to ignore both our traditions that guilt like belief is "personal and not a matter of mere association" and the obvious fact that "men adhering to a political party or other organization notoriously do not subscribe unqualifiedly to all of its platforms or asserted principles."

The fact is that once we allow any group which has some political aims or ideas to be driven from the ballot and from the battle for men's mind because some of its members are bad and some of its tenets are illegal, no group is safe. Today we deal with Communists or suspected Communists. In 1920, instead, the New York Assembly suspended duly elected legislators on the ground that, being Socialists, they were disloyal to the country's principles. In the 1830s the Masons were hunted as outlaws and subversives, and abolitionists were considered revolutionaries of the most dangerous kind in both North and South. Earlier still, at the time of the universally unlamented alien and sedition laws, Thomas Jefferson's party was attacked and its members were derisively called "Jacobins." Fisher Ames described the party as a "French faction" guilty of "subversion" and "officered, regimented and formed to subordination." Its members, he claimed, intended to "take arms against the laws as soon as they dare." History should teach us then, that in times of high emotional excitement minority parties and groups which advocate extremely unpopular social or governmental innovations will always be typed as criminal gangs and attempts will always be made to drive them out. It was knowledge of this fact, and of its great dangers, that caused the Founders of our land to enact the First Amendment as a guarantee that neither Congress nor the people would do anything to hinder or destroy the capacity of individuals and groups to seek converts and votes for any cause, however radical or unpalatable their principles might seem under the accepted notions of the time. Whatever the States were left free to do, the First Amendment sought to leave Congress devoid of any kind or quality of power to direct any type of national laws against the freedom of individuals to think what they please, advocate whatever policy they choose, and join with others to bring about the social, religious, political and governmental changes which seem best to them.

The Senate Judiciary committee holds hearings to determine if the executive surveillance operations carried out under the PATRIOT Act were a violation of constitutional law

Snowden leaks reveal that the NSA and CIA had been attempting to force corporations to provide a backdoor to encryption systems that would allow federal agents to bypass consumer encryption

Barenblatt v. United States
continued

Today's holding, in my judgment, marks another major step in the progressively increasing retreat from the safeguards of the First Amendment.

It is, sadly, no answer to say that this Court will not allow the trend to overwhelm us; that today's holding will be strictly confined to "Communists," as the Court's language implies. This decision can no more be contained than could the holding in *American Communications Assn. v. Douds*. In that case the Court sustained as an exercise of the commerce power an Act which required labor union officials to take an oath that they were not members of the Communist Party. The Court rejected the idea that the *Douds* holding meant that the Party and all

its members could be attainted because of their Communist beliefs. It went to great lengths to explain that the Act held valid "touches only a relative handful of persons, leaving the great majority of persons of the identified affiliations and beliefs completely free from restraint." "[W]hile this Court sits," the Court proclaimed, no wholesale proscription of Communists or their Party can occur. I dissented and said:

"Under such circumstances, restrictions imposed on proscribed groups are seldom static, even though the rate of expansion may not move in geometric progression from discrimination to arm-band to ghetto and worse. Thus, I cannot regard the Court's holding as one which merely bars Communists from holding union office and nothing more. For its reasoning would apply just as forcibly to statutes barring Communists and their respective sympathizers from election to political office, mere membership in unions, and in fact from getting or holding any job whereby they could earn a living."

My prediction was all too accurate. Today, Communists or suspected Communists have been denied an opportunity to work as government employees, lawyers, doctors, teachers, pharmacists, veterinarians, subway

> 66
>
> *If there is any fixed star in our constitutional constellation, it is that no official, high or petty, can prescribe what shall be orthodox in politics, nationalism, religion, or other matters of opinion or force citizens to confess by word or act their faith therein.*
>
> 99

2015

| Terrorist attacks in France reignite fears of domestic terrorist violence | The PATRIOT Act is replaced by the USA Freedom Act | Federal Courts order Apple, Inc. to create a new operation system that would enable federal investigators to bypass security on an iPhone. |

continued

conductors, industrial workers and in just about any other job. In today's holding they are singled out and, as a class, are subjected to inquisitions which the Court suggests would be unconstitutional but for the fact of "Communism."

Nevertheless, this Court still sits!

Justice Hugo Black went on to express his skepticism about the goals and function of the committee in general, viewing it as an organ for punishment, rather than a legitimate tool to discover and determine avenues for legislation.

Barenblatt v. United States
continued

Finally, I think Barenblatt's conviction violates the Constitution because the chief aim, purpose and practice of the House Un-American Activities Committee, as disclosed by its many reports, is to try witnesses and punish them because they are or have been Communists or because they refuse to admit or deny Communist affiliations. The punishment imposed is generally punishment by humiliation and public shame. There is nothing strange or novel about this kind of punishment. It is, in fact, one of the oldest forms of governmental punishment known to mankind; branding, the pillory, ostracism and subjection to public hatred being but a few examples of it.

To accomplish this kind of result, the Committee has called witnesses who are suspected of Communist affiliation, has subjected them to severe questioning, and has insisted that each tell the name of every person he has ever known at any time to have been a Communist, and, if possible, to give the addresses and occupations of the people named. These names are then indexed, published, and reported to Congress, and often to the press. The same technique is employed to cripple the job opportunities of those who strongly criticize the Committee or take other actions it deems undesirable.

The FCC publishes official rules of "neutrality"

2016

The EU establishes the General Data Protection Regulation (GDPR), described as the strongest digital data privacy law in the world

Though there are few specific references to a legal right to privacy in the Barenblatt trial, privacy was a core issue in the case. Individuals called before HUAC were compelled to reveal information about their beliefs, political views, and associations, and thus were essentially required, by law, to reveal private details about their lives. Further, the threat of punishment in the form of public humiliation, ridicule, loss of livelihood, and loss of public stature, was used to compel individuals called before HUAC to either reveal such details of their lives, history, and associations, thus constituting a fundamental violation of the principles used to justify the right to privacy on constitutional grounds. By ruling in favor of the governmental right to mitigate constitutional freedoms towards the goal of protecting security, the court established a controversial precedent that future legislators and jurists sought to undo towards reestablishing the right to privacy and civil liberties protections and this became the legacy of the Warren Court through the 1960s.

There were few opinion polls conducted in the McCarthy era to suggest how the public felt about McCarthy and the HUAC directly. A poll in 1951, by Gallup, found that only about a third of Americans knew who McCarthy was. This is after nearly a year of news covering him, following his 1950 speech and subsequent rise to become the face of the anti-communist effort. Those who had heard of McCarthy in 1951 were divided as to his favorability, with a small majority viewing him as unfavorable. Even at the height of McCarthy's celebrity, only 47 percent of Americans viewed him favorably.

It seems that public support was not the chief pillar of McCarthy's influence, but rather it was the panic that McCarthy inspired in the popular press, among academics and intellectuals, and among other legislators that helped disseminate the impression, within the public, that the issues McCarthy so passionately championed were worth more than idle consideration. This happened because McCarthy helped transform an underly-

2017   The "Vault 7" secrets, a leak of 9,000 CIA documents, reveal details of the CIA's attempts to break through encryption used by Internet

President Trump appoints Ajit Pai to head the FCC, who abolishes the FCC neutrality protections

ing fear into an attack on dissidence and leftist political/academic activity. Under threat, this facet of America spoke out, but the resulting outcry only made it appear as if McCarthy's assertions of the domestic threat were more real.

In the book *Joseph McCarthy: Reexamining the Life and Legacy of America's Most Hated Senator*, author Arthur Herman argues:

> *"It was those in the middle—people who might have gone to high school but not to college, who had to earn a living on their own without the benefit of a union or a professional degree, who were informed if not particularly well about what is happening in the world and in Korea—who were willing to give McCarthy the benefit of a doubt and believed he had found an issue, domestic communism, of genuine concern to them."*[18]

American opinions on communism, on the other hand, are more clearly defined in the polls of the era. In a series of Gallup Polls, 88 percent of Americans reported unfavorable views on communism in 1953, with a peak of 91 percent expressing this view in late 1954. The HUAC campaign against domestic communism did, it seems, result in a public opinion victory, with more and more Americans viewing communism and Russia with suspicion and skepticism thanks to the ongoing crusade. The image of communism would be rehabilitated through the 1960s and 70s, with only 29 percent viewing communism unfavorably in 1973, whereas the majority of Americans (55 percent) had shifted towards a more nuanced view, giving communism "mixed" reviews.[19]

The United States communist and socialist movements started in the early twentieth century. In sharp contrast to the authoritarian state-sponsored communism of China and the Russian Federation, the U.S. com-

Congress debates whether or not to renew the controversial Section 702 FISA Amendment used to authorize NSA domestic intelligence operations since 2008

munist and socialist movements were worker's rights movements, lobbying for unions and wage increases at the lowest levels of the nation's income spectrum. Though vilified in the 1940s and 50s, American communists and socialists struggled for years to call attention to the inherent inequities of America's capitalist system in which hierarchies of privilege and power create and maintain gross income inequality. In this way, the communist and socialist movements in America presaged the populist democratic movement represented by politicians like Bernie Sanders in the twenty-first century. By championing the rights of the marginalized, the U.S. Communist Party drew support from African Americans and the working class. Even as many Americans had come to view the U.S. Communist Party as a haven for anti-American subversives, the party and the ideals of communism and socialism, continued to appeal to many marginalized Americans and this played a role in the social transformation of the 1960s.

1788 State legislatures ratify the U.S. Constitution, establishing the basic precedent for all future constitutional law

1791 The U.S. Congress ratifies the Bill of Rights, creating the first 10 amendments to the United States Constitution

CONCLUSION

A majority of the 1959 Supreme Court justices felt that communism posed a legitimate, imminent threat to national security and, thus, the state had the right to violate First Amendment protections to address the issue. Though the court ruled to uphold Barenblatt's conviction, in subsequent decades a majority of Americans came to embrace the view that the government had gone too far in abridging personal freedoms to combat this alleged threat. The dissenting opinions in the case, delivered by Justices Earl Warren and Hugo Black respectively, were the most lasting remnants, presenting impassioned arguments on the importance of the First Amendment as a core American value and on the inherent danger posed when any one branch of the government violates its constitutional mandate, upending the checks and balances of the Constitution. Fear of radical Islamic terrorism in the twenty-first century has motivated legislative, intelligence agency, and military measures that, like HUAC activities in the 1950s, raise the issue of when and whether a threat to national security can justify violating constitutional rights. The 1959 case, and arguments on both sides, are, therefore, still vitally relevant in the effort to balance the needs and goals of the state against the rights and freedoms of the people.

1868 The 14th Amendment to the U.S. Constitution guarantees all citizens the right to due process under the law

1890 Warren and Brandeis publish "The Right to Privacy" in the *Harvard Law Review*

DISCUSSION QUESTIONS

- Do you agree with the court's ruling in *Barenblatt*, or with the dissenting opinion? Explain why.
- Should American citizens have the right to access information about or produced by radical terrorist organizations? Should the government be allowed to monitor persons who choose to do so?
- Is "Freedom of Association" an important right? Why or why not?
- Should the government be allowed to force an individual to reveal his or her personal feelings on a political issue? Why or why not?

Works Used

"A Declaration of Conscience." *United States Senate*. Senate Information Office. 2017. Web. 24 Oct. 2017.

Belknap, Michal R. *The Supreme Court under Earl Warren, 1953–1969*. Columbia, SC: U of South Carolina P, 2005.

"'Communists in Government Service,' McCarthy Says." *United States Senate*. Senate Information Office. 2017. Web. 24 Oct. 2017.

Herman, Arthur. *Joseph McCarthy: Reexamining the Life and Legacy of America's Most Hated Senator*. New York: The Free Press, 2000.

"Joseph R. McCarthy (1908–1957)." *George Washington University*. The Eleanor Roosevelt Papers. 2006. Web. 31 Oct. 2017.

Kingsbury, Alex. "Declassified Documents Reveal KGB Spies in the U.S." *US News*. U.S. News and World Report. July 17, 2009. Web. 5 Nov. 2017.

"Margaret Chase Smith—Declaration of Conscience." *United States Senate*. June 1, 1950. Web. 1 Nov. 2017.

"Senator J. William Fulbright, remarks in the senate." *Congressional Record*. U.S. Congress. Feb. 2, 1954. Web. 31 Oct. 2017.

1923   *Meyer v. Nebraska* establishes that the 14th Amendment guarantees privileges of citizenship

1928   *Olmstead v. United States* rules that wiretapping is not a form of search and seizure defined by the 14th Amendment

Smith, Tom W. "The Polls: American Attitudes Toward the Soviet
    Union and Communism." *Public Opinion Quarterly*. Vol. 47. No. 2.
    1983. Web. 6 Nov. 2017.
Wall, Wendy. "Anti-Communism in the 1950s." *Gilder Lehrman*. The
    Gilder Lehrman Institute of American History. 2007. Web. 24 Oct.
    2017.

1934 | The Federal Communications Commission (FCC) is established under the Federal Communications Act (FCA)

1942 | *Goldman v. United States* rules that using electronic listening devices does not violate the 14th Amendment

Estelle Griswold, executive director of the Planned Parenthood League, standing outside a center in April, 1963.

Introduction

This chapter introduces the constitutional right to privacy through the Supreme Court case of *Griswold v. Connecticut* in 1965, in which the court was asked to weigh in on the legality of a controversial Connecticut law that outlawed both birth control and the act of providing information about birth control to another individual. Although the case became a major milestone in privacy law, it was also about personal liberty and the degree to which the government has the right to dictate personal and private behavior. In the case, the court ruled against the Connecticut law, with Chief Justice Earl Warren, in his landmark opinion on the case, arguing that a combination of six different amendments (First, Third, Fourth, Fifth, Ninth, and Fourteenth) collectively constituted a legal, constitutional right to privacy. This decision had wide-reaching consequences, both establishing precedent for constitutional guarantees regarding privacy from governmental intrusion, and linking privacy rights with personal liberties in such a way that the case was essentially the beginning of the end for laws that prohibited various types of consensual sexual behavior among adults.

This chapter also explores how the landmark *Griswold* decision, marking a substantive shift towards privacy rights in the court, was later applied to other privacy issues, and specifically the perennial controversy over the constitutionality of police and federal surveillance. Excerpts from the 1967 case of *Katz v. United States*, in which government agents wiretapped a public telephone in an investigation of illegal gambling activities, demonstrate how the court's evolving focus on personal liberty shifted the onus to the state to demonstrate justification and appropriate oversight before potentially violating the constitutional right to privacy.

1951

Dennis v. United States rules that government limits to speech is legal only to prevent a threat to public safety or security

1959

Barenblatt v. United States rules that it's legal to order people to reveal personal details if national threat is perceived

Topics covered in this chapter include:
- Wiretapping and government surveillance
- The Fourth Amendment
- Technology and privacy rights
- Supreme Court cases on privacy rights
- Constitutional protection of privacy
- Marital right to privacy
- Personal liberties

This Chapter Discusses the Following Source Documents:
Griswold v. Connecticut, 381 U.S. 479 (1965)
Katz v. United States, 389 U.S. 347 (1967)
Eisenstadt v. Baird, 405 U.S. 438 (1972)

The Constitutional Right to Privacy
Griswold v. Connecticut (1965) and
Katz v. United States (1967)

Every society around the world, whether capitalist, communist, socialist, authoritarian, democratic, or theocratic, functions according to hierarchies of power that involve elite and subordinate classes. The United States is a capitalist nation that formed from an initial population of white Europeans and Christians. From this substrate, American society evolved to embrace a hierarchy of power that placed wealthy, white, Christian men at the top position. Below this upper echelon, a variety of marginalized subclasses developed, including the poor, members of racial minorities, and women. The most tumultuous periods in the history of a society occur when existing hierarchies are challenged or upended. The tumultuous 1950s, 60s, and 70s were marked by periodic challenges to the status-quo in American culture. The Civil Rights movement, the Women's Rights movement, the Anti-War movement, and the Worker's Rights movement occurred as a new generation was entering adulthood and as the fundamental values of American society were shifting. Reacting to a threat, those in society's elite participated in a sustained effort to repress the emerging youth and leftist movements of the era, and, though successful in some ways, this ultimately resulted in a gradual erosion of the relationship between the government and the people.

In the 1940s, a significant majority of Americans trusted the government to represent and uphold their interests and this continued into the early 60s. The American National Election Study of 1958, for instance, found 73 percent of Americans claiming they could trust the government most of the time. With a peak of trust in the government (77 percent) recorded in 1964, the ensuing years saw a precipitous decline that would continue, with various peaks and troughs, into the twenty-first century.[20] Trust in the government is a key factor when examining the evolution of policy and

1968 The Omnibus Crime Control Act holds that police needed to obtain a warrant before engaging in wire-

1969 Joseph Licklider creates the Advanced Research Projects Agency Network (ARPANET), which was

Invasion of privacy by a seaside camera obscura (left). George du Maurier cartoon from *Punch*, 17 October 1868. (Photo by Universal History Archive/Getty Images)

public opinion on national security and privacy rights. When Americans have faith in the federal government, they are more likely to approve of, or at least not to openly oppose, broader powers for federal agencies with regard to national security. When trust in the government declines, the public is more likely to turn to the courts and activism to urge policies that limit or reduce government powers. The 1960s saw a plethora of events and social movements that, together, transformed American culture. From the Civil Rights movement, to the Anti-War movement, the nation entered into a period of increasingly progressive politics and social activism and this groundswell of support for fundamental changes sent ripples through every level of society.

1971   The Pentagon Papers leaks from the press raise the issue of the Freedom of the Press versus the privacy of the government to conceal information about national security operations

1972   *Eisenstadt v. Baird* rules that the right to privacy applies to individuals

From 1953 to 1969, under Chief Justice Earl Warren, the Supreme Court responded to shifting public opinions on a number of key issues and delivered progressive decisions on a number of key cases. Among other decisions, the court abolished segregation in schools, ruled that mandatory prayer in schools violated religious freedom, and established the Miranda rights and public-representation systems for individuals accused of crimes.

On several occasions, the Warren Court had the opportunity to revisit the issue of personal privacy and national security. In the case of *Barenblatt v. United States*, a narrow majority of the court supported the idea that the federal government could violate otherwise protected amendment rights for the sake of protecting national security. On two other occasions, the court revisited the issue and, on both occasions, ruled in favor of civil liberties.

In the 1965 case of *Griswold v. Connecticut* the court was asked to consider the legality of the Connecticut "Comstock law," an 1879 law that prohibited the use of contraception and also made it illegal to encourage the use of contraception in others. Estelle Griswold director of Planned Parenthood, and Dr. C. Lee Buxton, from Yale Medical School, were arrested for providing access to illegal contraception tools and were sentenced according to state statutes. The case eventually came to the Supreme Court, where, in a 7–2 vote, the court ruled that the Connecticut law violated a "right to marital privacy."[21]

1974

The Watergate Scandal results in the revelation that the CIA had been conducting widespread surveillance of American dissidents and foreign leaders without judicial oversight

The Privacy Act is established

GRISWOLD V. CONNECTICUT
Source Document Excerpt

Amendment	Constitutional Right	Application in Terms of Right to Privacy
First Amendment	Freedom of speech and expression	Privacy of beliefs
Third Amendment	Freedom from government intrusion	Privacy of the home
Fourth Amendment	Freedom from unwarranted search and seizure	Privacy against government intrusion on personal property or personal communications
Fifth Amendment	Freedom from self-incrimination	Right to privacy of personal information
Ninth Amendment	Constitution cannot be used to deny rights retained by the people	Justification for reading the Bill of Rights to protect privacy
Fourteenth Amendment	Prohibits laws that deprive any person of life, liberty, or property without due process	Justification for prohibition of laws that violate privacy rights

In writing the majority opinion of the court, Justice William O. Douglas explained that, though there was no specific mention of the right to privacy within the constitution, support for such a right could be found within the various sections of the Bill of Rights, taken together. Douglas called this a "penumbra," referring to the shaded region just outside the shadow cast by an object, and argued that the interpretation of six different amendments provided collective legal justification for this interpretation of constitutional law.

Douglas wrote in the court's decision:

1975

Senator Frank Church leads a series of hearings about the secret NSA SHAMROCK operation involved intercepting communications from American citizens

1978

Congress passes the 1978 FISA Act

Griswold v. Connecticut
continued

...the First Amendment has a penumbra where privacy is protected from governmental intrusion. In like context, we have protected forms of "association" that are not political in the customary sense, but pertain to the social, legal, and economic benefit of the members. In *Schware v. Board of Bar Examiners,* we held it not permissible to bar a lawyer from practice because he had once been a member of the Communist Party. The man's "association with that Party" was not shown to be "anything more than a political faith in a political party," and was not action of a kind proving bad moral character.

Those cases involved more than the "right of assembly"—a right that extends to all, irrespective of their race or ideology. The right of "association," like the right of belief, is more than the right to attend a meeting; it includes the right to express one's attitudes or philosophies by membership in a group or by affiliation with it or by other lawful means. Association in that context is a form of expression of opinion, and, while it is not expressly included in the First Amendment, its existence is necessary in making the express guarantees fully meaningful.

The foregoing cases suggest that specific guarantees in the Bill of Rights have penumbras, formed by emanations from those guarantees that help give them life and substance. Various guarantees create zones of privacy. The right of association contained in the penumbra of the First Amendment is one, as we have seen. The Third Amendment, in its prohibition against the quartering of soldiers "in any house" in time of peace without the consent of the owner, is another facet of that privacy. The Fourth Amendment explicitly affirms the "right of the people to be secure in their persons, houses, papers, and effects, against unreasonable searches and seizures." The Fifth Amendment, in its Self-Incrimination Clause, enables the citizen to create a zone of privacy which government may not force him to surrender to his detriment. The Ninth Amendment provides: "The enumeration in the Constitution, of certain rights, shall not be construed to deny or disparage others retained by the people."

The Fourth and Fifth Amendments were described in *Boyd v. United States*, as protection against all governmental invasions "of the sanctity of a man's home and the privacies of life." We recently referred in *Mapp v. Ohio,* to the Fourth Amendment as creating a "right to privacy, no less important than any other right carefully and particularly reserved to the people."

1980 The Intelligence Oversight Act (IOA) updates legal standards

1981 President Reagan's E.O. authorized wiretapping

1986 The Electronic Communications Privacy Act is established

Griswold v. Connecticut
continued

We have had many controversies over these penumbral rights of "privacy and repose." These cases bear witness that the right of privacy which presses for recognition here is a legitimate one.

The present case, then, concerns a relationship lying within the zone of privacy created by several fundamental constitutional guarantees. And it concerns a law which, in forbidding the use of contraceptives, rather than regulating their manufacture or sale, seeks to achieve its goals by means having a maximum destructive impact upon that relationship. Such a law cannot stand in light of the familiar principle, so often applied by this Court, that a "governmental purpose to control or prevent activities constitutionally subject to state regulation may not be achieved by means which sweep unnecessarily broadly and thereby invade the area of protected freedoms."

Would we allow the police to search the sacred precincts of marital bedrooms for telltale signs of the use of contraceptives? The very idea is repulsive to the notions of privacy surrounding the marriage relationship.

We deal with a right of privacy older than the Bill of Rights—older than our political parties, older than our school system. Marriage is a coming together for better or for worse, hopefully enduring, and intimate to the degree of being sacred. It is an association that promotes a way of life, not causes; a harmony in living, not political faiths; a bilateral loyalty, not commercial or social projects. Yet it is an association for as noble a purpose as any involved in our prior decisions.

In defending the court's support of a more general right to privacy, Justice Arthur Goldberg quoted former Justice Louis Brandeis's dissenting opinion in *Olmstead*, arguing that the Bill of Rights and common law implicitly provide support for a "right to be let alone." Goldberg further argued:

1994 Netscape creates the "cookie" allowing computers to monitor Internet users

2001 The September 11 terrorist attacks result in Congress authorizing the Bush Administration to utilize military methods to combat terrorism

continued

The fact that no particular provision of the Constitution explicitly forbids the State from disrupting the traditional relation of the family—a relation as old and as fundamental as our entire civilization—surely does not show that the Government was meant to have the power to do so. Rather, as the Ninth Amendment expressly recognizes, there are fundamental personal rights such as this one, which are protected from abridgment by the Government, though not specifically mentioned in the Constitution.

In 1937, *Gallup* asked Americans how they felt about the "birth control" movement, and 61 percent of Americans said they approved of the right to birth control for those married people who wished to use it. When *Gallup* asked a similar question in 1939, 71 percent favored government clinics providing birth control information to individuals who wanted it, as opposed to 18 percent who disapproved. By the time of the *Griswold* decision, 81 percent of the public felt it should be legal to supply birth control information.[22]

For most Americans, the *Griswold* case wasn't about privacy as much as it was about personal liberty. The 1960s changed American attitudes about many of the social and cultural prohibitions that were largely artifacts of earlier eras. Americans were now more willing to defend long-standing practices, including sexuality without the goal of procreation, that were once conducted in secret, behind a façade of socially respectable Christian morals. It was an era in which Americans were learning to be more honest about who they were and so an era in which constitutional defenses of civil liberties were repeatedly tested, both in the courts and in the court of public opinion.

The *Griswold* case set the stage for numerous challenges against moral laws and statutes governing personal behavior and therefore raising questions of civil liberties. The fact that the court rested its defense of

The Bush administration secretly authorizes the President's Surveillance Program (PSP), utilizing E.O. 12333

The U.S. PATRIOT Act alters existing laws to facilitate better communication between the state's intelligence branches in the effort to combat terrorism

The Transportation Security Administration (TSA) is established, creating the "No Fly" and "Selectee" lists that limit the right to travel on airplanes in the United States

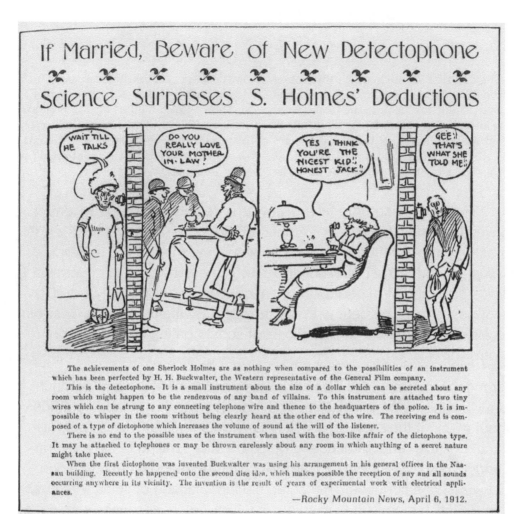

birth control on the issue of marital privacy was, however, initially an impediment to this effort. Between 1965 and 1972, the court upheld laws prohibiting contraception for unmarried people, as such laws did not violate the "marital privacy" principle established in the *Griswold* decision. This is despite the fact that there is no evidence to suggest that the public saw any justification for this. The public, in polls, demonstrated support for the overarching idea that individuals should be allowed access to birth

2005

The PATRIOT Act was reauthorized without substantial changes as Congress favors security concerns over warnings that the law creates the potential for civil liberties violations

The *New York Times* publishes articles resulting from leaks revealing the secret President's Surveillance Program (PSP) established by the Bush administration

control, and seemed to make little distinction between married and un-married individuals in this capacity.

The right of unmarried individuals to use birth control wasn't established until the 1972 case of *Eisenstadt v. Baird*, in which the court ruled that laws prohibiting birth control violated the equal protection clause. In this case, however, Justice William J. Brennan, one of the most liberal justices of the twentieth century, brought privacy back to the case in writing for the majority opinion:

EISENSTADT V. BAIRD
Source Document Excerpt

"If, under *Griswold*, the distribution of contraceptives to married persons cannot be prohibited, a ban on distribution to unmarried persons would be equally impermissible. It is true that, in *Griswold*, the right of privacy in question inhered in the marital relationship. Yet the marital couple is not an independent entity, with a mind and heart of its own, but an association of two individuals, each with a separate intellectual and emotional makeup. If the right of privacy means anything, it is the right of the individual, married or single, to be free from unwarranted governmental intrusion into matters so fundamentally affecting a person as the decision whether to bear or beget a child."

The constitutional justification for a right to privacy provided by the *Griswold* decision had far reaching impact on future decisions regarding the right to privacy in many other circumstances, other than potential intrusions on "marital privacy." In the 1967 case of *Katz v. United States*, the court applied the newly founded right to privacy to a case involving the balance of national security and personal liberty. The *Katz* case involved a gambler named Charles Katz who used a public phone to place illegal bets across state lines. The FBI had been monitoring the phone booth and recorded Katz' conversations and Katz was subsequently arrested and convicted. Though Katz' counsel claimed that the wiretap of the pub-

2007 The Bush Administration plans to make data taken from spy satellites available to law enforcement to be used to conduct domestic surveillance

2008 Congress passes Section 702, or the FISA Amendment Act, which is used to permit a massive NSA and CIA domestic surveillance program

lic phone violated Katz' Fourth Amendment rights prohibiting unreasonable search and seizure, the appeals court rejected this claim and allowed the conviction to stand.

The salient issue in the *Katz* case involved the determination of whether a wiretap was considered a type of "search and seizure." Prior court cases had established that law enforcement officers, at both the state and federal level, were required to demonstrate cause before being allowed to conduct a physical search of a person's residence or workplace. On two separate occasions, the 1928 *Olmstead* case and the 1942 *Goldman* case, the court ruled that intercepting verbal communications, through a phone or physically, did not constitute a "search" and, therefore, that such activities were permissible under the Fourth Amendment. This position, known as the "trespass doctrine," essentially limited the application of Fourth Amendment rights to situations in which government agents physically trespassed on a person's property or workplace. In the *Katz* case, the court was not only revisiting these previous decisions, but was also tasked with considering whether a person's expectation of privacy could extend to a public phone booth.

In a landmark ruling, the court ruled 7–1 in favor of *Katz*, establishing both that the Fourth Amendment applied to wiretapping and other forms of intercepting communications in an indirect or non-physical manner, and that a person's expectations of privacy were not limited to private spaces, but could legally extend to a public space as well.

Justice Potter Stewart delivered the majority opinion:

2012 The Obama Administration proposes a Consumer Privacy Bill of Rights guaranteeing individuals the right to greater control over the use of their digital data

2013 The *Guardian* and the *Washington Post* publish the first series of articles derived from leaked NSA and CIA documents delivered by Edward Snowden

KATZ V. UNITED STATES
Source Document Excerpt

We conclude that the underpinnings of *Olmstead* and *Goldman* have been so eroded by our subsequent decisions that the "trespass" doctrine there enunciated can no longer be regarded as controlling. The Government's activities in electronically listening to and recording the petitioner's words violated the privacy upon which he justifiably relied while using the telephone booth, and thus constituted a "search and seizure" within the meaning of the Fourth Amendment. The fact that the electronic device employed to achieve that end did not happen to penetrate the wall of the booth can have no constitutional significance.

The decision to broaden the scope of the Fourth Amendment to protect verbal communications as might be intercepted through a wiretap or listening device represents the court's attempt to adjust to the advancement of technology and changes in the way that American people used technology to handle their personal, private, and professional lives. This issue would be raised again and again as new technologies emerged, forcing legislators, lawmakers, and privacy advocates to contend with questions about what type of data may be considered personal or private, what constitutes a search when dealing with new types of technology and data, and when and how a person might legally have an expectation of privacy both within and outside of the home and/or office.[23]

As Justice Stewart wrote on the issue:

Katz v. United States
continued

The Government stresses the fact that the telephone booth from which the petitioner made his calls was constructed partly of glass, so that he was as visible after he entered it as he would have been if he had remained outside. But what he sought to exclude when he entered the booth was not the

The Senate Judiciary committee holds hearings to determine if the executive surveillance operations carried out under the PATRIOT Act were a violation of constitutional law

Snowden leaks reveal that the NSA and CIA had been attempting to force corporations to provide a backdoor to encryption systems that would allow federal agents to bypass consumer encryption

Katz v. United States
continued

intruding eye—it was the uninvited ear. He did not shed his right to do so simply because he made his calls from a place where he might be seen. No less than an individual in a business office, in a friend's apartment, or in a taxicab, a person in a telephone booth may rely upon the protection of the Fourth Amendment. One who occupies it, shuts the door behind him, and pays the toll that permits him to place a call is surely entitled to assume that the words he utters into the mouthpiece will not be broadcast to the world. To read the Constitution more narrowly is to ignore the vital role that the public telephone has come to play in private communication.

Recognizing that the state had legitimate interest, and that the officers involved had exercised appropriate practices in some aspects of their investigation, it remained to be determined under what conditions officers of the state could legally utilize electronic surveillance techniques. The court decided that such techniques could be used, legally, in much the same way that the law had long supported police searches and seizures of physical property: with independent judicial oversight.

In Justice Stewart's opinion:

Katz v. United States
continued

The question remaining for decision, then, is whether the search and seizure conducted in this case complied with constitutional standards. In that regard, the Government's position is that its agents acted in an entirely defensible manner: They did not begin their electronic surveillance until investigation of the petitioner's activities had established a strong probability that he was using the telephone in question to transmit gambling information to persons in other States, in violation of federal law. Moreover, the surveillance was limited, both in scope and in duration, to the

2015

Terrorist attacks in France reignite fears of domestic terrorist violence

The PATRIOT Act is replaced by the USA Freedom Act

Federal Courts order Apple, Inc. to create a new operation system that would enable federal investigators to bypass security on an iPhone.

continued

specific purpose of establishing the contents of the petitioner's unlawful telephonic communications. The agents confined their surveillance to the brief periods during which he used the telephone booth, and they took great care to overhear only the conversations of the petitioner himself.

Accepting this account of the Government's actions as accurate, it is clear that this surveillance was so narrowly circumscribed that a duly authorized magistrate, properly notified of the need for such investigation, specifically informed of the basis on which it was to proceed, and clearly apprised of the precise intrusion it would entail, could constitutionally have authorized, with appropriate safeguards, the very limited search and seizure that the Government asserts in fact took place. Only last Term we sustained the validity of such an authorization, holding that, under sufficiently "precise and discriminate circumstances," a federal court may empower government agents to employ a concealed electronic device "for the narrow and particularized purpose of ascertaining the truth of the ... allegations" of a "detailed factual affidavit alleging the commission of a specific criminal offense."

Discussing that holding, the Court in *Berger v. New York*, 388 U.S. said that "the order authorizing the use of the electronic device" in Osborn "afforded similar protections to those . . . of conventional warrants authorizing the seizure of tangible evidence". Through those protections, "no greater invasion of privacy was permitted than was necessary under the circumstances." Here, too, a similar judicial order could have accommodated "the legitimate needs of law enforcement" by authorizing the carefully limited use of electronic surveillance.

The Government urges that, because its agents relied upon the decisions in *Olmstead* and *Goldman*, and because they did no more here than they might properly have done with prior judicial sanction, we should retroactively validate their conduct. That we cannot do. It is apparent that the agents in this case acted with restraint. Yet the inescapable fact is that this restraint was imposed by the agents themselves, not by a judicial officer. They were not required, before commencing the search, to present their estimate of probable cause for detached scrutiny by a neutral magistrate. They were not compelled, during the conduct of the search itself, to observe precise

The FCC publishes official rules of "neutrality"

2016

The EU establishes the General Data Protection Regulation (GDPR), described as the strongest digital data privacy law in the world

Katz v. United States
continued

limits established in advance by a specific court order. Nor were they directed, after the search had been completed, to notify the authorizing magistrate in detail of all that had been seized. In the absence of such safeguards, this Court has never sustained a search upon the sole ground that officers reasonably expected to find evidence of a particular crime and voluntarily confined their activities to the least intrusive means consistent with that end. Searches conducted without warrants have been held unlawful "notwithstanding facts unquestionably showing probable cause," for the Constitution requires "that the deliberate, impartial judgment of a judicial officer . . . be interposed between the citizen and the police . . . ."

Over and again this Court has emphasized that the mandate of the [Fourth] Amendment requires adherence to judicial processes, and that searches conducted outside the judicial process, without prior approval by judge or magistrate, are per se unreasonable under the Fourth Amendment—subject only to a few specifically established and well-delineated exceptions.

It is difficult to imagine how any of those exceptions could ever apply to the sort of search and seizure involved in this case. Even electronic surveillance substantially contemporaneous with an individual's arrest could hardly be deemed an "incident" of that arrest. Nor could the use of electronic surveillance without prior authorization be justified on grounds of "hot pursuit." And, of course, the very nature of electronic surveillance precludes its use pursuant to the suspect's consent.

The Government does not question these basic principles. Rather, it urges the creation of a new exception to cover this case. It argues that surveillance of a telephone booth should be exempted from the usual requirement of advance authorization by a magistrate upon a showing of probable cause. We cannot agree. Omission of such authorization "bypasses the safeguards provided by an objective predetermination of probable cause, and substitutes instead the far less reliable procedure of an after-the-event justification for the . . . search, too likely to be subtly influenced by the familiar shortcomings of hindsight judgment."

And bypassing a neutral predetermination of the scope of a search leaves individuals secure from Fourth Amendment violations "only in the discretion of the police." These considerations do not vanish when the search in question is transferred from the setting of a home, an office, or a hotel room to that of a telephone booth. Wherever a man may be, he is

The "Vault 7" secrets, a leak of 9,000 CIA documents, reveal details of the CIA's attempts to break through encryption used by Internet

President Trump appoints Ajit Pai to head the FCC, who abolishes the FCC neutrality protections

continued

entitled to know that he will remain free from unreasonable searches and seizures. The government agents here ignored "the procedure of antecedent justification . . . that is central to the Fourth Amendment," a procedure that we hold to be a constitutional precondition of the kind of electronic surveillance involved in this case. Because the surveillance here failed to meet that condition, and because it led to the petitioner's conviction, the judgment must be reversed.

Since the 1928 *Olmstead* case, members of the court had described a "balancing" between the needs of the state to enforce laws and protect national security, and the constitutional rights of the individual. For many years, court decisions demonstrated a tendency to favor the needs of the state over the rights of the individual. In some cases, the courts adopted an "ends justify the means" stance, acknowledging that the state may have violated certain rights, but that the goal of preventing crime and protecting public security justified such actions. In *Katz*, the court reversed this position, holding that the rights of the individual must be preeminent unless the state could demonstrate, by following due process, the need to violate an individual's privacy or to violate other civil rights in an effort to enforce laws and enhance national security.

Congress debates whether or not to renew the controversial Section 702 FISA Amendment used to authorize NSA domestic intelligence operations since 2008

CONCLUSION

The *Griswold* case fundamentally altered privacy law in the United States. Whereas privacy had long been a matter of state laws and specific legal statutes, *Griswold* provided a broad constitutional guarantee. Many different state laws and statutes were invalidated by the *Griswold* decision and the belief that privacy should be considered a fundamental freedom—intended, though not explicitly stated by, the founders of the nation—gradually became a core aspect of American values. In *Katz*, the court made an equally meaningful ruling regarding the relationship between the individual and the state. Essentially, the court ruled that the Fourth Amendment freedom from unreasonable search and seizure applied to all telephone communication whether occurring in public or private. This was the final step in society's legal adjustment to the telephone, the legal recognition that the telephone was an essential tool for private communication, and so had to be protected in the same way as postal correspondence, or the private communications that occur within a person's home. For years after *Katz*, police, and federal agents submitted to the prevailing tide, seeking judicial court orders before engaging in electronic surveillance. However, this issue resurged as telephone communication gave way to email, social media, and cellular phones. Despite the *Katz* precedent, it was unclear whether or not the same protections extended to information transmitted digitally over the Internet, or cellular networks, which were corporate products owned by companies and not subjected to laws regarding public utilities. This debate, i.e., whether digital communication was a corporate product or a public utility, became a major part of the privacy debate in the twenty-first century.

1788   State legislatures ratify the U.S. Constitution, establishing the basic precedent for all future constitutional law

1791   The U.S. Congress ratifies the Bill of Rights, creating the first 10 amendments to the United States Constitution

DISCUSSION QUESTIONS

- Should the Internet be considered a utility similar to the telephone system? Why or why not?
- Who owns an email once it is created and sent? The sender? The receiver? The company providing email access? Explain.
- Do you agree with the court's ruling in the *Katz* case? Why or why not?
- What does the metaphor "penumbra" mean in the *Griswold* case?

Works Used

"Beyond Distrust: How Americans View Their Government." *Pew Research*. Pew Research Center. Nov. 23, 2015. Web. 24 Oct. 2017.

"*Griswold v. Connecticut* (1965)." *PBS*. Landmark Cases. 2007. Web. 24 Oct. 2017.

Iannacci, Nicandro. "*Katz v. United States*: The Fourth Amendment adapts to new technology." *Constitution Center*. Constitution Daily. National Constitution Center. Dec. 18, 2015. Web. 25 Oct. 2017.

"Public Attitudes about Birth Control." *Roper Center*. Roper Center for Public Opinion Research. Cornell University. 2017. Web. 10 Nov. 2017.

1868 The 14th Amendment to the U.S. Constitution guarantees all citizens the right to due process under the law

1890 Warren and Brandeis publish "The Right to Privacy" in the *Harvard Law Review*

Illustration titled "Freedom of the Press" shows a male newspaper owner and editor dressed as a female prostitute called "The Madam," taking money from a man labeled "Big Advertisers" as staff sit under a sign with the message "Obey the Madam." (Credit: Art Young)

1923   *Meyer v. Nebraska* establishes that the 14th Amendment guarantees privileges of citizenship

1928   *Olmstead v. United States* rules that wiretapping is not a form of search and seizure defined by the 14th Amendment

Introduction

In the previous chapter, we saw how the 1964 Supreme Court case *Griswold v. Connecticut* established a constitutional right to privacy, and the 1967 *Katz v. United States* case established an important ramification of this right, that the government must demonstrate justification before violating the privacy rights of individuals. The people have the right to privacy from the government, but does the government have the right to privacy from the people? In the 1971 Supreme Court case *New York Times Co. v. United States*, the Supreme Court was asked to evaluate the freedom of the press and to answer the question of whether the press had the right to publish information that might be damaging to the goals of the state.

This chapter examines the history and legacy of the 1971 *New York Times* case in which the *New York Times* newspaper published classified information about U.S. government policy during the Vietnam War that had been leaked to the press by whistleblower Daniel Ellsberg. These documents, called the "Pentagon Papers" in the press, revealed a long-term pattern of deception through four presidential administrations in which the executive branch, working with the military, deceived the American public and Congress regarding the nation's activities in Vietnam. The Richard Nixon administration argued that the publication of information from the leaked documents posed a threat to national security. However, after hearing arguments in the case, the court found that the government had failed to prove that the leaked information posed a threat to security and, therefore, ruled that the state had no justification to abridge constitutional guarantees regarding the freedom of the press.

1934

The Federal Communications Commission (FCC) is established under the Federal Communications Act (FCA)

1942

Goldman v. United States rules that using electronic listening devices does not violate the 14th Amendment

Topics covered in this chapter include:
- Freedom of the press
- Whistleblowers and government leaks
- State secrets
- Distrust of the government
- Supreme Court cases involving privacy rights

This Chapter Discusses the Following Source Document:
New York Times Co. v. United States, 403 U.S. 713 (1971)

Information Rights
New York Times Co. v. United States

The debate over the legal right to privacy began, in many ways, with the press. Prominent lawyers William Warren and Louis Brandeis, in their seminal 1890 paper *The Right to Privacy*, condemned what they saw as the invasive practices of tabloid journalists and argued that, given the increasing tendency of the press to invade the private domain, the courts should adopt and support a fundamental right, "to be let alone." In 1971, the Supreme Court was asked to examine another issue involving the press and privacy, though this time, the court was asked to balance governmental privacy against the freedom of the press.

Daniel Ellsberg, a former military analyst and employee of the RAND Corporation, sparked national controversy in 1971 when Ellsberg discovered, copied, and leaked more than 7000 pages of documents revealing secret governmental policies regarding the Vietnam War. Among other things, the documents within the papers revealed how the executive branch, working in secret with members of the military, had misled both Congress and the American public in pursuit of the executive agenda in Vietnam.[24] These documents, collectively called the "Pentagon Papers," were seen as a substantial threat by the Nixon administration, as the documents essentially demonstrated government overreach through four presidential administrations.

Speaking about the Pentagon Papers 40 years later, Ellsberg remarked:

> *...letting a small group of men in secret in the executive branch make these decisions—initiate them secretly, carry them out secretly and manipulate Congress, and lie to Congress and the public as to why they're doing it and what they're doing is a recipe for,*

1951 *Dennis v. United States* rules that government limits to speech is legal only to prevent a threat to public safety or security

1959 *Barenblatt v. United States* rules that it's legal to order people to reveal personal details if national threat is perceived

WHEN THE WHISTLE BLOWS

People like Daniel Ellsberg, Mark Felt, the FBI agent who leaked information leading to the Watergate Scandal, and Edward Snowden, the NSA analyst who revealed details of NSA surveillance techniques to the American people, are often called "whistleblowers," a term derived from activist Ralph Nader, who suggested the term to refer to persons who exposed wrongdoing or corruption, as opposed to terms like "informant" or "snitch," which have negative connotations. Beyond Nader's usage, the origin of the term is uncertain. Some have suggested it refers to English policemen, who would blow whistles to sound an alarm indicating a crime or other danger, while others have suggested that the term derives from the use of a whistle to call attention to an infraction in various types of sports.

a guarantee of Vietnams and Iraqs and Libyas, and in general foolish, reckless, dangerous policies."[25]

Ellsberg delivered the 7000 pages of illegally obtained documents to reporters at the *New York Times*, which shortly thereafter began publishing a series of articles based on the material. Within several days, the Nixon administration issued an executive order prohibiting the paper from publishing information about or contained within the illegally obtained material. With the *Times* temporarily banned from publishing as it fought the government's executive order in the courts, Ellsberg delivered the same documents to the *Washington Post*, which also began publishing information taken from the report. The Nixon administration sought another injunction to prevent the *Washington Post* from publishing information contained within the documents and both cases proceeded through the courts. Recognizing the pressing urgency of the case, the Supreme Court agreed to hear arguments on the issue less than two weeks after the controversy began.

One of the essential questions in the Pentagon Papers trial was whether the

1965 Griswold v. CT rules in favor of married couples' right to privacy

1967 Katz v. United States rules wiretaps a form of search and seizure

Willis Ware of RAND Corporation writes *Security and Privacy in Computer*

freedom of the press, as guaranteed by the First Amendment, was subordinate to the government's need to maintain secrecy in internal communications and information.

In previous court rulings, (*Dennis v. United States,* 1951 and *Brandenburg v. Ohio,* 1969) the court found that the government had the power to limit speech (or the freedom to publish) only if the speech in question advocated what the courts described as "imminent lawless action." While the court's rulings in these cases have been used to support censorship, the court's opinions in both cases make it clear that the overall approach was to favor First Amendment rights except in situations in which a person's speech or expression directly, and reasonably, can be seen as inciting action. Therefore, a person who calls for another person to be killed is not within his or her First Amendment rights in making such a request. A person who incites a group to loot, damage property, or injure other individuals, is similarly not protected by First Amendment protections in doing so.

In deciding the Pentagon Papers issue, therefore, the courts were forced to determine if publication of the material within the papers posed a threat to the public or not. It was

The Washington Post Headline After Winning Court Case 6/30/1971. William Frazee, Chief of the Presses, makes a 'V' for victory as he checks the first edition of *The Washington Post* after hearing the Supreme Court's decision allowing newspapers to resume publication of a top secret Pentagon study of the Vietnam War. A whoop of joy and applause was heard in the press room as the first run began rolling. (Credit: Bettman/Contributor/Getty Images.)

1968   The Omnibus Crime Control Act holds that police needed to obtain a warrant before engaging in wire-

1969   Joseph Licklider creates the Advanced Research Projects Agency Network (ARPANET), which was

further established that the government could not issue any "prior restraint" on speech until justification for such restrictions had been established, or, in other words, the government did not have the power to prohibit speech on the basis that such speech "might" lead to some security risk or danger, but had to be able to demonstrate an immediate danger before First Amendment rights could legally be abridged.

As Justice William O. Douglas wrote in his concurring opinion in the *Brandenburg* case:

> *The question in every case is whether the words used are used in such circumstances and are of such a nature as to create a clear and present danger that they will bring about the substantive evils that Congress has a right to prevent. It is a question of proximity and degree.*[26]

Therefore, although it was acknowledged that Ellsberg's behavior, in stealing and illegally distributing the Pentagon Papers, was a crime, the question was whether publication of the material posed a provable danger to national security and whether, therefore, there was any justification for Nixon's executive order barring publication.

The Court ruled 6–3 in favor of the *New York Times*, arguing that the government had failed to make a case justifying their request for an injunction.[27]

Justice Black wrote in support of the ruling:

1971 The Pentagon Papers leaks from the press raise the issue of the Freedom of the Press versus the privacy of the government to conceal information about national security operations

1972 *Eisenstadt v. Baird* rules that the right to privacy applies to individuals

NEW YORK TIMES, CO. V. UNITED STATES

Source Document Excerpt

Our Government was launched in 1789 with the adoption of the Constitution. The Bill of Rights, including the First Amendment, followed in 1791. Now, for the first time in the 182 years since the founding of the Republic, the federal courts are asked to hold that the First Amendment does not mean what it says, but rather means that the Government can halt the publication of current news of vital importance to the people of this country.

In seeking injunctions against these newspapers and in its presentation to the Court, the Executive Branch seems to have forgotten the essential purpose and history of the First Amendment. When the Constitution was adopted, many people strongly opposed it because the document contained no Bill of Rights to safeguard certain basic freedoms. They especially feared that the new powers granted to a central government might be interpreted to permit the government to curtail freedom of religion, press, assembly, and speech. In response to an overwhelming public clamor, James Madison offered a series of amendments to satisfy citizens that these great liberties would remain safe and beyond the power of government to abridge. Madison proposed what later became the First Amendment in three parts, two of which are set out below, and one of which proclaimed: "The people shall not be deprived or abridged of their right to speak, to write, or to publish their sentiments; and the freedom of the press, as one of the great bulwarks of liberty, shall be inviolable." The amendments were offered to curtail and restrict the general powers granted to the Executive, Legislative, and Judicial Branches two years before in the original Constitution. The Bill of Rights changed the original Constitution into a new charter under which no branch of government could abridge the people's freedoms of press, speech, religion, and assembly. Yet the Solicitor General argues and some members of the Court appear to agree that the general powers of the Government adopted in the original Constitution should be interpreted to limit and restrict the specific and emphatic guarantees of the Bill of Rights adopted later. I can imagine no greater perversion of history. Madison and the other Framers of the First Amendment, able men that they were, wrote in language they earnestly believed could never be misunderstood: "Congress shall make no law . . . abridging the freedom . . . of the press . . . ." Both the history and language of the First Amendment support the view that the press must be left free to publish news, whatever the source, without censorship, injunctions, or prior restraints.

The press was protected so that it could bare the secrets of government and inform the people. Only a free

1974

The Watergate Scandal results in the revelation that the CIA had been conducting widespread surveillance of American dissidents and foreign leaders without judicial oversight

The Privacy Act is established

New York Times, Co. v. United States
continued

and unrestrained press can effectively expose deception in government. And paramount among the responsibilities of a free press is the duty to prevent any part of the government from deceiving the people and sending them off to distant to die of foreign fevers and foreign shot and shell. In my view, far from deserving condemnation for their courageous reporting, the *New York Times* the *Washington Post*, and other newspapers should be commended for serving the purpose that the Founding Fathers saw so clearly. In revealing the workings of government that led to the Vietnam war, the newspapers nobly did precisely that which the Founders hoped and trusted they would do. The Government's case here is based on premises entirely different from those that guided the Framers of the First Amendment. The Solicitor General has carefully and emphatically stated:

"Now, Mr. Justice [BLACK], your construction of . . . [the First Amendment] is well known, and I certainly respect it. You say that no law means no law, and that should be obvious. I can only say, Mr. Justice, that to me it is equally obvious that 'no law' does not mean 'no law', and I would seek to persuade the Court that is true. . . . [T]here are other parts of the Constitution that grant powers and responsibilities to the Executive, and . . . the First Amendment was not intended to make it impossible for the Executive to function or to protect the security of the United States."

And the Government argues in its brief that in spite of the First Amendment, "[t]he authority of the Executive Department to protect the nation against publication of information whose disclosure would endanger the national security stems from two interrelated sources: the constitutional power of the President over the conduct of foreign affairs and his authority as Commander-in-Chief."

In other words, we are asked to hold that despite the First Amendment's emphatic command,

> " In the First Amendment the Founding Fathers gave the free press the protection it must have to fulfill its essential role in our democracy. The press was to serve the governed, not the governors. The Government's power to censor the press was abolished so that the press would remain forever free to censure the Government. "

1975 Senator Frank Church leads a series of hearings about the secret NSA SHAMROCK operation involved intercepting communications from American citizens

1978 Congress passes the 1978 FISA Act

continued

the Executive Branch, the Congress, and the Judiciary can make laws enjoining publication of current news and abridging freedom of the press in the name of "national security." The Government does not even attempt to rely on any act of Congress. Instead it makes the bold and dangerously far-reaching contention that the courts should take it upon themselves to "make" a law abridging freedom of the press in the name of equity, presidential power and national security, even when the representatives of the people in Congress have adhered to the command of the First Amendment and refused to make such a law. To find that the President has "inherent power" to halt the publication of news by resort to the courts would wipe out the First Amendment and destroy the fundamental liberty and security of the very people the Government hopes to make "secure." No one can read the history of the adoption of the First Amendment without being convinced beyond any doubt that it was injunctions like those sought here that Madison and his collaborators intended to outlaw in this Nation for all time.

The word "security" is a broad, vague generality whose contours should not be invoked to abrogate the fundamental law embodied in the First Amendment.

The guarding of military and diplomatic secrets at the expense of informed representative government provides no real security for our Republic. The Framers of the First Amendment, fully aware of both the need to defend a new nation and the abuses of the English and Colonial governments, sought to give this new society strength and security by providing that freedom of speech, press, religion, and assembly should not be abridged. This thought was eloquently expressed in 1937 by Mr. Chief Justice Hughes—great man and great Chief Justice that he was—when the Court held a man could not be punished for attending a meeting run by Communists.

"The greater the importance of safeguarding the community from incitements to the overthrow of our institutions by force and violence, the more imperative is the need to preserve inviolate the constitutional rights of free speech, free press and free assembly in order to maintain the opportunity for free political discussion, to the end that government may be responsive to the will of the people and that changes, if desired, may be obtained by peaceful means. Therein lies the security of the Republic, the very foundation of constitutional government."

1980   The Intelligence Oversight Act (IOA) updates legal standards

1981   President Reagan's E.O. authorized wiretapping

1986   The Electronic Communications Privacy Act is established

In the *New York Times* case, following in the landmark decisions delivered by the Warren Court in the 1950s and 1960s, the Supreme Court again established precedent that abridging civil liberties was only appropriate when and if the state could justify claims that doing so was necessary to protect national security. This was essentially a reversal of the Supreme Court's long-standing precedent of favoring state interests over civil rights, in cases involving crime and national security.

According to *New York Times* data, only 43 percent of the public agreed with the court's decision in *New York Times v. United States*[28], and this may have been a result of an intense campaign by the Nixon administration and other legislators of the era warning that the material within the documents posed a threat to national security. For the Nixon administration and many other legislators, the Pentagon Papers was a source of embarrassment that threatened to erode faith in the administration and the government as a whole. Whether this fear was well founded is unclear, but subsequent decades did see a further detachment between the American public and the government and a growing distrust in the policies, and accuracy of statements made by the nation's leaders.

1994 Netscape creates the "cookie" allowing computers to monitor Internet users

2001 The September 11 terrorist attacks result in Congress authorizing the Bush Administration to utilize military methods to combat terrorism

A copy of a declassified report known colloquially as "The Pentagon Papers." The 7,000-page document on the internal planning and policy decisions within the U.S. government regarding the Vietnam War gained fame when they were leaked and published in *The New York Times* in early 1971 by former RAND Corporation analyst, Daniel Ellsberg.

The Bush administration secretly authorizes the President's Surveillance Program (PSP), utilizing E.O. 12333

The U.S. PATRIOT Act alters existing laws to facilitate better communication between the state's intelligence branches in the effort to combat terrorism

The Transportation Security Administration (TSA) is established, creating the "No Fly" and "Selectee" lists that limit the right to travel on airplanes in the United States

CONCLUSION

The *New York Times* case and the Pentagon Papers proved a major embarrassment to the Nixon administration and arguably helped to precipitate a deepening distrust towards the federal government. Daniel Ellsberg, who stole and illegally leaked the documents to the press, was called a criminal by critics at the time, but later came to be seen by many as a hero for risking his own safety to expose governmental misconduct. Ellsberg's behavior, and the court ruling in the 1971 case, are relevant to modern debates about leaked governmental secrets and the ongoing effort to balance the government's ability to keep important information secret, against the public's right to know how their government functions with regard to important issues. In the 1971 case, the court reaffirmed the role of the free press, as an organ responsible for providing the public with accurate information and holding public officials responsible for their actions. These issues have new relevance in 2018, with the Trump administration openly hostile towards the mainstream media and urging supporters to seek information only from approved sources, thus calling the future of the free press into question.

2005

The PATRIOT Act was reauthorized without substantial changes as Congress favors security concerns over warnings that the law creates the potential for civil liberties violations

The *New York Times* publishes articles resulting from leaks revealing the secret President's Surveillance Program (PSP) established by the Bush administration

DISCUSSION QUESTIONS

- Is the mainstream media in the United States biased? Can you provide evidence to support your argument?
- Do you agree with the court's ruling in the *New York Times* case? Why or why not?
- Are there situations in which the government has the right to prevent the publication of certain information? Why or why not?
- Can you think of other examples of whistleblowers who have leaked government information? Were those situations similar or different from the Pentagon Papers leak? Explain why.

Works Used

"*Brandenburg v. Ohio.*" *Cornell Law School*. Supreme Court. June 9, 1969. Web. 31 Oct. 2017.

Cooper, Michael, and Sam Roberts. "After 40 Years, the Complete Pentagon Papers." *New York Times*. New York Times Co. June 7, 2011. Web. 25 Oct. 2017.

"*New York Times v. United States* (1971)." *Bill of Rights Institute*. Bill of Rights Institute. 2017. Web. 25 Oct. 2017.

"Public Approval of Major Court Decisions." *New York Times*. New York Times Co. 2012. Web. 31 Oct. 2017.

Sheehan, Neil. "Vietnam Archive: Pentagon Study Traces 3 Decades of Growing U.S. Involvement." *New York Times*. New York Times Co. June 13, 1971. Web. 25 Oct. 2017.

2007 The Bush Administration plans to make data taken from spy satellites available to law enforcement to be used to conduct domestic surveillance

2008 Congress passes Section 702, or the FISA Amendment Act, which is used to permit a massive NSA and CIA domestic surveillance program

RAND Corporation headquarters in Santa Monica, California

2012 The Obama Administration proposes a Consumer Privacy Bill of Rights guaranteeing individuals the right to greater control over the use of their digital data

2013 The *Guardian* and the *Washington Post* publish the first series of articles derived from leaked NSA and CIA documents delivered by Edward Snowden

Introduction

This chapter discusses the origins of "cybersecurity," the techniques, policies, and legal statutes regarding the privacy and security of digital data stored or transmitted through computers and computer networks. Long before the term "cybersecurity" had been coined, and before companies offered software and hardware to secure digital data, computer scientist Willis Ware, of the influential Rand Corporation research organization, foresaw many key aspects of the familiar digital security debate that would become common discourse today. The primary document for this chapter is an article published by Ware through Rand Corporation in April of 1967, "Security and Privacy in Computer Systems," in which Ware explains the ways in which the coming transition to digital data management would pose a host of new threats to both government data and the privacy of citizens.

Ware's 1967 report and subsequent testimony before Congress helped inspire a federal debate about digital security, and this led to the Privacy Act of 1974, which created the first laws regarding the ways in which federal agencies could collect and store data from citizens. In 1975, Ware and colleague Rein Turn published an updated version of "Security and Privacy in Computer Systems," this time focusing, largely, on what Ware and Turn saw as an urgent need for federal laws to protect consumer privacy in the deepening era of computer technology. Echoing issues still very much debated and often in the news today, Ware and Turn argued that federal laws were insufficient to protect the public, warned of the threat of cybercrime and cyberwarfare, and presaged that the coming computer age would create a threat to personal privacy beyond any that had been seen.

The Senate Judiciary committee holds hearings to determine if the executive surveillance operations carried out under the PATRIOT Act were a violation of constitutional law

Snowden leaks reveal that the NSA and CIA had been attempting to force corporations to provide a backdoor to encryption systems that would allow federal agents to bypass consumer encryption

Topics covered in this chapter include:
- Commercial/corporate privacy rights
- Digital privacy
- Ownership of digital data
- Cyberwarfare
- Cybercrime

This Chapter Discusses the Following Source Document:
Rein, Turn and Ware, Willis H. "Security and Privacy in Computer
   Systems." Rand Corporation. April 1967.

The Origins of Data Security
Privacy and Security in Computer Systems (1967 and 1975)

For decades, the RAND Corporation was one of the most powerful and influential think tanks in the nation. Created by the Air Force just after World War II, out of the recognition that the military needed the power to aggressively research new technological tools, the military research wing known as "Project RAND" became an independent research organization in 1948, though RAND was still deeply involved in military planning and research and the Air Force remained one of the organization's major clients. At the height of the RAND Corporation's influence, in the 1940s and 50s, the organization employed some of the best and brightest analysts and technology experts in the nation, including 29 Nobel Prize laureates. The RAND Corporation was responsible for many different technological and strategic innovations, including game theory, rational-choice theory, and the application of digital system's analysis to national military policy.[29]

Though RAND is both celebrated and maligned for its varied role in promoting American military policy, one of the most lasting contributions of the organization was in the field of computer science. RAND engineers and scientists made essential contributions to the development of personal and professional computing technology, and RAND became one of the earliest advocates for digital data protection and privacy rights.

Willis Ware, a pioneer in computer science who worked at RAND from the 1950s into the early 1990s, was one of the designers of the early computer system, "Johnniac," in 1953, and later became head of the organization's Computer Science division. Armed with an intimate knowledge of the industry and technology during a fundamental phase in the coming Digital Revolution, Ware was uniquely attuned to the potential benefits and risks that computer technology posed to both the public and the government.[30]

The FCC publishes official rules of "neutrality"

2016

The EU establishes the General Data Protection Regulation (GDPR), described as the strongest digital data privacy law in the world

In 1967, Willis Ware wrote a report on "Security and Privacy in Computer Systems," in which he identified and discussed a variety of potential threats to data stored in computer systems as such systems were increasingly being used by the government to store state secrets and military data and to store and process public records and other data on the American people. On the issue of privacy, Ware saw a system in which personal data was not given adequate protection and thus, in which, as what he termed the "computer age," commenced, new regulations would be needed to ensure that citizens could entrust data to computer systems without fear of having their data misused, abused, or of suffering other violations to their privacy.

SECURITY AND PRIVACY IN COMPUTER SYSTEMS
Source Document Excerpt

Though there apparently exist fragments of law and some precedents bearing on the protection of information, nonetheless the privacy situation is not so neatly circumscribed and tidy as the security situation. Privacy simply is not so tightly controlled. Within computer networks serving many companies, organizations, or agencies there may be no uniform governing authority; an incomplete legal framework; no established discipline, or perhaps not even a code of ethics among users. At present, there is not even a commonly accepted set of categories to describe levels of sensitivity for private information.

Great quantities of private information are being accumulated in computer files; and the incentives to penetrate the safeguards to privacy are bound to increase. Existing laws may prove inadequate, or may need more vigorous enforcement. There may be need for a monitoring and enforcement establishment analogous to that in the security situation. In any event, it can not be taken for granted that there now exist adequate legal and ethical umbrellas for the protection of private information.

The privacy problem is really a spectrum of problems. At one end, it may be necessary to provide only a very low level of protection to the information for only a very short time; at the opposite end, it may be necessary to invoke the most

The "Vault 7" secrets, a leak of 9,000 CIA documents, reveal details of the CIA's attempts to break through encryption used by Internet

President Trump appoints Ajit Pai to head the FCC, who abolishes the FCC neutrality protections

continued

sophisticated techniques to guarantee protection of information for extended periods of time. Federal regulations state explicitly what aspect of national defense will be compromised by unauthorized divulgence of each category of classified information. There is no corresponding particularization of the privacy situation; the potential damage from revealing private information is nowhere described in such absolute terms. It may be that a small volume of information leaked from a private file may involve inconsequential risk. For example, the individual names of a company's employees is probably not even sensitive, whereas the complete file of employees could well be restricted. Certainly the "big brother" spectre raised by recent Congressional hearings on "invasion of privacy" via massive computer files is strongly related to the volume of information at risk.[31]

Ware testified on computer privacy issues before Congress and his advocacy played a role in the development of the Privacy Act of 1974. This law established a code of conduct for the management of information stored in government databases, and governed the legal ways in which government agents were allowed to collect, maintain, use, and disseminate information on citizen data. The Privacy Act, for instance, prohibited the disclosure of federal records without prior, written consent of the individual, a rule that was still used to govern federal handling of consumer data in 2017.[32]

Though Ware's testimony helped to promote the act in the legislature, Ware and many other technology experts argued that the Privacy Act wasn't strong nor comprehensive enough to address the various potential threats to computer data. To express these concerns, in 1975, Ware and fellow computer expert Reid Turn wrote another influential report, "Privacy and Security in Computer Systems," later published in the pages of *American Scientist*.

In the report, Ware and Turn define computer privacy rights as:

Congress debates whether or not to renew the controversial Section 702 FISA Amendment used to authorize NSA domestic intelligence operations since 2008

─────────   *...the rights of the individual regarding the collection, processing, storage, dissemination, and use of information about his personal attributes and activities.*

─────────

From this, Ware and Turn describe principles that should be used to guide the creation of a new privacy law or policy:

Security and Privacy in Computer Systems
continued

1) There must be no personal data recordkeeping systems whose very existence is secret.

2) There must be a way for an individual to find out what information about him is on record and how it is used.

3) There must be a way for an individual to correct or amend a record of identifiable information about him.

4) There must be a way for an individual to prevent information about him that was obtained for one purpose from being used or made available for other purposes without his consent.

5) Any organization creating, maintaining, using, or disseminating records of identifiable personal data must guarantee the reliability of the data for their intended use and must take precautions to prevent misuse of the data.

Ware and Turn also discussed another issue with contemporary relevance; the potential for law enforcement or government agencies to subpoena information stored in computer databases for use in criminal or civil proceedings or investigations. Ware and Turn argued about this issue in 1975:

1788   State legislatures ratify the U.S. Constitution, establishing the basic precedent for all future constitutional law

1791   The U.S. Congress ratifies the Bill of Rights, creating the first 10 amendments to the United States Constitution

Security and Privacy in Computer Systems
continued

In contrast to privacy, which refers to the rights of the individual, confidentiality implies that the data themselves and the information they contain must be protected, and that their use must be confined to authorized purposes by authorized people.

Certain categories of personal information are given a confidential status by statutes and laws. For example, the personal data gathered in the United States decennial census are required to be kept confidential by Federal law. This means that no individually identified census responses may be disseminated to anyone outside the Census Bureau, and even within the Bureau only specially authorized employees are permitted access. Attorney-client information exchanges, certain medical and mental health information, and legal proceedings involving children and juveniles are other examples of information categories that are protected from general access by confidentiality provisions in Federal or state statutes.

Most categories of personal information do not enjoy any statutory protection, however; disclosure of such information may be compelled by legal process, such as subpoena issued by a court, legislative committee, or other official body that has jurisdiction in the locality where the data are kept. Personal information gathered by educational institutions and by research projects in social, political, and behavioral sciences are very susceptible to these procedures.

Ware and Turn thus recommended a separate provision of the code covering confidentiality, and setting limits on the degree to which a government agency or agent could access information stored in a computer and provided for another purpose:

1868 The 14th Amendment to the U.S. Constitution guarantees all citizens the right to due process under the law

1890 Warren and Brandeis publish "The Right to Privacy" in the *Harvard Law Review*

Security and Privacy in Computer Systems
continued

1) Protection should be limited to data identifiable with or traceable to specific individuals.

2) Protection should be specific enough to qualify for non-disclosure exemption under the Freedom of Information Act.

3) Protection should be available for data in the custody of all statistical reporting and research systems whether supported by federal funds or not.

4) Federal law should be controlling; no state statute should interfere with the protection provided.

5) Either the custodian or the individual about whom data are sought by legal process should be able to invoke the protection, but only the individual should be able to waive it.

Further, Ware and Turn recommended that an organization, individual, or institution gathering information should be responsible for:

Security and Privacy in Computer Systems
continued

1) Informing the individual subject whether he is legally required to supply the data requested or may refuse, and also of any specific consequences for him, which are known to the organization, or providing or not providing such data.

2) Guarantee that no use of individually identifiable data will be made that is not within the stated purposes of the system as reasonably understood by the individual, unless the informed consent of the individual has been explicitly obtained.

3) Guarantee that no data about an individual will be made available from the system in response to a compulsory legal process, unless the individual to whom the data pertains has been notified of the demand and has been afforded full access to the data before they are made available in response to the demand.33

1923   *Meyer v. Nebraska* establishes that the 14th Amendment guarantees privileges of citizenship

1928   *Olmstead v. United States* rules that wiretapping is not a form of search and seizure defined by the 14th Amendment

At the time that Ware and Turn published their report, few predicted that, in the 2010s, an average American citizen might carry in his or her pocket a machine capable of storing more personal data than the massive systems Ware and Turn were using in 1975 when they first envisioned the potential privacy threats of the Digital Age. Federal and state legislators did not pass the kind of privacy protections that Ware had long proposed and subsequent controversies regarding the collection, storage, and use of digital data—both by companies involved in collecting and selling consumer data (the "Big Data" controversy) and by the federal government as revealed by the NSA spying controversy that began in 2013—demonstrated just how prescient Ware's predictions had been.

Whether more comprehensive privacy policies are needed is still a matter of debate in 2017. Some critics of digital privacy laws argue that such laws might stifle economic development, given that a mass of American corporations have come to function primarily by collecting and selling data on consumers, whereas others argue that such laws should not impede government efforts to collect data that might be important to national security concerns. Both of these arguments are controversial and neither can be justified using data, but rely, instead, on subjective interpretations of the overall "need" for privacy or of the weight that privacy should be given in relation to other American ideals.

A report from *Pew Research Center* in 2017 indicated that 64 percent of Americans had personally experienced what they considered a violation of their private digital data. The study also showed that Americans were divided as to whether the government could or would protect their digital data, with 24 percent reporting no confidence at all in the government's ability to protect their data, and only 12 percent reporting a high level of confidence in government protections.[34] These statistics seem to indicate a popular mandate for privacy laws and, in fact, a majority of Americans, when asked, would support more comprehensive digital privacy

1934 The Federal Communications Commission (FCC) is established under the Federal Communications Act (FCA)

1942 *Goldman v. United States* rules that using electronic listening devices does not violate the 14th Amendment

Credit: Cagle Cartoons

protections. However, digital privacy remains a relatively low priority for voters compared to issues like education and national security, whereas the lobby against digital privacy laws is strong, well-funded, and contributes directly to many politicians who have opposed past legislative proposals. This combination of factors likely means that until something changes, new digital privacy laws will not be forthcoming, and the abuses and privacy violations predicted by Ware and colleagues in the 60s and 70s will continue unabated.

1945 The National Security Agency secretly creates Project SHAMROCK

1950 Senator Joseph McCarthy delivers a shocking speech claiming that more than 200 communist spies have infiltrated the U.S. government

CONCLUSION

In an era of "Big Data," where corporations collect and sell private data volunteered by consumers in return for access to digital entertainment and communication, and in which the Russian government hacked the Democratic National Convention, using information obtained to damage the Democratic party, the security and privacy concerns described by Ware in 1967, and expanded by Ware and Turn in 1975, are still very much relevant and vital today. Despite efforts on behalf of the government and by private companies and security experts helping to develop digital data security systems, the Digital Age has left Americans exposed to a vast and growing number of potential threats. With the federal government failing to create comprehensive digital rights laws, and few protections in place to guarantee privacy for those using digital tools and technology, many of Ware and Turn's fears have become reality.

1951 *Dennis v. United States* rules that government limits to speech is legal only to prevent a threat to public safety or security

1959 *Barenblatt v. United States* rules that it's legal to order people to reveal personal details if national threat is perceived

DISCUSSION QUESTIONS

- Should American citizens have a right to privacy regarding digital data? Why or why not?
- Have you ever experienced, or do you know someone who has experienced, a violation of digital privacy? If so, how did this occur?
- How is the digital privacy issue related to "net neutrality?"
- Would digital privacy laws limit corporate development of new technology? Why or why not?

Works Used

Olmstead, Kenneth, and Aaron Smith. "Americans and Cybersecurity." *Pew Research*. Pew Research Center: Internet and Technology. Jan. 26, 2017. Web. 31 Oct. 2017.

"Privacy Act of 1974." *Department of Justice*. U.S. Department of Justice Office of Privacy and Civil Liberties. 2017. Web. 25 Oct. 2017.

Schwarz, Benjamin. "America's Think Tank." *CJR*. Columbia Journalism Review. June 2008. Web. 25 Oct. 2017.

"The Passing of a Pioneer." *Purdue University*. Center for Education and Research in Information Assurance and Security. Nov. 26, 2013. Web. 25 Oct. 2017.

Turn, R., and W. H. Ware. "Privacy and Security in Computer Systems." RAND. RAND Corporation. Jan. 1975. Pdf. 25 Oct. 2017.

Ware, Willis H. "Security and Privacy in Computer Systems." *RAND*. RAND Corporation. Apr. 1967. Pdf. 31 Oct. 2017.

1965   *Griswold v. CT* rules in favor of married couples' right to privacy

1967   *Katz v. United States* rules wiretaps a form of search and seizure

Willis Ware of RAND Corporation writes *Security and Privacy in Computer*

Introduction

This chapter discusses the *Foreign Intelligence Surveillance (FISA) Act* of 1978, a legislative effort to reform the nation's intelligence agencies in the wake of one of the greatest intelligence industry controversies in U.S. history: the "Watergate" conspiracy that led to the resignation of President Richard Nixon. In 1972, a group of Nixon-administration employees and associates were discovered attempting to install listening devices in the offices of the Democratic National Committee at the Watergate Hotel, in hopes that information gleaned from the operation could be used to discredit Democratic opponents and help Nixon secure re-election. In was gradually revealed that, during his presidency, Nixon had utilized the intelligence community in a number of controversial ways.

Utilizing a dearth of regulations on intelligence agency surveillance, Nixon used the CIA and FBI to monitor the American youth and anti-war movements, and to spy on foreign heads of allied nations, without any congressional notification or judicial approval. After these activities were revealed to Congress, there was a passionate bipartisan outcry for intelligence industry reform. This resulted in the 1978 FISA Act, which struck a balance between reform and the need to maintain secrecy in intelligence industry activities. The primary source document for this chapter, excerpts from the original 1978 FISA Act bill, reveals some of the FISA provisions as originally envisioned by the legislature. The commentary of legislators, debating the act in an ensuing series of congressional hearings, demonstrate some of the concerns that critics voiced about the bill, including the fear that an unscrupulous executive leader could still utilize the weakness of FISA Act provisions to abuse intelligence powers in the same way that Nixon had during his controversial presidency.

1968 The Omnibus Crime Control Act holds that police needed to obtain a warrant before engaging in wire-

1969 Joseph Licklider creates the Advanced Research Projects Agency Network (ARPANET), which was

Topics covered in this chapter include:

- Wiretapping
- Intelligence reform
- Foreign intelligence law
- Distrust of the federal government
- Domestic surveillance

This Chapter Discusses the Following Source Document:
The Foreign Intelligence Surveillance Act of 1978. 50 USC 1801. Oct. 25, 1978.

Monitoring Dissidents
The FISA Act of 1978

Of the many factors that eroded American trust in the federal government between the 1960s and the twenty-first century, the presidency of Richard Nixon, and the scandals that led to Nixon becoming the first president to resign from office, were among the most damaging.

The 1971 Pentagon Papers controversy was an embarrassment to Nixon and his administration, though his public approval ratings remained high. What the public did not know at the time was that Nixon had authorized the creation of a special investigation unit within the White House, known later as the "White House Plumbers," who were charged with preventing leaks, like the one that resulted in the publication of the Pentagon Papers documents. The first task assigned to the Plumbers was to burglarize the office of a psychiatrist who had been treating Daniel Ellsberg, the man responsible for leaking the Pentagon Papers, and to search for information that could be used to discredit Ellsberg in the press. The operation was a failure.

On June 17, 1972, the plumbers engaged in another operation, attempting to install electronic listening devices in the offices of the Democratic National Committee at the Watergate hotel in Washington, D.C. Their intention was to gather information that could be used in the campaign to re-elect Nixon, possibly by finding data that could discredit his opponents or the Democratic Party as a whole. The mission did *not* go well. Police arrested five of the plumbers at the hotel, some of them former Nixon aides, and others easily connected to the administration or to the GOP.[35]

Richard Nixon won by a landslide in the November 1972 election, earning a 68 percent approval rating according to a Gallup Poll released after the election. However, soon after his second term began, details of the burglary and the subsequent attempts by members of Nixon's staff to conceal the involve-

1974

The Watergate Scandal results in the revelation that the CIA had been conducting widespread surveillance of American dissidents and foreign leaders without judicial oversight

The Privacy Act is established

ment of the White House, began to erode confidence in the presidency. By the summer of 1973, when the Watergate hearings were being broadcast across the country, Nixon's approval plummeted to 31 percent. Meanwhile, the percentage of Americans who believed Nixon should be removed from office increased from an estimated 19 percent in May–June of 1973, to 57 percent in August of 1974, just before Nixon, recognizing that he was likely going to be impeached, resigned from office.[36] Several members of Nixon's staff were arrested and charged with criminal offenses. Former Attorney General John Mitchell, one of Nixon's closest friends and his former law partner, became the first White House official ever to serve time in a federal prison when he was convicted of organizing funding for the Watergate break-in.

One of the most controversial revelations from the resulting investigation involved the Huston Plan, a domestic intelligence strategy developed by former intelligence officer and White House intelligence liaison Tom Charles Huston. Reviving echoes of the McCarthy Era, what few details of the plan were revealed to the public showed that Nixon had agreed to grant new powers to the National Security Agency (NSA), Central Intelligence Agency (CIA), and Federal Bureau of Investigation (FBI) to conduct domestic surveillance. This included surveilling foreign heads of state, political opponents in the Democratic Party, and those labeled as "subversives" for participating in the Anti-War movement.[37]

As of 2017, much of the Huston Plan is still classified under government secrecy guidelines and so there has been little opportunity for historians and political analysts to determine the degree to which the plan violated the rules of conduct for the agencies involved. What was discovered was that the CIA, acting against the organization's domestic charter, had been involved in a massive domestic spying operation, targeting the anti-war movement, with a special unit within the CIA reportedly maintaining files on at least 10,000 American citizens.[38]

1975   Senator Frank Church leads a series of hearings about the secret NSA SHAMROCK operation involved intercepting communications from American citizens

1978   Congress passes the 1978 FISA Act

A photographer takes a photo of evidence from the infamous Watergate break-in at the Democratic National Committee (DNC) headquarters at the Watergate Office Building in Washington, 17 June 1972. The US National Archives opened up and displayed some of the police evidence 13 June 2002 to mark the 30th anniversary of the historical crime. Seen (left to right) are arrest photo enlargements of the 4 Cubans from Miami, Valdez Martinez, Virgilio Gonzalez, Bernard Barker, and Frank Sturgis who committed the robbery, in the foreground are lights, film, a toolbag, a trenchcoat, and bugging equipment used in one of the most famous burglaries in political history. (Photo: Paul J. Richards/AFP/Getty Images)

Following the Supreme Court case of *Katz v. United States* in 1967, Congress drafted and approved a massive anti-crime bill, known as the Omnibus Crime Control Act (1968). The Omnibus Act clarified and broadened police powers in some arenas, but also included new, more stringent laws regarding electronic surveillance, guided by the court's decision in *Katz*. Under the provisions of the act, any agency conducting domestic surveillance was expected to obtain a warrant before engaging in any type of electronic surveillance operation.

1980 The Intelligence Oversight Act (IOA) updates legal standards

1981 President Reagan's E.O. authorized wiretapping

1986 The Electronic Communications Privacy Act is established

The Nixon scandal of the 1970s demonstrated that laws governing federal intelligence agencies were perhaps insufficient to prevent an unscrupulous executive administration from misusing and abusing the powers of the intelligence agencies. After Nixon's resignation, as details of his many questionable policies emerged, a movement for intelligence reform began to gain traction in congress. The result of this push was the 1978 Foreign Intelligence Surveillance Act (FISA), which established new rules for situations in which intelligence agencies, like the CIA or NSA, wished to investigate cases involving foreign governments or agents AND U.S. citizens.

The 1978 act established a new judicial body, the Foreign Intelligence Surveillance Court (FISC), that would be convened to hear petitions from federal agents regarding proposed surveillance programs. Information given to the court and the court's rulings would be classified under laws regarding state secrets and this, supporters asserted, would simultaneously preserve the need for secrecy in intelligence operations, while providing an additional level of oversight to prevent intelligence agencies from violating the rights of citizens to due process and constitutional protections. The FISA Act was thus a compromise between those who believed the powers of the intelligence agencies and the presidency, needed to be curtailed and those who argued that oversight would reduce the effectiveness of the nation's intelligence agencies.

As per the act, the process of designating the justices to the FISA court was to be left to the Supreme Court:

1994 Netscape creates the "cookie" allowing computers to monitor Internet users

2001 The September 11 terrorist attacks result in Congress authorizing the Bush Administration to utilize military methods to combat terrorism

THE FOREIGN INTELLIGENCE SURVEILLANCE ACT (FISA) OF 1978

Source Document Excerpt

The Chief Justice of the United States shall publicly designate 11 district court judges from at least seven of the United States judicial circuits of whom no fewer than 3 shall reside within 20 miles of the District of Columbia who shall constitute a court which shall have jurisdiction to hear applications for and grant orders approving electronic surveillance anywhere within the United States...

For the purposes of the law, electronic surveillance was described as:

FISA Act of 1978
continued

The acquisition by an electronic, mechanical, or other surveillance device of the contents of any wire or radio communication sent by or intended to be received by a particular known United States person who is in the United States, if the contents are acquired by intentionally targeting that United States person, under circumstances in which a person has a reasonable expectation of privacy and a warrant would be required for law enforcement purposes.

or:

FISA Act of 1978
continued

The installation or use of an electronic, mechanical, or other surveillance device in the United States for monitoring to acquire information, other than from a wire or radio communication, under circumstances in which a person has a reasonable expectation of privacy and a warrant would be required for law enforcement purposes.

The Bush administration secretly authorizes the President's Surveillance Program (PSP), utilizing E.O. 12333

The U.S. PATRIOT Act alters existing laws to facilitate better communication between the state's intelligence branches in the effort to combat terrorism

The Transportation Security Administration (TSA) is established, creating the "No Fly" and "Selectee" lists that limit the right to travel on airplanes in the United States

The FISA Act was controversial at its inception, with some worrying that the secrecy of the court and its proceedings eliminated the adversarial process necessary to ensure that investigations of Americans were carried out according to due process. Others raised concerns that the language of the legislation was sufficiently broad that it would be possible for the executive branch to abuse the FISA law to conduct surveillance beyond the limits intended by the legislature.

In Senate hearings conducted in two sessions, in February and June of 1978, Senators, legal scholars, federal employees, and experts on intelligence gave testimony to the Senate Intelligence Committee regarding the pros and cons of the FISA Act legislation.

Christopher Pyle, Professor of Constitutional Law and Mount Holyoke College, delivered a strong criticism of the proposed bill, reflecting the broader constitutional concerns that had been repeatedly raised by civil liberties advocates from the establishment of the Bill of Rights through the Nixon scandal. I was first confronted with the problem that faces this Committee ten years ago when, as an officer on the faculty of the Army Intelligence School, I had occasion to take a book down from my office shelf. Inside the cover was the faded imprint of a rubber stamp, which read:

"This publication is included in the counter-intelligence corps school library for research purposes only. Its presence on the library shelf does not indicate that the views expressed in the publication represent the policies or opinions of the Counter Intelligence Corps or the military establishment."

The book was the Constitution of the United States.

Over the years, I have reflected on the significance,

2005

The PATRIOT Act was reauthorized without substantial changes as Congress favors security concerns over warnings that the law creates the potential for civil liberties violations

The *New York Times* publishes articles resulting from leaks revealing the secret President's Surveillance Program (PSP) established by the Bush administration

and the symbolism, of that disclaimer. The men who stamped it there did not intend to disassociate themselves from the Constitution they had sworn to uphold; they had no strong feelings about the Constitution one way or the other. They simply responded—in an essentially mindless way— to pressures placed upon them by an outspoken Member of Congress who, in his zeal to ferret out Communism, sent his staff out to purge military libraries of "subversive" writings.

Today, of course, the situation is different. Congress is pressing the Executive branch to erase those disclaimers and I, for one, am glad of it. Yet I fear that Congress may achieve little more than cosmetic reform—new rubber stamps—proclaiming fealty to the Constitution in place of the old ones disclaiming it, while the same, essentially mindless behavior continues.

The gist of what I have to say today is that despite all of the effort that has gone into this bill, it may achieve little more than cosmetic reform. Indeed, it could be worse. It could turn into a "backdoor charter" authorizing many of the surveillance excesses Congress has so recently deplored.

The most disturbing aspect of the bill to me is its disregard for Fourth Amendment principles. The bill purports to extend traditional warrant procedures to foreign intelligence taps, bugs, and microwave intercepts, but, in fact, it does no such thing. Rather, it invents two new "pseudo-warrants," unlike anything

2007 The Bush Administration plans to make data taken from spy satellites available to law enforcement to be used to conduct domestic surveillance

2008 Congress passes Section 702, or the FISA Amendment Act, which is used to permit a massive NSA and CIA domestic surveillance program

the American judicial system has ever seen.

Probable cause to believe that a crime has been, is being, or is about to be committed is the sine qua non of a judicial search warrant. The Supreme Court has consistently condemned searches and seizures made without a search warrant, subject only to a few "jealously and carefully drawn" exceptions.

The only occasion on which a judge may issue a search warrant in the absence of probable cause is when a person refuses to comply with a reasonable inspection request by a public health, housing, or fire inspector. In these instances, direct advance notice to the subject of the search mitigates the invasion of privacy. Moreover, the Court orders required in Camara are really not search warrants at all, but "certificates of need" legitimizing inspections and lending the contempt powers of judges to inspectors to hasten their entry.

The fact that the Court has mislabelled these orders is no reason for Congress now to compound the error. Let there be no mistake about it: the "certificates of need" proposed in this bill cannot be called warrants without doing irreparable harm to the 200-year-old definition of a search warrant. If this Committee does nothing else to revise this bill, it should at least practice truth-in-labelling and replace the term "warrant" wherever it appears with the more accurate term "certificate of need." Then no one can accuse Congress of perpetrating a hoax on the American people and the departure from Fourth Amendment standards will be plain for all to see.

2012 The Obama Administration proposes a Consumer Privacy Bill of Rights guaranteeing individuals the right to greater control over the use of their digital data

2013 The *Guardian* and the *Washington Post* publish the first series of articles derived from leaked NSA and CIA documents delivered by Edward Snowden

One need not imagine how the certificates will be worded if the bill passes. John Mitchell's affidavit explaining the need for warrantless taps against the Jewish Defense League provides a perfect example:

"The surveillance of this telephone installation was authorized by the President of the United States acting through the Attorney General, in the exercise of his authority relating to the nation's foreign affairs and was deemed essential to protect this nation and its citizens against hostile acts of a foreign power and to obtain intelligence Information deemed essential to the security of the United States."

In short, anyone who believes that the certification procedures in this bill will protect liberty must believe that we will never again have an Attorney General like Prisoner No. 24171-157.[39]

The prisoner (No. 24171-157) referred to in Christopher Pyle's Senate testimony was John N. Mitchell, Nixon's former Attorney General. Pyle and other critics hoped that the intelligence reform push of the era would result in substantive reforms that would prevent future abuses of power like those committed under Nixon or under McCarthy's influence in the 1950s Communist witch hunts. By the time the FISA Act passed, the attempt to balance the demands of the state with the desire to prohibit state abuse of citizens, resulted in a law that failed to win the approval of critics on either side.

It is no accident that privacy and civil rights advocates repeatedly cite Watergate and the McCarthy era in formulating arguments in support of privacy protections. In both cases, politicians utilized broad interpretations of existing statutes and laws to grant themselves new powers and thus used the

The Senate Judiciary committee holds hearings to determine if the executive surveillance operations carried out under the PATRIOT Act were a violation of constitutional law

Snowden leaks reveal that the NSA and CIA had been attempting to force corporations to provide a backdoor to encryption systems that would allow federal agents to bypass consumer encryption

organs of national security (police and federal agents) to violate the privacy of their political enemies. This included other politicians and political "dissidents," like the anti-war protestors of the 60s and 70s, or the worker's rights activists in the Communist movement of the 40s and 50s. In the guise of protecting national security, the Nixon administration, and the McCarthy Senate used the state's intelligence powers to defend the status-quo of America's hierarchy against growing dissent within the populace.

Though the FISA Act represented the most effective compromise that the legislature could reach at the time, the proliferation of technology quickly raised concerns that FISA and other laws regarding surveillance were rapidly becoming obsolete. From the wiretaps of the Nixon era through the proliferation of personal computing, digital data replaced paper records as the primary method for storing data as well as the basic substrate of commerce and communication. As this reality dawned, legislators, activists, and jurists were forced to again return to the privacy and security debate.

Public opinion was mixed on Nixon and his legacy at the time of his resignation. Studies of public opinion at the time found that the impact of the Watergate scandal was negative for politics as a whole, rather than simply for Nixon. In addition, the influence of "big business" was a major issue in the Watergate hearings, and surveys found increasing skepticism and cynicism regarding the role of business in American society and especially about the influence of business on American politicians. The most notable trend in public opinion was an erosion of faith in government. With regards to the privacy debate, the gradual depiction of the government as detached from the American people, as potentially corrupt or engaged in untrustworthy foreign affairs or domestic activities, colored the way that Americans viewed their politicians and their government for decades after Nixon's resignation.[40]

2015

| Terrorist attacks in France reignite fears of domestic terrorist violence | The PATRIOT Act is replaced by the USA Freedom Act | Federal Courts order Apple, Inc. to create a new operation system that would enable federal investigators to bypass security on an iPhone. |

CONCLUSION

At the time it became law, the FISA Act of 1978 was an uneasy compromise, with some critics arguing that such a law would limit the effectiveness of the intelligence agencies, potentially posing a threat to national security, while critics on the other side argued that the secrecy of the act, and general lack of specificity in the law itself, left too much room for abuse. Domestic surveillance would become a hot topic again after it was revealed that the Bush Administration had utilized weaknesses in existing regulations to authorize domestic surveillance activities far more egregious and widespread than those conducted by Nixon.

The FCC publishes official rules of "neutrality"

2016

The EU establishes the General Data Protection Regulation (GDPR), described as the strongest digital data privacy law in the world

DISCUSSION QUESTIONS

- Should intelligence agencies need to obtain court approval before conducting surveillance on American citizens? Why or why not?
- Has the FISA Act been effective at preventing intelligence agency misconduct? Why or why not?
- Was it appropriate for the Nixon administration to use the intelligence agencies to monitor the anti-war movement? Why or why not?
- What modern controversies relate to intelligence agency misconduct and oversight?

Works Used

Brinkley, Douglas, and Luke A. Nichter. "Great mystery of the 1970s: Nixon, Watergate and the Huston Plan." *CNN*. CNN. June 17, 2015. Web. 25 Oct. 2017.

"Foreign Intelligence Surveillance Act of 1978." *U.S. Senate*. Subcommittee on Intelligence and the Rights of Americans. 1978. Web. 31 Oct. 2017.

Hersh, Seymour M. "Huge C.I.A. Operation Reported in U.S. Against Antiwar Forces, Other Dissidents in Nixon Years." *New York Times*. New York Times Company. Dec. 22, 1974. Web. 25 Oct. 2017.

Kohut, Andrew. "How the Watergate crisis eroded public support for Richard Nixon." *Pew Research*. Pew Research Center. Aug. 8, 2014. Web. 1 Nov. 2017.

Robinson, John P. "Public Opinion During the Watergate Crisis." *Communications Research*. Vol. 1, No. 4. Oct. 1974. Web. 9 Nov. 2017.

Savage, Charlie. "Classification Guide for FISA, the Protect America Act and the FISA Amendments Act." *New York Times*. New York Times, Co. Mar. 11, 2014. Web. 25 Oct. 2017.

"The Watergate Story." *Washington Post*. Washington Post LLC. 2017. Web. 25 Oct. 2017.

2017

The "Vault 7" secrets, a leak of 9,000 CIA documents, reveal details of the CIA's attempts to break through encryption used by Internet

President Trump appoints Ajit Pai to head the FCC, who abolishes the FCC neutrality protections

Introduction

The debate over privacy law in the United States begins with the 1890 article discussed in Chapter 1, *The Right to Privacy*, in which legal scholars Samuel Warren and Louis Brandeis defined privacy as "the right to be let alone." Over the years since Brandeis and Warren's article sparked the debate on privacy law, legal scholars examining the issue found many weaknesses with the notion of a "right to be let alone" as the basis for privacy law. Although this scholarly debate may have had little impact on the way that the public views privacy, the effort to advance and strengthen the concept of privacy has important ramifications when it comes to justifying claims of privacy in the legal sphere.

The primary source for this chapter is a 1980 article by Israeli legal scholar Ruth Gavison, "Privacy and the Limits of Law." Gavison makes a concerted effort to look at a host of situations in which people generally see privacy as an issue, from surveillance, to the intrusions of corporations or the media, to situations in which laws intrude on private behaviors within a person's home, trying to tease out the relevant thread tying those disparate issues together. From that, and an examination of other philosophical theories about privacy, Gavison advances an approach that defines privacy as the degree to which others have access to a person. This approach, Gavison argues, makes privacy a robust legal concept that can be evaluated and applied to judge various cases involving privacy law.

Topics covered in this chapter include:
- Privacy philosophy
- Legal definition of privacy
- Reductionism

This Chapter Discusses the Following Source Document:
Gavison, Ruth. "Privacy and the Limits of Law." *Yale Law Journal.* Vol. 89, No. 3. (Jan. 1980). 421–71.

1788 State legislatures ratify the U.S. Constitution, establishing the basic precedent for all future constitutional law

1791 The U.S. Congress ratifies the Bill of Rights, creating the first 10 amendments to the United States Constitution

Modernizing Privacy Philosophy
"Privacy and the Limits of Law" (1980)

In their seminal 1890 article, *The Right to Privacy*, future Supreme Court Justice Louis Brandeis and Boston lawyer Samuel Warren utilized common law to argue for a general legal right to privacy that could be used to protect citizens against intrusions by the state, the press, or other citizens. From this foundational work of scholarship, the legal right to privacy advanced through a series of court decisions and legislative debates, resulting in the 1967 case of *Griswold v. Connecticut,* which established, nearly 80 years after Brandeis and Warren first raised the issue, a constitutional right to privacy. This then laid the foundation for the 1968 Omnibus Crime Control Act, the Privacy Act of 1974, the FISA Act of 1978, and other legal and legislative efforts to codify and define the limits of this emerging right within the context of U.S. laws and in keeping with the goals of the state to uphold the law and ensure national security.

While a majority of the American people already accepted the importance of privacy, in principle, the philosophical debate was important to the evolution of public opinion in several keys ways. First, influential scholarly thought about privacy could potentially filter into public conceptions over the longer term. Second, legal philosophy helped define the legal approach to philosophy in the courts and thus helped to determine whether and how legal policy would develop to resemble, as close as possible, the ways in which the public conceived of privacy and wished to see their rights protected.

By 1980, legal scholars and philosophers in the "reductionist" school suggested that calls to protect privacy in the legal system inevitably involved some other interest. When a criminal claimed his or her privacy rights had been violated, therefore, it could be argued that the interest in this claim was motivated by a desire to avoid punishment, and not by a legitimate

1868 The 14ᵗʰ Amendment to the U.S. Constitution guarantees all citizens the right to due process under the law

1890 Warren and Brandeis publish "The Right to Privacy" in the *Harvard Law Review*

interest in privacy as an independent right or value. Arguments like these raised questions about the legitimacy of privacy as a right or legal principle.

Israeli Political scholar Ruth Gavison contributed to this debate with her article, "Privacy and the Limits of Law," published in the 1980 edition of the *Yale Law Journal*. Gavison, who earned her doctorate in legal philosophy from the University of Oxford in 1975, made privacy law one of the focuses of her doctorate studies and later, as a Law professor at the Hebrew University of Jerusalem, also advanced theories on human rights and ethnic conflict.[41]

As Gavison introduces the subject:

PRIVACY AND THE LIMITS OF LAW
by Ruth Gavison
Yale Law Journal, 1980
Source Document Excerpt

Our interest in privacy, I argue, is related to our concern over our accessibility to others: the extent to which we are known to others, the extent to which others have physical access to us, and the extent to which we are the subject of others' attention. This concept of privacy as a concern for limited accessibility enables us to identify when losses of privacy occur. Furthermore, the reasons for which we claim privacy in different situations are similar. They are related to the functions privacy has in our lives: the promotion of liberty, autonomy, selfhood, and human relations, and furthering the existence of a free society.

From there, Gavison advances the need for a "neutral" concept of privacy that could be used to evaluate situations in which a loss of privacy has been claimed:

1923
Meyer v. Nebraska establishes that the 14th Amendment guarantees privileges of citizenship

1928
Olmstead v. United States rules that wiretapping is not a form of search and seizure defined by the 14th Amendment

"Privacy and the Limits of Law"
continued

"Privacy" is a term used with many meanings. For my purposes, two types of questions about privacy are important. The first relates to the *status* of the term: is privacy a situation, a right, a claim, a form of control, a value? The second relates to the *characteristics* of privacy: is it related to information, to autonomy, to personal identity, to physical access? Support for all of these possible answers, in almost any combination, can be found in the literature.

The two types of questions involve different choices. Before resolving these issues, however, a general distinction must be drawn between the concept and the value of privacy. The concept of privacy identifies losses of privacy. As such, it should be neutral and descriptive only, so as not to preempt question we might want to ask about such losses. Is the loser aware of the loss? Has he consented to it? Is the loss desirable? Should the law do something to prevent or punish such losses?

This is not to imply that the neutral concept of privacy is the most important, or that it is only legitimate to use "privacy" in this sense. Indeed, in the context of legal protection, privacy should also indicate a value. The coherence and usefulness of privacy as a value is due to a similarity one finds in the reasons advanced for its protection, a similarity that enables us to draw principles of liability for invasions. These reasons identify those aspects of privacy that are considered desirable. When we claim legal protection for privacy, we mean that only those aspects should be protected, and we no longer refer to the "neutral" concept of privacy. In order to see which aspects of privacy are desirable and thus merit protection as a value, however, we must begin our inquiry in a non-preemptive way by starting with a concept that does not make desirability, or any of the elements that may preempt the question of desirability, part of the notion of privacy. The value of privacy can be determined only at the conclusion of discussion about what privacy is, and when-and why-losses of privacy are undesirable.

In this section I argue that it is possible to advance a neutral concept of privacy, and that it can be shown to serve important functions that entitle it to prima facie legal protection. The coherence of privacy in the third context—as a legal concept—relies on our understanding of the functions and value of privacy; discussion of the way in which the legal system should consider privacy is therefore deferred until later sections.

1934   The Federal Communications Commission (FCC) is established under the Federal Communications Act (FCA)

1942   *Goldman v. United States* rules that using electronic listening devices does not violate the 14th Amendment

Gavison's neutral concept, based on privacy as a measure of access to a person, can be divided into three components:

1) Information about the individual (secrecy)

2) Attention paid to the individual (anonymity)

3) Physical access to the individual (solitude)

"Privacy and the Limits of Law" continued

In its most suggestive sense, privacy is a limitation of others' access to an individual. As a methodological starting point, I suggest that an individual enjoys perfect privacy when he is completely inaccessible to others.

This may be broken into three independent components: in perfect privacy, no one has any information about X, no one pays any attention to X, and no one has physical access to X.

Perfect privacy is, of course, impossible in any society. The possession or enjoyment of privacy is not an all or nothing concept, however, and the total loss of privacy is as impossible as perfect privacy. A more important concept, then, is loss of privacy. A loss of privacy occurs as others obtain information about an individual, pay attention to him, or gain access to him. These three elements of secrecy, anonymity, and solitude are distinct and independent, but interrelated, and the complex concept of privacy is richer than any definition centered around only one of them.

The complex concept better explains our intuitions as to when privacy is lost, and captures more of the suggestive meaning of privacy. At the same time, it remains sufficiently distinctive to exclude situations that are sometimes labeled "privacy," but that are more related to notions of accountability and interference than to accessibility.

From the development of Gavison's neutral concept, she demonstrates how the three interrelated concepts (secrecy, anonymity, solitude) manifest in various types of situations.

1945 The National Security Agency secretly creates Project SHAMROCK

1950 Senator Joseph McCarthy delivers a shocking speech claiming that more than 200 communist spies have infiltrated the U.S. government

"Privacy and the Limits of Law"
continued

The interrelations between the three elements may be seen when we consider the different aspects of privacy that may be involved in one situation. For instance, police attempt to learn of plans to commit crimes. Potential criminals may raise a privacy claim concerning this information, but are unlikely to gain much support. The criminal's desire that information about his plans not be known creates a privacy claim, but not a very convincing one. We might be more receptive, however, to another privacy claim that criminals might make concerning attention and observation, or the opportunity to be alone. If constant surveillance were the price of efficient law enforcement, we might feel the need to rethink the criminal law. The fact that these are two independent claims suggests that concern for the opportunity to have solitude and anonymity is related not only to the wish to conceal some kind of information, but also to needs such as relaxation, concentration, and freedom from inhibition.

Yet another privacy concern emerges when we talk about the right against self-incrimination. Again, the sense of the concern is not simply the information itself; we do not protect the suspect against police learning the information from other sources. Our concern relates to the way the information is acquired: it is an implication of privacy that individuals should not be forced to give evidence against themselves. Similarly, evidentiary privileges that may also be defended in terms of privacy do not reflect concern about the information itself. The concern here is the existence of relationships in which confidentiality should be protected, so that the parties know that confidences shared in these relationships will not be forced out.

> *A loss of privacy occurs as others obtain information about an individual, pay attention to him, or gain access to him. These three elements of secrecy, anonymity, and solitude are distinct and independent, but interrelated, and the complex concept of privacy is richer than any definition centered around only one of them.*

1951 *Dennis v. United States* rules that government limits to speech is legal only to prevent a threat to public safety or security

1959 *Barenblatt v. United States* rules that it's legal to order people to reveal personal details if national threat is perceived

On the need for a new privacy concept, Gavison argues against previous concepts of privacy as either:

1) A "right to be let alone"

2) Interference in liberty

3) As a matter of "human dignity"

The "right to be let alone" concept of privacy advanced by Brandeis and Warren became the foundation for U.S. privacy laws over the next century and was repeatedly cited by privacy advocates and lawmakers attempting to address the issue.

The "human dignity" approach mentioned by Gavison refers to the work of New York University Law Professor Edward J. Bloustein who, in a 1964 article on the subject, argued for a definition of privacy that drew on concepts of dignity and individuality. As he writes in his conclusion:

> *The man who is compelled to live every minute of his life among others and whose every need, thought, desire, fancy or gratification is subject to public scrutiny, has been deprived of his individuality and human dignity. Such an individual merges with the mass. His opinions, being public, tend never to be different; his aspirations, being known, tend always to be conventionally accepted ones; his feelings, being openly exhibited, tend to lose their quality of unique personal warmth and to become the feelings of every man. Such a being, although sentient, is fungible; he is not an individual.*[42]

1965 | *Griswold v. CT* rules in favor of married couples' right to privacy

1967 | *Katz v. United States* rules wiretaps a form of search and seizure

Willis Ware of RAND Corporation writes *Security and Privacy in Computer*

Gavison thus argues that none of these approaches is sufficient to encompass the variety of situations in which individuals have an inherent sense of privacy or in which individuals see their privacy as having been violated:

"Privacy and the Limits of Law"
continued

There is one obvious way to include all the so-called invasions of privacy under the term. Privacy can be defined as "being let alone," using the phrase often attributed—incorrectly—to Samuel Warren and Louis Brandeis. The great simplicity of this definition gives it rhetorical force and attractiveness, but also denies it the distinctiveness that is necessary for the phrase to be useful in more than a conclusory sense. This description gives an appearance of differentiation while covering almost any conceivable complaint anyone could ever make. A great many instances of "not letting people alone" cannot readily be described as invasions of privacy. Requiring that people pay their taxes or go into the army, or punishing them for murder, are just a few of the obvious examples.

For similar reasons, we must reject Edward Bloustein's suggestion that the coherence of privacy lies in the fact that all invasions are violations of human dignity. We may well be concerned with invasions of privacy, at least in part, because they are violations of dignity. But there are ways to offend dignity and personality that have nothing to do with privacy. Having to beg or sell one's body in order to survive are serious affronts to dignity, but do not appear to involve loss of privacy.

To speak in privacy terms about claims for noninterference by the state in personal decisions is similar to identifying privacy with "being let alone." There are two problems with this tendency. The first is that the typical privacy claim is not a claim for noninterference by the state at all. It is a claim for state interference in the form of legal protection against other individuals, and this is obscured when privacy is discussed in terms of noninterference with personal decisions. The second problem is that this conception excludes from the realm of privacy all claims that have nothing to do with highly personal decisions, such as an individual's unwillingness to have a file in a central data bank. Moreover, identifying privacy as noninterference with private action, often to avoid an explicit return to "substantive due process," may obscure the nature of the legal decision and draw attention away from important considerations. The limit of state interference with individual

1968 The Omnibus Crime Control Act holds that police needed to obtain a warrant before engaging in wire-

1969 Joseph Licklider creates the Advanced Research Projects Agency Network (ARPANET), which was

"Privacy and the Limits of Law"
continued

action is an important question that has been with us for centuries. The usual terminology for dealing with this question is that of "liberty of action." It may well be that some cases pose a stronger claim for noninterference than others, and that the intimate nature of certain decisions affects these limits. This does not justify naming this set of concerns "privacy," however. A better way to deal with these issues may be to treat them as involving questions of liberty, in which enforcement may raise difficult privacy issues.

Gavison, therefore, argues that the neutral definition of privacy she favors could not have been applied to the Supreme Court case of *Griswold v. Connecticut*, which is, in fact, the case that defined the constitutional right to privacy in U.S. law. In the case, a majority of justices agreed that a Connecticut law outlawing contraception was a violation of "marital privacy." This, Gavison argues, may be a misapplication of the concept of privacy, as the issue in question was actually whether the state had the right to interfere with a person's private decision to use contraception.

The question of whether the state has the right to interfere with personal decisions that do not affect the state is also, Gavison argues, an important determination. In the *Griswold* case, Gavison argues that a legal claim against the law might have taken the form of an argument that such a law was a violation of personal liberty, rather than privacy. However, though a law prohibiting contraception might not be seen as a violation of privacy in itself, Gavison raised the issue of enforcement, and argues that enforcing such a law would require that police ascertain information about a person's private life and behavior and thus enforcing an anti-contraception law would itself constitute a violation of privacy according to the neutral, access-oriented approach.

In the section of her article entitled, "The Limits of Law," Gavison argues:

1971   The Pentagon Papers leaks from the press raise the issue of the Freedom of the Press versus the privacy of the government to conceal information about national security operations

1972   *Eisenstadt v. Baird* rules that the right to privacy applies to individuals

"Privacy and the Limits of Law"
continued

One of the advantages of this analysis is that it draws attention to—and explains—the fact that legal protection of privacy has always had, and always will have, serious limitations. In many cases, the law cannot compensate for losses of privacy, and it has strong commitments to other ideals that must sometimes override the concern for privacy. Consequently, one cannot assume that court decisions protecting privacy reflect fully or adequately the perceived need for privacy in our lives.

In attempting to tackle the difficult philosophical issues surrounding the evolution of privacy as a concept, Gavison builds upon, and attempts to improve upon, the basic "right to be let alone" principle that long-informed legal discussions on the subject. In doing so, Gavison also attempted to provide a framework both for future philosophical discussions on the issue, and also for legal protections. She argues, in her conclusion:

"Privacy and the Limits of Law"
continued

There is much to be said for making an explicit legal commitment to privacy. Such a commitment would affirm that privacy is not just a convenient label, but a central value.

1974

The Watergate Scandal results in the revelation that the CIA had been conducting widespread surveillance of American dissidents and foreign leaders without judicial oversight

The Privacy Act is established

CONCLUSION

Gavison's access theory of privacy demonstrates how legal scholarship had advanced since Brandeis and Warren's 1890 article and the "right to be let alone" theory of privacy rights. For the generation of jurists, lawyers, and judges studying law in the late twentieth century, Gavison's access theory of privacy was an influential work that greatly shaped scholarly thought on the subject. Gavison demonstrated how many of the exceptions raised by reductionist philosophers arguing against the concept of privacy as a distinct right or value could be eliminated by adopting a more rigorous legal definition that was both coherent and specific enough to be evaluated in different situations.

1975   Senator Frank Church leads a series of hearings about the secret NSA SHAMROCK operation involved intercepting communications from American citizens

1978   Congress passes the 1978 FISA Act

DISCUSSION QUESTIONS

- Do you agree with Gavison's definition of privacy as a matter of access to an individual? Why or why not?
- What is the difference between privacy and personal liberty? Give some examples.
- Gavison rejects Bloustein's theory of privacy as a matter of "human dignity," do you agree with her criticism of this idea? Why or why not?
- Is it important to create a legal definition of privacy? Why or why not?

Works Used

Bloustein, Edward J. "Privacy as an Aspect of Human Dignity: An Answer to Dean Prosser." *NYUL Review*. New York University Law Review. 1964. Web. 31 Oct. 2017.

Gavison, Ruth. "Privacy and the Limits of Law." *Yale Law Journal*. Vol. 89, No. 3. (Jan. 1980). 421–71.

"Prof. Ruth Gavison." *HUJI*. Hebrew University of Jerusalem. The Faculty of Law. 2017. Web. 31 Oct. 2017.

1980 The Intelligence Oversight Act (IOA) updates legal standards

1981 President Reagan's E.O. authorized wiretapping

1986 The Electronic Communications Privacy Act is established

1994 Netscape creates the "cookie" allowing computers to monitor Internet users

2001 The September 11 terrorist attacks result in Congress authorizing the Bush Administration to utilize military methods to combat terrorism

Introduction

The debate over privacy rights has followed several separate trajectories. One important aspect of this ongoing debate has been an effort to advance privacy law to adjust to new technology and the ways that technological innovation changes the management of private information. This aspect of the privacy debate saw the courts, legislature, and the public struggling to cope with the evolution of telephone communication, which was initially thought of as a new corporate product (available primarily to the wealthy), but gradually became so integrated into society that telephone communication came to be seen as a public utility, regulated and managed in the public interest. Over the years, the courts and legislature struggled to decide whether messages delivered over telephones were protected as private communications, and if using electronic listening devices or wiretaps constituted a "search and seizure" for legal purposes. The advancement of computers brought a host of new technological innovations in the realm of personal communication and the storage of private data.

The 1974 Privacy Law regulated the ways in which the government collected and managed digital data from citizens, but left many unresolved issues. In this chapter, we examine the next phase in the effort to adjust privacy laws to emerging technology in the form of the 1986 *Electronic Communications Privacy Act*. The primary document for this chapter, the official text of the 1986 law, provides an example of how the legislature was attempting to ensure that existing privacy protections could be expanded to cover emerging modes of communication.

The Bush administration secretly authorizes the President's Surveillance Program (PSP), utilizing E.O. 12333

The U.S. PATRIOT Act alters existing laws to facilitate better communication between the state's intelligence branches in the effort to combat terrorism

The Transportation Security Administration (TSA) is established, creating the "No Fly" and "Selectee" lists that limit the right to travel on airplanes in the United States

Topics covered in this chapter include:
- Wiretapping
- Commercial/corporate privacy rights
- The Fourth Amendment of the Bill of Rights
- Commercial invasion of privacy
- Technology and privacy rights
- Legislation on digital privacy

This Chapter Discusses the Following Source Document:
Electronic Communications Privacy Act of 1986 (ECPA) 18 U.S.C. 2510-22.

Adjusting to Technology
The Electronic Communications Privacy Act (1986)

The ongoing effort to balance the needs and interests of the state (law enforcement, confidentiality of government data, intelligence activities) with the needs and interests of the public (personal privacy, personal liberty) has been a central feature of the historic debate on privacy laws in the United States. It is also possible, however, to examine the history of privacy law in another way, as a gradual evolution of the nation's efforts to adjust, legally, procedurally, and ethically, to advances in technology.

The first Supreme Court case related to the right to privacy, *Olmstead v. United States* (1928) dealt with two issues:

1) Whether there was a legal justification for a right to privacy.

2) Whether "wiretapping" was a form of search and seizure.

At the time, the court ruled that wiretapping was *not* a form of search, and this decision was based on the legal language of precedent to that point. As per the 1928 ruling, a search could only be said to have taken place if:

1) there had been a physical intrusion on a person's property or workplace; or

2) if the investigation involved intercepting written communications or correspondence delivered through the United States Postal System.

2007

The Bush Administration plans to make data taken from spy satellites available to law enforcement to be used to conduct domestic surveillance

2008

Congress passes Section 702, or the FISA Amendment Act, which is used to permit a massive NSA and CIA domestic surveillance program

Examining this second point, the basic idea was that the precepts of the Federal Postal Service guaranteed confidentiality and, this, therefore, was the justification for extending search and seizure protections to communications delivered through the post. At the time, there had been no laws or statutes granting the same level of protection to telephone communication and this was, in part, because telephones were corporate consumer products and not, at the time, governed by a federal authority.

In 1928, Census Bureau data indicates that about 40.9 percent of American households had telephones, an increase from 35 percent in 1920, which was the first year for which the Census Bureau recorded statistics on telephone ownership. By the time the Supreme Court ruled, in the 1967 case of *Katz v. United States*, that wiretapping was a form of search and seizure, over 87 percent of households had telephones.[43]

Whereas, in 1920, the telephone might still be considered a relatively new medium or a luxury afforded only to some, by the 1960s telephones were a familiar aspect of public and professional life. By 1967, it was generally understood that the telephone was integral to American life, essential for private communication, and therefore that telephone conversations should be given at least the same degree of protection as correspondence delivered through the Postal Service. The degree to which a type of communication is protected, therefore, has to do with the length of time the medium has been part of the public sphere, whether the medium in question is privately- or publicly-owned, and on a general consensus about the importance of the medium to public life.

The next major leap in communication technology initiated what some historians and sociologists have described as a new era in human life, the "Digital" or "Computer" age, marked by the invention, proliferation, and integration of digital data and digital processing tools into various aspects of human life. Beginning in the 1970s, pioneers in computing, like Willis Ware of the RAND Corporation, had already petitioned the government to estab-

2012 The Obama Administration proposes a Consumer Privacy Bill of Rights guaranteeing individuals the right to greater control over the use of their digital data

2013 The *Guardian* and the *Washington Post* publish the first series of articles derived from leaked NSA and CIA documents delivered by Edward Snowden

lish privacy protections governing the collection, storage, and transmission of digital data.

Public opinion polls from the era indicate that Americans were also deeply concerned about potential government intrusion and/or interception of private information. A Harris poll from 1983, for instance, found that 84 percent of Americans believed that the government might use televisions to spy on citizens, while 70 percent expressed concern that the government could collect and use private information to intimidate and thus control the citizenry.[44]

The federal government, responding to public pressure and a gradual recognition that digital data was becoming a more important factor in American life, addressed this issue in 1986 with the Electronic Communications Privacy Act (ECPA). This law was a first attempt to update protections for oral, written, and telephone communication to cover other emerging modes of electronic communication.

ELECTRONIC COMMUNICATIONS PRIVACY ACT (ECPA)
Source Document

Title I Typically referred to as the "Wiretap Act," prohibits the interception, use, or disclosure, of any "wire, oral, or electronic communication," and prohibits the use of such data as evidence in criminal or civil proceedings except in cases where officers of the law or government had properly obtained legal permission. Title I also elucidated the proper procedures for federal, state, and other government investigators to obtain judicial authorization for intercepting communications.

Title II The Stored Communications Act (SCA) protects the privacy of files stored by both service providers (companies offering electronic communication and data storage services) and the records that companies and agencies compiled and held regarding individual users. This included information such as a subscriber's name, billing records, and IP addresses.

The Senate Judiciary committee holds hearings to determine if the executive surveillance operations carried out under the PATRIOT Act were a violation of constitutional law

Snowden leaks reveal that the NSA and CIA had been attempting to force corporations to provide a backdoor to encryption systems that would allow federal agents to bypass consumer encryption

Electronic Communications Privacy Act (ECPA)
continued

Title III Concerns the use of "pen register" or "trap and trace" devices that could be used to record dialing, routing, addressing, and signaling information used to transmit wire or electronic communications. The third section further provided legal procedures for federal investigators to obtain court orders to utilize trap and trace or registering devices in investigations.[45]

Few lawmakers at the time would likely have been able to foresee the degree to which digital communication would become integral to public life, even, in many cases, eclipsing traditional modes of communication entirely. The effectiveness of the ECPA was the subject of debate in 1986 and the pace of technological development was such that, within a short time after the law was passed, numerous exceptions and problems with the law had been identified.[46] Thus, beginning in 1994, Congress attempted, on several occasions, to update the ECPA to address the emergence of new technologies and to better codify the specific rules governing various types of digital media.

During the 1990s, most of the major changes involving privacy rights regarded attempts, by the Federal Communications Commission (FCC), and advocacy groups, to create stronger protections regarding digital data. Most of this development did not have to do much with national security, but rather, concerned the corporate use of digital data. For instance, in 1994 the web-company Netscape invented a new type of program called a "cookie" that essentially allowed the company to monitor the behavior of Internet users online. Data collected about users was then sold to other companies to create targeted ads and this, in the 2000s and 2010s, became one of the most controversial privacy issues of the era.[47]

2015

| Terrorist attacks in France reignite fears of domestic terrorist violence | The PATRIOT Act is replaced by the USA Freedom Act | Federal Courts order Apple, Inc. to create a new operation system that would enable federal investigators to bypass security on an iPhone. |

In 1995, concerned about corporate threats to personal user data, the European Union (EU) adopted Directive 95/46/EC or the "…protection of individuals with regard to the processing of personal data and on the free movement of such data."[48] This was the world's strongest digital privacy law of the era and the EU continued, over subsequent years, to develop far stronger privacy protections than the United States. You could remove "in the same period" here. There are many reasons why U.S. digital privacy protections never reached the level of protection supported in the EU, but the primary reason is the power and influence of the nation's corporate lobbyists and, especially, the corporate rights lobby's influence over Republican lawmakers.

American conservatives have long been suspicious of government regulation, seeing it as a form of "interference" in personal liberty. Such thinkers opposed proposals to create government regulations on the telephones in the early twentieth century and have similarly opposed efforts to regulate digital data and commerce. A pro-business argument on the issue of corporate data privacy will typically hold that free-market competition will solve the issue. An argument from this perspective might say that, if digital privacy is important to consumers, then companies that establish privacy policies will flourish, whereas those that refuse to do so will fail.

In relation to privacy and privacy law, the free market provides little incentive for companies to voluntarily enact the strongest possible privacy protections if such laws do nothing to improve the bottom line of their core business and increase profits. Rather, companies that

The FCC publishes official rules of "neutrality"

2016

The EU establishes the General Data Protection Regulation (GDPR), described as the strongest digital data privacy law in the world

stand to benefit from using consumer data are often slow to be proactive in preserving privacy rights and only react when consumers or consumer advocates push back, industry standards and practices shift or legislation is passed.

Throughout the 1990s and 2000s, corporate use of data has been a major factor in the right to privacy debate in the United States. It wasn't until after the events of September 11, 2001, however, that Americans were able to see the possible connections between corporate privacy and national security. In essence, after the terrorist attacks on the United States, typically referred to simply as "9/11," the U.S. government adopted a renewed focus on national security. A slew of executive orders and congressional bills provided new powers to the military and intelligence community to investigate issues involving terrorism and radical militants. Many of the digital rights provisions in the ECPA were thus altered by subsequent amendments and new laws and the relative lack of rules regarding corporate use of consumer data also became an important feature of the ensuing debate. Using executive powers, the state asked (and in some cases forced) companies that had been collecting data on users to surrender data to the state for use in investigations. This blurred the lines between privacy from corporate entities (the issue that gave rise to the U.S. debate over legal privacy rights) and privacy from the state. The free-market freedoms granted to Internet providers and web service companies thus enabled the data collected to become part of a state database, which provides an example of the intimate links between privacy in the public realm and the private realm.

2017

The "Vault 7" secrets, a leak of 9,000 CIA documents, reveal details of the CIA's attempts to break through encryption used by Internet

President Trump appoints Ajit Pai to head the FCC, who abolishes the FCC neutrality protections

CONCLUSION

The 1986 Electronic Communications Privacy Act (ECPA) was already outdated by the time the bill became law. Few legislators of the era foresaw how digital communication would evolve in U.S. society, becoming essential for personal communication, work, education, and many other facets of daily life. Whether or not the Internet, and other forms of digital communication, should be considered a public utility is still a contentious debate in American culture, with some arguing that corporations should remain largely unregulated to promote investment and innovation, whereas others argue that the Internet and other digital technologies have become so essential to modern life that they are no longer optional technologies. The 1986 ECPA was updated on several occasions, but was ultimately insufficient to prevent corporate and governmental invasions of privacy that many Americans felt violated their privacy rights.

Congress debates whether or not to renew the controversial Section 702 FISA Amendment used to authorize NSA domestic intelligence operations since 2008

DISCUSSION QUESTIONS

- Should the Internet be considered a public utility? Why or why not?
- Should Americans have a right to privacy in digital communication? Why or why not?
- Can you give an example of how privacy from corporations and private entities relates to privacy rights from governmental intrusion?
- How would you formulate an effective privacy law that would cover modern technology? Do you think such a law would be effective?

Works Used

Communications: Telephone and Telegraph Systems (Series R 1-92). *Census*. United States Census Bureau. Pdf. 26 Oct. 2017.

"Electronic Communications Privacy Act of 1986 (ECPA)." *Justice Information Sharing*. U.S. Department of Justice, Office of Justice Programs. July 20, 2013. Web. 26 Oct. 2017.

Helft, Miguel, and Claire Cain Miller. "1986 Privacy Law Is Outrun by the Web." *New York Times*. New York Times Co. Jan. 9, 2011. Web. 26 Oct. 2017.

Mahtesian, Charles. "Privacy in Retreat, A Timeline." *NPR*. National Public Radio. Law. June 11, 2013. Web. 1 Nov. 2017.

Schwarz, Hunter. "Sales are spiking for '1984,' but it has a long history in politics." *CNN*. CNN. Jan. 26, 2017. Web. 26 Oct. 2017.

1788 State legislatures ratify the U.S. Constitution, establishing the basic precedent for all future constitutional law

1791 The U.S. Congress ratifies the Bill of Rights, creating the first 10 amendments to the United States Constitution

Introduction

This chapter discusses the legal provisions governing electronic
surveillance operations by the National Security Agency (NSA)
before the 9/11 terrorist attacks on the United States. The NSA and
Central Intelligence Agency (CIA) are authorized to engage in foreign
intelligence operations, conducting investigations of foreign nationals
within the United States and abroad. Laws governing the behavior of
intelligence agency operatives had been designed, up to 2000, to ensure
that intelligence operations involving U.S. citizens followed protocols to
ensure due process. Under the FISA Act of 1978, intelligence agencies
were expected to obtain permission from the FISA Courts for various
types of surveillance activities, and it was, therefore, intended that
the courts would recognize and prevent any activities that violated the
rights of U.S. citizens unless such a violation was deemed reasonable
under the law.

The source document for this chapter, a 2000 report from the NSA
"Legal Standards for the Intelligence Community in Conducting
Electronic Surveillance (2000)," was the 2000 version of a mandatory
annual reporting system established first in 1980, under the
Intelligence Authorization Act, which was intended to make
intelligence activities more transparent for legislative oversight.
According to the law, every intelligence agency needed to report their
activities to Congress annually to receive authorization for continued
operation. Interestingly, in the 2000 report from the NSA, the "overall
framework" for intelligence activities is described as having been
derived from President Ronald Reagan's Executive Order 12333. As per
this executive order, intelligence agencies were directed to prioritize
collecting foreign intelligence information, but were required to do so
using the least intrusive methods when such activities involved the

1868 | The 14th Amendment to the U.S. Constitution guarantees all citizens the right to due process under the law

1890 | Warren and Brandeis publish "The Right to Privacy" in the *Harvard Law Review*

surveillance of U.S. persons in the United States or abroad.

Topics covered in this chapter include:
- Foreign intelligence
- FISA Act of 1978
- Executive Orders
- The Ronald Reagan Administration
- The War on Terror
- The 9/11 terrorist attacks on the United States

This Chapter Discusses the Following Source Document:
Legal Standards for the Intelligence Community in Conducting
Electronic Surveillance. NSA. Feb. 2000.

Calm Before the Storm
Legal Standards for the Intelligence Community in Conducting Electronic Surveillance (2000)

In 1980, Congress passed the Intelligence Oversight Act, which updated the nation's legal standards regarding the activities undertaken by the nation's intelligence branches. Along with this act was the Intelligence Authorization Act (IAA), which was, generally speaking, a legislative effort to make the nation's intelligence agencies more amenable to congressional oversight.

Essentially, the IAA holds that all operations carried out by intelligence agencies must be approved by the president and all operations must subsequently be reported to congress.[49] The IAA needed to be renewed each year and the nation's intelligence agencies, therefore, delivered reports to congress on the state of intelligence and on recommendations for policy changes.

Headquarters of the NSA at Fort Meade, Maryland

1934

The Federal Communications Commission (FCC) is established under the Federal Communications Act (FCA)

1942

Goldman v. United States rules that using electronic listening devices does not violate the 14th Amendment

In 2000, in conjunction with the requirements of the 2000 version of Intelligence Authorization Act, the National Security Administration (NSA) delivered a report to Congress entitled "Legal Standards for the Intelligence Community in Conducting Electronic Surveillance." In the report, the authors define electronic surveillance and discuss existing legal protections in U.S. law:

LEGAL STANDARDS FOR THE INTELLIGENCE COMMUNITY IN CONDUCTING ELECTRONIC SURVEILLANCE
NSA, February 2000
Source Document Excerpt

Electronic surveillance is conducted by elements of the Intelligence Community for foreign intelligence and foreign counterintelligence purposes. Because of its potential intrusiveness and the implications for the privacy of United States persons, such surveillance is subject to strict regulation by statute and Executive Order, and close scrutiny. The applicable legal standards for the collection, retention, or dissemination of information concerning U.S. persons reflect a careful balancing between the needs of the government for such intelligence and the protection of the rights of U.S. persons, consistent with the reasonableness standard of the Fourth Amendment, as determined by factual circumstance.

In the act of balancing, the report goes on to explain, the government places more stringent restrictions on any intelligence gathering activity targeting U.S. citizens, then on intelligence activities targeting foreign citizens potentially involved in espionage or acting outside of the United States. These provisions were specifically delineated in the Foreign Intelligence Surveillance Act (FISA) of 1978 and described by the NSA as follows:

1945 The National Security Agency secretly creates Project SHAMROCK

1950 Senator Joseph McCarthy delivers a shocking speech claiming that more than 200 communist spies have infiltrated the U.S. government

Legal Standards for the Intelligence Community in Conducting Electronic Surveillance
continued

The Act further mandates the filing of an application approved by the Attorney General setting forth probable cause that the target of the proposed electronic surveillance is either a foreign power or an agent of a foreign power as defined by the statute. The purpose must be to gather foreign intelligence information, and a certification to that effect by a senior Executive Branch official must accompany every application. If a U.S. person, acting as an agent of a foreign power, is the target of the proposed surveillance, the government must satisfy a more stringent standard than that which pertains when the target is not a U.S. person. It is sufficient in the case of a non-U.S. person to show that the information to be acquired is merely related to the national defense or security of the United States of the conduct of foreign affairs; where a U.S. person is involved, the contents of the application must include a showing that the acquisition of such information is necessary to national defense or security or the conduct of foreign affairs.

In addition, FISA requires the government generally to minimize the amount of information acquired or retained and prohibits, with limited exception, the dissemination of nonpublic information about nonconsenting U.S. persons, consistent with the need of the United States to obtain, produce, and disseminate foreign intelligence information. The Attorney General, as required by statute, has adopted and filed with the Court specific procedures designed to effectuate the statutory minimization procedures. These procedures are also reported to the intelligence committees of Congress. Among other things, the procedures ensure that the surveillance technique employed minimizes the likelihood of acquiring information, and the amount of information acquired, concerning U.S. persons. The procedures also limit the retention of incidentally acquired information concerning U.S. persons. Finally, the procedures restrict the dissemination of U.S. person-identifying information to the statutorily prescribed bases.

1951
Dennis v. United States rules that government limits to speech is legal only to prevent a threat to public safety or security

1959
Barenblatt v. United States rules that it's legal to order people to reveal personal details if national threat is perceived

As described in the above excerpt, the FISA Act and other laws/statutes regarding the right to privacy of U.S. citizens establish stringent guidelines for intelligence gathering operations. Essentially then, up to 2000, any domestic intelligence operation involving U.S. citizens required intelligence agencies to demonstrate the violations of privacy were "necessary" to national interests.

The report also describes intelligence agency policies under E.O. 12333 (United States Intelligence Activities), a 1981 Executive Order delivered by President Reagan that was designed to strengthen communication and information sharing between the various branches of the nation's intelligence agencies.

As described in the report:

Legal Standards for the Intelligence Community in Conducting Electronic Surveillance
continued

While FISA provides the statutory basis for conducting electronic surveillance within the United States for foreign intelligence purposes, E.O. 12333 establishes the overall framework for the conduct of intelligence activities by U.S. intelligence agencies, including the use of electronic surveillance. The Order, which was issued by President Reagan in 1981, governs the conduct of intelligence activities applicable to all intelligence agencies, and also identifies specific responsibilities for each of the agencies.

The overall scheme of the Order is premised upon the determination that the "[c]ollection of [foreign intelligence information] is a priority objective and will be pursued in a vigorous, innovative and responsible manner that is consistent with the Constitution and applicable law and respectful of the principles upon which the United States was founded." Primary among these principles is the need to respect the rights of U.S. persons. The Order mandates that intelligence agencies "shall use the least intrusive collection techniques feasible within the United States or directed against U.S. persons abroad."

1965
Griswold v. CT rules in favor of married couples' right to privacy

1967
Katz v. United States rules wiretaps a form of search and seizure

Willis Ware of RAND Corporation writes *Security and Privacy in Computer*

The terrorist attacks of September 11, 2001 marked a major turning point in American history and public policy. From 2001 on, the nation would be embroiled in a military, ideological and economic war to combat the rise of terrorism around the world. For many in the American public, the attacks were revelatory, demonstrating the danger of a threat that many had not embraced as a realistic danger to American citizens. Many were outraged, frightened, confused, and perplexed as they learned, through media and governmental statements, the depth and nature of the problem as it existed.

Because terrorism is difficult, if not impossible, to combat using traditional military strategies, the government relied on intelligence activity and this led to the development of secret programs designed to expand the role of intelligence agencies in the domestic security system. In 2001, President George W. Bush authorized, in a controversial executive order, a new intelligence regime known as the President's Surveillance Program (PSP) that granted the NSA new powers to conduct domestic surveillance, while limiting existing oversight procedures in an effort to hasten the pace of NSA investigations.

The public was not aware of the program until 2007 and, in 2009, the Departments of Justice and Defense released an unclassified report detailing some aspects of the order. The report divulges that the program targeted and intercepted (without judicial oversight) communications between 500–1000 people with suspected, though largely unproven, connections to the terrorist organization al-Qaeda, suspected of conducting the 2001 terrorist attack.[50] More controversial was the fact that the program essentially authorized the NSA to intercept cellular communications across the board, with no initial limits or oversight. The NSA further intercepted at least 1.7 billion emails per day that could later be mined and analyzed for suspicious words, phrases, and patterns that might be used to locate terrorists.[51]

1968   The Omnibus Crime Control Act holds that police needed to obtain a warrant before engaging in wire-

1969   Joseph Licklider creates the Advanced Research Projects Agency Network (ARPANET), which was

The President's Surveillance Program was not an act of Congress and, in fact, was established without congressional oversight. Later information revealed that President Reagan's E.O. 12333, or "Twelve-Triple-Three," as it came to be known, was the underlying legal justification for most of the domestic surveillance programs initiated after 9/11. Under 12333, the NSA installed massive wiretaps capable of recording all of the telephone calls of entire geographic areas. It was later revealed, for instance, that the NSA recorded every telephone call in the Bahamas. It was later discovered that the NSA used the legal language of 12333 to warrant the creation of an internal search engine covering more than 850 billion phone and Internet records and containing unrestricted access to "unfiltered private information of millions of Americans."[52]

Because the public was unaware of the President's Surveillance Program at the time, it is unclear how public opinion fell on whether the Bush administration was justified in establishing secret surveillance programs towards the goal of combating national security threats. In 2000, before the terrorist attacks, the public was divided in support for the Bush Administration. Bush entered his first term with around 50 percent support and saw a massive boost in support after the terrorist attacks as the nation rallied behind the presidency. Over time, opinion of Bush declined precipitously as the ensuing war resulted in more memorable failures than victories. By December of 2008, only 11 percent of Americans said, in a *Pew Research* report, that Bush would be remembered as an "outstanding" president. A full 64 percent believed the Bush administration would be
remembered primarily for its failures and 34 percent said Bush would be remembered as a poor president. However, Pew researchers said, of Bush's legacy, "He helped to shape the post-9/11 climate of opinion that was broadly accepting of a muscular approach to U.S. national security."[53]

1971 The Pentagon Papers leaks from the press raise the issue of the Freedom of the Press versus the privacy of the government to conceal information about national security operations

1972 *Eisenstadt v. Baird* rules that the right to privacy applies to individuals

Americans weren't aware of the privacy issues at stake when the "War on Terror" began and so did not know how Bush's aggressive foreign policy proposals would impact this area of U.S. law. As the Bush administration proceeded into the second term, and the constitutionality of Bush-era policies came to the courts and through legislative scrutiny, the public, the press, and the legislature would debate how the events of 2000 and 2001 were changing the civil liberties landscape.

Credit: Cagle Cartoons

1974 The Watergate Scandal results in the revelation that the CIA had been conducting widespread surveillance of American dissidents and foreign leaders without judicial oversight

The Privacy Act is established

CONCLUSION

The 9/11 terrorist attacks on the United States were the beginning of a new era in both privacy law and domestic intelligence activity. Few Americans were aware of how the Bush administration's initial reaction to the terrorist attacks substantively changed American privacy rights at the time, but it was later revealed that Executive Order 12333 was used to authorize a massive domestic surveillance program without congressional or judicial oversight. The generality of the language used by Reagan in crafting EO 12333 provided room for interpretation that allowed the Bush administration to create a surveillance that many later saw as a violation of American privacy rights. This demonstrates the inherent dangers in allowing executive orders to determine intelligence industry policy. Just as in the controversy over Nixon's secret domestic surveillance programs, the Bush administration operated outside of Congress and the courts, thus eliminating layers of potential oversight designed to prevent the executive branch, or the nation's security and intelligence agencies, from violating the constitutional rights of the people.

1975   Senator Frank Church leads a series of hearings about the secret NSA SHAMROCK operation involved intercepting communications from American citizens

1978   Congress passes the 1978 FISA Act

DISCUSSION QUESTIONS

- Have the NSA and other intelligence agencies adhered to the principles explained in the 2000 report by the NSA?
- Did Bush's surveillance program violate the principles of the FISA Act? Why or why not?
- How were the Bush administration's intelligence policies similar to those of the Nixon administration? Were there significant differences between the way that the two administrations handled domestic surveillance? Explain.
- Should intelligence agencies use different policies when conducting surveillance on American citizens than when conducting surveillance on foreign individuals? Why or why not?

Works Used

"Bush and Public Opinion." *Pew Research*. Pew Research Center. Dec. 18, 2008. Web. 7 Nov. 2017.

Emmons, Alex. "Obama Opens NSA's Vast Trove of Warrantless Data to Entire Intelligence Community, Just in Time for Trump." *The Intercept*. First Look Media. Jan. 13, 2017. Web. 1 Nov. 2017.

"NSA Spying: How it Works." *EFF*. Electronic Frontier Foundation. 2013. Web. 26 Oct. 2017.

"Public Law 96-100-Nov. 2., 1979." *U.S. Senate*. United States Senate Intelligence Committee. 1979. Pdf. 26 Oct. 2017.

"Unclassified Report on the President's Surveillance Program." Offices of Inspectors General. July 10, 2009. Web. 26 Oct. 2017.

1980 | The Intelligence Oversight Act (IOA) updates legal standards

1981 | President Reagan's E.O. authorized wiretapping

1986 | The Electronic Communications Privacy Act is established

1994 Netscape creates the "cookie" allowing computers to monitor Internet users

2001 The September 11 terrorist attacks result in Congress authorizing the Bush Administration to utilize military methods to combat terrorism

Introduction

This chapter discusses the changes to U.S. privacy laws included in the 2001 *Uniting and Strengthening America by Providing Appropriate Tools Required to Intercept and Obstruct Terrorism Act*, better known by the acronym *USA PATRIOT Act*. Crafted in such a way as to make it difficult for critics to decipher the actual legal changes created by the law, while simultaneously creating an acronym that would associate the law with patriotism and nationalism in the minds of the public, the controversial 2001 law altered the function of the FISA Court, (discussed in Chapter 8) enabled rapid, unsupervised sharing of information between intelligence agencies, and fundamentally altered the chain of authority regarding the investigation and prevention of terrorism.

The source document for this chapter is an article written for *Wired* magazine in October of 2001, by security and technology expert Declan McCullagh entitled "Terror Act Has Lasting Effects." An opponent of the bill, McCullagh's short examination helps to tease out many of the more controversial provisions in the law, raising issues that are still relevant in 2018, after the PATRIOT Act was abandoned but replaced with laws that preserved most of the expanded powers granted to intelligence agencies and law enforcement agencies in the original 2001 law. As McCullagh describes in his article, only a single senator, Russell Feingold, opposed the PATRIOT Act in 2001, arguing that the law posed a danger to privacy rights. Feingold was largely ignored at the time, though his concerns were validated in subsequent years as the interpretation of the PATRIOT Act resulted in intelligence oversight that many felt violated the privacy rights of American citizens.

The Bush administration secretly authorizes the President's Surveillance Program (PSP), utilizing E.O. 12333

The U.S. PATRIOT Act alters existing laws to facilitate better communication between the state's intelligence branches in the effort to combat terrorism

The Transportation Security Administration (TSA) is established, creating the "No Fly" and "Selectee" lists that limit the right to travel on airplanes in the United States

Topics covered in this chapter include:
- Foreign intelligence
- Domestic surveillance
- Executive Orders
- The PATRIOT Act of 2001
- The War on Terror
- The 9/11 terrorist attacks on the United States

This Chapter Discusses the Following Source Document:
McCullagh, Declan. "Terror Act Has Lasting Effects." *Wired*. Conde Nast. Oct. 26, 2001.

Privacy Surrenders to Patriotism
The PATRIOT Act (2001)

It has been well documented that the 2001 terrorist attacks resulted in a surge of nationalism in the United States and many journalists and analysts of the era noted that, historically, when a national crisis and especially a military threat occurs, public support of the president and government tends to increase.

Gallup Poll data, for instance, showed that 46 percent of Americans believed that terrorism was the nation's most important problem in 2001 and, just after the attacks, 88 percent of people reported confidence in the U.S. government to protect citizens from terrorism. That percentage fell to 78 percent by 2004, then to 73 percent by 2006, and then to 59 percent in 2015. Essentially, then, in the immediate wake of the terrorist attacks, Americans suddenly viewed national security as the nation's top concern and a majority rallied behind the president and expressed belief that the government would address the situation appropriately.

Specifically looking at the way Americans felt about the balance between civil liberties (including the right to privacy) and national security, in late 2001, 47 percent of Americans said, in a Gallup Poll, that the government should take steps necessary to prevent terrorism even if civil liberties were violated. This surge in public confidence in the government was not a lasting trend and, even in the few months that followed directly after the September 2001 terrorist attacks, a slim majority (49 percent) still believed that the government should not violate civil liberties even to combat terrorism. By 2002, the percentage of Americans believing it was permissible for the government to violate civil liberties to enhance national security had fallen to 33 percent and, by 2012, only 25 percent held this view.[54]

2007 | The Bush Administration plans to make data taken from spy satellites available to law enforcement to be used to conduct domestic surveillance

2008 | Congress passes Section 702, or the FISA Amendment Act, which is used to permit a massive NSA and CIA domestic surveillance program

Hijacked United Airlines Flight 175 from Boston crashes into the south tower of the World Trade Center and explodes at 9:03 a.m. on September 11, 2001 in New York City. The crash of two airliners hijacked by terrorists loyal to al Qaeda leader Osama bin Laden and subsequent collapse of the twin towers killed some 2,800 people. (Photo: Spencer Platt/Getty Images)

2012 The Obama Administration proposes a Consumer Privacy Bill of Rights guaranteeing individuals the right to greater control over the use of their digital data

2013 The *Guardian* and the *Washington Post* publish the first series of articles derived from leaked NSA and CIA documents delivered by Edward Snowden

In 2001, operating from the momentary surge in public support, the Bush administration and the U.S. Congress enacted laws that gave intelligence agencies new powers to conduct surveillance and placed limitations on oversight procedures previously in place.

The first new presidential program created to enhance national security was the Presidential Surveillance Program (PSP), which authorized the NSA to intercept and collect emails, cellular telephone data, and other types of digital data from U.S. citizens without independent review. The second came in the form of the controversial Uniting and Strengthening America By Providing Appropriate Tools Required to Intercept and Obstruct Terrorism Act of 2001 (USA PATRIOT Act).

The PATRIOT Act provided law enforcement agents and agencies new powers, though most of the powers ascribed were derived from existing laws, and it also removed some safeguards and provisions requiring independent oversight in cases involving surveillance. In addition to debate over congress's apparent tendency to adopt paragraph-length names for new legislative initiatives, the USA PATRIOT Act (or "terror act") as it was sometimes called, sparked intense, immediate disagreement within the public and among legal experts. Whereas some saw the act as a necessary development given the nature of the threat presented by foreign terrorist organizations others felt that the act was an overreach by the administration and constituted a potential threat to civil liberties.

In this 2001 article from *Wired*, journalist Declan McCullagh discusses the newly introduced USA PATRIOT Act and examines some of the concerns that the act raised regarding civil liberties and privacy.

The Senate Judiciary committee holds hearings to determine if the executive surveillance operations carried out under the PATRIOT Act were a violation of constitutional law

Snowden leaks reveal that the NSA and CIA had been attempting to force corporations to provide a backdoor to encryption systems that would allow federal agents to bypass consumer encryption

TERROR ACT HAS LASTING EFFECTS
by Declan McCullagh
Wired, October 26, 2001
Source Document Excerpt

WASHINGTON—Legislators who sent a sweeping anti-terrorism bill to President Bush this week proudly say that the most controversial surveillance sections will expire in 2005.

Senate Judiciary chairman Patrick Leahy (D-Vermont) said that a four-year expiration date "will be crucial in making sure that these new law enforcement powers are not abused." In the House, Bob Barr (R-Georgia) stressed that "we take very seriously the sunset provisions in this bill."

But the Dec. 2005 expiration date embedded in the USA Act—which the Senate approved 98 to 1 on Thursday—applies only to a tiny part of the mammoth bill.

After the president signs the measure on Friday, police will have the permanent ability to conduct Internet surveillance without a court order in some circumstances, secretly search homes and offices without notifying the owner, and share confidential grand jury information with the CIA.

Also exempt from the expiration date are investigations underway by Dec. 2005, and any future investigations of crimes that took place before that date.

On Thursday, Attorney General John Ashcroft vowed to publish new guidelines as soon as the president signs the bill, which is expected to happen Friday. "I will issue directives requiring law enforcement to make use of new powers in intelligence gathering, criminal procedure and immigration violations," Ashcroft said.

President Bush said this week that he looks forward to signing the USA Act, which his administration requested in response to the Sept. 11 hijackings, "so that we can combat terrorism and prevent future attacks."

During the Senate debate Thursday, the lone critic of the bill was Russ Feingold (D-Wisconsin), who introduced an unsuccessful series of pro-privacy amendments earlier this month.

"We in this body have a duty to analyze, to test, to weigh new laws that the zealous and often sincere advocates of security would suggest to us," Feingold said. "This is what I have tried to do with this anti-terrorism bill. And that is why I will vote against this bill."

Feingold said the USA Act "does not strike the right balance between

2015

Terrorist attacks in France reignite fears of domestic terrorist violence

The PATRIOT Act is replaced by the USA Freedom Act

Federal Courts order Apple, Inc. to create a new operation system that would enable federal investigators to bypass security on an iPhone.

continued

empowering law enforcement and protecting constitutional freedoms."

But not one of his colleagues joined him in dissent. Sen. Chuck Schumer (D-New York) seemed to speak for the rest of the Senate when saying "the home front is a war front" and arguing that police needed new surveillance powers.

Sen. Mary Landrieu (D-Louisiana) did not vote.

Other sections of the USA Act, which the House approved by a 357 to 66 vote on Wednesday, that do not expire include the following:

• Police can sneak into someone's house or office, search the contents, and leave without ever telling the owner. This would be supervised by a court, and the notification of the surreptitious search "may be delayed" indefinitely. (Section 213)

• Any U.S. attorney or state attorney general can order the installation of the FBI's Carnivore surveillance system and record addresses of Web pages visited and email correspondents—without going to a judge. Previously, there were stiffer legal restrictions on Carnivore and other Internet surveillance techniques. (Section 216)

• Any American "with intent to defraud" who scans in an image of a foreign currency note or e-mails or transmits such an image will go to jail for up to 20 years. (Section 375)

• An accused terrorist who is a foreign citizen and who cannot be deported can be held for an unspecified series of "periods of up to six months" with the attorney general's approval. (Section 412)

• Biometric technology, such as fingerprint readers or iris scanners, will become part of an "integrated entry and exit data system" with the identities of visa holders who hope to enter the U.S. (Section 414)

• Any Internet provider or telephone company must turn over customer information, including phone numbers called—no court order required—if the FBI claims the "records sought are relevant to an authorized investigation to protect against international terrorism." The company contacted may not "disclose to any person" that the FBI is doing an investigation. (Section 505)

• Credit reporting firms like Equifax must disclose to the FBI any information that agents request in connection with a terrorist investigation—without police needing to seek a court order first. Current law permits this only in espionage cases. (Section 505)

The FCC publishes official rules of "neutrality"

2016

The EU establishes the General Data Protection Regulation (GDPR), described as the strongest digital data privacy law in the world

"Terror Act Has Lasting Effects"
continued

• The current definition of terrorism is radically expanded to include biochemical attacks and computer hacking. Some current computer crimes—such as hacking a U.S. government system or breaking into and damaging any Internet-connected computer—are covered. (Section 808)

• A new crime of "cyberterrorism" is added, which covers hacking attempts causing damage "aggregating at least $5,000 in value" in one year, any damage to medical equipment or "physical injury to any person." Prison terms range between five and 20 years. (Section 814)

• New computer forensics labs will be created to inspect "seized or intercepted computer evidence relating to criminal activity (including cyberterrorism)" and to train federal agents. (Section 816)

McCullagh's article was written in 2001 and so McCullagh did not know, to what extent, the government would or would not abuse the powers granted in the act, nor did anyone know, at the time, the full extent of the domestic spying program that was already underway (separate from the PATRIOT Act, but arguably constituting a much more egregious violation of privacy rights).

In addition to the civil liberties concerns expressed by McCullagh and other journalists and analysts at the time, the PATRIOT Act raised a number of issues affecting the rights of Americans in other spheres.

For instance, the American Civil Liberties Union (ACLU) wrote an article in 2002 examining the way that the PATRIOT Act redefined the meaning of the term "domestic terrorism.[55]" In the article, the ACLU suggests that, given the redefinition of the term, protesters representing groups like Greenpeace and Operation Rescue could, if the government chose, be seen as domestic terrorists and, therefore, could be subject to arrest, forfeiture of personal assets, and a variety of other possible penalties that

2017

The "Vault 7" secrets, a leak of 9,000 CIA documents, reveal details of the CIA's attempts to break through encryption used by Internet

President Trump appoints Ajit Pai to head the FCC, who abolishes the FCC neutrality protections

would not apply under general criminal codes. Furthermore, because of the language of the law, such penalties could be imposed without a prior hearing. The essence of the ACLU's argument was, therefore, that the PATRIOT Act, in presenting a generalized, catchall definition of terrorism, opened the door for abuses that vastly restricted the right to protest and dissent.

Despite the protests of civil liberties advocates, Americans were not extremely concerned by the PATRIOT Act in the years immediately following the bill becoming law. In a 2003 Gallup Poll, only 21 percent of Americans believed the Bush Administration had gone "too far" in restricting liberties, whereas 55 percent believed the administration had done "about right." Between 2002 and 2003, however, polls did demonstrate a shift in public opinion. The percentage of Americans who believed the Bush Administration had gone "too far" in 2002, around 11 percent, almost doubled when the same question was asked in 2003, and 21 percent voiced the same concern.[56] However, in 2004, about 64 percent believed that the government had either done "about right" or had not gone far enough to enhance national security and so, in the two years following the act becoming law, a significant majority of Americans were generally not concerned about the PATRIOT Act's potential impact on civil liberties.

Several intersecting factors influenced public opinion on the PATRIOT Act in the few turbulent years following the September 11 attacks and during the initial invasion of Iraq and the beginning of the "War on Terror."

First, a surge in nationalism resulted in an increasing tendency to equate support for the government with patriotism and criticism of the government with supporting terrorism. Therefore, organizations like the American Civil Liberties Union (ACLU), were increasingly portrayed in a negative light by those who supported the PATRIOT Act as a necessary and timely rebalancing of the relationship between national security and civil liberties.

Congress debates whether or not to renew the controversial Section 702 FISA Amendment used to authorize NSA domestic intelligence operations since 2008

Second, the PATRIOT Act was an impenetrable and dense legal document, and this made it extremely difficult for ordinary Americans without specialized legal training to fully understand the issues surrounding the act's provisions. Therefore, claims on both sides needed to be taken at face value as few were able to interpret the act for themselves.

This second factor, a general inability to understand the act, was demonstrated by 2004 Gallup Poll data demonstrating that only 13 percent of Americans said they were "very familiar" with the law, whereas 46 percent claimed to be "somewhat" familiar. Most notably, a full 41 percent reported being either "not too" or "not at all" familiar with the PATRIOT Act and its implications for U.S. law.

The Gallup data from 2004 also indicates that Americans' attitudes about the act changed when asked about specific provisions. For instance, 71 percent disapproved of the provision that federal agents could secretly search a U.S. citizen's home and would not have to disclose the search for an indeterminate period. Similarly, 51 percent opposed requiring businesses, including hospitals, bookstores, and libraries to turn over records to investigators without informing patients, clients, or customers.[57]

Numerous public opinion polls, from 2001 to 2017, show that a majority of Americans believe it is NOT necessary for the government to infringe on liberties to fight terrorism, and that a strong majority also views personal privacy as an important right and value. Given this, it would seem logical that Americans, in general, would disapprove of the PATRIOT Act, or, at least, some of the more controversial provisions of the law. However, faced with claims that the PATRIOT Act was a necessary tool to combat terrorism, and claims that such a law might have prevented the terrorist attacks of 9/11, or that without it, Americans faced an imminent threat from terrorism, Americans were, in general, willing to accept the threat to their civil liberties out of the fear that not doing so would place them in danger.

1788 State legislatures ratify the U.S. Constitution, establishing the basic precedent for all future constitutional law

1791 The U.S. Congress ratifies the Bill of Rights, creating the first 10 amendments to the United States Constitution

President George W. Bush signing the PATRIOT Act, October 10, 2001.
(Credit: https://www.flickr.com/photos/usnationalarchives)

1868 The 14th Amendment to the U.S. Constitution guarantees all citizens the right to due process under the law

1890 Warren and Brandeis publish "The Right to Privacy" in the *Harvard Law Review*

CONCLUSION

What the PATRIOT Act of 2001 did, on the most basic level, was to expand the powers of the state, intelligence agencies, and law enforcement to combat terrorism. Because terrorism is loosely defined as any act using violence or intimidation, especially when targeting civilians, towards some political goal, determining whether an investigation should be subject to standard law or the expanded laws designed to combat terrorism, was largely up to interpretation. In the years from 2001 to 2018, it became clear that defining terrorism is a highly subjective and politicized activity. For instance, attacks by white supremacists on African Americans are not typically defined as "terrorist" attacks despite the fact that such attacks meet the basic requirements for the definition. The PATRIOT Act did not eliminate privacy protections in place in 2000, but the act did, because of its generality, allow for interpretations that resulted in many different intelligence agencies and government activities that were later seen as violating the privacy rights of American citizens.

1923 *Meyer v. Nebraska* establishes that the 14th Amendment guarantees privileges of citizenship

1928 *Olmstead v. United States* rules that wiretapping is not a form of search and seizure defined by the 14th Amendment

DISCUSSION QUESTIONS

- Which, if any, of the issues raised by McCullagh in his article is the most concerning in terms of privacy rights? Explain.
- Should attacks by white supremacists also be considered terrorist attacks in the United States? Why or why not?
- Is it possible to create a more specific, rigorous definition of terrorism? How might such a definition be worded to create legal guidelines?
- Were the PATRIOT Act and other Bush Era policies effective responses to the threat of terrorism? Is terrorism less of an issue now than it was in 2001? Why or why not?

Works Used

"How the USA PATRIOT Act Redefines 'Domestic Terrorism.'" *ACLU*. American Civil Liberties Union. Dec. 6, 2002. Web. 26 Oct. 2017.

Moore, David W. "Public Little Concerned About PATRIOT Act." *Gallup*. Gallup News. Sept. 9, 2003. Web. 1 Nov. 2017.

Newport, Frank. "Gallup Review: U.S. Public Opinion on Terrorism." *Gallup News*. Gallup. Nov. 17, 2015. Web. 26 Oct. 2017.

Saad, Lydia. "Americans Generally Comfortable with PATRIOT Act." *Gallup*. Gallup News. Mar. 2, 2004. Web. 1 Nov. 2017.

1934

The Federal Communications Commission (FCC) is established under the Federal Communications Act (FCA)

1942

Goldman v. United States rules that using electronic listening devices does not violate the 14th Amendment

1945 The National Security Agency secretly creates Project SHAMROCK

1950 Senator Joseph McCarthy delivers a shocking speech claiming that more than 200 communist spies have infiltrated the U.S. government

Introduction

Ever since the publication of George Orwell's seminal 1949 novel *Nineteen Eighty-Four*, politicians, political activists, and critics of governmental policy have used imagery, terminology, and concepts from the novel to call attention to issues of alleged governmental overreach, authoritarianism, and, especially, government surveillance of citizens. In *Nineteen Eighty-Four*, an authoritarian government controls the citizenship of a dystopian future Earth through the use of constant surveillance and by outlawing dissidence and dissident thoughts and language. Known as "Big Brother," the malevolent surveillance-state of Orwell's future exists in a world where the desire to enhance security and social order has eliminated personal liberty, free expression, the independent press, and has eroded free will to such a state that most in the populace voluntarily surrender their freedom.

This chapter examines the use of Orwellian imagery and vocabulary to criticize government surveillance or policies seen as providing too much power to the state to dominate the populace. Such accusations have been part of political discourse in the United States and Europe since the 1950s, occurring repeatedly in response to revelations of controversial domestic surveillance programs, or other secret policies seen as authoritarian. In the source document for this chapter, an article by John Markoff and John Schwartz, "Many Tools of Big Brother Are Now Up and Running," in a December 2002 issue of the *New York Times*, Markoff and Schwartz describe how Internet and digital technology, coupled with changes to intelligence industry policies and privacy laws, were being used to create a surveillance program, known as Total Information Awareness (TIA) that resembled the omnipresent surveillance networks of Orwell's dystopian novel.

1951 *Dennis v. United States* rules that government limits to speech is legal only to prevent a threat to public safety or security

1959 *Barenblatt v. United States* rules that it's legal to order people to reveal personal details if national threat is perceived

Topics covered in this chapter include:
- The Bush Administration
- The PATRIOT Act of 2001
- Terrorism
- Digital privacy
- Domestic surveillance

This Chapter Discusses the Following Source Document:
Markoff, John and Schwartz, John. "Many Tools of Big Brother Are Now Up and Running." *New York Times*. New York Times Co. Dec. 23, 2002.

The Orwellian Age
Big Brother and the Privacy Debate (1949-2018)

In 2017, Internet bookseller Amazon reported that the 1949 novel *Nineteen Eighty-Four*, by author George Orwell, had surged to the top of the best-seller list. Orwell's novel, a dystopian fiction set in an imagined 1984, explores the lives of characters living in Airstrip One (formerly England), which is part of a massive superstate known as Oceania. The world imagined by Orwell was one in which a totalitarian regime dominates the population, restricting free speech and even the freedom of thought, and elements of Orwell's novel are periodically applied to politics, generally in situations where a government is seen as having exercised too much control over the people.

In the novel, the government, known as "Big Brother," has created its own language, known as Newspeak, which is tightly controlled and only contains terms and words that fit within the government's values and ideology. The Newspeak language is a reduced, controlled, simplified language representing what Orwell viewed as a linguistic dimension of social control. By limiting language to Newspeak (which replaces Oldspeak), the government eliminates dissent by removing the language necessary to express dissenting ideas. From there, Orwell's Big Brother proceeded to exact control by creating its own "facts" and discarding any contradictory information down a "memory hole." Individuals who exercise independent thought can be accused of "thought crimes" and arrested by the Thought Police, who report to the "Ministry of Truth." The fictional autocracy of Orwell's imagined 1984 is a society controlled by a government that controls news, and therefore controls information and thus controls the minds of the people.

The connections that some have made between *Nineteen Eighty-Four* and the Trump administration can be found in Trump's repeated habit of

1968 The Omnibus Crime Control Act holds that police needed to obtain a warrant before engaging in wire-

1969 Joseph Licklider creates the Advanced Research Projects Agency Network (ARPANET), which was

citing false information about a variety of issues. Orwell's *Nineteen Eighty-Four* began to sell in large numbers after Trump's then Press Secretary Sean Spicer made several demonstrably false claims about the size of the crowd at Trump's inauguration. Journalists immediately called attention to the mistake made by Spicer and asked the administration to clarify. Defending the claims (which were repeated by Trump himself), White House Adviser Kellyanne Conway said that Spicer had given "alternative facts.[58]" Author Peter Stansky, who wrote a biography of Orwell, called the "alternative facts" phrase, "very Orwellian, very 'Newspeak.'"

Immediately after the now infamous Conway interview, *Nineteen Eighty-Four* hit the bestseller list.[59]

Whereas Trump's handling of information, news, and data inspired many comparisons to Orwell, the dawning of a new "Orwellian age" has been predicted again and again by anti-establishment theorists and civil libertarians years before Trump's controversial presidency began.

In the wake of the 2001 terrorist attacks, the Bush Administration and Congress enacted a number of new amendments to existing laws that were designed to reportedly aid in combating radical terrorism. These included a secret, and still largely unrevealed program called the Presidential Surveillance Program (PSP), which authorized a massive domestic surveillance program by using legal terminology in several existing laws and executive orders. The existence of this program was largely unknown to the public until 2007 and so debate over the legality, ethics, and justifiability of the program wouldn't inform public debate until after the program officially ended. In October of 2001, Congress adopted the USA PATRIOT Act, a series of reforms, new laws, and extensions to existing laws, approved by bipartisan vote and intended to strengthen the nation's national security with regard to terrorism.

1971 | The Pentagon Papers leaks from the press raise the issue of the Freedom of the Press versus the privacy of the government to conceal information about national security operations

1972 | *Eisenstadt v. Baird* rules that the right to privacy applies to individuals

The USA PATRIOT Act was controversial in 2001 and sparked passionate objections from privacy and civil liberties advocates. Although many claimed that the PATRIOT Act was the first step towards an Orwellian police state, some noted that numerous facets of other laws, established long before the PATRIOT Act, had already granted sufficient leeway for the executive branch to conduct mass surveillance.

In this article from the December 23, 2002 edition of the *New York Times*, journalists John Markoff and John Schwartz discuss how the Internet, and the lack of effective protections against governmental intrusion or interception of digital data, had created the basic technology already needed for a national surveillance network.

MANY TOOLS OF BIG BROTHER ARE NOW UP AND RUNNING
by John Markoff and John Schwartz
The New York Times, **December 23, 2002**
Source Document

In the Pentagon research effort to detect terrorism by electronically monitoring the civilian population, the most remarkable detail may be this: Most of the pieces of the system are already in place.

Because of the inroads the Internet and other digital network technologies have made into everyday life over the last decade, it is increasingly possible to amass Big Brother-like surveillance powers through Little Brother means. The basic components include everyday digital technologies like email, online shopping and travel booking, A.T.M. systems, cellphone networks, electronic toll-collection systems and credit-card payment terminals.

In essence, the Pentagon's main job would be to spin strands of software technology that would weave these sources of data into a vast electronic dragnet.

Technologists say the types of computerized data sifting and pattern matching that might flag suspicious activities to government agencies and coordinate their surveillance are not much different from programs already

1974

The Watergate Scandal results in the revelation that the CIA had been conducting widespread surveillance of American dissidents and foreign leaders without judicial oversight

The Privacy Act is established

"Many Tools of Big Brother Are Now Up and Running"
continued

in use by private companies. Such programs spot unusual credit card activity, for example, or let people at multiple locations collaborate on a project.

The civilian population, in other words, has willingly embraced the technical prerequisites for a national surveillance system that Pentagon planners are calling Total Information Awareness. The development has a certain historical resonance because it was the Pentagon's research agency that in the 1960's financed the technology that led directly to the modern Internet. Now the same agency—the Defense Advanced Research Projects Agency, or Darpa—is relying on commercial technology that has evolved from the network it pioneered.

The first generation of the Internet— called the Arpanet—consisted of electronic mail and file transfer software that connected people to people. The second generation connected people to databases and other information via the World Wide Web. Now a new generation of software connects computers directly to computers.

And that is the key to the Total Information Awareness project, which is overseen by John M. Poindexter, the former national security adviser under President Ronald Reagan. Dr.

Poindexter was convicted in 1990 of a felony for his role in the Iran-contra affair, but that conviction was overturned by a federal appeals court because he had been granted immunity for his testimony before Congress about the case.

Although Dr. Poindexter's system has come under widespread criticism from Congress and civil liberties groups, a prototype is already in place and has been used in tests by military intelligence organizations.

Total Information Awareness could link for the first time such different electronic sources as video feeds from airport surveillance cameras, credit card transactions, airline reservations and telephone calling records. The data would be filtered through software that would constantly look for suspicious patterns of behavior.

The idea is for law enforcement or intelligence agencies to be alerted immediately to patterns in otherwise unremarkable sets of data that might indicate threats, allowing rapid reviews by human analysts. For example, a cluster of foreign visitors who all took flying lessons in separate parts of the country might not attract attention. Nor would it necessarily raise red flags if all those people reserved airline tickets for the same day. But a system

1975
Senator Frank Church leads a series of hearings about the secret NSA SHAMROCK operation involved intercepting communications from American citizens

1978
Congress passes the 1978 FISA Act

continued

that could detect both sets of actions might raise suspicions.

Some computer scientists wonder whether the system can work. "This wouldn't have been possible without the modern Internet, and even now it's a daunting task," said Dorothy Denning, a professor in the Department of Defense Analysis at the Naval Postgraduate School in Monterey, Calif. Part of the challenge, she said, is knowing what to look for. "Do we really know enough about the precursors to terrorist activity?" she said. "I don't think we're there yet."

The early version of the Total Information Awareness system employs a commercial software collaboration program called Groove. It was developed in 2000 by Ray Ozzie, a well-known software designer who is the inventor of Lotus Notes. Groove makes it possible for analysts at many different government agencies to share intelligence data instantly, and it links specialized programs that are designed to look for patterns of suspicious behavior.

Total Information Awareness also takes advantage of a simple and fundamental software technology called Extended Markup Language, or XML, that is at the heart of the third generation of Internet software. It was created by software designers at companies like Microsoft, Sun Microsystems and I.B.M., as well as independent Silicon Valley programmers.

The markup language allows data that has long been locked in isolated databases, known in the industry as silos, to be translated into a kind of universal language that can be read and used by many different systems. Information made compatible in this way can be shared among thousands, or even hundreds of thousands, of computers in ways that all of them can understand.

It is XML, a refinement of the Internet's original World Wide Web scheme, that has made it possible to consider welding thousands of databases together without centralizing the information. Computer scientists said that without such new third-generation Web technologies, it would have never been possible to conceive of the Total Information Awareness system, which is intended to ferret out the suspicious intentions of a handful of potential terrorists from the humdrum everyday electronic comings and goings of millions of average Americans.

Civil libertarians have questioned whether the government has the legal or constitutional grounds to conduct such electronic searches. And other critics have called it an outlandishly futuristic and ultimately unworkable scheme on technical grounds.

1980 The Intelligence Oversight Act (IOA) updates legal standards

1981 President Reagan's E.O. authorized wiretapping

1986 The Electronic Communications Privacy Act is established

"Many Tools of Big Brother Are Now Up and Running"
continued

But on the latter point, technologists disagree. "It's well grounded in the best current theory about scalable systems," said Ramana Rao, chief technology officer at Inxight, a Sunnyvale, Calif., company that develops text-searching software. "It uses all the right buzzwords."

People close to the Pentagon's research program said Dr. Poindexter was acutely aware of the power and the invasiveness of his experimental surveillance system. In private conversations this summer, according to several Department of Defense contractors, he raised the possibility that the control of the Total Information Awareness system should be placed under the jurisdiction of an independent, nongovernmental organization like the Red Cross because of the potential for abuse.

Dr. Poindexter declined to be interviewed for this article. A Darpa spokeswoman, Jan Walker, wrote in an email reply to questions that "we don't recall ever talking about" having a nongovernmental organization operate the Total Information Awareness program and that "we've not held any discussions with" such an organization.

The idea of using an independent organization to control a technology that has a high potential for abuse has been raised by previous administrations. An abortive plan to create a backdoor surveillance capability in encrypted communications, known as Clipper, was introduced by the Clinton administration in 1993. It called for keys to the code to be held by an organization independent of the F.B.I. and other law enforcement agencies.

Speaking of Dr. Poindexter, John Arquilla, an expert at the Naval Postgraduate School in Monterey on unconventional warfare, said, "The admiral is very concerned about the tension between security and civil liberties." He added that because of the changing nature of warfare and the threat of terrorism, the United States would be forced to make trade-offs between individuals' privacy and national security.

"In an age of terror wars, we have to learn the middle path to craft the security we need without incurring too great a cost on our civil liberties," he said.

Computer scientists who work with Darpa said that Dr. Poindexter was an enthusiastic backer of a Darpa-sponsored advisory group that had been initiated by a Microsoft researcher, Eric Horvitz, in October 2001 in the wake of the Sept. 11 terrorist attacks.

1994 Netscape creates the "cookie" allowing computers to monitor Internet users

2001 The September 11 terrorist attacks result in Congress authorizing the Bush Administration to utilize military methods to combat terrorism

continued

The group, which was composed of 41 computer scientists, policy experts and government officials, met three times to explore whether it was possible to employ sophisticated data-mining technologies against potential terrorist attacks while protecting individuals' privacy.

A number of the scientists proposed "black box" surveillance systems that would alert human intelligence analysts about suspicious patterns. Once the alerts were issued in such a system, they suggested, legal processes like those used for wiretapping could be employed.

But a number of the scientists and policy experts who attended the meetings were skeptical that technical safeguards would be adequate to ensure that such a system would not be abused.

The debate is a healthy one, said Don Upson, who is senior vice president of the government business unit of a software company in Fairfax, Va., webMethods, and the former secretary of technology for Virginia.

"I'm glad Darpa is doing this because somebody has to start defining what the rules are going to be" about how and when to use data, he said. "I believe we're headed down the path of setting the parameters of how we're going to use information."

Former Rear Admiral John Poindexter's Total Information Awareness program did not work out, however. First, enough members of Congress saw the potential for privacy and civil rights abuse within the program that Congress voted to prohibit the TIA system from collecting data on American citizens. The program was later renamed "Terrorism Information Awareness," and had a far more limited scope. Though there are no opinion polls measuring public opinion on the program itself, legislators reported an outpouring of concern from their constituents and this became the linchpin that resulted in the program being cancelled.

The Bush administration secretly authorizes the President's Surveillance Program (PSP), utilizing E.O. 12333

The U.S. PATRIOT Act alters existing laws to facilitate better communication between the state's intelligence branches in the effort to combat terrorism

The Transportation Security Administration (TSA) is established, creating the "No Fly" and "Selectee" lists that limit the right to travel on airplanes in the United States

For one thing, the Information Awareness Office adopted, as its logo, the image of the Eye of Providence (the eye above a pyramid also seen on U.S. currency) directing its gaze onto planet earth. This logo, argued Annie Jacobsen, author of *The Pentagon's Brain: An Uncensored History of DARPA*, fueled conspiracy theories about the TIA program and seemed to many, to lend credence to the claims of privacy advocates that the proposed program would pose the greatest threat to civil liberties of any previous government program. Less than a year after the program was initiated, DARPA pulled funding and the program was cancelled.[60]

Poindexter fared little better than his failed program, as, in 2003, Poindexter drew ire when two senators, Byron L. Dorgan of North Dakota and Ron Wyden of Oregon revealed, to the press, details of a plan developed by Poindexter to create a website where investors could bet on future

terrorist attacks, coups, and assassinations. According to a *New York Times* article on the controversy, defense agency officials at first attempted to defend Poindexter's betting ring, describing it as "using the marketplace to assess the probability of events, much like predicting elections or commodity prices." However, these defenses did not persuade the Defense department to continue the $3 million program and it was quickly shut down. Within a few weeks, the Bush Administration announced that Poindexter would resign from his post. Speaking about the issue to the *Times*, Senator Patrick J. Leahy of Vermont said, "The problem is more than the fact that Admiral Poindexter was put in charge of these projects. The problem is that these projects were just fine with the administration until the public found out about them."

2005

The PATRIOT Act was reauthorized without substantial changes as Congress favors security concerns over warnings that the law creates the potential for civil liberties violations

The *New York Times* publishes articles resulting from leaks revealing the secret President's Surveillance Program (PSP) established by the Bush administration

Since the 1949 publication of *Nineteen Eighty-Four*, the phrase "Big Brother" has been adopted into the English-speaking lexicon as a way to refer to governments or authority figures exerting extensive control or intruding into the lives of individuals through surveillance. In Orwell's fictional future, the phrase "Big Brother is Watching," referred to the omnipresent technological eyes and ears constantly surveilling the citizens in Orwell's dystopian world. In the case of the Total Information Awareness program, the public and at least some lawmakers agreed that such a program was perhaps "too Orwellian" even for combatting terrorism. Yet the idea behind the program did not die with Poindexter's career. In 2012, journalists uncovered the fact that, even as Poindexter's DARPA had been developing their version of TIA, the NSA was developing the same technology. Between 2001 and 2012, the NSA's program collected so much data that the NSA has constructed a 1 million-square-foot facility in Utah to store and process its trove of digital information.[61]

Allusions to "Orwellian" government policies and references to politicians and government agents as representations of some sort of emerging Big Brother have been part of the political rhetoric for some time. The same sorts of allegations were used frequently to refer to Nixon's domestic spying program in the 1960s, and the American counterculture of the 1960s frequently used terms from Orwell to describe the perception of an oppressive

Logo of Information Awareness Office, US federal agency formed after the attacks of September 11, 2001.

2007 — The Bush Administration plans to make data taken from spy satellites available to law enforcement to be used to conduct domestic surveillance

2008 — Congress passes Section 702, or the FISA Amendment Act, which is used to permit a massive NSA and CIA domestic surveillance program

bureaucracy operating through clandestine agents. This perception was partially based in truth as the spying program was extensive and investigations have revealed, for instance, that the CIA of the era did recruit young agents posing as college students to infiltrate and report on the youth and Anti-War movements.

Though the concepts of "Big Brother," or depictions of some or another government or government policy as "Orwellian" have become perennial in American politics, the similarities seen in the Bush-era expansion of government surveillance programs was, for many, the most apt usage of the comparison since Nixon. At a 2003 meeting organized by MoveOn. org and the American Constitution Society, Former Vice President Al Gore agreed, arguing:

> *Where Civil Liberties are concerned, they have taken us much farther down the road toward an intrusive, "Big Brother"-style government—toward the dangers prophesized by George Orwell in his book "1984"—than anyone ever thought would be possible in the United States of America.*

In speaking about the balance of national security and personal liberty, Gore then returned to the foundation of privacy rights:

> *Almost eighty years ago, Justice Louis Brandeis wrote "Those who won our independence by revolution were not cowards. . . They did not exalt order at the cost of liberty." Those who won our independence, Brandeis asserted, understood that "courage [is] the secret of liberty" and "fear [only] breeds repression." Rather than defending our freedoms, this Administration has sought to abandon them. Rather than accepting our traditions of openness*

2012 The Obama Administration proposes a Consumer Privacy Bill of Rights guaranteeing individuals the right to greater control over the use of their digital data

2013 The *Guardian* and the *Washington Post* publish the first series of articles derived from leaked NSA and CIA documents delivered by Edward Snowden

and accountability, this Administration has opted to rule by secrecy and unquestioned authority. Instead, its assaults on our core democratic principles have only left us less free and less secure.[62]

The Senate Judiciary committee holds hearings to determine if the executive surveillance operations carried out under the PATRIOT Act were a violation of constitutional law

Snowden leaks reveal that the NSA and CIA had been attempting to force corporations to provide a backdoor to encryption systems that would allow federal agents to bypass consumer encryption

CONCLUSION

The Total Information Awareness program was eventually cancelled after significant public and legislative resistance to the proposal, but the basic tools used to create the program endured, and were integrated into NSA and CIA surveillance programs still in use as of 2018. Language from Orwell's novel was frequently used to describe Bush-era surveillance and privacy-rights policies, and was subsequently used by critics of Obama-era continuations and expansion of many of those same intelligence operations. During the first year of the Donald Trump administration in 2017, Trump's presidency was also frequently described as "Orwellian," but not because of Trump's surveillance programs. Rather, accusations of Orwellian-ism directed at Trump were based on the president's attacks on the legitimacy of the media and his strategy of using propaganda and misinformation to obfuscate criticism of his performance, history, and policies.

2015

Terrorist attacks in France reignite fears of domestic terrorist violence	The PATRIOT Act is replaced by the USA Freedom Act	Federal Courts order Apple, Inc. to create a new operation system that would enable federal investigators to bypass security on an iPhone.

DISCUSSION QUESTIONS

- Was the Total Information Awareness program, in fact, Orwellian? Explain your answer.
- Should the government have the right to conduct unwarranted domestic surveillance to combat terrorism? Why or why not?
- Have there been other examples of Orwellian policies, laws, or political activities that have occurred since the Bush administration? Give specific examples.
- Should the tools used to create TIA be abandoned or should they be used by modern intelligence agencies? Explain your answer.

Works Used

Bradner, Eric. "Conway: Trump White House offered 'alternative facts' on crowd size." *CNN Politics*. CNN. Jan. 23, 2017. Web. 26 Oct. 2017.

Flock, Elizabeth. "George Orwell's '1984' is a best-seller again. Here's why it resonates now." *PBS News Hour*. News Hour Productions LLC. Jan. 25, 2017. Web. 26 Oct. 2017.

Gore, Al. "Freedom and Security." *Alternet*. Nov. 9, 2003. Web. 26 Oct. 2017.

Harris, Shane. "Giving in to the Surveillance State." *New York Times*. New York Times, Co. Aug. 22, 2012. Web. 1 Nov. 2017.

Kessler, Matt. "The Logo That Took Down a DARPA Surveillance Project." *Atlantic*. Atlantic Monthly Group. Dec. 22, 2015. Web. 1 Nov. 2017.

The FCC publishes official rules of "neutrality"

2016

The EU establishes the General Data Protection Regulation (GDPR), described as the strongest digital data privacy law in the world

2017

The "Vault 7" secrets, a leak of 9,000 CIA documents, reveal details of the CIA's attempts to break through encryption used by Internet

President Trump appoints Ajit Pai to head the FCC, who abolishes the FCC neutrality protections

Introduction

This chapter explores the difference between journalism and punditry, which is a type of political writing or speaking that involves giving authoritative opinions to influence public opinion in favor of a certain viewpoint or policy. Whereas journalism seeks to *inform* the public, punditry seeks to *influence* the public. The source document in this chapter is an article written by conservative pundit Heather Mac Donald in the conservative publication *National Review*. Mac Donald's article was in response to an American Civil Liberties Union (ACLU) suit against the Transportation Security Administration (TSA), a new government agency empowered to enhance security in the U.S. air travel industry under the Bush administration and in response to the 9/11 terrorist attacks. The ACLU filed suit on behalf of numerous citizens who argued that the TSA's "no-fly" and "selectee" lists violated laws ensuring due process by allowing the TSA to add names to the list without providing reason or justification for doing so. Mac Donald criticizes the ACLU suit and other complaints made by privacy-advocates regarding Bush-era security and anti-terrorism initiatives and argues that such complaints are largely the result of hypersensitivity to minor inconveniences.

Examining Mac Donald's criticism of the ACLU and privacy advocates in general, in comparison to the way that the mainstream media provided coverage of the ACLU suit and other privacy-rights complaints and claims criticizing Bush-era policies, illustrates the differences between punditry and journalism as types of political writing. Mac Donald's criticisms, for instance, take the form of insults and insinuations about the character of individuals complaining about privacy rights violations and threats, whereas mainstream media report on the same issue, summarize the complaints made by privacy advocates, as well as responses from defenders of the controversial

Congress debates whether or not to renew the controversial Section 702 FISA Amendment used to authorize NSA domestic intelligence operations since 2008

policies, and provide readers with information that might be used (by anyone interested in doing so) to check the accuracy of the information provided in the article.

Topics covered in this chapter include:
- Journalism
- Political pundits
- The TSA No-Fly and Selectee Lists
- The American Civil Liberties Union
- The War on Terror
- The PATRIOT Act
- Domestic surveillance

This Chapter Discusses the Following Source Document:
Mac Donald, Heather. "Privocrats vs. National Security." *National Review*. National Review, Inc. May 18, 2004.

Dividing the Republic
Punditry and Journalism

The term "pundit," often used to describe political commentators, is derived from the Sanskrit word "pandita," meaning "wise individual," and the word entered the American lexicon as a term for "learned teacher." Over the years, the word pundit has come to have a different meaning, referring to a person who provides authoritative opinions on political or social issues in the mass media. In times of political controversy, Americans have many different options for information. Each year, political scientists and researchers publish numerous articles on various social and political issues, providing reasoned analyses and statistical data that can help to clarify difficult or complex subjects. This is not, however, a practical way to get rapid information on a subject and so, most data in political debates comes from two main sources, journalists and pundits.

The goals and approach of a journalist is different from that of a pundit. For one thing, legitimate journalists are expected to adhere to certain codes of conduct, at least when reporting on an issue rather than writing an op-ed or opinion piece:

——————— The Society of Professional Journalists has adopted a code of ethics, including the following broad principles[63]:

• Seek Truth and Report it: Ethical journalism should be accurate and fair. Journalists should be honest and courageous in gathering, reporting and interpreting information

• Minimize harm: Ethical journalist treats sources, subjects, colleagues and members of the public as human beings deserving of respect.

1868 | The 14th Amendment to the U.S. Constitution guarantees all citizens the right to due process under the law

1890 | Warren and Brandeis publish "The Right to Privacy" in the *Harvard Law Review*

> • *Act Independently: The highest and primary obligation of ethical journalism is to serve the public.*
>
> • *Be Accountable and Transparent: Ethical journalism means taking responsibility for one's work and explaining one's decisions to the public.*

Journalists succeed by finding stories that attract readers and bring prestige to their companies or publications by uncovering new, captivating issues or by finding new angles on familiar issues. For investigative journalists, the goal is to "break" stories and this often involves revealing information that could potentially damage the careers of public figures.

To provide an example, in 2016, the *New York Times* broke the story about Donald Trump's part ownership of a university that defrauded hundreds of students, while the newspaper also broke the story about Hillary Clinton's email controversy, which became one of the issues cited most by Trump in his criticisms of Clinton during the campaign.[64] The information discovered by *Times* journalists helped shape public opinion in the campaign, in one instance benefitting Trump and in the other, Clinton. This is the function of a journalist, to report information.

Journalism has been called the "Fourth Estate," an unofficial branch of the government that helps to bridge the gap between politics and the people. By holding politicians and public figures responsible for their actions, journalism also functions as a check on the powers of the state. Journalists succeed in their careers by finding titillating or captivating stories and it is, therefore, in a journalist's selfish interests to seek out corruption and expose misbehavior wherever it occurs, and not simply on one or the other side of an ideological debate. Further, legitimate journalists are expected, when reporting on news, to provide sources for the claims contained within their articles and, when possible, to direct readers or viewers to sources of further, more detailed information on a topic. By helping the

1923   *Meyer v. Nebraska* establishes that the 14th Amendment guarantees privileges of citizenship

1928   *Olmstead v. United States* rules that wiretapping is not a form of search and seizure defined by the 14th Amendment

public to fact check when they are so inclined, journalists play an important function in facilitating education and the dissemination of legitimate information.

Pundits, by contrast, publish information or give speeches in support of a specific stance on a political or social issue. In some cases, pundits might be motivated by personal opinion, whereas, in other cases, an institution or organization pays pundits to promote a certain viewpoint and so are responsible for gathering information and for shaping and framing data in such a way as to support that organization. There are many kinds of pundits, from the content creators at popular conservative websites like *Breitbart* to many of the privacy "crusaders" who write essays and op-ed pieces about constitutional threats. Punditry can serve an important role in society and, in fact, some journalists also act as pundits in writing opinion and editorial pieces. The essential difference between the two fields is one of purpose. Journalism may be self-serving or may serve the public, whereas punditry serves a cause or promotes a view or political product and is, therefore, a kind of informational advertising.

The balance between national security and personal privacy has always been a controversial topic, but the controversy reached a new zenith in the years after the 9/11 terrorist attacks, when the Bush Administration and Congress enacted legislation and executive orders ostensibly aimed at strengthening national security that some critics believed removed safeguards against governmental invasions of privacy and violations of civil liberties. As journalists covered the issue, presenting statements from many different angles of the debate, pundits delivered hundreds of articles defending their chosen side on the issue.

1934

The Federal Communications Commission (FCC) is established under the Federal Communications Act (FCA)

1942

Goldman v. United States rules that using electronic listening devices does not violate the 14th Amendment

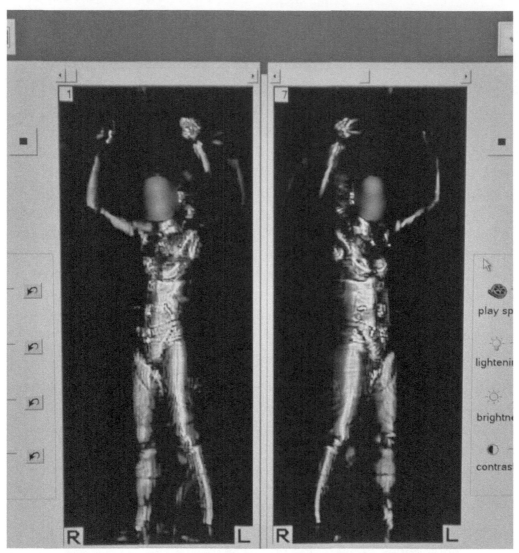

An unidentified volunteer allows her image to be viewed as she is scanned by the TSA (Transportation Security Administration) Millimeter Wave Passenger Imaging Technology on March 5, 2009, at Ronald Reagan National Airport in Washington, DC. Passenger privacy is ensured through the anonymity of the image. The officer attending the passenger cannot view the image, and the officer viewing the image is remotely located and cannot see the passenger. Additionally, the image cannot be stored, transmitted or printed and is deleted immediately after being viewed. Finally, the facial area of the image has been blurred to further ensure privacy. (Credit: Paul J. Richard/AFP/Getty Images)

1945 The National Security Agency secretly creates Project SHAMROCK

1950 Senator Joseph McCarthy delivers a shocking speech claiming that more than 200 communist spies have infiltrated the U.S. government

Because the 9/11 attacks involved hijacking commercial airplanes, one of the chief goals for the Bush Administration was to enhance security in the nation's air travel industry. This resulted in the creation of the Transportation Security Administration (TSA), a branch of the Department of Homeland Security (DHS) officially created on November 19, 2001 and empowered to create new security screening techniques and policies, to place federal marshals on commercial flights, and to investigate passengers to identify potential terrorist threats. This coincided with another controversial development: the creation of the "No Fly List," the "Selectee List," and the "Terrorist Watch List," created and maintained by the then newly established Terrorist Screening Center (TSC). The No-Fly List is a list of individuals compiled by the federal government who, for a variety of reasons, are not allowed to fly on commercial airlines. The Selectee List contains the names of individuals who are not prohibited from flying, but who have been targeted for extra security precautions before being allowed to board a flight.

The creation of the No-Fly List and Selectee List became a controversial topic, with some critics arguing that the lack of due process, when adding someone to the list, was a violation of constitutional rights. Some whose names appeared on the list complained to their legal representatives about being stopped or subjected to interrogation seemingly without cause. Some of these complaints were later brought to the American Civil Liberties Union (ACLU) and the legal experts from the ACLU sued the federal government with the goal of reforming the policies used to create the lists.

In this 2004 article in the conservative publication *National Review*, pundit Heather Mac Donald criticizes the ACLU suit and the individuals who believed the No-Fly List or Selectee List constituted a violation of civil liberties.

1951 *Dennis v. United States* rules that government limits to speech is legal only to prevent a threat to public safety or security

1959 *Barenblatt v. United States* rules that it's legal to order people to reveal personal details if national threat is perceived

PRIVOCRATS VS. NATIONAL SECURITY
by Heather Mac Donald
National Review, May 18, 2004
Source Document

Casualties in the privacy wars

The country's "privacy advocates" are jeopardizing national security. Most recently, they have sued to halt the government's efforts to keep terrorists off of airlines. But the privocrats' assault on essential antiterror policies long predates this latest suit: In fact, they were responsible for much of the paralysis in the nation's counterterrorism community before 9/11. Unfortunately, even after 9/11, the privacy advocates keep pressing their extreme arguments and—all too often—winning.

The recent litigation against the government's "no-fly" list, brought by the ACLU, is a peerless example of privacy charlatanry. The seven plaintiffs' names resemble those on a list of suspected terrorists whom the government wants to block from flying. When the plaintiffs try to board an airplane, they are often asked to produce additional identification and are briefly detained while their identification is verified. Security agents have searched their luggage and used the ubiquitous magnetic wand to scan their bodies for weapons.

And that is all. None of the plaintiffs has ever missed a flight because of the additional security procedures. Their biggest complaints? They can't use curbside check-in or the e-ticket self-service check-in; one woman didn't get her assigned window seat. They all felt embarrassed by having been more closely scrutinized in front of other passengers.

Out of this set of minor inconveniences, the ACLU has manufactured major constitutional infractions. The government's application of the no-fly list deprives the plaintiffs of liberty and property in violation of the Fifth Amendment, the ACLU charges, and subjects them to unreasonable searches and seizures in violation of the Fourth Amendment. Unless a federal court immediately blocks the operation of the no-fly list, pleads the ACLU, the plaintiffs will suffer "irreparable injury."

The ACLU's tactics are by now familiar to anyone who has watched the privacy advocates in action. The drill runs as follows: Elevate a fleeting inconvenience to the status of a constitutional violation. Next: Take an absolutist view of individual rights, while

1965   Griswold v. CT rules in favor of married couples' right to privacy

1967   Katz v. United States rules wiretaps a form of search and seizure

Willis Ware of RAND Corporation writes *Security and Privacy in Computer*

continued

conceding almost no countervailing interest in public security. The annoyance of a few hundred passengers subjected to additional screening trumps, in the ACLU's view, the interests of 380 million other Americans in not getting blown up or used as a cruise missile mid-flight. Finally: Cut the government no slack in its efforts to protect citizens—any good-faith error in administering antiterror systems immediately becomes a breach of the Bill of Rights.

According to the ACLU's logic, millions of air passengers suffer constitutional abuse every day: most of us have been wanded, our bags have been searched, we sometimes don't get our assigned seats, and there may be no self-check-in kiosks at our airport, or those kiosks may be malfunctioning.

While the ACLU takes on the no-fly list, a coalition of privacy advocates, from the Electronic Privacy Information Center on the left to Americans for Tax Reform on the right, has already blocked an important reform of airline-security procedures on similarly specious grounds. The advocates claim that the proposed Computer Assisted Passenger Pre-screening System (CAPPS II) violates privacy rights by asking an air traveler to provide his name, address, date of birth, and phone number upon making a reservation. The government wants that information in order to verify that passengers are who they say they

are and are not listed in government intelligence files. Such information is hardly private. Commercial data banks daily traffic in such basic consumer identifiers and far more, from our purchasing preferences to our mortgage amount and credit-card balance. And with the exception of birth date, airline passengers have long given the required CAPPS II information when reserving a seat.

Nevertheless, the privacy agitators have stalled CAPPS II, and airlines are refusing to cooperate with the Transportation Security Administration for fear of being accused of violating their passengers' privacy.

The list of security casualties in the privacy wars goes on. Last year, the advocates killed groundbreaking research to spot terrorist planning with computer analysis—the Total Information Awareness program. As a result, the computing-research world has given up trying to develop cutting-edge tools for terror preemption, lest they, too, face the wrath of the privocrats.

The privacy crusade is based on imaginary injury and indifference to the real terror threat. It's time for public officials to stand up to the privacy charlatans and defend their commonsensical antiterror protections as lawful and essential to national defense.

1968   The Omnibus Crime Control Act holds that police needed to obtain a warrant before engaging in wire-

1969   Joseph Licklider creates the Advanced Research Projects Agency Network (ARPANET), which was

In her article, MacDonald refers to those advocating for civil liberties protections as "privacy charlatans," "agitators," and "privocrats." Her intention is to foster the negative impression that such individuals are simply hypersensitive to what she calls "minor inconveniences." The essence of the article, then, is to simplify the issue into an ideological dichotomy consisting of those who want strong national security and those who do not, which is, not only an unrealistic characterization of a complex debate but is tinged with punditry in appealing to the publication's conservative audience.

When journalists covered the ACLU's 2004 suit, the resulting impression of the issue was more nuanced and less instigatory. According to *CNN* and *Times* articles on the subject, the plaintiffs in the case were *not* advocating for the elimination of a No-Fly List in principle, but objected to the way in which the list was constructed. David Fathi, an ACLU lawyer of Iranian descent told CNN reporters in 2004, "If the government is going to put your name on a list and call you a security risk, the government should have to tell you why."

Another one of the plaintiffs in the case, attorney David Nelson of St. Louis, claimed he had been stopped more than 30 times, without explanation, and had been unable to discover why his name had been added to the list. Although the government offered a "redress" system for those who believed they had been wrongfully added to the list, critics argued that the system in place did not meet the standards of "due process" required by U.S. law. "We have no problem with the government doing whatever it can to make us safe," ACLU representative Randy Shuford told CNN, "We support those efforts wholeheartedly, with the caveat that it has to be done in a way that does not trump or trample upon constitutional rights."[65]

When addressing controversial and highly charged issues, there is a tendency for pundits to overly simplify an issue and to present it as a contest between political theories, groups, or different "types of people," or to

1971

The Pentagon Papers leaks from the press raise the issue of the Freedom of the Press versus the privacy of the government to conceal information about national security operations

1972

Eisenstadt v. Baird rules that the right to privacy applies to individuals

attack, characterize, and disparage those whose views differ from their own. The ACLU is, by definition, an activist organization whose primary goal is to safeguard the nation's civil liberties. In identifying and challenging laws and policies that might have implications for civil rights, the ACLU is performing its clearly stated and transparent purpose. Although a person may or may not agree with the ACLU's stance on a specific issue, the information provided by the ACLU is meant to ensure that politicians always consider civil rights when enacting policies and that the public is made aware of any present, future, or potential threats to civil rights. This also does *not* mean that the ACLU or other "privocrats" are not concerned about national security.

The many thousands of Americans who helped to shape the nation's privacy protections from the nineteenth century to the twenty-first century were no less patriotic or dismissive of national security concerns. This effort involved both conservatives and progressives, activists and ideologues, republicans and democrats, and journalists and pundits. The protection of civil liberties was a primary goal for the founders of the United States and the very impetus for the decision to divide from England was, in part, motivated by the desire to escape a political system in which the state had unfettered powers to limit the liberties of the people.

Gallup polls from 2004, the same year that MacDonald's article appeared in *National Review,* indicated that approximately 31 percent of Americans believed that the government should take all steps necessary to prevent terrorism, even if it meant violating civil liberties. This is essentially the position that MacDonald supports and so her punditry could be seen as representing this facet of the populace. However, this is less than half of the percentage of Americans (65 percent) who said they believed the government should take necessary steps to fight terrorism, but *not* at the expense of civil liberties.[66] The fight that the "privocrats" were engaged in, is therefore the effort to represent the concerns of this 65 percent, who want *both* security *and* privacy, rather than one or the other.

1974

The Watergate Scandal results in the revelation that the CIA had been conducting widespread surveillance of American dissidents and foreign leaders without judicial oversight

The Privacy Act is established

CONCLUSION

Pundits like Heather Mac Donald play a public role in advancing the views of organizations or special interests they represent by writing or speaking on issues from a specific perspective. Punditry can be found in print, on TV, and on talk radio programs from both a progressive and conservative perspective. Legitimate, ethical journalism functions differently, providing information that citizens can use to form perspectives on key issues. Bush-era security policies inspired a wealth of passionate punditry, and this helped to shape public opinion, especially for those whose world views were deeply entrenched on either the right or left. However, for those undecided or still struggling to understand the issues at play, punditry is often more misleading than informative.

1975 Senator Frank Church leads a series of hearings about the secret NSA SHAMROCK operation involved intercepting communications from American citizens

1978 Congress passes the 1978 FISA Act

DISCUSSION QUESTIONS

- How does Mac Donald's article differ from a journalistic perspective on the same issue? Provide examples.
- Do you agree with Mac Donald's characterization of the ACLU suit against the Bush administration? Why or why not?
- Should the TSA be required to provide reasons for adding individuals to the No-Fly or Selectee lists? Explain your answer.
- What are some additional examples of pundits or punditry in the modern media?

Works Used

Meserve, Jeanne, and Phil Hirschkorn. "ACLU Sues U.S. over 'No-Fly' List." *CNN*. CNN. Apr. 6, 2004. Web. 26 Oct. 2017.

Newport, Frank. "Gallup Review: U.S. Public Opinion on Terrorism." *Gallup*. Gallup LLC. Nov. 17, 2004. Web. 26 Oct. 2017.

"SPJ Code of Ethics." *SPJ*. Society of Professional Journalists. Sept. 6, 2014. Web. 26 Oct. 2017.

Victor, Daniel. "Clinton and Trump Revealed: Our Best Investigative Reporting on the 2016 Campaign." *New York Times*. New York Times Co. Nov. 4, 2016. Web. 26 Oct. 2017.

1980 The Intelligence Oversight Act (IOA) updates legal standards

1981 President Reagan's E.O. authorized wiretapping

1986 The Electronic Communications Privacy Act is established

1994 Netscape creates the "cookie" allowing computers to monitor Internet users

2001 The September 11 terrorist attacks result in Congress authorizing the Bush Administration to utilize military methods to combat terrorism

Introduction

The PATRIOT Act of 2001, discussed in Chapter 12, was controversial at its inception, and the controversy surrounding the law deepened with each year that the PATRIOT Act remained in place. Between 2001 and 2005, supporters of the PATRIOT Act promoted the idea that Americans simply needed to sacrifice some level of privacy and personal liberty for the government to effectively fight terrorism. Whether or not this sacrifice is really necessary for combating terrorism is the essential disagreement in the long-standing debate between 2001 and 2018. In 2005, several of the most controversial provisions in the original PATRIOT Act were set to automatically expire. This was a feature built into the original act by legislators, realizing that some of the law's more extreme measures should be temporary and renewed only if the need for them remained.

This chapter examines changing public and political attitudes about the PATRIOT Act as demonstrated by the congressional debate over the 2005 reauthorization of some of the act's most contentious provisions. The primary source for this chapter, excerpts from the congressional testimony given during the reauthorization hearings, provides arguments from both sides of the issue, including Gregory Nojeim of the American Civil Liberties Union (ACLU), who argued for reform instead of straightforward reauthorization, and conservative pundit Heather Mac Donald who argued in support of straightforward reauthorization and whose article "Privocrats vs. National Security" is disscussed in Chapter 14. The debate elucidates many of the controversies surrounding the PATRIOT Act itself and also demonstrates the polarization of political attitudes between the more extreme arguments from both sides of the ideological divide.

The Bush administration secretly authorizes the President's Surveillance Program (PSP), utilizing E.O. 12333

The U.S. PATRIOT Act alters existing laws to facilitate better communication between the state's intelligence branches in the effort to combat terrorism

The Transportation Security Administration (TSA) is established, creating the "No Fly" and "Selectee" lists that limit the right to travel on airplanes in the United States

Topics covered in this chapter include:
- Foreign intelligence
- The War on Terror
- The 9/11 terrorist attacks on the United States
- The PATRIOT Act of 2001
- Political punditry

This Chapter Discusses the Following Source Document:
Hearing Before the Select Committee on Intelligence of the United States Senate. Senate Hearing 109-341. April 19, 27, and May 24, 2005.

Trying Security
The 2005 PATRIOT Act Hearings

Public opinion on the PATRIOT Act is difficult to assess for a number of reasons. For one thing, Americans are, in general, poorly informed and largely inattentive to public affairs. Researchers looking into public opinion typically find that Americans demonstrate limited awareness even of key issues that have been part of longstanding policy debates. Second, the text of the PATRIOT Act was so impenetrable that, at the time of the bill's publication, even legal scholars complained that the implications of the law were difficult to ascertain.[67]

In 2001 and 2002, with the nation still reeling from the tragedy of 9/11 and the sociopolitical revelation of a threat that few contemplated before the attack, more Americans were, on average, willing to give their government the benefit of the doubt on how best to address the issue.

On January 25–27, 2002, 47 percent of Americans were comfortable with the government taking whatever steps were needed to combat terrorism, according to a Gallup poll, even if such actions violated civil liberties, as opposed to 49 percent who argued that the government should not violate civil liberties to combat terrorism. By 2005, 65 percent were opposed to the government violating civil liberties to combat terrorism, as compared to 31 percent who approved.

This demonstrates that, on average and in principle, a majority of Americans, even immediately after the terrorist attacks, did not want the government to violate civil liberties even to combat terrorism. However, opinion on whether the policies that the government enacted constituted violations of civil liberties varied more widely. In June of 2015, Gallup Polls found that 41 percent of people felt the government's policies violated their civil liberties, as opposed to 55 percent who believed that policies enacted to that point had not resulted in a violation of their

2007 The Bush Administration plans to make data taken from spy satellites available to law enforcement to be used to conduct domestic surveillance

2008 Congress passes Section 702, or the FISA Amendment Act, which is used to permit a massive NSA and CIA domestic surveillance program

rights.[68] After the publication of the PATRIOT Act, objections came first from legislators, legal experts, and privacy advocates who saw, within the act, a potential erosion of due process, privacy, and other constitutional protections designed to prevent governmental abuse. Over the years from 2001 to 2005, articles and analysis on the issue resulted in subtle shifts in public opinion.

In December of 2004, a *Pew Research* poll found that 33 percent believed the PATRIOT Act was a necessary tool that helped the government find terrorists, whereas 39 percent believed the act went too far and posed a threat to civil liberties, with 28 percent reportedly feeling uncertain about the issue.[69]

The PATRIOT Act included 342 pages of dense exposition and, recognizing the difficulty in analyzing the law, lawmakers determined that 16 of the most controversial provisions would automatically expire in 2005 and would thereafter need to be reauthorized or abandoned. This resulted in a series of public hearings that allowed critics and supporters to voice support, criticisms, and concerns with the law as it then existed.[70]

Sec. 216 of the PATRIOT Act of 2001 permits phone calls to be recorded without a warrant or notification. (Credit: David Drexler/flickr.)

Among other concerns, the hearings focused on several of the most controversial provisions up for review, including:

Section 213: The so-called "sneak and peek" provision that allowed federal agents to search a home or business, in secret, and to delay notifying the owner for an unspecified period of time.

Section 215: The "library records" provi-

2012 The Obama Administration proposes a Consumer Privacy Bill of Rights guaranteeing individuals the right to greater control over the use of their digital data

2013 The *Guardian* and the *Washington Post* publish the first series of articles derived from leaked NSA and CIA documents delivered by Edward Snowden

sion, which allowed investigators to secretly force libraries, doctors, and other companies to release records related to a customer or client.

Section 505: Allowed federal agents to obtain records under the authorization of the "national security letter," rather than obtaining an independent court order.[71]

Associate Professor Orin Kerr of George Washington University Law School gave a moderate account of the act and defended the basic law within:

HEARING BEFORE THE SELECT COMMITTEE ON INTELLIGENCE
Source Document Excerpt

The public debate over the USA PATRIOT Act has been based on a number of major misunderstandings about the scope and effect of the law. Millions of Americans believe that the PATRIOT Act profoundly reshaped the balance between privacy and security in a post-9/11 world.

That is simply wrong. The truth is that the law is much more modest: Most of the PATRIOT Act consists of minor adjustments to a set of preexisting laws, such as the Foreign Intelligence Surveillance Act and the Electronic Communications Privacy Act. The PATRIOT Act left the basic framework of preexisting law intact, offering mostly minor changes to the set of statutory privacy laws Congress first enacted in the 1970's and 1980's. I explained this in greater depth in a law review article published in January 2003, and stand by that view today.

Fortunately, the gap between the perception and the reality of the PATRIOT Act is beginning to narrow. In recent months, critics of the PATRIOT Act have come to acknowledge that most of the Act is consensus legislation that does not raise civil liberties concerns. For example, in an April 5, 2005 press release the American Civil Liberties Union acknowledged that:

Most of the voluminous PATRIOT Act is actually unobjectionable from a civil liberties point of view and . . . the law makes important changes that give law enforcement agents the tools they need to protect against terrorist attacks. A few provisions . . . must be revised. . . .

The Senate Judiciary committee holds hearings to determine if the executive surveillance operations carried out under the PATRIOT Act were a violation of constitutional law

Snowden leaks reveal that the NSA and CIA had been attempting to force corporations to provide a backdoor to encryption systems that would allow federal agents to bypass consumer encryption

Hearing Before the Select Committee on Intelligence
continued

Although it is unfortunate that this acknowledgment appeared as late as it did, the ACLU's recognition that the PATRIOT Act debate is actually quite narrow is an important step to understanding PATRIOT Act reform. It reveals that the differences among pre-PATRIOT Act law, the law under the PATRIOT Act, and proposals to reform the PATRIOT Act tend to be relatively small. Of course, any legislative proposals that impact government power to conduct criminal or intelligence surveillance must be treated with the greatest consideration and care. Finding the right balance that both gives the government the power it needs to investigate terrorist threats and preserves our precious civil liberties is a very difficult task. At the same time, the effect of the PATRIOT Act and the scope of proposed amendments to it are much narrower than press accounts would lead one to believe.

Gregory Nojeim, of the American Civil Liberties Union, raised the issue that some provisions of the PATRIOT Act, especially concerning the expansion of intelligence authority powers, had been sealed under the justification of government secrecy.

Hearing Before the Select Committee on Intelligence
continued

Secrecy permeates the PATRIOT Act, particularly in its expansions of intelligence authorities. Many powers are accompanied by statutory gag orders. Moreover, the administration has taken the posture that information that is embarrassing to it must be kept secret for reasons of national security. For these reasons, it has been extremely difficult to uncover information about how the PATRIOT Act has been used, and even information about whether particular sections have been used at all. The ACLU has repeatedly sought this information in letters, requests under the Freedom of Information Act (FOIA) and in FOIA litigation.

Despite the efforts of the executive branch to cover up information about how controversial provisions of the PATRIOT Act have been used, some information has become public. This information is disturbing in and of itself, and may be emblematic of

2015

| Terrorist attacks in France reignite fears of domestic terrorist violence | The PATRIOT Act is replaced by the USA Freedom Act | Federal Courts order Apple, Inc. to create a new operation system that would enable federal investigators to bypass security on an iPhone. |

continued

other abuses that have not yet become public. Appended to this testimony are some examples of abuses of intelligence powers expanded under the PATRIOT Act, and of the chill on the exercise of First Amendment rights that such powers can create.

On the more concerning powers granted to federal and law enforcement agencies, Nojeim argued:

Hearing Before the Select Committee on Intelligence
continued

A power to secretly obtain records of ordinary Americans—i.e., Americans who are not suspected of involvement with any foreign government or terrorist organization—outside of a criminal investigation is a vast power. The government bears the burden in showing such a power "actually materially enhances security." If the government sustains this burden, it is clear, as even Attorney General Gonzales has acknowledged, that additional safeguards must be added.

Recommendation: Congress should bring intelligence records powers (national security letters and FISA records search orders) back into line with basic constitutional freedoms. Congress should enact the SAFE Act, which restores the requirement of individual suspicion, provides a right to challenge records demands, limits the secrecy order and provides for a right to challenge the secrecy order.

The SAFE Act ("Security and Freedom Enhancement Act," S. 737) restores the requirement of "specific and articulable facts giving reason to believe" the records involve an "agent of a foreign power" for both FISA records demands and national security letters. In addition, the SAFE Act makes explicit the right to file a motion to quash the records demands because they are unreasonable, contrary to law, or seek privileged information. The SAFE Act also sets standards for a judicially imposed, temporary secrecy order that can be challenged by the recipient of a records demand. Finally, the SAFE Act provides a right to notice, and an opportunity to challenge, before information from a FISA records search or national security letter search can be used in a court proceeding.

The FCC publishes official rules of "neutrality"

2016

The EU establishes the General Data Protection Regulation (GDPR), described as the strongest digital data privacy law in the world

Hearing Before the Select Committee on Intelligence
continued

As the Attorney General concedes is necessary, Congress should certainly make clear what the government has now conceded should be the law—that the secrecy order does not prevent recipients from discussing records demands internally or obtaining legal advice. Without public scrutiny, the potential for unreasonable "fishing expeditions" using a secret, unreviewable records power is simply too great.

A government search or electronic surveillance of a home or office generally requires a warrant based on probable cause of crime under the Fourth Amendment. As a general rule, the owner of the home or office is entitled to notice of the search. Foreign intelligence searches have been an exception to this rule. They do not require criminal probable cause and forbid notice to the owner.

The special power to secretly search a home or office, without ever notifying the owner, is among the most intrusive domestic surveillance powers available to the Federal Government. Such "black bag jobs" were the hallmark of national security investigations run amok, including COINTELPRO and other investigations of civil rights activists, anti-war activists, and other Americans who in the end were guilty of nothing more than peacefully opposing government policies.

The inappropriate use of a secret search power, without court oversight, led directly to warrantless wiretaps of civil rights leaders and, eventually, an unauthorized "black bag job" at the Watergate, sending a shock wave through the Nation and prompting thorough and searching reviews of the intelligence community. These reviews led Congress to enact important reforms of intelligence powers, including the passage of the Foreign Intelligence Surveillance Act (FISA) and the creation of this committee.

While FISA secret searches and wiretaps pre-date the PATRIOT Act, two vital protections that cabined such searches until 2001 have been seriously eroded by amendments that are subject to the December 31, 2005 sunset. First, section 218 of the PATRIOT Act allowed the government to obtain a FISA secret search order even where the "primary purpose" of the search was not foreign intelligence.

Second, for searches of so-called "lone wolf" terror suspects, section 6001 of the Intelligence Reform and Terrorism Prevention Act of 2004 eliminated, for the first time, the basic requirement applied by the Foreign Intelligence Surveillance Court for all FISA secret searches and surveillance: that probable causes exists that the target of the search is a foreign power or agent of foreign power.

The "Vault 7" secrets, a leak of 9,000 CIA documents, reveal details of the CIA's attempts to break through encryption used by Internet

President Trump appoints Ajit Pai to head the FCC, who abolishes the FCC neutrality protections

In conclusion, Nojeim summarized the general concerns over the civil liberties issues found within the provisions of the act:

Hearing Before the Select Committee on Intelligence continued

The PATRIOT Act provisions that pose the greatest challenges share certain common themes. As a result of gag orders, or delayed notification, they permit surveillance with a far greater degree of secrecy than is common in most government investigations. They do not allow affected parties the opportunity to challenge government orders before a judge. Finally, because the substantive standards for some forms of surveillance have been modified, weakened, or even eliminated, the role of the Foreign Intelligence Surveillance Court in checking government abuse has been made less meaningful.

This committee's review of the PATRIOT Act and related legal measures in the ongoing effort to combat terrorism is needed to ensure continued public support for the government's efforts to safeguard national security. The controversy over the PATRIOT Act reflects the concerns of millions of Americans for preserving our fundamental freedoms while safeguarding national security. To date, resolutions in opposition to parts of the PATRIOT Act and other actions that infringe on fundamental rights have been passed in in 377 communities in 43 states including five state-wide resolutions.

Such widespread concern, across ideological lines, reflects the strong belief of Americans that security and liberty need not be competing values. Congress included a "sunset provision" precisely because of the dangers represented by passing such far-reaching changes in American law in the aftermath of the worst terrorist attack in American history. Now is the time for Congress to complete the work it began when it passed the PATRIOT Act, by bringing the PATRIOT Act back in line with the Constitution.

James X. Dempsey, Executive Director of the Center for Democracy & Technology, supported the ACLU position in the trial. Concluding at the end of his testimony:

Congress debates whether or not to renew the controversial Section 702 FISA Amendment used to authorize NSA domestic intelligence operations since 2008

Hearing Before the Select Committee on Intelligence
continued

In the debate over the PATRIOT Act, civil libertarians did not argue that the government should be denied the tools it needs to monitor terrorists' communications or otherwise carry out effective investigations. Instead, privacy advocates urged that those powers be focused and subject to clear standards and judicial review. The tragedy of the response to September 11 is not that the government has been given new powers—it is that those new powers have been granted without standards or checks and balances.

Of course, the FBI should be able to carry out roving taps during intelligence investigations of terrorism, just as it has long been able to do in criminal investigations of terrorism. But the PATRIOT Act standard for roving taps in intelligence cases lacks important procedural protections applicable in criminal cases.

Of course, the law should clearly allow the government to intercept transactional data about Internet communications (something the government was doing before the PATRIOT Act anyhow). But the pen register/trap and trace standard for both Internet communications and telephones, under both the criminal wiretap law and under FISA, is so low that judges are reduced to mere rubber stamps, with no authority to even consider the factual basis for a surveillance application.

Of course, prosecutors should be allowed to use FISA evidence in criminal cases (they did so on many occasions before the PATRIOT Act) and to coordinate intelligence and criminal investigations (there was no legal bar to doing so before the PATRIOT Act). But FISA evidence in criminal cases should not be shielded from the adversarial process (as it has been in every case to date).

We need limits on government surveillance and guidelines for the use of information not merely to protect individual rights but to focus government activity on those planning violence. The criminal standard and the principle of particularized suspicion keep the government from being diverted into investigations guided by politics, religion or ethnicity. Meaningful judicial controls do not tie the government's hands—they ensure that the guilty are identified and that the innocent are promptly exonerated.

1788 State legislatures ratify the U.S. Constitution, establishing the basic precedent for all future constitutional law

1791 The U.S. Congress ratifies the Bill of Rights, creating the first 10 amendments to the United States Constitution

Conservative pundit Heather Mac Donald argued strongly in favor of renewing provisions of the PATRIOT Act, charging those who raised concerns of manufacturing and fabricating issues that led to a national panic, where none legitimately exists:

Hearing Before the Select Committee on Intelligence continued

The most powerful weapon against terrorism is intelligence. The United States is too big a country to rely on physical barriers against attack; the most certain defense is advanced knowledge of terrorist plans.

In recognition of this fact, Congress amended existing surveillance powers after 9/11 to ready them for the terrorist challenge. The signal achievement of these amendments, known as the PATRIOT Act, was to tear down the regulatory "wall" that had prevented anti-terrorism intelligence agents and anti-terrorism criminal agents from sharing information. That wall was neither constitutionally nor statutorily mandated, but its effect was dire: it torpedoed what was probably the last chance to foil the 9/11 plot in August 2001. Thanks to the PATRIOT Act, all members of the anti-terrorism community can now collaborate to prevent the next terrorist strike before it happens.

Besides dismantling the wall, the PATRIOT Act made other necessary changes to surveillance law: it extended to terrorism investigators powers long enjoyed by criminal investigators, and it brought surveillance law into the 21st century of cell phones and email. Where the act modestly expands the government's authority, it does so for one reason only: to make sure that the government can gather enough information to prevent terrorism, not just prosecute it after the fact.

Each modest expansion of government power in the PATRIOT Act is accompanied by the most effective restraint in our constitutional system: judicial review. The act carefully preserves the traditional checks and balances that safeguard civil liberties; 4 years after its enactment, after constant monitoring by the Justice Department's Inspector General and a host of hostile advocacy groups, not a single abuse of government power has been found or even alleged.

This record of restraint is not the picture of the act most often presented in the media or by government critics, however. The PATRIOT Act has been the target of the most successful disinformation campaign in recent memory. From the day of its passage, law enforcement critics have portrayed

1868 The 14th Amendment to the U.S. Constitution guarantees all citizens the right to due process under the law

1890 Warren and Brandeis publish "The Right to Privacy" in the *Harvard Law Review*

Hearing Before the Select Committee on Intelligence
continued

it as an unprecedented power grab by an administration intent on trampling civil rights.

As lie after lie accumulated, the administration failed utterly to respond. As a result, the public is wholly ignorant about what the law actually does. Hundreds of city councils have passed resolutions against the act; it is a safe bet that none of them know what is in it. The Committee is to be congratulated for taking the time to get the truth out.

MacDonald went on to list "strategies," used by who she calls "anti-PA-TRIOT Act demagogues" to discredit portions of the PATRIOT Act. Arguing that the "commonsensical reforms of existing investigative power have called forth a crescendo of hysteria," MacDonald goes on to argue that the entire act has been the target of a "misinformation campaign," and argues that what actually drives objections to the act is a fear of government secrecy and argues further that "Speed and secrecy are of the essence in preventing an attack."

Over three days of debate and deliberation, the U.S. Congress heard arguments for and against the PATRIOT Act, as well as proposals for updates and amendments to the act. Prior to the hearings, newly sworn in Attorney General Alberto Gonzales reported he was willing to hear arguments, but believed, prior to the hearings, that the PATRIOT Act had been successful and that the 16 provisions set to automatically expire should be renewed.

In all, investigations of the PATRIOT Act and its history, between 2001 and 2005, revealed that most of the provisions in the law had not resulted in identified breaches of civil liberties and that, in cases where civil liberty violations had been noted, circumstances outside the provisions of the PATRIOT Act contributed to the situation. The renewed PATRIOT Act was approved in Congress, with a few minor changes: including requirements

1923 *Meyer v. Nebraska* establishes that the 14th Amendment guarantees privileges of citizenship

1928 *Olmstead v. United States* rules that wiretapping is not a form of search and seizure defined by the 14th Amendment

for the FBI director to approve any attempts to access library or book-store records and a 15-day limit for a "roving wiretap" operation before federal investigators were required to report to a judge on the investigation.

When ideologues accuse organizations like the ACLU of mounting a misinformation campaign, it is uncertain what the perceived goals of such a campaign might be. The ACLU and other privacy and civil liberties advocates have embraced the mission to identify not only *existing* threats to civil liberties, but also *potential* threats. Imagine, for instance, that the powers of the PATRIOT Act, and the Presidents Surveillance Program, and the Executive Order 12333, were to fall into the hands of an unstable president who came to believe that a conspiracy of opposing party politicians and the press posed a threat to national security. Given the powers already in place, the technologies that exist, and the wording of laws authorizing and restricting intelligence powers, that president could direct agencies to conduct what many might view as unethical surveillance activities targeting American citizens who have not been justifiably proven to have taken part in any illegal act or any act that threatens security. The purpose of the ACLU is to identify these potential dangers, rather than to call attention to civil liberties risks only after abuse has occurred.

The reauthorization of the PATRIOT Act in 2005 did not specifically reflect public opinion on the issue. In December of 2004, only 33 percent viewed the act as a "necessary tool that helps the government find terrorists," whereas 39 percent believed the law "goes too far and poses threat to civil liberties." By January of 2006, there had been a small increase in support, with 39 percent expressing the view that the PATRIOT Act was a necessary tool. Over time, support for the bill waned and studies indicated that the more people knew about the law, the less they were willing to support it.[72]

1934

The Federal Communications Commission (FCC) is established under the Federal Communications Act (FCA)

1942

Goldman v. United States rules that using electronic listening devices does not violate the 14th Amendment

There was evidence, despite the eventual reauthorization, that concerns about the civil liberties implications of the act had begun to spread among politicians. Whereas Democratic Senator Russel D. Feingold of Wisconsin had been the only senator to vote against the bill in 2001, when the bill came up for reauthorization, more than 40 Democrats and 4 Republicans joined together to oppose the bill until certain compromises had been reached.[73]

The following year, in 2006, new revelations about the surveillance activities carried out under the Bush administration came to light. The controversy surrounding these revelations raised public concern on the issue and inspired a new and more informed debate about the potential dangers of the government's surveillance programs.

1945 The National Security Agency secretly creates Project SHAMROCK

1950 Senator Joseph McCarthy delivers a shocking speech claiming that more than 200 communist spies have infiltrated the U.S. government

Credit: Cagle Cartoons

1951 *Dennis v. United States* rules that government limits to speech is legal only to prevent a threat to public safety or security

1959 *Barenblatt v. United States* rules that it's legal to order people to reveal personal details if national threat is perceived

CONCLUSION

Following three hearings on PATRIOT Act reauthorization in 2005, Congress voted to renew the act with only minor reforms, representing a gesture to privacy advocates, but without satisfying the concerns of most critics of the original bill. Two sections of the bill: Section 206, which allowed for roving wiretaps; and Section 215, which forced libraries and businesses to provide customer records upon request, were set to automatically expire in 2009, at which time there would be another set of hearings to decide whether to reauthorize the expiring provisions. Despite reauthorization succeeding—largely thanks to the prevailing opinion that the act had been instrumental at preventing terrorist attacks in the United States—opposition to the PATRIOT Act and suspicion of Bush-administration policies in general, had increased dramatically since 2001. Whereas only one senator, Russell Feingold, opposed the PATRIOT Act in 2001, more than 40 Democrats and 4 Republicans opposed all or at least some sections of the bill when it came up for review in 2005. It is noteworthy that the reauthorization came the year *before*, the public and members of Congress became more widely aware of the secret domestic surveillance operations conducted by the Bush administration since 2001.

1965

Griswold v. CT
rules in favor of
married couples'
right to privacy

1967

Katz v. United States
rules wiretaps a form
of search and seizure

Willis Ware of RAND
Corporation writes *Security
and Privacy in Computer*

DISCUSSION QUESTIONS

- Do you believe the PATRIOT Act was effective in combating terrorism? Why or why not?
- Do you agree with Mac Donald's assertion that secrecy is necessary to prevent terrorism? Explain your answer.
- Did the PATRIOT Act violate the checks and balances of the American political system? Explain your answer.
- Did the Bush administration effectively combat terrorism? Why or why not?

Works Used

Best, Samuel J., and Monika L. McDermott. "Measuring Opinions vs. Non-Opinions—The Case of the USA PATRIOT Act." *The Forum*. Vol. 5 (2007), No. 2, Article 7. Web. 26 Oct. 2017.

"Civil Liberties." *Gallup*. Gallup, Inc. 2016. Web. 26 Oct. 2017.

"Public Remains Divided Over the PATRIOT Act." *Pew Research*. Pew Research Center. Feb. 15, 2011. Web. 26 Oct. 2017.

Stolberg, Sheryl Gay. "Once-Lone Foe of PATRIOT Act Has Company." *New York Times*. New York Times Co. Dec. 19, 2005. Web. 1 Nov. 2017.

Zetter, Kim. "PATRIOT Act Gets a Hearing." *Wired*. Conde Nast. Apr. 6, 2005. Web. 26 Oct. 2017.

1968 The Omnibus Crime Control Act holds that police needed to obtain a warrant before engaging in wire-

1969 Joseph Licklider creates the Advanced Research Projects Agency Network (ARPANET), which was

1971 The Pentagon Papers leaks from the press raise the issue of the Freedom of the Press versus the privacy of the government to conceal information about national security operations

1972 *Eisenstadt v. Baird* rules that the right to privacy applies to individuals

Introduction

Between 2001 and 2005, numerous privacy advocates and critics of the PATRIOT Act and other Bush-era security policies, argued that the laws, as they had been formulated, created the potential for abuse such that it was possible for Bush or another executive to use current laws to commit gross violations of privacy rights across the United States. However, until 2005, there had been no proof that any widespread violations had actually occurred. In 2004, a government leak resulted in the *New York Times* learning of a secret surveillance program authorized by Bush. In good faith, the *Times* agreed to postpone publishing information from the leak, giving the administration time to address existing security concerns related to information within the leak. The *Times* published their first article on the issue in December of 2005, revealing how Bush used the PATRIOT Act, an interpretation of presidential powers in Article II of the constitution, and the congressional Authorized Use of Military Force (AUMF) to justify ordering intelligence agencies to conduct surveillance on American citizens without the supervision of the FISA Courts as defined in the 1978 FISA Act (see Chapter 8).

The leak was a major embarrassment to the Bush Administration, with several prominent senators and representatives calling for an investigation. The Bush administration responded by claiming that the program was legal and had been properly authorized according to existing presidential powers and the AUMF, and that such a program, if it had been in place, might have prevented the 9/11 attacks. The source document for this chapter is an op-ed article, "Spies, Lies and Wiretaps," published in the *New York Times* in January of 2006. In the article, the *Times* editors argue that the administration failed to justify violating 30 years of law to establish the secret program and argue

1974

The Watergate Scandal results in the revelation that the CIA had been conducting widespread surveillance of American dissidents and foreign leaders without judicial oversight

The Privacy Act is established

that the program, despite defenses from the administration, violated the 1978 FISA law.

Topics covered in this chapter include:
- FISA Act of 1978
- Congressional Authorization on the Use of Military Force
- George W. Bush administration
- The War on Terror
- The 9/11 terrorist attacks on the United States
- Domestic surveillance

This Chapter Discusses the Following Source Document:
"Spies, Lies and Wiretaps." *New York Times.* New York Times, Co. Jan. 29, 2006.

The President's Surveillance Program
The 2005 Domestic Surveillance Controversy

In 2004, *New York Times* reporters discovered evidence of a secret surveillance program, known as the "Terrorist Surveillance Program," authorized in a 2002 executive order from President Bush. The program was later shown to be only one part of a much larger program, the "President's Surveillance Program," which was revealed to the press in 2007. Reacting to the 2004 leak, the Bush administration asked the *New York Times* not to publish any articles on the program, citing security concerns. Representatives of the *Times* met with representatives from the White House and, the *Times* agreed to wait one year before publishing their first articles. On December 16, 2005, the *Times* published the first of a series of articles, alleging that the NSA had been authorized to collect information on U.S. citizens without court-approved warrants. The following day, Bush delivered a national address stating:

> *Yesterday the existence of this secret program was revealed in media reports, after being improperly provided to news organizations. As a result, our enemies have learned information they should not have, and the unauthorized disclosure of this effort damages our national security and puts our citizens at risk. Revealing classified information is illegal, alerts our enemies, and endangers our country.*[74]

In explaining the program, the administration claimed that existing safeguards were sufficient to protect civil liberties and that the Justice Department was still required to seek a warrant to monitor communications occurring entirely within the United States. Spokespersons for the White House said further that the program had been an important tool in pre-

1980 | The Intelligence Oversight Act (IOA) updates legal standards

1981 | President Reagan's E.O. authorized wiretapping

1986 | The Electronic Communications Privacy Act is established

venting terrorist attacks. Officials whose names were not disclosed for security reasons told *Times* reporters, that the program had helped to uncover a plot by Iyman Faris, an Ohio trucker who pled guilty of planning to attack the Brooklyn Bridge as part of an al-Qaeda plot in 2003.[75]

In early 2006, Senator Arlen Specter of Pennsylvania announced his intention to hold hearings to determine if the surveillance program violated constitutional law. Prior to the Terrorist Surveillance Program, NSA operatives seeking to establish wiretaps or intercept electronic information linked to U.S. citizens would have needed permission by a FISA court. The program thus eliminated the FISA court requirement, based on presidential powers delineated in Article II of the constitution and expanded by the congressional Authorized Use of Military Force (AUMF), granted to the Bush administration in September 2001, immediately after the terrorist attacks.

New York Times coverage of the controversy provided ample room to both defenders and critics of the program and Bush administration officials made several claims to support their use of the program. Notably:

- The NSA program could have prevented 9/11;
- The AUMF authorization from Congress provided justification for the program;
- Investigating terrorism required the reduction of requirements from "probable cause" to "reasonable suspicion";
- The NSA program did not violate any current laws;
- The program had targeted only reasonable suspects.

Many of the claims made by the Bush Administration to justify the program were questionable and none were based on incontrovertible evidence or proof. The 9/11 Commission Report, issued in 2004, revealed, for instance, that the CIA issued repeated warnings about an imminent attack from al-Qaeda and that the failure to address the threat was due to ineffective administrative policy, rather than insufficient intelligence.[76]

1994   Netscape creates the "cookie" allowing computers to monitor Internet users

2001   The September 11 terrorist attacks result in Congress authorizing the Bush Administration to utilize military methods to combat terrorism

In January of 2006, the editorial board of the *New York Times* published an Op-Ed article criticizing many of the claims made by the Bush Administration in defense of the secret surveillance program. The Bush administration strongly disapproved of the coverage and claimed, on numerous occasions, that the press was essentially aiding terrorists by uncovering details of the program. Bush, speaking about the resulting media coverage, told CNN reporters, "The fact that somebody leaked this program causes great harm to the United States. There is an enemy out there. They read newspapers."[77]

SPIES, LIES & WIRETAPS
New York Times, **January 29, 2006**
Source Document

A bit over a week ago, President Bush and his men promised to provide the legal, constitutional and moral justifications for the sort of warrantless spying on Americans that has been illegal for nearly 30 years. Instead, we got the familiar mix of political spin, clumsy historical misinformation, contemptuous dismissals of civil liberties concerns, cynical attempts to paint dissents as anti-American and pro-terrorist, and a couple of big, dangerous lies.

The first was that the domestic spying program is carefully aimed only at people who are actively working with Al Qaeda, when actually it has violated the rights of countless innocent Americans. And the second was that the Bush team could have prevented the 9/11 attacks if only they had thought of eavesdropping without a warrant.

Sept. 11 could have been prevented. This is breathtakingly cynical. The nation's guardians did not miss the 9/11 plot because it takes a few hours to get a warrant to eavesdrop on phone calls and e-mail messages. They missed the plot because they were not looking. The same officials who now say 9/11 could have been prevented said at the time that no one could possibly have foreseen the attacks. We keep hoping that Mr. Bush will finally lay down the bloody banner of 9/11, but Karl Rove, who emerged from hiding recently to talk about domestic spying, made it clear that will not happen—because the White House thinks it can make Democrats look as though they do not want to defend America. "President Bush believes if Al Qaeda is calling somebody in America, it is in our national security interest to know

The Bush administration secretly authorizes the President's Surveillance Program (PSP), utilizing E.O. 12333

The U.S. PATRIOT Act alters existing laws to facilitate better communication between the state's intelligence branches in the effort to combat terrorism

The Transportation Security Administration (TSA) is established, creating the "No Fly" and "Selectee" lists that limit the right to travel on airplanes in the United States

"Spies, Lies & Wiretaps"
continued

who they're calling and why," he told Republican officials. "Some important Democrats clearly disagree."

Mr. Rove knows perfectly well that no Democrat has ever said any such thing and that nothing prevented American intelligence from listening to a call from Al Qaeda to the United States, or a call from the United States to Al Qaeda, before Sept. 11, 2001, or since. The 1978 Foreign Intelligence Surveillance Act simply required the government to obey the Constitution in doing so. And FISA was amended after 9/11 to make the job much easier.

Only bad guys are spied on. Bush officials have said the surveillance is tightly focused only on contacts between people in this country and Al Qaeda and other terrorist groups. Vice President Dick Cheney claimed it saved thousands of lives by preventing attacks. But reporting in this paper has shown that the National Security Agency swept up vast quantities of email messages and telephone calls and used computer searches to generate thousands of leads. F.B.I. officials said virtually all of these led to dead ends or to innocent Americans. The biggest fish the administration has claimed so far has been a crackpot who wanted to destroy the Brooklyn Bridge with a blowtorch—a case that F.B.I.

officials said was not connected to the spying operation anyway.

The spying is legal. The secret program violates the law as currently written. It's that simple. In fact, FISA was enacted in 1978 to avoid just this sort of abuse. It said that the government could not spy on Americans by reading their mail (or now their email) or listening to their telephone conversations without obtaining a warrant from a special court created for this purpose. The court has approved tens of thousands of warrants over the years and rejected a handful.

As amended after 9/11, the law says the government needs probable cause, the constitutional gold standard, to believe the subject of the surveillance works for a foreign power or a terrorist group, or is a lone-wolf terrorist. The attorney general can authorize electronic snooping on his own for 72 hours and seek a warrant later. But that was not good enough for Mr. Bush, who lowered the standard for spying on Americans from "probable cause" to "reasonable belief" and then cast aside the bedrock democratic principle of judicial review.

Just trust us. Mr. Bush made himself the judge of the proper balance between national security and Americans' rights, between the law and presidential power. He wants Americans to accept, on faith, that he is doing it right. But even if

2005

The PATRIOT Act was reauthorized without substantial changes as Congress favors security concerns over warnings that the law creates the potential for civil liberties violations

The *New York Times* publishes articles resulting from leaks revealing the secret President's Surveillance Program (PSP) established by the Bush administration

continued

the United States had a government based on the good character of elected officials rather than law, Mr. Bush would not have earned that kind of trust. The domestic spying program is part of a well-established pattern: when Mr. Bush doesn't like the rules, he just changes them, as he has done for the detention and treatment of prisoners and has threatened to do in other areas, like the confirmation of his judicial nominees. He has consistently shown a lack of regard for privacy, civil liberties and judicial due process in claiming his sweeping powers. The founders of our country created the system of checks and balances to avert just this sort of imperial arrogance.

The rules needed to be changed. In 2002, a Republican senator—Mike DeWine of Ohio—introduced a bill that would have done just that, by lowering the standard for issuing a warrant from probable cause to "reasonable suspicion" for a "non-United States person." But the Justice Department opposed it, saying the change raised "both significant legal and practical issues" and may have been unconstitutional. Now, the president and Attorney General Alberto Gonzales are telling Americans that reasonable suspicion is a perfectly fine standard for spying on Americans as well as non-Americans—and they are the sole judges of what is reasonable.

So why oppose the DeWine bill? Perhaps because Mr. Bush had already secretly lowered the standard of proof—and dispensed with judges and warrants—for Americans and non-Americans alike, and did not want anyone to know.

War changes everything. Mr. Bush says Congress gave him the authority to do anything he wanted when it authorized the invasion of Afghanistan. There is simply nothing in the record to support this ridiculous argument.

The administration also says that the vote was the start of a war against terrorism and that the spying operation is what Mr. Cheney calls a "wartime measure." That just doesn't hold up. The Constitution does suggest expanded presidential powers in a time of war. But the men who wrote it had in mind wars with a beginning and an end. The war Mr. Bush and Mr. Cheney keep trying to sell to Americans goes on forever and excuses everything.

Other presidents did it. Mr. Gonzales, who had the incredible bad taste to begin his defense of the spying operation by talking of those who plunged to their deaths from the flaming twin towers, claimed historic precedent for a president to authorize warrantless surveillance. He mentioned George Washington, Woodrow Wilson

2007 The Bush Administration plans to make data taken from spy satellites available to law enforcement to be used to conduct domestic surveillance

2008 Congress passes Section 702, or the FISA Amendment Act, which is used to permit a massive NSA and CIA domestic surveillance program

"Spies, Lies & Wiretaps"
continued

and Franklin D. Roosevelt. These precedents have no bearing on the current situation, and Mr. Gonzales's timeline conveniently ended with F.D.R., rather than including Richard Nixon, whose surveillance of antiwar groups and other political opponents inspired FISA in the first place. Like Mr. Nixon, Mr. Bush is waging an unpopular war, and his administration has abused its powers against antiwar groups and even those that are just anti-Republican.

The Senate Judiciary Committee is about to start hearings on the domestic spying. Congress has failed, tragically, on several occasions in the last five years to rein in Mr. Bush and restore the checks and balances that are the genius of American constitutional democracy. It is critical that it not betray the public once again on this score.

Subsequent reporting revealed that the establishment of the program caused a rift within the Bush Administration, with some believing that the program was necessary and justifiable and others believing that the surveillance program crossed constitutional lines.

In March of 2004, while then Attorney General John Ashcroft was confined to a hospital recovering from an illness, acting Attorney General James Comey refused to reauthorize one component of the president's wiretapping program, believing the provision to be illegal. White House council Alberto Gonzales then visited Ashcroft in the hospital in an effort to convince Ashcroft to override Comey, but Comey heard of Gonzales' visit and also arrived at the hospital. Ashcroft backed Comey, with Ashcroft, Comey, FBI Director Robert Mueller, and several other officials threatening to resign if Bush insisted on authorizing the program over their objections. Though the details of this controversial meeting were never explained in public, the report revealed the deep divisions, even within the Bush administration, over the surveillance program.

2012 The Obama Administration proposes a Consumer Privacy Bill of Rights guaranteeing individuals the right to greater control over the use of their digital data

2013 The *Guardian* and the *Washington Post* publish the first series of articles derived from leaked NSA and CIA documents delivered by Edward Snowden

Subsequent investigations of the President's Surveillance Program revealed that the NSA did not focus solely on telephone communications, but also intercepted telephone metadata (such as a person's call logs), as well as Internet data and metadata (emails, Internet searches, shopping history, etc.). The fact that the program included the interception of metadata raised new questions regarding the constitutionality of the program. When collecting telephone and Internet content, i.e., listening in on calls or reading emails, such surveillance could, as the administration suggested, be limited to individuals who the NSA had reason to believe had contacts with individuals in Afghanistan or some organization. The collection of metadata, however, could not, in principle, meet those same requirements. To find meaningful data from metadata requires collecting massive amounts of metadata and then filtering the data to find data of interest. Essentially then, although it might be claimed that interception of calls and emails is a form of "targeted" electronic surveillance, the collection of metadata is, by its nature, a bulk surveillance program outside the

Satellite tower collecting data.

The Senate Judiciary committee holds hearings to determine if the executive surveillance operations carried out under the PATRIOT Act were a violation of constitutional law

Snowden leaks reveal that the NSA and CIA had been attempting to force corporations to provide a backdoor to encryption systems that would allow federal agents to bypass consumer encryption

scope of what could, legally, have been authorized by a FISA court. This revelation thus essentially proved that the program was conducted outside of legal bounds at the time.[78]

Many of the problems identified by the *New York Times* editors in their commentary on the issue proved prescient, as further disclosures and investigations (between 2007 and 2017) revealed previously unknown dimensions to the program not revealed in the initial leaks. In August of 2006, a federal judge ruled that the domestic spying program was unconstitutional. Attorney General Gonzales defended the program and proponents claimed that ending the NSA initiative might pose a grave danger to national security, but the legal challenge, delivered by U.S. District Court Judge Anna Diggs Taylor, in a 44-page memorandum, argued that the program violated the rights of free speech and privacy and ordered an immediate halt to the program.[79] Further legal challenges followed and, in 2007, the Bush Administration announced that control of NSA surveillance activities would be returned to the FISA courts.

In a May 2006 Gallup Poll report, 51 percent said they disapproved of the Bush Administration's surveillance programs, or at least, in the bulk collection of telephone data that had been revealed at the time. However, researchers noted, over subsequent years, a distinct partisan preference. In 2006, more Republicans approved of the program whereas revelations during the subsequent Obama Administration, that the same programs had continued, drew far more criticism from Republicans who were, apparently, willing to view the program as a violation when conducted under a Democrat Administration. Similarly, fewer Democrats disapproved of the same surveillance methods under Obama than they had under Bush.[80]

The 2006 press leaks were the first in a series of leaks that essentially justified years of warnings and objections from the ACLU and other civil liberties advocates. Although administration officials had essentially argued, for years, that the administrative and intelligence community response to

2015

| Terrorist attacks in France reignite fears of domestic terrorist violence | The PATRIOT Act is replaced by the USA Freedom Act | Federal Courts order Apple, Inc. to create a new operation system that would enable federal investigators to bypass security on an iPhone. |

terrorism had been within the limits imposed by the Constitution, details of the NSA program that had been secretly authorized proved that this had not been the case.

The FCC publishes official rules of "neutrality"

2016

The EU establishes the General Data Protection Regulation (GDPR), described as the strongest digital data privacy law in the world

CONCLUSION

After the existence of the President's Surveillance Program was exposed to the public, details of the program slowly emerged over the next several years. These details revealed that the program was broader and more invasive than the initial leaks suggested and that the NSA had not only conducted unwarranted surveillance on telephone communication, but had also been collecting "metadata," essentially revealing that the program was not, as the administration claimed after the initial leak, specifically targeting individuals with connections to terrorism or terrorist groups. As criticism of the Bush administration intensified, defenders of the program succeeded in obfuscating the issue through claims that all measures undertaken by the administration had been necessary to combat terrorism and that, without such extreme measures, the nation would be faced with an imminent threat of another terrorist attack.

2017

The "Vault 7" secrets, a leak of 9,000 CIA documents, reveal details of the CIA's attempts to break through encryption used by Internet

President Trump appoints Ajit Pai to head the FCC, who abolishes the FCC neutrality protections

DISCUSSION QUESTIONS

- Did the President's Surveillance Program violate constitutional rights? Why or why not?
- Do you agree with the *New York Times* arguments regarding the Bush administration's justification for the President's Surveillance Program? Why or why not?
- Was the Bush administration's surveillance program similar to the domestic surveillance activities that occurred during the Nixon administration? Why or why not?
- Does the United States need privacy laws or laws regarding domestic surveillance? Explain your position on this issue.

Works Used

"Bush defends NSA spying program." *CNN*. CNN, Inc. Jan. 1, 2006. Web. 27 Oct. 2017.

Mears, Bill, and Andrea Koppel. "NSA eavesdropping program ruled unconstitutional." *CNN*. CNN, Inc. Aug. 17, 2006. Web. 27 Oct. 2017.

"President's Radio Address." *The White House*. Dec. 17, 2005. Web. 2 Nov. 2017.

Risen, James, and Lichtblau, Eric. "Bush Lets U.S. Spy on Callers Without Courts." *New York Times*. Dec. 16, 2005. Web. 26 Oct. 2017.

Sanchez, Julian. What the Ashcroft "Hospital Showdown on NSA spying was all about." *Ars Technica*. Conde Nast. July 29, 2013. Web. 26 Oct. 2017.

"The 9/11 Commission Report." *9/11 Commission*. National Commission on Terrorist Attacks. 2004. Web. 2 Nov. 2017.

Congress debates whether or not to renew the controversial Section 702 FISA Amendment used to authorize NSA domestic intelligence operations since 2008

1788 State legislatures ratify the U.S. Constitution, establishing the basic precedent for all future constitutional law

1791 The U.S. Congress ratifies the Bill of Rights, creating the first 10 amendments to the United States Constitution

Introduction

Skepticism about the Bush administration and its policies increased steadily from 2001 through the final years of Bush's second term. The revelation, in 2005 and 2006, that the Bush administration had started a secret, illegal, domestic spying program that monitored the telephone calls and Internet communications of American citizens drove suspicion of the administration to a peak and caused a nationwide paranoia about government surveillance. This chapter examines one of the consequences of this increasing scrutiny in the form of a failed effort to create a new Department of Homeland Security (DHS) division that would have been able to share data from military satellites and aircraft sensors, with local law enforcement agencies.

The existence of the program was revealed to the public, and to members of Congress, when the *Wall Street Journal* published an article about the proposed program in August of 2007. Critics and privacy advocates immediately took exception to the program, while numerous members of Congress were immediately skeptical, having learned of the program through the *Wall Street Journal*, rather than being informed by either DHS or the administration. The primary source document for this chapter, excerpts from House of Representatives hearings on the issue in September of 2007, summarize the concerns of civil libertarians and privacy advocates, and the defense of administration and DHS officials who felt the program would provide a needed boost to law enforcement around the country.

Topics covered in this chapter include:
- Foreign intelligence
- Domestic surveillance

1868 The 14th Amendment to the U.S. Constitution guarantees all citizens the right to due process under the law

1890 Warren and Brandeis publish "The Right to Privacy" in the *Harvard Law Review*

- Department of Homeland Security
- The George W. Bush administration
- The War on Terror
- The Barack Obama administration

Eyes Everywhere
The National Applications Office Controversy (2007)

On August 15, 2007, the *Wall Street Journal* published an article on a new program, created through the Bush Administration, the Department of Homeland Security (DHS), and the Office of the Director of National Intelligence, that would have given police and local law enforcement agencies access to data collected by satellite and aircraft sensors. Speaking to *Washington Post* reporters, Jeffrey T. Richelson of the National Security Archive in Washington explained that the data in question included high resolution real-time imagery, electromagnetic and infrared sensor data, and readings from ground penetrating radar. According to statements, the spy network was capable of seeing through cloud cover and penetrating buildings and underground bunkers and thus would prove an invaluable asset to law enforcement efforts to combat smuggling, illegal immigration, and terrorism.[81]

At the time, data from the nation's satellite network was already not limited to intelligence applications and the same data had been used for scientific applications, such as to create topographic maps or monitor volcanic activity, and had also been made available to local law enforcement agencies on a "case-by-case" basis.

Charles Allen, of the DHS, told the *Washington Post*, "These systems are already used to help us respond to crises. We anticipate that we can also use it to protect Americans by preventing the entry of dangerous people and goods into the country, and by helping us examine critical infrastructure for vulnerabilities."

The program was formally authorized by Director of National Intelligence Mike McConnell in a May, 2007 memo sent to Director of DHS Michael Chertoff, and based on a 2005 study from the National Reconnaissance Office. To coordinate the program, the DHS planned to create a new

1934 The Federal Communications Commission (FCC) is established under the Federal Communications Act (FCA)

1942 *Goldman v. United States* rules that using electronic listening devices does not violate the 14th Amendment

sub-agency, the National Applications Office (NAO), within the DHS, which would be responsible for coordinating state and local requests for data from the network. The DHS and Office of the Director of National Intelligence would be, according to the report, responsible for coordinating oversight.

Immediately after the article in the *Wall Street Journal*, privacy advocates raised serious objections to the program and Kate Martin, of the Center for National Security studies called the program "Big Brother in the sky," referencing the authoritarian police state in George Orwell's dystopian 1949 novel *Nineteen Eighty-Four*.

As a result, the House Committee on Homeland Security delayed the program to give time for legislators to review any potential constitutional infringements posed by the proposal. The open hearing was held on September 6, 2007 and featured testimony by Chief Intelligence Officer (DHS) Charles Allen, Chief Privacy Officer (DHS) Hugo Teufel, and Dan Sutherland, the DHS Civil Rights and Civil Liberties Officer.[82]

Representative Bennie G. Thompson of Mississippi led the hearings, and summarized the concerns of the committee with regard to the program:

TURNING SPY SATELLITES ON THE HOMELAND:
THE PRIVACY AND CIVIL LIBERTIES IMPLICATIONS OF THE NATIONAL APPLICATIONS OFFICE
House Hearing, 110 Congress, September 6, 2007
Source Document Excerpt

The committee is meeting today to receive testimony on "Turning Spy Satellites on the Homeland: The Privacy and Civil Liberties Implication of the National Applications Office." The Department chose Congress'

1945 The National Security Agency secretly creates Project SHAMROCK

1950 Senator Joseph McCarthy delivers a shocking speech claiming that more than 200 communist spies have infiltrated the U.S. government

continued

August recess as a time to announce, with great fanfare, the creation of a new National Applications Office, referred to as the NAO, to facilitate the use of spy satellites to protect the homeland.

For the first time in our Nation's history, the Department plans to provide satellite imagery to State and local law enforcement officers to help them secure their communities. Although I am all for information sharing with our first preventers, it has to happen the right way. Whether the National Applications Office is the right way remains to be seen.

What was perhaps most disturbing about the Department's announcement, moreover, is that it wasn't an announcement at all. This authorizing committee did not learn about the National Applications Office from you, Mr. Allen, but from the *Wall Street Journal*. There was no briefing, no hearing, no phone call from anyone on your staff to inform any member of this committee of why, how, or when satellite imagery would be shared with police and sheriffs' offices nationwide.

Apparently, we weren't the only ones left in the dark. Despite my repeated requests that the Department take privacy and civil liberties seriously, the privacy officer and civil rights and civil liberties officer were not brought into the National Applications Office

development process until this spring, more than a year and a half after the National Applications Office started coming together. This is unacceptable. The rigorous privacy and civil liberties protection must be baked into from the beginning, and your Department's experts on these topics were shut out.

Furthermore, the National Applications Office will be up and running in less than 4 weeks. How the working group responsible for developing the rules for State and local use of spy satellite imagery will complete their work in this time is beyond me. Indeed, they only recently began their work.

We are here today to help to ensure that privacy and civil liberties at the Department do not remain the afterthoughts that they have apparently been. I want to know from our Department witnesses the scope of the program, its legal basis, and specifically how constitutional protections will be incorporated. I note, however, we will be doing it with one hand tied behind our back.

Last week, we invited the Department's Office of General Counsel to send an attorney to explain all this. What we got instead was a letter from the Department's Acting General Counsel stating, I do not feel that it would be useful for me to participate as a witness.

1951

Dennis v. United States rules that government limits to speech is legal only to prevent a threat to public safety or security

1959

Barenblatt v. United States rules that it's legal to order people to reveal personal details if national threat is perceived

Turning Spy Satellites on the Homeland: The Privacy and Civil Liberties Implications of the National Applications Office continued

We frankly don't need the Acting General Counsel's advice on determining who will be a useful witness and who will not. I had a reason and a purpose for asking him to testify, and his absence creates a new question that I will seek to have answered later.

I firmly agree that America must use the tools at its disposal to prevent another terrorist attack on our soil, but we must do so within the confines of the law. Sharing spy satellite information with our State and local law enforcement simply goes too far more noncontroversial applications. As Martin of the Center for National Security Studies has stated, this potentially gives rise to a Big Brother in the Sky. Like Ms. Martin, I am not convinced that the potential impact of all this has been fully considered or that adequate protections are in place.

In a prepared statement, Chief Intelligence Officer Charles Allen of the DHS explained the basis and operation of the program:

Turning Spy Satellites on the Homeland: The Privacy and Civil Liberties Implications of the National Applications Office continued

National Technical Means (NTM)—such as overhead imagery from satellites—have been used for decades, lawfully and appropriately, to support a variety of domestic uses by the US government's scientific, law enforcement and security agencies. The NAO, when operational, will facilitate the use of remote sensing capabilities to support a wide variety of customers, many of whom previously have relied on ad hoc processes to access these intelligence capabilities. The NAO will provide not only a well-ordered, transparent process for its customers but also will ensure that full protection of civil rights, civil liberties and privacy are applied to the use of these remote sensing capabilities.

Once initially operational this fall, the NAO will facilitate the use of NTM for civil applications and homeland security purposes. A third domain, law

1965   *Griswold v. CT* rules in favor of married couples' right to privacy

1967   *Katz v. United States* rules wiretaps a form of search and seizure

Willis Ware of RAND Corporation writes *Security and Privacy in Computer*

continued

enforcement, will be a part of the NAO, but will not be operational on October 1 to allow additional time to closely examine any unique aspects of law enforcement requirements in light of privacy and civil liberties. In doing so, it will build on the outstanding work of the Civil Applications Committee, known as the "CAC," which was established in 1975 to advance the use of the capabilities of the Intelligence Community for civil, non-defense uses. My staff and I have worked closely with the CAC to ensure that the stand-up of the NAO—with a broadened mandate to include the homeland security and law enforcement communities—will still support civil and scientific need for geospatial imagery, at an even more robust level.

Background of the National Applications Office

From its inception, the CAC has helped civil and scientific users understand how NTM can assist their missions and how to gain access to information normally in the hands of the intelligence agencies. With the CAC's assistance, for example, scientists have used historical and current satellite imagery to study issues such as environmental damage, land use management, and for similar purposes of research. The CAC also has used imagery to study glaciers and examine the effects of global climate change.

Similarly, some homeland security and law enforcement users in the past routinely accessed imagery and other technical intelligence directly from the Intelligence Community, especially in response to natural disasters such as hurricanes and forest fires. The Department of Homeland Security (DHS), for example, used overhead imagery in 2005 to examine areas damaged by Hurricanes Katrina and Rita to determine areas most in need of assistance. The DHS US Secret Service has used overhead imagery to identify areas of vulnerability based on topography and to build large maps to support its security planning. DHS and Federal law enforcement agencies have used imagery to identify potential vulnerabilities of facilities used for high-profile events such as the Super Bowl. These are all valid, lawful uses of NTM that enhance our ability to protect our nation—whether the threats are man-made or naturally occurring. The objective of the NAO is to bring all of these requirements for imagery support under one oversight body, where they are not only prioritized but also reviewed to determine whether requirements are appropriate and lawful. Allow me to state categorically, the NAO will have no relationship or interaction with either the FISA or the Terrorist Surveillance Programs.

1968 The Omnibus Crime Control Act holds that police needed to obtain a warrant before engaging in wire-

1969 Joseph Licklider creates the Advanced Research Projects Agency Network (ARPANET), which was

Turning Spy Satellites on the Homeland: The Privacy and Civil Liberties Implications of the National Applications Office
continued

Let me provide background on the decision to establish the NAO. The Director of National Intelligence (DNI) and the Director of the U.S. Geological Survey commissioned an independent study group in early 2005 to review the current and future role of the CAC and to study whether the Intelligence Community was employing NTM capabilities effectively for homeland security and law enforcement purposes.

The study group, led by Mr. Keith Hall, formerly Director of the National Reconnaissance Office, concluded that, unlike civil users, many homeland security and law enforcement agencies lacked a federal advocate for the use of NTM. In addition, the study group determined that many agencies, especially at the state and local level, did not know what remote sensing capabilities the Intelligence Community possessed that might be useful to them or how to request NTM in support of their missions. The study group's bottom line was that there was "an urgent need for action because opportunities to better protect the nation are being missed." It recommended unanimously that the DNI establish a new program to employ effectively the Intelligence Community's NTM capabilities not only for civil purposes,

but also for homeland security and law enforcement uses as well.

In response to the study group's recommendations, the DNI designated the Secretary of Homeland Security as Executive Agent in late spring 2007 to establish the new program in the form of the NAO. As it becomes initially operational this fall, the NAO will work with the Intelligence Community to improve access to NTM for domestic users in the homeland security and civil applications communities at all levels of government, who, heretofore, have not had a structured process to request such intelligence. DHS, as executive agent, will operate the NAO. A National Applications Executive Committee, co-chaired by the DNI and DHS, will be established to provide senior interagency oversight and guidance. This interagency forum will ensure the NAO adequately serves those government customers who have lawful and appropriate requirements for geospatial intelligence, to include classified satellite imagery and derived products.

Day-to-Day Activities
On a day-to-day basis, the NAO will work with civil applications, homeland security, and in the future on a case-by-case basis, law enforcement customers,

1971 The Pentagon Papers leaks from the press raise the issue of the Freedom of the Press versus the privacy of the government to conceal information about national security operations

1972 *Eisenstadt v. Baird* rules that the right to privacy applies to individuals

continued

to articulate their requirements, determine how our satellite imagery systems may be able to satisfy them, and submit any validated requests to the National Geospatial Intelligence Agency (NGA) for review, approval and collection tasking. The NAO also will be able to access, through NGA, commercially available imagery to meet many customer needs.

The NAO will be advised and supported by three working groups representing customer domains: civil applications, homeland security, and law enforcement. It should be noted that the law enforcement working group will be stood up over the next year, after closely examining any unique aspects of law enforcement requirements in light of privacy and civil liberties. All three domain working groups will include representatives from the DHS Privacy Office and the DHS Office for Civil Rights and Civil Liberties as well as an attorney assigned directly to the NAO.

In addition to its day-to-day business of helping its customers gain access to NTM, the NAO will help customers take advantage of educational opportunities to learn about the Intelligence Community remote sensing capabilities, including their benefits and limitations. The NAO also will serve as an advocate in Intelligence Community discussions about future technology investments that might benefit the civil applications, homeland security, and law enforcement domains.

Privacy and Civil Liberties

Since its inception, we have considered privacy and civil liberties to be at the forefront of the planning for the NAO. The independent study group in 2005 clearly articulated the need to protect privacy and civil liberties as a guiding principle in its findings. In my view, the NAO—when operational—will strengthen privacy and civil liberties. The NAO will be subject to direct oversight by privacy and civil liberties offices within both the Department of Homeland Security and the Office of the Director of National Intelligence.

In addition, the NAO will have its own legal advisor. At the executive level, the DNI's Civil Liberties Protection Officer and its Office of General Counsel, as well as DHS's Chief Privacy Officer and Officer for Civil Rights and Civil Liberties Officer, will serve as advisors to the National Applications Executive Committee, which will provide executive oversight and guidance for the NAO. The President's Privacy and Civil Liberties Oversight Board will have oversight of the use of NTM for combating terrorism.

In addition, all requests from the NAO for the use of classified satellite

1974 The Watergate Scandal results in the revelation that the CIA had been conducting widespread surveillance of American dissidents and foreign leaders without judicial oversight

The Privacy Act is established

Turning Spy Satellites on the Homeland: The Privacy and Civil Liberties Implications of the National Applications Office
continued

imagery will continue to abide by current NGA processes and be vetted by NGA attorneys and policy staff to determine legal appropriateness before collection tasking occurs. This review provides a supplemental level of oversight in addition to the strong protections already embedded in the NAO. In this way, both DHS and NGA will ensure adherence to applicable law and regulation, and intelligence oversight rules. DHS and NGA are bound by intelligence oversight rules, explained in Executive Order 12333, that protect the privacy and civil liberties of US persons. Further, DHS and NGA are required to report any violations of law or other questionable activities to the Intelligence Oversight Board of the President's Foreign Intelligence Advisory Board including violations of E.O. 12333. Finally, both DHS and NGA are subject to oversight by the House and Senate intelligence committees.

Conclusion

I assure you and the American people that the appropriate use of these NTM capabilities will make the nation safer while maintaining the privacy and civil liberties of Americans. The NAO will continue long-standing practices of employing these capabilities with full regard and protection for the privacy and civil liberties of Americans. The rules for lawful and appropriate use of such capabilities have not changed.

Under all conditions, and especially in our increasingly uncertain homeland security environment in which we face a sustained and heightened threat, it is essential that our government use all its capabilities to assure the safety and well-being of its citizens. The NAO brings a critical and sensitive national capability to bear. It does so with full respect for the law and the rights our citizens cherish. I request your support for this vital national program.

Representative Al Green, of Texas, questioned DHS Chief Intelligence Officer Charles Allen regarding the historic basis of right to privacy laws and the constitutionality of the proposed program:

1975

Senator Frank Church leads a series of hearings about the secret NSA SHAMROCK operation involved intercepting communications from American citizens

1978

Congress passes the 1978 FISA Act

Turning Spy Satellites on the Homeland: The Privacy and Civil Liberties Implications of the National Applications Office continued

Friends, if I may, I would like to share with you briefly this thought. This country was founded, in part, because of the unfettered access that the king's men had to our property, to our papers; and it was that unfettered access that caused people to venture across the ocean and come here so that they could establish a system that would give them the kind of privacy that we enjoy to this day.

The Founding Fathers were really brilliant men and—well, of course, there were some women involved—who understood the need and necessity for a fourth amendment. The Supreme Court has held in Kyllo versus the U.S. that thermal imagery is subject to the fourth amendment. The fourth amendment really is kind of the cornerstone, if you will, of the home being the castle. If we allow the unfettered access by way of satellite technology, which is unchartered space for us, we really don't know exactly where this will end. We know where we are. And if we allow it based upon custom and tradition, meaning we have always done what we are doing, we allow it based upon the notion that we have in-house people who will review this and our in-house people will tell us whether we are making mistakes or not, I think we are making a mistake.

It is not a question of whether it has been done before. The question is whether what was done before was constitutional. The question is whether what will be done is constitutional. So we are at a point where, in my opinion, we have to ask ourselves, do we have the kinds of checks and balances that the Constitution envisions, not the kinds of checks and balances that the executive branch envisions?

We just found that Dr. King's wife, Mrs. King, was being surveilled unconstitutionally by the executive branch. We have discovered that a Congressperson had his papers taken from his office unconstitutionally. The question is: Is this constitutional and are there checks and balances as envisioned by the executive branch? To have the NGA under the executive branch—and let me pause for a second and get this on the record—is the NGA under the executive branch? Does everybody agree that it is?

Mr. Allen: Yes.

Mr. Green: All right. If the NGA is under the executive branch, it is not comparable even to the FISA courts. It is at best an executive remedy. The

1980 | The Intelligence Oversight Act (IOA) updates legal standards

1981 | President Reagan's E.O. authorized wiretapping

1986 | The Electronic Communications Privacy Act is established

Turning Spy Satellites on the Homeland: The Privacy and Civil Liberties Implications of the National Applications Office continued

constitution requires a broader remedy that envisions the judiciary being a part of something as pervasive as what we are capable of doing with the satellites. My question is: Why don't we have the NGA or something comparable to the NGA under another branch of government? This is kind of the clearinghouse; do you agree?

Mr. Allen: I believe, sir, you are talking about the National Applications Office.

Mr. Green: No. The National Applications Office, as I understand it, it will go to the NGA and the NGA will review and approve the collections of information. Is this not true?

Mr. Allen: That is not exactly the way it will work. Because the National Application's Office, working with both civil agencies, science agencies, as well as the Homeland Security and potentially law enforcement—

Mr. Green: If I may, sir, please. Let me abridge your comments. Will not the National Applications Office receive the request?

Mr. Allen: They will receive the request and it will prioritize it.

Mr. Green: If I may, please. Will not the National Applications Office then take the request to the NGA?

Mr. Allen: After explicit, significant legal review.

Mr. Green: Yes, but they take it to the NGA. And will not the NGA then give a yea or nay?

Mr. Allen: Another review, yes. If there is a difference, it will be resolved between the two organizations.

Mr. Green: A rose by any name— that which we call a rose by any name still smells just as sweet. Call it NGA, call it National Application; either office is under the auspices of the executive, true?

Mr. Allen: Both offices will fall under the executive branch.

Mr. Green: That creates a great amount of consternation in the minds of constitutional scholars. I believe it does. Why not have NGA— or if we want to talk about the National Applications Office, why not have this under the auspices of the judiciary, something comparable to FISA? Probably I shouldn't say comparable to FISA, but something— something comparable to what FISA was envisioned to be. Why not have

1994 Netscape creates the "cookie" allowing computers to monitor Internet users

2001 The September 11 terrorist attacks result in Congress authorizing the Bush Administration to utilize military methods to combat terrorism

continued

it on the judiciary? The President appoints these FISA judges. Why can't we have some other entity outside of the executive to perform these as a clearinghouse?

Mr. Allen: I believe that no other element can really understand the customers or—

Mr. Green: I beg to differ.

Mr. Allen: —or priorities.

Mr. Green: I beg to differ. If you are saying there are not other people that have the intelligence and intellect to understand the Constitution of the United States of America, then we need to do away with the Supreme Court.

Mr. Allen: That is not what I said. You didn't let me answer.

Mr. Green: Let me give you more time.

Mr. Allen: There are limits to physics. What we have is an application for civil and homeland security purposes. And the National Applications Office is going to bring into order and focus already existing processes. It will have a broader customer set, as Congresswoman Harman noted, but it will all be done in accordance with the Constitution, in accordance with the laws, and there will be checks and balances.

Mr. Green; If I may, please, sir. I have to intercede because I have little time. It will be done according to the executive branch's interpretation. And that, many times, will conflict with the Constitution, which is why you have another branch to give another opinion that can supersede the executive branch's interpretation. Listen, I am imploring, I beseech you, I beg that you please give some consideration to the notion that we need a third branch of government or another branch of government involved.

Barry Steinhardt, Director of the ACLU program on technology and liberty, also expressed concerns over possible constitutional protections and raised the issue of the "posse comitatus" Act of 1878 that prohibits the use of federal military personnel or technology to enforce domestic policies. The act, which only applied to U.S. Army technology was enacted to prohibit a potentially authoritarian executive branch from using the tools created for national defense against the citizens of the nation.

The Bush administration secretly authorizes the President's Surveillance Program (PSP), utilizing E.O. 12333

The U.S. PATRIOT Act alters existing laws to facilitate better communication between the state's intelligence branches in the effort to combat terrorism

The Transportation Security Administration (TSA) is established, creating the "No Fly" and "Selectee" lists that limit the right to travel on airplanes in the United States

Turning Spy Satellites on the Homeland: The Privacy and Civil Liberties Implications of the National Applications Office
continued

The government's use of spy satellites to monitor its own people, and let me emphasize that. This is to monitor the American people. This is not weather phenomena. This is not our National infrastructure, bridges or the like. This is people who are being monitored here, represents another large and disturbing step towards what amounts to a surveillance society.

Our response, especially the Congressional response to this new technology, will serve as an important test case for how wisely we handle the introduction of powerful new technologies.

Congress needs to act before this new technology, this new tool is turned inward on the American people. We need to establish a regime of checks and balances and law that protects us against their misuse.

The chairman and this Committee have taken an important first step in calling the Department of Homeland Security to account and holding this hearing. You have our thanks, Mr. Chairman. But it has been interesting. I have heard a lot of discussion this morning about the respective roles of the three branches of government here. Most of the discussion about the

two other of branches of government beyond the executive branch, that is the legislative branch and the judicial branch, have come from the members of this Committee.

One of the things that I find disturbing about this discussion this morning, not the Committee's participation in it but the Department's, is the degree to which you have been told by the Department of Homeland Security, "trust us; we can handle all of this powerful technology, and we will handle it in a manner that is consistent with our principles and consistent"—they haven't even said consistent with the laws, but I suppose that is implied.

I guess I am from the Ronald Reagan school here, trust but verify. You need to verify that in fact this technology will not be misused. And one way in which you can verify that is to establish a clear legal framework for how this technology can in fact be used. As Mrs. Harman said earlier, the capabilities here are extraordinary. They go far beyond what the human eye can process. These are very powerful technologies, everything from thermal imaging that you discussed a little bit this morning, to infrared, to ultrawide band. We can tick them all off. But the point is, these are extraordinarily powerful technologies,

2005

The PATRIOT Act was reauthorized without substantial changes as Congress favors security concerns over warnings that the law creates the potential for civil liberties violations

The *New York Times* publishes articles resulting from leaks revealing the secret President's Surveillance Program (PSP) established by the Bush administration

continued

and they go well beyond what you and I could see if we happened, for example, to be in a helicopter. We need to have laws that make it clear how these technologies can be trained inward on the American people.

Now, there is a very good starting base for all this, and it has been referenced here this morning, and that is Posse Comitatus. In my written testimony, we discuss this in greater length, and with the Committee's permission, we will make available to you a memorandum from our legal counsel on the applicability of Posse Comitatus here. But it is important to remember what the basic principle of the Posse Comitatus and the ensuing Federal statutes was. The notion that military is not to be trained on the American public; it is for our National defense. It is not to be used for law enforcement purposes. These are the Department of Defense satellites. These offices are within the Department of Defense. This is the military. And we need to be very careful that Posse Comitatus and that principle that we not use the military we have trained on the American public; these are not folks who are trained or capable in protecting the rights of Americans. That is why we have set them apart and said, you protect us from foreign enemies, but we do not use you for domestic law enforcement. So I think Posse Comitatus raises important questions.

We have four recommendations for the Committee which I will just highlight now. The first is that Congress should demand and the Department of Homeland Security should impose a moratorium on the domestic use of these satellites and enactment of this program. The moratorium should not be lifted until the Congress receives answers to the key questions that you have already begun to ask and the many other questions that will arise as you learn more details. But that moratorium is extraordinarily important. There is no hurry here. You have heard, if it is necessary to use this, for example, to track a hurricane or even to look at another natural disaster, there is already sufficient authority for that.

Secondly, Congress should not authorize the enactment of this program before enacting statutory checks and balances to ensure not only the proper

Our response, especially the Congressional response to this new technology, will serve as an important test case for how wisely we handle the introduction of powerful new technologies.

2007 The Bush Administration plans to make data taken from spy satellites available to law enforcement to be used to conduct domestic surveillance

2008 Congress passes Section 702, or the FISA Amendment Act, which is used to permit a massive NSA and CIA domestic surveillance program

Turning Spy Satellites on the Homeland: The Privacy and Civil Liberties Implications of the National Applications Office continued

oversight of this program but that the potentially enormously powerful surveillance tools that are at play here be used properly. This measure should include rules for when domestic satellite use is permissible and be combined with judicial oversight.

Lastly, the Congress should strengthen and make truly independent the chief privacy officer and civil rights officers of the Department of Homeland Security. As Representative Thompson pointed out in his letter to Secretary Chertoff, those bodies, those offices appear to have been marginalized through this process. I think this morning's testimony made that clear as well. It is possible to give these bodies true independent authority where they report equally to the Congress as they do to the Secretary of their agencies, that it is possible to get beyond a discussion which is purely internal to the agency to have those officers report to you, report to the American public, and make sure that our civil liberties and privacy is in fact being protected.

On April 12, 2008, the *Washington Post* reported that the Bush Administration planned to initiate the program over concerns of House Democrats. Homeland Security Secretary Michael Chertoff wrote letters to Representatives Thompson and Jane Harman of California arguing that there was no basis to suggest that the program posed a danger to civil liberties. Representative Harman told *Washington Post* reporters that she was reluctant to trust the administration given the 2005 revelations about the NSA's domestic wiretapping program.[83]

In October of 2008, the *Wall Street Journal* reported that the first phase of the controversial program had been set in motion, despite continued objections over the possible civil liberties implications. According to the *Journal's* report, the Government Accountability Office had issued an unpublished report detailing similar concerns and claiming that there were insufficient assurances to guarantee that the National Applications Office would adhere to existing laws, or could potentially prevent misuse.[84]

2012 The Obama Administration proposes a Consumer Privacy Bill of Rights guaranteeing individuals the right to greater control over the use of their digital data

2013 The *Guardian* and the *Washington Post* publish the first series of articles derived from leaked NSA and CIA documents delivered by Edward Snowden

The 2008 presidential election resulted in the election of Barack Obama to serve as the 44th President of the United States. In reviewing the policies enacted under Bush, the Obama Administration decided to continue the domestic spy-satellite expansion program, though newly appointed Homeland Security Secretary Janet Napolitano was asked to review the program to identify civil liberties concerns. It was announced in June of 2009 that Napolitano had decided to cancel the program. The decision reportedly came after Napolitano consulted with local law enforcement officials, with the consensus being that local law enforcement did not view the program as a significant priority.

Shortly before the decision to cancel the program was announced, Representative Jane Harman had introduced legislation that would have prevented the DHS from using space-based satellite imagery in domestic surveillance. In a statement introducing her bill, Harman again referenced Orwell's *Nineteen Eighty-Four*:

Imagine, for a moment, what it would be like of one of these satellites were directed on your neighborhood or home, a school or place of worship— and without an adequate legal framework or operation procedures in place for regulating their use. I dare say the reaction might be that Big Brother has finally arrived, and the black helicopters can't be far behind.[85]

The Senate Judiciary committee holds hearings to determine if the executive surveillance operations carried out under the PATRIOT Act were a violation of constitutional law

Snowden leaks reveal that the NSA and CIA had been attempting to force corporations to provide a backdoor to encryption systems that would allow federal agents to bypass consumer encryption

CONCLUSION

During the hearing, the concerns voiced by state representatives and the ACLU reveal how trust in the Bush White House had eroded over Bush's two terms as president. Despite these concerns, the administration announced that the program would go ahead as planned. Opposition intensified, however, with the Government Accountability Office (GAO) echoing similar concerns. The program was, therefore, postponed, and after Barack Obama won the historical November 2008 election, the program was abandoned. The proposed National Applications Office (NAO) is only one of many Bush-era laws and executive policies that drew concern from privacy experts and advocates, but the depth of resistance and skepticism from opponents of the plan echoes the loss of faith in Bush's overall policy and a deepening distrust of governmental motives and methods that remains one of the nation's vital issues in 2018.

2015

Terrorist attacks in France reignite fears of domestic terrorist violence

The PATRIOT Act is replaced by the USA Freedom Act

Federal Courts order Apple, Inc. to create a new operation system that would enable federal investigators to bypass security on an iPhone.

DISCUSSION QUESTIONS

- Did the National Applications Office proposal pose a danger to privacy rights? Explain your position.
- What are some other examples of technology that pose or could pose a danger to privacy?
- What is your impression of the testimony by Chief Intelligence Office Charles Allen from the Department of Homeland Security?
- Do you agree with ACLU Director Barry Steinhardt's concerns about the NAO program? Why or why not?

Works Used

Gorman, Siobhan. "Satellite-Surveillance Program to Begin Despite Privacy Concerns." *Wall Street Journal.* Oct. 1, 2008. Web. 27 Oct. 2017.

Hsu, Spencer S. "Administration Set to Use New Spy Program in U.S." *Washington Post*. The Washington Post Company. Apr. 12, 2008. Web. 27 Oct. 2017.

Meyer, Josh. "Homeland Security said to kill spy satellite plan." *Los Angeles Times*. Los Angeles Times. June 23, 2009. Web. 28 Oct. 2017.

"Turning Spy Satellites on the Homeland: The Privacy and Civil Liberties Implications of the National Applications Office." *FAS*. Federation of American Scientists. Sept. 6, 2007. Web. 27 Oct. 2017.

Warrick, Joby. "Domestic Use of Spy Satellites to Widen." *Washington Post*. The Washington Post Company. Aug. 16, 2007. Web. 27 Oct. 2017.

The FCC publishes official rules of "neutrality"

2016

The EU establishes the General Data Protection Regulation (GDPR), described as the strongest digital data privacy law in the world

2017

The "Vault 7" secrets, a leak of 9,000 CIA documents, reveal details of the CIA's attempts to break through encryption used by Internet

President Trump appoints Ajit Pai to head the FCC, who abolishes the FCC neutrality protections

Introduction

By 2008, the long list of controversies surrounding the Bush administration's post-9/11 security strategy had made it clear that privacy rights, as they existed in the pre-9/11 world, no longer prevail. This chapter provides a snapshot of the academic debate over the present and future of privacy rights in the post-911 world. The primary source document is one half of a debate series published in the pages of *The Economist,* in which business executive Neil Livingstone debated privacy rights with former Attorney General Bob Barr. The article encapsulates one of the main dichotomies in the debate, between those who felt that the realities of terrorism necessitated surrendering privacy rights as previously known, whereas others argued that such a sacrifice was not legitimately necessary, and that the government needed to establish clear privacy regulations within its broader framework for combating the terrorist threat.

In the article, entitled, "Privacy Is Dead, at Least in the Traditional Sense. Get Over It," Livingstone parroted the talking points of the Bush administration's defenders after the revelation of Bush's secret telephone and Internet surveillance program. The argument can be distilled to three contentious claims: 1) that the nature of terrorism requires strategies that violate privacy rights as previously understood; 2) that without such methods, America would suffer more terrorist attacks, like 9/11; and 3) that those who aren't doing anything wrong have nothing to fear from the government and so shouldn't be concerned about the government intercepting their telephone and Internet communications. These three claims proved convincing to many Americans and, especially, to conservative politicians, but not to the majority of the public or privacy advocates. Former Attorney General Barr rebutted the points made by Livingstone in his side

Congress debates whether or not to renew the controversial Section 702 FISA Amendment used to authorize NSA domestic intelligence operations since 2008

of the debate, and asserted that the role of the government was not simply to protect the citizenry, but rather to safeguard the rights and freedoms of American society. By failing to protect the established right to privacy, Barr believes that the government has failed this basic function.

Topics covered in this chapter include:
- The War on Terror
- The 9/11 terrorist attacks on the United States
- The George W. Bush administration
- Domestic surveillance

This Chapter Discusses the Following Source Document:
Livingstone, Neil C. "The Proposition's Closing Statement: Privacy Is Dead, at Least in the Traditional Sense. Get Over It." *The Economist*. Economist Newspaper, ltd. Feb. 13, 2008.

Debating Privacy
The Scholarly Debate Over the State of Privacy (2001-2018)

In 2008, *The Economist* published a debate series in which experts in chosen fields presented pro and con arguments on some of the pressing national security and public policy issues of the era.

In a series on privacy and security, American business executive and author on national security issues Neil C. Livingstone debated privacy rights with former Attorney General and former U.S. Representative Bob Barr of Georgia. The essential issue in the debate was whether emerging issues in national security, given the proliferation of the Internet as a tool in commerce, business, education, and government, required surrendering certain civil liberties.

In his article: *The Proposition's Closing Statement*, Livingstone presents the argument for the position that modern realities necessitate surrendering privacy, beginning with the intentionally inflammatory assertion: Privacy is dead, at least in the traditional sense. Get over it.[86]

THE PROPOSITION'S CLOSING STATEMENT:
PRIVACY IS DEAD, AT LEAST IN THE TRADITIONAL SENSE. GET OVER IT
by Neil C. Livingstone
The Economist, February 13, 2008
Source Document

I know this is not a popular assertion, nor is it what this audience wants to hear, but it is time to reframe the debate and become serious about what we can do to harness the new technologies reconfiguring the world and eroding our privacy and enlist them in an effort to erect a new privacy paradigm.

1868 The 14th Amendment to the U.S. Constitution guarantees all citizens the right to due process under the law

1890 Warren and Brandeis publish "The Right to Privacy" in the *Harvard Law Review*

"The Proposition's Closing Statement: Privacy is Dead, At Least in the Traditional Sense. Get Over It"
continued

In his rebuttal, my opponent, Mr. Barr, cites the words of Justice Louis Brandeis in his dissenting opinion to the 1928 Olmstead decision, to the effect that privacy is the most "comprehensive" and "valued" right of "civilised men". I have, by contrast, in my earlier remarks suggested that the right to life is even more valued and fundamental, and must be protected and guaranteed, to the extent possible, before rights like privacy can be fully appreciated and prized. Moreover, Mr. Barr failed to note that Justice Brandeis, in the very same passage in his dissent to Olmstead, described privacy as "the right to be let alone." [87]

By that standard, I am fully in agreement with Mr. Barr. I believe that all citizens should be left alone unless they are engaged in criminal or antisocial conduct. This does not mean, however, that we should not monitor certain activities, technologies and movements to ensure that people are not guilty of malicious behaviour, nor should we hesitate to develop databases to protect society from the transgressions of known or would-be terrorists and criminals. What is wrong, for example, in protecting families with young children by maintaining national databases, available to the public, of convicted paedophiles, including their addresses? Only those who have been convicted of crimes against children would be included in such an inventory and the great mass of citizens would not be harmed in any way; they would only benefit from such information.

Let us turn our attention to the internet. The internet cannot function without vast amounts of data and certain personal information stored online. However, if our information is properly stored and protected, and access to it is appropriately controlled, how much real privacy have we lost? Haven't we lost vastly more privacy if our identities are stolen or the computer systems we depend on are incapacitated by denial of service attacks? Credit cards make our lives immeasurably simpler and more convenient, yet they, too, depend on validation codes and full owner information. Do we want financial fraud and theft to flourish because we want to restrict the amount and kind of information needed in the verification process? In short, if we are identified, but not compromised, what have we lost?

There are vast criminal cyber-networks in existence today seeking to acquire and sell the intellectual property on which much of our national economy depends. Other malicious

1923   *Meyer v. Nebraska* establishes that the 14th Amendment guarantees privileges of citizenship

1928   *Olmstead v. United States* rules that wiretapping is not a form of search and seizure defined by the 14th Amendment

continued

actors regularly hope to compromise our national security by breaking into highly sensitive and restricted computer sites. Should we not do everything in our power to police such activities and preserve both the utility and efficacy of the internet, even if it means that we may have to scrutinise all users in order to identify what my opponent has referred to as the bad guys? There may be no other alternative. If there is, I would like Mr. Barr to put it forward, since his arguments are long on feel-good rhetoric and short on substance.

Returning to my introductory comments, if citizens are not misusing the internet or telephonic communications, or attempting to board an aircraft in the hopes of hijacking it, to cite only a few examples, then they have nothing to fear from government scrutiny. With this in mind, I am not suggesting that some actions and activities should not remain private and beyond the ordinary interest of the government. But these should be activities that are inherently private, like most intimate relations, medical records and the inviolability of the home (without a court order). But activities that occur in the public sphere must be subjected to more scrutiny in order to protect society and ensure their safe and uncompromised operation. As I have suggested in my earlier statements, if a citizen desires to live below the radar, then he or she should not use the internet, try to board an aircraft, make a purchase with a credit card, or place phone calls. I, for one, am happy to subject myself to reasonable government scrutiny, and to provide certain personal data, in order to do all of these things conveniently and without serious disruption.

The new technologies that many seem to fear, I believe, may in the end actually do more to liberate us than enslave us. The global access to information technologies will make it more and more difficult for repressive and dictatorial governments to oppress their citizens without fear of exposure and international sanction. The internet has played a major role in political reform and empowering ordinary citizens in China. Surveillance cameras are already liberating citizens, especially the elderly, from the constant fear of crime. Universal access to DNA information, opposed by many civil libertarians, would go a long way to ensuring many innocent people are not convicted of crimes they did not commit.

Surveillance of communications and the movements of certain individuals are great tools in fighting terrorism and ensuring the security and happiness of our citizens. Just think, if the US intelligence community had more aggressively collected information prior to 9/11, and had properly connected

1934 The Federal Communications Commission (FCC) is established under the Federal Communications Act (FCA)

1942 *Goldman v. United States* rules that using electronic listening devices does not violate the 14th Amendment

"The Proposition's Closing Statement: Privacy is Dead, At Least in the Traditional Sense. Get Over It"
continued

the so-called "dots", we might not be at war today in Iraq and Afghanistan. Moreover, this debate would probably not be taking place because the new security procedures which my opponent rails against would not have been implemented.

In closing, to be a defender of reasonable and commonsense security does not mean that one has to become the enemy of privacy. Quite the contrary; my opponent, if his views were to prevail, would so diminish and undermine security that privacy also would soon become a casualty of his folly.

I have enjoyed the opportunity of taking what is the more unpopular and seemingly less sympathetic position in this debate. I understand that many of you are cynical and skeptical about the demands of security versus privacy in the contemporary world. I would only ask that you carefully consider my arguments and try to expand the way you view this complex debate before making a final judgment.

In a rebuttal to Mr. Livingston's article, Mr. Barr asserts that the primary duty of the government is not simply to provide security, but to "serve as guardian of the rights guaranteed the citizens under the founding documents and principles of the nation."

This, Barr concludes, includes but is not limited to the duty to protect citizens from harm. Were the only primary duty of the government to provide security services, Barr argues, then all existing privacy protections, such as prohibitions against reading mail, or prohibitions against unwarranted wiretapping, or prohibitions against other invasions of personal privacy, would also be subordinate to interests in national security.

Therefore, if the premise that the government's chief duty is national security is taken as fact, there exists no justification to bar the government from any activity, even those prohibited by existing laws and legal

1945 | The National Security Agency secretly creates Project SHAMROCK

1950 | Senator Joseph McCarthy delivers a shocking speech claiming that more than 200 communist spies have infiltrated the U.S. government

precedent, that have been developed as checks against the power of the government to intrude on the lives of citizens.

In concluding his argument, Barr noted that authoritarian regimes have long used the justification of security to justify curtailing rights and argues that the only way to prevent this pattern is to establish and defend fundamental checks and oversight on the activities and powers of the state to intrude on the lives of citizens or to determine when and how a citizen's rights might be curtailed in the name of national security.[88]

The *Economist* debate series over the right to privacy came at a time when Americans were gradually coming to realize that the voluntary participation in web commerce and culture, whether online shopping, using social media, or using web-based databases for education or governmental purposes, had essentially meant that users were routinely surrendering ownership of their personal data to commercial entities. The legal ownership of digital data was, therefore, among the central privacy issues of the era, dealing not only with potential government intrusion and misuse of personal information, but equally with the issue of whether corporations providing services had the right to record, maintain, and use data provided by users to further corporate economic interests. This debate would become part of a broader controversy over ownership of digital data, with lobbyists and activists petitioning the government to enact legislation that would protect the basic rights of individuals to own personal data even when voluntarily transmitted, through a company, over the Internet. For several years, corporate invasions of privacy would remain the privacy rights topic du jour, until leaks revealed the Obama Administration's surveillance activities in 2013, reigniting the debate over intelligence reform.

In 2008, the National Research Council released a comprehensive, book-length report *Protecting Individual Privacy in the Struggle Against Terrorists*, which included, in an appendix, a comprehensive analysis of public

1951 *Dennis v. United States* rules that government limits to speech is legal only to prevent a threat to public safety or security

1959 *Barenblatt v. United States* rules that it's legal to order people to reveal personal details if national threat is perceived

opinion on the security vs. privacy debate since the beginning of the War on Terror to 2008.

Drawing data from over 30 different public survey organizations the authors found an overall increase in support for protecting privacy and civil liberties even at the expense of investigating terrorism. This overall shift in public opinion was seen as related to the dwindling sense of an imminent threat to safety as well as to the fact that subsequent violent events had been linked to individual actors rather than organized terrorist groups or cells. The researchers found that reports on surveillance activities resulted in surges of interest in protecting civil liberties, whereas news of terrorist attacks, around the world, coincided unsurprisingly with a surge in support for stronger security measures.[89]

The patterns in public interest measured by the many polling organizations that attempted to measure public opinion between 2001 and 2008 show that Americans remained highly concerned with their civil liberties and privacy rights, but that the War on Terror had inspired a high-level concern over national security as well. Opinion polls found a high level of concern for civil liberties in the abstract, and lower levels of concern in specific instances of potential government overreach. Americans were less concerned, on average, about whether presidential administrations had, or were continuing to, violate laws to enhance security. The relative lack of "outrage" among the public regarding state policies that clearly posed a threat to civil liberties was most likely related to the fact that the ACLU and other rights advocate groups had not yet been able to clearly identify egregious examples of government policies infringing on the rights of citizens. Although examples existed, then, the widely-reported examples represented relatively minor violations of rights, rather than obvious, glaring abuses of power.

Essentially, the Bush administration, using the AUMF congressional authorization of military powers, coupled with Executive Order 12333 and

1965   *Griswold v. CT rules in favor of married couples' right to privacy*

1967   *Katz v. United States rules wiretaps a form of search and seizure*

Willis Ware of RAND Corporation writes Security and Privacy in Computer

the PATRIOT Act, had demonstrably exceeded the constitutional authority vested in the presidency to establish intelligence operations beyond the scope that violated constitutional law. These programs put into place a system that could, under certain circumstances, be used by the government to vastly curtail the rights of the people regarding search and seizure, due process, and privacy. However, though Americans were deeply concerned about their civil liberties, there was a tendency to view these threats as "potential" and, therefore, the government's assertion that the public could trust them to use potentially dangerous technologies and powers, had been sufficient to convince enough of the public to support or at least not actively oppose such initiatives. Had the Bush administration used the NSA to not only surveil, but to arrest dissidents, the public might have been more willing to see the Bush-era expansions of powers as a threat akin to that posed by the Nixon administration's illegal wiretapping in the 1960s. As far as the public was aware, such abuses had not occurred, or, at least, had not affected people other than the "bad" people that the Bush administration claimed they had specifically targeted. The issue was, therefore, one of potential versus imminent danger and of constitutional principles rather than constitutional remedies to existing abuses.

1968 The Omnibus Crime Control Act holds that police needed to obtain a warrant before engaging in wire-

1969 Joseph Licklider creates the Advanced Research Projects Agency Network (ARPANET), which was

CONCLUSION

Most of the claims made by Livingstone in defense of the domestic surveillance program were repeated so often by defenders of the administration that the claims took on the appearance of established fact. For instance, the oft-echoed claim that without domestic surveillance there would be another 9/11 or that a domestic surveillance program might have *prevented* 9/11, was convincing to many Americans, but was not based on legitimate data. The Bush administration was not able to provide any significant evidence to justify this claim or to legitimize the statement that such a system was necessary to effectively counter terrorism. Likewise, the fears of privacy advocates had not been borne out in the form of egregious abuses by the government. Debates like that between Livingstone and Barr reflect the frequent sparring of ideological positions, but with neither position tied to practical examples.

1971   The Pentagon Papers leaks from the press raise the issue of the Freedom of the Press versus the privacy of the government to conceal information about national security operations

1972   *Eisenstadt v. Baird* rules that the right to privacy applies to individuals

DISCUSSION QUESTIONS

- Do you agree with Barr or Livingstone in the debate? Explain your position.
- Is domestic surveillance necessary to combat terrorism? Why or why not?
- Should law-abiding citizens who have nothing to fear from the government be concerned about domestic surveillance? Why or why not?
- Do you believe that domestic surveillance would have prevented 9/11? Explain your answer.

Works Used

Barr, Bob. "The Opposition's closing statement." *The Economist*. Feb. 13, 2008. Web. 26 Oct. 2017.

Livingstone, Neil C. "The Proposition's closing statement." *The Economist*. The Economist Newspaper Limited. Feb. 13, 2008. Web. 28 Oct. 2017.

National Research Council. *Protecting Individual Privacy in the Struggle Against Terrorists*. Washington D.C.: The National Academies Press, 2008.

1974

The Watergate Scandal results in the revelation that the CIA had been conducting widespread surveillance of American dissidents and foreign leaders without judicial oversight

The Privacy Act is established

1975

Senator Frank Church leads a series of hearings about the secret NSA SHAMROCK operation involved intercepting communications from American citizens

1978

Congress passes the 1978 FISA Act

Introduction

This chapter looks at the corporate consequences of America's security over the privacy approach developed by the Bush administration and continued under the Obama administration. Cloud computing, a system that uses virtual computer networks to store data and to increase processing power, was becoming one of the hottest digital technologies in the 2010s and American companies offering cloud computing and storage services were looking to expand into European markets. However, European consumers were wary of storing their data with American companies because, under the PATRIOT Act, American intelligence agencies had unfettered and unregulated access to data stored and processed through American companies. Between 2010 and 2012, American companies operating in Europe struggled to attract consumers, unable to reassure companies that data stored would be protected from U.S. governmental interception or intrusion.

In the source document for this chapter, a press release from the Obama White House, the Obama administration tries to assuage the fears of European consumers, exploring what the White House calls five "myths" about law enforcement access to personal information. Drawing on several specific instances of data management issues, the press release claims that, as of 2012, the United States protected privacy to the same, if not in some cases a higher degree, than European nations. Among other points used to demonstrate this claim, the White House cites the Cybercrime Convention, which established cooperative data sharing between law enforcement agencies, but also includes a layer of privacy protection protocols more comprehensive than many employed in European nations.

Topics covered in this chapter include:
- Foreign intelligence
- The PATRIOT Act
- Corporate data privacy
- International commerce
- The War on Terror
- Cybercrime and cyberwarfare
- Digital privacy rights
- The Obama administration

This Chapter Discusses the Following Source Document:
"Five Myths Regarding Privacy and Law Enforcement Access to Personal Information in the European Union and the United States." U.S. Department of State. Dec. 4, 2012.

Reassuring Consumers
The European Cloud Computing Controversy

Cloud computing and cloud-based data storage are technological tools developed through a series of innovative discoveries that can be traced back to the 1960s, when the potential of computer networks was first being realized. Joseph Licklider, known as "Lick," was a computer scientist considered a pioneer in the theory that gave rise to the Internet.

In 1962, Licklider released a series of memos discussing what he called an "Intergalactic Computer Network," imagined as a massive, international network that users could utilize to collaborate on data across international lines. Licklider was one of the individuals responsible for creating the Advanced Research Projects Agency Network (ARPANET) in 1969, which was the forerunner of the Internet and the basis for later technology that became part of the World Wide Web.[90]

Private corporations were responsible for making many of Licklider's theories into reality. The 1999 Salesforce.com website, for instance, delivered applications via a central website, thus serving as an early example of a web-based collaborative environment, while the 2002 Amazon Web Services program took this a step further, offering virtual storage and computation services. These stepping stones eventually led to the basic technology for what is now often called "the cloud," a series of virtual networks that can be used to store and retrieve data as well as to collaborate on data from different areas.

Essentially, the cloud is a way of referring to a network linked, in such a way, that vast amounts of data could be stored within the network, rather than on a single computer or server. The cloud thus replaces the need for physical storage with distributed virtual storage, which enables a user to access her or his files from remote locations, but also to store or transfer more data than might be possible using traditional file storage or transfer systems.[91]

The Bush administration secretly authorizes the President's Surveillance Program (PSP), utilizing E.O. 12333

The U.S. PATRIOT Act alters existing laws to facilitate better communication between the state's intelligence branches in the effort to combat terrorism

The Transportation Security Administration (TSA) is established, creating the "No Fly" and "Selectee" lists that limit the right to travel on airplanes in the United States

29 OCT 69	2100	LOADED OP. PROGRAM FOR BEN BARKER BBN	CSK
	22:30	Talked to SRI Host to Host	CSK
		Left op. imp. program running after sending a host dead message to imp.	CSK

First ARPANET IMP log: the first message ever sent via the ARPANET, 10:30 p.m., 29 October 1969. This IMP Log excerpt, kept at UCLA, describes setting up a message transmission from the UCLA SDA Sigma 7 Host computer to the SRI SDS 940 Host computer.

Between 2002 and 2012, cloud computing services developed into one of the most profitable Internet services industries and the companies offering cloud services gradually began to expand into European markets. This led to concern, in the European Union (EU), that the U.S. guidelines on privacy were insufficient to the kinds of protections that the EU had established regarding digital privacy.

At a 2011 celebration of the launch of the Microsoft 365 program, head of Microsoft U.K. Gordon Frazer was asked, "Can Microsoft guarantee that EU-stored data, held in EU-based datacenters, will not leave the European Economic Area under any circumstances—even under a request by the PATRIOT Act?"

Frazer responded, as reported by *Zdnet* that "Microsoft cannot provide those guarantees. Neither can any other company." This statement sparked

2005

The PATRIOT Act was reauthorized without substantial changes as Congress favors security concerns over warnings that the law creates the potential for civil liberties violations

The *New York Times* publishes articles resulting from leaks revealing the secret President's Surveillance Program (PSP) established by the Bush administration

a major debate in Europe and ultimately led to the adoption of new EU privacy guidelines for digital data aimed in part at establishing a legal basis to prohibit U.S. security agencies from collecting data from EU users.[92]

Cloud computing service providers, like Google and Microsoft, then pressured the federal government to provide security guarantees to protect their overseas business interests. A January 30, 2012 report from Gartner indicated that the cloud computing market in Western Europe was worth an estimated $47 billion and some critics argued that EU companies had been purposefully stoking fears about U.S. data protection in an effort to prevent U.S. companies from capitalizing on the lucrative EU cloud data market.

In response, the European Commission released a proposal for a new data protection scheme that would require any agency planning on extracting data from the cloud to provide notice before collecting the data in question. Secondly, the new privacy proposal included a "right to be forgotten" provision, meaning that customers would have the right to have their data removed from various systems at their request.[93] Whether to adopt "right to be forgotten" legislation became a major debate in the United States as well, related to broader concerns over whether a person had the right to remove him or herself from "the grid" of the web.

In December of 2012, the U.S. State Department issued a report, entitled, "Five Myths Regarding Privacy and Law Enforcement Access to Personal Information in the European Union and the United States," as part of an effort to reassure EU consumers regarding the use of U.S. based cloud computing services.

2007   The Bush Administration plans to make data taken from spy satellites available to law enforcement to be used to conduct domestic surveillance

2008   Congress passes Section 702, or the FISA Amendment Act, which is used to permit a massive NSA and CIA domestic surveillance program

FIVE MYTHS REGARDING PRIVACY AND LAW ENFORCEMENT ACCESS TO PERSONAL INFORMATION IN THE EUROPEAN UNION AND THE UNITED STATES

U.S. Department of State, December 4, 2012
Source Document

Cloud computing is one of the Internet's great innovations, enabling individuals and small and medium size enterprises to enjoy state-of-the-art data processing services that until very recently were available only to large businesses. Cloud computing is now key to the functioning of smart phones, tablets, and the other wireless devices with which most people access the Internet. Consequently, cloud computing allows users to access cloud services from locations around the world irrespective of national borders. The ability of cloud consumers to exploit the full value of this innovation has been increasingly threatened over the last year by misplaced assertions that use of cloud services provided by a company subject to the U.S. legal process will routinely expose customer data to seizure by U.S. law enforcement authorities. As this controversy jeopardizes opportunities on both sides of the Atlantic and around the world for needed economic and employment growth, the record needs to be set straight.

The transatlantic privacy discussion is too often based on myths about the U.S. legal system—myths that obscure our fundamental commitment to privacy and the extensive legal protections we provide to data. Contrary to concerns raised by some, electronic data stored in the United States—including data of foreign nationals—receives protections from access by criminal investigators equal to or greater than the protections provided within the European Union.

This document dispels these myths and discusses certain aspects of U.S. laws that are often mischaracterized abroad, and that discourage citizens of other countries from storing their data with U.S. cloud providers.

Myth 1: The United States Cares Less about Privacy than the European Union.

Reality: The United States was founded on—and its modern-day laws, regulations, and practices reflect—a core belief in the importance of protecting citizens from government

2012 The Obama Administration proposes a Consumer Privacy Bill of Rights guaranteeing individuals the right to greater control over the use of their digital data

2013 The *Guardian* and the *Washington Post* publish the first series of articles derived from leaked NSA and CIA documents delivered by Edward Snowden

continued

intrusion. Our most important legal document—our Constitution—set forth, more than two hundred years ago, a Bill of Rights that provided protection from unreasonable searches and seizures, and that continues to protect privacy today, including the privacy of electronic communications. The United States and the European Union are united in our common values regarding the fundamental importance of privacy protections and our deeply rooted commitment to continue to safeguard these values in the digital age.

Myth 2: The European Union Does a Better Job of Protecting Data from Law Enforcement Access than the United States.

Reality: Privacy protections limiting U.S. law enforcement access to electronic communications, a key area of modern data privacy concern, are among the highest in the world. They provide protections that are at least equivalent to—and often superior to— those provided by the laws and practices in many EU Member States.

Myth 3: U.S. Law Enforcement Authorities Are Less Protective of the Privacy Interests of Foreign Nationals than of U.S. Citizens.

Reality: In the key area of law enforcement acquisition of electronic communications, the stringent U.S. statutes protecting the privacy of email and voice communications apply equally to foreign nationals and U.S. citizens. Moreover, the United States does not discriminate with regard to judicial redress to obtain access to personal data collected for criminal investigations, and provides opportunities for any person, regardless of citizenship, to correct such data if it is believed to be inaccurate, as explained below.

Myth 4: The PATRIOT Act Gives the U.S. Government Carte Blanche to Access Private Data Stored in the "Cloud" or Elsewhere.

Reality: The PATRIOT Act continues to be the subject of serious misinterpretation and mischaracterization. Although portions of the Act updated existing investigative tools, the PATRIOT Act did not eliminate the pre-existing, highly protective restrictions on U.S. law enforcement access to electronic communications information in criminal investigations—restrictions that are, as noted above, no less stringent than those found within the EU.

Myth 5: The Advent of "Cloud Computing" Changes Everything.

Reality: Even before the "cloud" became a popular concept, data

The Senate Judiciary committee holds hearings to determine if the executive surveillance operations carried out under the PATRIOT Act were a violation of constitutional law

Snowden leaks reveal that the NSA and CIA had been attempting to force corporations to provide a backdoor to encryption systems that would allow federal agents to bypass consumer encryption

Five Myths regarding Privacy and Law Enforcement Access to Personal Information in the European Union and the United States
continued

was stored remotely and U.S. laws anticipated the need to protect such data. As a result, U.S. law has carefully regulated law enforcement requests for remotely stored data and other records since long before even the Internet—for this is an issue that predates both the Internet and cloud computing.

1. Myth: The United States Cares Less about Privacy than the European Union.

Reality: The United States was founded on—and its laws reflect—a core belief in the importance of protecting citizens from government intrusion. Our most important legal document—our Constitution—established, more than two hundred years ago, a federal government with limited powers and extensive checks and balances. Our Bill of Rights ensures the freedom to speak, assemble, and worship freely. It also provides protection from self incrimination, as well as from unreasonable searches and seizures. Each of these constitutionally guaranteed civil liberties protects important aspects of a person's privacy.

The approach to privacy in many parts of the European Union has evolved more recently, and reflects a different set of legal traditions and historical developments—indeed, traditions and developments that vary even among Member States—so it is understandable that there are differences in our respective schemes. Nonetheless, our systems share many common principles, including the recognition in the International Covenant on Civil and Political Rights (ICCPR) that "[n]o one shall be subjected to arbitrary or unlawful interference with his privacy, family, home or correspondence." The United States and the European Union are united in our common values regarding the fundamental importance of privacy protections and our deeply rooted commitment to continue to safeguard these values in the digital age.

2. Myth: The European Union Does a Better Job of Protecting Data from Law Enforcement Access than the United States.

Reality: As discussed below, the United States provides numerous protections from law enforcement access to electronic communications, a key area of modern data privacy concern. In addition, the United States

2015

Terrorist attacks in France reignite fears of domestic terrorist violence

The PATRIOT Act is replaced by the USA Freedom Act

Federal Courts order Apple, Inc. to create a new operation system that would enable federal investigators to bypass security on an iPhone.

continued

has an extensive and highly effective system of layered oversight, including criminal prosecutions of government officials who access computer systems without authorization or for an unauthorized purpose. These protections match, and indeed in many instances exceed, protections available under EU law.

The United States Provides Broad Protections for the Privacy of Electronic Communications

The United States was a pioneer in safeguarding the privacy of telephone and email communications in criminal investigations. With very limited exceptions, law enforcement agents in the United States are prohibited from intercepting the contents of voice and email communications in criminal investigations unless an independent judicial authority finds that stringent evidentiary and procedural requirements have been met. In particular, specific information must be presented to an independent judicial authority establishing probable cause to believe that specific named individuals are using or will use the targeted telephone or other device to commit specific identified offenses.

Law enforcement agents must also demonstrate the specific need for the proposed electronic surveillance and provide a detailed discussion of the other investigative procedures that have been tried and failed, are reasonably unlikely to succeed if tried, or are too dangerous to employ. This is to ensure that such intrusive techniques are not resorted to in situations where traditional investigative techniques would suffice to expose the crime.

U.S. law also ensures that such authority is used only as long as necessary. For example, if an interception request is ultimately approved, criminal investigators are only permitted to intercept the subject communications for a maximum of 30 days, unless the time period is specifically extended by a court. In addition, throughout the limited period of interception, the investigators must actively minimize the interception of all non-pertinent communications.

These standards for conducting criminal investigations are among the highest in the world. The laws and practices in EU Member States are often far more permissive than in the United States when it comes to accessing the contents of telephone and email communications. For instance, not all EU Member States require independent court orders to authorize the interception of voice or email communications, and many Member States authorize interception if the communications are "relevant," a lower standard than probable cause and all

The FCC publishes official rules of "neutrality"

2016

The EU establishes the General Data Protection Regulation (GDPR), described as the strongest digital data privacy law in the world

Five Myths regarding Privacy and Law Enforcement Access to Personal Information in the European Union and the United States
continued

the other U.S. requirements. Indeed, publicly available figures indicate a heavier reliance by EU law enforcement authorities on electronic surveillance to intercept the contents of private voice and email communications by several EU Member States, including Italy, Germany, France, and the Netherlands, than by the United States. When relative population sizes are taken into account, the disparity in the use of electronic surveillance by the United States and EU Member States becomes even more apparent.

The United States also is a world leader in protecting the privacy of stored email communications sought in criminal investigations. Before the contents of stored email communications can be divulged, U.S. law enforcement authorities must, at a minimum, obtain a court order or grand jury subpoena. In most cases, however, U.S. authorities obtain a search warrant from an independent judicial authority authorizing the seizure. To obtain such a warrant, the agents must present specific evidence establishing probable cause to believe that the particular email account will contain evidence of the crime under investigation (and not just that the account is under the control of a suspected criminal). This is essentially the same standard used when a U.S. judge decides whether to authorize the search of someone's home. Moreover, if a warrant is constitutionally required, defects in applying for one, or failure to obtain one, may result in a ban on the prosecution's use of the evidence, no matter how incriminating it is. (This is known as the "exclusionary rule" under U.S. constitutional law.) The United States is not aware of any other country in the world that employs a more stringent evidentiary standard in this context.

The exacting nature of these U.S. privacy protections has been evident in cases where European law enforcement authorities have requested U.S. assistance in obtaining stored email correspondence from U.S.-based Internet service providers, and have shared with the U.S. government how onerous they find the U.S. legal requirements in comparison to their own domestic legal standards.

Significantly, law enforcement officials in the United States may be prosecuted criminally or sued for money damages civilly if they illegally intercept voice or email communications. U.S. service providers

The "Vault 7" secrets, a leak of 9,000 CIA documents, reveal details of the CIA's attempts to break through encryption used by Internet

President Trump appoints Ajit Pai to head the FCC, who abolishes the FCC neutrality protections

continued

are also barred from voluntarily providing traffic or subscriber data or the content of stored email communications to U.S. government agents in response to informal requests (i.e., requests not accompanied by a formal legal order directing production of the data), except in very limited circumstances. U.S. providers that violate this ban are subject to civil suit and penalties. In a recent comparative survey of global practices, the United States and Japan were determined to be the only two countries studied that prohibited service providers from voluntarily disclosing customer data to their governments in response to informal requests (except in those limited cases). The other countries in the study included Denmark, France, Germany, Spain, and the United Kingdom.

The United States Has Adopted an Extensive Regime of Layered Oversight of Privacy Protections

Privacy protection in the United States is ensured not only by these strict legal standards for gathering evidence but also by a layered system of oversight and enforcement of privacy protections, including criminal prosecutions.

Pursuant to EU laws, Member States are required to establish public data protection authorities with "complete independence" in the exercise of the functions entrusted to them. The absence of such data protection authorities in the United States is sometimes cited as evidence that the European Union does a better job of protecting privacy. However, the model adopted within the European Union is not the only, or necessarily the optimal, legal structure for ensuring independent and effective oversight. Even the European Commission has observed in recent proposed legislation that Member State data protection authorities, notwithstanding their "complete independence," have been "unable to ensure consistent and effective application of the [EU data protection] rules."94 In contrast, the multilayered privacy protection system long adopted in the United States has proven to be robust and effective.

One of the keys to the success of the U.S. system is that the extensive system of checks and balances between the powers exercised by the different branches of our government (executive, legislative, and judicial) mandated by our Constitution ensures that none of these branches acts in "complete independence" from the others. Strong protections in specific legislation and the check of judicial authority establish bulwarks for the protection of data. Rather than a weakness in the protection of privacy, these rigorous checks and balances in the U.S. system of government are enduring strengths.

Congress debates whether or not to renew the controversial Section 702 FISA Amendment used to authorize NSA domestic intelligence operations since 2008

Five Myths regarding Privacy and Law Enforcement Access to Personal Information in the European Union and the United States
continued

Moreover, within the executive branch itself, there is a multi-layered system of oversight authorities, which includes Chief Privacy Officers in federal agencies specifically charged to ensure compliance with applicable privacy laws and regulations. In addition, there are more than 70 Inspectors General, many of whose appointments are subject to congressional confirmation, assigned to various U.S. government agencies. These Inspectors General separately conduct, coordinate, and supervise audits and investigations of their respective agencies, including on data protection and privacy issues. Federal law provides that agency heads may not prevent an Inspector General from initiating or carrying out an investigation and often requires Inspectors General to report the results of their reviews to Congress.

Pursuant to our constitutional framework, the legislative branch also plays an important oversight role in ensuring compliance with privacy laws and regulations. The Government Accountability Office—an agency within the legislative branch—regularly investigates executive branch agencies, including compliance with privacy and data protection laws and policies. In addition, numerous congressional committees have an oversight role with respect to the executive branch, including privacy and data protection issues. These congressional committees have regularly conducted hearings on privacy-related issues, including the PATRIOT Act.

In addition to administrative and congressional oversight and enforcement, the United States has a strong and documented record of criminal prosecutions of government officials for unauthorized access to data or access for an unauthorized purpose, with prison sentences possible in the most serious cases. We are not aware of any similar record of prosecutions elsewhere in the world.

Finally, the judicial branch also acts as a check on both the executive branch and the legislative branch. The stringent oversight that the judicial branch exercises over the executive branch and its investigative techniques regarding electronic communications, as discussed above, is another example of the checks and balances inherent in the U.S. system.

3. Myth: U.S. Law Enforcement Authorities Are Less Protective of the Privacy Interests of Foreign Nationals than of U.S. Citizens.

1788 State legislatures ratify the U.S. Constitution, establishing the basic precedent for all future constitutional law

1791 The U.S. Congress ratifies the Bill of Rights, creating the first 10 amendments to the United States Constitution

continued

Reality: This myth rests on a misunderstanding of U.S. law—with regard to both protections and remedies. First, in the key area of electronic communications, the stringent statutes protecting the privacy of email and voice communications in criminal investigations, discussed above, apply equally to foreign nationals and U.S. citizens. Second, the United States does not discriminate between U.S. citizens and foreign nationals with regard to judicial redress to obtain access to personal data collected for criminal investigations, and provides opportunities for any person, regardless of citizenship, to correct such data if it is believed to be inaccurate. There are several U.S. laws that specifically provide judicial redress options for individuals who suffer damages pertaining to data protection and privacy violations, including in the context of law enforcement operations. These include the Electronic Communications Privacy Act, the Computer Fraud and Abuse Act, the Federal Tort Claims Act, and the Mandatory Victims Restitution Act. The judicial redress options under these laws are equally available to foreign nationals and U.S. citizens.

In the United States, the Privacy Act of 1974 allows individuals to access and correct information that federal government agencies have obtained about them and it provides for judicial redress to enforce those rights. The fact that the Privacy Act applies only to U.S. citizens and aliens who are lawful permanent residents of the United States is sometimes mistakenly cited as evidence that U.S. law gives preferential treatment to U.S. citizens in this regard. However, law enforcement records collected for criminal investigations are regularly exempted from these provisions of the Privacy Act, in a manner similar to analogous exemptions in EU data protection laws. Consequently, foreign nationals and U.S. citizens are on equal footing with regard to access and correction of exempt criminal law enforcement records under the Privacy Act.

Notwithstanding these exemptions, foreign nationals and U.S. citizens alike can invoke other administrative processes to correct their law enforcement investigation data. For instance, anyone, regardless of citizenship, may seek review of the accuracy of data maintained by the applicable Department component. If an individual is dissatisfied with the component's response, the individual may appeal to the Justice Department's Office of Privacy and Civil Liberties, which will review the component's determination as a matter of administrative discretion. If he or she is still dissatisfied, the Department may permit the individual to file a

1868 The 14th Amendment to the U.S. Constitution guarantees all citizens the right to due process under the law

1890 Warren and Brandeis publish "The Right to Privacy" in the *Harvard Law Review*

Five Myths regarding Privacy and Law Enforcement Access to Personal Information in the European Union and the United States
continued

statement of disagreement regarding the accuracy of the information and request that it be included in the file. In addition to the procedures for correcting criminal investigative files, Department regulations allow any person regardless of citizenship to request access to his or her own criminal history data in FBI files and request correction of any errors.

Finally, the Freedom of Information Act gives any person, regardless of citizenship, the right to request access to records and information that a federal agency maintains about him or her. All agencies of the U.S. executive branch are required to disclose records upon receiving a written request, absent an applicable exemption. Anyone, regardless of citizenship, can go to court to enforce this requirement.

4. Myth: The PATRIOT Act Gives the U.S. Government Carte Blanche to Access Private Data Stored in the "Cloud" or Elsewhere.

Reality: The PATRIOT Act has been the subject of serious misinterpretation and mischaracterization. The portions of the Act relevant here updated existing investigative tools in order to make investigations of terrorism and other national security threats more efficient and effective, while retaining important protections for privacy and civil liberties. The PATRIOT Act maintained highly protective restrictions on U.S. law enforcement access to electronic communications information.

Moreover, U.S. law, including revisions concerning investigative authorities implemented by the PATRIOT Act, does not go as far as the expansive authorities granted to law enforcement authorities in a number of EU Member States to collect data stored in the cloud and elsewhere. For example, in some Member States, government officials are authorized to issue warrants for the interception of content (wiretaps) without any independent court approval, and in the case of one Member State, whenever determined necessary for national security, prevention and detection of serious crime, or safeguarding the economic well-being of the country.

In addition, these authorities in the United States are available only in certain limited circumstances and are subject to important constraints. For example, under the authority to obtain "business records" that was amended by

1923   *Meyer v. Nebraska* establishes that the 14th Amendment guarantees privileges of citizenship

1928   *Olmstead v. United States* rules that wiretapping is not a form of search and seizure defined by the 14th Amendment

continued

the PATRIOT Act, the government may obtain such records only if it first gets a court order, and only if the judge finds that the records sought are relevant to an authorized investigation to protect against international terrorism or clandestine intelligence activities. The Attorney General approves guidelines that establish the circumstances under which a national security investigation may be opened. Finally, the recipient of such a business records order may challenge the legality of the order in court.

National Security Letters are another authority that was amended by the PATRIOT Act, and they also are the subject of significant misunderstanding. The authority to issue National Security Letters is available only where the records sought are relevant to an authorized investigation to protect against international terrorism or clandestine intelligence activities. Furthermore, the law specifically limits the type of information that may be obtained with a National Security Letter. For example, National Security Letters may be issued to wire or electronic communications service providers only to obtain limited, non-content information (e.g., names, addresses, length of service, and billing records). National Security Letters do not permit the government to obtain the content of

communications. Although a National Security Letter may require that the recipient not disclose the National Security Letter to the subscriber or account holder, the provider that receives the letter may challenge that requirement in court.

In short, the PATRIOT Act did not fundamentally alter the protections U.S. law affords to communications information. Moreover, the United States is hardly exceptional with respect to establishing special procedures to govern national security investigations—the laws of most, if not all countries in Europe provide similar mechanisms to facilitate rapid access to information by government authorities under such circumstances. International practice, no less than the language of the relevant laws themselves, has shown the U.S. legal framework provides a greater level of protection than the laws of many other countries.

5. Myth: The Advent of "Cloud Computing" Changes Everything.

Reality: "Cloud computing" may be a recently developed term, but, of course, data exists on physical servers. As has always been the case since the development of the Internet, data transmitted over the Internet is stored on a server located in a particular

1934 The Federal Communications Commission (FCC) is established under the Federal Communications Act (FCA)

1942 *Goldman v. United States* rules that using electronic listening devices does not violate the 14th Amendment

Five Myths regarding Privacy and Law Enforcement Access to Personal Information in the European Union and the United States
continued

country or countries, and the rules establishing access to the data by U.S. law enforcement authorities have not changed. Moreover, even before the "cloud" became a popular concept, U.S. laws anticipated the need to protect data that was stored remotely. A part of the Electronic Communications Privacy Act, called the Stored Communications Act, contains specific provisions that protect data stored with remote computing services by establishing procedures for law enforcement to request and obtain such information from providers.

Beyond this, the United States also places stringent restrictions on the extra-territorial collection of data by law enforcement. The issue of when an entity present in a jurisdiction can be compelled to produce data that is in its possession or control—but which is stored in another jurisdiction—predates not only the "cloud," but computers themselves. As a result, the United States has restricted such law enforcement requests since long before the advent of cloud computing or the Internet—for this is an issue that predates both. Such requests are vetted at high levels within the U.S. Department of Justice and can be challenged in court.

The U.S. approach is consistent with internationally agreed upon rules in this context. In 2001, the Council of Europe Cybercrime Convention, which the United States, Japan, and 34 European states have ratified, set out a legal framework for law enforcement and judicial access to computer data. The procedural law provisions of the Convention obligate each party to enact legislation enabling its authorities to search or similarly access a computer system in its territory in order to seize data stored therein. In addition, the Convention requires each party to enact legislation enabling its authorities to compel production, from any individual person or legal person (typically a corporation) in its territory, of computer data that is stored in a computer system or storage medium that is in the person's possession or control. The geographic scope of this rule is left to domestic law to define; countries may choose to limit it to data in the party's territory, but the Convention does not prohibit a party from applying it to data in the possession or control of a person within the party's territory even where the data itself is located outside the party's territory.

In this manner, the Cybercrime Convention establishes a regime

1945   The National Security Agency secretly creates Project SHAMROCK

1950   Senator Joseph McCarthy delivers a shocking speech claiming that more than 200 communist spies have infiltrated the U.S. government

continued

for effective and swift international cooperation for law enforcement purposes, in recognition of the reality that both crime and computer data travel quickly across borders. Importantly, countries that are parties to the Convention are required to ensure that implementation and application of its rules, including production orders for data stored on remote servers, are subject to appropriate legal safeguards for the protection of human rights and liberties within their domestic legal systems. As a result of these and other provisions, the Cybercrime Convention has provided a secure and effective international framework for ensuring that electronic data is available to law enforcement authorities when needed for the investigation and prosecution of crimes, in a manner consistent with applicable international human rights commitments.

Moreover, a recent comparative survey of global practices determined that law enforcement authorities in all ten of the countries studied—including Denmark, France, Germany, Spain, and the United Kingdom, as well as the United States—have comparable legal authorities to obtain data from cloud servers located within their territory.95 Significantly, however, and as noted above, the United States has an internal procedure severely restricting the exercise of this extra-territorial jurisdiction in any criminal case.

In contrast, EU Member States routinely seek and obtain direct access to data located in the United States, including data on U.S.–based cloud servers. In fact, in one case, Belgian authorities imposed criminal sanctions on a U.S.–based Internet company for refusing to disclose the personal data of certain e-mail users directly to a Belgian prosecutor. Although the case is proceeding, the Supreme Court of Belgium has held that Belgian law, specifically section 88ter of the Belgian Criminal Code of Procedure, permitted the prosecutor to unilaterally compel the production of such data, despite the fact that both the company and the data were located entirely outside of Belgium.

Given the extent to which personal communications and business transactions have moved online, it is not surprising that records of such activities have become increasingly relevant to law enforcement investigations of all types, ranging from money laundering to human trafficking to child pornography. However, the perception that the United States is somehow unique or more aggressive than EU counterparts in seeking access to such data for law enforcement purposes is inaccurate, as shown above. In sum, then, data stored in the United States is at least as protected from law enforcement access—and in many cases more protected—than data stored within the EU.

1951 *Dennis v. United States* rules that government limits to speech is legal only to prevent a threat to public safety or security

1959 *Barenblatt v. United States* rules that it's legal to order people to reveal personal details if national threat is perceived

In an article about the release, Robert Holleyman, President and CEO of the technology lobbyist organization the Software Alliance (BSA) said of the DOS release, "The State Department has injected a constructive dose of reality into the transatlantic privacy discussion. Left unchecked, myths about US privacy law would distort the marketplace and stunt the growth of cloud computing services that offer huge social and economic benefits for citizens, consumers, businesses, and governments alike. The truth is America has a strong system of privacy protections—and those protections apply to foreign citizens, not just US citizens."[96]

Although the State Department argued that EU privacy concerns were largely unfounded, privacy advocates continued to assert that the PATRIOT Act and other post-war powers granted to federal agencies constituted a potential, if not imminent threat, to anyone utilizing cloud computing, either in the U.S. or abroad. Further, it was argued by privacy advocates that the rules and laws were still unclear and that consumers, therefore, had little knowledge regarding their rights and privacy protections. For instance, an April 2012 report from *Consumer Reports* indicated that 71 percent of consumers were concerned about online data collection, while a *Times* survey from the same year found that 82 percent of California residents were concerned about corporate data collection.[97]

Ongoing concerns over data security, from both government agencies and corporate entities, motivated the White House, under the Obama Administration, to support a proposal for a "Consumer Privacy Bill of Rights," governing the behavior of corporations regarding data provided by users. The proposed bill would have included the following basic rights:

- Individual Control over personal data companies collect and on how companies may use their data.
- Transparency in privacy guidelines
- Respect for Context, or the right to expect companies to use data in

1965   *Griswold v. CT* rules in favor of married couples' right to privacy

1967   *Katz v. United States* rules wiretaps a form of search and seizure

Willis Ware of RAND Corporation writes *Security and Privacy in Computer*

ways consistent with the context in which it was given.
- Security: The right to secure and responsible handling of data.
- Access and Accuracy: The right to access and correct personal data.
- Focused Collection: The right to reasonable limits on the collection and retention of data.
- Accountability: The right to have data handled by companies with appropriate measures in place to assure they adhere to the principles in the Consumer Privacy Bill of Rights.

The Obama administration's efforts to translate the Consumer Privacy Bill of Rights into law failed due to lobbying and influence from corporate entities concerned that such measures would reduce their potential profit from the collection, sale, and use of consumer data. Whether U.S. security policies translated into weaker overall consumer protections remained unclear as well, though the issue continued to resurge in the following years.

Despite the attempt to reassure EU consumers, concerns over privacy rights in the U.S. motivated stronger and stronger consumer protections in the European Union.[98] In 2016, the EU replaced its existing privacy laws with a new General Data Protection Regulation (GDPR), described in a 2016 article in *Fortune* as the world's toughest privacy laws. Among the changes brought by the GDPR included:
- Companies face fines of up to 4 percent of their global profits if they break privacy rules.
- Consumers have the right to transfer their data between service providers.
- Privacy terms and conditions need to be presented in clear and understandable language.
- Consumers have the right to know if there data has been hacked.
- Consumers have the right to tell companies to stop using their personal data once they close their accounts.

1968 The Omnibus Crime Control Act holds that police needed to obtain a warrant before engaging in wire-

1969 Joseph Licklider creates the Advanced Research Projects Agency Network (ARPANET), which was

- Consumers have the right to tell marketing companies to stop compiling profiles of them based on their personal data.
- EU countries will need to establish age of consent for signing-up for web services like Facebook (between 13 and 16).[99]

To understand how the policies in the GDPR might translate into actual corporate consequences, consider a 2014 case in which Google was found guilty in an EU court of violating EU privacy policies. Google opted to pay the fine, which under laws at the time amounted to $204,000, rather than change the way that it was handling consumer data. Under the GDPR, Google's fine in that case would have been more than $1 billion.[100]

The Obama administration's contention that the United States had equivalent privacy laws to the EU in 2012 might have been an open debate. However, since that time the EU has strengthened privacy laws, while the United States has favored corporate rights over consumer rights. The difficulty in establishing stronger consumer rights policies in the United States is a function of the nation's extremely powerful corporate lobby. Even when a vast majority of consumers object to a lack of corporate regulation, U.S. legislators rarely establish stronger protections. The standard argument is that such laws hinder development and reduce the incentive for corporations to invest in innovation.

In a 2015 interview with *Los Angeles Times*, Neil Richards, a professor of law at Washington University in Saint Louis said, "Every developed country in the world has a general privacy law—except us. What we have instead is a mishmash of state laws based on what the market will bear." In that same interview, Nancy Kim, Law Professor at the California Western School of Law," said, "Americans care a lot about privacy too. The difference is that Europeans haven't bought into the 'market knows best' philosophy. In the U.S., the words 'free market' and 'free speech' are powerful rhetorical tools that businesses use to fend off regulation."

1971 The Pentagon Papers leaks from the press raise the issue of the Freedom of the Press versus the privacy of the government to conceal information about national security operations

1972 *Eisenstadt v. Baird* rules that the right to privacy applies to individuals

While Americans were, therefore, more willing, than their EU counterparts to place their trust in corporations, the San Diego Privacy Rights Clearinghouse reported in 2005 that the 4700 corporate data breaches known to have occurred by 2005 resulted in 895 million corporate consumer records being put at risk. Companies in the United States had further failed to adopt stronger internal methods for protecting data, such as encryption, preferring to save on the cost of stronger protections.[101]

Examining the relationship between consumer data and national security, the frequency of corporate data leaks indicates that corporations are not adequately able to protect the data they collect on their users and customers. Given this, loose data protection regimes could pose a security threat in that enemies of the state might violate corporate security programs to obtain data on Americans that could be used in various espionage or military operations. Further, revelations that the NSA and CIA had been obtaining consumer data directly from the companies that managed and transferred that data, revealed that privacy laws were also insufficient to prohibit state surveillance through the corporate management level of the data stream. This backdoor approach sparked outrage and concern from those who found fault with the government's intelligence policies, but the situation was also intimately tied to the U.S. failure to make consumer privacy a legislative priority.

1974

The Watergate Scandal results in the revelation that the CIA had been conducting widespread surveillance of American dissidents and foreign leaders without judicial oversight

The Privacy Act is established

CONCLUSION

Many of the claims made by the White House regarding the strength of U.S. privacy protections compared to the European Union (EU) were questionable though based, at least in part, on accurate depictions of laws to that point. Rather than reassuring European consumers, however, the campaign from the United States simply became part of an EU movement to create stronger privacy laws. Between 2012 and 2016, the European Union gradually adopted the strongest privacy laws in the world, far stronger than any policy or statute adopted in the United States. The Obama administration attempted to address the growing privacy-rights controversy by proposing a consumer bill of rights regarding privacy protection and by pushing for changes to digital privacy laws, but these efforts were largely symbolic as the powerful anti-regulation lobby and security-minded supporters of domestic surveillance derailed the effort and prevented the digital privacy bill of rights from becoming law.

1975   Senator Frank Church leads a series of hearings about the secret NSA SHAMROCK operation involved intercepting communications from American citizens

1978   Congress passes the 1978 FISA Act

DISCUSSION QUESTIONS

- Should the U.S. government adopt a digital privacy bill of rights? Should these rights be protected by law?
- Were European consumers overreacting about U.S. privacy laws? Why or why not?
- Are U.S. companies able to protect data from consumers effectively? Explain your answer.
- Do you believe that the U.S. government is committed to protecting privacy? Explain your answer.

Works Used

Freeland, Amy. "Data Privacy Protection Discrepancies Could Hamper U.S. Cloud Provider Growth in Europe." *NTTCOM*. NTT Communications. Jan. 30, 2012. Web. 27 Oct. 2017.

"J.C.R. Licklider." *Internet Hall of Fame*. Internet Society. 2016. Web. 27 Oct. 2017.

Lazarus, David. "Europe and U.S. have different approaches to protecting privacy of personal data." *Los Angeles Times*. Dec. 22, 2015. Web. 2 Nov. 2017.

Meyer, David. "Google should have been fined $1B over privacy policy, says EU justice chief." *Gigaom*. Knowingly, Inc. Jan. 21, 2014. Web. 2 Nov. 2017.

Meyer, David. "Here Come the World's Toughest Privacy Laws." *Fortune*. Fortune Inc. Apr. 14, 2016. Web. 2 Nov. 2017.

Mohamed, Arif. "A history of cloud computing." *Computer Weekly*. TechTarget. March 2009. Web. 27 Oct. 2017.

1980 The Intelligence Oversight Act (IOA) updates legal standards

1981 President Reagan's E.O. authorized wiretapping

1986 The Electronic Communications Privacy Act is established

Sarno, David. "Consumer Reports, Times polls find broad data privacy concerns." *LATimes*. Los Angeles Times. Apr. 3, 2012. Web. 27 Oct. 2017.

Singer, Natasha. "Why a Push for Online Privacy Is Bogged Down in Washington." *New York Times*. New York Times, Co. Feb. 28, 2016. Web. 27 Oct. 2017.

"State Department Dispels Cloud Myths with Facts about US Privacy Protections." *BSA*. Software Alliance. Dec. 4, 2012. Web. 27 Oct. 2017.

Whittaker, Zack. "Microsoft admits PATRIOT Act can access EU–based cloud data." *ZDNet*. CBS Interactive. June 28, 2011. Web. 27 Oct. 2017.

1994 Netscape creates the "cookie" allowing computers to monitor Internet users

2001 The September 11 terrorist attacks result in Congress authorizing the Bush Administration to utilize military methods to combat terrorism

Introduction

This chapter describes the beginning of the infamous Snowden leaks of 2013, in which former CIA and NSA contractor Edward Snowden stole and leaked 1.5 million classified documents to the press detailing aspects of the Obama administration's ongoing domestic surveillance and bulk data collection activities. The revelations demonstrated that not only had the Obama administration essentially continued the domestic surveillance program started by Bush, but that the administration had deepened and expanded the program. Among other revelations, the Snowden files revealed that the NSA and CIA had been empowered to collect telephone, Internet, and cellular data on essentially the entire American public, that companies like Verizon and Apple had provided data to the government without notifying customers, and that the U.S. government had been monitoring foreign heads of state and conducting espionage operations against allied leaders in the EU.

The source document for this chapter are excerpts from a Senate Judiciary Committee hearing on the legality of the surveillance programs under the Obama administration. Especially controversial were two provisions, Section 215 of the PATRIOT Act, (see Chapter 12) which had been secretly interpreted to authorize the bulk collection of cell phone data, and Section 702 of FISA, (see Chapter 8) which has been used by the NSA to justify collecting communications from overseas without judicial oversight. The July 2013 hearings heard testimony from Jameel Jaffer, of the ACLU, as well as Senator Patrick Leahy of Vermont, criticizing the programs, whereas Deputy Attorney General James Cole and former NSA counsel Stewart Baker defended the programs undertaken by the NSA and argued that such measures were both necessary to prevent terrorism and had been effective tools for enhancing national security.

The Bush administration secretly authorizes the President's Surveillance Program (PSP), utilizing E.O. 12333

The U.S. PATRIOT Act alters existing laws to facilitate better communication between the state's intelligence branches in the effort to combat terrorism

The Transportation Security Administration (TSA) is established, creating the "No Fly" and "Selectee" lists that limit the right to travel on airplanes in the United States

Topics covered in this chapter include:

- The PATRIOT Act
- FISA Act of 1978
- Domestic surveillance
- The NSA
- The War on Terror
- Bulk data collection
- Corporate data protections
- Government leaks

This Chapter Discusses the Following Source Document:
"Strengthening Privacy Rights and National Security: Oversight of FISA Surveillance Programs." Senate Hearing 113-334. July 31, 2013.

National Insecurity
The Snowden Leaks (2013)

In 2012, former NSA and CIA contractor Edward Snowden stole over 1.5 million classified files from the NSA. Snowden, who began working in the IT department of the NSA in 2006, also worked for both the CIA and NSA in his position as a private contractor for Dell computers. During his time working with the NSA and CIA, Snowden came across a trove of documents detailing NSA and CIA operations involving the surveillance of American citizens. In a statement recorded later regarding his reasons, Snowden claimed:

"I'm just another guy who sits there day to day in the office, watching what's happening, and goes, 'This is something that's not our place to decide.' The public needed to decide whether these programs or policies are right or wrong."

In December of 2012, Snowden contacted Glenn Greenwald, columnist for *The Guardian* newspaper and Barton Gellman, of the *Washington Post* and, in March of 2013, Snowden began delivering documents to the two journalists. Fleeing the United States for Hong Kong, realizing that he would soon be arrested once news of the leak emerged, Snowden arranged to meet with reporters in early June.

On June 5, 2013, *The Guardian* published the first article derived from information contained within Snowden's leaked documents, entitled "NSA collecting phone records of millions of Verizon customers daily." The article revealed that, under a secret order from the FISA court, the Verizon telecommunications company had been required to give the NSA information on all telephone calls in its system, on a daily ongoing basis. The document thus provided proof that the Obama administration had been indiscriminately collecting the communications records of millions of Americans, regardless of whether the targets of the program were

2007 The Bush Administration plans to make data taken from spy satellites available to law enforcement to be used to conduct domestic surveillance

2008 Congress passes Section 702, or the FISA Amendment Act, which is used to permit a massive NSA and CIA domestic surveillance program

Former intelligence contractor Edward Snowden poses for a photo during an interview in an undisclosed location in December 2013 in Moscow, Russia. Snowden who exposed extensive details of global electronic surveillance by the National Security Agency has been in Moscow since June 2012 after getting temporary asylum in order to evade prosecution by authorities in the U.S. (Photo by Barton Gellman/Getty Images)

suspected of any illegal activity or links with foreign powers. The order to collect the data, reporters revealed, had been authorized by using the provisions of the PATRIOT Act, 50 USC, section 1861, empowering agencies to collect "business data."[102]

Over the next few weeks, the *Washington Post* and *The Guardian* published a series of articles revealing new findings from their ongoing analysis of the documents provided by Snowden. With each new revelation, privacy advocates and legislators voiced their concerns while the Obama administration insisted that all of the activities conducted under the NSA and CIA programs targeted only those individuals suspected of terrorism.

The day after the first article was published, reporters revealed details of the controversial program PRISM, which collected email, voice, text, and video data from Microsoft, Yahoo, Facebook, Apple, and Google.[103] Shortly thereafter it was revealed that the NSA had secretly monitored the phone records and calls of 35 world leaders. The news came after German Chancellor Angela Merkel publicly accused the United States of wiretapping her office phone.[104]

2012 The Obama Administration proposes a Consumer Privacy Bill of Rights guaranteeing individuals the right to greater control over the use of their digital data

2013 The *Guardian* and the *Washington Post* publish the first series of articles derived from leaked NSA and CIA documents delivered by Edward Snowden

It was also revealed that the Government Communications Headquarters (GCHQ) in Britain had worked with the NSA, utilizing the same surveillance network to gather information. In cases where bulk collection of data was insufficient, the documents revealed that the NSA used a variety of methods, including brute force hacking, to steal data from Internet service companies like Google and Yahoo.

The Snowden leaks, in some ways, embroiled the Obama administration and the U.S. government as a whole, in a massive, seemingly never-ending scandal. Numerous elected representatives in Congress saw the leaks as evidence that President Obama had exceeded his constitutional authority and powers. Companies that had been forced to relinquish customer data were angered that the leaks exposed their culpability and were concerned that consumers would turn away because of privacy concerns. Further, although some companies had voluntarily agreed to provide data, the revelation that the NSA had forcibly and secretly infiltrated their systems to steal data also angered many company leaders.

The revelation that the United States and United Kingdom had used their powers to spy on foreign heads of state caused another set of problems for the Obama administration. According to a *Guardian* article, German Chancellor Angela Merkel had a heated exchange with President Obama after the German magazine *Der Spiegel* broke the story that the NSA had been tapping Merkel's private mobile phone. Merkel reportedly compared the U.S. operation to the Stasi, the Nazi secret police, in an angry confrontation with Obama after the story was published. In the weeks that followed, leaders in the European Union met in numerous meetings to determine how to respond to the actions carried out by the NSA and British intelligence, as Obama apologized to foreign leaders who had been targeted but defended the necessity of the NSA program as a whole.[105]

Some viewed Snowden as a hero and patriot, whereas others called for his arrest, or even execution. Rumors began to surface accusing

The Senate Judiciary committee holds hearings to determine if the executive surveillance operations carried out under the PATRIOT Act were a violation of constitutional law

Snowden leaks reveal that the NSA and CIA had been attempting to force corporations to provide a backdoor to encryption systems that would allow federal agents to bypass consumer encryption

Snowden of being a foreign spy and, as he fled to Hong Kong and later Russia, seeking asylum in South America, the theory that Snowden had been a Russian agent was also circulated through the press, though without any corroborating evidence. The *New York Observer* ran an article about Snowden written by conservative, security columnist John Schindler alleging that Snowden was, in Schindler's words, "a Kremlin-Controlled Pawn."

In Congress, revelations about the secret spy program inspired both anger and concern. Senators Rand Paul, Ron Wyden, Mark Udall, and Richard Blumenthal proposed a surveillance reform bill, while Representatives Jim Sensenbrenner, Justin Amash, and John Conyers also proposed bills to the House containing various suggestions for intelligence and surveillance reform laws. Although many senators and representatives seemed shocked by the revelations, Senator John McCain was more realistic about the issue. Speaking to CNN, McCain argued,

"The Republican and Democrat chairs, and …members of the Intelligence Committee have been very well briefed on these programs. We passed the PATRIOT Act. We passed specific provisions of the act that allowed for this program to take place, to be enacted in operation. Now, if members of Congress did not know what they were voting on, then I think that's their responsibility a lot more than it is the government's." [106]

In July, the Senate Judiciary Committee held a hearing entitled: "Strengthening Privacy Rights and National Security: Oversight of FISA Surveillance Programs," Democratic Vermont Senator Patrick Leahy, who also authored a new oversight program, the FISA Accountability and Privacy Protection Act of 2013, served as chairman during the hearings. In his opening statements, Leahy summarized the situation:

2015

Terrorist attacks in France reignite fears of domestic terrorist violence	The PATRIOT Act is replaced by the USA Freedom Act	Federal Courts order Apple, Inc. to create a new operation system that would enable federal investigators to bypass security on an iPhone.

STRENGTHENING PRIVACY RIGHTS AND NATIONAL SECURITY:
OVERSIGHT OF FISA SURVEILLANCE PROGRAMS
Source Document

Today, the Judiciary Committee will scrutinize Government surveillance programs conducted under the Foreign Intelligence Surveillance Act, or FISA. In the years since September 11th, Congress has repeatedly expanded the scope of FISA and has given the Government sweeping new powers to collect information on law-abiding Americans, and we must carefully consider now whether those laws may have gone too far.

Last month, many Americans learned for the first time that one of these authorities—Section 215 of the USA PATRIOT Act—has for years been secretly interpreted—to authorize the collection of Americans' phone records on an unprecedented scale. Information was also leaked about Section 702 of FISA, which authorizes the NSA to collect the communications of foreigners overseas.

Now, first, let me make it very clear. I do not condone the way these and other highly classified programs were disclosed, and I am concerned about the potential damage to our intelligence-gathering capabilities and national security. It is appropriate to hold people accountable for allowing such a massive leak to occur. We need to examine how to prevent this type of breach in the future.

In the wake of these leaks, the President said that this is an opportunity to have an open and thoughtful debate about these issues. And I welcome that statement because this is a debate that several of us on this Committee in both parties have been trying to have for years. Like so many others, I will get the classified briefings, but then, of course, you cannot talk about them. There are a lot of these things that should be and can be discussed. And if we are going to have the debate that the President called for, the executive branch has to be a full partner. We need straightforward answers, and I am concerned that we are not getting them.

Just recently, the Director of National Intelligence acknowledged that he provided false testimony about the NSA surveillance programs during a Senate hearing in March, and his office had to remove a fact sheet from its website after concerns were raised about its accuracy. And I appreciate

The FCC publishes official rules of "neutrality"

2016

The EU establishes the General Data Protection Regulation (GDPR), described as the strongest digital data privacy law in the world

Strengthening Privacy Rights and National Security: Oversight of FISA Surveillance Programs
continued

that it is difficult to talk about classified programs in public settings, but the American people expect and deserve honest answers.

It also has been far too difficult to get a straight answer about the effectiveness of the Section 215 phone records program. Whether this program is a critical national security tool is a key question for Congress as we consider possible changes to the law. Some supporters of this program have repeatedly conflated the efficacy of the Section 215 bulk metadata collection program with that of Section 702 of FISA, even though they are entirely different. Now, I do not think that is a coincidence when we have people in Government make that comparison, but it needs to stop. I think the patience of the American people is beginning to wear thin, but what has to be of more concern in a democracy is the trust of the American people is wearing thin.

I asked General Alexander—and I understand he cannot be here today because he is at a convention in Las Vegas, I guess for hackers. But I asked General Alexander about the effectiveness of the Section 215 phone records program at an Appropriations Committee hearing last month, and he agreed to provide a classified list

of terrorist events that Section 215 helped to prevent, and I have reviewed that list. Although I agree that it speaks to the value of the overseas content collection implemented under Section 702, it does not do the same for Section 215. The list simply does not reflect dozens or even several terrorist plots that Section 215 helped thwart or prevent—let alone 54, as some have suggested.

These facts matter. This bulk collection program has massive privacy implications. The phone records of all of us in this room—all of us in this room—reside in an NSA database. I have said repeatedly that just because we have the ability to collect huge amounts of data does not mean that we should be doing so. In fact, it has been reported that the bulk collection of Internet metadata was shut down because it failed to produce meaningful intelligence. We need to take an equally close look at the phone records program. If this program is not effective, it has to end. And so far I am not convinced by what I have seen.

I am sure that we will hear from witnesses today who will say that these programs are critical in helping to identify and connect the so-called dots. But there are always going to be dots

2017

The "Vault 7" secrets, a leak of 9,000 CIA documents, reveal details of the CIA's attempts to break through encryption used by Internet

President Trump appoints Ajit Pai to head the FCC, who abolishes the FCC neutrality protections

continued

to collect, analyze, and try to connect. The Government is already collecting data on millions of innocent Americans on a daily basis based on a secret legal interpretation of a statute that does not on its face appear to authorize this kind of bulk collection. So what is going to be next? And when is enough enough?

I think Congress has to carefully consider the powerful surveillance tools that we grant to the Government. We have to ensure that there is stringent oversight, accountability, and transparency.

Jameel Jaffer, Deputy Legal Director for the American Civil Liberties Union Foundation in New York, gave the following statement on the civil liberties implications of the NSA programs revealed by the Snowden leaks:

Strengthening Privacy Rights and National Security: Oversight of FISA Surveillance Programs
continued

Over the last 2 months, it has become clear that the NSA is engaged in far-reaching, intrusive, and unlawful surveillance of Americans' telephone calls and electronic communications. The surveillance programs we are talking about this morning are the product of both defects in the law and defects in the current oversight system. FISA affords the Government sweeping power to monitor the communications of innocent people. Excessive secrecy has made congressional oversight difficult and public oversight impossible. Intelligence officials have repeatedly misled the public, Congress, and the courts about the nature and scope of the Government's surveillance activities. The ordinary federal courts have improperly used procedural doctrines to place the NSA's activities beyond the reach of the Constitution. And structural features of the FISA Court have prevented that Court from serving as an effective guardian of individual rights.

Surveillance supposedly undertaken to protect our democracy now presents a threat to it. It is not simply that this surveillance has dramatic implications for individual privacy, though plainly it does. Pervasive surveillance is also poisonous for free speech and free association. People who know the Government could be monitoring their

Congress debates whether or not to renew the controversial Section 702 FISA Amendment used to authorize NSA domestic intelligence operations since 2008

Strengthening Privacy Rights and National Security: Oversight of FISA Surveillance Programs
continued

every move, their every phone call, or their every Google search will comport themselves differently. They will hesitate before visiting controversial websites. They will hesitate before joining controversial advocacy groups. And they will hesitate before exercising rights that the Constitution guarantees.

Now, individually those hesitations may appear to be inconsequential, but the accumulation of those hesitations over time will alter the nature of our democracy. It will alter citizens' relationship to one another, and it will alter their relationship to their Government. That much is clear from the history of many other countries. And it is what the Church Committee warned of more than 30 years ago. That warning should have even more resonance today because in recent decades the intelligence agencies' resources have grown, statutory and constitutional limitations have been steadily eroded, and the technology of surveillance has become exponentially more powerful.

Because the problem Congress confronts today has many roots, there is no single solution to it. But should take certain steps right away.

First, it should amend FISA to prohibit "dragnet" monitoring of Americans' communications. Amendments of that kind should be made to the FISA Amendments Act, to FISA's so-called business 37 records provision—that is, Section 215—and to the national security letter authorities.

Second, Congress should end the unnecessary and corrosive secrecy that has obstructed congressional and public oversight. It should require the Government to publish basic statistical information about the Government's use of foreign intelligence authorities. It should ensure that the gag orders associated with national security letters are limited in scope and duration and imposed only when absolutely necessary. And it should require the publication of FISA Court opinions that evaluate the meaning, scope, or constitutionality of the foreign intelligence laws.

Finally, Congress should ensure that the Government's surveillance activities are subject to meaningful judicial review. It should clarify by statute the circumstances in which individuals can challenge Government surveillance in ordinary federal

1788 State legislatures ratify the U.S. Constitution, establishing the basic precedent for all future constitutional law

1791 The U.S. Congress ratifies the Bill of Rights, creating the first 10 amendments to the United States Constitution

continued

courts. It should provide for open and adversarial proceedings in the FISC, in the FISA Court, when the Government's surveillance applications raise those kinds of novel issues of statutory or constitutional interpretation. And it should enact legislation to ensure that the state secrets privilege is not used to place the Government's surveillance activities beyond the reach of the courts.

Deputy Attorney General for the U.S. Department of Justice James M. Cole summarized the government's position on the NSA programs, bulk data collection, and the need to continue such programs in the ongoing effort to combat terrorism.

Strengthening Privacy Rights and National Security: Oversight of FISA Surveillance Programs
continued

With these programs and other intelligence activities, we are constantly seeking to achieve the right balance between the protection of national security and the protection of privacy and civil liberties. We believe these two programs have achieved the right balance.

First of all, both programs are conducted under public statutes passed and later reauthorized by Congress. Neither is a program that has been hidden away or off the books. In fact, all three branches of Government play a significant role in the oversight of these programs. The judiciary—through the Foreign Intelligence Surveillance Court—plays a role in authorizing the programs and overseeing compliance; the executive branch conducts extensive internal reviews to ensure compliance; and Congress passes the laws, oversees our implementation of those laws, and determines whether or not the current laws should be reauthorized and in what form.

Let me explain how this has worked in the context of the 215 program. The 215 program involves the collection of metadata from telephone calls. These are telephone records maintained by the phone companies. They include the number the call was dialed from, the number the call was dialed to, the date

1868 The 14th Amendment to the U.S. Constitution guarantees all citizens the right to due process under the law

1890 Warren and Brandeis publish "The Right to Privacy" in the *Harvard Law Review*

Strengthening Privacy Rights and National Security: Oversight of FISA Surveillance Programs
continued

and time of the call, and the length of the call. The records do not include the names or other personal identifying information, they do not include cell site or other location information, and they do not include the content of any phone calls. These are the kinds of records that under longstanding Supreme Court precedent are not protected by the Fourth Amendment.

The short court order that you have seen published in the newspapers only allows the Government to acquire the phone records; it does not allow the Government to access or use them. The terms under which the Government may access or use the records is covered by another, more detailed court order that the DNI declassified and released today. That other court order, called the "primary order," provides that the Government can only search the data if it has a "reasonable, articulable suspicion" that the phone number being searched is associated with certain terrorist organizations. The order also imposes numerous other restrictions on NSA to ensure that only properly trained analysts may access the data and that they can only access it when the reasonable, articulable suspicion predicate has been met and documented. The documentation of the analyst's justification is important so

that it can be reviewed by supervisors before the search and audited afterwards to ensure compliance. In the criminal context, the Government could obtain the same types of records with a grand jury subpoena, without going to the court. But here, we go to the court every 90 days to seek the court's authorization to collect the records. In fact, since 2006, the court has authorized the program on 34 separate occasions by 14 different judges. As part of that renewal process, we inform the court whether there have been any compliance problems, and if there have been, the court will take a very hard look and make sure we have corrected those problems. As we have explained before, the 11 judges on the FISA Court are far from a rubber stamp; instead, they review all of our pleadings thoroughly, they question us, and they do not approve an order until they are satisfied that we have met all statutory and constitutional requirements.

In addition to the judiciary, Congress also plays a significant role in this program. The classified details of this program have been extensively briefed to both the Judiciary and Intelligence Committees and their staffs on numerous occasions. If there are any significant issues that arise with the 215 program, we would report those to

1923
Meyer v. Nebraska establishes that the 14th Amendment guarantees privileges of citizenship

1928
Olmstead v. United States rules that wiretapping is not a form of search and seizure defined by the 14th Amendment

continued

the two Committees right away. Any significant interpretations by the FISA Court would likewise be reported to the Committees under our statutory obligations, including opinions of any significant interpretation, along with any of the court orders that go with that.

In addition, Congress plays a role in reauthorizing the provision under which the Government carries out this program and has done so since 2006. Section 215 of the PATRIOT Act has been renewed several times since the program was initiated—including most recently for an additional 4 years in 2011. In connection with those recent renewals, the Government provided a classified briefing paper to the House and Senate Intelligence Committees to be made available to all Members of Congress. The briefing paper and a second updated version of it set out the operation of the programs in detail, explained that the Government and the FISA Court had interpreted the Section 215 authorization to authorize the bulk collection of telephone metadata, and stated that the Government was, in fact, collecting such information. The DNI also declassified and released those two papers today.

We also made offers to brief any member on the 215 program, and the availability of the paper and the opportunity for oral briefings were communicated through "Dear Colleague" letters issued by the Chairs of the Intelligence Committees to all Members of 7 Congress. Thus, although we could not talk publicly about the program at the time—since it was properly classified—the executive branch took all reasonably available steps to ensure that Members of Congress were appropriately informed about the programs when they renewed it.

I understand that there have been recent proposals to amend Section 215 authority to limit the bulk collection of telephone metadata. As the President has said, we welcome a public debate about how best to safeguard both our national security and the privacy of our citizens. Indeed, we will be considering in the coming days and weeks further steps to declassify information and help facilitate that debate, just as we have done this morning in releasing the primary order and the congressional briefing papers. In the meantime, however, we look forward to working with the Congress to determine in a careful and deliberate way what tools can best be structured and secured to secure the Nation and at the same time protect our privacy and civil liberties.

1934 The Federal Communications Commission (FCC) is established under the Federal Communications Act (FCA)

1942 *Goldman v. United States* rules that using electronic listening devices does not violate the 14th Amendment

Stewart A. Baker, former General Counsel for the NSA, and Partner at the firm of Steptoe and Johnson LLP, gave a rebuttal to the emerging concerns over the NSA program:

Strengthening Privacy Rights and National Security: Oversight of FISA Surveillance Programs
continued

Just two points about this program I think are important to begin with.

First, the kind of information that is being gathered here—phone numbers, phone records, billing records, in essence—is the sort of information for which a million subpoenas a year are served by law enforcement on phone companies today. This is not data that is kept out of the hands of Government by existing procedures and not the kind of data that has been abused in obvious ways since they have been doing this since the beginning of billing records almost a century ago. So this is not extraordinarily sensitive information.

And neither is this an unchecked program. I think, having looked at the order that was declassified this morning and having heard the procedures that have been described in the past, it is pretty clear that the people who are reviewing these records are subject to more scrutiny, more checks, more discipline than any of the other law enforcement agencies that have subpoenaed a million records from the phone companies each year.

The problem, obviously, from the discussion here is that the Government gathered the information and put it in a database first, and that is an unusual step. The question is: What could we do other than that? If we leave this with the phone companies and try to gather the information from the phone companies, first, they will get rid of this information when they choose to, when it is no longer of interest to them, which would be in a matter of months. We have no guarantee it will be there when we need it. We have no ability to search across the records of each of those phone companies to do the kind of analysis that we need to do to find the folks that have been found with this program.

And, finally, I suppose we could pay them to put it in a format and keep it for a period of time that we thought was necessary to run this program, but then you have created a database that every divorce lawyer in America is going to say, "Well, that is AT&T's data. I am just going to subpoena it." This is not something that we really want to do. Who is going to search it? Is the phone company going to search it?

1945 The National Security Agency secretly creates Project SHAMROCK

1950 Senator Joseph McCarthy delivers a shocking speech claiming that more than 200 communist spies have infiltrated the U.S. government

continued

Are we going to ask China Mobile to do searches for national security targets on the data that they are storing? Or are we going to give the Government access to the servers? Which is, of course, what caused the flap over the 702 program in the first place.

So I think there are real problems with leaving this in the hands of the private companies, and that is why as a practical matter the Government chose the route that it did.

The other problem obviously is that this has been kept secret, and I have to say the fact is—and I have spent a lifetime doing this—you cannot do intelligence in public because the targets are the most interested in how you do it and what the limitations you have imposed on yourself may be. And, therefore, disclosing the limitations, arguing about exactly how we are going to do this reveals to the people we are trying to gather intelligence on, who in many cases are trying to kill us, exactly what it is that we are trying to

do. So there is a big cost to doing this in public and to having the kinds of disclosures that we are having.

Last thought, and I have heard Senator Blumenthal's proposal and Judge Carr's proposal. I have to express some doubts about the idea of appointing a counsel from outside the Government to represent—I do not know—well, that is the first question. Who or what is this person supposed to be representing? Are they representing the terrorists? Are they representing the Court? Are they representing some abstract interest in civil liberties? Or are we just going to let them decide? You know, we got rid of the independent counsel law precisely because we were uneasy about having private parties just make up their own public policy without any check from political decision makers or without any client. And I fear we are getting into the same situation if we start appointing counsel to represent something in the context of these cases.

General Keith Alexander, then Director of the National Security Agency, was not present at the hearings as he was, at the time, attending a digital security conference in Las Vegas. However, Alexander commented on the issue during the conference, claiming that the surveillance program had disrupted "dozens" of terrorist attacks. Rory Carroll, writing in *The Guardian*, quoted Alexander as stating, "The assumption is our people are just

1951 *Dennis v. United States* rules that government limits to speech is legal only to prevent a threat to public safety or security

1959 *Barenblatt v. United States* rules that it's legal to order people to reveal personal details if national threat is perceived

out there wheeling and dealing. Nothing could be further from the truth. We have tremendous oversight over these programs. We can audit the actions of our people 100%, and we do that." Alexander explained further that only 35 vetted NSA analysts had the authority to query the database derived from the program and argued that the FISA courts were not, in fact, a "rubber stamp," but rather an independent source of oversight that controlled and monitored the NSA's activities.[107]

For anyone familiar with the information leaked and then released about how the Bush Administration used Executive Order 12333, the congressional Authorization for the Use of Military Force (AUMF), and sections of the PATRIOT Act to authorize STELLAR WIND and the President's Surveillance Program, the rhetoric and consternation that followed in the wake of the Snowden leaks might have seemed familiar. The Snowden documents revealed, incontrovertibly, that the Obama administration had continued the same types of operations undertaken by the Bush administration and, in some cases, had expanded on the state's intelligence gathering activities, in clear violation of constitutional protections and law. Just as occurred after each revelation of similar constitutional violations under the Bush administration, many citizens and lawmakers were willing to believe that such activities were necessary to prevent terrorism, or at least, were unwilling to push the government to end its activities just in case such measures were, as intelligence industry representatives claimed, necessary to national security.

The press, meanwhile, was split on the legality, ethics, and morality of Snowden's actions. In *The New Yorker*, columnist Jeffrey Toobin called him a "grandiose narcissist who deserves to be in prison," and asked, "…whether the government can function when all of its employees (and contractors) can take it upon themselves to sabotage the programs they don't like. That's what Snowden has done." Whereas David Brooks, in the *New York Times*, argued "…for society to function well, there have to be

1965   *Griswold v. CT* rules in favor of married couples' right to privacy

1967   *Katz v. United States* rules wiretaps a form of search and seizure

Willis Ware of RAND Corporation writes *Security and Privacy in Computer*

basic levels of trust and cooperation, a respect for institutions and deference to common procedures. By deciding to unilaterally leak secret NSA documents, Snowden had betrayed all of these things."[108]

Among those who offered qualified support was Conor Friedersdorf, who wrote in *The Atlantic*, offering a philosophical argument against those who claimed Snowden revealed a legitimately kept secret:

> *Think of what it means to argue that ongoing surveillance on almost all Americans is a legitimate secret, and that it's illegitimate to render its covertness "no longer possible." If that policy is a legitimate secret, it means ...*
>
> *•that seizing and storing the phone records of all Americans would never be openly debated in Congress.*
>
> *•that the propriety of the policy would never be a campaign issue, and could not be raised by challengers in Congressional races.*
>
> *•that it would never be subject to challenge in open court.*[109]

Former White House domestic policy adviser William Galston, appearing in the *Lawfare* legal blog said on the issue:

> *"The driving principle of our constitution is the fear of tyranny. Madisonian institutionalism is designed to prevent dangerous concentrations of power, in part, by setting constitutional institutions against one another, in part by allowing the people to see and assess what is being done in their name. I am increasingly skeptical that our surveillance state meets either of these tests."*[110]

1968 The Omnibus Crime Control Act holds that police needed to obtain a warrant before engaging in wire-

1969 Joseph Licklider creates the Advanced Research Projects Agency Network (ARPANET), which was

In a *Time* magazine article on the Snowden leaks, journalist Adam Cohen compared and contrasted Snowden to another famous "whistle-blower," Daniel Ellsberg, who leaked the Pentagon Papers to the press. On Snowden's legacy, Cohen wrote:

—————— *"Ellsberg is also widely regarded as a hero today because history moved his way. There is general agreement now that it was high time we pulled out of Vietnam—and that there was little real damage to national security from the release of the Pentagon Papers. The more it appears that what the NSA has been doing is wrong, the more Snowden will look like a whistle-blower. History's verdict on Snowden will turn on whether he got the balance right: whether it turned out that we were more at risk of becoming a surveillance state than we were of terrorism."*[111]

As for Snowden's public image, reactions to the Snowden leaks were mixed and sharply divided along ideological and demographic lines. In January of 2014, a *Pew Research* poll found that 57 percent of 18 to 29-year-olds believed that the leaks served the public trust, which was the exact opposite of the 65+ group, in which 57 percent believed the leaks had harmed the nation.

While a majority of Americans believed that Snowden's actions were wrong, the ensuing debate did cause a significant spike in concern over civil liberties and governmental abuses of power. The government's response to the controversy was to assert, as Obama did in speeches about the issue, that there needed to be a balance between privacy and security and that the NSA program preserved the correct balance. A majority of Americans, in the immediate wake of the NSA revelations did not agree with this assessment, or at least felt that the methods used were not the only possible methods to achieve the goal of securing the nation. In the same *Pew* report, researchers

1971 The Pentagon Papers leaks from the press raise the issue of the Freedom of the Press versus the privacy of the government to conceal information about national security operations

1972 *Eisenstadt v. Baird* rules that the right to privacy applies to individuals

found that a significant majority in all age groups—78 percent of 18-29-year-olds, 74 percent of 30-49-year-olds, 65 percent of 50-64-year-olds, and 62 percent of 65+-year-olds—believed, whether they agreed with Snowden's methods, that Americans should not be required to give up their privacy and freedom to be safe from terrorism.[112]

Speaking about public opinion, William Galston noted in his interview with *Lawfare:*

————————— *"While the framing of survey questions on this topic affects the results, it is probably the case that a majority of Americans is prepared to accept current policies. But that's Hamilton's point: fear can drive us to subordinate liberty to security. Obama is right: there are real tradeoffs here, and we can't have 100 percent of everything we value. It is time for us to ask ourselves—as a country—whether the balance we're striking is the right one. To do that, the people and their representatives must be in possession of the facts—and empowered to discuss them freely. Our government should stop asking us to sacrifice democratic deliberation on the altar of secrecy."*

1974

The Watergate Scandal results in the revelation that the CIA had been conducting widespread surveillance of American dissidents and foreign leaders without judicial oversight

The Privacy Act is established

CONCLUSION

The Snowden leaks resulted in a surge of public concern regarding privacy and data security and validated the warnings that the ACLU and other privacy advocates had long held about the state of privacy in the post-9/11 world. Whereas a majority of Americans already felt that the government had gone too far in curtailing privacy rights, the Snowden leaks made it clear to many that this belief was legitimate. Opinions on Snowden varied more widely, with many viewing him as a criminal who had violated the oaths he'd taken to serve his country, whereas others lauded him as a hero for exposing governmental misconduct. Obama gave a statement on the issue, essentially echoing the familiar assertion that fighting terrorism required a trade-off in the form of surrendering some degree of privacy. Though the scandal proved an embarrassment to the Obama administration, congressional hearings resulted in few substantive changes over subsequent years.

1975 Senator Frank Church leads a series of hearings about the secret NSA SHAMROCK operation involved intercepting communications from American citizens

1978 Congress passes the 1978 FISA Act

DISCUSSION QUESTIONS

- How do the actions of Snowden compare to the actions of Nixon-era whistleblower Daniel Ellsberg? How do the two situations contrast?
- Do you agree with President Obama that fighting terrorism required a trade-off in terms of personal privacy? Explain your answer.
- Is it dangerous to reveal to the public that the government had been intercepting communications from the entire American public? Why or why not?
- What does the phrase "rubber stamp" mean in terms of criticism of the FISA Court?

Works Used

Ball, James. "NSA monitored calls of 35 world leaders after US official handed over contacts." *The Guardian*. Guardian News and Media. Oct. 25, 2015. Web. 27 Oct. 2017.

Bever, Lindsey. "Top 10 commentaries on the NSA leaks and whistleblower Edward Snowden." *The Guardian*. Guardian News and Media. June 13, 2013. Web. 3 Nov. 2017.

Cohen, Adam. "Edward Snowden: A Modern-Day Daniel Ellsberg, Except for One Key Difference." *Time*. Time Inc. June 10, 2013. Web. 3 Nov. 2017.

DeSilver, Drew. "Most young Americans say Snowden has served the public interest." *Pew Research Center*. Jan. 22, 2014. Web. 27 Oct. 2017.

Friedersdorf, Conor. "Choose One: Secrecy and Democracy Are Incompatible." *The Atlantic*. Atlantic Monthly Group. June 12, 2013. Web. 3 Nov. 2017.

1980 The Intelligence Oversight Act (IOA) updates legal standards

1981 President Reagan's E.O. authorized wiretapping

1986 The Electronic Communications Privacy Act is established

Greenwald, Glenn. "NSA collecting phone records of millions of Verizon customers daily." *The Guardian*. Guardian News and Media. June 6, 2013. Web. 27 Oct. 2017.

Gabbatt, Adam. "US senators press officials on NSA surveillance programs—live." *The Guardian*. Guardian News and Media. July 31, 2013. Web. 27 Oct. 2017.

Liptak, Kevin. "Senators should have known about snooping, says McCain." *CNN*. CNN Politics. June 9, 2013. Web. 2 Nov. 2017.

"NSA slides explain the PRISM data-collection program." *Washington Post*. Washington Post Company, LLC. June 6, 2013. Web. 27 Oct. 2017.

Traynor, Ian, and Paul Lewis. "Merkel compared NSA to Stasi in heated encounter with Obama." *The Guardian*. Guardian News and Media. Dec. 17, 2013. Web. 2 Nov. 2017.

Wittes, Benjamin. "William Galston on the NSA Controversies." *Lawfare*. The Lawfare Institute. June 12, 2013. Web. 3 Nov. 2017.

1994 Netscape creates the "cookie" allowing computers to monitor Internet users

2001 The September 11 terrorist attacks result in Congress authorizing the Bush Administration to utilize military methods to combat terrorism

Introduction

Encryption is a process that involves translating information into another form or format to conceal or protect sensitive data. This chapter explores the controversy surrounding private and corporate encryption programs and software and the debate over whether or not the government should have the right to access commercial encryption systems. The encryption debate has raised the following issues: 1) Do companies have the right to create encryption systems that prohibit government agents from accessing information? 2) Do consumers have the right to protect their own data against governmental intrusion? Some security-focused theorists and intelligence industry advocates believe that any encryption system used by a company or sold to consumers should include a "back door" that would allow investigators or government agents to access information stored on the system. Critics of this idea argue that citizens have the right to hide their data from governmental surveillance and have the right to ask companies for products that allow them to do so. Further, some critics argue that government "back doors" compromise security systems, providing a weakness that hackers and foreign agents could exploit.

The source document for this chapter is a 2013 article in *Salon*, "Is Online Privacy A Right?," written by columnist David Sirota. Sirota explores the Obama administration's effort to force tech companies to provide back door access to encryption systems, as well as a similar effort to force web companies to divulge encrypted passwords used by consumers. Sirota also discusses the history of the encryption debate stretching back to the 1990s, revealing how government agencies had long sought methods to break through corporate and private data protection regimes. Sirota concludes that the encryption debate should occur in Congress and criticizes the Obama administration for

The Bush administration secretly authorizes the President's Surveillance Program (PSP), utilizing E.O. 12333

The U.S. PATRIOT Act alters existing laws to facilitate better communication between the state's intelligence branches in the effort to combat terrorism

The Transportation Security Administration (TSA) is established, creating the "No Fly" and "Selectee" lists that limit the right to travel on airplanes in the United States

attempting to settle such an essential privacy rights issue outside of public scrutiny, by basing the anti-encryption efforts on White House policy and executive orders, rather than legislation.

Topics covered in this chapter include:
- Corporate data protections
- Government leaks
- Digital privacy
- Encryption

This Chapter Discusses the Following Source Document:
Sirota, David. "Is Online Privacy A Right?" *Salon*. Salon Media Group. July 29, 2013.

The Right to Hide
National Security vs. the Free Market

Cryptography is an ancient field that involves the development of ciphers or codes, systems used to conceal or to prevent unauthorized access to information. From this field came the processes of "encryption," which involves converting information into a code, and "decryption," in which the code is translated back to its original form.

One of the earliest examples of encryption found by historians came from Assyria in 1500 B.C.E. in the form of a coded message describing a coveted recipe for a pottery glaze. Many of the earliest known uses of encryption come, in fact, from the commercial realm. Just as the Assyrian merchants sought to protect their glazing recipes, so, too, the Chinese used codes to protect manufacturing secrets for the development of silk. Thus, before there were copyright laws and other ways of protecting intellectual property, encryption and decryption were used to protect trade secrets from the ancient version of what might today be called "corporate espionage."

Of course, the uses of encryption go far beyond commercial applications. Historians have similarly found a section in the *Kama Sutra*, which was written in the fourth century C.E., that advises men and women involved in secret, personal communication, to use codes to conceal the nature of their correspondence.[113] This, then, is one of the earliest examples of the use of cryptography to protect personal privacy.

In ancient Rome, Julius Caesar, not trusting the messengers who would deliver his letters, used a "substitution cipher" to camouflage his correspondence. Caesar used a "shift by three" cipher, in which every letter "A" was replaced by a letter "D," while every "B" was replaced by an "E," and so on through the alphabet. Only recipients who knew to "shift back by three," would, therefore, be able to read his messages. Caesar, as a

2007 The Bush Administration plans to make data taken from spy satellites available to law enforcement to be used to conduct domestic surveillance

2008 Congress passes Section 702, or the FISA Amendment Act, which is used to permit a massive NSA and CIA domestic surveillance program

military leader and later emperor, thus used encryption to conceal information about the state's military activities and other state secrets, constituting an early use of encryption for the purposes of state security. This was thus a forerunner of the mathematical codes used to protect military data in later centuries, like the famous Enigma machine used by the German military in World War II, which used an alpha-numeric system to translate potentially sensitive military orders into strings of complex codes that, for years, baffled the state's enemies.[114]

A cipher, or cryptographic algorithm, is a mathematical function used to translate data (called plaintext) into another kind of data, known as ciphertext. Creating ciphertext can involve relatively simple operations, such as substituting one symbol for another, known as a "substitution cipher," but may also involve the use of extremely complex algorithms that convert information through a number of interrelated steps and stages. Whatever method is used, the steps must be exact and clearly defined. This is because, once plaintext has been converted into ciphertext, it must be possible for the text to be "decrypted," or translated back to its original form. This process requires a "key," which is a set of instructions regarding the steps needed to perform the decryption.

In the ancient, pre-digital world, encryption and decryption involved the creation and use of written codes and tables, serving as the keys that were used to translate and retranslate data. Encryption became immeasurably more complex once computers could be used to rapidly convert data through complex algorithms and, this led to the massive, room-sized encryption and decryption machines that characterized information warfare in World War II. This gradually became the norm and, in the modern, technological world, encryption, like many other aspects of the ways in which humans handle and manage data, is largely an automated process.

2012 The Obama Administration proposes a Consumer Privacy Bill of Rights guaranteeing individuals the right to greater control over the use of their digital data

2013 The *Guardian* and the *Washington Post* publish the first series of articles derived from leaked NSA and CIA documents delivered by Edward Snowden

The proliferation of consumer computing technology brought about so many basic changes in society that it constitutes what some historians see as the dawn of a new age, called the "Information Age" or "Digital Age." For cryptographers, and those with a vested interest in the privacy of information, advancement of computing technology led both to a proliferation of more complex encryption methods and systems, but also to a vast increase in the need, or at least demand, for encryption technologies and services. This is because life in the Digital Age, for many around the world, involves transmitting potentially sensitive data through largely unprotected systems vulnerable to all manner of potential intrusion. Basic encryption technology thus became a consumer, tech product and, by 2017, people around the world carried, in their pockets, devices thousands of times more powerful at encrypting and decrypting data than the tools used to hide military secrets in World War II.

Encryption is a privacy tool, whether utilized by the state, by a company, or by an individual seeking to protect his or her private information. It is not surprising, therefore, that encryption became a major subject in the privacy versus security debate of the twenty-first century.

In 2000, former FBI Director Louis Freeh urged lawmakers to pass legislation that would require technology companies using encryption to provide a "backdoor" for government agents who might need access to that same data for the purposes of conducting investigations. Freeh's interest in the issue lasted after he left the FBI in June of 2011 and he continued campaigning, in speeches and papers written to Congress, for regulating corporate encryption. In 2002, Freeh appeared before the Senate intelligence community, arguing that:

"Robust and commercially available encryption products are proliferating, and no legal means has been provided to law enforcement to deal with this problem, as was recently done by Parliament

The Senate Judiciary committee holds hearings to determine if the executive surveillance operations carried out under the PATRIOT Act were a violation of constitutional law

Snowden leaks reveal that the NSA and CIA had been attempting to force corporations to provide a backdoor to encryption systems that would allow federal agents to bypass consumer encryption

> *in the United Kingdom. Terrorists, drug traffickers, and criminals have been able to exploit this huge vulnerability in our public safety matrix."*[115]

Corporate representatives were wary of creating "backdoor" access to their data. For one thing, such a system compromised security by creating an inherent vulnerability that could be exploited or abused beyond the intended purposes of the need for investigative access. For another, encryption was rapidly developing into a corporate product and some were concerned that the need to provide backdoor access to the state limited the marketability of such products. In the arena of corporate encryption, therefore, the privacy versus security conflict became a contest between security and corporate freedom.

In a 2016 article published in the *Lawfare* blog, Stanford University political scientist Amy Zegart wrote:

> *"The government has compelling interests to keep Americans safe from terrorist attack. But the government also has compelling interests to safeguard the sources of American power over the long term. And increasingly the sources of national power in the twenty-first century are economic, not military."*[116]

Exactly at what point Americans embraced the idea that the free market was a symbol of American identity is unclear, but the zealous belief in this idea has played a major role in the development of American law and policy. Politicians in the United States are uniquely reluctant to limit corporate rights, because, in the United States, such limitations have been associated with a host of un-American values, such as socialism, communism, and "big government."

2015

| Terrorist attacks in France reignite fears of domestic terrorist violence | The PATRIOT Act is replaced by the USA Freedom Act | Federal Courts order Apple, Inc. to create a new operation system that would enable federal investigators to bypass security on an iPhone. |

America's conviction to preserving corporate freedom pervades nearly every facet of American life and society. Yale University lecturer in American Studies James Berger argues in a 2015 article in *Salon*, that this tendency to favor corporate rights even constitutes the nation's most blatant media bias with every newspaper in the nation having an entire section dedicated to "business" whereas none had a similar section dedicated to "labor."[117]

The campaign for national security exceptions and backdoors was not, in fact, a twenty-first century concern, but played a role in the earliest attempts by legislators to address the legality of electronic communication. There was, for instance, an attempt by future Vice President Joe Biden to include law enforcement "backdoors" in the 1968 Omnibus Crime Bill, though this effort failed and the provision was stricken from the bill before it became law, largely due to protests from corporate rights advocates who argued such a measure was unnecessarily restrictive. So, Louis Freeh, the FBI director who took on Biden's mantle in the lobby for backdoor access in the 2000s, also failed to gain traction for his essential security policy past the legislators and lobbyists who feared and fought against corporate regulation. Even in the few months after 9/11, when national security zealotry was at a fever pitch, Freeh was unable to build enough support to mandate his backdoor access proposals.

The consumer encryption market got a massive boost in the 2000s when newspapers revealed that the Bush administration had been secretly intercepting digital data from millions of Americans. Another surge occurred in 2013 when the Snowden leaks revealed that the Obama administration had done pretty much the same thing, and had even expanded, rather than restricting, domestic surveillance by the state. Digital privacy advocates like the Freedom of the Press Foundation and the Electronic Frontier Foundation began promoting the use of personal encryption as the best way for consumers to take control of their own data.

The FCC publishes official rules of "neutrality"

2016

The EU establishes the General Data Protection Regulation (GDPR), described as the strongest digital data privacy law in the world

Also in 2013, investigative journalists revealed that the federal government had attempted to force U.S. companies to provide backdoor access, or master "encryption keys," that would have provided federal agents with access to virtually all of the data streaming through the Internet. This effort prompted a new debate in the arena of personal privacy, asking whether citizens had the right to protect their own data, and whether the government had the right to restrict encryption systems or to force corporations handling data, and promising privacy to consumers, to relinquish data at the government's request. Although it was unknown at the time which companies had submitted to the government's demands and which hadn't, this emerging issue, the balance between corporate rights and national security, became a contentious new dimension in the broader privacy debate.

In a July 2013 issue of *Salon*, journalist David Sirota's article "Is Online Privacy a Right?" poses fundamental questions about ownership of data, the legality of encryption, and the evolving effort to balance personal privacy, corporate freedom, and national security.

IS ONLINE PRIVACY A RIGHT?
by David Sirota
Salon, July 29, 2013
Source Document

Keep Calm, and Encrypt—this slogan, a play off Britain's World War II posters, is the privacy-seeker's new motto in the age of mass surveillance and data mining. The idea is that even with the expansion of surveillance, some data can still be kept away from eavesdroppers, as long as it is properly encrypted. It is the assumption behind whistleblower Edward Snowden's insistence on only communicating via encrypted conduits and it is the basis for watchdog groups like the Freedom of the Press Foundation to help reporters learn how to communicate through such conduits with their sources.

Using encryption is clearly a smart move in this Orwellian era. After all, even with the NSA's impressive codebreaking abilities, secure encryption still works. In fact, when done properly, it works so well to preserve privacy and lock data away from snoops that the government

The "Vault 7" secrets, a leak of 9,000 CIA documents, reveal details of the CIA's attempts to break through encryption used by Internet

President Trump appoints Ajit Pai to head the FCC, who abolishes the FCC neutrality protections

continued

has now kicked off an aggressive campaign to turn the concept of "secure encryption" into an oxymoron.

Specifically, the Obama administration has launched an initiative to force tech companies to give the NSA a set of Internet-wide skeleton keys. The radical move, which would let law enforcement agencies access vast troves of encrypted information, adds significant questions to the ongoing debate over privacy. It begs us to ask not only whether the government has a right to vacuum up millions of Americans' private data, but also to ask whether the security-conscious among us should even be allowed to retain the right to make data truly secure?

The word right is important here—the Fourth Amendment of the Constitution does not only bar unreasonable searches and seizures nor does it only mandate probable cause for searches. In addition to all that, it enshrines "the right of the people to be secure in their persons, houses, papers, and effects." In the digital age, it shouldn't be a stretch to assume that such a precept means a basic right to access tools that keep personal property, including data and intellectual property, secure.

That tool is encryption—aka software and hardware that codes data

so that it is locked and inaccessible to everyone except those who are specifically given a key. But as CNET's Declan McCullagh reports, "The U.S. government has attempted to obtain the master encryption keys that Internet companies use to shield millions of users' private Web communications from eavesdropping." Accurately describing the move as "a technological escalation" in the government's effort to conduct mass surveillance, McCullagh goes on to explain why this is such a big deal:

An increasing amount of Internet traffic flowing through those fiber cables is now armored against surveillance using SSL encryption...

"Strongly encrypted data are virtually unreadable," NSA director Keith Alexander told the Senate earlier this year.

Unless, of course, the NSA can obtain an Internet company's private SSL key. With a copy of that key, a government agency that intercepts the contents of encrypted communications has the technical ability to decrypt and peruse everything it acquires in transit, although actual policies may be more restrictive.

A day after this dispatch, McCullaugh went on to report that, according to "two industry sources,"

Congress debates whether or not to renew the controversial Section 702 FISA Amendment used to authorize NSA domestic intelligence operations since 2008

"Is Online Privacy A Right?"
continued

the government is also demanding "that major Internet companies divulge users' stored passwords...which (are) typically stored in encrypted form."

It should go without saying that such powerful digital skeleton keys in the hands of national security agencies makes the term "secure encryption" meaningless and consequently turns the Fourth Amendment's first clause into a worthless platitude. And while we do not yet know whether these skeleton keys are in those agencies' hands, the reaction from the tech industry is hardly reassuring, especially considering what National Journal calls its history of "willing and even eager cooperation" with the NSA.

For instance, Apple, Yahoo, AOL, Verizon, AT&T, Time Warner Cable, and Comcast all declined to answer CNET's specific questions about whether they had obeyed the government's new request.

CNET also reports that Microsoft first "would not say whether the company has received requests from the government" but then tried to defend itself by claiming that "we can't see a circumstance in which we would provide" a skeleton key to law enforcement agencies. This, of course, was contradicted by The Guardian's recent report showing that "Microsoft

has collaborated closely with U.S. intelligence services to allow users' communications to be intercepted, including helping the National Security Agency to circumvent the company's own encryption."

Meanwhile, as McCullagh notes, while its possible some of the other large tech firms may have thought about resisting government demands for the skeleton keys, "smaller companies without well-staffed legal departments might be less willing to put up a fight" against such requests. Of course, appalling as this all is, it shouldn't be particularly surprising considering both the general history of the government's posture toward encryption and the specific politician near the top of the Obama administration.

Back in the early 1990s, programmer Phil Zimmerman released his "Pretty Good Protection" (PGP) encryption code first in book form and then on the Internet. According to *U.S. News and World Report*, that move was met with Justice Department-led grand jury investigation "for possible violation of federal arms-export laws." Why? Because encryption was viewed by the government as a weapon and once it was on the Internet, the magazine noted it meant Zimmerman's

1788 State legislatures ratify the U.S. Constitution, establishing the basic precedent for all future constitutional law

1791 The U.S. Congress ratifies the Bill of Rights, creating the first 10 amendments to the United States Constitution

continued

"'cryptography for the masses' has slipped out of America."

At the time, a U.S. intelligence official justified the harassment of Zimmerman by bluntly stated that the government was concerned not about Americans' privacy, but about the fact that PGP would allow more people to guarantee that privacy.

"The ability of just about everybody to encrypt their messages is rapidly outrunning our ability to decode them," the official told the magazine, lamenting that "it's a lot harder to eavesdrop on a worldwide web than it is to tap a cable."

For his part, Zimmerman explained his decision to publish PGP as a response to the threat of congressional efforts to effectively outlaw secure encryption—efforts led by none other than now-Vice President Joe Biden.

That's right, back in 1991, Biden inserted language into an omnibus crime bill that "providers of electronic communications services and manufacturers of electronic communications service equipment shall ensure that communications systems permit the government to obtain the plain text contents of voice, data, and other communications." Zimmerman says that if the language "had become real law, it would have forced manufacturers of secure communications equipment to insert special trap doors in their products, so that the government can read anyone's encrypted messages."

Though the three-year grand jury investigation ended up with no charges against Zimmerman, and though Biden's language was removed from the final bill, it was the beginning of an ongoing campaign by government officials to try to ban, restrict or otherwise undermine truly secure, privacy-protecting encryption.

That campaign has now culminated in the Obama administration's heavy-handed push for Internet-wide skeleton keys. It is a classic—if abhorrent—political workaround. Unable to convince rank-and-file members of Congress to openly vote against privacy and pass legislation outlawing secure encryption, anti-privacy/pro-surveillance ideologues have resorted to circumventing the democratic process by convincing the executive branch to try to simply bully tech companies into submission.

Though unstated, the government's presumption in its anti-encryption crusade is that Americans should have no right to access technology that cannot be infiltrated by law enforcement agencies. The logic is that in critical national security cases, the government needs to be able to guarantee that it can access all data in

1868   The 14th Amendment to the U.S. Constitution guarantees all citizens the right to due process under the law

1890   Warren and Brandeis publish "The Right to Privacy" in the *Harvard Law Review*

"Is Online Privacy A Right?"
continued

order to save lives.

But here's the thing: because of a recent court decision that weakens the Fifth Amendment, search warrants can now force suspects to give up their passwords and encryption keys, under penalty of punishment. That means along with their already impressive codebreaking capacity, law enforcement agencies already have substantial legal power to access encrypted data. There's just one caveat: those agencies often have to at least submit to judicial oversight and obtain a warrant to use some of those extraordinary powers.

In light of that, the government's new push for master keys and all passwords is almost certainly a move to try to reduce that minimal judicial oversight. It is security and law enforcement agencies attempting obtain the tools necessary to silently access encrypted data on an ongoing basis—a "collect it all" system that seems deliberately designed to be used without a warrant.

Public officials will no doubt say all of this is for our own safety. But there's little evidence that outlawing or undermining encryption is going to make us any safer, just like, according to top congressional officials, there's little evidence that the NSA's mass surveillance has thwarted major terrorist plots.

Additionally, even if one thinks the case for skeleton keys is valid and worthy of at least some discussion, the fact that there hasn't been an open debate about it in Congress should be troubling. After all, the executive branch is just unilaterally trying to intimidate tech companies into putting backdoors in encryption—and worse, in a devious way that attempts to leave the public believing that such backdoors do not exist.

Sure, some might argue that the official requirement for warrants will preclude skeleton keys from being abused and that therefore citizens will still be protected from invasive surveillance. But that argument shouldn't be comforting. In the age of warrantless surveillance, it should be the opposite: a reminder of why the availability and preservation of truly secure encryption is more necessary than ever.

Despite pressure from the state, many of the companies involved in encryption efforts refused to provide "backdoor" access to investigators. Encryption opponents routinely argue that such technologies are an

1923
Meyer v. Nebraska establishes that the 14th Amendment guarantees privileges of citizenship

1928
Olmstead v. United States rules that wiretapping is not a form of search and seizure defined by the 14th Amendment

Wire tap device for eavesdropping through a wall, door, etc., a microphone and hearing aid trick. The mic picks up sound and the hearing aid magnifies the reception. (Photo: Bettman/Contributor/Getty Images)

impediment to effective policing and the need to prevent terrorism and foreign attacks, whereas privacy advocates argue that consumers have the right to protect their own data using whatever technology is available. A law prohibiting individuals from creating their own codes and encrypting their own data would not likely pass constitutional tests and there have been no serious efforts to establish such a law. Instead, the government placed pressure on corporations that, if inclined to provide access, would essentially be providing access to corporate assets, rather than private property, and thus to data protected under a different set of laws and regulations.

1934

The Federal Communications Commission (FCC) is established under the Federal Communications Act (FCA)

1942

Goldman v. United States rules that using electronic listening devices does not violate the 14th Amendment

It is important to note that the companies encrypting data do not, as a matter of course and so far, as has been publicly revealed, also create "backdoor" master keys that provide access to any and all encrypted data running through their systems. Some argued, therefore, that what the government was demanding of tech companies was to intentionally create a vulnerability that could potentially be abused.

In 2015, tech experts at Massachusetts Institute of Technology (MIT) argued against providing backdoors to encryption on the basis that the existence of a "master key" in government hands essentially meant that it might be possible for someone to steal the master key from the government, or from the companies forced to create master keys. The researchers, therefore, argue that the very existence of such keys, no matter what company or agency has possession, means that, eventually, the key could be stolen, with disastrous potential consequences for the individuals using encryption to protect personal or financial data.[118] Government agents argue that the federal government would be able to secure the sensitive "master key," though tech and security experts are unsure whether this is the case. Essentially, the MIT researchers argued, creating a master key is like hiding one's keys under a doormat. Although it might remain safe for some time, eventually someone will find it.

In a June 2017 article in *Wired*, security journalist Brian Barrett discussed the security situation in reference to the increasing phenomenon of government data leaks. Barrett references, for instance, the March 2017 leak of 9000 documents involving a secret CIA hacking scheme known as the "Vault 7" secrets, and another high-profile leak of NSA data delivered to the press by a group known as the "Shadow Brokers" as evidence that data stored by government agencies, even those charged with intelligence and information secrecy, is neither secret, nor safe. These high-profile leaks of secret, government information led Barrett to make another argument against "master key" proposals, arguing, "Why entrust a key to someone who gets robbed frequently?"[119]

1945   The National Security Agency secretly creates Project SHAMROCK

1950   Senator Joseph McCarthy delivers a shocking speech claiming that more than 200 communist spies have infiltrated the U.S. government

CONCLUSION

The Snowden leaks of 2013, as well as government leaks in subsequent years, strengthened the arguments of encryption advocates and critics of the "back door" access proposals in that such leaks demonstrated that the federal government was unable to effectively protect data stored in federal systems. Between 2013 and 2018, legislators did not adopt any laws that would mandate the creation of back doors or master key systems to provide government agencies with access to data stored in commercial or private systems. The combination of public distrust and intense lobbying on behalf of web and technology companies effectively stalled such an effort. However, information in the Snowden leaks revealed that the NSA and other intelligence agencies had developed numerous strategies to bypass private encryption between 2001 and 2018, though the success of the methods used remained largely uncertain.

1951 *Dennis v. United States* rules that government limits to speech is legal only to prevent a threat to public safety or security

1959 *Barenblatt v. United States* rules that it's legal to order people to reveal personal details if national threat is perceived

DISCUSSION QUESTIONS

- Should companies have to provide a back door to federal agents and law enforcement? Why or why not?
- Do citizens have the right to hide their own data from the government? Explain.
- Can the federal government be trusted to protect private data from American citizens? Why or why not?
- Would you be more likely to use a company that provided access to the government, or one that prohibited government access without prior permission? Explain your answer.

Works Used

Abelson, Harold, et al. "Keys Under Doormats: Mandating Insecurity by Requiring Government Access to All Data and Communications." *MIT.* Computer Science and Artificial Intelligence Laboratory Technical Report. July 6, 2015. Web. 29 Oct. 2017.

Barrett, Brian. "The Encryption Debate Should End Right Now." *Wired.* Conde Nast. June 30, 2017. Web. 29 Oct. 2017.

Berger, James. "This is the media's real bias—pro-business, pro-corporate, pro-CEO." *Salon.* Salon Media Inc. Oct. 30, 2015. Web. 3 Nov. 2017.

"History of Encryption." *SANS Institute.* Information Security Reading Room. 2001. Pdf. 28 Oct. 2017.

McCullagh, Declan. "Former FBI chief takes on encryption." *CNET.* CBS Interactive. Oct. 15, 2002. Web. 28 Oct. 2017.

Waddell, Kaveh. "The Long and Winding History of Encryption." *The Atlantic.* Atlantic Monthly Group. Jan. 13, 2016. Web. 28 Oct. 2017.

Zegart, Amy. "The Security Debate We Need to Have." *Lawfare.* Lawfare Institute. Feb. 23, 2016. Web. 3 Nov. 2017.

1965 | *Griswold v. CT* rules in favor of married couples' right to privacy

1967 | *Katz v. United States* rules wiretaps a form of search and seizure

Willis Ware of RAND Corporation writes *Security and Privacy in Computer*

Introduction

This chapter continues the discussion regarding encryption introduced in the previous chapter by explaining some of the many methods that the NSA and other intelligence agencies were using between 2001 and 2013 in their effort to break through encryption systems used by individuals and companies to protect consumer data. One of the methods the NSA used was to try and influence the adoption of international encryption standards, which are standardized methods for coding and developing algorithms. International standards organizations maintain detailed information on standards for various industries that both guide the development of new products and provide a method to judge the quality of new products against the official standards for the industry. Chapter 21 discussed the revelation in 2013 that the NSA had attempted to convince international standards organizations in the encryption fields to adopt standards developed within the NSA that contained an inherent security weakness that would enable the NSA to penetrate any encryption system developed according to those standards.

The source document for this chapter is an article from the September 6, 2013 issue of *The New Yorker*, by technology columnist Matt Buchanan, entitled "How the N.S.A. Cracked the Web." In the article, Buchanan discusses a series of documents found within the Snowden leaks (see Chapter 20) detailing various NSA efforts to break through commonly-used encryption systems. These efforts included hacking or using brute force methods. Buchanan also reports that the full extent of the NSA's encryption breaking programs remained largely unknown. According to documents revealed by Snowden, the NSA had been able to find some way to access data protected by some Internet-level encryption systems, but it was unclear whether or not the agency

1968 The Omnibus Crime Control Act holds that police needed to obtain a warrant before engaging in wire-

1969 Joseph Licklider creates the Advanced Research Projects Agency Network (ARPANET), which was

had been able to bypass the encryption used on 2013 generation smart phones or personal computers. Buchanan also discusses the controversy surrounding the NSA working to undermine encryption standards and discusses unsubstantiated reports that major communication and web companies were providing back door access to encrypted data, though the names of collaborating companies had not yet been revealed.

Topics covered in this chapter include:
- Corporate data protections
- Government leaks
- Digital privacy
- Encryption

This Chapter Discusses the Following Source Document:
Buchanan, Matt. "How the N.S.A. Cracked the Web." *The New Yorker*. Conde Nast. Sept. 6, 2013.

Brute Force
The Encryption Debate

From the 1960s to the 2010s, one of the sub-debates within the broader privacy versus security debate has been whether companies had the right to encrypt data such that even federal investigators would be unable to gain access. There have been repeated proposals, from those who favor state needs over corporate rights, to force companies to create "master keys" or "backdoors" that would provide state agents with immediate access to all encrypted data flowing through a network or web service portal. It was revealed in the press, in 2013, that the National Security Agency (NSA) and the Government Communications Headquarters (GCHQ), a branch of British intelligence, had been secretly pressuring corporations to provide backdoor access. At the same time, the NSA and GCHQ were developing a secret battery of tools that would allow them to bypass web security systems and encryption.[120]

One method that the NSA and other intelligence agencies have used to gain access to encrypted data is to exert control over what are known as "international encryption standards." Encryption standards are a form of technical standards, which are industry-based norms, criteria, methods, and practices. Standards are created as a basis for quality evaluation. Therefore, standards in automobile manufacturing can be used as a measure to judge how closely a manufacturer adheres to the standards set for the field. The standards for a certain field are developed through research and debate. Trade unions and professional organizations can propose standards, whereas countries also have standards organizations, like the American National Standards Institute (ANSI), composed of experts who review research and methods used in a field and compile and publish standards for various practices. There is also an International Standards Organization (ISO) that creates and monitors a set of international standards for products, services and systems to ensure quality, safety, and efficiency.

1974 The Watergate Scandal results in the revelation that the CIA had been conducting widespread surveillance of American dissidents and foreign leaders without judicial oversight

The Privacy Act is established

In many cases, standards are optional rather than mandatory, but the standards set by standards organizations serve an important function, providing a way for other professionals and consumers to judge the quality through comparisons to the various standards set within an industry. Encryption has its own set of standards, based around a core group of methods that can be used, in a variety of variations, to create data encryption services and products for a variety of applications. In 2013, the NSA released a new proposed encryption system known as "Simon and Speck," based on a combination of the Speck block cipher and a "sister algorithm" known as "Simon." The NSA then promoted this new encryption standard to the ANSI and eventually to the ISO for adoption as the new international standard.

In marketing their Simon and Speck system to the ISO, the NSA claimed that their powerful algorithms would help to create a more secure global standard, thus reducing the likelihood of hostile foreign or even terrorist interception of data; critics believed that the NSA's motivations were not as the agency claimed. The NSA, having developed Simon and Speck, also had the capability to break the system. Therefore, had Simon and Speck developed into a global standard, the NSA would have had access to any encryption system built to comply with the Simon and Speck mold. Documents revealed in the infamous Snowden leak in 2013 demonstrated this, with budget documents from the NSA calling for funding to "insert vulnerabilities into commercial encryption systems." The Snowden documents further revealed that the Simon and Speck system was not the first time that the NSA had its hands in the standards process. In the 2000s, the NSA had been involved in promoting standards for an encryption component called Dual Elliptic Curve (Dual EC), that was successfully adopted as a global standard. Within the Snowden documents, NSA communications made it clear that the agency considered the adoption of Dual EC a success and described how NSA representatives guided the debate over the system until it had been adopted. The documents further showed that the NSA paid the private security

1975   Senator Frank Church leads a series of hearings about the secret NSA SHAMROCK operation involved intercepting communications from American citizens

1978   Congress passes the 1978 FISA Act

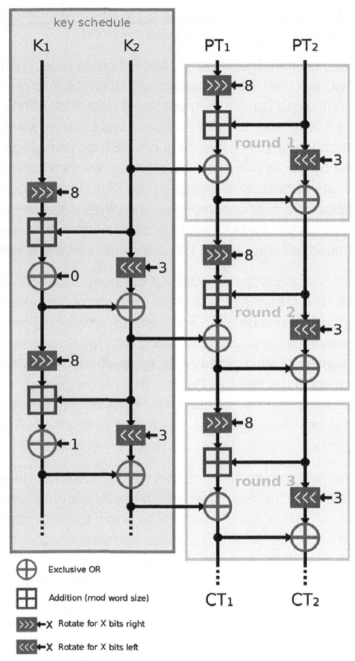

3 rounds of Speck with 2-word key schedule.

company RSA $10 million to include Dual EC in a software development kit distributed to security programmers around the world.

Mathematicians proved, in 2007, that Dual EC could hide a backdoor, enabling individuals with the appropriate key to eavesdrop on encrypted communications using Dual EC without being detected. Although such activities were not proven, the ISO dropped Dual EC from its list of recommended technologies. For their part, the NSA denied allegations that the Simon and Speck system was intended to provide a backdoor. A German delegate to the ISO meetings on the Simon and Speck proposal argued, "How can we expect companies and citizens to use security algorithms from ISO standards if those algorithms come from a source that has compromised security-related ISO standards just a few years ago?"

Suspicion and criticism from international partners resulted in a compromise, with the NSA retracting most of the versions of Simon and Speck it had submitted for consideration and, instead, advancing only the two strongest versions of the techniques, along with full documentation of the organization's internal attempts to break the system. Chris Mitchell of the British delegation to the ISO told Reuters that he supported the system, arguing that no one had so far been able to break the algorithms, but also acknowledged that "trust, particularly for U.S. government participants in standardization, is now non-existent."[121]

Another secret revealed in the Snowden leaks showed that the NSA and GCHQ had teams of "hackers," experts in digital security, who had been trying to develop "brute force" methods to break through corporate encryption protections. Experts, however, debated whether this effort was likely to be fruitful. For instance, digital security expert Micah Lee, writing in his blog in 2013 demonstrated that the mathematics behind encryption are powerful and that, therefore, when appropriate encryption keys are used, encryption systems can essentially be unbeatable. For instance, the generation of a random 128-bit key (common in basic

1994 Netscape creates the "cookie" allowing computers to monitor Internet users

2001 The September 11 terrorist attacks result in Congress authorizing the Bush Administration to utilize military methods to combat terrorism

computing in the 2010s), involved 2 to the power of 128 possible keys. Therefore, imagining that the NSA could gather 2 trillion computers (a physical impossibility), each of which could test 100,000 keys a second, the time required to brute force through a 128-bit encryption would require 27 billion millennia. Putting it another way, Lee argues that, even if all the world's computing power were directed at cracking a single message in this way, the sun would burn out before the message would be decoded.[122]

This, however, refers to the act of trying to brute force attack an entirely random 128-bit encryption system, and this is not the method most people use to create passwords, nor the method that the NSA would likely use to try and break through private encryption. In 2015, for instance, the security company Kaspersky Lab discovered that a group, known as the "Equation" had been hiding malware (malicious programs) in commercial hard drives, and that these hidden malware programs essentially allowed an external operator to access data placed into the hard drive. Some security specialists thus theorized that the program might have been part of the NSA initiative revealed in the Snowden documents claiming a series of methods used to break through encryption protections, though this allegation was never confirmed.[123] The German newspaper, *Der Spiegel*, reported in 2014 on some of the techniques the NSA was attempting to develop to break through widely used encryption schemes like the Advanced Encryption Standard (AES) encryption program, though it was uncertain whether the organization ever managed to achieve that goal.

Finally, the Snowden documents also revealed that a number of prominent Internet companies had been forced or had willingly complied with NSA requests for customer data. It was revealed that Google, Hotmail, Yahoo, and Facebook, had worked with the government to create vulnerabilities that could be used to access consumer data. The $250 million-per-year program had been ongoing for more than a decade before information on the

The Bush administration secretly authorizes the President's Surveillance Program (PSP), utilizing E.O. 12333

The U.S. PATRIOT Act alters existing laws to facilitate better communication between the state's intelligence branches in the effort to combat terrorism

The Transportation Security Administration (TSA) is established, creating the "No Fly" and "Selectee" lists that limit the right to travel on airplanes in the United States

program was leaked to the press, but revealed some of the more insidious methods that had been developed over the years.[124] In some cases, companies had been directed to cooperate by the courts. For instance, documents in the Snowden trove revealed that Microsoft, which owned the video chat program Skype, had been forced to provide the NSA with access to all Skype communications beginning in February of 2011, under a FISA court order.[125]

In this article, *How the N.S.A. Cracked the Web*, from a September 6, 2013 issue of *The New Yorker*, Matt Buchanan gathers information from tech and web security experts exploring how the still poorly understood secret efforts to crack Internet security took place and which encryption methods had been rendered vulnerable to attack:

HOW THE N.S.A CRACKED THE WEB
by Matt Buchanan
The New Yorker, September 6, 2013
Source Document

It's been nearly three months since Edward Snowden started telling the world about the National Security Agency's mass surveillance of global communications. But the latest disclosures, by the *Guardian*, *New York Times*, and *ProPublica* are perhaps the most profound yet: the N.S.A. and its partner agency in the United Kingdom, the Government Communications Headquarters, possess significant capabilities to circumvent widely used encryption software in order to access private data.

Encryption poses a problem for intelligence agencies by scrambling data with a secret code so that even if they, or any other third-party, manages to capture it, they cannot read it—unless they possess the key to decrypt it or have the ability to crack the encryption scheme. Encryption has become only more pervasive in the decade since the N.S.A.'s "aggressive, multipronged effort to break widely used Internet encryption technologies" began in 2000. When you log into Gmail or Facebook, chat over iMessage, or check your bank account, the data is

2005

The PATRIOT Act was reauthorized without substantial changes as Congress favors security concerns over warnings that the law creates the potential for civil liberties violations

The *New York Times* publishes articles resulting from leaks revealing the secret President's Surveillance Program (PSP) established by the Bush administration

continued

typically encrypted. This is because encryption is vital for everyday Web transactions; if for instance, you were to log in to your Gmail account using a park's open wireless network and your username and password were transmitted in plain form, without being encrypted, your credentials could potentially be captured by anyone using that same network.

Both the *Times* and the *Guardian* write that the N.S.A. and the G.C.H.Q. have "cracked much of the encryption" on the Web. But we don't know precisely how much: the *Times* writes that the "full extent of the N.S.A.'s decoding capabilities is known only to a limited group of top analysts from the so-called Five Eyes: the N.S.A. and its counterparts in Britain, Canada, Australia and New Zealand." But it deploys "custom-built, superfast computers to break codes," and it works with "technology companies in the United States and abroad to build entry points into their products."

While the *Times* and the *Guardian* do not make clear precisely which encryption schemes the N.S.A. and its partners have rendered effectively useless—and which companies the agency has partnered with—there are some hints about what the N.S.A. has accomplished with Bullrun, its project to defeat network encryption.

The N.S.A. has apparently possessed "groundbreaking capabilities" against encrypted voice and text communication since 2010, which the *Guardian* says made "'vast amounts' of data collected through internet cable taps newly 'exploitable.'" The N.S.A. appears to have found a way around some Internet-level encryption protocols that use outdated standards, but are nonetheless ubiquitous: the *Guardian* writes, "The agency has capabilities against widely used online protocols, such as HTTPS, voice-over-IP and Secure Sockets Layer." And the *Times* notes that the "most intensive efforts have focused on the encryption in universal use in the United States, including Secure Sockets Layer, or SSL; virtual private networks, or V.P.N.s; and the protection used on fourth-generation, or 4G, smartphones." The hypertext transfer protocol (H.T.T.P.) is the basis for Web communication—it's the "http" in your browser's address bar. S.S.L. is one of the most common cryptographic protocols on the Web and is supported by nearly all Web sites. (It's also used by instant-messaging and other programs to secure transmissions over the Internet.) H.T.T.P.S. is essentially the application of the S.S.L. protocol to H.T.T.P., making online services like e-mail and banking secure. A virtual private network enables a user to have a private connection

2007 The Bush Administration plans to make data taken from spy satellites available to law enforcement to be used to conduct domestic surveillance

2008 Congress passes Section 702, or the FISA Amendment Act, which is used to permit a massive NSA and CIA domestic surveillance program

"How the N.S.A Cracked the Web"
continued

on a public network in which their transmissions are protected. Under normal circumstances, the use of these protocols would shield data from the N.S.A.'s dragnet surveillance of communications.

Cryptographic and security experts have been able to piece together some ideas about the extent of the agency's capabilities. Mike Janke, the C.E.O. of the encrypted-communications company Silent Circle—which shut down its encrypted e-mail service a few weeks ago—said over the phone that, based on information and literature he has seen, he believes the N.S.A. developed "a massive push-button scale" ability to defeat or circumvent S.S.L. encryption in virtually real time. He added, "the reality of it is that most of the security world has known that lower level encryption—S.S.L., H.T.T.P.S., V.P.N.s—are highly susceptible to being defeated because of their architecture." Bruce Schneier, who has seen the Snowden documents, wrote that the N.S.A. has circumvented common Web encryption "primarily by cheating, not by mathematics." Instead of busting the algorithms that power encryption schemes, Schneier is suggesting that the N.S.A. has found a way around it. Matthew Green, a prominent crypto researcher, suggests that the N.S.A. may have compromised the encryption software

that implements the algorithms that determine how data is scrambled—in particular, software made by Microsoft and used by many Web servers for encryption. The *Times* writes that the "the agency maintains an internal database of encryption keys for specific commercial products, called a Key Provisioning Service, which can automatically decode many messages." Intriguingly, it adds, "independent cryptographers say many are probably collected by hacking into companies' computer servers, where they are stored." If the agency possesses the keys, there is no need to crack the encryption algorithm.

Thomas Drake, an N.S.A. whistleblower who was profiled by Jane Mayer in the magazine, said over the phone that he believes the 2010 breakthrough was possibly more dramatic and may refer to the defeat of "some of the main-line encryption" algorithms in wide use, like the R.S.A. algorithm or the Advanced Encryption Standard at 256-bit level. (The length of the key used to encrypt and decrypt information, measured in bits, is one of many aspects of what determines how hard an encryption scheme is to crack: 128-bit encryption is now relatively easy; 2048-bit is much harder.) This kind of capability was hinted at in James Bamford's piece a year ago about the N.S.A.'s massive new data

2012 The Obama Administration proposes a Consumer Privacy Bill of Rights guaranteeing individuals the right to greater control over the use of their digital data

2013 The *Guardian* and the *Washington Post* publish the first series of articles derived from leaked NSA and CIA documents delivered by Edward Snowden

continued

center in Utah.

The most damning aspect of the new disclosures is that the N.S.A. has worked to make widely used technology less secure. The *Times* reports that in 2006, the N.S.A. intentionally introduced a vulnerability into an encryption standard adopted by both the National Institute of Standards and Technology and the International Organization for Standardization. This is deeply problematic, Green writes, because the cryptographic industry is "highly dependent on NIST standards." The N.S.A. also uses its Commercial Solutions Center, which invites companies, including start-ups, to show their technology to the agency under the guise of improving security, in order to "leverage sensitive, cooperative relationships with specific industry partners" and covertly make those products more susceptible to N.S.A.'s surveillance. Schneier, who has reviewed the documents, describes the process thusly: "Basically, the NSA asks companies to subtly change their products in undetectable ways: making the random number generator less random, leaking the key somehow, adding a common exponent to a public-key exchange protocol, and so on." This is why the N.S.A. specifically asked the *Times* and *Guardian* to not publish their articles and the documents detailing the program warn explicitly and repeatedly of the need for secrecy:

"Do not ask about or speculate on sources or methods."

The *Times* notes that the N.S.A. expects to "gain full unencrypted access to an unnamed major Internet phone call and text service" sometime this year. The Guardian further specifies that it is a "major internet peer-to-peer voice and text communications," which sounds like it might be Skype—owned by Microsoft and previously named as an N.S.A. partner. Drake said that he was certain that Skype has been "compromised." And, in one instance, the *Times* notes that "after the government learned that a foreign intelligence target had ordered new computer hardware, the American manufacturer agreed to insert a back door into the product before it was shipped." This is worse than the legal mandate the N.S.A. and the F.B.I. pushed for in the nineties to force technology companies to build backdoors into their products, because, as Chris Soghoian, the principal technologist for the American Civil Liberties Union said, "with a secret backdoor you'll think it's secure," rather than simply avoiding the technology. Schneier writes, "My guess is that most encryption products from large U.S. companies have NSA-friendly back doors, and many foreign ones probably do as well." The pervasive effort to engineer backdoors into commercial technology strikes upon a

The Senate Judiciary committee holds hearings to determine if the executive surveillance operations carried out under the PATRIOT Act were a violation of constitutional law

Snowden leaks reveal that the NSA and CIA had been attempting to force corporations to provide a backdoor to encryption systems that would allow federal agents to bypass consumer encryption

"How the N.S.A Cracked the Web"
continued

broader question, raised by Soghoian: "Can we rely on technology provided by corporations with extensive relations with the U.S. government?"

Despite the scope of the N.S.A.'s program, and its apparent success against Internet-level encryption, strong encryption schemes do remain uncracked by the N.S.A, and they are "your best bet" for privacy, said Janke. Pretty Good Privacy, a common encryption program, if used with the latest algorithms, remains safe, he added, as does the encryption used in Z.R.T.P., which is used by Silent Circle's voice and text products to encrypt communications. Janke believes in their security in large part because "it's good enough for the government to approve it for their use." Soghoian says that the "the kind of stuff we need is already available, it's just not in our browsers and not with Google and Facebook." (However, in response to the N.S.A. revelations, Google has fast-tracked its plan to encrypt data as it zips between its own data centers to prevent it from being subject to intelligence-agency prying.) Janke notes that on a local level, TrueCrypt, a hard-drive encryption program, along with Apple's native hard-disk encryption tool both remain unbroken. Though Drake said he would only trust 2048-bit level encryption schemes and that he relies largely on open-source

software, he would not reveal how he protects his own communications. "I just don't want others to know how I protect myself," he said. "I literally do not trust anything commercial."

In response to the latest revelations, Representative Rush Holt of New Jersey has introduced a bill, the Surveillance State Repeal Act, which would, among other things, bar the N.S.A. from installing such backdoors into encryption software. While a statement from the Director of National Intelligence, James Clapper—published after the reports by the Times and the Guardian—said that the fact that the N.S.A. works to crack encrypted data was "not news," Holt said, correctly, that "if in the process they degrade the security of the encryption we all use, it's a net national disservice."

The upshot is that it is now known that "the N.S.A. cannot be trusted on the issue of cyber security," said Soghoian. He continued, "My sincere hope is that the N.S.A. loses its shine. They're the bad guy; they're breaking into systems; they're exploiting vulnerabilities." It's conceivable that they have good intentions. And yet, Soghoian continued, "they act like any other hacker. They steal data. They read private communications." With that methodology, how easy can it be,

2015

Terrorist attacks in France reignite fears of domestic terrorist violence

The PATRIOT Act is replaced by the USA Freedom Act

Federal Courts order Apple, Inc. to create a new operation system that would enable federal investigators to bypass security on an iPhone.

continued

though, to give the agency the benefit of the doubt? As many have, Thomas Drake compared the worldview of what he calls the "rogue agency" to the total surveillance of George Orwell's "1984," in which the only way to escape was "to cower in a corner. I don't want to live like that. I've already lived that and it's not pleasant."

The Snowden leaks reinvigorated the encryption debate and the revelation that companies guaranteeing privacy to their customers had willingly (or forcibly) given customer data to the NSA constituted a major public relations problem for some of the nation's largest Internet service corporations. In *ProPublica* journalists indicated that some of the companies involved, Google, Yahoo, and Facebook, had petitioned the government to reveal more details about the secret requests that the NSA and GCHQ had made to their companies. With the NSA able to provide court orders from FISA, despite an inability to demonstrate reasonable suspicion to suggest that such information gathering would aid in any specific investigation, the companies felt caught between their promises to consumers and the need to aid in any legal investigation.

The Snowden leaks, however, resulting in a short-lived surge of public concern about state snooping and empowered companies to take a more affirmative stance on privacy rights. Microsoft released a statement in December of 2013, promising to fight any NSA information requests in the courts as well as to commit to a higher level of encryption for consumer data. Google Inc. and Yahoo made similar promises to their customers, to resist state requests for consumer data while also investing in encryption systems capable of standing up to the NSA's encryption assault.

Further, reporters revealed that a small handful of companies had already refused to comply with NSA requests, citing privacy concerns. For in-

The FCC publishes official rules of "neutrality"

2016

The EU establishes the General Data Protection Regulation (GDPR), described as the strongest digital data privacy law in the world

stance, the email encryption companies Lavabit and Silent Circle, shut down their email programs rather than submitting to NSA demands.

In a letter to customers about the decision to end their encrypted service, Lavabit founder Ladar Levison wrote,

"Without Congressional action or a strong judicial precedent, I would strongly recommend against anyone trusting their private data to a company with physical ties to the United States."

In a statement on the issue sent to *ProPublica* by the Office of the Director of National Intelligence in 2013, the agency argued:

> *"It should hardly be surprising that our intelligence agencies seek ways to counteract our adversaries' use of encryption. Throughout history, nations have used encryption to protect their secrets, and today, terrorists, cybercriminals, human traffickers and others also use code to hide their activities. Our intelligence community would not be doing its job if we did not try to counter that."*[126]

The Snowden leaks did lead to tension between consumers and the companies providing data services, but also to an erosion of faith in the ability of companies and the government to adequately protect data. *Pew Research* reports from 2015 indicate that only 6 percent of Americans reported feeling "very confident" in government agencies to keep records private and secure, while 76 percent reported being either "not too confident" or "not at all confident" that records of their activities would remain secure from online advertisers, while 69 percent reported little confidence in the privacy and security of social media sites. Overall, only 9 percent of Americans believed they still had "a lot" of control over how much

2017   The "Vault 7" secrets, a leak of 9,000 CIA documents, reveal details of the CIA's attempts to break through encryption used by Internet

President Trump appoints Ajit Pai to head the FCC, who abolishes the FCC neutrality protections

information is collected about them and how such information was being used.

Similarly, the revelations of corporate and government interception changed public behavior online. Though only 7 percent made any serious changes to their Internet or cellphone use out of fear of being tracked, a significantly larger number of Americans engaged in what *Pew Research* analysts called "obfuscation tactics" to protect their personal information. For instance, nearly 23 percent had decided against using a website that asked for their name, while 24 percent had given inaccurate or misleading information about themselves online.[127] However, by 2017, Americans were still divided, overall, on whether the state should be able to break encryption to investigate crimes or handle national security issues. A 2017 *Pew* poll found that 46 percent believed that the government should have the ability to access encrypted data, whereas 44 percent wanted companies to use encryption tools that were unbreakable by law enforcement or state agencies.[128]

As with many other facets of the privacy and security debate, the divide in public perception is related to an overall lack of clarity and an inability to resolve key questions. Although the public, in general, values privacy and does not want anyone, including the government, to intrude on their privacy or encroach on their civil liberties, it is impossible for most Americans to determine when and if the government is telling the truth when it says that it needs to use or have certain tools to combat existing dangers. Therefore, the question of encryption is determined to a large extent on whether Americans were willing to trust the government and whether they believed, as the government claimed, that encryption posed a danger to national security.

Congress debates whether or not to renew the controversial Section 702 FISA Amendment used to authorize NSA domestic intelligence operations since 2008

CONCLUSION

The Snowden leaks and reports on government efforts to undermine data encryption intensified the debate over digital security and privacy rights, but did little to influence policy. The surge in public concern did motivate new policies from companies competing for consumers as web service providers sought to appeal to security and privacy-minded customers by marketing their commitment to privacy, even from the government. The public remained largely divided on the encryption issue, and nearly evenly split on whether the government should be allowed and empowered to bypass encryption in cases involving national security issues.

United States President George W. Bush shakes hands with U.S. Senator Arlen Specter after signing H.R. 3199, the USA PATRIOT Improvement and Reauthorization Act of 2005 in the East Room of the White House.

1788 State legislatures ratify the U.S. Constitution, establishing the basic precedent for all future constitutional law

1791 The U.S. Congress ratifies the Bill of Rights, creating the first 10 amendments to the United States Constitution

DISCUSSION QUESTIONS

- Should encryption systems include a back door or master key to allow federal agents to access encrypted information? Why or why not?
- Should Americans use encryption to protect their personal data? Explain your answer.
- Should web and Internet-service companies voluntarily provide consumer information to the government? Why or why not?
- Should a company notify consumers if the courts or federal government order the company to turn over customer records? Explain your position.

Works Used

Ball, James, Borger, Julian, and Glenn Greenwald. "Revealed: how US and UK spy agencies defeat internet privacy and security." *The Guardian*. Guardian News and Media. Sept. 6, 2013. Web. 29 Oct. 2017.

Brandom, Russell. "Someone (probably the NSA) has been hiding viruses in hard drive firmware." *The Verge*. Vox Media. Feb. 16, 2015. Web. 3 Nov. 2017.

"Inside the NSA's War on Internet Security." *Der Spiegel*. Spiegel Online. Dec. 28, 2014. Web. 4 Nov. 2017.

Larson, Jeff. "Revealed: The NSA's Secret Campaign to Crack, Undermine Internet Security." *ProPublica*. ProPublica, Inc. Sept. 5, 2013. Web. 29 Oct. 2017.

Lee, Micah. "No Really, the NSA Can't Brute Force Your Crypto." *Micahflee.com*. Micah Lee's Blog.

1868 The 14th Amendment to the U.S. Constitution guarantees all citizens the right to due process under the law

1890 Warren and Brandeis publish "The Right to Privacy" in the *Harvard Law Review*

Madden, Mary, and Lee Rainie. "Americans' Attitudes About Privacy, Security and Surveillance." *Pew Research*. Pew Research Center. Internet and Technology. May 20, 2015. Web. 3 Nov. 2017.

Menn, Joseph. "Distrustful U.S. allies force spy agency to back down in encryption fight." *Reuters*. Thomson Reuters. Sept. 21, 2017. Web. 3 Nov. 2017.

Olmstead, Kenneth and Aaron Smith. "Americans and Cybersecurity." *Pew Research*. Pew Research Center. Jan. 26, 2017. Web. 4 Nov. 2017.

Perlroth, Nicole, Larson, Jeff, and Scott Shane. "N.S.A. Able to Foil Basic Safeguards of Privacy on Web." *New York Times*. New York Times Company. Sept. 5, 2013. Web. 29 Oct. 2017.

1923 *Meyer v. Nebraska* establishes that the 14th Amendment guarantees privileges of citizenship

1928 *Olmstead v. United States* rules that wiretapping is not a form of search and seizure defined by the 14th Amendment

Introduction

This chapter discusses the efforts of privacy advocates, such as the ACLU, and a number of senators and representatives, such as Oregon Senator Ron Wyden, to promote privacy rights reform in the U.S. Congress, or through executive policy. Wyden, a pioneer in privacy rights and a long-time champion of progressive reforms in his home state, initially supported the PATRIOT Act (see Chapter 12) and the overall shift towards security-minded policies that it heralded, but later came to be one of the PATRIOT Act's strongest and most dedicated critics. In Wyden's estimation, the PATRIOT Act had essentially opened the door to a whole host of abuses and governmental programs that violated decades of advocacy and legislation on personal privacy. He strongly opposed reauthorizing the PATRIOT Act's most controversial provisions in 2007 and again in 2011 and had worked to create several bills designed to strengthen privacy law, though each effort failed to gain sufficient support to become law.

The source document for this chapter is a December 2013 article from *The New Yorker*, "State of Deception: Why Won't the President Rein in the Intelligence Community?" written by political journalist Ryan Lizza. In the comprehensive article, featuring interviews with Wyden and other legislators and a detailed account of many different privacy rights controversies over the years, Lizza traces the history of Wyden's career and rise to become one of the chief opponents of the post-privacy national security policies used by Bush and Obama. Lizza then discusses some of the factors that had mitigated public support for intelligence and privacy policy reform over the years.

1934

The Federal Communications Commission (FCC) is established under the Federal Communications Act (FCA)

1942

Goldman v. United States rules that using electronic listening devices does not violate the 14th Amendment

Topics covered in this chapter include:

- The PATRIOT Act
- The ACLU
- The 9/11 terrorist attacks
- Privacy rights legislation
- The Snowden leaks
- NSA spying

This Chapter Discusses the Following Source Document:
Lizza, Ryan. "State of Deception: Why Won't the President Rein in the Intelligence Community?" *The New Yorker*. Conde Nast. Dec. 16, 2013.

The Advocates
Privacy Advocates

By the time the infamous Edward Snowden leaks revealed, to the world, details about the United States' domestic surveillance programs, Senator Ron Wyden of Oregon, had been campaigning for intelligence-industry reform and increased privacy protections for more than a decade. In the 2000s and 2010s, Wyden led efforts to curtail state surveillance programs, to increase transparency, to strengthen judicial oversight, and to enhance civil liberties protections, becoming one of the strongest congressional critics of the Bush and Obama-era intelligence policies.

Born in Wichita, Kansas, Wyden obtained a political science degree from Stanford University, and a Juris Doctorate from the Oregon School of Law. Remaining in Oregon, Wyden specialized in nonprofit and social

CodePink protesters hold signs in the audience as Richard Salgado, director of law enforcement and information security matters for Google, Inc, testifies before the Senate Judiciary Committee's Privacy, Technology, and the Law Subcommittee November 13, 2013 in Washington, DC. The committee heard testimony on the topic of The Surveillance Transparency Act of 2013. (Photo by Win McNamee/Getty Images)

1951 *Dennis v. United States* rules that government limits to speech is legal only to prevent a threat to public safety or security

1959 *Barenblatt v. United States* rules that it's legal to order people to reveal personal details if national threat is perceived

services law, working with the Oregon Legal Service Center for the Elderly and other organizations, and teaching courses in gerontology. Wyden ran for election to the House of Representatives in 1980, for Oregon's third district, winning his first election with 71 percent of the vote at only 31 years old. A popular politician in his district, Wyden won reelection seven times, serving from 1981 to 1996, before he decided to leave the house, running for a disputed Senate seat against Republican Gordon Smith. In the 1996 election, Wyden won a close race, defeating Smith by 2 percent of the vote. As a Senator, Wyden made a name for himself as a progressive politician, especially on Civil Rights issues. He was the first senator to endorse same-sex marriage rights and was an early supporter of the Open Internet movement.

Wyden was one of only 10 senators to vote against reauthorizing the PATRIOT Act in 2006, and he campaigned against the 2011 reauthorization as well, arguing, on both occasions, that provisions of the bill were being used to violate civil liberties. Journalists at the *Washington Post* noted that Wyden had been giving "dire but vague" warnings about threats to personal privacy for years, but that few in the public were aware of the meaning of his warnings until the Snowden leaks revealed the details of the government's surveillance programs.[129] In 2011, Wyden gave a speech to the Senate about the "so-called" Secret Law, an interpretation of PATRIOT Act provisions, secretly developed and used by the federal government that, Wyden argued, posed a threat to personal liberties:

> *M. President, the United States Senate is now preparing to pass another four-year extension of the USA PATRIOT Act. I have served on the Intelligence Committee for a decade, and I want to deliver a warning this afternoon: when the American people find out how their government has secretly interpreted the PATRIOT Act, they will be stunned and they will*

1965
Griswold v. CT rules in favor of married couples' right to privacy

1967
Katz v. United States rules wiretaps a form of search and seizure

Willis Ware of RAND Corporation writes *Security and Privacy in Computer*

be angry. And they will be asking senators, "Did you know what this law actually permits?" "Why didn't you know before you voted on it?" The fact is that anyone can read the plain text of the PATRIOT Act, and yet many members of Congress have no idea how the law is being secretly interpreted by the executive branch, because that interpretation is classified.

It's almost as if there are two PATRIOT Acts, and many members of Congress haven't even read the one that matters. Our constituents, of course, are totally in the dark. Members of the public have no access to the executive branch's secret legal interpretations, so they have no idea what their government thinks this law means.[130]

Wyden's campaign was largely ignored until the 2013 leaks from Edward Snowden revealed details of the secret interpretation of PATRIOT Act law that Wyden had been campaigning against. The Snowden controversy lingered throughout 2014 and into 2015, dominating public debate and shifting public opinion, but arguably not to the degree that Wyden and other committed privacy advocates might have hoped.

In this article by from the December 16, 2013 issue of *The New Yorker*, journalist Ryan Lizza follow's Wyden's career through the U.S. House of Representatives and the U.S. Senate and investigates the Obama administration's gradual embrace of the national security policies of the previous administration.

1968 The Omnibus Crime Control Act holds that police needed to obtain a warrant before engaging in wire-

1969 Joseph Licklider creates the Advanced Research Projects Agency Network (ARPANET), which was

STATE OF DECEPTION:
WHY WON'T THE PRESIDENT REIN IN THE INTELLIGENCE COMMUNITY?

by Ryan Lizza

The New Yorker, **December 16, 2013**

Source Document

On March 12, 2013, James R. Clapper appeared before the Senate Select Committee on Intelligence to discuss the threats facing America. Clapper, who is seventy-two, is a retired Air Force general and Barack Obama's director of National Intelligence, in charge of overseeing the National Security Agency, the Central Intelligence Agency, and fourteen other U.S. spy agencies. Clapper is bald, with a gray goatee and rimless spectacles, and his affect is intimidatingly bureaucratic. The fifteen-member Intelligence Committee was created in the nineteen-seventies, after a series of investigations revealed that the N.S.A. and the C.I.A. had, for years, been illegally spying on Americans. The panel's mission is to conduct "vigilant legislative oversight" of the intelligence community, but more often it treats senior intelligence officials like matinée idols. As the senators took turns at the microphone, greeting Clapper with anodyne statements and inquiries, he obligingly led them on a tour of the dangers posed by homegrown extremists, far-flung terrorist groups, and emerging nuclear powers.

"This hearing is really a unique opportunity to inform the American public to the extent we can about the threats we face as a nation, and worldwide," Dianne Feinstein, a California Democrat and the committee's chairman, said at one point. She asked committee members to "refrain from asking questions here that have classified answers." Saxby Chambliss, a Georgia Republican, asked about the lessons of the terrorist attack in Benghazi. Marco Rubio, a Florida Republican, asked about the dangers of Egypt's Muslim Brotherhood.

Toward the end of the hearing, Feinstein turned to Senator Ron Wyden, of Oregon, also a Democrat, who had a final question. The two senators have been friends. Feinstein held a baby shower for Wyden and his wife, Nancy Bass, before the birth of twins, in 2007. But, since then, their increasingly divergent views on intelligence policy have strained the relationship. "This is an issue where we just have a difference of opinion," Wyden told me. Feinstein often uses the committee to bolster the tools that spy agencies say they need

1971 The Pentagon Papers leaks from the press raise the issue of the Freedom of the Press versus the privacy of the government to conceal information about national security operations

1972 *Eisenstadt v. Baird* rules that the right to privacy applies to individuals

continued

to protect the country, and Wyden has been increasingly concerned about privacy rights. For almost a decade, he has been trying to force intelligence officials like Clapper to be more forthcoming about spy programs that gather information about Americans who have no connection to terrorism.

Wyden had an uneasy kind of vindication in June, three months after Clapper's appearance, when Edward Snowden, a former contractor at the N.S.A., leaked pages and pages of classified N.S.A. documents. They showed that, for the past twelve years, the agency has been running programs that secretly collect detailed information about the phone and Internet usage of Americans. The programs have been plagued by compliance issues, and the legal arguments justifying the surveillance regime have been kept from view. Wyden has long been aware of the programs and of the agency's appalling compliance record, and has tried everything short of disclosing classified information to warn the public. At the March panel, he looked down at Clapper as if he were about to eat a long-delayed meal.

Wyden estimates that he gets about fifteen minutes a year to ask questions of top intelligence officials at open hearings. With the help of his intelligence staffer, John Dickas, a thirty- five-year-old from Beaverton, Oregon, whom Wyden calls "the hero of the intelligence-reform movement," Wyden often spends weeks preparing his questions. He and Dickas look for opportunities to interrogate officials on the gaps between what they say in public and what they say in classified briefings. At a technology conference in Nevada the previous summer, General Keith Alexander, the director of the N.S.A., had said that "the story that we have millions or hundreds of millions of dossiers on people is absolutely false." Wyden told me recently, "It sure didn't sound like the world I heard about in private." For months, he tried to get a clarification from the N.S.A. about exactly what Alexander had meant. Now he had the opportunity to ask Clapper in public. As a courtesy, he had sent him the question the day before.

Wyden leaned forward and read Alexander's comment. Then he asked, "What I wanted to see is if you could give me a yes or no answer to the question 'Does the N.S.A. collect any type of data at all on millions or hundreds of millions of Americans?'"

Clapper slouched in his chair. He touched the fingertips of his right hand to his forehead and made a fist with his left hand.

"No, sir," he said. He gave a quick shake of his head and looked down at the table.

1974

The Watergate Scandal results in the revelation that the CIA had been conducting widespread surveillance of American dissidents and foreign leaders without judicial oversight

The Privacy Act is established

"State of Deception: Why Won't the President Rein in the Intelligence Community?"
continued

"It does not?" Wyden asked, with exaggerated surprise.

"Not wittingly," Clapper replied. He started scratching his forehead and looked away from Wyden. "There are cases where they could inadvertently perhaps collect, but not wittingly."

Wyden told me, "The answer was obviously misleading, false." Feinstein said, "I was startled by the answer." In Washington, Snowden's subsequent leaks created the most intense debate about the tradeoffs between national security and individual liberty since the attacks of September 11th. The debate will likely continue. According to Feinstein, Snowden took "millions of pages" of documents. Only a small fraction have become public. Under directions that the White House issued in June, Clapper declassified hundreds of pages of additional N.S.A. documents about the domestic-surveillance programs, and these have only begun to be examined by the press. They present a portrait of an intelligence agency that has struggled but often failed to comply with court-imposed rules established to monitor its most sensitive activities. The N.S.A. is generally authorized to collect any foreign intelligence it wants—including conversations from the cell phone of Germany's Chancellor, Angela Merkel—but domestic surveillance is governed by strict laws. Since 2001, the N.S.A. has run four surveillance programs that, in an effort to detect terrorist plots, have swept up the contents of the phone and Internet communications of hundreds of thousands of Americans, and collected the telephone and Internet metadata of many more Americans. (Metadata is data about data. For telephone records, it can include numbers dialled, the date, time, and length of calls, and the unique identification of a cell phone. Internet metadata can include e-mail and I.P. addresses, along with location information, Web sites visited, and many other electronic traces left when a person goes online.)

Soon after the March hearing, Dickas called a senior member of Clapper's staff and requested that Clapper acknowledge that his statement had been wrong. Through his staff member, Clapper declined. In July, however, after Snowden's leaks, Clapper finally wrote to the committee and offered a formal retraction: "My response was clearly erroneous, for which I apologize." Wyden told me, "There is not a shred of evidence that the statement ever would've been corrected absent the Snowden disclosures."

1975   Senator Frank Church leads a series of hearings about the secret NSA SHAMROCK operation involved intercepting communications from American citizens

1978   Congress passes the 1978 FISA Act

continued

Wyden is now working on a bill that would ban the mass collection of phone records and reform the court that oversees the N.S.A.'s domestic surveillance. Feinstein, who has resisted most of Wyden's efforts at disclosure over the years, has put forward her own legislation, which would authorize the N.S.A. to continue bulk collection. Wyden dismisses her bill as "cosmetic stuff that just puts the old wine in a new bottle." Feinstein counters that it "puts some very stringent parameters on" the program. She adds, "Senator Wyden also calls it a 'surveillance program.' It's not a surveillance program—it is a data-collection program."

Feinstein and Clapper insist that Wyden's latest proposals would deprive the N.S.A. of crucial tools that it uses to disrupt terrorist plots. President Obama has been mostly silent on the issue. In August, he appointed a five-person panel to review intelligence policy, and the group is scheduled to issue recommendations by the end of the year. His decisions about what changes to endorse could determine whether his Presidency is remembered for rolling back one of the most controversial national-security policies of the Bush years or codifying it.

Wyden, who said that he has had "several spirited discussions" with Obama, is not optimistic. "It really seems like General Clapper, the intelligence leadership, and the lawyers drive this in terms of how decisions get made at the White House," he told me. It is evident from the Snowden leaks that Obama inherited a regime of dragnet surveillance that often operated outside the law and raised serious constitutional questions. Instead of shutting down or scaling back the programs, Obama has worked to bring them into narrow compliance with rules—set forth by a court that operates in secret—that often contradict the views on surveillance that he strongly expressed when he was a senator and a Presidential candidate.

"These are profoundly different visions," Wyden said, referring to his disagreements with Obama, Feinstein, and senior intelligence officials. "I start with the proposition that security and liberty are not mutually exclusive." He noted that General Alexander had an "exceptionally expansive vision" of what the N.S.A. should collect. I asked Wyden for his opinion of the members of the review panel, most of whom are officials with ties to the intelligence establishment. He smiled and raised his eyebrows. An aide said, "Hope springs eternal."

I—Is it Legal?

In 1961, when John F. Kennedy took office, he inherited a scheme from his

---

1980 | The Intelligence Oversight Act (IOA) updates legal standards

1981 | President Reagan's E.O. authorized wiretapping

1986 | The Electronic Communications Privacy Act is established

"State of Deception: Why Won't the President Rein in the Intelligence Community?"
continued

predecessor, Dwight Eisenhower, to invade Cuba with a small band of exiles and overthrow Fidel Castro. The plot, devised by the C.I.A. and carried out in April of that year, was a disaster: the invading forces, shepherded by C.I.A. operatives, were killed or captured, and Castro's stature increased.

The failed plot is richly documented in a 1979 book, "Bay of Pigs: The Untold Story," written by Senator Wyden's father, Peter. At the time of its release, the book, which won an Overseas Press Club award, was the most comprehensive account of the Bay of Pigs fiasco. (During a six-hour interview with Peter Wyden, Castro marvelled that the author "knows more about it than we do.") One recent morning, when Ron Wyden and I were sitting in his office discussing the N.S.A., he leaped out of his chair and walked across the room to a small bookshelf. "I want to show you something," he said, and handed me a tattered copy of his father's book. It describes how the C.I.A.'s arrogance and obsessive secrecy, combined with Kennedy's naïveté, led a young President to embrace a wildly flawed policy, resulting in an incident that the author likens to "Waterloo staged by the Marx Brothers." In Ron Wyden's view, the book explains a great deal about

the modern intelligence community and his approach to its oversight.

Wyden, a former college-basketball player, is a gangly six feet four and speaks in an incongruous high-pitched voice. He grew up in Palo Alto, California, and graduated from Stanford, where his mother was a librarian. He went to law school at the University of Oregon and, in 1972, worked as a volunteer on the campaign of Senator Wayne Morse. Morse, an Oregon Democrat, had been one of two senators to vote against the Gulf of Tonkin Resolution, eight years earlier, and became an outspoken opponent of the Vietnam War. The position had cost him the '68 race; the Republican Bob Packwood won. "Perhaps more than any other political figure I've either been around or studied, Morse embodied a sense of independence," Wyden said. "I thought, This is what public service is supposed to be about."

Wyden was Morse's expert on issues important to seniors in Oregon, and he later set up the Oregon chapter of the Gray Panthers, an organization that fought for seniors' rights. One of the earliest national newspaper stories about Wyden, which ran in the *Times* on January 7, 1979, described a victory that elderly Oregonians won in

1994 Netscape creates the "cookie" allowing computers to monitor Internet users

2001 The September 11 terrorist attacks result in Congress authorizing the Bush Administration to utilize military methods to combat terrorism

continued

the state legislature, where a Wyden-backed plan to allow non-dentists to fit and sell dentures was approved. "I think the measure really shows that senior citizens have bulging political biceps," Wyden told the *Times*.

The next year, at thirty-one, Wyden won a U.S. House seat in a Portland district. Although he focused on domestic issues, he entered politics just as major changes were taking place in the intelligence agencies. In the nineteen- seventies, a Senate committee chaired by Frank Church revealed widespread abuses at the N.S.A., the C.I.A., and other agencies, including active programs to spy on Americans. An N.S.A. program called Project SHAMROCK, which started shortly after the Second World War, had persuaded three major American telegraph companies to hand over most of their traffic. By the time the program was shut down, in 1975, the N.S.A. had collected information on some seventy-five thousand citizens. For many years, the information was shared with the C.I.A., which was running its own illegal domestic-intelligence program, Operation CHAOS.

The Church committee recommended not only sweeping reform of the laws governing the intelligence community but also a new system of oversight. Senator Walter Mondale, a member of the committee, said he worried about "another day and another President, another perceived risk and someone breathing hot down the neck of the military leader then in charge of the N.S.A." Under those circumstances, he feared, the N.S.A. "could be used by President 'A' in the future to spy upon the American people." He urged Congress to "very carefully define the law." In 1978, Congress passed the Foreign Intelligence Surveillance Act, or FISA, which forbade the intelligence agencies to spy on anyone in the U.S. unless they had probable cause to believe that the person was a "foreign power or the agent of a foreign power." The law set up the Foreign Intelligence Surveillance Court, and, in 1976, Congress created the Senate Select Committee on Intelligence. The N.S.A. and other spy agencies are instructed to keep the committee, as well as a similar one in the House, "fully and currently informed."

In 1995, Packwood resigned, after numerous women accused him of sexual harassment and assault, and Wyden won a special election, in 1996, to replace him. In early 2001, he landed a spot on the Intelligence Committee. His father had told him about how the intelligence community had stonewalled his requests for basic information for his book. Wyden soon encountered that opacity himself, he told me, especially after September 11th: "That really changed the debate."

The Bush administration secretly authorizes the President's Surveillance Program (PSP), utilizing E.O. 12333

The U.S. PATRIOT Act alters existing laws to facilitate better communication between the state's intelligence branches in the effort to combat terrorism

The Transportation Security Administration (TSA) is established, creating the "No Fly" and "Selectee" lists that limit the right to travel on airplanes in the United States

"State of Deception: Why Won't the President Rein in the Intelligence Community?"
continued

On October 13, 2001, fifty computer servers arrived at the N.S.A.'s headquarters, in Fort Meade, Maryland. The vender concealed the identity of the N.S.A. by selling the servers to other customers and then delivering the shipments to the spy agency under police escort. According to a 2009 working draft of a report by the N.S.A.'s inspector general, which Snowden provided to Glenn Greenwald, of the Guardian, their arrival marked the start of four of the most controversial surveillance programs in the agency's history—programs that, for the most part, are ongoing. At the time, the operation was code-named STARBURST.

In the days after 9/11, General Michael Hayden, the director of the N.S.A., was under intense pressure to intercept communications between Al Qaeda leaders abroad and potential terrorists inside the U.S. According to the inspector general's report, George Tenet, the director of the C.I.A., told Hayden that Vice-President Dick Cheney wanted to know "if N.S.A. could be doing more." Hayden noted the limitations of the FISA law, which prevented the N.S.A. from indiscriminately collecting electronic communications of Americans. The agency was legally vacuuming up just

about any foreign communications it wanted. But when it targeted one side of a call or an e-mail that involved someone in the U.S. the spy agency had to seek permission from the FISA court to conduct surveillance. Tenet later called Hayden back: Cheney wanted to know what else the N.S.A. might be able to do if Hayden was given authority that was not currently in the law.

Hayden resurrected a plan from the Clinton years. In the late fall of 1999, a large body of intelligence suggested that Osama bin Laden was planning multiple attacks around New Year's Eve. The Clinton Administration was desperate to discover links between Al Qaeda operatives and potential terrorists in the U.S., and N.S.A. engineers had an idea that they called "contact chaining." The N.S.A. had collected a trove of telephone metadata. According to the N.S.A. report, "Analysts would chain through masked U.S. telephone numbers to discover foreign connections to those numbers."

Officials apparently believed that, because the U.S. numbers were hidden, even from the analysts, the idea might pass legal scrutiny. But the Justice Department thought otherwise, and

2005

The PATRIOT Act was reauthorized without substantial changes as Congress favors security concerns over warnings that the law creates the potential for civil liberties violations

The *New York Times* publishes articles resulting from leaks revealing the secret President's Surveillance Program (PSP) established by the Bush administration

continued

in December of 1999 it advised the N.S.A. that the plan was tantamount to electronic surveillance under FISA: it was illegal for the N.S.A. to rummage through the phone records of Americans without a probable cause. Nonetheless, the concept of bulk collection and analysis of metadata was born. During several meetings at the White House in the fall of 2001, Hayden told Cheney that the FISA law was outdated. To collect the content of communications (what someone says in a phone call or writes in an e-mail) or the metadata of phone and Internet communications if one or both parties to the communication were in the U.S., he needed approval from the fisa court. Obtaining court orders usually took four to six weeks, and even emergency orders, which were sometimes granted, took a day or more. Hayden and Cheney discussed ways the N.S.A. could collect content and metadata without a court order.

The Vice-President's lawyer, David Addington, drafted language authorizing the N.S.A. to collect four streams of data without the FISA court's permission: the content of Internet and phone communications, and Internet and phone metadata. The White House secretly argued that Bush was allowed to circumvent the FISA law governing domestic surveillance thanks to the extraordinary power granted by Congress's resolution, on September 14th, declaring war against Al Qaeda. On October 4th, Bush signed the surveillance authorization. It became known inside the government as the P.S.P., the President's Surveillance Program. Tenet authorized an initial twenty-five million dollars to fund it. Hayden stored the document in his office safe.

Over the weekend of October 6, 2001, the three major telephone companies—A. T. & T., Verizon, and BellSouth, which for decades have had classified relationships with the N.S.A.—began providing wiretap recordings of N.S.A. targets. The content of e-mails followed shortly afterward. By November, a couple of weeks after the secret computer servers were delivered, phone and Internet metadata from the three phone companies began flowing to the N.S.A. servers over classified lines or on compact disks. Twenty N.S.A. employees, working around the clock in a new Metadata Analysis Center, at the agency's headquarters, conducted the kind of sophisticated contact chaining of terrorist networks that the Clinton Justice Department had disallowed. On October 31st, the cover term for the program was changed to STELLARWIND.

Nearly everyone involved wondered whether the program was legal. Hayden didn't ask his own general

2007

The Bush Administration plans to make data taken from spy satellites available to law enforcement to be used to conduct domestic surveillance

2008

Congress passes Section 702, or the FISA Amendment Act, which is used to permit a massive NSA and CIA domestic surveillance program

"State of Deception: Why Won't the President Rein in the Intelligence Community?"
continued

counsel, Robert Deitz, for his opinion until after Bush signed the order. (Deitz told Hayden he believed that it was legal.) John Yoo, a Justice Department lawyer, wrote a legal opinion, the full text of which has never been disclosed, arguing that the plan was legal. When Deitz tried to obtain the text, Addington refused his request but read him some excerpts over the phone. Hayden never asked for the official legal opinion and never saw it, according to the inspector general's report. In May, 2002, the N.S.A. briefed Judge Colleen Kollar-Kotelly, the incoming chief of the Foreign Intelligence Surveillance Court, about the program. She was shown a short memo from the Department of Justice defending its legality, but wasn't allowed to keep a copy. The N.S.A.'s inspector general later said he found it "strange that N.S.A. was told to execute a secret program that everyone knew presented legal questions, without being told the underpinning legal theory."

Meanwhile, Wyden, on the Intelligence Committee, found himself involved in the first debate about the U.S.A. PATRIOT Act, a law that the Bush White House pushed through Congress in October, 2001, and which included major changes to FISA. Tucked into the bill, in Section 215, was something called the "business records" provision. It allowed the government to seize "any tangible thing" from a company as long as officials proved to the FISA court that the item was "sought for an investigation to protect against international terrorism."

Of the many new powers that Congress granted law enforcement through the PATRIOT Act—roving wiretaps, delayed-notice search warrants—this was not the most controversial provision at the time. It was often innocuously described as the "library records" provision, conjuring the notion that the government should know if someone is checking out bomb-making books. Some members of Congress were satisfied with the wording because Representative Jim Sensenbrenner, a Republican who was the chairman of the Judiciary Committee, and who wrote the PATRIOT Act, had defeated an effort by the Bush White House to make the provision even more expansive. Wyden voted for the legislation, which included the most substantial modifications of FISA since 1978, when it was enacted, but he helped attach "sunsets" to many provisions, including Section 215, that hadn't been thoroughly examined: in five years, Congress would have to vote again, to reauthorize them. As Wyden

2012 The Obama Administration proposes a Consumer Privacy Bill of Rights guaranteeing individuals the right to greater control over the use of their digital data

2013 The *Guardian* and the *Washington Post* publish the first series of articles derived from leaked NSA and CIA documents delivered by Edward Snowden

continued

later wrote, "The idea was that these provisions would be more thoughtfully debated at a later, less panicked time." The PATRIOT Act passed overwhelmingly. (Russ Feingold, of Wisconsin, was the only senator to oppose it.)

Three months later, the Defense Department started a new program with the Orwellian name Total Information Awareness. T.I.A. was based inside the Pentagon's Information Awareness Office, which was headed by Admiral John Poindexter. In the nineteen-eighties, Poindexter had been convicted, and then acquitted, of perjury for his role in the Iran-Contra scandal. He wanted to create a system that could mine a seemingly infinite number of government and private-sector databases in order to detect suspicious activity and preëmpt attacks. The T.I.A. system was intended to collect information about the faces, fingerprints, irises, and even the gait of suspicious people. In 2002 and 2003, Wyden attacked the program as a major affront to privacy rights and urged that it be shut down.

In the summer of 2003, while Congress debated a crucial vote on the future of the plan, Wyden instructed an intern to sift through the Pentagon's documents about T.I.A. The intern discovered that one of the program's ideas was to create a futures market

in which anonymous users could place bets on events such as assassinations and terrorist attacks, and get paid on the basis of whether the events occurred. Wyden called Byron Dorgan, a Democratic senator from North Dakota, who was also working to kill the program. "Byron, we've got what we need to win this," he told him. "You and I should make this public." Twenty-four hours after they exposed the futures-market idea at a press conference, Total Information Awareness was dead. Poindexter soon resigned.

It was Wyden's first real victory on the Intelligence Committee. "If you spend enough time digging into these documents and doing the work, it can pay off," Wyden told me. "The one advantage that I have, being on the Intelligence Committee, is a chance to get access to information. But you really have to fight for it."

In the first season of "Homeland," the Showtime drama about the C.I.A. and terrorism, the protagonist, an agent named Carrie Mathison, conducts warrantless surveillance on an American whom she suspects is a terrorist. Saul Berenson, her boss at the C.I.A., realizes that it's problematic, so he persuades a judge on the FISA court to give the operation the court's legal imprimatur. Like many of the show's plot twists, the episode seemed implausible. But it is

The Senate Judiciary committee holds hearings to determine if the executive surveillance operations carried out under the PATRIOT Act were a violation of constitutional law

Snowden leaks reveal that the NSA and CIA had been attempting to force corporations to provide a backdoor to encryption systems that would allow federal agents to bypass consumer encryption

"State of Deception: Why Won't the President Rein in the Intelligence Community?"
continued

a pale shadow of what happened with the Bush-era surveillance programs. Between 2001 and 2007, according to the inspector general's report, before the four STELLARWIND programs had all gained a legal legitimacy, the N.S.A. wiretapped more than twenty-six hundred American telephones and four hundred American e-mail accounts, and collected phone and Internet metadata from hundreds of millions more.

During that time, an expanding circle of people in Washington, including members of Congress, lawyers at the Justice Department, reporters, and, eventually, the public, gradually became aware of the Bush programs. Jay Rockefeller, then the top Democrat on the Intelligence Committee, was one of the first officials to express dissent. On July 17, 2003, Rockefeller came back shaken from a White House meeting with Cheney, who had briefed him on the N.S.A. programs. While Congress was shutting down the Total Information Awareness program, the four phone- and Internet-spying programs under STELLARWIND had been up and running for about two years. Rockefeller drafted a handwritten letter to Cheney. "Clearly, the activities we discussed raise profound oversight issues," he

wrote. "As you know, I am neither a technician nor an attorney. Given the security restrictions associated with this information, and my inability to consult staff or counsel on my own, I feel unable to fully evaluate, much less endorse these activities. As I reflected on the meeting today, and the future we face, John Poindexter's TIA project sprung to mind, exacerbating my concern regarding the direction the Administration is moving with regard to security, technology, and surveillance."

Some Administration officials were concerned, too. In early March of 2004, Deputy Attorney General James Comey, who was serving as the acting Attorney General while John Ashcroft was in the hospital, determined that three of the four STELLARWIND programs were legal, but that the program involving the bulk collection of Internet metadata was not. Cheney summoned Comey to the White House and tried to change his mind, telling him that his decision would put thousands of lives at risk. Comey wouldn't budge. Bush then sent two top White House aides to the hospital to visit Ashcroft, who was in the intensive-care unit after surgery. Ashcroft refused to overrule Comey, and the White House decided that Alberto Gonzales, Bush's counsel,

2015

Terrorist attacks in France reignite fears of domestic terrorist violence

The PATRIOT Act is replaced by the USA Freedom Act

Federal Courts order Apple, Inc. to create a new operation system that would enable federal investigators to bypass security on an iPhone.

continued

would sign a new authorization instead. Addington called Hayden the following day to make sure that he would accept the document despite the opposition of the Justice Department. "Will you do it?" he asked, according to the N.S.A. report. Hayden told me that he agreed, because he "had multiple previous such orders from D.O.J." and "strong congressional support," and also had in mind "the deaths of nearly two hundred Spaniards that morning in an Al Qaeda terrorist attack in Madrid."

Lawyers many tiers below the Attorney General slowly became aware that the N.S.A. was working on something that people referred to simply as "the program." Not long after Comey's refusal, one Justice lawyer, Thomas M. Tamm, picked up a pay phone in a Metro station and called the *Times*. He told the newspaper everything he knew about STELLARWIND. As the paper began investigating Tamm's allegations, the N.S.A. decided that the STELLARWIND programs needed a legal justification that carried more weight than a letter from the President. Like the C.I.A.'s Saul Berenson in "Homeland," the agency asked the FISA court to make the programs legal. (As of March 26th, the Internet-metadata program had been suspended.) According to the N.S.A. report, lawyers at the N.S.A. and the Justice Department "immediately began efforts to re-create this authority."

Over the summer, on two consecutive Saturdays, Hayden met with Judge Kollar-Kotelly, of the FISA court, to press for new authority to run the Internet-metadata program. On July 14, 2004, she gave her assent. She cited a contentious 1979 Supreme Court case, *Smith v. Maryland*, which held that police could place a type of monitor called a "pen register" on a suspect's phone without a warrant. But the order didn't target a single device; it allowed the N.S.A. to collect the metadata of all U.S. devices communicating with devices outside the U.S. According to the N.S.A. report, "The order essentially gave N.S.A. the same authority to collect bulk Internet metadata that it had under the P.S.P.," Bush's original, warrantless plan. (Later, Judge Kollar-Kotelly reportedly expressed misgivings about the N.S.A.'s misuse of the program, even shutting it down at one point, when she learned that the N.S.A. might have been overstepping its authority.)

On December 16, 2005, the *Times* broke the news about some aspects of the President's four-pronged surveillance program. After the story appeared, Bush addressed the country to defend the P.S.P., calling it the "Terrorist Surveillance Program." He claimed that it had been "thoroughly reviewed by the Justice Department and N.S.A.'s top legal officials," and that N.S.A. analysts "receive extensive training to insure they perform their

The FCC publishes official rules of "neutrality"

2016

The EU establishes the General Data Protection Regulation (GDPR), described as the strongest digital data privacy law in the world

"State of Deception: Why Won't the President Rein in the Intelligence Community?"
continued

duties consistent with the letter and intent of the authorization." Wyden didn't know whether to be more shocked by the details of the N.S.A. program or by the way he learned about it. "I read about it in the *New York Times*," he told me.

The *Times* had uncovered many details about the two programs that collected the content of e-mails and phone calls, and won a Pulitzer for its investigation, but the two metadata programs run by the N.S.A. were still largely unknown, even to most members of the Senate Intelligence Committee. Some details of the metadata programs soon appeared in the *Times*, in *USA Today*, and in a story by Seymour Hersh in this magazine. But the Bush Administration never officially confirmed the existence of the programs, which remained secret until this year.

II—Obama Signs On

Even without a full picture of the programs, two senators who were not on the Intelligence Committee became intense critics of N.S.A. domestic surveillance: Barack Obama and Joe Biden. In May, 2006, after the USA Today article appeared, Biden said it was frightening to learn that the government was collecting telephone records. "I don't have to listen to your phone calls to know what you're doing," he told CBS News. "If I know every single phone call you made, I'm able to determine every single person you talked to. I can get a pattern about your life that is very, very intrusive."

Obama's objections to domestic surveillance stretched back even further. In 2003, as a Senate candidate, he called the PATRIOT Act "shoddy and dangerous." And at the 2004 Democratic Convention, in the speech that effectively launched his eventual campaign for President, he took aim at the "library records" provision of the law. "We worship an awesome God in the blue states, and we don't like federal agents poking around our libraries in the red states," he declared. In 2005, when he arrived in Washington, Obama became one of Wyden's new allies in his attempts to reform the law. The PATRIOT Act was up for reauthorization, and, at Wyden's urging, the Senate was trying to scale back the "library records" section. One of the first bills that Obama co-sponsored, the Security and Freedom Enhancement Act, would have required that the government present "specific and articulable facts" if it wanted a court order for records, a much higher standard than the existing one.

2017

The "Vault 7" secrets, a leak of 9,000 CIA documents, reveal details of the CIA's attempts to break through encryption used by Internet

President Trump appoints Ajit Pai to head the FCC, who abolishes the FCC neutrality protections

continued

Obama and several other senators, including John Kerry, now the Secretary of State, and Chuck Hagel, the current Secretary of Defense, laid out their legal case against the provision in a letter to colleagues on December 14, 2005. The government could "obtain library, medical and gun records and other sensitive personal information under Section 215 of the PATRIOT Act on a mere showing that those records are relevant to an authorized intelligence investigation," they wrote. It allowed "government fishing expeditions targeting innocent Americans. We believe the government should be required to convince a judge that the records they are seeking have some connection to a suspected terrorist or spy." The following day, on the Senate floor, Obama said that the provision "seriously jeopardizes the rights of all Americans and the ideals America stands for."

The Bush White House fought Obama's changes, but offered a few minor concessions. Most notably, a business that received a demand for records could challenge in court a nondisclosure agreement that accompanied the demand. That was enough to placate some Democrats, including Obama. Wyden objected that the change did nothing to address Obama's concerns, but the reauthorization of the PATRIOT Act passed the Senate on March 1, 2006.

Wyden, eight other Democrats, and one Independent voted against it; Obama and Biden voted for it. Bush signed the law on March 9th.

Wyden later learned that, while he and Obama were fighting to curtail Section 215, the N.S.A.'s lawyers were secretly arguing before the FISA court that the provision should allow the N.S.A. to legally collect the phone records of all Americans. The lawyers, encouraged by their success in retroactively legalizing the Internet-metadata program, believed that they could persuade the FISA court to force phone companies to regularly hand over their entire databases. At the FISA court, there are no lawyers challenging the government's arguments; all the N.S.A. needed to do was convince a single judge. Had Obama's language been adopted, the N.S.A.'s case would have collapsed.

Just after noon on May 24, 2006, the FISA court issued a secret opinion ratifying the N.S.A.'s audacious proposal. It became known as the Business Records Order. That bland language concealed the fact that the court's opinion dramatically reinterpreted the scope of the "library records" provision. The FISA court essentially gave the N.S.A. authority to place a pen register on everyone's phone. Anytime an American citizen makes a call, it is logged into an N.S.A.

Congress debates whether or not to renew the controversial Section 702 FISA Amendment used to authorize NSA domestic intelligence operations since 2008

"State of Deception: Why Won't the President Rein in the Intelligence Community?"
continued

database. The court required some new oversight by the Justice Department and new rules for accessing the database, but it was a nearly complete victory for the agency. The change was unknown to most members of Congress, including Obama and Wyden, who had just finished debating the PATRIOT Act. "What do I know?" Wyden would tell people who asked him about sensitive national- security issues. "I'm only on the Intelligence Committee."

At the time, the public and Congress were understandably focused on Bush's warrantless wiretapping, and only a few officials understood the full details of the phone-metadata program. Wyden began asking questions. In June, 2006, after some stonewalling, the Bush Administration began providing summary briefings to the committee about the program. Wyden wasn't allowed to bring any staff, and the N.S.A. didn't respond to many of his follow-up questions. It wasn't until the next January, after the Democrats took over Congress and were able to change the rules so that Wyden could bring Dickas to the briefings, that he fully understood what the agency was doing with the Business Records Order. He was stunned. "Look at the gap between what people think the law is and how it's been secretly interpreted," he said.

"Holy Toledo!"

The National Counterterrorism Center is in an X-shaped building, known as Liberty Crossing, that is disguised as a suburban office park. It sits on a hill a few miles from C.I.A. headquarters, in northern Virginia. The center was created in 2003, at the recommendation of the 9/11 Commission, which concluded that the attacks might have been prevented if the F.B.I. and the C.I.A. had done a better job of sharing intelligence. At the base of the flagpole at the N.C.T.C.'s main entrance is a concrete jigsaw puzzle that represents the organization's central mission: fitting together the seemingly random pieces of intelligence that flow into Liberty Crossing from the N.S.A., the C.I.A., the F.B.I., and other agencies.

The director of the N.C.T.C. since 2011 has been Matthew G. Olsen, a former federal prosecutor. He is a young-looking fifty-one, despite his hair, which has thinned and become grayer since he took his current job. Down the hall from his office is a door marked "Weapons, Tactics, and Targets Group," which is part of the N.C.T.C.'s Directorate of Intelligence. The N.C.T.C. helps prepare the target lists, sometimes called kill lists, of

1788 State legislatures ratify the U.S. Constitution, establishing the basic precedent for all future constitutional law

1791 The U.S. Congress ratifies the Bill of Rights, creating the first 10 amendments to the United States Constitution

continued

terrorists who must be approved by Obama as legitimate threats in order to be the object of C.I.A. drone strikes. In a recent dissertation about the N.C.T.C., a former C.I.A. analyst, Bridget Rose Nolan, quoted a colleague who described the process as: "You track 'em, we whack 'em." The day after I visited, in mid-November, a drone over Pakistan that sought to strike a terrorist compound fired three missiles that Pakistani officials claimed hit a madrassa and killed six people.

Olsen is one of the few high-level national-security officials to have dealt with the legal issues of the N.S.A.'s programs in both the Bush and the Obama Administrations, and he offers a fair reflection of how the current President and his top advisers approach them. In September, 2006, Olsen moved to the Justice Department's new National Security Division, which was charged with overseeing the increasingly complex FISA cases concerning the N.S.A. He led a hundred lawyers in what was then called the Office of Intelligence Policy Review, which did all the preparatory work for the FISA court. Olsen started four months after the court secretly legalized the phone-metadata program. "I didn't know any of it before I took the job," he told me. "Only a handful of people in the entire government knew anything about it."

Two weeks into the job, Olsen received his first assignment from lawyers at the N.S.A. The N.S.A. had been lobbying the FISA court to approve its four domestic-surveillance programs. The two metadata programs had been O.K.'ed; now Olsen and his colleagues had to persuade the FISA judge to make the phone and e-mail wiretapping programs legal. He did not see the job as especially controversial. "It was a huge policy debate, one of the biggest ones post-9/11, and we're still having it," he said. "But at the time I felt like a lawyer who'd been handed a problem at a very tactical level: How do we figure this out? What are the legal rules we're applying? What are the facts? How do we work with the N.S.A.?" He added, "I thought the goal was actually quite laudable. I was pleased to have the opportunity to work on an important thing, and I thought, Yes, if we could figure out a way to put this on a more firm legal footing, whether through judicial authority or legislative authority, that would be quite an important achievement, and it would be better for the country."

The legal case for phone and Internet wiretapping was harder to make than the arguments concerning metadata. The Supreme Court had ruled in 1979 that metadata was not covered by the Fourth Amendment, but the content of phone calls and e-mails certainly was. Since 9/11, the N.S.A. had largely

1868 The 14th Amendment to the U.S. Constitution guarantees all citizens the right to due process under the law

1890 Warren and Brandeis publish "The Right to Privacy" in the *Harvard Law Review*

"State of Deception: Why Won't the President Rein in the Intelligence Community?"
continued

ignored the law requiring it to get a warrant for each domestic target whose content it collected. The FISA court was not impressed with Olsen's attempt to justify legalizing the program. It issued new rules that vastly reduced the amount of collection from foreign phone and Internet sources. Olsen and his team tried different legal theories, but the court balked. Eventually, he and his colleagues decided that Bush would have to go to Congress instead and ask for legislation to amend the FISA law.

In 2008, Olsen helped lobby Congress to approve a new system that would curtail the fiSA court's role and allow the N.S.A. to intercept enormous numbers of communications to and from the U.S. The FISA court had only to review and certify the over-all system that the N.S.A. would use; it no longer had to approve each target. Congress passed the FISA Amendments Act of 2008 on July 9th. All four Bush programs now had legal cover.

In the Senate Intelligence Committee, only Wyden and Feingold voted against the new FISA law. They were troubled by the central provision—Section 702—which created the new system governing N.S.A. surveillance of phone and Internet content. "I am one of the few members of this body who has been fully briefed on the warrantless-wiretapping program," Feingold said at the time, in a speech on the Senate floor. "I can promise that if more information is declassified about the program in the future, as is likely to happen . . . members of this body will regret that we passed this legislation." Wyden was reassured when Obama was elected President. Although Obama had voted for the new law, he promised at the time of the vote that, if he became President, his Attorney General would immediately "conduct a comprehensive review of all our surveillance programs."

In February of 2009, days after Obama was sworn in, Olsen and Benjamin Powell, a Bush holdover and the general counsel for the Office of the Director of National Intelligence, went to the White House to brief the new President and Eric Holder, the new Attorney General, on the N.S.A.'s programs. There was no way to know how Obama would react. During the campaign, Holder, who was serving as a top legal adviser to Obama, had said that Bush's original surveillance program operated in "direct defiance of federal law." Obama had sponsored the legislation curbing the authority of the business-records provision, which was

1923 *Meyer v. Nebraska* establishes that the 14th Amendment guarantees privileges of citizenship

1928 *Olmstead v. United States* rules that wiretapping is not a form of search and seizure defined by the 14th Amendment

continued

now crucial to the N.S.A. Greg Craig, Obama's White House counsel, was also at the meeting. Because Obama had not been a member of the Intelligence Committee, much of the information was new to him. Powell, who led the briefing, and Olsen also had some news: the FISA court had just ruled that the phone-records program had so many compliance issues that the court was threatening to shut it down. The court was waiting for a response from the new Administration about how to proceed.

Olsen had recently discovered that for the previous two and a half years, the period when the phone-metadata program was supposed to have followed strict new procedures laid out by the FISA court, the N.S.A. had been operating it in violation of those procedures—and had misled the court about it. The N.S.A. was supposed to search its archive of metadata only after it had determined that there was a "reasonable, articulable suspicion"—RAS—to believe that the phone number or other search term was related to terrorism.

RAS was the thin wall between a legal program with some oversight and one with the potential for domestic spying and tremendous privacy violations. It was what prevented an analyst from querying the database for his girlfriend's personal information or for a Tea Party activist's network of contacts or for a journalist's sources. Since 2006, in numerous filings before the FISA court, the N.S.A. had falsely sworn that every search term was RAS-approved. The agency had built a list of some eighteen thousand phone numbers and other search terms that it continuously checked against the metadata as it flowed into the N.S.A.'s servers. Of these, it turned out, fewer than two thousand had legal legitimacy. Thousands of the unauthorized search terms were associated with Americans. On January 15th, Olsen had informed the FISA court of the problem.

Reggie Walton, the FISA judge overseeing the program at that time, wrote, in an opinion on January 28th, that he was "exceptionally concerned" that the N.S.A. had been operating the program in "flagrant violation" of the court's orders and "directly contrary" to the N.S.A.'s own "sworn attestations." Walton was considering rescinding the N.S.A.'s authority to run the program, and was contemplating bringing contempt charges against officials who misled the court or perhaps referring the matter to "appropriate investigative offices." He gave Olsen three weeks to explain why the court shouldn't just shut down the program. The controversy was known at the court as the "'big business' records matter."

1934 The Federal Communications Commission (FCC) is established under the Federal Communications Act (FCA)

1942 *Goldman v. United States* rules that using electronic listening devices does not violate the 14th Amendment

"State of Deception: Why Won't the President Rein in the Intelligence Community?"
continued

At the White House, Olsen and Powell told Obama of the problems. "I want my lawyers to look into this," Obama said. He pointed at Holder and Craig. Olsen believed that the N.S.A. simply had difficulty translating the court's legal language into technical procedures; it could all be fixed. Wyden believed that the court never should have allowed the N.S.A. to collect the data in the first place. In his view, the court's unusually harsh opinion gave Obama an opportunity to terminate the program.

"That was a very, very significant moment in the debate," Wyden told me. "Everybody who had been raising questions had been told, 'The FISA court's on top of this! Everything that's being done, the FISA court has given the O.K. to!' And then we learned that the N.S.A. was routinely violating the court orders that authorized bulk collection. In early 2009, it was clear that the N.S.A.'s claims about bulk-collection programs and how carefully those programs were managed simply were not accurate."

On February 17th, about two weeks after the White House briefing, Olsen, in a secret court filing, made the new Administration's first official statement about Bush's phone-metadata program:

"The government respectfully submits that the Court should not rescind or modify the authority." He cited a sworn statement from Keith Alexander, who had replaced Hayden as the director of the N.S.A. in 2005, and who insisted that the program was essential. "Using contact chaining," Olsen wrote, "N.S.A. may be able to discover previously unknown telephone identifiers used by a known terrorist operative . . . to identify hubs or common contacts between targets of interest who were previously thought to be unconnected, and potentially to discover individuals willing to become US Government assets."

Judge Walton replied that he was still troubled by the N.S.A.'s "material misrepresentations" to the court, and that Alexander's explanation for how they happened "strains credulity." He noted that the FISA court's orders "have been so frequently and systemically violated that it can fairly be said that" the N.S.A. program "has never functioned effectively" and that "thousands of violations" occurred. The judge placed new restrictions on the program and ordered the agency to conduct a full audit, but he agreed to keep it running. Olsen, and Obama, had saved Bush's surveillance program.

1945 The National Security Agency secretly creates Project SHAMROCK

1950 Senator Joseph McCarthy delivers a shocking speech claiming that more than 200 communist spies have infiltrated the U.S. government

continued

It was the first in a series of decisions by Obama to institutionalize some of the most controversial national-security policies of the Bush Administration. Faced with a long list of policies to roll back—torture, the wars in Afghanistan and Iraq, the use of the prison at Guantánamo Bay to hold suspected terrorists—reining in the N.S.A.'s surveillance programs might have seemed like a low priority. As core members of Al Qaeda were killed, the danger shifted to terrorists who were less organized and more difficult to detect, making the use of the N.S.A.'s powerful surveillance tools even more seductive. "That's why the N.S.A. tools remain crucial," Olsen told me. "Because the threat is evolving and becoming more diverse."

Feinstein said, "It is very difficult to permeate the vast number of terrorist groups that now loosely associate themselves with Al Qaeda or Al Nusra or any other group. It is very difficult, because of language and culture and dialect, to really use human intelligence. This really leaves us with electronic intelligence."

The N.S.A.'s assurances that the programs were necessary seemed to have been taken at face value. The new President viewed the compliance problems as a narrow issue of law; it was the sole responsibility of the FISA court, not the White House, to oversee the programs. "Far too often, the position that policy makers have taken has been that if the intelligence agencies want to do it then the only big question is 'Is it legal?'" Wyden said. "And if government lawyers or the fisa court secretly decides that the answer is yes, then the intelligence agencies are allowed to go ahead and do it. And there never seems to be a policy debate about whether the intelligence agencies should be allowed to do literally anything they can get the fisa court to secretly agree to."

Any doubts about the new Administration's position were removed when Obama turned down a second chance to stop the N.S.A. from collecting domestic phone records. The business-records provision of the PATRIOT Act was up for renewal, and Congress wanted to know the Administration's position.

It was one thing to have the Justice Department defend the program in court. But now Obama had to decide whether he would publicly embrace a section of the PATRIOT Act that he had criticized in his most famous speech and that he had tried to rewrite as a senator. He would have to do so knowing that the main government program authorized by the business-records provision was beset by problems. On September 14th, Obama publicly revealed that he wanted the provision renewed without

1951 *Dennis v. United States* rules that government limits to speech is legal only to prevent a threat to public safety or security

1959 *Barenblatt v. United States* rules that it's legal to order people to reveal personal details if national threat is perceived

"State of Deception: Why Won't the President Rein in the Intelligence Community?"
continued

any changes. "At the time of the U.S.A. PATRIOT Act, there was concern that the F.B.I. would exploit the broad scope of the business-records authority to collect sensitive personal information on constitutionally protected activities, such as the use of public libraries," a Justice Department official wrote in a letter to Congress, alluding to one of Obama's former concerns. "This simply has not occurred." The letter, which was unclassified, did not explain the details of the metadata program or the spiralling compliance issues uncovered by the court.

Wyden's early hope, that Obama represented a new approach to surveillance law, had been misguided. "I realized I had a lot more to do to show the White House that this constant deferring to the leadership of the intelligence agencies on fundamental policy issues was not going to get the job done," he said.

III—A Question of Privacy

In December, 2009, Wyden met with Vice-President Biden and explained his case against the bulk collection of phone records and the Administration's Bush-like secrecy about the programs. By now Wyden had become known for his independent streak, which some colleagues saw as grandstanding. On the Intelligence Committee, staffers complained that his readiness to question his colleagues' commitment to the Constitution was so self-righteous that it sometimes backfired when he was trying to garner support.

"I was trying to convey the urgency of the situation," Wyden said of his meeting with Biden. "There was an opportunity here to strike a balance that did more to protect liberty and security." As the deadline to renew the business-records provision approached, the Administration finally agreed to provide the entire Congress with details about the metadata programs. On December 14th, the Justice Department sent a five-page classified document explaining them. Most members of the House and the Senate were learning about them for the first time. The document was kept in secure rooms for a limited period of time; no copies were allowed and no notes could be removed. If members of Congress had any questions, executive-branch officials were available at designated times to chat.

In general, the document described the programs accurately. But, in a section on "compliance issues," the Administration withheld significant

1965 *Griswold v. CT* rules in favor of married couples' right to privacy

1967 *Katz v. United States* rules wiretaps a form of search and seizure

Willis Ware of RAND Corporation writes *Security and Privacy in Computer*

continued

details. Months earlier, the phone-metadata program had come close to being stopped. Obama officials reported this episode to Congress in far less dire terms. "There have been a number of technical compliance problems and human implementation errors in these two bulk collection programs"—phone and Internet metadata—"discovered as a result of Department of Justice reviews and internal N.S.A. oversight," the document said. There were no "intentional or bad-faith violations," just glitches in "implementation of highly sophisticated technology in a complex and ever-changing communications environment," which occasionally "resulted in the automated tools operating in a manner that was not completely consistent" with the FISA court's orders. The Administration assured Congress that everything had been fixed. The N.S.A. had even created a new position, director of compliance, to keep an eye on things.

The debate ended on Christmas Day, 2009, when Umar Farouk Abdulmutallab, a twenty-three-year-old Nigerian man, on a flight from Amsterdam to Detroit, tried to detonate a bomb hidden in his underwear as the plane landed. Although he burned the wall of the airplane's cabin—and his genitals—he failed to set off the device, a nonmetallic bomb made by Yemeni terrorists. Many intelligence officials said that the underwear bomber was a turning point for Obama.

"The White House people felt it in their gut with a visceralness that they did not before," Michael Leiter, who was then the director of the National Counterterrorism Center, said. The center was sharply criticized for not detecting the attack. "It's not that they thought terrorism was over and it was done with," Leiter said, "but until you experience your first concrete attack on the homeland, not to mention one that becomes a huge political firestorm—that changes your outlook really quickly." He added, "It encouraged them to be more aggressive with strikes"—drone attacks in Yemen and Pakistan—"and even stronger supporters of maintaining things like the PATRIOT Act."

Obama also became more determined to keep the programs secret. On January 5, 2010, Holder informed Wyden that the Administration wouldn't reveal to the public details about the N.S.A.'s programs. He wrote, "The Intelligence Community has determined that information that would confirm or suggest that the United States engages in bulk records collection under Section 215, including that the Foreign Intelligence Surveillance Court (FISC) permits the collection of 'large amounts of information' that includes 'significant amounts

1968 The Omnibus Crime Control Act holds that police needed to obtain a warrant before engaging in wire-

1969 Joseph Licklider creates the Advanced Research Projects Agency Network (ARPANET), which was

"State of Deception: Why Won't the President Rein in the Intelligence Community?"
continued

of information about U.S. Persons,' must remain classified." Wyden, in his reply to Holder a few weeks later, expressed his disappointment with the letter: "It did not mention the need to weigh national security interests against the public's right to know, or acknowledge the privacy impact of relying on legal authorities that are being interpreted much more broadly than most Americans realize." He said that "senior policymakers are generally deferring to intelligence officials on the handling of this issue."

Rather than rely on private channels to persuade the White House to change course, he decided he would have to be more publicly aggressive from his perch on the Intelligence Committee. On February 24, 2010, the Senate, without debate, passed a one-year extension of the expiring PATRIOT Act provisions. The following day, the House passed the measure, 315–97. Obama signed it into law two days later. James Sensenbrenner, the author of the original PATRIOT Act, wrote recently in the Los Angeles Times that he and a majority of his colleagues in Congress did not know how the law was being used before they voted to endorse it.

Both politically and personally, the year 2010 was a turning point

for Wyden. He won reelection that November, receiving fifty-seven per cent of the vote, with the slogan "Ron Wyden: Different. Like Oregon." In December, he was treated successfully for prostate cancer. But Russ Feingold, his friend and mentor on surveillance issues, was defeated by a Tea Party opponent. "It was a huge loss," Wyden told me. "Senator Feingold and I talked at that time about how the mantle of liberty and privacy issues was going to be carried on without him."

High-profile Tea Party libertarians such as Rand Paul, from Kentucky, and Mike Lee, from Utah, joined the Senate, and they prompted discussions about national-security law within the Republican Party. "We're still a minority in the Republican caucus, but people are beginning to think about some of these things," Senator Paul told me recently. In the House, there were dozens of small-government conservatives who opposed just about everything George W. Bush had been for, on both foreign and domestic policy.

In addition, in 2011 Mark Udall, a Democratic senator from Colorado, joined the Intelligence Committee. For years, Udall had served in the House and had a record as a skeptic about many post-9/11 security policies. "I

1971 The Pentagon Papers leaks from the press raise the issue of the Freedom of the Press versus the privacy of the government to conceal information about national security operations

1972 *Eisenstadt v. Baird* rules that the right to privacy applies to individuals

continued

voted against the original PATRIOT Act," Udall told me. "I have a strong civil-libertarian streak and background. I'm well aware of some of the mistakes that we've made historically, whether it's the Alien and Sedition Acts or the internment of Japanese-Americans or the warrantless wiretapping that went on under the previous Administration. As I watched that unfold in the last decade, I was more and more aware of Franklin's great admonition that a society that will trade essential liberty for short-term security deserves neither." Paul and Wyden joked that they might finally have enough senators to start what they called the Ben Franklin caucus.

In early 2011, as Udall prepared for the new debate over the PATRIOT Act, he was shocked by what he learned. "It raised a series of red flags for me," Udall said. "It made me realize that, much as I was enthralled by and impressed by what we do, I had also an equally important role to play, which was to ask questions, to provide oversight, and to remember the lessons of the past—which are that the intelligence community, without oversight, without limits, will do everything it possibly can to get everything it possibly can get its hands on. And we've come to regret that, historically."

On May 26, 2011, Wyden delivered what he considered to be one of the most important speeches of his career. He is a strident and tenacious debater, a policy nerd who can overwhelm his opponents with details. "I've served on the Intelligence Committee for over a decade," he said, standing in the well of the Senate during another debate over the PATRIOT Act. "And I want to deliver a warning this afternoon: when the American people find out how their government has secretly interpreted the PATRIOT Act, they are going to be stunned and they are going to be angry. And they're going to ask senators, 'Did you know what this law actually permits?' 'Why didn't you know before you voted on it?'" He reviewed the history of secret intelligence operations that inevitably became public: the C.I.A.'s illegal surveillance in the sixties, the Church committee's investigation of the N.S.A.'s Project SHAMROCK, Iran-Contra, and Bush's warrantless-wiretapping program. As Wyden recalled the history of each scandal, Dickas placed blown-up versions of news headlines on an easel: "Huge C.I.A. Operation Reported in U.S. Against Antiwar Forces, Other Dissidents in Nixon Years," "Senators Reveal U.S. Spies Read Millions of Telegrams," "Bush Lets U.S. Spy on Callers Without Courts."

After each episode that Wyden described, he asked, "Did the program stay a secret?," and responded, "No." The truth always comes out, he added,

1974 The Watergate Scandal results in the revelation that the CIA had been conducting widespread surveillance of American dissidents and foreign leaders without judicial oversight

The Privacy Act is established

"State of Deception: Why Won't the President Rein in the Intelligence Community?"
continued

and, when it does, "the result is invariably a backlash and an erosion of public confidence in these government agencies."

The 2011 PATRIOT Act extension passed the Senate later that day, and this time the controversial provisions were extended until 2015. But twenty-three senators—including Paul and Lee—and a hundred and fifty-three members of the House voted against the law. Wyden and Paul's Ben Franklin caucus was growing.

Even as the Obama Administration publicly defended the PATRIOT Act and the shaky FISA opinions that propped up the secret surveillance regime, behind the scenes the N.S.A. was being challenged by the FISA court for violating its rules. Defending the programs on behalf of the Obama Administration again fell to Matthew Olsen, who now had a new job, as the N.S.A.'s general counsel.

In the spring of 2011, Olsen learned that the agency's program for collecting the content of e-mails and phone calls—the one that he had worked on in 2006 and which was now known as Section 702—had a major problem. The N.S.A. had assured the FISA court that it did not intentionally capture domestic communications, and that, if it unintentionally did so, it had court-sanctioned procedures for disposing of them. That wasn't true. The agency was actually collecting the domestic communications of tens of thousands of Americans: in some cases, the N.S.A. told the court, its filtering devices couldn't weed out the material it was allowed to collect from the stuff it wasn't. The agency called the problem "unintentional" and a "failure" of the N.S.A.'s "technical means." The FISA court called it unconstitutional. Judge John D. Bates declared that the practice violated not only the specific federal law governing surveillance but the Fourth Amendment, which protects Americans against unreasonable search and seizure.

The FISA court also repeatedly rebuked the N.S.A. for its collection of Internet metadata. In one opinion, the court said that for years the "N.S.A. exceeded the scope of authorized acquisition continuously." It also declared that the N.S.A.'s description of the program had been "untrue," and that the government had engaged in "unauthorized" and "systemic overcollection," had searched the system using terms that were "non-compliant with the required RAS approval process," and had improperly

1975 Senator Frank Church leads a series of hearings about the secret NSA SHAMROCK operation involved intercepting communications from American citizens

1978 Congress passes the 1978 FISA Act

continued

disseminated intelligence about Americans derived from the database. In fact, the court said, almost every record "generated by this program included some data that had not been authorized for collection." The court also noted that the N.S.A. program had conducted "unauthorized 'electronic surveillance'" and had asked a FISA judge to "authorize the government to engage in conduct that Congress has unambiguously prohibited."

Wyden, who had read the court opinions and knew the troubled history of the Internet-data program, pressed his advantage. Throughout the year, in correspondence that remains secret, he repeatedly challenged the N.S.A.'s contention that the program was effective. In late 2011, with little explanation, and despite the fact that, just months earlier, the N.S.A. had sworn in court and to Congress that the program was essential, the N.S.A. sent Wyden and other members of the Senate Intelligence Committee a notification that it was indefinitely suspending the program.

On the face of it, the Congress of 2011–12 had been a success for Wyden. He had new allies on the left and the right. He had shut down a program that was collecting huge amounts of Internet data about Americans. During Olsen's confirmation hearing as the director of the N.C.T.C., Wyden

forced Olsen to admit publicly that the FISA court made interpretations of law in secret. In July, 2012, Wyden successfully lobbied for the director of National Intelligence to publicly acknowledge that, "on at least one occasion . . . some collection carried out pursuant to the Section 702" law was "unreasonable under the Fourth Amendment."

Yet three of the four original Bush programs—the phone-metadata program and the content-collection programs—were still running, and, through Olsen's years of work, the N.S.A. seemed finally to be governing them all within the confines of the court's rules. The PATRIOT Act had been renewed, and, in 2012, the FISA amendments, which codified the content-collection program in law, were also reauthorized. In March, 2013, Wyden had his dramatic encounter with Clapper, but, at the time, the public didn't know that Clapper hadn't told the truth. Despite Wyden's victories, any momentum for intelligence reform seemed dead.

But there was one person who was troubled by Clapper's testimony. "Seeing someone in the position of James Clapper baldly lying to the public without repercussion is the evidence of a subverted democracy," Edward Snowden said later, in a Q. & A. on the Guardian Web site. At some point

| **1980** | The Intelligence Oversight Act (IOA) updates legal standards | **1981** | President Reagan's E.O. authorized wiretapping | **1986** | The Electronic Communications Privacy Act is established |

"State of Deception: Why Won't the President Rein in the Intelligence Community?"
continued

during this period, Snowden also came upon the N.S.A. inspector general's secret report about the history of the President's Surveillance Program and STELLARWIND. It was rich with details: the secret computer servers that were delivered under police escort, Hayden's dealings with Cheney's staff, the facts about the Justice Department's rebellion, the decision to take the legally dubious programs and fit them under the umbrella of the PATRIOT Act. Snowden later told the Times that, after he read the report, he decided that he would release it—and thousands of other documents—to the press. "If the highest officials in government can break the law without fearing punishment or even any repercussions at all," he told the paper, "secret powers become tremendously dangerous."

On October 26th, a warm and clear Saturday in Washington, a few hundred protesters gathered in front of Union Station for what organizers called the Stop Watching Us Rally Against Mass Surveillance. A man wearing a giant papier-mâché Obama mask roamed the plaza in a trenchcoat and sunglasses holding an oversized "Obama-Cam." There were signs about "NSA Doublespeak" and demands that the government "stop sniffing my packets," a tech reference to intercepting data as it moves across the Internet. Two protesters held up a large flag depicting the artist Shepard Fairey's famous Obama drawing with the words "Yes We Scan," a play on the President's campaign slogan. Wyden couldn't attend, but he posted a short video message on YouTube, saying, "This is a once-in-a-lifetime opportunity to stand up and protect the privacy of millions of law-abiding Americans. Please know that it's the voices of people like you that are going to make a difference in the fight for real, meaningful surveillance reform."

It was Wyden's kind of crowd: geeky, libertarian, passionate, and baffled that the rest of the public wasn't as outraged as they were. He insisted to me afterward that a movement for reform was building. Snowden's disclosures had vindicated him, he said, and he predicted that they would change the way the N.S.A. operated: "I hope that they see now that the truth always comes out in America, that the deceptions and misleading statements that they engaged in for years are just not going to pass as gospel in the future."

Such a movement is less evident in Congress. A couple of days after

continued

the rally, on October 29th, the Senate Intelligence Committee retreated to its secret chambers, on the second floor of the Hart Office Building. The room has vaulted doors and steel walls that keep it safe from electronic monitoring; the electricity supply to the room is reportedly filtered, for the same reason. The committee's fifteen members, eight Democrats and seven Republicans, debated Feinstein's intelligence-reform bill, the fiSA Improvements Act, for three hours. As Congress and the public have digested the details of Snowden's disclosures, the legislative debate has narrowed to three big questions: Should Congress reform the e-mail and phone tapping allowed by Section 702 to insure that the communications of innocent Americans are not getting swept up in the N.S.A.'s targeting of terrorists? Should the N.S.A. end the bulk collection of phone metadata now authorized by Section 215? Should the FISA court be reformed to make it less deferential to the government?

The committee's answer to all three questions was no. By a vote of 11–4, it endorsed the Feinstein bill. Wyden, Udall, and Martin Heinrich, a Democrat from New Mexico elected last year and the newest member of Wyden's Franklin caucus, voted against the bill. (Tom Coburn, a Republican from Oklahoma, also voted no, because he thought the bill was too restrictive.) "There's three of us out of

eight on our side," Wyden told me later. "That's a lot better than meeting in a phone booth." But the majority of the committee declared, in a report, that the compliance issues at the N.S.A. were "uniformly unintentional, self-identified, and reported to the Court and to Congress." The majority added, "Up until these programs were leaked, their implementation by N.S.A. was an example of how our democratic system of checks and balances is intended to, and does, work."

The following day, Wyden said of the Feinstein bill, "They're wrapping the status quo in this really sparkly gift-wrapping paper and everybody's going, 'Oh, this is beautiful.' They're going to look inside and see the changes are skin-deep, there's not really much there." He added, "People get on this committee and the first thing the intelligence community tries to do is get them to be ambassadors for the intelligence community rather than people doing vigorous oversight. The intelligence community basically takes everybody aside and says, 'Here's the way it works. . . .' There's no discussion about privacy issues or questions about civil liberties—those usually get thrown in afterward."

Feinstein took strong exception to Wyden's characterization: "I've been on the committee for twelve years now, and, when I went on, I knew I had a

The Bush administration secretly authorizes the President's Surveillance Program (PSP), utilizing E.O. 12333

The U.S. PATRIOT Act alters existing laws to facilitate better communication between the state's intelligence branches in the effort to combat terrorism

The Transportation Security Administration (TSA) is established, creating the "No Fly" and "Selectee" lists that limit the right to travel on airplanes in the United States

"State of Deception: Why Won't the President Rein in the Intelligence Community?"
continued

lot to learn. I asked a lot of questions, I read a lot of material, I went out to the N.S.A. You learn what questions to ask, you write letters asking questions, you raise the questions in a meeting. I don't think there's anything that Senator Wyden has asked me to do that I haven't done. If he's got a better way, he's got substantial seniority on the committee, he ought to suggest it."

Feinstein argued that opponents of the surveillance programs have forgotten the lessons of 9/11. "Nothing is dimmed in my mind," she said of a recent trip to Ground Zero. "I saw the part of the steel structure that the planes went through. I saw the white roses on the names etched in bronze in the fountain." She added, "They will come after us again, if they can."

An updated version of Wyden's bill is now making its way through the Judiciary Committee, where it has been introduced by the chairman, Patrick Leahy. The bill would end the bulk collection of phone records, tighten the rules for Section 702, and create a Constitutional Advocate at the FISA court to provide a view in opposition to the government's. At the moment, neither Feinstein's nor Wyden's legislation has the support of sixty senators, the number it needs to

get to the floor for a vote. Obama could make the difference. "The President will sign our bill," Feinstein told me. She said that her staff worked closely with the White House in drafting it.

In August, at the height of the frenzy over Snowden's disclosures, Obama delivered remarks at the White House suggesting that he was wrestling with whether, as President, he had struck the proper balance on surveillance policy: "Keep in mind that, as a senator, I expressed a healthy skepticism about these programs. And, as President, I've taken steps to make sure they have strong oversight by all three branches of government and clear safeguards to prevent abuse and protect the rights of the American people. But, given the history of abuse by governments, it's right to ask questions about surveillance— particularly as technology is reshaping every aspect of our lives."

In practice, Obama has not wavered from the position taken by the N.S.A.'s lawyers and embraced by Feinstein and the majority of the Intelligence Committee. "The system generally has worked," Matthew Olsen told me. "One way to think about the current debate is the degree to which, as a lawyer or as a citizen, you have confidence in

2005

The PATRIOT Act was reauthorized without substantial changes as Congress favors security concerns over warnings that the law creates the potential for civil liberties violations

The *New York Times* publishes articles resulting from leaks revealing the secret President's Surveillance Program (PSP) established by the Bush administration

continued

our government institutions to operate effectively and trust our system of court oversight, congressional oversight, and executive-branch responsibilities."

The history of the intelligence community, though, reveals a willingness to violate the spirit and the letter of the law, even with oversight. What's more, the benefits of the domestic-surveillance programs remain unclear. Wyden contends that the N.S.A. could find other ways to get the information it says it needs. Even Olsen, when pressed, suggested that the N.S.A. could make do without the bulk-collection program. "In some cases, it's a bit of an insurance policy," he told me. "It's a way to do what we otherwise could do, but do it a little bit more quickly."

In recent years, Americans have become accustomed to the idea of advertisers gathering wide swaths of information about their private transactions. The N.S.A.'s collecting of data looks a lot like what Facebook does, but it is fundamentally different. It inverts the crucial legal principle of probable cause: the government may not seize or inspect private property or information without evidence of a crime. The N.S.A. contends that it needs haystacks in order to find the terrorist needle. Its definition of a haystack is expanding; there are indications that, under the auspices of the "business records" provision of the PATRIOT Act, the intelligence community is now trying to assemble databases of financial transactions and cell-phone location information. Feinstein maintains that data collection is not surveillance. But it is no longer clear if there is a distinction.

"My phone numbers, I assume, are collected like everybody else's," Feinstein said. "But so what? It does not bother me. By the Supreme Court decision in 1979, the data is not personal data. There's a Google Map that allows somebody to burgle my house, it's so clear and defined, and I can't do anything about it."

Wyden said that the continued leaks from Snowden help build momentum for changing the law. "We pick up more support as more and more of this comes out," he told me. "After a decade, we think this is the best opportunity for reform that we're going to have, certainly in my lifetime, and we're not going to let it go by."

2007 The Bush Administration plans to make data taken from spy satellites available to law enforcement to be used to conduct domestic surveillance

2008 Congress passes Section 702, or the FISA Amendment Act, which is used to permit a massive NSA and CIA domestic surveillance program

In 2013 and 2014, the intelligence reformers and privacy advocates enjoyed the highest levels of popular support recorded to that point. Public opinion polls from those years demonstrate that the public was both increasingly concerned about civil liberties and increasingly skeptical that the government was acting in the best interest of the public. A few of the most notable polls showed:

- *Washington Post* (2013)—66 percent of Americans were concerned about NSA data collection.
- *Washington Post* (2014)—74 percent agree NSA spying is an invasion of privacy rights. 77 percent of Republicans believe the program violates privacy (as opposed to 50 percent in 2006).
- *Pew Research* (2014)—53 percent of Americans oppose NSA collection of phone and Internet data, with 40 percent approving of the practice to combat terrorism.
- *Liszt Grove Research* (Nov 2013)—59 percent of Americans support intelligence reform and 63 percent want greater oversight on surveillance and spying programs.[131]

Wyden's 2013 campaign for intelligence reform failed, as had his efforts in previous years, largely because the lobby contending that the programs in place were necessary to combat terrorism held sway over the legislature and a significant portion of the public. The Snowden leaks motivated a short-term surge of concern about privacy and civil liberties in the public, but the momentum of this movement was insufficient to empower privacy advocates to enact significant reform and resulted, instead, in cosmetic reforms that reinforced the status quo. In addition, although a majority of Americans disapproved of the NSA's activities, did not feel that such activities were needed to combat terrorism, and were concerned about civil liberties violations, the issue remained a relatively low priority for many Americans.

2012 The Obama Administration proposes a Consumer Privacy Bill of Rights guaranteeing individuals the right to greater control over the use of their digital data

2013 The *Guardian* and the *Washington Post* publish the first series of articles derived from leaked NSA and CIA documents delivered by Edward Snowden

By 2015, interest in establishing stronger privacy protections had returned, in most polls, to pre-Snowden levels. For privacy advocates, this posed a continued challenge as legislators like Wyden and privacy groups like the Electronic Frontier Foundation (EFF) struggled not only to promote new policies and legislation, but also to help the public see the depths and nature of the problem as they saw it. This effort became more important in the summer of 2015 as congress debated over a proposal, by Republican Mitch McConnell, for a "clean" or unchanged reauthorization of the PATRIOT Act, including the 215 provision that had been used as the justification for the NSA's most controversial programs.

The Senate Judiciary committee holds hearings to determine if the executive surveillance operations carried out under the PATRIOT Act were a violation of constitutional law

Snowden leaks reveal that the NSA and CIA had been attempting to force corporations to provide a backdoor to encryption systems that would allow federal agents to bypass consumer encryption

CONCLUSION

The profile of Ron Wyden's career and the broad failure to create meaningful intelligence reform after 2001 demonstrate how political punditry, campaigning, lobbying, and the pervasive fear of the nebulous threat posed by terrorism and extremism divided the public and prevented the kind of consensus needed for a stronger political movement to take hold. Privacy advocates like Wyden compiled an extensive list of privacy violations (both realized and potential) that occurred under the Bush and Obama administrations, and argued that neither administration nor the government's intelligence community representatives had been able to justify their policy priorities or demonstrate the effectiveness of the most controversial methods in play. Despite this, and despite years of campaigning for public support, fear and uncertainty kept the issue on the back burner for most Americans.

2015

| Terrorist attacks in France reignite fears of domestic terrorist violence | The PATRIOT Act is replaced by the USA Freedom Act | Federal Courts order Apple, Inc. to create a new operation system that would enable federal investigators to bypass security on an iPhone. |

DISCUSSION QUESTIONS

■ Should the government adopt more stringent privacy protections? Why or why not?

■ Do you agree with Wyden's assessment of the PATRIOT Act, or with the defense of the act presented by both the Bush and Obama administrations?

■ Would Wyden's intelligence reform legislation have helped protect the public against government surveillance? Why or why not?

■ Do you trust the government to be honest with the public regarding their domestic surveillance programs? Explain your answer.

Works Used

Fahrenthold, David A. "With NSA revelations, Sen. Ron Wyden's vague privacy warnings finally become clear." *Washington Post.* Washington Post Company. July 28, 2013. Web. 29 Oct. 2017.

"In Speech, Wyden Says Official Interpretations of PATRIOT Act Must be Made Public." *Ron Wyden.* Ron Wyden Senator for Oregon. May 26, 2011. Web. 29 Oct. 2017.

Tien, Lee. "Update: Polls Continue to Show Majority of Americans Against NSA Spying." *EFF.* Electronic Frontier Foundation. Jan. 22, 2014. Web. 29 Oct. 2017.

The FCC publishes official rules of "neutrality"

2016

The EU establishes the General Data Protection Regulation (GDPR), described as the strongest digital data privacy law in the world

2017

The "Vault 7" secrets, a leak of 9,000 CIA documents, reveal details of the CIA's attempts to break through encryption used by Internet

President Trump appoints Ajit Pai to head the FCC, who abolishes the FCC neutrality protections

Introduction

This chapter discusses the PATRIOT Act renewal debate of 2015, which came at a time when a new radical organization, known as ISIL, ISIS, or the Islamic State, had supplanted Al-Qaeda as the most famous terrorist group in the United States. Following a devastating series of attacks in Europe connected to the group, Republican Senator Mitch McConnell led an effort to immediately reauthorize the expiring provisions in the PATRIOT Act, most notably the controversial Section 215 that authorizes the collection of "bulk data" on American citizens. As this debate was proceeding, two radicals attempted to attack an art show in Texas where artists organized by anti-Islam activists designed to showcase art that is offensive to individuals of the Muslim faith. Two American Muslims tried to attack the event, and both were killed by a local SWAT team while fleeing the scene.

The source document for this chapter is the article, "NSA Data Collection: Necessary, or Unconstitutional?", written by conservative columnist Fred Fleitz in the *National Review*. In his commentary, Fleitz echoes the same sentiments that have long been voiced by supporters of domestic surveillance programs and metadata collection, that such a system, despite potential risks to personal privacy, is necessary to counter the unique danger of terrorism. Fleitz repeatedly references the Garland, Texas, attack at the anti-Islam art show as evidence to support reauthorizing bulk data collection under Section 215, and argues that opposition to the NSA, the PATRIOT Act, and Section 215 was the result of exaggerated fears and overreaction to the Snowden leaks of 2013 (see Chapter 12).

Congress debates whether or not to renew the controversial Section 702 FISA Amendment used to authorize NSA domestic intelligence operations since 2008

Topics covered in this chapter include:

- Islamophobia
- The PATRIOT Act
- The NSA
- Bulk data collection
- Domestic surveillance
- The War on Terror

This Chapter Discusses the Following Source Document:
Fleitz, Fred. "NSA Data Collection: Necessary, or Unconstitutional."
National Review. National Review, Inc. May 11, 2015.

The Case for Bulk Data
PATRIOT Act Renewal (2015)

The debate over NSA spying intensified approaching the summer of 2015 as the PATRIOT Act again came up for renewal. One issue that played a major role in the debate was the recent surge in radical violence in Iraq, Syria, and Afghanistan, which occurred as the United States was beginning to withdraw troops from the region and handing security over to native military and security forces. Chief among these concerns, for residents of the United States and much of Europe, was the emergence of the Syrian fundamentalist group known as the Islamic State.

The Islamic State gained international infamy in 2014 when the organization captured and executed several U.S. and European journalists, publishing videos of the executions online. Over the next year, the organization was nearly constantly in the news, linked to terrorist attacks in Europe and engaged in a military campaign to capture portions of Iraq, Syria, and Afghanistan from government forces.[132]

In January of 2015, a small group of militants linked to the Islamic State attacked the headquarters of the

Silent vigil to condemn the gun attack at French satirical magazine *Charlie Hebdo* office in Paris, which killed 12 people on January 7, 2015.

1868 The 14th Amendment to the U.S. Constitution guarantees all citizens the right to due process under the law

1890 Warren and Brandeis publish "The Right to Privacy" in the *Harvard Law Review*

NAMING THE ISLAMIC STATE

The Islamic State is a conservative, anti-modernist organization based in Syria, and also known as the Islamic State of Iraq and the Levant (ISIL) or the Islamic State of Iraq and Syria (ISIS). In the Middle East, the organization is more generally known as "Daesh" or "Da'ish," which is an acronym for the Arabic description, "al-Dawla al-Islamiya fil Iraq wa al-Sham." The term Daesh sounds similar to an Arabic verb meaning to crush or trample something and so the Islamic State strenuously objects to the use of the term Daesh when referring to them, even going so far as to threaten to cut the tongues out of individuals referring to them as "Daesh." Encouraged by the group's vehement objection to the term, "Daesh" has become common among Arabic-speaking opponents of the group.

satirical French magazine *Charlie Hebdo*, killing ten journalists and two police officers.[133] The attack was in response to the magazine's publication of cartoons depicting the Islamic prophet Muhammad, which anti-modernist Islamic radicals considered a violation of sacred principles prohibiting idolatry, which, over centuries came to also mean any artistic representations of the religion's holy figures.[134] This and other high-profile attacks in Europe brought the threat of terrorism back to the forefront of the public debate. Reinvigorated fear of terrorism thus led to a shift, away from civil liberties concerns and back to support for stronger national security programs.

It was within this resurgence of fear that the PATRIOT Act came up for reauthorization again and legislators, activists, and policy experts debated whether to reauthorize some of the act's most controversial provisions. Most notably, much of the debate centered around Section 215, the section used to authorize the now infamous bulk data collection by the NSA. Republican Senator Mitch McConnell became the most prominent voice in the "pro-215" camp, arguing that the program, whatever its privacy implications, had been an important tool in combating

1923
Meyer v. Nebraska establishes that the 14th Amendment guarantees privileges of citizenship

1928
Olmstead v. United States rules that wiretapping is not a form of search and seizure defined by the 14th Amendment

A member of the Iraqi forces walks past a mural bearing the logo of the Islamic State (IS) group in a tunnel that was reportedly used as a training centre by the jihadists, on March 1, 2017, in the village of Albu Sayf, on the southern outskirts of Mosul. Iraqi forces launched a major push on February 19 to recapture the west of Mosul from the Islamic State jihadist group, retaking the airport and then advancing north. (Photo: AHMAD AL-RUBAYE/AFP/ Getty Images)

terrorism and needed to be renewed or the nation would face an imminent terrorist threat.

In May of 2015, the conservative, anti-Islam organization Stop Islamization of America (SIOA) decided to hold a "First Annual Muhammad Art Exhibit and Contest," featuring paintings, drawing, and other depictions of the prophet Muhammad in defiance of conservative Islamic prohibitions of such activities and in with the *Charlie Hebdo* artists and editors who were victims of the January 2015 attacks in France. The exhibit, held at the Curtis Culwell Center in Garland, Texas, was controversial and pur-

1934   The Federal Communications Commission (FCC) is established under the Federal Communications Act (FCA)

1942   *Goldman v. United States* rules that using electronic listening devices does not violate the 14th Amendment

posefully inflammatory, but gained support from free speech advocates and many national and international critics of Islam. During the event, two men (later identified as American citizens who had taken an interest in radical Islam), attempted to attack the art show using a battery of legally-obtained weapons. After a shootout, in which one security guard was injured by one of the shooters, the two attackers abandoned their attack and attempted to flee, but were killed by members of the SWAT team while fleeing.

In this article from the conservative *National Review*, former CIA analyst and Vice President of the Center for Security Policy, Fred Fleitz summarizes the upcoming legislative effort and presents an argument for retaining bulk data collection.

"NSA DATA COLLECTION: NECESSARY, OR UNCONSTITUTIONAL?
by Fred Fleitz
National Review, **May 11, 2015**
Source Document

Although the Obama administration refuses to say that the attempted massacre by two heavily armed assailants at a "draw Mohammed" contest in Garland, Texas, was an act of terrorism directed by ISIS, there is little doubt this was the case. One of the heavily armed attackers had been in touch through Twitter with jihadists in Australia and Somalia who were associated with ISIS and who had called for attacks on the Garland event. ISIS also seemed to know about the attack in advance and immediately claimed responsibility for it.

Pamela Geller, the organizer of the "draw Mohammed" contest, wrote this week that whether ISIS leaders actually directed the attack or only had foreknowledge of it is a distinction without a difference, since ISIS has called for attacks on the United States and published manuals explaining how homegrown Islamist terrorists can construct bombs and kill infidels.

The Garland attack was stopped in a matter of seconds—but only because

continued

of a heavy police presence assigned to the event and a traffic cop who somehow killed both assailants with his service revolver even though they were wearing body armor. However, this will certainly not be the last attack in the United States by homegrown terrorists inspired or directed by ISIS and al-Qaeda. There may not be heavy security in place the next time ISIS attacks.

This is why Senator Mitch McConnell recently introduced a "clean"—that is, with no changes at all—reauthorization of the PATRIOT Act, which extends three of its provisions on electronic-surveillance programs used to protect our country against terrorist attacks. The most controversial is the NSA metadata program enacted in Section 215 of the PATRIOT Act.

Opponents of the 215 program claim it is an unconstitutional violation of privacy rights and say that it has played no role in protecting the United States from terrorist attacks. Both of these claims are untrue.

Under the metadata program, the NSA collects large numbers of phone records—not the contents of phone calls—and uses them to make connections between terror suspects. The program is subject to stro ng oversight by the executive branch, Congress, and the courts and is used only for national-security investigations. Only 22 people at the NSA are allowed access to these metadata, and they are barred from any data-mining, even in connection with an investigation.

While its detractors refuse to admit it, the 215 program has been a successful tool in stopping terrorist attacks. It has been strongly defended by many intelligence officials and members of Congress, including Senator Dianne Feinstein (D., Calif.), vice chairman of the Senate Intelligence Committee, who said during a January 14, 2014, Judiciary Committee hearing that this program had helped stop terrorist plots to bomb the New York City subways, the New York Stock Exchange, and a Danish newspaper.

Former deputy CIA director Michael Morell said in a December 27, 2013, *Washington Post* op-ed: "Had the [metadata] program been in place more than a decade ago, it would likely have prevented 9/11. And it has the potential to prevent the next 9/11."

Although 35 of 38 court decisions have found the 215 program to be constitutional, its opponents like to quote a December 2013 opinion by D.C. District Court Judge Richard Leon, which questioned its constitutionality. Instead of shutting down the program,

1951 *Dennis v. United States* rules that government limits to speech is legal only to prevent a threat to public safety or security

1959 *Barenblatt v. United States* rules that it's legal to order people to reveal personal details if national threat is perceived

"NSA Data Collection: Necessary, or Unconstitutional?" continued

however, Leon stayed his decision pending a government appeal. When this appeal was heard by a D.C. Circuit Court of Appeals panel last November, the judges did not accept the challengers' contentions that the 215 program violated the Fourth Amendment's protection against unreasonable searches.

Opponents of the 215 program are now praising a decision on May 7 by a New York Court of Appeals panel that found that the program was not authorized by the PATRIOT Act. However, this decision fell far short of what the ACLU was seeking in the case, since the court did not order the 215 program halted, noting that the debate in Congress could render the issue moot. The court also did not find the 215 program to be unconstitutional or a violation of privacy rights, although it said it could revisit these issues if Congress passes new legislation to reauthorize the program. Indeed, if the 215 program continues, legal challenges to it are likely to be eventually decided by the Supreme Court.

Despite the continuing need for the 215 program, it is in trouble because Republicans are sharply divided on it.

Much of the opposition from both sides of the political spectrum is a result of the deluge of Snowden leaks.

The release of so much information out of context led to a media frenzy and wild claims that American intelligence is illegally spying on Americans. Both intelligence officials and the White House did a poor job at defending the program, and conspiracy theories flourished.

And, of course, there also is in America a venerable history of suspicion of government and government secrecy. Senator Rand Paul (R., Ky.) has said that America's Founding Fathers would be "appalled" at the 215 program. Actually, Senator Paul is probably right, if only because the Founding Fathers lived in the era of wooden ships and simple firearms and had no notion of modern warfare and weapons of mass destruction. I suspect they would be appalled at many aspects of modern society.

In an April 25 National Review article, Senator Mike Lee (R., Utah) made a similar argument when he expressed his concerns about the U.S. governments gathering data "to paint a fairly complete picture of the private lives of every person in this country." In fact, although there is no evidence that the NSA has ever done or ever intended to do such a thing, it is being done, and on a huge scale, by Google, Facebook, other social-media sites, and data brokers. According to a March 9, 2014,

1965   *Griswold v. CT* rules in favor of married couples' right to privacy

1967   *Katz v. United States* rules wiretaps a form of search and seizure

Willis Ware of RAND Corporation writes *Security and Privacy in Computer*

continued

60 Minutes report, Acxiom, a data broker, claims that it has on average 1,500 pieces of information each on more than 200 million Americans. If Senator Lee is really worried about privacy threats, he should focus on the unregulated gathering of such data on Americans by technology companies.

From what people have told me as I've traveled around the country giving talks on this topic, I know that a major factor driving Republicans to oppose the 215 program is Obama-administration policies and scandals. These abuses include the effort by the IRS to discriminate against conservative groups, and the Justice Department's seizing the phone records and e-mails of Fox News correspondent James Rosen and his parents. Many Republicans complain that they have been repeatedly lied to by the Obama administration—about Obamacare, the 2012 attacks on the U.S. consulate in Benghazi, the Iran nuclear talks, and other issues.

As a result, some Republican members of Congress are loath to extend an intelligence program that they fear could be used by the Obama administration against its political enemies. Although I understand this concern, the realities are that the 215 program is subject to intense oversight and has been an effective counterterrorism tool. Abuse of this program is purely theoretical. Shutting it down because of the Obama administration's scandals and failings makes no sense.

At the other end of the political spectrum, the metadata program has been broadly opposed by the Left and by electronic-privacy advocates. However, this opposition goes beyond the metadata program: These groups are also pushing for granting privacy rights to foreign citizens on foreign soil (which President Obama tacitly supports), negotiating international treaties banning Internet spying, and preventing the NSA from exploiting software vulnerabilities.

President Obama has struggled to deal with controversy sparked by the Snowden leaks. In August 2013, he named a panel to look at reforming NSA collection, though he eventually ignored most of its recommendations, probably because they were so radical and naïve. These included recommendations similar to those by the Left mentioned above, such as extending the Privacy Act of 1974 to non-U.S. persons; calling for U.S. electronic surveillance to be guided by Article 12 of the Universal Declaration of Human Rights and Article 17 of the International Covenant on Civil and Political Rights; codes of conduct between intelligence agencies on electronic surveillance against foreign

1968 The Omnibus Crime Control Act holds that police needed to obtain a warrant before engaging in wire-

1969 Joseph Licklider creates the Advanced Research Projects Agency Network (ARPANET), which was

"NSA Data Collection: Necessary, or Unconstitutional?"
continued

citizens, and barring U.S. intelligence agencies from cracking Internet encryption methods and penetrating computer software.

People who make such recommendations are oblivious to the reality that we need aggressive intelligence collection to keep our nation safe in a dangerous world. They also do not understand that adopting such standards would severely undermine or shut down many crucial intelligence-collection programs but would be completely ignored by America's enemies and adversaries.

President Obama also instructed intelligence officials to defend the 215 program and work to block legislative language that would overly restrict it. This led Jeb Bush to remark last month, "I would say the best part of the Obama administration has been his continuance of the protections of the homeland using the big metadata programs, the NSA being enhanced." However, Bush may need to retract this statement. According to a House Intelligence Committee source, the White House gave up on defending the metadata program late last year in response to its supporters on the left, especially deep-pocketed Democratic contributors in Silicon Valley.

Congress also has struggled with NSA reform. Last May, the House passed the 2014 USA Freedom Act, which would put significant restrictions on the 215 program, including a mandate that metadata be retained by the phone companies, not the NSA. Although I viewed this as a bad bill, I endorsed it in a June 23, 2014, National Review article because I believed that, regardless of the merits and capabilities of the metadata program, it has been so damaged by fear-mongering attacks by the press and some politicians that it could not continue in its current form.

Unfortunately, the House version of the USA Freedom Act was made substantially worse by Patrick Leahy, then-chairman of the Senate Judiciary Committee, who added restrictions that would effectively kill the metadata program and interfere with the operation of the Foreign Intelligence Surveillance Court.

Because of Leahy's changes to the House version of the 2014 USA Freedom Act, it did not garner a filibuster-proof majority last November, and the Senate failed to pass it. The top members of the Senate Intelligence Committee—then-chairman Feinstein and Saxby Chambliss—said Leahy's bill went too far. Former CIA director Michael Hayden and former attorney general

1971 The Pentagon Papers leaks from the press raise the issue of the Freedom of the Press versus the privacy of the government to conceal information about national security operations

1972 *Eisenstadt v. Baird* rules that the right to privacy applies to individuals

continued

Michael Mukasey condemned the bill in a November 17, 2014, *Wall Street Journal* op-ed titled "NSA Reform That Only ISIS Could Love."

The challenge for Congress now is to pass legislation to extend the metadata program before it expires at the end of this month. Members of Congress and staff have been working over the past three months to devise a 2015 version of the USA Freedom Act. On April 30, the House Judiciary Committee approved this bill by a vote of 25 to 2. An identical version has been sponsored in the Senate by Senators Leahy and Lee.

The House's 2015 USA Freedom Act is slightly better than the 2014 Senate version. The metadata program would continue, although the data would be held by phone companies. NSA searches of metadata databases would be narrowed. The bill also would create a panel of experts to advise the Foreign Intelligence Surveillance Court on privacy, civil liberties, and technological matters. Significant FISC decisions would be declassified.

The bill includes concessions to the House Intelligence Committee, such as allowing the NSA authority to conduct surveillance for 72 hours without obtaining a warrant on foreign targets who enter the United States, and to monitor domestic targets on whom it has a probable-cause warrant when they travel overseas. The NSA will also be allowed to use the PATRIOT Act to collect data domestically in an emergency.

The Left and privacy groups are split over the 2015 version of the USA Freedom Act. Some have endorsed it, because they believe that it is the best they can get and that it will open the door to greater reform down the road. These groups are pressuring Congress to remove the concessions made to the House Intelligence Committee. Several of these groups have stepped up their efforts to amend the bill in the light of the May 7 New York Court of Appeals decision.

Others on the left, such as the ACLU and the *New York Times*, do not support the 2015 USA Freedom Act, since they would prefer that the electronic-surveillance provisions of the PATRIOT Act be allowed to expire.

Senator McConnell has enlisted freshman Senator Tom Cotton (R., Ark.) to help push a clean reauthorization of the PATRIOT Act, which would retain the 215 program in its current form. Cotton, who now serves on the Senate Intelligence Committee and who supported the House version of the USA Freedom Act when he was a member of that body last year, has become a rising star in the Senate because of his outspoken opposition to the Obama administration's nuclear diplomacy with Iran. He reportedly is

1974

The Watergate Scandal results in the revelation that the CIA had been conducting widespread surveillance of American dissidents and foreign leaders without judicial oversight

The Privacy Act is established

"NSA Data Collection: Necessary, or Unconstitutional?"
continued

holding classified meetings with other Republican senators to explain the metadata program and to dispel the misinformation about it spread by its opponents.

Senators Richard Burr (R., N.C.), Jeff Sessions (R., Ala.), and Marco Rubio (R., Fla.) have also spoken out in defense of the NSA and in support of McConnell's PATRIOT Act bill. Rubio suggested during a May 7 floor speech that if the 215 program isn't reauthorized and there is then another terrorist attack within the United States, Congress will be under fire to explain whether the program could have helped prevent such an attack.

With three GOP senators already running for president, the 215 program has become an issue in the presidential campaign. Senator Paul has criticized Rubio and Bush for supporting the program and opposes the 2015 USA Freedom Act, preferring that the PATRIOT Act be repealed. Senator Ted Cruz (R., Tex.) also opposes the metadata program but supports the USA Freedom Act. Senator Burr, the chairman of the Senate Intelligence Committee, has criticized Paul and Cruz for their attacks on the 215 program as weakening their standing on national defense; Burr claims that their position "tells me that they don't want to learn what bulk data collection is."

Security-minded Republicans therefore must work to strengthen the House bill and fend off efforts by Democrats and libertarians to weaken it. We may hope that growing concerns about future ISIS terrorism in the United States will allow Republican congressional leaders to limit the damage to the metadata program from the House bill and move it in McConnell's direction. McConnell's bill, which I strongly support, is unlikely to pass. The Snowden leaks and anti-NSA hysteria have done too much damage to the 215 program for it to continue without substantial changes. Moreover, support for the House bill is probably too strong to allow the McConnell version to become law.

Passage of the 2015 USA Freedom Act is far from an ideal outcome, since this bill would needlessly undermine an effective counterterrorism tool that is needed to protect our country. But this may be only a short-term setback for American national security: Already the shock of the Snowden leaks is fading, and the grandstanding against the NSA by Senator Paul, other libertarians, and the Left is becoming tiresome. This could mean the metadata program might be revised in a few years under a new Republican president.

1975 Senator Frank Church leads a series of hearings about the secret NSA SHAMROCK operation involved intercepting communications from American citizens

1978 Congress passes the 1978 FISA Act

continued

Unfortunately, before that time comes, there is a real danger of an ISIS terrorist attack in the United States if Congress seriously weakens the metadata program. Congress needs to think long and hard about such an outcome as it moves ahead with legislation on this issue this month.

The debate over whether to renew controversial sections of the PATRIOT Act also brought another important question to the American public's attention; i.e., whether the PATRIOT Act, which had been in place for nearly 15 years, had been effective in combating terrorism?

Though Fleitz argues that, without bulk data collection, there will be a "real danger of an ISIS terrorist attack in the United States," reports on the program call this claim into question. In May of 2015, the Office of the Inspector General released part of a report reviewing FBI use of metadata collected through Section 215, indicating that, despite years of nearly unfettered data collection, the FBI had not derived any significant actionable intelligence from the program.[135] This coincided with unclassified government documents described in the *New York Times* suggesting that the NSA's "Stellar Wind" program, which authorized broad NSA surveillance of American Internet and phone data, has similarly resulted in not many terrorist arrests or any other identifiable boon to public safety.[136] Supporters therefore claimed that the effectiveness of the PATRIOT Act

| 1980 | The Intelligence Oversight Act (IOA) updates legal standards | 1981 | President Reagan's E.O. authorized wiretapping | 1986 | The Electronic Communications Privacy Act is established |

could not be fully understood, because of the necessary secrecy needed to protect ongoing investigations, but this, after 15 years, was no longer sufficient to sway legislators.

Further, despite numerous references to the Garland, Texas, attempted shooting as justification for the continuation of the PATRIOT Act, the incident proved nothing about the effectiveness of NSA bulk collection methods or even about the broader effectiveness of the PATRIOT Act as a whole. Recognizing that the art contest was purposefully inflammatory and would offend millions around the world, a heavy police presence was sanctioned, and it was this, a combination of common sense precautions and the effectiveness of local policing, that resulted in the death of the two perpetrators. Although the attempted attack might, therefore, have helped to reignite fears about potential terrorist attacks, there was no clear way for the public, or supporters of the act, to link NSA activities or PATRIOT Act provisions to the attempted shooting.

The alternative USA Freedom Act, was intended as a compromise between critics and supporters of the PATRIOT Act. Providing moderate privacy regulations that altered some facets of the PATRIOT Act, McConnell and other supporters of the original law felt the act might weaken national security. Meanwhile, for Ron Wyden, Rand Paul, and other privacy advocates in the legislature, the Freedom Act didn't provide adequate controls to ensure that the civil liberties threats under the PATRIOT Act would be prevented in the future.

1994 Netscape creates the "cookie" allowing computers to monitor Internet users

2001 The September 11 terrorist attacks result in Congress authorizing the Bush Administration to utilize military methods to combat terrorism

1966 © The Herb Block Foundation

The Bush administration secretly authorizes the President's Surveillance Program (PSP), utilizing E.O. 12333

The U.S. PATRIOT Act alters existing laws to facilitate better communication between the state's intelligence branches in the effort to combat terrorism

The Transportation Security Administration (TSA) is established, creating the "No Fly" and "Selectee" lists that limit the right to travel on airplanes in the United States

CONCLUSION

For years, critics called the effectiveness and necessity of domestic surveillance into question and, for years, supporters were unable to provide evidence to prove that the programs had been effective, but instead, based their defense on the unsubstantiated claim that without bulk data collection and mass surveillance, there would be an imminent threat. Fleitz repeatedly references the Garland, Texas, art show attack as evidence for the necessity of Section 215, but this argument has no substance. The two attackers were killed by police using standard police methods and intelligence gathering capabilities and the case had no connection to NSA activities, or bulk data collection. Despite passionate defenses by McConnell and his allies, backed up by pundits like Fleitz, the popularity of the PATRIOT Act had declined to such a level by 2015 that it was unclear whether supporters would be able to reauthorize the act's most controversial provisions.

2005

The PATRIOT Act was reauthorized without substantial changes as Congress favors security concerns over warnings that the law creates the potential for civil liberties violations

The *New York Times* publishes articles resulting from leaks revealing the secret President's Surveillance Program (PSP) established by the Bush administration

DISCUSSION QUESTIONS

■ Was Fleitz' argument in favor of bulk data collection convincing? Why or why not?

■ Are there any significant connections between bulk data collection and the Garland, Texas anti-Islamic art show incident?

■ What is the most convincing point made by Fleitz in his article?

■ What is your impression of the Garland, Texas art contest? Was it a meaningful statement on freedom of expression? Why or why not?

Works Used

"A Review of the FBI's Use of Section 215 Orders: Assessment of Progress in Implementing Recommendations and Examination of Use in 2007 through 2009." *Office of the Inspector General.* Department of Justice. May 2015. Pdf. 30 Oct. 2017.

Rayner, Gordon, Samuel, Henry, and Martin Evans. "Charlie Hebdo attack: France's worst terrorist attack in a generation leaves 12 d-ead." *The Telegraph.* Telegraph UK. Jan. 7, 2015. Web. 30 Oct. 2017.

Savage, Charlie. "Declassified Report Shows Doubts About Value of N.S.A.'s Warrantless Spying." *New York Times.* New York Times Company. Apr. 24, 2015. Web. 30 Oct. 2017.

"What is 'Islamic State'?" *BBC News.* BBC. Dec. 2, 2015. Web. 30 Oct. 2017.

"Why Islam prohibits images of Muhammad." *The Economist.* The Economist Newspaper Limited. Jan. 19, 2015. Web. 31 Oct. 2017.

2007

The Bush Administration plans to make data taken from spy satellites available to law enforcement to be used to conduct domestic surveillance

2008

Congress passes Section 702, or the FISA Amendment Act, which is used to permit a massive NSA and CIA domestic surveillance program

2012 The Obama Administration proposes a Consumer Privacy Bill of Rights guaranteeing individuals the right to greater

2013 The *Guardian* and the *Washington Post* publish the first series of articles derived from leaked NSA and CIA documents

Introduction

This chapter discusses the intelligence reform movement from 2013 to 2015 that eliminated the PATRIOT Act and replaced it with the *USA Freedom Act*, a compromised reform bill that essentially maintained most of the surveillance activities legal under the PATRIOT Act and, in some cases, expanded the capabilities of intelligence agencies to conduct legal domestic surveillance. The Freedom Act began life as a legitimate effort for intelligence reform. However, compromise in the House of Representatives altered the bill's original provisions and the resulting law was a compromise that provided symbolic minor changes to appease privacy advocates and those concerned about the privacy implications of the programs revealed in the Snowden leaks (see Chapter 12). Critics of the bill immediately pointed out that the legal language of the act was sufficiently vague so that intelligence agencies could interpret the law in such a way as to essentially continue their activities unabated.

The source document for this chapter is the August 2015 article in *Salon* by Elsa Givan, in which Givan interviews Internet security expert Micah Lee, who helped journalist Glenn Greenwald to protect and store the Snowden leak documents. Lee argues that the lack of public support for stronger intelligence reform was due to the fact that the public, by and large, had limited specific understanding about domestic surveillance and the activities undertaken by the NSA. Essentially, Lee argues that the highly technical nature of some of the issues at play had prevented the public from grasping the actual implications and, thus, complicated the efforts of privacy advocates to build public support behind reform. Given the lack of understanding, the visceral fear generated by those who claimed that the existence of mass surveillance was the only thing standing in the way of terrorist attacks, held sway.

The Senate Judiciary committee holds hearings to determine if the executive surveillance operations carried out under the PATRIOT Act were a

Snowden leaks reveal that the NSA and CIA had been attempting to force corporations to provide a backdoor to encryption systems that would allow

Topics covered in this chapter include:

- The Snowden leaks
- Government leaks
- The USA Freedom Act
- The PATRIOT Act
- Domestic surveillance
- Bulk data collection
- The NSA

This Chapter Discusses the Following Source Document:
Givan, Elsa. "'I Had No Idea What I Was Getting Into': Glenn Greenwald's Security Guru on Edward Snowden's Secrets, Obama's Surveillance State." *Salon*. Aug. 2015.

The Snowden Effect
The USA Freedom Act (2015)

In June of 2015 Congress passed the USA Freedom Act, hailed by supporters as a meaningful overhaul of federal policy that addressed the most significant concerns in the PATRIOT Act. This view, however, was not universal. Many privacy advocates, while acknowledging that the Freedom Act changes were a positive first step, argued that the act did not go far enough and was not a substantive basis for a renewed right to privacy.[137]

The Freedom Act, as it was originally conceived by Representative Jim Sensenbrenner, completely eliminated the NSA bulk data collection program. In interviews, Sensenbrenner argued that security agencies had misused the powers granted by the PATRIOT Act and said it was time, "to put their metadata program out of business."[138]

There had been other efforts to pass bipartisan intelligence reform, such as a 2013 bill proposed by Senator Ron Wyden and allies that also would have called for an immediate end to bulk data collection, while proposing substantive reforms of the FISA court system to grant greater oversight and create an adversarial dimension to the court.[139] This proposal failed to win enough support and Wyden and other senators agreed to support Sensenbrenner's Freedom Act, which they hoped would accomplish some (though not all) of the same goals.

By the time the Freedom Act passed through Congress, negotiation and compromise had significantly weakened the legal language of the bill and, therefore, the potential impact on intelligence activities. For instance, the original provision banning bulk data had been eliminated in favor of a less stringent provision requiring agencies to provide "reasonable" justification before collecting bulk data related to a certain issue or suspect. The Freedom Act also extended Section 215, the roving wiretaps provision, and

The FCC publishes official rules of "neutrality"

2016

The EU establishes the General Data Protection Regulation (GDPR), described as the strongest digital data privacy law in the world

the lone wolf surveillance authority, until 2019.

Critics of the bill, like *Guardian* journalist Spencer Ackerman, argued that the language in the final bill still provided the NSA and other agencies of the state the room for interpretation that could be used to essentially continue surveillance programs largely unaltered. The provisions demanding FISA oversight for instance, were also part of the PATRIOT Act and yet, using controversial interpretations, the government enabled the NSA to bypass the FISA court entirely in establishing the Stellar Wind program. Critics, therefore, saw no reason to believe that the Freedom Act's changes would be strong enough to substantively change NSA or other intelligence agency behavior.[140] Furthermore, despite court rulings that certain activities carried out under the PATRIOT Act were unconstitutional, the Freedom Act essentially legalized many of these same activities, to the dismay of privacy advocates.

In an August 2015 article in *Salon*, journalist Elsa Givan interviewed computer security engineer and software designer Micah Lee, a founding member of the Freedom of the Press Foundation and previously a technology and security expert for the Electronic Frontier Foundation. Lee helped *Guardian* journalist Glenn Greenwald analyze and secure the documents received from Snowden and was Greenwald's digital security advisor, helping to keep the data safe while Greenwald and other journalists published articles on the contents.

In the article, Lee discusses the Snowden leaks, NSA spying methods and programs, and proposes that a lack of information and understanding among the American people is the reason that interest in privacy hadn't coalesced into a meaningful push for stronger privacy protections.

2017

The "Vault 7" secrets, a leak of 9,000 CIA documents, reveal details of the CIA's attempts to break through encryption used by Internet

President Trump appoints Ajit Pai to head the FCC, who abolishes the FCC neutrality protections

'I HAD NO IDEA WHAT I WAS GETTING INTO': GLENN GREENWALD'S SECURITY GURU ON EDWARD SNOWDEN'S SECRETS, OBAMA'S SURVEILLANCE STATE

by Elsa Givan

Salon, August 2015

Source Document

Micah Lee is the 21st-century power player—not a gray-haired politician in a Brooks Brothers suit, but a casual, slightly awkward technologist. As Lee is quick to point out, there's one reason why that role has changed.

"It's all on the Internet," he explains, "but... people just don't understand how the Internet works." According to Lee, people tacitly accept violations of their Internet privacy rights because they simply don't understand what rights are being violated.

"It's very dysfunctional from a government reform standpoint," Lee continues as he sips his Americano. "A lot of what the [National Security Administration] does with dragnet surveillance is very blatantly breaking the Fourth Amendment right of every American. But they have their own rules." He shrugs.

Lee looks like any Berkeley grad student stopping in at Café Yesterday before heading to campus. He's tall, lanky, and sports a T-shirt, jeans, and a canvas messenger bag. He could be any regular 29-year-old, but he's not—he's the technological brilliance behind First Look Media's The Intercept and the initial contact for Edward Snowden's 2013 intelligence leaks.

Lee began his career after dropping out of Boston University to pursue activism. He honed his technical skills as a method of protest and eventually landed a job at the Electronic Frontier Foundation. Now, Lee works as a technology analyst at The Intercept.

"I have a kind of unique job," says Lee, "we actually just released First Look code. So [for example] one of the things I also help do is redact documents securely and make sure we don't have any hidden information that we meant to not publish when publishing documents." The early 2014 redaction failure of the New York Times is a good example of just why Lee's work is so crucial.

Congress debates whether or not to renew the controversial Section 702 FISA Amendment used to authorize NSA domestic intelligence operations since 2008

"'I Had No Idea What I Was Getting Into': Glenn Greenwald's Security Guru on Edward Snowden's Secrets, Obama's Surveillance State"
continued

And, according to Lee, there are still quite a few documents left that must be effectively redacted if they're ever to be released for public consumption. "Yeah, there's still a lot of documents," he quips in reference to his 2013 trip to Rio de Janeiro. He visited Intercept journalist Glenn Greenwald and secured his computers containing the remainder of the unreleased Snowden documents.

In fact, Lee was the first person Snowden contacted after struggling to connect with Greenwald. Lee proceeded to facilitate Snowden's contact with journalist and filmmaker Laura Poitras, who later broke one of the lead stories on the Snowden documents in the Washington Post. Why did Lee take Snowden's initial anonymous encrypted email seriously when he admitted to receiving many each day?

"He sounded..." Lee pauses. "Sane," he finally says, laughing nervously. "I had no idea what I was getting into."

Since the recent expiration of key PATRIOT Act provisions that the NSA claimed created legality for its metadata collection program and the subsequent passage of the USA Freedom Act, Snowden and his intelligence leaks have come to the forefront of public debate once again. "The legal reforms that have been passing have not been very substantial," says Lee. "But there's definitely a shift in debate even if there isn't a very big shift in reform." In the days preceding the vote on the reauthorization of the PATRIOT Act, many administration officials and members of Congress made public statements regarding the potential dangers of expiration. Even President Obama warned that expiration would threaten national security.

Lee sighs when asked about these statements.

"The legal justification for surveillance has always been terrorism," he says. "I think that the reason why the PATRIOT Act provisions expired... is because there hasn't actually been a very big terrorism problem recently... plus the Snowden documents have just shown how incredibly overboard the government has gone in surveilling everyone. So I think that those two combined make it so that just calling "terrorism" doesn't always work anymore."

Even so, threats of terrorism still carry considerable weight in American

1788 State legislatures ratify the U.S. Constitution, establishing the basic precedent for all future constitutional law

1791 The U.S. Congress ratifies the Bill of Rights, creating the first 10 amendments to the United States Constitution

continued

political discourse, as evidenced by the passage of the Freedom Act shortly after the PATRIOT Act's expiration. Although the Freedom Act has been touted as a substantial reform to illegal surveillance, many have criticized it as insufficient or even counterproductive.

Lee refers to the Freedom Act as "kind of horrible," explaining that "[The Freedom Act] for the first time tries to address mass surveillance but also for the first time legalizes chunks of mass surveillance that have always been illegal... [mass surveillance is] being addressed in a very bad way that's sort of legitimizing all of the stuff that shouldn't be legitimate."

Is there hope for legitimately resolving privacy issues, both on a domestic and international level, for U.S. citizens? Not even slightly, according to Lee.

"In terms of legislation, we're never going to get privacy for everybody and the most we could ever ask for would be 'it's not okay to spy on Americans but it's perfectly okay to spy on anyone else in the world.' If the NSA were going to change things to start complying with the Constitution and the law, they would have to stop spying on Americans but they could continue to spy on the other 7 billion people. And... I don't think that [a cessation of domestic spying] is even ever going to happen."

The main issue, according to Lee, is that substantial efforts at reform have been largely rendered ineffective. "All of the oversight of the intelligence community that got set up in the 1970s... was a really big deal [at the time]... fast-forward 30, 40 years and it's all backwards now."

"The FISA Court is a rubber stamp and Congress is... just defending what NSA is doing against people who are trying to reform it." Lee appears visibly frustrated at the lack of what he refers to as "meaningful oversight."

In order to strengthen these weak reforms, Lee suggests that the FISA Court stop using "secret legal interpretations" that "[go] against democracy." He also urges Congress to "be a bit more adversarial to the intelligence community" and "regularly audit for abuse." These reforms are all much easier said than done, though—a point he makes before trailing into a glum silence.

Lee is also appalled by the Obama administration's stance on surveillance and press freedom. "There's definitely a different climate doing investigative journalism now than there used to be... the Obama administration has just gone overboard with Espionage Act charges on Snowden and several other sources and journalists."

1868 The 14th Amendment to the U.S. Constitution guarantees all citizens the right to due process under the law

1890 Warren and Brandeis publish "The Right to Privacy" in the *Harvard Law Review*

"'I Had No Idea What I Was Getting Into': Glenn Greenwald's Security Guru on Edward Snowden's Secrets, Obama's Surveillance State"
continued

"The Espionage Act under the Obama administration is being used against journalists and sources when it's never been used like that in history," he finishes grimly.

In 2014, President Obama asserted that Snowden shouldn't have leaked the NSA documents because the issue of illegal surveillance would have inevitably been brought up through secret review processes.

When asked if he agrees with this assertion, Lee looks entertained. "No," he says, laughing. "I don't see any evidence that the Obama administration was going to bring up surveillance issues, especially considering that the Obama administration has just been expanding surveillance."

This expansion under the Obama administration was actually the driving factor in Snowden's decision to leak, Lee continues. He explains that Snowden considered being a whistleblower "for a long time" under the Bush administration but held out when President Obama was elected because he anticipated positive change. "When things got a lot worse [under the Obama administration], that was when he decided to do it."

When asked more broadly about whistleblowers, Lee hesitates before giving a concrete answer. "Just because you have access to information about a lot of corruption or a lot of crimes doesn't necessarily…." He trails off. "I mean, I think that it's good; I think that it's necessary for democracy… because whistleblowers are often times the only way that information can get out. It's just a hard decision…." He stops again.

"Because it might ruin your life."

It's not just potential whistleblowers and journalists who are at risk either— average Americans are all potential targets for warrantless surveillance and hacking.

"Everybody is really, really insecure," he laments.

"It's definitely not just NSA and FBI… you have to worry about. There's a lot of off-the-shelf hacking products… it's easy to dismiss this stuff as being like 'it's really complicated, so it's only NSA and CIA that do it,' but it's really not that complicated. You can download free software hacking tools and spend a weekend learning how to use them and then hack a bunch of people."

1923
Meyer v. Nebraska establishes that the 14th Amendment guarantees privileges of citizenship

1928
Olmstead v. United States rules that wiretapping is not a form of search and seizure defined by the 14th Amendment

continued

At the same time, it's often difficult for most Americans to find the motivation to protect their information when the process seems more trouble than it's worth. "I think that it's a legit criticism that it's really complicated and hard," Lee echoes. But he goes on to argue that "everyone has a right to privacy in the United States and everyone also has a right to free speech, but just because you don't have anything to say doesn't mean that you don't have that right anymore."

"I think that it's really important to stand up for your privacy rights because otherwise they're going to go away. They've already basically gone away, and the only way to have privacy anymore is to take it into your own hands."

In preparation for this interview, The Qui Vive attempted to set up encrypted email and found it to be less complicated than expected (which was still quite complicated). There's a steep learning curve in regards to the vernacular used around encryption, but it's not impossible to understand and implement.

For those looking to start with something easier, Lee recommends Signal, an iPhone app that sends encrypted messages and makes encrypted phone calls. He also advocates for the use of OTR (Off-The-Record) messaging, an encrypted chat service.

However, using third party hosts (i.e., Google, Apple, Microsoft) for increased security can lead to an "obnoxious tradeoff," according to Lee. "The Third Party Doctrine... [is] the Justice Department's legal opinion that when people's private information is held by a third party, it's not really their private information. So that means that if you store your messages with your friends on Facebook... it's not violating your rights if [the government goes] to Facebook and [gets] those messages... I don't think that this is gonna change. As long as companies and news organizations don't host their own services... third parties will be the ones getting requests, [since] it's a lot less risky for leak investigators to send requests to third parties than it is to send requests to journalists."

The face of journalism has changed rapidly as technology has proliferated. Lee anticipates that as print media dies and online media becomes the dominant form of journalism, news organizations will begin to track their audience in the same way that companies like Facebook and Google do.

"News organizations are gonna be... spying on all of their readers and advertising [to them]... young

---

1934 The Federal Communications Commission (FCC) is established under the Federal Communications Act (FCA)

1942 *Goldman v. United States* rules that using electronic listening devices does not violate the 14th Amendment

"'I Had No Idea What I Was Getting Into': Glenn Greenwald's Security Guru on Edward Snowden's Secrets, Obama's Surveillance State"
continued

journalists should be aware of [this trend] and try and fight it."

Lee also believes that journalism has become more difficult and risky since the advent of the modern surveillance state. "It used to be that when journalists had sensitive sources, they could make a phone call from a pay phone and it was pretty anonymous... now nobody can make a phone call without being tracked... nobody can send emails without being tracked. Nobody can meet in person and carry their cell phone with them without being tracked."

With the Third Party Doctrine and such constant tracking, being an anonymous source in the twenty-first century is nearly impossible.

Lee's comments emphasize that the state of privacy rights in the United States is much worse than people think. After the Snowden leaks died down, most Americans went back to daily life without much thought. But security issues are only becoming more pertinent, our rights are only being invaded more acutely, and the risk of illegal government overreach is only increasing. The Freedom Act essentially legalized the parts of the PATRIOT Act that were abused to justify the NSA metadata program and later ruled illegal. If we write the Fourth Amendment out of the law, does its status as a constitutional right really matter?

It's frightening to consider that the answer could be no.

What was clear from studies of public opinion in 2014 and 15 was that Americans were, in general, very concerned about their privacy and were simultaneously losing faith that the government could be trusted to handle sensitive data.

In May of 2015, a *Pew Research* report on privacy, NSA surveillance, and national security revealed that 54 percent of the people (including 56 percent of Republicans, 48 percent of Democrats, and 57 percent of independents) disapproved of NSA phone and Internet data collection.

1945 The National Security Agency secretly creates Project SHAMROCK

1950 Senator Joseph McCarthy delivers a shocking speech claiming that more than 200 communist spies have infiltrated the U.S. government

Since 2001, security-minded legislators and intelligence industry representatives had echoed a singular sentiment: that the threats facing the nation required citizens to compromise their privacy rights and potentially their civil liberties. This claim did not change, significantly, over the years, but the idea that fighting terrorism required surrendering liberties never gained majority support among the people.

In the Spring of 2014, Pew researchers found that 74 percent of Americans, across partisan lines, did not believe that national security required surrendering civil liberties. This was an increase from another Pew poll in 2004 in which a lesser majority, 60 percent, held the same view. Pew researchers found that 87 percent of Americans were aware of the NSA surveillance programs (in 2014) and that 61 percent had become less confident that the programs served the public interest. However, the 2015 Pew report also showed divergence on more specific issues. For instance, 49 percent of Americans stated they did not feel the government had gone far enough to protect the country from terrorism, whereas only 37 percent believed the nation had gone "too far" in restricting civil liberties. [141]

Americans are deeply afraid of terrorism and so wary of going too far in restricting the government's tools ostensibly used to combat radicals and terrorist groups. However, the public also rejects the basic premise that sacrificing civil liberties is *necessary* to fight terrorism. This was true immediately after the 9/11 attacks and remained true in 2015, with an even larger proportion of Americans asserting that national security should not require surrendering civil liberties. If there is a public mandate that can be derived from public opinion polls between 2001 and 2015, it is that the American people want their government to fight terrorism, but question the way in which the government has engaged in this fight thus far.

Heading into 2016, Americans continued to demonstrate mixed and often conflicting opinions about personal privacy and national security. The subsequent year, notable for the controversial campaign of businessman

1951 *Dennis v. United States* rules that government limits to speech is legal only to prevent a threat to public safety or security

1959 *Barenblatt v. United States* rules that it's legal to order people to reveal personal details if national threat is perceived

outsider Donald Trump, saw a broad priority shift for American news media and activist organizations. In facing the rise of a new brand of anti-modernist conservatism in the United States, privacy was subordinated to the preeminent issues of the campaign season: immigration, jobs, and international trade.

1965 *Griswold v. CT* rules in favor of married couples' right to privacy

1967 *Katz v. United States* rules wiretaps a form of search and seizure

Willis Ware of RAND Corporation writes *Security and Privacy in Computer*

CONCLUSION

The USA Freedom Act was not an ideal outcome for privacy advocates. The momentum against domestic surveillance that existed after the 2013 Snowden leaks hit the press had been weakened by uncertainty, misinformation, fear, and several years of intensive terrorist attacks around the world. Despite broad public disapproval of domestic surveillance in general, the issue remained a moderate or minor priority for most Americans. Entering 2016, attention shifted away from the Obama administration entirely, and towards the controversial 2016 election season in which the many minor and major controversies surrounding Donald Trump's propagandistic presidential campaign supplanted most of the other issues that had been discussed in American politics to that point.

1968 The Omnibus Crime Control Act holds that police needed to obtain a warrant before engaging in wire-

1969 Joseph Licklider creates the Advanced Research Projects Agency Network (ARPANET), which was

DISCUSSION QUESTIONS

- Was the USA Freedom Act a substantial improvement over the PATRIOT Act? Explain your answer.
- Are security expert Micah Lee's arguments about the overall lack of public interest/outrage about domestic surveillance and loss of privacy rights convincing? Why or why not?
- Do you agree with the majority of Americans who disapprove of domestic surveillance? Why or why not?
- Do you think that the Espionage Act applies to the Snowden case? Explain your answer.

Works Used

Ackerman, Spencer. "Fears NSA will seek to undermine surveillance reform." *The Guardian*. Guardian News and Media. June 1, 2015. Web. 30 Oct. 2017.

Gao, George. "What Americans think about NSA surveillance, national security and privacy." *Pew Research*. Pew Research Center. Factank. May 29, 2015. Web. 29 Oct. 2017.

Greenwald, Glenn. "On PATRIOT Act Renewal and USA Freedom Act: Glenn Greenwald Talks With ACLU's Jameel Jaffer. *The Intercept*. First Look Media. May 27, 2015. Web. 29 Oct. 2017.

Lewis, Paul, and Dan Roberts. "NSA reform bill to trim back US surveillance unveiled in Congress." *The Guardian*. Guardian News and Media. Sept. 25, 2013. Web. 30 Oct. 2017.

Roberts, Dan. "PATRIOT Act author prepares bill to put NSA bulk collection 'out of business.'" *The Guardian*. Guardian News and Media. Oct. 10, 2013. Web. 30 Oct. 2017.

1971   The Pentagon Papers leaks from the press raise the issue of the Freedom of the Press versus the privacy of the government to conceal information about national security operations

1972   *Eisenstadt v. Baird* rules that the right to privacy applies to individuals

Introduction

In December of 2015, FBI agents were investigating a domestic terrorist attack in which a married couple attacked a government center in San Bernardino, California, and discovered an Apple iPhone belonging to one of the suspects. The FBI then contacted Apple to ask the company to help access the phone's contents without triggering a security feature that would erase all data on the phone if an incorrect password was attempted too many times within a short period of time. Apple told the FBI that they would be happy to help, but that they did not have a system in place that would allow the company to bypass the security on the phone. The FBI then asked Apple to build a program that would provide a "back door" to the phone's security, a process discussed in Chapter 21. Apple refused on the basis that building such a program would essentially mean providing the FBI with the ability to unlock any iPhone and because the existence of a "master key" program like the one the FBI wanted was too dangerous to Apple customers, who might be compromised if the master key program fell into the wrong hands. A federal judge then ordered Apple to comply with the FBI order, citing precedent in the 1789 *All Writs Act,* which gives the government the power to compel citizens to obey rules in ways not explicitly described in existing laws.

The source for this chapter is an article written by journalist Danny Lewis in a February 2016 issue of *Smithsonian Magazine*, entitled, "What the All Writs Act of 1789 Has to Do with the iPhone." Lewis focuses less on the contemporary controversy and more on the history of the 1789 All Writs Act, other historic attempts to use the law by the federal government, and the legal implications of using the more than 200-year-old law to compel a modern company to essentially work for the state.

1974

The Watergate Scandal results in the revelation that the CIA had been conducting widespread surveillance of American dissidents and foreign leaders without judicial oversight

The Privacy Act is established

Topics covered in this chapter include:
- Encryption
- Corporate rights
- Digital privacy
- Domestic terrorism

This Chapter Discusses the Following Source Document:
Lewis, Danny. "What the All Writs Act of 1789 Has to Do with the iPhone." *Smithsonian*. Smithsonian Institution. Feb. 24, 2016.

The Writ to Refuse
The Apple Inc. iPhone Controversy (2016)

In December of 2015, 28-year-old U.S. born Syed Rizwan Farook and his wife, 29-year-old Pakistan-born Tashfeen Malik, attacked the Inland Regional Center of San Bernardino County, during an employee holiday party. Armed with semi-automatic rifles, pistols, and pipe bombs, Farook and Malik killed 16 people and injured 24 before both were killed by police after a chase and shootout. In the wake of the tragedy, police struggled to figure out whether Farook and Malik were members of a radical cell, or were "lone-wolf" radicals inspired by, but not belonging to, a larger group. The international radical group known as the Islamic State (also known as ISIS or ISIL or the Daesh) issued a statement through the organization's *Amaq News Agency* claiming responsibility for the attack, and

U.S. President Barack Obama is seen on television in the home of Helen Medina, during his nationally-televised address from the White House about terrorism following the attack on the Inland Regional Center on December 6, 2015 in San Bernardino, California. Medina hid in her home as the police engaged in a gun battle with terror suspects on her street; police killed the terror suspects that attacked the Center in San Bernardino that left 14 people dead and 21 injured on December 2. (Photo: Joe Raedle/Getty Images)

1980 The Intelligence Oversight Act (IOA) updates legal standards

1981 President Reagan's E.O. authorized wiretapping

1986 The Electronic Communications Privacy Act is established

investigators were concerned that Farook and Malik might have been part of a larger terrorist cell.

As part of the investigation, the FBI obtained an iPhone 5 belonging to one of the two assailants and hoped to gain access to the phone to learn more about the assailants. The iPhone discovered among the assailants' possessions had a security feature, generally called a "self-destruct" mechanism, that automatically erased all data from the phone if an incorrect password was entered 10 times. In an effort to avoid possibly erasing the data stored on the device, the FBI contacted Apple, Inc., asking the company to help bypass the phone's security. Apple explained to investigators that the company did not have a tool that could be used to bypass the self-destruct mechanism and so the FBI asked Apple to create a new, specialized software program that would run off of the phone's RAM and would allow investigators to enter possible passcodes without activating the self-destruct mechanism built into the iPhone's operating system. Apple refused the request on the principle that building such a program would be akin to building a master key that could potentially be used to unlock any iPhone. The FBI then took their case to the courts.

In February of 2016, Justice Sheri Pym of the US District Court of Central California, issued a court order requiring Apple, Inc. to comply with the FBI request. This ruling, based on an obscure legal precedent known as the "All Writs Act" of 1789, demonstrated considerable creativity on the part of the courts and raised interesting legal questions about ownership of digital data and the rights and responsibilities of corporations.[142]

In this article, from *Smithsonian Magazine* on February 24, 2016, New York technology journalist Danny Lewis describes the current and historic use of the "All Writs Act," and discusses the possible consequences of the federal ruling on the San Bernardino case.

WHAT THE ALL WRITS ACT OF 1789 HAS TO DO WITH THE IPHONE:
HOW A LAW SIGNED BY GEORGE WASHINGTON IS BEING APPLIED BY GOOGLE

by Danny Lewis

Smithsonian Magazine, **February 24, 2016**

Source Document

The ongoing battle between the United States government and Silicon Valley tech companies over encryption exploded last week when a federal judge ordered Apple to unlock an iPhone. In doing so, the government invoked a 227-year-old law signed by President George Washington, himself. But what does one of the United States' earliest laws have to do with the latest in communications technology?

To make a long story short, Apple has so far refused to comply with government agents, who have demanded that the company helps break the encryption on the iPhone that belonged to one of the San Bernardino shooters responsible for killing 14 people in California, last year. Since the attacks, the F.B.I. has received a warrant for the information on the iPhone, but they have been stymied by its encryption, which is why they're looking for Apple's help. In an attempt to make Apple create a backdoor into the phone's operating system, the U.S. government has invoked the All Writs Act of 1789.

The legal issues around the All Writs Act are complex, but at its core, it gives federal judges the power to issue orders to compel people to do things within the limits of the law, Eric Limer writes for *Popular Mechanics*. In its original form, the All Writs Act was part of the Judiciary Act of 1789, which established the federal justice system from the Supreme Court down to the lower federal courts. The All Writs Act allows federal judges the power to issue court orders, which makes sense considering that "writs" is an old-fashioned term for "formal order." At one point in history, writs were fairly common, but over the centuries, courts have tended to use them only in extraordinary circumstances where there are no other laws that apply to the situation at hand, such as this case, where the government wants access to information in a password-protected cell phone. The vagueness built into the All Writs Act has leant itself to new readings throughout American history, Laura Sydell reports for *NPR*.

"The law actually seems to be keeping up with technology by being

The Bush administration secretly authorizes the President's Surveillance Program (PSP), utilizing E.O. 12333

The U.S. PATRIOT Act alters existing laws to facilitate better communication between the state's intelligence branches in the effort to combat terrorism

The Transportation Security Administration (TSA) is established, creating the "No Fly" and "Selectee" lists that limit the right to travel on airplanes in the United States

"What the All Writs Act of 1789 Has to do With the iPhone: How a Law Signed by George Washington is Being Applied by Google" continued

so broad that we're just reinterpreting it all the time," Irina Raicu, director of the Internet Ethics Program at Santa Clara University's Markkula Center for Applied Ethics, tells Sydell.

The government has cited the All Writs Act in the past, from a 1977 ruling forcing phone companies to help set up devices that record all numbers called from a specific phone line to the Wireless Communications and Public Safety Act of 1999 which required all cellphone providers to be able to geolocate their customers' phones. The writ does have its limits: a federal judge ruled in 2005 that the All Writs Act could not be used to force a phone company to allow real-time tracking of a phone without a warrant, Eric

Lichtblau and Katie Benner report for the *New York Times*.

Whatever the result of this current case, the dispute will have major legal implications for the fight over encryption in the future. While the F.B.I. says the court-ordered bypass, which would have Apple create software to disable the feature that wipes the data on the phone after 10 incorrect password attempts, would only be used in this particular case, Apple's chief, Timothy D. Cook recently fired off an open letter arguing that allowing this would set a dangerous legal precedent for user privacy in the future

In the open letter issued by Apple CEO Tim Cook, Cook explains the company's perspective on the issue, the potential security issues involved and claims that the company's primary interest is in ensuring the future security of Apple's products, while also taking a stand against what Cook calls "governmental overreach." Critics doubted that Apple was as concerned with customer privacy as with protecting the technological innovations built into the company's devices.

In his open letter to Apple's customers, Cook asserts that encryption is an essential *consumer* technology: The best measure available to consumers to prevent cybercrime and the exposure of potentially damaging

2005

The PATRIOT Act was reauthorized without substantial changes as Congress favors security concerns over warnings that the law creates the potential for civil liberties violations

The *New York Times* publishes articles resulting from leaks revealing the secret President's Surveillance Program (PSP) established by the Bush administration

personal data. While acknowledging the legitimacy of the FBI's goals, and the company's desire to help to prevent terrorism, Cook explains that the FBI's request is not simply for Apple Inc. to bypass security on a single device, but rather, to create a key that could be used to unlock any device. This backdoor key, Cook argues, is too dangerous to customer safety to create and Cook expresses doubt that the government, Apple, or any other entity would be capable of keeping such a program safe and out of the hands of cybercriminals. Furthermore, he argues that there exists no clear legal precedent that would allow the government to compel a company to create a product dangerous to their own customers.

Cook's argument, that the FBI was asking "...for something we simply do not have, and something we consider too dangerous to create," gets to the heart of the long-standing debate over the legality of encryption and whether corporations had a responsibility to help or facilitate access for government and law enforcement. Cook essentially argues that there should be no "master key" available to anyone, whether a company or a government agency, because the very existence of such a mechanism poses too great a risk to personal privacy. Consider, for instance, that a data breach at Apple, Inc, or one from the federal government (of which there have been many) could result in the master key program falling into the hands of hackers or cybercriminals.

Further, privacy advocates have long warned about the dangers of enabling the state to develop powers or technologies that might be used to curtail basic liberties, unless proper safeguards to prevent misuse had already been developed and established. This effort, despite sometimes generating controversy, is in keeping with the fundamental founding principles of the United States. Therefore, while Apple's CEO says, "...we believe the FBI's intentions are good," placing limits on governmental abilities is not only about whether the people trust their current government, but are meant to address the future as well, when unforeseen cir-

2007
The Bush Administration plans to make data taken from spy satellites available to law enforcement to be used to conduct domestic surveillance

2008
Congress passes Section 702, or the FISA Amendment Act, which is used to permit a massive NSA and CIA domestic surveillance program

cumstances might lead to an administration willing and able to use such tools for oppression.

A third issue also arises from the government's use of the All Writs Act, which simply states that the federal government is empowered to "issue all writs necessary or appropriate in aid of their respective jurisdiction and agreeable to the usages and principles of law." Writing about the issue in *The Guardian*, journalists Neil Richards and Woodrow Hartzog argue that the All Writs Act is "…a piece of Swiss Army knife legislation that the FBI is trying to turn into a giant sword."

Hartzog and Richards explain that the act was part of a series of clauses meant to establish the legal right for the government to exceed the powers given within the constitution, but only to the point at which the government utilized powers "necessary and appropriate" to the situation. The power to compel a company to create new software isn't included in the FBI's legal mandate and Judge Sheri Pym therefore utilized a catchall rule to argue that the FBI could legally exceed the powers given to the agency by existing U.S. law. Hartzog and Richard thus argue:

> *"If the FBI wants new powers to break the security of our digital technologies, let it demand a law from Congress. And then we can submit that law to the courts to make sure it is constitutional."*[144]

The government's attempts to force Apple to create new software also raises another important issue involving civil liberties; whether the state has the right to compel a company, or a person, to work in service of the state? In other words, can the government simply order a car manufacturer, or a baker, or an oil painter, or a watchmaker, to create something for the government? What if the person has moral or ethical objections to the request? What if the person simply doesn't want to work for the government? Does a person or company have the right to refuse? In the case

2012 The Obama Administration proposes a Consumer Privacy Bill of Rights guaranteeing individuals the right to greater control over the use of their digital data

2013 The *Guardian* and the *Washington Post* publish the first series of articles derived from leaked NSA and CIA documents delivered by Edward Snowden

of the Apple Inc. controversy, the courts ruled that the FBI had the right to compel Apple Inc. to work for the state. The justification or reasons for the FBI's request may have played a role in this specific case, but such considerations are immaterial to the broader question, which has far reaching civil liberties implications.[145]

In the end, after Apple's refusal, the FBI announced that it had found another way to bypass the phone's security system and the issue of whether Apple would be forced to comply became moot. The case, however, raised a host of important questions regarding privacy and security that were never resolved. Apple was widely praised by some for standing up to the government's perceived overreach, while also criticized by those who believed the company was refusing to help a government agency combat a legitimate, imminent threat to national security. Others believed that Apple's decision was based purely on the desire to protect company secrets and so criticized Apple for placing the company's well-being ahead of security and public concerns. Whether Cook and Apple, Inc. were motivated by "selfish" concerns, or were legitimately interested in the broader privacy and civil liberties issues is also unimportant in exploring the significance of the case. Whatever the reasons, the civil liberties questions raised by the case are important in determining when and to what degree national security concerns can be used to compel behavior.

Public opinion on the Apple issue was mixed and complex. In a 2016 article in *The Atlantic*, journalist Krishnadev Calamur explored opinion polls on the issue. In a *Pew Research* poll, 51 percent believed that Apple should comply with the government's orders, though Calamur raised an interesting point in noting that the way in which the question was raised influenced the way people responded to the issue. The original question asked:

The Senate Judiciary committee holds hearings to determine if the executive surveillance operations carried out under the PATRIOT Act were a violation of constitutional law

Snowden leaks reveal that the NSA and CIA had been attempting to force corporations to provide a backdoor to encryption systems that would allow federal agents to bypass consumer encryption

───────── *"As you may know, the FBI has said that accessing the iPhone is an important part of their ongoing investigation into the San Bernardino attacks, while Apple has said that unlocking the iPhone could compromise the security of other user's information, do you think Apple:*

Should unlock the iPhone

Should NOT unlock the iPhone

Don't know/refused."

In answer to the question phrased in this way, 51 percent said Apple should unlock the phone. However, in a Reuters/Ipsos poll, the question was phrased:

───────── *"Apple is opposing a court order to unlock a smart phone that was used by one of the shooters in the San Bernardino attack. Apple is concerned that if it helps the FBI this time, it will be forced to help the government in future cases that may not be linked to national security, opening the door for hackers and potential future data breaches for smartphone users. Do you agree or disagree with Apple's decision to oppose the court order?"*

When phrased in this way, 46 percent supported Apple, and 35 percent supported the government, with 20 percent uncertain about the issue.[146]

The difference in phrasing of the two questions could be seen as constituting a shift in focus as well. When emphasis is placed on the FBI's justification in the specific case, more Americans supported the FBI's argument, whereas, when emphasis was placed on Apple's objections,

2015

Terrorist attacks in France reignite fears of domestic terrorist violence

The PATRIOT Act is replaced by the USA Freedom Act

Federal Courts order Apple, Inc. to create a new operation system that would enable federal investigators to bypass security on an iPhone.

more respondents were willing to accept Apple's position on the issue. In March, a *Wall Street Journal* poll demonstrated a nearly even split on the issue, with Republicans favoring the government by a margin of 57 to 37 percent, while Democrats favored Apple by a margin of 50 to 40 percent. Independent voters, however, strongly sided with Apple, by a margin of 58 to 28 percent.[147]

While the Bernardino iPhone case was proceeding, the Department of Justice (DOJ) also called on Apple to help bypass security on an iPhone belonging to a drug dealer involved in a conspiracy case in New York City. In the case, the DOJ again attempted to argue that the All Writs Act gave them the power to compel Apple to comply with their request and Apple attorneys again refused to help unlock the device. Federal Judge James Orenstein rejected the DOJ's request, holding that the All Writs Act could not legitimately be used to order a company to manipulate its products.

"The implications of the government's position are so far-reaching—both in terms of what it would allow today and what it implies about Congressional intent in 1789—as to produce absurd results."[148]

Be Careful What You Say—Be On Your Guard, WWII Careless Talk poster. (Photo by The National Archives/SSPL/Getty Images)

The FCC publishes official rules of "neutrality"

2016

The EU establishes the General Data Protection Regulation (GDPR), described as the strongest digital data privacy law in the world

CONCLUSION

The Apple iPhone controversy of 2016 intensified the existing debate over encryption and the right to hide from governmental intrusion. Apple Inc. refused to comply with the government's order, despite the court ruling that used the All Writ's Act as precedent, arguing that the existence of a master key like the one that federal government wanted was too dangerous to consumers and violated privacy rights protections. The suit never came to trial, as the FBI claimed later that they had discovered another way to bypass the phone's security mechanisms. Studies of public opinion about the incident found that the public was broadly supportive of the FBI's desire to conduct a thorough investigation, especially because the case involved domestic terrorism, but that, in general, the public remained skeptical of the federal government's overall commitment to privacy and/or ability to properly secure sensitive information.

2017

The "Vault 7" secrets, a leak of 9,000 CIA documents, reveal details of the CIA's attempts to break through encryption used by Internet

President Trump appoints Ajit Pai to head the FCC, who abolishes the FCC neutrality protections

DISCUSSION QUESTIONS

- Should American citizens have the right to use encryption products that the government cannot bypass? Why or why not?
- Was the *All Writs Act* an appropriate legal justification for the request made by the FBI? Explain your answer.
- Do you trust the federal government to have a master key that would allow federal agents to bypass security on any phone? Why or why not?
- Was Apple Inc. justified in refusing the FBI's request? Why or why not?

Works Used

Ackerman, Spencer, Thielman, Sam, and Danny Yadron. "Apple case: judge rejects FBI request for access to drug dealer's iPhone." *The Guardian*. Guardian News and Media. Feb. 29, 2016. Web. 4 Nov. 2017.

"A Message to Our Customers." *Apple*. Apple, Inc. Feb. 16, 2016. Web. 31 Oct. 2017.

Calamur, Krishnadev. "Public Opinion Supports Apple Over the FBI—or Does it?" *The Atlantic*. Atlantic Monthly Group. Feb. 24, 2016. Web. 4 Nov. 2017.

Musil, Steven. "Apple has support of independent voters in FBI iPhone battle." *CNET*. Mar. 8, 2016. Web. 4 Nov. 2017.

Richards, Neil, and Woodrow Hartzog. "*Apple v. the FBI*: why the 1789 All Writs Act is the wrong tool." *The Guardian*. Guardian News and Media. Feb. 24, 2016. Web. 30 Oct. 2017.

Sorkin, Amy Davidson. "The Dangerous All Writs Act Precedent in the Apple Encryption Case." *The New Yorker*. Conde Nast. Feb. 19, 2016. Web. 31 Oct. 2017.

Zetter, Kim. "Magistrate Orders Apple to Help FBI Hack San Bernardino Shooter's Phone." *Wired*. Conde Nast. Feb. 16, 2016. Web. 31 Oct. 2017.

Congress debates whether or not to renew the controversial Section 702 FISA Amendment used to authorize NSA domestic intelligence operations since 2008

1788 State legislatures ratify the U.S. Constitution, establishing the basic precedent for all future constitutional law

1791 The U.S. Congress ratifies the Bill of Rights, creating the first 10 amendments to the United States Constitution

Introduction

In 2016, Congress began debating another key issue in the domestic surveillance arena, Section 702, or the FISA Amendment Act of 2008. The FISA Amendments Act retconned the FISA system (see Chapter 8) right after leaks revealed that the Bush administration had undertaken a secret domestic surveillance program. When Bush's surveillance program was revealed to Congress and the public in 2006/07, legal scholars immediately noted that the program violated constitutional law and the FISA Act of 1978, despite the administration's argument that alternative interpretations of previous executive orders and the PATRIOT Act, made the program legal. With Section 702, the Bush administration not only legalized the illegal activities that occurred between 2002 and 2008 as part of this secret program, but also granted immunity to individuals who might otherwise have been guilty of violating the law by participating in the program. Declassified documents from the Bush-era made it clear that despite the administration claiming that the program was legal, even within the administration at the time, key officials felt the program violated constitutional rights and laws.

This chapter looks at the beginning of the debate (in 2016) over whether or not to renew the controversial Section 702 amendment. By January of 2018, the issue was still unresolved, though domestic surveillance stalwart and majority leader Mitch McConnell spent weeks campaigning on behalf of renewal, with President Donald Trump throwing his weight behind the renewal camp as well. With neither McConnell nor Trump commanding high approval ratings, their support did little to alter the general sense of skepticism among the public or legislators who'd grown wary over the years about the effectiveness of domestic surveillance on the whole. The source

1868 The 14th Amendment to the U.S. Constitution guarantees all citizens the right to due process under the law

1890 Warren and Brandeis publish "The Right to Privacy" in the *Harvard Law Review*

document for this chapter, excerpts from the May 10, 2016 hearings over the act within the Committee on Judiciary of the U.S. Senate, demonstrate that the concerns of privacy advocates and the warnings of supporters had changed little since 2002. Overall, a lack of specific data on the effectiveness of Section 702 or domestic surveillance, in general, made the Section 702 debate a contest between ideological perspectives.

Topics covered in this chapter include:
- The FISA Act of 1978
- The FISA Amendment of 2008
- The PATRIOT Act
- The Bush Administration
- The Obama Administration
- The Trump Administration
- Domestic surveillance
- Bulk data collection
- Congressional hearings

This Chapter Discusses the Following Source Document:
"Oversight and Reauthorization of the FISA Amendments Act: The Balance Between National Security, Privacy and Civil Liberties." Senate Committee of the Judiciary. May 10, 2016.

The Debate Continues
Section 702 Renewal (2016-2018)

In 2016, Congress debated whether to reauthorize another of the many controversial laws regarding domestic and bulk surveillance, Section 702 or the FISA Amendment Act of 2008. A review of the path from the original 1978 law to the 2016 reauthorization debate shows how the periodic resurgence of interest in intelligence reform repeatedly failed to limit domestic surveillance.

The 1978 Foreign Intelligence Surveillance Act (FISA) was meant to limit the freedom that had previously been afforded to intelligence agencies. The law was the result of a long-term intelligence reform movement in the 1960s and 70s, which gained a boost in public and legislative support after the Watergate scandal and subsequent discovery of the many questionable ways in which the Nixon administration had used the state's intelligence agencies.

The Foreign Intelligence Surveillance Court (FISC) was controversial at its inception for a number of reasons. First, recognizing that foreign intelligence requires secrecy, Congress determined that the hearings and rulings of the court would be kept secret and this worried some civil rights activists who worried that without outside oversight the court might turn into a "rubber stamp" for the intelligence agencies. Second, the FISC justices, who are selected from among federal trial judges by the Chief Justice of the United States, only hear arguments from the federal government and thus the court does not adhere to the "adversarial" process established in the U.S. judicial system to protect the rights of the accused.

Another concern, among critics of the 1978 bill, was that requirements for obtaining a court order to conduct surveillance under FISA were less stringent than the requirements for obtaining a court order to conduct

1934

The Federal Communications Commission (FCC) is established under the Federal Communications Act (FCA)

1942

Goldman v. United States rules that using electronic listening devices does not violate the 14th Amendment

Senator Richard Blumenthal, D-Conn., chairs the Senate Judiciary Committee hearing on 'The Report of the Privacy and Civil Liberties Oversight Board on Reforms to the Section 215 Telephone Records Program and the Foreign Intelligence Surveillance Court' on Wednesday, Feb. 12, 2014. (Photo by Bill Clark/CQ Roll Call)

surveillance under the 1968 Omnibus Crime Bill. Critics worried that federal agencies (like the FBI) might use the FISA Act to bypass the more stringent laws regarding domestic surveillance activities. To prevent this, the FISA Act was written using narrow language that required investigators to provide reasonable justification that the investigation they intended to undertake involved foreign entities, individuals, or nations.

In the wake of the September 11, 2001 terrorist attacks, Congress and the Bush Administration set about conducting an overhaul of U.S. military and intelligence industry policy. Capitalizing on a limited surge in public support for aggressive anti-terrorism action, Congress passed the PATRIOT Act of 2001, while Congress empowered the administration to claim additional powers under the Authorization to Use Military Force (AUMF). It was later revealed that the administration had used a secret

1945 The National Security Agency secretly creates Project SHAMROCK

1950 Senator Joseph McCarthy delivers a shocking speech claiming that more than 200 communist spies have infiltrated the U.S. government

interpretation of the PATRIOT Act, coupled with the AUMF, and Executive Order 12333, to establish the President's Surveillance Program. This was then used to authorize a massive domestic spying program that involved intercepting phone and Internet data from millions of American citizens.

The President's Surveillance Program became known to the public, there was a short-term movement in favor of intelligence reform as constitutional law experts argued that the program violated constitutional law. In 2008, Congress addressed this controversy by amending the FISA law of 1978 with the controversial "FISA Amendments Act," or "Section 702," which was marketed to the public as "intelligence reform," but essentially legalized the kind of surveillance conducted by the Bush administration since 2001 and granted immunity for individuals involved in such activities prior to the amendment.

The FISA Amendment Act, or Section 702, was renewed under the Obama Administration in 2012, just before the Snowden leaks revealed the depth of the government's domestic surveillance programs. The Snowden leaks again motivated a short-lived intelligence reform movement, which resulted in the PATRIOT Act being replaced by the Freedom Act of 2015. The USA Freedom Act, like Section 702, was marketed as intelligence reform, but resulted in few substantive changes while still providing sufficient legal justification for the Obama administration to continue its domestic surveillance activities.

Section 702 expires on December 31, 2017 and Congress has therefore been debating whether to renew the controversial provision since 2015. On May 10, 2016, the Committee on Judiciary of the U.S. Senate met for a hearing, entitled "Oversight and Reauthorization of the FISA Amendments Act: The Balance Between National Security, Privacy and Civil Liberty," to determine the fate of Section 702. Led by Republican Senator Chuck Grassley of Indiana and Democratic Senator Patrick Leahy of Vermont, the committee heard testimony from The Brennan Center for

1951 *Dennis v. United States* rules that government limits to speech is legal only to prevent a threat to public safety or security

1959 *Barenblatt v. United States* rules that it's legal to order people to reveal personal details if national threat is perceived

Justice, the IronNet cybersecurity company, and the Privacy and Civil Liberties Oversight Board.

In a repeat of the ideological arguments presented at previous hearings regarding the expansion of surveillance powers under the former PATRIOT Act and the original FISA Amendments Act, those favoring reauthorization of Section 702 primarily took the stance that Section 702, like other efforts to expand surveillance capabilities, was warranted and necessary given the nature of the terrorist threat. Those in favor of reform argued that the law, as currently written, does not effectively protect civil liberties.

OVERSIGHT AND REAUTHORIZATION OF THE FISA AMENDMENTS ACT:
THE BALANCE BETWEEN NATIONAL SECURITY, PRIVACY AND CIVIL LIBERTIES
Senate Committee of the Judiciary
May 10, 2016
Source Document

ARGUMENTS IN FAVOR OF RENEWAL

Kenneth L. Wainstein, Partner, Cadwalader, Wickersham & Taft LLP. Former Assistant Attorney General and Homeland Security Advisor from 2008 to 2009

THE THREAT OF TERRORISM

Before going into the intricacies of the FISA Amendments Act and its reauthorization, it's important to remind ourselves about the national security threats—and particularly, the threat from international terrorism— that this legislation addresses. Since the attacks of September 11, 2001, we and our allies have been at war with terrorist organizations around the globe—including al Qaeda and its affiliates and the Islamic State (ISIS)— as well as with individuals—like the San Bernardino shooters—whom these organizations have inspired. While we have significantly degraded their effectiveness with strikes against their leadership and operational personnel, they continue to pose a serious threat to the U.S. and our allies.

1965 *Griswold v. CT* rules in favor of married couples' right to privacy

1967 *Katz v. United States* rules wiretaps a form of search and seizure

Willis Ware of RAND Corporation writes *Security and Privacy in Computer*

continued

Although many institutional and operational improvements have contributed to that progress over the past decade, none has been more instrumental than the overall enhancement in our intelligence capabilities. We can see the fruits of that effort regularly in the newspaper. Every successful strike against ISIS leaders happens because we have sound intelligence telling us where and when we can find the targets. And every plot prevention happens because we now have a developed network of surveillance capabilities, human assets and international partnerships that provides us insight into our adversaries' planning and operations that we simply did not have before 9/11.

EFFECTIVENESS OF SECTION 702

The most significant provision in the FISA Amendments Act is Section 702, which authorizes the FISA Court to approve surveillance of categories of terrorist suspects and other foreign intelligence targets overseas without requiring the government to provide an individualized application as to each particular target. The statute prescribes a new, streamlined process by which categories of overseas targets are approved for surveillance. Under this process, the Attorney General and the Director of National Intelligence (DNI) provide the FISA Court annual certifications identifying the categories of foreign intelligence targets to be subject to this surveillance and certifying that all statutory requirements for that surveillance have been met. The Intelligence Community designs "targeting procedures" for the surveillance categories, which are the operational steps it takes to determine whether each individual surveillance target is outside the United States and therefore subject to this non-individualized collection process. It also draws up "minimization procedures" that lay out the limitations on the handling and dissemination of any information from that surveillance that may identify or relate to U.S. 6 persons. The government submits the Attorney General and DNI certifications as well as the targeting and minimization procedures for review by the FISA Court. The FISA Court then decides whether to approve the surveillances, based on its assessment whether all statutorily required steps have been taken in compliance with FISA and the Fourth Amendment.

This process succeeds in bringing the operation of FISA back in line with its original intent. It allows the government to conduct overseas surveillance without individualized court approval while at the same time giving the FISA Court an important role in ensuring that this authority is used only against those non-U.S.

1968 The Omnibus Crime Control Act holds that police needed to obtain a warrant before engaging in wire-

1969 Joseph Licklider creates the Advanced Research Projects Agency Network (ARPANET), which was

"Oversight and Reauthorization of the FISA Amendments Act: The Balance Between National Security, Privacy and Civil Liberties"

continued

persons who are "reasonably believed to be located outside the United States."

INTELLIGENCE AGENCY OVERSIGHT

Over the past few years, the leaks by Edward Snowden and the government's transparency efforts have revealed an Intelligence Community committed to compliance with the law. Since 2008, the government has informed the FISA Court of incidents in which the NSA collected information in non-compliance with the FAA. As the government explained, all of these incidents were apparently mistakes and oversights, and none reflected intentional misuse of the FAA authority—a conclusion that was echoed by the findings of the Privacy and Civil Liberties Oversight Board ("PCLOB"), which conducted its own review of the Executive's intelligence collection operations under Section 702 and found that "internal and external compliance programs have not to date identified any intentional attempts to circumvent or violate the procedures or the statutory requirements." The absence of any findings of intentional misconduct over the past eight years is a testament to the Intelligence Community's commitment to compliance.

Matthew G. Olsen, Former Director of the National Counterterrorism Center

THE THREAT OF TERRORISM

Several factors are driving this trend toward the increasing pace and scale of terrorist violence. First, the sheer number of number of Europeans and other Westerners who have gone to Syria to fight in the conflict and to join ISIS is supplying a steady flow of operatives to the group. More than 6,000 Europeans—including many French, German, British, and Belgian nationals—have travelled to Syria to join the fight. This is part of the total of approximately 40,000 foreign fighters in the region. Among the Europeans who have left for Syria, several hundred fighters have returned to their home countries, typically battle-hardened, trained, and further radicalized. The number of Americans who have travelled to Syria or Iraq, or have tried to, exceeds 250.

We should also recognize the potential for an ISIS-directed attack in the United States. While the principal threat from ISIS in the United States is from homegrown, ISIS-inspired actors, the fact that so many Americans have travelled to Syria and Iraq to fight,

1971 The Pentagon Papers leaks from the press raise the issue of the Freedom of the Press versus the privacy of the government to conceal information about national security operations

1972 *Eisenstadt v. Baird* rules that the right to privacy applies to individuals

continued

along with thousands more from visa waiver countries in Europe, raises the real danger that these individuals could be deployed here to conduct attacks similar to the attacks in Paris and Brussels.

Second, ISIS has developed more advanced tactics in planning and executing these attacks. In both Brussels and Paris, the operatives staged coordinated attacks at multiple sites, effectively hampering police responses. The militants exploited weaknesses in Europe's border controls in order to move relatively freely from Syria to France and Belgium. The group has also moved away from previous efforts to attack symbolically significant targets—such as the 2014 attack on a Jewish museum in Brussels—and appears to have adopted the guidance of a senior ISIS operative in the group's online magazine, who directed followers "to stop looking for specific targets" and to "hit everyone and everything." Further, the explosives used in Paris and likely in Brussels indicate the terrorists have achieved a level of proficiency in bomb making.

Third, existing networks of extremists in Europe are providing the infrastructure to support the execution of attacks there. The investigations of the Paris and Belgium attacks have revealed embedded radical networks that supply foreign fighters to ISIS in Syria and operatives and logistical support for the terrorist attacks in those cities. While such entrenched and isolated networks are not present in the United States, ISIS continues to target Americans for recruitment, including through the use of focused social media, in order to identify and mobilize operatives here.

Looking more broadly, the rise of ISIS should be viewed as a manifestation of the transformation of the global jihadist movement over the past several years. We have seen this movement diversify and expand in the aftermath of the upheaval and political chaos in the Arab world since 2010. Instability and unrest in large parts of the Middle East and North Africa have led to a lack of security, border control, and effective governance. In the last few years, four states—Iraq, Syria, Libya, and Yemen—have effectively collapsed. ISIS and other terrorist groups exploit these conditions to expand their reach and establish safe havens.

EFFECTIVENESS OF SECTION 702

Based on its review of classified information, the PCLOB identified approximately 30 specific cases in which Section 702 information was the initial catalyst that identified previously unknown terrorist

1974

The Watergate Scandal results in the revelation that the CIA had been conducting widespread surveillance of American dissidents and foreign leaders without judicial oversight

The Privacy Act is established

"Oversight and Reauthorization of the FISA Amendments Act: The Balance Between National Security, Privacy and Civil Liberties"
continued

operatives or plots. In the typical case, Section 702 information was based on targeted surveillance of a specific foreign individual overseas based on the government's reasonable belief the individual was involved with terrorist activities. This narrowly focused surveillance led to the discovery of a specific plot. The government next engaged in a short, intensive period of further investigation, leading to the identification of associates and the arrest of the plotters. As a result, Section 702 led to the arrest of more than 100 individuals on terrorism-related offenses. These paradigmatic cases demonstrate the critical importance of the authority Congress established under Section 702.

Two specific cases, now declassified, highlight the value of Section 702.

In September 2009, NSA analysts relied on Section 702 to target an email address used by a suspected al-Qaeda courier in Pakistan. Based on this surveillance, NSA discovered a message sent to an individual 6 in the United States, subsequently identified as Najibullah Zazi, who was urgently seeking advice on how to make explosives. Further investigation revealed that Zazi and a group of

operative had imminent plans to detonate explosives in the New York City subway. The FBI and local law enforcement officials arrested Zazi and his confederates and stopped the attack before it could be executed.

In another example, NSA conducted surveillance under Section 702 of an email address used by a suspected extremist in Yemen. This surveillance led NSA to discover a connection between the extremist and an unknown person in Kansas City, Missouri, who was then identified as Khalid Ouazzani. The follow-up investigation revealed that Ouazzani was connected to other al-Qaeda associates in the United States, who were part of an earlier plot to bomb the New York Stock Exchange. All of these individuals were prosecuted and pled guilty to terrorism offenses

ARGUMENTS IN FAVOR OF REFORM

Elizabeth Goitein, Co-Director of the Liberty and National Security Program at the Brennan Center for Justice of the New York University School of Law.

1975   Senator Frank Church leads a series of hearings about the secret NSA SHAMROCK operation involved intercepting communications from American citizens

1978   Congress passes the 1978 FISA Act

continued

ON GOVERNMENT SURVEILLANCE

The government uses Section 702 to engage in two types of surveillance. The first is "upstream collection," whereby a huge proportion of communications flowing into and out of the United States is scanned for selectors associated with designated foreigners. Although the data are first filtered in an attempt to weed out purely domestic communications, the process is imperfect and domestic communications are inevitably acquired. The second type of Section 702 surveillance is "PRISM collection," under which the government provides selectors, such as e-mail addresses, to U.S.–based electronic communications service providers, who must turn over any communications to or from the selector. Using both approaches, the government collected more than 250 million Internet transactions a year as of 2011.

Due to the changes wrought by Section 702, it can no longer be said that FISA is targeted at foreign threats. To describe surveillance that acquires 250 million Internet communications a year as "targeted" is to elevate form over substance. And on its face, the statute does not require that the targets of surveillance pose any threat, or that the purpose of the program be the collection of threat information.

It is certainly possible that the government is choosing to focus its surveillance more narrowly than Section 702 requires. The certifications that the government provides to the FISA Court—which include the foreign intelligence categories at which surveillance is aimed, and could therefore shed some light on this question—have not been publicly disclosed by the government. Even if actual practices stop short of what the law allows, however, the available statistics suggest a scope of surveillance that is difficult to reconcile with claims of narrow targeting. Moreover, one certification, listing the foreign nations and factions about which foreign intelligence could be sought, was leaked; it included most of the countries in the world, ranging from U.S. allies to small countries that play little role on the world stage.

More important, Americans' privacy should never depend on any given administration's voluntary self-restraint. Nor should it depend on additional requirements layered on by the FISA Court, given that the court's membership changes regularly and its judges generally are not bound by others' decisions. Section 702 establishes the boundaries of permissible surveillance, and it clearly allows collection of communications between Americans and foreigners who pose no threat to the U.S. or its

1980 The Intelligence Oversight Act (IOA) updates legal standards

1981 President Reagan's E.O. authorized wiretapping

1986 The Electronic Communications Privacy Act is established

"Oversight and Reauthorization of the FISA Amendments Act: The Balance Between National Security, Privacy and Civil Liberties"
continued

interests. That creates an enormous opening for unjustified surveillance.

CONSTITUTIONAL ISSUES

The warrantless acquisition of millions of Americans' communications presents deep Fourth Amendment concerns. The communications being obtained under Section 702, like any emails or phone calls, include not only mundane conversations, but the most private and personal confidences, as well as confidential business information and other kinds of privileged exchanges. Since the Supreme Court decided Katz v. United States in 1967, the government has been required to obtain a warrant to wiretap Americans' communications.13 Moreover, in a subsequent case, the Court made clear that this requirement applied in domestic national security cases as well as criminal cases.

A. "Incidental" Collection

The government nonetheless justifies the warrantless collection of international communications under Section 702 on the ground that the targets themselves are foreigners overseas, and the Supreme Court has held (in a different context) that the government does not need a warrant to search the property of a non-U.S. person abroad. Although the communications obtained under Section 702 sometimes involves both foreigners and Americans, the FISA Court has held that the right to conduct warrantless surveillance of the foreign target entails the right to "incidentally" collect the communications of those in contact with the target.

But there is nothing "incidental" about the collection of Americans' communications under Section 702. Indeed, with one exception, Section 702 wrought no change to the government's authority to collect foreign-to-foreign communications. The primary change brought about by Section 702 was to eliminate the requirement of an individual court order when a foreign target communicates with an American. The legislative history makes clear that facilitating the capture of communications to, from, or about Americans was a primary purpose, if not the primary purpose, of the statute.

In any event, outside of Section 702, the case law does not support the existence of a right to warrantless "incidental" collection. In criminal cases, courts have held that the

continued

government need not obtain separate warrants for everyone in contact with the target. But they have emphasized the existence of a warrant for the target (which affords some vicarious protection to those in contact with him) and the application of strict minimization procedures. In the Section 702 context, there is no warrant to help mitigate "incidental" collection, and the minimization procedures are significantly weaker than those that apply in the domestic criminal context.

B. The Foreign Intelligence Exception

Alternatively, the FISA Court (and, more recently, a district court following its lead) has relied on the "foreign intelligence exception" to the Fourth Amendment's warrant requirement. The Supreme Court has never recognized this exception, and there is significant controversy over its scope. The FISA Court has construed the exception extremely broadly, stating that it applies even if the target is an American and even if the primary purpose of collection has no relation to foreign intelligence.

In the era before FISA, however, several federal courts of appeal had the opportunity to review foreign intelligence surveillance, and they articulated a much narrower version of the exception. They held that it

applies only if the target is a foreign power or agent thereof, and only if the acquisition of foreign intelligence is the primary purpose of the surveillance. They also emphasized the importance of close judicial scrutiny (albeit after-the-fact) in cases where the target challenges the surveillance. While these cases addressed surveillance activities that differed in many respects from Section 702, it is clear that Section 702 surveillance would not pass constitutional muster under the standards they articulated.

A detailed analysis of the case law is beyond the scope of this testimony, but the Brennan Center's report, "What Went Wrong with the FISA Court," engages in such an analysis and explains why the foreign intelligence exception does not justify Section 702 surveillance.

C. The Reasonableness Test

Even if a foreign intelligence exception applies, the surveillance still must be "reasonable" under the Fourth Amendment. The "reasonableness" inquiry entails weighing the government's interests against the intrusion on privacy.

In undertaking this analysis, courts generally accept that the government's interest in protecting national security is of the highest order—as it certainly is. But to determine the reasonableness

The Bush administration secretly authorizes the President's Surveillance Program (PSP), utilizing E.O. 12333

The U.S. PATRIOT Act alters existing laws to facilitate better communication between the state's intelligence branches in the effort to combat terrorism

The Transportation Security Administration (TSA) is established, creating the "No Fly" and "Selectee" lists that limit the right to travel on airplanes in the United States

"Oversight and Reauthorization of the FISA Amendments Act: The Balance Between National Security, Privacy and Civil Liberties"
continued

of a surveillance scheme, one must also ask whether it goes further than necessary to accomplish the desired end. For instance, how does it further national security to allow the targeting of foreigners who have no known or suspected affiliation with foreign governments, factions, or terrorist groups? How does it further national security to permit the FBI to search for Americans' communications to use in prosecutions having nothing to do with national security?

EFFECTIVENESS OF OVERSIGHT

The substantive legal restrictions on collecting information about Americans are looser than they have been since before 1978. At the same time, the amount of data available to the government and the capacity to store and analyze that data are orders of magnitude greater than they were during the period of J. Edgar Hoover's worst excesses. History teaches us that this combination is an extraordinarily dangerous one.

To date, there is only limited evidence of intentional abuse of Section 702 authorities. There have, however, been multiple significant

instances of non-compliance by the NSA with FISA Court orders. Notably, these include cases in which the NSA did not detect the noncompliance for years, and the agency's overseers had no way to uncover the incidents in the meantime. Given that these incidents went unreported for years even when the agency was not trying to conceal them, it is not clear how overseers would learn about intentional abuses that agency officials were making every effort to hide. In other words, regardless of whether intentional abuse is happening today, the potential for abuse to take place—and to go undiscovered for long periods of time—is clearly present.

Inadvertent failures to adhere to privacy protections are a concern in their own right. On multiple occasions in the past decade, the FISA Court has had occasion to rebuke the NSA for repeated, significant, and sometimes systemic failures to comply with court orders. These failures took place under multiple foreign intelligence collection authorities (including Section 702) and at all points of the programs: collection, dissemination, and retention.

It is unclear whether these failures occurred because the NSA

2005

The PATRIOT Act was reauthorized without substantial changes as Congress favors security concerns over warnings that the law creates the potential for civil liberties violations

The *New York Times* publishes articles resulting from leaks revealing the secret President's Surveillance Program (PSP) established by the Bush administration

continued

was not putting sufficient effort into compliance, because the NSA lacked the technical capability to ensure consistent compliance, or some other reason. Whatever the explanation, the fact that the agency's many failures to honor privacy protections were inadvertent is of limited comfort when the NSA is asking Congress and the American public to entrust it with extensive amounts of private data.

ARGUMENTS FOR REFORM

Having discussed the concerns surrounding Section 702 surveillance, it is important to address the arguments that have been put forward for its necessity. These arguments have varying degrees of merit, but none of them forecloses the possibility of reforms.

A. Restoring FISA's Original Intent?

Executive branch officials have argued that Section 702 was necessary to restore the original intent behind FISA, which was being subverted by changes in communications technology. These officials note that FISA in 1978 required the government to obtain an individual court order when collecting any communications involving Americans that traveled by wire, but required an individual court order to obtain satellite communications only when all of the communicants were inside the U.S. Asserting that "'wire' technology was the norm for domestic calls, while "almost all transoceanic communications into and out of the United States were carried by satellite, which qualified as 'radio' (vs. 'wire') communications," they infer that Congress intended to require the government to obtain an order when acquiring purely domestic communications, but not when obtaining communications between foreign targets and Americans. This intent was undermined when fiber-optic cables later became the standard method of transmission for international calls.

The problem with this theory is two-fold. First, it would have been quite simple for Congress to state that FISA orders were required for purely domestic communications and not for international ones. Instead, Congress produced an elaborate, multi-part definition of "electronic surveillance" that relied on particular technologies rather than the domestic versus international nature of the communication. Second, it is not correct that "almost all" international communications were carried by satellite; the available evidence indicates that one third to one half of international communications were carried by wire.

2007 The Bush Administration plans to make data taken from spy satellites available to law enforcement to be used to conduct domestic surveillance

2008 Congress passes Section 702, or the FISA Amendment Act, which is used to permit a massive NSA and CIA domestic surveillance program

"Oversight and Reauthorization of the FISA Amendments Act: The Balance Between National Security, Privacy and Civil Liberties"
continued

A more plausible explanation for the original FISA's complex scheme—one with much stronger support in the legislative history—was put forward by David Kris, a former head of the Justice Department's National Security Division. Mr. Kris concluded that Congress intended to require a court order for international wire communications obtained in the U.S., and that the purpose behind its definitional acrobatics was to leave legislation covering surveillance conducted outside the U.S. and NSA satellite surveillance for another day. Although Congress never followed up, the legislative history of FISA made clear that the gaps in the statute's coverage of NSA's operations "should not be viewed as congressional authorization for such activities as they affect the privacy interests of Americans."

A related argument in support of Section 702 is that certain purely foreign-to-foreign communications, which Congress never intended to regulate, now travel through the United States in ways that bring them within FISA's scope. In practice, this appears to be a fairly discrete (albeit thorny) problem that applies to one category of communication: e-mails between foreigners that are stored on U.S. servers. 84 Section 702, however, goes far beyond what would be necessary to solve that problem. Moreover, there is a flip side to this issue: changes in technology have also caused certain purely domestic communications to travel outside the U.S. in ways that remove them from FISA's scope. Purely domestic communications once traveled on copper wires inside the U.S., and FISA thus required a court order to obtain them. Today, digital data may be routed anywhere in the world—and U.S. Internet Service Providers may store domestic communications on overseas servers—rendering these communications vulnerable to surveillance under Executive Order 12333, which has far fewer safeguards. Any legislation that attempts to solve the former problem should address the latter one as well.

B. Thwarting Terrorist Plots

Executive officials have stated, and the PCLOB and the president's Review Group on Intelligence and Communications Technologies have found, that Section 702 surveillance played a role in detecting and thwarting a number of terrorist plots. That is, after all, the most important function the statute is intended to

2012 The Obama Administration proposes a Consumer Privacy Bill of Rights guaranteeing individuals the right to greater control over the use of their digital data

2013 The *Guardian* and the *Washington Post* publish the first series of articles derived from leaked NSA and CIA documents delivered by Edward Snowden

continued

serve; if it did not accomplish this goal, it presumably should go the way of the now-discontinued Section 215 bulk collection program, which, by most reliable reports, added little counterterrorism value.

Whether Section 702 is useful is thus a question of critical importance. It is not, however, the only question that must be answered. There is also the question of whether effective surveillance could be conducted in a manner that entails less intrusion on the privacy of law-abiding Americans and foreigners. Indeed, in the few cases that have been made public—including those of Najibullah Zazi, Khalid Ouazzani, David Headley, Agron Hasbajrami, and Jamshid Muhtorov—it appears that the targets of the Section 702 surveillance were known or suspected to have terrorist affiliations. These cases therefore do not support, for example, the idea that the NSA needs the ability to target any foreigner overseas.

We must also ask whether the costs to our liberties are too high. It is commonly said that if terrorists succeed in undermining our values, they win. But while this notion is often invoked, it is also often forgotten. The United States was founded on a set of core principles, and none of these was more important than the right of the citizens to be free from undue intrusions by the government on their privacy. Our Constitution promises us that law-abiding citizens will be left alone. It is incumbent upon us as a nation to find ways of addressing the terrorist threat that do not betray this promise.

TRANSPARENCY

Within constitutional bounds set by our nation's courts, it is up to the American people—speaking through their representatives in Congress—to decide how much surveillance is too much. But they cannot do this without sufficient information. While a significant amount of information about Section 702 has been declassified in recent years, critical information remains unavailable. For instance, the certifications setting forth the categories of foreign intelligence the government seeks to collect—but not the individual targets—have not been released, even in redacted form. Unlike the NSA and the CIA, the FBI does not track or report how many times it uses U.S. person identifiers to query databases containing Section 702 data. The list of crimes for which Section 702 data may be used as evidence has not been disclosed. Nor have the policies governing when evidence used in legal proceedings is considered to be "derived from" Section 702 surveillance. The length of time that the FBI may retain data that has been reviewed but whose value has not been determined remains secret.

The Senate Judiciary committee holds hearings to determine if the executive surveillance operations carried out under the PATRIOT Act were a violation of constitutional law

Snowden leaks reveal that the NSA and CIA had been attempting to force corporations to provide a backdoor to encryption systems that would allow federal agents to bypass consumer encryption

"Oversight and Reauthorization of the FISA Amendments Act: The Balance Between National Security, Privacy and Civil Liberties"
continued

Perhaps most strikingly, despite multiple requests from lawmakers dating back several years, the NSA has yet to disclose an estimate of how many Americans' communications are collected under Section 702. The NSA has previously stated that generating an estimate would itself violate Americans' privacy, ostensibly because it might involve reviewing communications that would otherwise not be reviewed. In October of last year, a coalition of more than thirty advocacy groups—including many of the nation's most prominent privacy organizations—sent a letter to the Director of National Intelligence urging that the NSA go forward with producing an estimate. The letter noted that, as long as proper safeguards were in place, the result would be a net gain for privacy. Recently, a bipartisan group of fourteen House Judiciary Committee members sent the DNI a letter making the same request.

This basic information is necessary for Americans to evaluate the impact of Section 702 on their privacy. It is also necessary because most Americans are not lawyers, and when they hear that a surveillance program is "targeted" only at foreigners overseas and that any acquisition of Americans' communications is "incidental," they may reasonably assume that there is very little collection of their own calls and e-mails. An estimate of how many communications involving Americans are collected would help to pierce the legalese and give Americans a truer sense of what the program entails.

In short, Section 702 is a public statute that is subject to the democratic process, and the democratic process cannot work when Americans and lawmakers lack critical information. More transparency is urgently needed so that the country can begin an informed public debate about the future of foreign intelligence surveillance.

The testimony delivered by Elizabeth Goitein, of the Brennan Center for Justice was based, in part, on a study conducted by the Brennan Center on the implementation and effectiveness of Section 702 between 2008 and 2016, with the experts at the center determining that the law, as it ex-

2015

| Terrorist attacks in France reignite fears of domestic terrorist violence | The PATRIOT Act is replaced by the USA Freedom Act | Federal Courts order Apple, Inc. to create a new operation system that would enable federal investigators to bypass security on an iPhone. |

ists, is not sufficient to protect civil liberties. In a comprehensive analysis of data on the issue, Goitein and Faiza Patel, the report's primary authors, provide evidence of deep concerns revealed in the courts and by data leaks detailing NSA, CIA, and FBI activities under the program and recommend abandoning or substantially reforming the program rather than reauthorizing 702 in its current form.[149]

In the debate over the issue, supporters of reauthorization argue that the Privacy and Civil Liberties Oversight Board (PCLOB) had not discovered sufficient evidence of intentional misuse of Section 702 powers to warrant concerns that the law had been abused, misused, or was insufficient to protect civil liberties. Goitein admits, in her written testimony, that there has been little evidence to suggest intentional misuse, but suggests that the potential for abuse still exists. Two members of the PCLOB also testified at the May 10 hearings, both recommending reforms to the current law before reauthorization.

The only existing evidence of intentional misuse of NSA data comes from a 2013 letter from Inspector General George Ellard delivered to Senator Charles Grassley of the Senate Committee on the Judiciary, providing brief descriptions of 12 instances in which the NSA had detected intentional misuse by NSA employees. In most of the cases reviewed, civilian employees of the NSA had used the classified data to conduct surveillance on their husbands/wives, romantic partners, or to essentially stalk individuals in whom the employees had taken an apparent romantic interest. Most of the instances reported by the NSA ended when the employee "retired" and thus none resulted in prosecution.[150]

After the legislative election of 2016, the House and Senate were unable to develop reform or reauthorization proposals that garnered majority support. Various House and Senate proposals have been crafted, some including substantial reforms, and others calling for "clean" reauthorization without significant changes. Long-time privacy advocates Ron

The FCC publishes official rules of "neutrality"

2016

The EU establishes the General Data Protection Regulation (GDPR), described as the strongest digital data privacy law in the world

Wyden and Rand Paul were among those senators who promoted serious changes to the law requiring federal agents to adhere more closely to due process and Fourth Amendment restrictions. Senator Kamala Harris and Senator Dianne Feinstein were also among those in the Senate urging for stronger civil liberties protections before the bill should be renewed.[151]

The year 2017 was also the first year of the Donald Trump presidency and so provided some hints on how Trump would cope with national security issues. The Trump administration, which came to power amidst a populist surge in the United States, resulted in a pro-business government that offered little direct influence on the privacy versus security debate during the first year of Trump's presidency. The administration announced that it supported "full and permanent" reauthorization of Section 702, thus aligning the presidency with Senator Mitch McConnell and the pro-domestic surveillance wing of the conservative legislature.

While marketing himself as an anti-establishment figure, most of Trump's policy positions, with regard to security, have fallen within the bounds of establishment GOP priorities, though he has also advanced a number of extreme proposals that stretch the boundaries of GOP traditionalism. For instance, Trump's assertion that immigration poses a threat to national security is a repeat of a very old, anti-modernist strain of conservative thought that uses immigrants as scapegoats for loosely connected national issues. The same phenomenon motivated the 1882 Chinese Exclusion Act, with conservative politicians blaming Chinese immigrants for a loss of jobs and alleging that immigrants were largely criminals, despite no evidence to support such claims, and therefore using Chinese immigrants as scapegoats for deeper economic and social problems. Trump's anti-immigrant stance is, therefore, in keeping with traditional conservative thought and strategy, though his proposal to build a $21 billion wall along the Mexican border departs from traditional GOP tactics in that GOP traditionalists would typically avoid engaging in a massive public

2017

The "Vault 7" secrets, a leak of 9,000 CIA documents, reveal details of the CIA's attempts to break through encryption used by Internet

President Trump appoints Ajit Pai to head the FCC, who abolishes the FCC neutrality protections

works project that has questionable potential effectiveness. Trump has, therefore, demonstrated a general tendency to align with basic, conservative ideology, though, on occasion, he also supports more radical policies. How this will translate to future debates over privacy and security remains to be seen.

Congress debates whether or not to renew the controversial Section 702 FISA Amendment used to authorize NSA domestic intelligence operations since 2008

CONCLUSION

The 1978 FISA Amendment Act was intended to prevent a president from misusing the powers of the intelligence agencies in such a way as to violate the rights and liberties of the American people. The law was a reaction to the revelation that Richard Nixon had engaged in unwarranted, unlawful, domestic surveillance, using the CIA and FBI to investigate subversives in the youth movement and to spy on political opponents so as to gain an electoral advantage. Bush violated the FISA Act when he empowered the NSA to collect data on all American citizens, to be analyzed later to search for terrorists, thus violating not just the letter, but the spirit of the law as well. Section 702 made this legal, and granted immunity to Bush and his associates who'd violated the law to start their domestic surveillance program in the first place. The 2016–2018 debate over whether or not to renew Section 702 is, therefore, a return, full circle, to the very beginning of the domestic surveillance controversy. The wild card in the continuing privacy debate is President Donald Trump, who has been critical both of the nation's intelligence agencies and of domestic surveillance, in specific. It remains unclear whether Trump will alter this stance, as he has done with many other pre-election positions, to align with conservative mainstream thought, or whether he will take a different direction than GOP leaders of the past.

1788 State legislatures ratify the U.S. Constitution, establishing the basic precedent for all future constitutional law

1791 The U.S. Congress ratifies the Bill of Rights, creating the first 10 amendments to the United States Constitution

DISCUSSION QUESTIONS

- Should Trump maintain or change the existing laws regarding privacy and domestic surveillance? Why or why not?
- What testimony provided at the hearings over Section 702 were most influential? Give reasons.
- Was it ethical for the Bush administration to grant immunity to individuals who might have broken the law by establishing the President's Surveillance Program? Why or why not.
- Do you believe that the FISA Act as it was originally written would hamper the state's ability to prevent terrorism? Why or why not?

Works Used

Goitein, Elizabeth, and Faiza Patel. "What Went Wrong with the FISA Court." *Brennan Center*. Brennan Center for Justice. New York University School of Law. 2015. Web. 31 Oct. 2017.

Matishak, Martin. "Trump's rhetoric hampers his aides' surveillance push." *Politico*. Politico LLC. Oct. 8, 2017. Web. 4 Nov. 2017.

Nakashima, Ellen, and Karoun Demirjian. "Divided Senate intelligence panel advances spy-bill renewal without major changes." *Washington Post*. Washington Post Company. Oct. 25, 2017. Web. 1 Nov. 2017.

"NSA Inspector Generals Letter to Senator Charles Grassley." *NSA*. National Security Administration. Sept. 11, 2013. Pdf. 31 Oct. 2017.

Olmstead, Kenneth. "Most Americans think the government could be monitoring their phone calls and emails." *Pew Research*. Pew Research Center. Sept. 27, 2017. Web. 5 Nov. 2017.

1868 The 14th Amendment to the U.S. Constitution guarantees all citizens the right to due process under the law

1890 Warren and Brandeis publish "The Right to Privacy" in the *Harvard Law Review*

1923

Meyer v. Nebraska establishes that the 14th Amendment guarantees privileges of citizenship

1928

Olmstead v. United States rules that wiretapping is not a form of search and seizure defined by the 14th Amendment

Introduction

This chapter recapitulates and deepens the historical discussion of privacy rights, philosophy, and law presented in the previous chapters of the book. Beginning with revisiting the landmark 1890 *Right to Privacy* law review by Brandeis and Warren, and exploring the motivation behind the article and the source of the "right to be let alone" perspective, the chapter proceeds to touch on a variety of important points about the way that privacy is conceptualized in the American popular imagination. This includes a discussion of the data privacy and ownership debate, as well as a review of some of the most influential philosophical definitions and privacy concepts in history, from the right to be let alone to the pragmatic approach to privacy as protecting the space and freedom for individuals to develop private rituals in their lives.

The source document for this chapter is a 2016 article by jurist Urs Gasser from the *Harvard Law Review*, entitled, "Recoding Privacy Law: Reflections on the Future Relationship Among Law, Technology and Privacy," in which Gasser presents his own summary on the history of privacy law considering the technological transformations of the digital age. Gasser calls for a paradigm shift, reimagining the relationships between technology and civil liberties and between privacy and the law such that the legal debates on the future of privacy will be less rooted in the arguments, precedent, and traditions of the pre-digital world, and will better reflect the integration of technology and personal life that pervades the modern era.

1934 The Federal Communications Commission (FCC) is established under the Federal Communications Act (FCA)

1942 *Goldman v. United States* rules that using electronic listening devices does not violate the 14th Amendment

Topics covered in this chapter include:

- The FISA Act of 1978
- The FISA Amendment of 2008
- The PATRIOT Act
- The Bush Administration
- The Obama Administration
- The Trump Administration
- Domestic surveillance
- Bulk data collection
- Congressional hearings

This Chapter Discusses the Following Source Document:
Gasser, Urs. "Recoding Privacy Law: Reflections on the Future Relationship Among Law, Technology and Privacy." *Harvard Law Review*. Dec. 9, 2016.

The Existence of Privacy
The Philosophy of Privacy

In 1880, when Judge Thomas Cooley published a famous treatise on constitutional law, Cooley wrote, "The right to one's person may be said to be a right of complete immunity: The right to be let alone." The question facing Cooley was whether *attempting* to touch a person, rather than actually touching the person, was an injury, and Cooley argued that it was an injury. Whether Cooley felt such a "right" could be extended to cover other instances of alleged privacy violations is unclear, but, in 1890, former lawyer Samuel Warren and his one-time roommate and law partner Louis Brandeis, who later became a Supreme Court justice, used Cooley's "right to be let alone" as part of their basis for a general right to privacy derived from common law.

Warren's interest in privacy was inspired by personal concerns. Mr. Warren's daughter, who recently married, was the subject of a number of tabloid news stories ferreting out gossip about the family, who were, at the time, among Boston's wealthy elite and so frequently the subject of tabloid gossip. Objecting to the way the papers had, in Warren's view, violated his daughter's privacy on her wedding day, Warren enlisted the help of Brandeis and the two delivered a powerful argument for right to privacy law that inspired more than a century of scholarship and debate on the issue.

In a 1960 article *Privacy*, written by William M. Prosser in the *California Law Review*, Prosser notes:

> *"All this is a most marvelous tree to grow from the wedding of the daughter of Mr. Samuel D. Warren. One is tempted to surmise that she must have been a very beautiful girl. Resembling, perhaps, that fabulous creature, the daughter of a Mr. Very, a*

1951 *Dennis v. United States* rules that government limits to speech is legal only to prevent a threat to public safety or security

1959 *Barenblatt v. United States* rules that it's legal to order people to reveal personal details if national threat is perceived

The title page of *General Principles of Constitutional Law* (1880)

1965 *Griswold v. CT* rules in favor of married couples' right to privacy

1967 *Katz v. United States* rules wiretaps a form of search and seizure

Willis Ware of RAND Corporation writes *Security and Privacy in Computer*

confectioner in Regent Street, who was so wonderous fair that her presence in the shop caused three or four hundred people to assemble every day in the street before the window to look at her, so that her father was forced to send her out of town, and counsel was led to inquire whether she might not be indicted as a public nuisance. This was the face that launched a thousand lawsuits. "[152]

Brandeis and Warren's article was the beginning of a long-term effort to establish a right to privacy within the U.S. legal system and the fundamental arguments raised by Warren and Brandeis have been cited by numerous scholars, legislators, and privacy advocates speaking or writing about the issue over the next century. This dynamic effort was based on the intuitive belief that privacy is a fundamental human value, but, as scholars studied the issue, it became clear that it was exceedingly difficult to define and codify privacy and so to create a legal definition robust enough to cover all instances in which individuals, in their lives, intuitively saw privacy issues. Subsequent jurists, legal scholars, and philosophers thus endeavored to answer this basic question: What is privacy and why is it important?

THE LIMITS OF PRIVACY

Philosophers and legal scholars generally agree that privacy rights are never absolute. This is because humans live in societies and being part of a society necessarily involves surrendering some personal liberty. At one point in human history, it was possible for a person to live a more or less solitary existence in an ungoverned portion of the world. Such an individual would not, of course, have any legal right to privacy, nor any other legal rights, because legal rights require participation in a society that has laws.

1968 The Omnibus Crime Control Act holds that police needed to obtain a warrant before engaging in wire-

1969 Joseph Licklider creates the Advanced Research Projects Agency Network (ARPANET), which was

Thus, in the ancient world, a person seeking absolute isolation and privacy might have lived outside of national boundaries, staking a personal claim to a portion of what humanity calls "nature." This kind of existence may provide nearly absolute privacy, but also means relying entirely on one's own skills and capabilities. If an isolated hermit becomes ill, for instance, he or she might die from the illness because they have no access to trained physicians, might starve from an inability to obtain food, or might have his or her property or assets taken by individuals who are healthier, stronger, or are part of a larger group. Living within a society provides substantial benefits, including access to a pool of skills and capabilities beyond that which any one person would likely possess. However, living within a group also requires compromise and the willingness to surrender some degree of privacy and personal liberty.

Brandeis and Warren recognized that the legal right to privacy was not absolute, even when it concerned their shared enemy: the press. They argued, therefore, that an individual who chooses to run for public office must accept a higher level of scrutiny, because the public has the right to know even personal information about a person who seeks to become a leader in their society. Politicians and other public figures therefore implicitly accept a contract when attempting to become a representative of the people, and this contract involves surrendering the right to privacy at least concerning information germane to public needs or interest.[153]

The right to privacy, therefore, depends on the degree to which one *participates* in society. Many debates about privacy rights center on the question of whether and when a person has a right to privacy from the government, and this, too, is situational and a matter of degree. The government is an institution that has an implicit contract with the citizenry to provide services and ensure public safety and this may require, in certain conditions, the need to violate the privacy of some citizens. Consider a situation in which the spread of an illness poses a threat to public health.

1971   The Pentagon Papers leaks from the press raise the issue of the Freedom of the Press versus the privacy of the government to conceal information about national security operations

1972   *Eisenstadt v. Baird* rules that the right to privacy applies to individuals

A police CCTV camera observes a woman walking in the Embankment area of central London, 04 April 2007. A system of 'talking' CCTV cameras which let operators shout at people who misbehave is being extended across England, fueling fears of a 'Big Brother' society. Under the scheme, local council workers in local control centres monitor pictures from the cameras and can berate passers-by if they feel they are doing something wrong. (Photo by Leon Neal/AFP/ Getty Images)

It can be argued that a person does not have the right to refuse a state health department examination, even though forcing someone to undergo a medical procedure might, in other circumstances, be considered an unacceptable violation of privacy. This right, it could be argued, is subordinated to the need of the society when and if a person's behavior poses a threat to public safety.

ADVANCING THE CONCEPT OF PRIVACY

Recognizing that concepts of privacy, at least for the purpose of establishing laws, needed to be able to blend the subjective value that people place on privacy with more practical concerns regarding situations in which one needs to balance personal liberty with the collective benefit,

1974

The Watergate Scandal results in the revelation that the CIA had been conducting widespread surveillance of American dissidents and foreign leaders without judicial oversight

The Privacy Act is established

philosophers and legal scholars have studied the nature of privacy and its relationship to law and have tried to generate more robust definitions.

In studying the issue, some scholars have concluded that privacy is not a coherent concept, and some have even argued that the very existence of privacy is an illusion. Criticisms regarding the philosophical or legal coherence of privacy as a concept tend to fall into one of several categories:

• Privacy is not an independent right as claims of privacy can equally be classified as examples of other rights. For instance, the dissemination of the private contents of a letter is covered under copyright law, and there is, therefore, no need to protect such actions under separate privacy laws.

• Cases in which individuals claim privacy rights do not share common characteristics and so there is no concept of privacy that holds in all cases in which individuals claim the right.

• Privacy is a personal preference, rather than a moral issue.

Such arguments, whatever their philosophical grounding, fail to match up with the way that people, in general, *feel* about privacy. Whether this is irrational or a subjective matter of personal preference, there is a shared intuition about the importance of privacy as a feature of human existence. Therefore, numerous philosophers and other scholars have thus attempted to answer the objections of skeptics by formulating more comprehensive concepts of privacy that can be used to meet the conditions of various real-world privacy rights claims and legal disputes.

Privacy as an Expression of Dignity
In 1964, Edward J. Bloustein argued that it was possible to connect disparate claims of privacy, seen in court cases, to derive a general concept involving integrity, dignity, autonomy, and independence. Respect for these values, Bloustein argues, could therefore constitute respect for a

1975   Senator Frank Church leads a series of hearings about the secret NSA SHAMROCK operation involved intercepting communications from American citizens

1978   Congress passes the 1978 FISA Act

broader right to privacy derived as a person's capability to maintain their own human dignity. Therefore, in Bloustein's view, privacy cases involving wiretapping, eavesdropping, dissemination of confidential information, and surveillance could all be related to the desire to protect oneself from injury against one's individual freedom and sense of dignity.[154]

Privacy as a Function of Personal Access

Israeli legal scholar Ruth Gavison, in her 1980 article "Privacy and the Limits of Law," presents a concept of privacy divided into three separate categories:

1) Information about the individual (secrecy)

2) Attention paid to the individual (anonymity)

3) Physical access to the individual (solitude)

Gavison thus argues that a change in state, with regards to any of the three categories, can be called a violation of privacy and argues that privacy is thus coherent in that the goals of controlling access involve a person's internal concepts of autonomy and the social goal of promoting a free society. Thus, in Gavison's view, privacy has social and personal functions and the degree to which individuals conceive of themselves as independent and free, and conceive of their society as promoting these benefits, is related to how the individual and the state function so as to permit individuals to restrict access to themselves.

Building on this same tradition of thought, University of Washington scholar Adam D. Moore argues that privacy can be defined as a series of rights involving the "control of access." This, Moore argues can be a matter of control over physical things, such as a person's body or property, or to information, such as medical or financial data about an individual. Laws regarding privacy, therefore, can grant "access control rights" to certain physical bodies, such as one's own body and (to a more limited extent) to other physical bodies

1980 The Intelligence Oversight Act (IOA) updates legal standards

1981 President Reagan's E.O. authorized wiretapping

1986 The Electronic Communications Privacy Act is established

with which one has a relationship. Laws can also grant access control rights to objects, like houses or other personal property and to intellectual or informational property, such as ideas, communications, or personal records.[155]

Privacy as a Function of Intimacy

In her 1992 book *Privacy, Intimacy and Isolation*, scholar Julie Inness rejects the attempts of other scholars to define privacy as a matter of restricting access or gaining seclusion and, instead, forwards a definition of privacy as "the state of possessing control over a realm of intimate decisions, which includes decisions about intimate access, intimate information, and intimate actions." Intimacy, Inness argues, is not an inherent quality of a certain act but rather is a function of a person's intentions. Privacy is thus cultural, social, and personal, and regards the way a person chooses to construct personal relationships.[156]

Other scholars also argued in favor of a link between privacy and intimacy, at times blending the concept with other concepts involving access such as to formulate a theory of privacy as a matter of restricted access towards the goal of controlling one's intimate life. Privacy, as a function of intimacy, therefore exists as a way for an individual to control his or her ability to create intimate relationships and these relationships, are necessary to human life and wellbeing.

Privacy as a Mechanism for Forming and Maintaining Identity

In a 2003 article in *Seton Hall Law Review*, bioethics research fellow Jonathan Kahn advances a definition of privacy as a legal principle of identity maintenance. Kahn argues that literature on privacy provides justification for a definition of privacy as a system that protects individuals from "the intrusive nature of the (external) market." The marketplace of ideas that Kahn refers to is the competition of ideas that occurs in public discourse, in which ideas and ideologies compete in the formation of collective culture. Privacy, Kahn argues, is a combined theory of social interaction with the marketplace of ideas that is itself the means for creating notions of

1994 | Netscape creates the "cookie" allowing computers to monitor Internet users

2001 | The September 11 terrorist attacks result in Congress authorizing the Bush Administration to utilize military methods to combat terrorism

dignity and identity. Privacy is, therefore, not defined by dignity and identity but is a means of social interaction that gives rise to these concepts.

"Thus, when Justice Brandeis construes the wiretaps in *Olmstead* as menacing the 'spiritual nature' of man, he is articulating a concern for more than the mere protection of secrets. He argues that the Constitution should be invoked to protect a sphere in which the individual can freely maintain and develop his identity."

Thus, Kahn argues that many of the due process cases involving Fourth Amendment protections display, in commentary by jurists and lawyers, concern for institutions like family and child rearing seen as central to human life. Kahn believes that these arguments are essentially about the right of an individual to maintain his or her identity. He argues further that the idea of identity maintenance is the concept that Brandeis and Warren invoked when referring to privacy rights as a matter of "inviolate personality."[157]

Pragmatic Concepts of Privacy

In a 2002 article in *California Law Review*, professor of law Daniel Solove takes a more pragmatic approach to the question, arguing for what he conceives as a "bottom-up contextualized approach toward conceptualizing privacy."

First, Solove argues that the effort of defining privacy according to necessary or core characteristics is inherently flawed and argues that privacy might be better conceived as a concept of "family resemblances," drawn from the philosophy of Wittgenstein, such that the concepts might not have a single characteristic, but, instead, "Draw from a common pool of similar elements." Then, Solove argues that by focusing on pragmatism, or the "consequences of ideas" theories can adapt to changing conditions better than theories based on general principles. Solove argues therefore, that it is possible to understand privacy according to the activ-

The Bush administration secretly authorizes the President's Surveillance Program (PSP), utilizing E.O. 12333

The U.S. PATRIOT Act alters existing laws to facilitate better communication between the state's intelligence branches in the effort to combat terrorism

The Transportation Security Administration (TSA) is established, creating the "No Fly" and "Selectee" lists that limit the right to travel on airplanes in the United States

ities, customs, norms, and traditions of people and thus that privacy is a cultural and historical product that can be understood by looking at the types of situations in which people generally invoke the idea of privacy. For his exploration, Solove uses the family, the body, and the home as examples.

Protecting privacy, therefore, is about preventing disruptions to certain practices, with the term "privacy" being a general term used to refer to practices that a person wishes to protect. From there, he argues that the value of privacy is also not universal in all contexts, but depends, in each specific context, on the social importance of the practice involved.

For instance, Solove holds that the Supreme Court ruling, from the 1891 case of *Union Pacific v. Botsford*, in which the court stated, "No right is held more sacred, or is more carefully guarded by the common law, than the right of every individual to the possession and control of his own person," is referring to the privacy of bodily practices, such as the right to conceal certain body parts, to keep a disease or physical condition secret, as well as norms of touching and interpersonal contact. The home, likewise, is often viewed as the primary domain of the right to privacy, but this, Solove argued, is not because the home is a private space but rather because individuals seek to protect practices that now occur in the home, such as intimate relations and the ability to retreat from the public eye, though this had not, historically, been the reality of home life for many individuals and that the concept of a person's home as their "castle" primarily applied only to white, wealthy homeowners for most of history. It is, therefore, not that the home is a private space in some objective, absolute sense, but rather that the home is one of many spaces in which certain types of private practices can be employed. It is, therefore, the private practices that are associated with the home that are used to develop the concept of privacy within the home.[158]

2005

The PATRIOT Act was reauthorized without substantial changes as Congress favors security concerns over warnings that the law creates the potential for civil liberties violations

The *New York Times* publishes articles resulting from leaks revealing the secret President's Surveillance Program (PSP) established by the Bush administration

PRIVACY FOR THE PEOPLE

Most Americans probably don't care much how philosophers and legal scholars debate the issue of privacy. Americans *believe* in privacy, regardless of how the concept is defined. The measure of public interest in the subject is revealed through numerous opinion polls and social science studies and evinced by the millions that, each year, campaign for privacy rights or engage the legal system to protect their privacy against different types of intrusions. American belief in privacy endures over the decades, despite the fact that most Americans would most likely be unable to provide a detailed definition or to explain why they feel they should have it. However, most Americans also understand that privacy is not absolute and that it is sometimes necessary to sacrifice privacy for the common good.

It might be argued that a basic, commonsensical definition of privacy might be something like, "the right to be let alone, except when there is good reason to intrude on one's privacy." The bit about a "good reason," is the most subjective and that has been the subject of many legal and policy debates. Supreme Court cases on privacy, for instance, often revolve around these issues; when is a reason good enough to violate privacy and who has the authority to decide when a reason is good enough?

So, while some believe that the FISA Court is the proper authority to decide when the NSA's reasons are good enough to warrant spying on American citizens, others do not believe that the court is sufficiently independent or unbiased to serve as a proper legal authority. This is still the subject of impassioned debate and legal tests and so, whether the court is a proper authority is still, by many measures, undecided.

As for deciding when a reason is "good enough," consider that most Americans would probably agree that it is permissible for police to forcibly violate the privacy of a person's home (by means of breaking in, etc.) if the police hear gunshots coming from inside the home. How about if the

2007 The Bush Administration plans to make data taken from spy satellites available to law enforcement to be used to conduct domestic surveillance

2008 Congress passes Section 702, or the FISA Amendment Act, which is used to permit a massive NSA and CIA domestic surveillance program

police don't *hear* gunshots, but receive reports of gunshots being fired? What if police hear a second-hand rumor that a person has been shooting a gun in their house? At what point is violating a person's privacy no longer permissible? Is it a function of sufficient evidence? Reasonable belief? How to you define "sufficient" and "reasonable" for the purposes of determining when it is okay to violate a person's privacy?

On some level, each person decides when he or she feels it is necessary to compromise their right to privacy, though an individual's personal feelings on the matter may not match up with the rights as protected by law, or with the majority consensus on the issue, or with the traditions of their family, or community, or culture. While a sense of privacy may be subjective, the formulation of traditions, practices, and norms surrounding privacy are social matters that arise from the organization and gradual evolution of societies and cultures.

Personal concepts of privacy become part of a collective marketplace of ideas, gradually generating the sense of a majority consensus, which then influences legislators and policy advocates, who then promote or personally engage in the process of creating laws, which eventually results in court cases where the limits of various privacy laws can be tested in various situations and with regard to other laws and values. Privacy rights are thus a hodgepodge of laws, legal precedent, and statutes, which may or may not match up with how any specific individual feels his or her rights should be defined or protected. If the person feels strongly enough, he or she may campaign to change the law, or to inspire a shift in public consensus on an issue. This is, after all, how the American legal debate started, with Samuel Warren's anger that the tabloid press had violated his daughter's privacy.

As society evolves and changes, the consensus and laws regarding privacy change to reflect broader shifts in popular culture. For instance, for much of history and in many parts of the world, a man's right to privacy

2012 The Obama Administration proposes a Consumer Privacy Bill of Rights guaranteeing individuals the right to greater control over the use of their digital data

2013 The *Guardian* and the *Washington Post* publish the first series of articles derived from leaked NSA and CIA documents delivered by Edward Snowden

might have been seen as nearly absolute when it came to a man's behavior inside his home or with regards to his family. A man in such a culture might abuse his wife and/or children without any reprisal or consequence, at least so long as such activities took place within the man's "castle," and away from direct public scrutiny. Though this still occurs and some men may still claim this level of privacy rights with regard to their families or homes, this level of privacy, with regards to home and family, is no longer protected by law, nor embraced in the ethical public consensus. U.S. law and American popular culture has embraced the idea that domestic abuse and child abuse are not acceptable behavior, even in the privacy of a person's home, and that it is therefore proper, permissible, and beneficial for society for individuals or the state to intervene in order to prevent such behavior, even if doing so means violating a man's expectations of privacy.

How strongly a person feels about privacy rights is related to the degree to which the person feels that their rights are threatened. For instance, many Americans are aware that the NSA currently has the capability, and claims legal justification, to intercept mobile phone conversations from just about any American citizen. Most Americans disapprove of this, but not to the degree that this issue tops their list of governmental priorities. However, how would this situation change if Americans were *certain* they were being listened to? Imagine for instance, if it was possible to hear the agent listening into a conversation, such that one was acutely aware of the surveillance. Would this generate a more passionate objection from the public? Most likely it would, because such a situation would create an imminent, visceral sense of an immediate threat to one's privacy.

Likewise, individuals who occupy power positions—either because of wealth, political connections, or some other factor determining social/societal power—are generally more willing to trust the state when it comes to their rights, largely because such individuals feel a sense of power with regard to

The Senate Judiciary committee holds hearings to determine if the executive surveillance operations carried out under the PATRIOT Act were a violation of constitutional law

Snowden leaks reveal that the NSA and CIA had been attempting to force corporations to provide a backdoor to encryption systems that would allow federal agents to bypass consumer encryption

their society and government. Individuals who feel marginalized and detached from their society are more likely to view their government with fear and/or suspicion, and might, therefore, be less likely to trust the state when it comes to their rights. Interest in privacy is, therefore, a function of how a person views him or herself in relation to their society, the degree to which a person trusts his or her leaders/government/fellow humans, and the degree to which a person feels his or her privacy is threatened.

Privacy is easily surrendered, when another threat becomes preeminent. A threat to public safety or national security, therefore, provides justification for violating privacy and a person is generally more willing to accept this, if such violations are seen as necessary to combat some other danger or fear. Thus, fear of terrorism overwhelms the fear of the state invading one's personal privacy and a tradeoff is made. Though potential state surveillance is not the ideal state, Americans have accepted this because the alternative, they are told, is the imminent threat of radical, terrorist violence.

DATA OWNERSHIP

In his 1597 *Meditationes Sacrae*, Sir Francis Bacon wrote the famous phrase "*Scientia potentia est*," which is usually translated as "knowledge is power." Knowledge, which in the twenty-first century is also often called "data," has different value to different entities. U.S. intelligence agencies collect data on American citizens as a tool towards their goal of ensuring public safety and security. The intelligence community, therefore, resists any attempt to curtail their data-gathering capabilities as such restrictions, at least in theory, makes this task more difficult. Similarly, when the first electronic surveillance methods were put in place, police and federal agents used such tools with impunity, regardless of potential violations of privacy, to locate and capture criminals and it wasn't until the courts decided that such activities violated constitutional rights that limits were placed on police surveillance.

2015

Terrorist attacks in France reignite fears of domestic terrorist violence	The PATRIOT Act is replaced by the USA Freedom Act	Federal Courts order Apple, Inc. to create a new operation system that would enable federal investigators to bypass security on an iPhone.

Whether police and federal agencies have the right to data depends, at least to some degree, over whether a person *owns* his or her data. When a person writes a letter, and delivers the letter through the U.S. Postal Service, the data contained within the letter is owned by the author, or both the author and recipient. Laws, therefore, require police to justify taking possession of a letter, as this activity involves claiming property that belongs to another individual. The courts later decided that a person speaking into a telephone essentially "owns" the data transmitted through the phone, along with the recipient of that data. Therefore, laws were put into place that required agents to justify taking this informational "property" from the original owners.

Many Americans were aware, in 2017, that they did not own data transmitted through the Web or other digital tools in the same way that they might have owned data transmitted through traditional communication mediums, like the telephone or postal service. This data, because it is transmitted through portals and infrastructure belonging to corporations, is partially owned by the companies that facilitate such communications. This is part of another important aspect of the privacy debate, the proliferation of technology and the process of adjusting laws and regulations to extend privacy protections to new media.

In this article, Urs Gasser, Executive Director of the Berkman Klein Center for Internet & Society at Harvard University, discusses the history of privacy law in relation to emerging technology and explores moral and normative issues emerging from this ongoing debate.

The FCC publishes official rules of "neutrality"

2016

The EU establishes the General Data Protection Regulation (GDPR), described as the strongest digital data privacy law in the world

RECODING PRIVACY LAW:
REFLECTIONS ON THE FUTURE RELATIONSHIP AMONG LAW, TECHNOLOGY AND PRIVACY

Commentary by Urs Gasser
Reprinted in *Harvard Law Review*, December 9, 2016
Source Document

The history of privacy is deeply intertwined with the history of technology. A wealth of scholarly literature tracks and demonstrates how privacy as a normative concept has evolved in light of new information and communication technologies since the early modern period, when face-to-face interactions were challenged by urbanization and the rise of mass communication. In the beginning of the nineteenth century, a combination of societal changes, institutional developments, and technological advancements gave birth to a series of new threats to privacy. At the time, innovative technologies—including telegraph communications and portable cameras—were among the key drivers (interacting with other factors, such as increased literacy rates) that led to growing concerns about privacy protection. These developments also set the stage for Samuel Warren and later-Justice Louis Brandeis's highly influential 1890 article The Right to Privacy, which was written, in large part, in response to the combined negative effects of the rise of the "yellow press"

and the adaptation of "instantaneous photography" as privacy-invading practices and technologies. Similarly, advancements in information and communication technologies in the twentieth century, combined with other developments such as the rise of the welfare state, challenged existing notions of information privacy and led to renegotiations of the boundaries between the private and public spheres.

The development, adaptation, and use of innovative technologies that enabled and increased the collection and use of personal information later in the twentieth century were also among the key drivers that led to the birth of modern information privacy law in the early 1970s. Starting in the United States and then extending to Europe, the increased use of computers for information processing and storage by government agencies was an important factor that led to the first generation of modern privacy and data protection laws. Anchored in a set of Fair Information Practices, many of these laws were expanded, adjusted, and supplemented over the

2017

The "Vault 7" secrets, a leak of 9,000 CIA documents, reveal details of the CIA's attempts to break through encryption used by Internet

President Trump appoints Ajit Pai to head the FCC, who abolishes the FCC neutrality protections

continued

following decades in light of evolving technologies and changing institutional practices, which—together with other factors—resulted in an ever-growing cascade of privacy concerns. In the 1990s, for instance, the widespread adoption of internet technology as a global information and communication medium and the rise of the database industry led to a wave of legislative and regulatory interventions aimed at dealing with emerging privacy problems. More recent and more ambitious information-privacy reforms, such as the revision of the influential OECD Privacy Guidelines at the international level, the General Data Protection Regulation in the EU, and the proposed Consumer Privacy Bill of Rights Act in the United States, seek to update existing privacy norms for the digital age—again driven, in part, by new technologies and applications such as cloud computing and Big Data, among others.

Reflecting across centuries and geographies, one common thread emerges: advancements in information and communication technologies have largely been perceived as threats to privacy and often led policymakers to seek, and consumers to demand, additional privacy safeguards in the legal and regulatory arenas. This perspective on technology as a challenge to existing notions of, and safeguards for, information privacy is also reflective of the mindset of contemporary law and policymaking. Whether considering the implications of Big Data technologies, sensor networks and the Internet of Things, facial recognition technology, always-on wearable technologies with voice and video interfaces, virtual and augmented reality, or artificial intelligence, recent policy reports and regulatory analyses have identified privacy challenges as among the most pressing concerns.

In considering this fundamentally defensive stance that privacy law has taken historically with regard to technology, it is important to note that law in the broader context of information and communication technology often transcends its traditional role as a constraint on behavior acting through the imposition of sanctions. In areas such as intellectual property and antitrust, law seeks to engage with technology in a more nuanced way by enabling or in some cases leveling desired innovative or disruptive activity.

With this understanding of law as a functionally differentiated response system, and an acknowledgment that legal responses to technological innovation should not be understood as a simple stimulus-response mechanism, it is possible to identify a series of response patterns when examining the evolution of privacy law vis-à-vis

Congress debates whether or not to renew the controversial Section 702 FISA Amendment used to authorize NSA domestic intelligence operations since 2008

Recoding Privacy Law: Reflections on the Future Relationship Among Law, Technology and Privacy
continued

technological change. At a general level, three analytically distinct, but in practice often overlapping, response modes can be identified.

(1) When dealing with innovative technologies, the legal system—including privacy law—by default seeks to apply the old rules to the (new) problem resulting from the new technology and its uses (subsumption). U.S. courts' application of privacy torts, for instance, when addressing complaints about improper collection, use, or disclosure by digital businesses such as Google and Facebook—largely relying on tort conceptions of privacy advanced in the late nineteenth century—is an illustration of this default response mode.

(2) Where subsumption is considered insufficient given the novelty of issues raised by a new technology, the legal system might resort to innovation within its own system. One version of this response mode is to "upgrade" existing (privacy) norms gradually, typically by setting new precedent or by adjusting or complementing current norms (gradual innovation). Proposals to introduce a tort for the misuse of personal information by data traders, to provide legal recognition of data harms by extending developments from other areas of the law such as torts and contracts, and to enact a Consumer Privacy Bill of Rights Act, are examples of gradual legal innovations that leave core elements of the current regulatory approach unchanged.

(3) A more radical, paradigm-shifting approach is more deeply layered law reform where not only individual norms are updated but also entire approaches or instruments are changed. Examples in this category include proposals to reimagine privacy regimes based on models that emerged in the field of environmental law, to create an alternative dispute resolution scheme such as a "cyber court" system to deal with large-scale privacy threats in the digital age, or to introduce a "Digital Millennium Privacy Act" that would provide immunity for those companies willing to subscribe to a set of information fiduciary duties, to name just three illustrations.

Perhaps the most interesting, and arguably the most promising, approach to reprogramming privacy law in a more fundamental sense is linked to a potential paradigm shift: embracing the multifaceted, functional role of law and reframing technology, broadly defined, no longer (only) as a threat to privacy, but as part of the

1788 State legislatures ratify the U.S. Constitution, establishing the basic precedent for all future constitutional law

1791 The U.S. Congress ratifies the Bill of Rights, creating the first 10 amendments to the United States Constitution

continued

solution space. Precursors of such a potential shift date back to the 1970s, when researchers started to develop technical mechanisms under the header of "Privacy-Enhancing Technologies" (PETs) in response to privacy challenges associated with new information and communication technologies. Originally focused on identity protection and technical means to minimize data collection and processing without losing a system's functionality, the scope of PETs and the available instruments have broadened over time to include encryption tools, privacy-preserving analysis techniques, data management tools, and other techniques covering the entire lifecycle of personal data. Starting in the 1990s, PETs as one instrument in the toolbox were put into a larger context by the introduction of Privacy by Design as a "systematic approach to designing any technology that embeds privacy into the underlying specification or architecture." Still remaining a somewhat amorphous approach, Privacy by Design as an umbrella philosophy (as well as certain types of PETs) promotes a means to manage privacy challenges resulting from a wide range of emerging technologies, and has been adopted by law and policymakers on both sides of the Atlantic, with the EU General Data Protection Regulation among the most prominent examples.

Law's relatively recent "discovery" of technology as an approach to address the very privacy challenges technology (co-)creates has potential. The approach's promise manifests itself not so much at the mechanical level of individual techniques and tools. Rather, it becomes visible when considering the types of perspectives an approach situated at the law/ technology interface opens up when dealing with the privacy challenges of the digital age. Projecting from the past into the future, approaches like Privacy by Design signal a departure from binary notions of privacy and ad hoc balancing tests of competing interests toward more holistic and rigorous privacy risk assessment models that rely on modeling approaches from information security and an understanding of privacy that is informed by recent theoretical advances across different disciplines. A growing body of interdisciplinary research demonstrates the theoretical and practical promise of holistic analytical frameworks for a modern privacy analysis that incorporates recent research from fields such as computer science, statistics, law, and the social sciences. This promise does not mean that a blended approach has no issues; to the contrary, there are significant limitations including, among others, internal constraints, incentive misalignments, and broader

1868 The 14th Amendment to the U.S. Constitution guarantees all citizens the right to due process under the law

1890 Warren and Brandeis publish "The Right to Privacy" in the *Harvard Law Review*

Recoding Privacy Law: Reflections on the Future Relationship Among Law, Technology and Privacy
continued

normative challenges. Yet these challenges are properly understood as issues of operationalization and ought not automatically foreclose a reconceptualization of the relevant solution space.

In addition to advancing new tactical methods to conceptualize and evaluate privacy risk, embedding technology into (privacy) law can boost the development of new solutions to more strategically manage a broad range of privacy risks. Research initiatives across the country show how emerging technical privacy solutions, including sophisticated tools for data storage and access control, as well as advanced tools for data analysis and release, can play in concert with legal, organizational, and other safeguards to manage privacy risks across the different stages of the lifecycle of data. Consider, for instance, the important role encryption plays in securing access to and storage of data, or the technological development of a personal data store that enables individuals to exercise fine-grained control over where information about them is stored and how it is accessed. Differential privacy is a new formal mathematical framework for addressing privacy challenges associated with the statistical analysis of information maintained in databases.

Secure multiparty computation, to add another example, is a method that enables parties to carry out a joint computation over their data in such a way that no single entity needs to hand a dataset to any other explicitly. While some of these technologies are still in development, others have been tested out in practice and are already recommended as best practices in selected fields of application.

In the digitally networked world, the regulation of information privacy has an inherently technical dimension. Such technological aspects have been the focus of intense study by computer scientists, resulting in a rich theoretical literature as well as practical tools for protecting privacy, but such discussion has by and large occurred in a space separate from the sphere of legal norms, regulations, policies, ethics codes, and best practices. A number of trends make it important and urgent to overcome the silos that have been created, to foster knowledge sharing between the two spheres, and to embrace technological approaches to support legal privacy across the different functions mentioned before.

Technological advances, for instance, are enabling new and sophisticated attacks that were unforeseen at the

1923 *Meyer v. Nebraska* establishes that the 14th Amendment guarantees privileges of citizenship

1928 *Olmstead v. United States* rules that wiretapping is not a form of search and seizure defined by the 14th Amendment

continued

time that legal standards for privacy protection were drafted. Computer scientists have developed approaches that are robust not only against known modes of attack, but also against unknown future attacks, and are therefore well suited to address challenges posed by new technological threats to privacy.

Further, legal standards can result in wide variations in treatment of data across contexts, depending on the jurisdictions, industry sectors, actors, and categories of information involved. New frameworks for evaluating privacy threats based on both legal and scientific standards for privacy protection could be used to provide more comprehensive, consistent, and robust data privacy protection, thereby furthering end goals of the law.

Finally, traditional legal approaches for protecting privacy while transferring data, making data-release decisions, and drafting data-sharing agreements, among other activities, are time-intensive and not readily scalable to Big Data contexts. Technological approaches can be designed with compliance with legal standards and practices in mind, in order to help automate data-sharing decisions and ensure consistent privacy protection at a massive scale. These and related examples indicate how law and technology can advance the state of the practice through a mutually productive relationship. Taken together, the development of privacy tools that aim to integrate legal and technical approaches could help pave the way for a more strategic and systematic way to conceptualize and orchestrate the contemporary interplay between law and technology in the field of information privacy. In concrete terms, this path could urge actors to incorporate modern legal and technological approaches in their privacy analysis frameworks and to adopt tiered-access models that integrate both legal and technical tools for privacy protection. When demonstrating a privacy technology's compliance with legal standards for privacy protection, policymakers and technologists could seek to employ a hybrid of legal and technical reasoning. And regulatory systems and institutions could support additional research on policy reasoning, accountable systems, and computable policies for automating compliance with legal requirements and enforcement of privacy policies. Such integrated approaches recognize the rich roles that law can play alongside the technical space and hint at how more robust and effective privacy protections can emerge by melding different instruments and methods—both at the conceptual and implementation levels.

1934 The Federal Communications Commission (FCC) is established under the Federal Communications Act (FCA)

1942 *Goldman v. United States* rules that using electronic listening devices does not violate the 14th Amendment

Recoding Privacy Law: Reflections on the Future Relationship Among Law, Technology and Privacy
continued

These developments might ultimately culminate in a more deeply layered recoding of privacy law that leverages the synergies between technological and legal perspectives and instruments and transcends the traditional response patterns discussed earlier in this Commentary in order to cope with the complex privacy-relevant challenges of our future. For example, in light of substantial definitional gaps between various technological and legal approaches to privacy, updating the law to better support new privacy technologies could require a fundamental reframing away from traditional legal notions such as "Personally Identifiable Information" and "de-identification." Furthermore, legal standards could be redesigned to focus on the ends rather than the means of privacy protection, which are likely to continue to evolve rapidly. Rather than implicitly or explicitly endorsing traditional approaches like de-identification, updated legal standards might, for instance, adopt more general descriptions of the intended privacy goal, which would provide a clearer basis for demonstrating whether new classes of emerging privacy technologies are sufficient.

However, such a strategy requires significant investments in interdisciplinary education, research, and collaboration. Programs designed to stimulate collaboration and interdisciplinary learning have been developed at universities. Furthermore, technology positions in government, such as the Chief Technologist position at the Federal Trade Commission, and advisory panels such as the President's Council of Advisors on Science and Technology, recognize the need for experts in computer science to inform the regulation of privacy and to serve as promising examples of cross-disciplinary communication and knowledge sharing in policy circles. Similarly, it is becoming increasingly important for technologists to understand legal and policy approaches to privacy protection so that they can implement measures that advance the specific goals of legal and regulatory privacy standards. Doing so will likely require policymakers to develop mechanisms and resources for communicating their shared understanding of the interface between law and technology to privacy practitioners. There is much yet to be uncovered: development of novel systems of governance requires not only interdisciplinary mutual understandings, but also deep inquiry into the most effective role for law and

1945 The National Security Agency secretly creates Project SHAMROCK

1950 Senator Joseph McCarthy delivers a shocking speech claiming that more than 200 communist spies have infiltrated the U.S. government

continued

legal governance in such a dynamic, fast-changing system.

Reimagining the relationship between technology and privacy law in the digital age should be seen as a key component of a larger effort aimed at addressing the current digital privacy crisis more holistically. Under contemporary conditions of complexity and uncertainty, the solution space for the multifaceted privacy challenges of our time needs to do more than treat the symptoms of discrete privacy ills. It needs to combine approaches, strategies, and instruments that span all available modes of regulation in the digital space, including technology, markets, social norms, and the law. If pursued diligently and collaboratively, such a turn toward privacy governance could result in a future-oriented privacy framework that spans a broad set of norms, control mechanisms, and actors—"a system of information privacy protection that is much larger, more complex and varied, and likely more effective, than individual information privacy rights." Through such nuanced intervention, the legal system (understood as more than merely a body of constraining laws) can more proactively play a key role in coordinating the various elements and actors in the new governance regime, and—above all—in ensuring the transparency, accountability, and legitimacy that allow democratic governance to flourish.

Ownership of digital data has not been legally established in part because companies fight against this effort, recognizing that such regulations would reduce their potential profit from buying and selling customer information. Federal agencies have benefitted from this by claiming the right to intercept data that has been transmitted through commercial channels and so is no longer protected by laws governing personal data. Federal agencies have also fought against efforts to establish digital privacy laws because such regulations would limit the tools at their disposal, essentially making their jobs more difficult. Despite promises to the contrary, corporate and state agencies interested in collecting data are not likely to voluntarily surrender this ability. Until such time as the public decides that digital privacy is a top priority and so puts pressure on legislators to es-

1951

Dennis v. United States rules that government limits to speech is legal only to prevent a threat to public safety or security

1959

Barenblatt v. United States rules that it's legal to order people to reveal personal details if national threat is perceived

tablish laws to this effect, entities interesting in collecting and using data from Americans will continue to engage in this practice.

A COMPLEX DYNAMIC

The philosophy of privacy law is a complex and evolving subject. As Mr. Gasser demonstrates, the evolution of technology has created a wealth of new challenges, in the form of legal loopholes, and new challenges emerging from a growing dependence on data as a primary currency in the modern economy. On the national security side of the debate, it has been argued that the nature of modern threats to safety and security, namely the rise of antimodernist, conservative, radical groups, demands stronger, more wide-reaching intelligence capabilities and so necessitates a reimagining of privacy that places greater trust in the beneficence of the state.

Whether these claims are true is a matter of perspective and personal opinion. Currently, the public is divided on the issue, uncertain of whether to trust the state and the corporations that transmit and facilitate their communications and recreational activities, or whether to support protections that reinstate privacy laws as they existed in the era before terrorism and before the Big Data market came into being. How this debate evolves, in coming years, may depend largely on personal philosophy and the degree to which Americans embrace some concept of privacy as important in their own lives.

1965

Griswold v. CT rules in favor of married couples' right to privacy

1967

Katz v. United States rules wiretaps a form of search and seizure

Willis Ware of RAND Corporation writes *Security and Privacy in Computer*

CONCLUSION

Gasser's vision for an updated legal approach to privacy is unlikely to come to fruition while the privacy debate is still heavily influenced by fears of terrorist attacks and by corporate lobbying towards the goal of maintaining the "big data" market. Americans, in general, express dismay that they have seemingly lost control of their own private information. Further, as the Trump administration has proven to favor corporate over consumer rights, and to favor national security over civil liberties, the possibility of reform is remote. The primary factor that will decide whether or not the United States ever returns to an era in which privacy is given legal and commercial priority will depend on how deeply the American public embraces privacy as a priority or comes to object to the ways in which the general lack of privacy protections affects their lives.

1968 The Omnibus Crime Control Act holds that police needed to obtain a warrant before engaging in wire-

1969 Joseph Licklider creates the Advanced Research Projects Agency Network (ARPANET), which was

DISCUSSION QUESTIONS

- Do you agree with Urs Gasser's belief that technology has fundamentally altered the nature of privacy? Explain your answer.
- Which of the approaches to privacy summarized in this chapter is most appealing? Which is least appealing?
- What does the idiom "knowledge is power" have to do with the digital data debate?
- Can you create your own definition of privacy? How is this definition different or similar to other definitions presented in this chapter?

Works Used

Bloustein, Edward J. "Privacy as an Aspect of Human Dignity: An Answer to Dean Prosser." *New York University Law Review*. 1964. Web. 4 Nov. 2017.

Inness, Julie C. *Privacy, Intimacy, and Isolation*. New York: Oxford UP, 1996. Web. 4 Nov. 2017.

Kahn, Jonathan. "Privacy as a Legal Principle of Identity Maintenance." *Seton Hall Law Review*. Vol. 33. 2003. Web 4 Nov. 2017.

Moore, Adam D. "Defining Privacy." *Journal of Social Philosophy*. Vol. 39, No. 3. 2008. Web. 4 Nov. 2017.

Prosser, William L. "Privacy." *California Law Review*. Vol. 48, Iss 3, Article 1. August 1960. Web. 6 Nov. 2017.

Solove, Daniel J. "Conceptualizing Privacy." *California Law Review*. Vol. 90, Iss 4, Article 2. July 2002. Web. 4 Nov. 2017.

Warren, Samuel, and Louis Brandeis. "The Right to Privacy." *Harvard Law Review*. Vol. IV, No. 5. Dec. 15, 1890. Web. 31 Oct. 2017.

1971 The Pentagon Papers leaks from the press raise the issue of the Freedom of the Press versus the privacy of the government to conceal information about national security operations

1972 *Eisenstadt v. Baird* rules that the right to privacy applies to individuals

It is easy to find evidence to support the argument that Americans, as a whole, value privacy. It is equally easy to find evidence to support the argument that Americans, as a whole, are willing to sacrifice privacy when they feel there is sufficient reason to do so. It is also true that public opinion is changing and that the shift of American politics, in 2017, may bring about new attitudes on privacy and security as well.

THE ANTIMODERNIST MOVEMENT

In November 2016, Donald J. Trump won a close electoral victory to claim the presidency. His victory surprised career campaign operatives in both parties as well as many seasoned poll watchers. The election of Trump resulted in a surge in activist politics in the United States, as many Americans questioned his fitness as commander-in-chief with no prior experience in public service or the military. The Trump agenda—To Make America Great Again—included vague promises of change and a retreat from many of the previous administration's domestic and international initiatives.

As of November, 2017, Trump's position on national security has been to support the conservative mainline embodied by Mitch McConnell and other establishment Republicans in the legislature. For instance, on the issue of the controversial Section 702 provision, which was used to authorize mass surveillance by the NSA, the administration favored reauthorization and making the section permanent, thus siding with the standard GOP position on the issue. Whereas Trump's support of 702 thus signals the administration's trust in the conservative GOP mainline, his personal commentary on surveillance is a departure from this position.

President Trump has alleged that the Obama administration illegally spied on him and "tapped" his phones and, though the

1974

The Watergate Scandal results in the revelation that the CIA had been conducting widespread surveillance of American dissidents and foreign leaders without judicial oversight

The Privacy Act is established

administration backed off of the claim and never provided a source or any corroborating evidence, his comments resulted in a brief surge of interest in intelligence reform, as pro-Trump anti-establishment followers joined the ranks of libertarian and Democratic reformers.

Arthur Rizer of the libertarian R Street Institute told *Politico* in October, "Now you have this third party. You have the Twitter account of the president. Trump has created the perfect storm where you have these unlikely allies coming together because they're seeing boogeymen everywhere."[159]

Polling organizations did not attempt to measure public opinion on Section 702 directly, though polling groups have found that public interest in privacy remains high, across partisan lines, and that most Americans still believe it is unacceptable for the government to monitor American citizens. Interestingly, in September of 2017, *Pew Research* found that 37 percent of U.S. adults feel it is "very likely" that the government is monitoring their phone calls and emails, while an additional 33 percent feel it is somewhat likely. The report also showed that suspicion of government surveillance held across party lines, and, therefore, that the idea that the government was, is, and will be intercepting phone calls and Internet communications matriculated through society. It remained to be seen, however, if this broadening suspicion would in any way influence government policy on the issue.[160]

DIGITAL PRIVACY IN THE TRUMP ADMINISTRATION
Whereas the Trump administration has not made a significant, official impact on the privacy rights debate, Trump has established himself as "pro-business" in the traditional Republican manner and, by appointing former Verizon executive Ajit Pai to run the Federal Communications Commission (FCC), has made it clear that his administration will favor corporate freedom over consumer rights in

1975   Senator Frank Church leads a series of hearings about the secret NSA SHAMROCK operation involved intercepting communications from American citizens

1978   Congress passes the 1978 FISA Act

regard to the ownership of digital data. Pai opposes measures like net neutrality and digital rights movements aimed at providing citizens with the ability to control their own data and favors the idea that the free market will solve this problem without government intervention.[161] Though the history of corporate behavior vis-à-vis digital privacy would seem to indicate this is not the case, Pai has embraced the idea that regulation stifles innovation and so, like Trump, promises a pro-business approach to managing federal communication regulations.

Americans, in general, do not much approve of this approach. A report from *Pew Research* showed that 91 percent of consumers agreed or strongly agreed with the statement that Americans had lost control of how personal information was collected and used by companies. Approximately 74 percent reported it was "very important" to them to control who was able to access information about them, whereas 65 percent said it was important to control who collected information about them.[162]

Current laws do not allow customers to control their own data or to control who has access to their data and so the failure of the FCC and the legislature to establish such measures of protection and, in fact, Ajit Pai's assertion that he will dismantle existing privacy and neutrality rules in favor of broader corporate freedom to "innovate," is not in keeping with the desires of the American people. This is one example, therefore, of an imbalance in current privacy law favoring companies and businesses over consumer interest and over the weight of public opinion.

Experts in the field also feel, in general, that too much weight had been given to corporate freedom in the privacy debate. A *Pew Research* survey of 2,511 Internet and digital technology experts demonstrated broad concern for privacy rights and a general consensus that the

1980 | The Intelligence Oversight Act (IOA) updates legal standards

1981 | President Reagan's E.O. authorized wiretapping

1986 | The Electronic Communications Privacy Act is established

current situation was one in which corporations would continue to exploit data without controls and that the evolution of the free market alone would not address this. Whereas experts had different ideas about the future of privacy rights in the Digital Age, one of the common views expressed was that privacy was no longer a right of American citizens, but had become a commodity that needed to be purchased. A full 55 percent of respondents in the study did not believe that a privacy-rights regime or infrastructure would be created in the coming decade.

Joe Touch, Director of the Information Sciences Institute at the University of Southern California said, regarding the future of digital privacy:

————— *"Privacy is in direct opposition to the business models of the largest Internet companies. The Internet does not require a login, birthdate, or username, yet these companies continue to create 'walled gardens' that do—to create the information that fuels their revenue stream... The issue is not about policymakers and corporations, but rather, whether the public will continue to be comfortable exposing that information. Such norms already vary widely, and I continue to be surprised at the extent to which posts within the frame of a personal video screen, and thus to the entire world, exceed what would be posted—by the same person—to their own front door. I think we have not yet seen the backlash of the current norms of personal public exposure; we might when that generation shifts from being 'kids just posting stuff' to being in the position of establishing and protecting their company's reputation as managers."* [163]

1994 Netscape creates the "cookie" allowing computers to monitor Internet users

2001 The September 11 terrorist attacks result in Congress authorizing the Bush Administration to utilize military methods to combat terrorism

HAVE AMERICAN OPINIONS ON PRIVACY CHANGED?

Between 2002 and 2015, *Gallup* asked Americans how they felt about the government's efforts to fight terrorism, with regard to their civil liberties. In January of 2002, 47 percent favored the government taking all steps necessary, even if such steps violated civil liberties, whereas 49 percent believed that the government should stop short of violating civil liberties. This was just a few months after the September 11 terrorist attacks and marked the apex of public support for potentially invasive national security policies. Even in this impassioned moment, with fear of terrorism reaching near hysterical levels across the country, a slight majority still favored protecting liberties over ensuring public safety.

The percentage of Americans who believed it was permissible for the government to violate civil liberties to combat terrorism fell to 33 percent by September of 2002, then to 29 percent in April of 2003, then to 25 percent in August of 2011. Between 2011 and 2015, the percentage of those who believed it was permissible to violate liberties *increased* for the first time since Gallup began measuring the trend, with 30 percent supporting this position in June of 2015. What motivated this shift? In May of 2015 Islamic State radicals launched a series of attacks in Europe and Americans perceived a more imminent threat, and this motivated a short-lived surge in support for more invasive national security measures.[164]

Through the first 17 years of the twenty-first century, Americans have remained broadly supportive of civil rights and privacy protections. There have been short-term swings in one or the other direction, but without any specific and sustained momentum. When terrorist attacks or mass shootings occur in the United States, there is typically a brief surge of public support for stronger security measures, but such surges are typically short-lived and rapidly decohere as the media and other

The Bush administration secretly authorizes the President's Surveillance Program (PSP), utilizing E.O. 12333

The U.S. PATRIOT Act alters existing laws to facilitate better communication between the state's intelligence branches in the effort to combat terrorism

The Transportation Security Administration (TSA) is established, creating the "No Fly" and "Selectee" lists that limit the right to travel on airplanes in the United States

public figures abandon the recent attack for the next emerging issue. Similarly, revelations about specific privacy or civil rights violations, by government agencies or corporations, motivates short-term shifts in favor of privacy and liberties, but such trends rarely impact the overall momentum of public interest.

Though events around the world also influence public opinion on privacy and security, not all events are afforded equal interest. Americans, in general, see themselves as part of what the Trump administration calls "Western" culture, an imprecise cultural distinction based on the spread of white Europeans, Christianity, certain philosophical traditions linked to ancient Rome and Greece, and related to the historical patterns of European colonialism. Americans react more strongly to events occurring in other Western nations than they do to events occurring in other cultural regions. Therefore, terrorist attacks in Europe make Americans more aware of the potential threat to persons like them, while attacks in Africa, such as the long-lasting terrorist violence linked to Boko Haram, do not result in significant changes in public support for national security measures.

On more specific issues, and when measured over shorter spans of time, public opinion polls may give the impression of directional shifts in public opinion. For instance, 11 percent of people polled by *Gallup* in June of 2002 said that the government had gone too far in restricting civil liberties to fight terrorism. This was before the public was generally aware of the way in which the Bush administration had interpreted laws to engage in domestic surveillance. In May of 2006, just after details of government surveillance programs carried out under the PATRIOT Act had been revealed, 41 percent thought the government had gone too far.

2005

The PATRIOT Act was reauthorized without substantial changes as Congress favors security concerns over warnings that the law creates the potential for civil liberties violations

The *New York Times* publishes articles resulting from leaks revealing the secret President's Surveillance Program (PSP) established by the Bush administration

Gallup polls in 2014, 2015, and 2016 asked Americans how satisfied they were with government surveillance. In 2014, immediately after the Snowden leaks, 63 percent were either somewhat or very dissatisfied, whereas in 2015, 59 percent felt the same and, in 2016, 52 percent expressed the same view.[165] During this short, three-year period, there were numerous widely publicized terrorist attacks in Europe, and these helped to build support for surveillance programs, though not sufficiently to represent a broader shift in opinion.

Research also indicates that American opinions on privacy change according to a number of specific variables. A 2013 Pew study showed that when respondents were asked whether they approved of NSA surveillance, the percentage jumped from 25 to 37 percent when the question added the information that the program was "approved by courts." Similarly, while in 2015 only 26 percent said they favored NSA data collection, when the question was asked with the qualification that the data collection was "...part of anti-terrorism efforts," the proportion who approved jumped to 35 percent. Results like these indicate that Americans are more trusting of the government when they feel that the powers of the government are balanced by the courts. Similarly, they are not supportive of surveillance overall, but are far more likely to accept it when told that it is directly correlated to the struggle against terrorism.

What is clear is that, despite back and forth surges in public opinion, a majority of Americans disapprove of the privacy situation as it currently exists, both with respect to government invasions and corporate use of consumer data. For instance, a *Pew Report* from 2016 indicated that 65 percent of Americans felt there were not adequate limits on "what telephone and internet data the government can collect." This belief was consistent across all demographic groups and the researchers found further that individuals reporting that they

2007
The Bush Administration plans to make data taken from spy satellites available to law enforcement to be used to conduct domestic surveillance

2008
Congress passes Section 702, or the FISA Amendment Act, which is used to permit a massive NSA and CIA domestic surveillance program

know "a lot" about government surveillance were more distinctly concerned, with 74 percent arguing there were not adequate protections. A full 88 percent of Americans claimed they felt it was important not to have someone watch or listen to them without permission, with 67 percent claiming this was "very important."

In a 2013 issue of the *Statesman Journal*, covering the blowout from the Snowden revelations, journalist Dick Hughes opined, "...the surveillance revelations have largely been met with a gigantic snore from the public. Maybe average Americans don't care about privacy anymore. They loudly carry on cell-phone conversations that are overheard by their neighbors and could easily be intercepted by ne'er-do-wells. They spill their personal financial data across public wi-fi networks. They share the most intimate details of their lives through Facebook and other social media."[166]

Contrary to Hughes's assertion, public opinion research demonstrates that Americans have a strong and enduring interest in privacy even if, situationally, they are not motivated to actively fight against threats to their privacy rights. The malaise that Hughes perceived, in the days immediately following the Snowden revelations, is complex and has to do with the fact that Americans were not immediately aware of the significance of the Snowden leaks and that, despite the revelations, Americans had not felt personally violated by the surveillance programs that were revealed. Opposition to policy is correlated directly with the degree to which a person perceives an immediate, personal threat. Therefore, the revelation that Americans had been under surveillance, while unacceptable in principle, did not motivate a strong backlash because Americans had not been able to perceive the threat as personal.

2012 The Obama Administration proposes a Consumer Privacy Bill of Rights guaranteeing individuals the right to greater control over the use of their digital data

2013 The *Guardian* and the *Washington Post* publish the first series of articles derived from leaked NSA and CIA documents delivered by Edward Snowden

Bob Briscoe of British Telecom told *Pew Research*, "Lack of concern about privacy stems from complacency because most people's life experiences teach them that revealing their private information allows commercial (and public) organizations to make their lives easier (by targeting their needs), where as the detrimental cases tend to be very serious but relatively rare."[167]

In the case of corporate invasions of privacy, Americans might not approve, but as Internet exchange has become essential to daily life, Americans accept the potential violations as a price of accessing the information economy and because such invasions enable conveniences. In terms of national security, Americans do not approve of changes to privacy, but begrudgingly accept them because they have been told that doing so is necessary to prevent terrorism.

Joe Kochan, chief operating officer for US Ignite, a company developing gigabit-ready digital experiences and applications, told *Pew* researchers, "I do not believe that there is a 'right balance' between privacy, security, and compelling content. This will need to be a constantly negotiated balance—one that will swing too far in one direction or another with each iteration… Public norms will continue to trend toward the desire for more privacy, while people's actions will tend toward giving up more and more control over their data."[168]

Over the longer term, it is difficult to make generalizations about the broader trends in public opinion. A general scarcity of data makes it difficult to determine how the public felt about things like government surveillance during periods when surveillance wasn't a major news issue. There was a surge of public concern about surveillance in the 1970s, surrounding the Nixon administration, and similar peaks in public skepticism about intelligence policies in the 2000s and 2010s, again related to leaks about secret domestic surveillance programs.

The Senate Judiciary committee holds hearings to determine if the executive surveillance operations carried out under the PATRIOT Act were a violation of constitutional law

Snowden leaks reveal that the NSA and CIA had been attempting to force corporations to provide a backdoor to encryption systems that would allow federal agents to bypass consumer encryption

Beyond this, it is difficult to determine whether there has been an overall direction of opinion on the issue in the twentieth century.

What can be seen from more long-term studies is that Americans have, in general, lost trust in the government. From nearly 80 percent saying they trusted the government "always" or "most of the time" in the late 1960s, there has been an inexorable decline. In May of 2017, Pew Researchers measured that only 20 percent of Americans trusted the government, with 4 percent saying they trusted the government "always" and 16 saying they trusted the government "most of the time." This occurred in the midst of a contentious presidency that resulted in the lowest approval ratings for a president ever recorded, with 59 percent of Americans disapproving of Trump's presidential performance in October of 2017.[169]

REJECTING IDEOLOGICAL POLARITY AND MOVING TOWARDS THE FUTURE

In a 2015 report on privacy and security, authors Mary Madden and Lee Rainie introduced the results of their study with this summary on the state of affairs:

> *The cascade of reports following the June 2013 government surveillance revelations by NSA contractor Edward Snowden have brought new attention to debates about how best to preserve Americans' privacy in the digital age. At the same time, the public has been awash with news stories detailing security breaches at major retailers, health insurance companies and financial institutions. These events—and the doubts they inspired—have contributed to a cloud of personal "data insecurity" that now looms over many Americans' daily decisions*

2015

Terrorist attacks in France reignite fears of domestic terrorist violence	The PATRIOT Act is replaced by the USA Freedom Act	Federal Courts order Apple, Inc. to create a new operation system that would enable federal investigators to bypass security on an iPhone.

and activities. Some find these developments deeply troubling and want limits put in place, while others do not feel these issues affect them personally. Others believe that widespread monitoring can bring some societal benefits in safety and security or that innocent people should have "nothing to hide."[170]

The overall impression is one of confusion and uncertainty, with some Americans reporting deeply held beliefs whereas others express conflicting opinions or are otherwise undecided. The uncertainty of the American people means, essentially, that the petitions of advocates, activists, politicians, pundits, journalists, and presidents are still relevant in the war of public opinion.

There is a tendency, in the political banter that surrounds complex issues, for individuals to depict trending issues as contests between two sides. There is a fictional division of "pro-security" people versus "pro-privacy" seen in the way that some journalists, but especially partisan ideologues and pundits, portray the issue. This perception is false and does not legitimately reflect American attitudes on the topic. Privacy is an American issue, beyond politics, and is an important issue for conservatives, liberals, Republicans, Democrats, Socialists, Communists, and even anarchists.

The confusion of the American people results from conflicting, but nearly equally compelling points made on various sides of the debate:

- Corporate entities argue that allowing them to partially own and collect digital data will enable them to build more convenient and beneficial products.

- The intelligence industry argues that reduced privacy protections

The FCC publishes official rules of "neutrality"

2016

The EU establishes the General Data Protection Regulation (GDPR), described as the strongest digital data privacy law in the world

will enable better efforts to prevent terrorism.

• Privacy advocates argue that changes to the law have reduced privacy protections and leave the American public vulnerable to government and corporate abuse.

All of these statements are, from a certain perspective, true.

• Companies able to collect personal data on users profit from this data and can use those profits to fund new products. Data from users likewise allows companies to tailor products and advertisements to the needs of their consumers and this does increase convenience, though at the expense of privacy.

• The capability to conduct mass, bulk surveillance does provide a potentially powerful tool for federal agents combating crime and threats to national security. The massive trove of data could potentially make the intelligence community more effective. While it is unclear whether this has been the case, the argument is sound in principle. In theory, if police and feds were able to watch and listen to all Americans all of the time, they would be far more effective in combating crime. The problem is, most Americans aren't willing to allow this, even if it means that there would be less crime.

• Privacy advocates are correct when they claim that privacy protections have been eroded by amendments and laws such that Americans are more vulnerable to potential governmental abuse. Whether this has actually happened is open to debate, but privacy advocates are correct when they identify the potential for this to occur.

2017

The "Vault 7" secrets, a leak of 9,000 CIA documents, reveal details of the CIA's attempts to break through encryption used by Internet

President Trump appoints Ajit Pai to head the FCC, who abolishes the FCC neutrality protections

Privacy is not a liberal issue, nor are the organizations that struggle to protect civil rights simply part of some broad liberal agenda. Civil liberties advocates perform their function in society when they identify and disseminate information on any potential or existing threats to civil liberties. The information they provide to the public debate, which comes in the form of journalistic reports as well as opinion and commentary, is biased towards protecting civil liberties because this is the function of these organizations within society. This does not mean that all of the threats perceived by all civil liberties advocates are equally legitimate. It simply means that liberties advocates provide information that can help people decide how they feel about issues.

It is important to keep in mind that those who argue from the national security standpoint, or the standpoint of corporations, may bring up legitimate points about the benefits of the system as it currently exists. Internet tech and national security are the basis of multi-trillion-dollar industries, stretching into many facets of the American economy. Regulation threatens these monetary interests as well and companies and individuals arguing against regulation often have economic motivations to consider. These motivations should be considered by everyone attempting to weigh arguments on the issue, because the divided loyalties of individuals arguing against regulation might affect how convincing such arguments seem to American citizens. This does not mean that the claims made by security-advocates are invalid or necessarily corrupt, but simply that one should consider, when weighing these arguments, whether there are undisclosed motivations at play.

Ultimately, deciding how one feels about security and privacy is a personal choice and will be based on a number of highly subjective considerations such as:

Congress debates whether or not to renew the controversial Section 702 FISA Amendment used to authorize NSA domestic intelligence operations since 2008

- whether a person trusts his or her government, or trusts the corporations marketing products and services

- whether a person believes that such entities can police themselves or need to be tightly controlled

- whether a person feels that he or she will be personally affected by the current state of privacy laws

- whether a person feels that terrorism is a threat that requires sacrifices of personal liberty to ensure domestic safety.

These are questions that have no single answer and depend on a person's relationship to the state, to his community, and to the cultural norms of his or her family and society. Ultimately, resolving the issue may be an impossible goal as the realities of the world continue to change. Bryan Padgett, research systems manager for a major US entertainment company, theorized about the future in a survey by *Pew Research*:

> *"The current two-sided security versus privacy pendulum will be replaced by a third option— perhaps independent warehouses of data controlled by independent parties, fed by data providers, and accessed by government only when necessary. With increasing amounts of data being generated for and by all users worldwide, it will continue to be used for good and bad in increasing amounts... I can see a future where it is accepted that anonymity has fallen by the wayside as the online world and the real world become even more fused; however, along with the loss of anonymity, the ability to remove and*

1788   State legislatures ratify the U.S. Constitution, establishing the basic precedent for all future constitutional law

1791   The U.S. Congress ratifies the Bill of Rights, creating the first 10 amendments to the United States Constitution

prevent others from seeing and/or using your data (or data about you) will emerge to become clearer and easier to manage from a single entity. If that comes to pass, it would only come from a government or international agreement, with academia and the private sector creating the technical solution that allows it to work."

Brandeis and Warren argued that privacy was a matter of "inviolate personality," and the American people are still in the process of deciding what parts of their personality are so precious as to deserve protection and what parts are permissibly accessible for other interests. The line that Americans will draw around their private spaces or private practices will differ according to personal taste, generation, and many other factors. There is, it can be argued, a general sense that the current state of privacy is not acceptable and that the American government has, in a broad sense, lost the trust of the people. The rise of antimodernist conservatism may deepen this distrust moving forward and this may mean that the privacy debate gains new momentum, in one direction or another. Alternately, the privacy debate may remain, for the time being, a relatively low priority for a public consumed by income inequality, race relations, and the threat of radical militancy. It is clear that interest in privacy is neither new, nor new to the American experiment, and this debate therefore constitutes one strain of an ongoing effort to translate the principles of the American founders to the emerging digital language and to adjust those founding principles that Americans still deem worthy of preservation, to the changing values of an increasingly global and multicultural world.

1868 The 14th Amendment to the U.S. Constitution guarantees all citizens the right to due process under the law

1890 Warren and Brandeis publish "The Right to Privacy" in the *Harvard Law Review*

Credit: Cagle Cartoons

NOTES

1. Solove, Daniel. "Conceptualizing Privacy." *California Law Review*. Vol. 90, Iss 4. July 2002.

2. Hardwick, Daniel W. "Defining Privacy." *Notre Dame Journal of Law, Ethics & Public Policy*. Vol. 14, Iss 2 Jan. 1, 2012.

3. Shapiro, Fred, and Pearse, Michelle. "The Most-Cited Law Review Articles of All Time." *Michigan Law Review*. Vol. 110, Iss 8. 2012.

4. Howell, Bill. *Alaska Beer: Liquid Gold in the Land of the Midnight Sun*. Charleston, SC: American Palate, 2015.

5. Metcalfe, Philip. *Whispering Wires: The Tragic Tale of an American Bootlegger*. Portland, OR: Inkwater Press, 2007.

6. *"Olmstead v. United States 277 U.S. 438 (1928)." Justia*. Justia. 2017. Web. 31 Oct. 2017.

7. Solove, Daniel J., Rotenberg, Marc, and Paul M. Schwartz. *Privacy, Information, and Technology*. New York: Aspen Publishers, 2006.

8. Gray, David. *The Fourth Amendment in an Age of Surveillance*. New York: Cambridge University Press, 2017.

9. Stephens, Otis H. and Richard A. Glen. *Unreasonable Searches and Seizures: Rights and Liberties Under the Law*. Santa Barbara: ABC-CLIO, 2006.

10. "Senator J. William Fulbright, remarks in the senate," *Congressional Record*.

11. "Joseph R. McCarthy (1908-1957)," *George Washington University*.

12. "Communists in Government Service," *United States Senate*.

13. Kingsbury, "Declassified Documents Reveal KGB Spies in the U.S."

14. Wall, "Anti-Communism in the 1950s."
15. "A Declaration of Conscience," *United States Senate*.
16. "Margaret Chase Smith Declaration of Conscience," *United States Senate*.
17. Kruse, "A stern Senate speech won't stop Trump. It didn't stop McCarthy."
18. Herman, *Joseph McCarthy: "Reexamining the Life and Legacy of America's Most Hated Senator."*
19. Smith, "The Polls: American Attitudes Toward the Soviet Union and Communism."
20. "Beyond Distrust," *Pew Research*.
21. "Griswold v. Connecticut (1965)," *PBS*.
22. "Public Attitudes about Birth Control," *Roper Center*.
23. Iannacci, *"Katz v. United States."*
24. Sheehan, "Vietnam Archive: Pentagon Study Traces 3 Decades of Growing U.S. Involvement."
25. Cooper and Roberts, "After 40 Years, the Complete Pentagon Papers."
26. *"Brandenburg v. Ohio," Cornell Law School.*
27. "New York Times V. United States (1971)," *Bill of Rights Institute*.
28. "Public Approval of Major Court Decisions," *New York Times*.
29. Schwarz, "America's Think Tank."
30. "The Passing of a Pioneer," *Purdue University*.
31. Ware, "Security and Privacy in Computer Systems."
32. "Privacy Act of 1974," *Department of Justice*.
33. Turn and Ware, "Privacy and Security in Computer Systems."
34. Olmstead and Smith, "Americans and Cybersecurity."
35. "The Watergate Story," *Washington Post*.
36. Kohut, "Howe the Watergate crisis eroded public support for Richard Nixon."

37.   Brinkley and Nichter, "Great mystery of the 1970s: Nixon, Watergate and the Huston Plan."

38.   Hersh, "Huge C.I.A. Operation Reported in U.S. Against Antiwar Forces, Other Dissidents in Nixon Years."

39.   "Foreign Intelligence Surveillance Act of 1978," *U.S. Senate*.

40.   Robinson, "Public Opinion During the Watergate Crisis."

41.   "Prof. Ruth Gavison," *The Hebrew University of Jerusalem*.

42.   Bloustein, "Privacy As an Aspect of Human Dignity."

43.   "Communications: Telephone and Telegraph Systems (Series R 1-92)," *Census Bureau*.

44.   Schwarz, "Sales are spiking for '1984,' but it has a long history in politics."

45.   "Electronic Communications Privacy Act of 1986," *Justice Information Sharing*.

46.   Helft and Miller, "1986 Privacy Law Is Outrun by the Web."

47.   Mahtesian, "Privacy in Retreat, A Timeline."

48.   "31995l0046," *European Union Official Journal*.

49.   "Public Law 96-100-Nov. 2, 1979," *U.S. Senate*.

50.   "Unclassified Report on the President's Surveillance Program," Offices of Inspectors General.

51.   "NSA Spying," *Electronic Frontier Foundation*.

52.   Emmons, "Obama Opens NSA's Vast Trove of Warrantless Data to Entire Intelligence Community, Just in Time for Trump."

53.   "Bush and Public Opinion," *Pew Research*.

54.   Newport, "Gallup Review: U.S. Public Opinion on Terrorism."

55.   "How the USA PATRIOT Act Redefines "Domestic Terrorism," *ACLU*.

56.   Moore, "Public Little Concerned About PATRIOT Act."

57.   Saad, "Americans Generally Comfortable with PATRIOT Act."

58.   Bradner, "Conway: Trump White House offered 'alternative facts' on crowd size."

59. Flock, "George Orwell's '1984' is a best-seller again. Here's why it resonates now."
60. Kessler, "The Logo That Took Down a DARPA Surveillance Project."
61. Harris, "Giving IN to the Surveillance State."
62. Gore, "Freedom and Security."
63. "SPJ Code of Ethics," *Society of Professional Journalists*.
64. Victor, "Clinton and Trump Revealed."
65. Meserve and Hirschkorn, "ACLU Sues U.S. over 'No-Fly' List."
66. Newport, "Gallup Review: U.S. Public Opinion on Terrorism."
67. Best and McDermott, "Measuring Opinions vs. Non-Opinions—The Case of the USA PATRIOT Act."
68. "Civil Liberties," Gallup.
69. "Public Remains Divided Over the PATRIOT Act," *Pew Research*.
70. Zetter, "PATRIOT Act Gets a Hearing."
71. "PATRIOT Act"
72. "Public Remains Divided Over the PATRIOT Act," *Pew Research*.
73. Stolberg, "Once-Lone Foe of PATRIOT Act Has Company."
74. "President's Radio Address," *The White House*.
75. Risen and Lichtblau, "Bush Lets U.S. Spy on Callers Without Courts."
76. "The 9/11 Commission Report," *9-11 Commission*.
77. "Bush defends NSA spying program," CNN.
78. Sanchez, "What the Ashcroft "Hospital Showdown" on NSA spying was all about."
79. Mears and Koppel, "NSA eavesdropping program ruled unconstitutional."
80. Newport, "Americans Disapprove of Government Surveillance Programs."
81. Warrick, "Domestic Use of Spy Satellites to Widen."
82. "Turning Spy Satellites on the Homeland," *Federation of Ameri-*

can Scientists.

83. Hsu, "Administration Set to Use New Spy Program in U.S."

84. Gorman, "Satellite-Surveillance Program to Begin Despite Privacy Concerns."

85. Meyer, "Homeland Security said to kill spy satellite plan."

86. Livingstone, "The Proposition's closing statement."

87. Barr, "The Opposition's closing statement."

88. *Protecting Individual Privacy in the Struggle Against Terrorists*, National Research Council.

89. "J.C.R. Licklider," *Internet Hall of Fame.*

90. Mohamed, "A history of cloud computing."

91. Whittaker, "Microsoft admits PATRIOT Act can access EU-based cloud data."

92. Freeland, "Data Privacy Protection Discrepancies Could Hamper U.S. Cloud Provider Growth in Europe."

93. "State Department Dispels Cloud Myths with Fact about US Privacy Protections," *BSA.*

94. Sarno, "Consumer Reports, Times polls find broad data privacy concerns."

95. Singer, "Why a Push for Online Privacy Is Bogged Down in *Washington.*"

96. Meyer, "Here Come the World's Toughest Privacy Laws."

97. Meyer, "Google should have been fined $1B over privacy policy, says EU justice chief."

98. Lazarus, "Europe and U.S. have different approaches to protecting privacy of personal data."

99. Greenwald, "NSA collecting phone records of millions of Verizon customers daily."

100. "NSA slides explain the PRISM data-collection program," Washington Post.

101. Ball, "NSA monitored calls of 35 world leaders after US official

handed over contacts."

102. Traynor and Lewis, "Merkel compared NSA to Stasi in heated encounter with Obama."

103. Liptak, "Senators should have known about snooping, says McCain."

104. Gabbatt, "US senators press officials on NSA surveillance programs—live."

105. Bever, "Top 10 commentaries on the NSA leaks and whistleblower Edward Snowden."

106. Friedersdorf, "Choose One: Secrecy and Democracy Are Incompatible."

107. Wittes, "William Galston on the NSA Controversies."

108. Cohen, "Edward Snowden: A Modern-Day Daniel Ellsberg, Except for One Key Difference."

109. DeSilver, "Most young Americans say Snowden has served the public interest."

110. Waddell, "The Long and Winding History of Encryption."

111. "History of Encryption," *SANS Institute*.

112. McCullagh, "Former FBI chief takes on encryption."

113. Zegart, "The Security Debate We Need to Have."

114. Berger, "This is the media's real bias – pro-business, pro-corporate, pro-CEO."

115. Abelson, et al, "Keys Under Doormats."

116. Barrett, "The Encryption Debate Should End Right Now."

117. Perlroth, Larson, and Shane, "N.S.A. Able to Foil Basic Safeguards of Privacy on Web."

118. Menn, "Distrustful U.S. allies force spy agency to back down in encryption fight."

119. Lee, "No Really, the NSA Can't Brute Force Your Crypto."

120. Brandom, "Someone (probably the NSA) has been hiding viruses in hard drive firmware."

121. Ball, Borger, and Greenwald, "Revealed: how US and UK spy agencies defeat internet privacy and security."
122. "Inside the NSA's War on Internet Security," *Der Spiegel*.
123. Larson, "Revealed: The NSA's Secret Campaign to Crack, Undermine Internet Security."
124. Madden and Rainie, "Americans' Attitudes About Privacy, Security and Surveillance."
125. Olmstead and Smith, "Americans and Cybersecurity."
126. Fahrenthold, "With NSA revelations, Sen. Ron Wyden's vague privacy warnings finally become clear."
127. "In Speech, Wyden Says Official Interpretations of PATRIOT Act Must be Made Public," *Ron Wyden*.
128. Tien, "Update: Polls Continue to Show Majority of Americans Against NSA Spying."
129. "What *Is* 'Islamic State'?," *BBC News*.
130. Rayner, Samuel, and Evans, "Charlie Hebdo attack: France's worst terrorist attack in a generation leaves 12 dead."
131. "Why Islam prohibits images of Muhammad," *The Economist*.
132. "A Review of the FBI's Use of Section 215 Orders," *Office of the Inspector General*.
133. Savage, "Declassified Report Shows Doubs About Value of N.S.A.'s Warrantless Spying."
134. Greenwald, "On PATRIOT Act Renewal and USA Freedom Act: Glenn Greenwald Talks with ACLU's Jameel Jaffer."
135. Roberts, "PATRIOT Act author prepares bill to put NSA bulk collection 'out of business'."
136. Lewis and Roberts, "NSA reform bill to trim back US surveillance unveiled in Congress."
137. Ackerman, "Fears NSA will seek to undermine surveillance reform."
138. Gao, "What Americans think about NSA surveillance, national

security and privacy."

139. Zetter, "Magistrate Orders Apple to Help FBI Hack San Bernardino Shooter's Phone."

140. "A Message to Our Customers," *Apple Inc.*

141. Richard and Hartzog, "Apple v the FBI: why the 1789 All Writs Act is the wrong tool."

142. Sorkin, "The Dangerous All Writs Act Precedent in the Apple Encryption Case."

143. Calamur, "Public Opinion Supports Apple Over the FBI—or Does it?"

144. Musil, "Apple has support of independent voters in FBI iPhone battle."

145. Ackerman, Thielman, and Yadron, "Apple case: judge rejects FBI request for access to drug dealer's iPhone."

146. Goitein and Patel, "What Went Wrong with the FISA Court."

147. "NSA Inspector Generals Letter to Senator Charles Grassley," NSA.

148. Nakashima and Demirjian, Divided Senate intelligence panel advances spy-bill renewal without major changes."

149. Prosser, "Privacy."

150. Warren and Brandeis, "The Right to Privacy."

151. Bloustein, "Privacy as an Aspect of Human Dignity."

152. Moore, "Defining Privacy."

153. Inness, "Privacy, Intimacy, and Isolation."

154. Kahn, "Privacy as a Legal Principle of Identity Maintenance."

155. Solove, "Conceptualizing Privacy."

156. Matishak, "Trump's rhetoric hampers his aides' surveillance push."

157. Olmstead, "Most Americans think the government could be monitoring their phone calls and emails."

158. Brodkin, "Ajit Pai not concerned about number of pro-net

neutrality comments."

159. Rainie, "The state of privacy in post-Snowden America."
160. Rainie and Anderson, "The Future of Privacy."
161. "Civil Liberties," *Gallup*.
162. Ibid
163. Hughes, "Do checks and balances matter in surveillance?"
164. Rainie and Anderson, "The Future of Privacy."
165. Ibid
166. "Public Trust in Government: 1958-2017."
167. Madden and Rainie, "Americans' Attitudes About Privacy, Security and Surveillance."

Primary & Secondary Sources

The Right to Privacy by Samuel Warren and Louis Brandeis
Harvard Law Review 1890

The Bootlegger, the Wiretap, and the Beginning of Privacy by
Karen Abbott *The New Yorker* July 5, 2017

Goldman v. United States, 316 U.S. 129 (1942) United States
Supreme Court. (Excerpts and commentary based on the Court's ruling
and opinions)

Barenblatt v. United States, 360 U.S. 109 (1959) United States
Supreme Court. (Excerpts and commentary based on the Court's ruling
and opinions)

New York Times Co. v. United States, 403 U.S. 713 (1971) United
States Supreme Court. (Excerpts and commentary based on the Court's
ruling and opinions)

Security and Privacy in Computer Systems by William H. Ware
Rand Corporation Study April 1967

The Foreign Intelligence Surveillance Act of 1978 (FISA). U.S.
Department of Justice.

Katz v. United States 389 U.S. 347 (1967) United States Supreme
Court. (Excerpts and commentary based on the Court's ruling and
opinions)

Privacy and the Limits of Law by Ruth E. Gavison, *Yale Law
Journal* January 1980

Electronic Communications Privacy Act of 1986 Public Law, Federal Record

Legal Standards for the Intelligence Community in Conducting Electronic Surveillance (2000) National Security Agency (NSA) Report to Congress on Legal Standards for Electronic Surveillance

USA PATRIOT Act Excerpts from the Hearing Before the Select Committee on Intelligence of the United States Senate One Hundred Ninth Congress. First Session. USA PATRIOT Act. April 19, 2005; April 27, 2005; and May 24, 2005.

Terror Act Has Lasting Effects by Declan McCullagh *Wired* October 26, 2001

Many Tools Of Big Brother Are Now Up And Running. *The New York Times* December 23, 2002

Privocrats vs. National Security *National Review* May 18, 2004

Spies, Lies and Wiretaps *The New York Times* January 29, 2006

Turning Spy Satellites On The Homeland: The Privacy And Civil Liberties Implications Of The National Applications Office. Excerpt from the Hearing of the Committee on Homeland Security, House of Representatives, One Hundred Tenth Congress, First Session, September 6, 2007.

The Proposition's Closing Statement by Neil C. Livingstone *The Economist* February 13, 2008

Five Myths Regarding Privacy and Law Enforcement Access to Personal Information in the European Union and the United States The State Department December 2012

Glossary

A

(AES) Advanced Encryption Standard An encryption algorithm for securing sensitive but unclassified material by US Government agencies and, as a consequence, may eventually become the de facto encryption standard for commercial transactions in the private sector.

AG Attorney General

B

Backdoor A means of access to a computer program that bypasses security mechanisms. A programmer may sometimes install a backdoor so that the program can be accessed for troubleshooting or other purposes.

Big Data Analytics The process of examining large amounts of data of a variety of types (big data) to uncover hidden patterns, unknown correlations, and other useful information.

Bulk Data An electronic collection of data composed of information from multiple records, whose primary relationship to each other is their shared origin from a single or multiple databases.

C

Church Committee An 11-member investigating body of the Senate (a Senate Select Committee) that studied governmental operations with respect to Intelligence Activities. It published 14 reports that contain a wealth of information on the formation, operation, and abuses of US intelligence agencies. The reports were published in 1975 and 1976, after which recommendations for reform were debated in Congress and in some cases enacted.

CIA Central Intelligence Agency

Cloud Computing A model for enabling ubiquitous, convenient, on-demand network access to a shared pool of configurable computing resources (e.g., networks, servers, storage, applications, and services) that can be rapidly provisioned and released with minimal management effort or service provider interaction.

CLPP Board Civil Liberties and Privacy Protection Board

(CMP) Continuous Monitoring Program Maintaining ongoing awareness of information security, vulnerabilities, and threats to support organizational risk management decisions.

Counter-intelligence Information gathered and activities conducted to identify, deceive, exploit, disrupt, or protect against espionage, other intelligence activities, sabotage, or assassinations conducted for or on behalf of foreign powers, organizations or persons, or their agents, or international terrorist organizations or activities.

Counter-proliferation Those actions (e.g., detect and monitor, prepare to conduct counter-proliferation operations, offensive operations, weapons of mass destruction, active defense, and passive defense) taken to defeat the threat and/or use of weapons of mass destruction against the United States, our military forces, friends, and allies.

D

Data Mining The process of collecting, searching through, and analyzing a large amount of data within a database, to discover patterns of relationships.

Decryption The process of converting encrypted data back to its original form, so it can be understood.

DHS Department of Homeland Security

DIAA Defense Information Assurance Agency

Diffie-Hellman Key Exchange Algorithm Cryptographic algorithm used for secure key exchange. The algorithm allows two users to exchange a symmetric secret key through an insecure wired or wireless channel and without any prior secrets.

(DRM) Digital Rights Management/(IRM) Information Rights Management A collection of systems and software applications used to protect the copyrights of documents and electronic media. These include digital music and movies, as well as other data that is stored and transferred digitally. DRM is important to publisher of electronic media because it helps to control the trading, protection, monitoring, and tracking of digital media, limiting the illegal propagation of copyrighted works.

DISA Defense Information Systems Agency

DNI Director of National Intelligence

DOD Department of Defense

DOJ Department of Justice

DTRA Defense Threat Reduction Agency

E
Einstein 3 An advanced, network-layer intrusion detection system (IDS) which analyzes Internet traffic as it moves in and out of United States Federal Government networks. EINSTEIN filters packets at

the gateway and reports anomalies to the United States Computer Emergency Readiness Team (US-CERT) at the Department of Homeland Security.

Encryption The conversion of data into a form, called a ciphertext (encrypted text), that cannot be easily understood by unauthorized people.

Executive Order Official documents, numbered consecutively, through which the President of the United States manages the operations of the Federal Government.

Executive Order 12333 Under section 2.3, intelligence agencies can only collect, retain, and disseminate information about a "US person" (US citizens and lawful permanent residents) if permitted by applicable law, if the information fits within one of the enumerated categories under Executive Order 12333, and if it is permitted under that agency's implementing guidelines approved by the Attorney General. The EO has been amended to reflect the changing security and intelligence environment and structure within the US Government.

F

FBI Federal Bureau of Investigation

(FISA) Foreign Intelligence Surveillance Act As amended, establishes procedures for the authorization of electronic surveillance, use of pen registers and trap-and-trace devices, physical searches, and business records for the purpose of gathering foreign intelligence.

(FISC) Foreign Intelligence Surveillance Court A special court for which the Chief Justice of the United States designates 11 federal district court judges to review applications for warrants related to national security investigations.

FTC Federal Trade Commission

I

Identifier/Selector Communication accounts associated with a target (e.g., e-mails address, phone number)

IAD Information Assurance Directorate of the National Security Agency Intelligence Community Seventeen-member group of Executive Branch agencies and organizations that work separately and together to engage in intelligence activities, either in an oversight, managerial, support, or participatory role necessary for the conduct of foreign relations and the protection of the national security of the United States.

M

Meta-data A characterization or description documenting the identification, management, nature, use, or location of information resources (data).

(MLAT) Mutual Legal Assistance Treaty An understanding and agreement between two countries that wish to mutually cooperate regarding investigation, prosecution, and enforcement of the provisions of the laws of the agreeing countries. The MLAT also specifies the grounds on which a request by either nation may be rejected or denied by the other nation.

N

NAS National Academy of Sciences

(NIPF) National Intelligence Priorities Framework DNI's guidance to the Intelligence Community on the national intelligence priorities approved by the President. The NIPF guides prioritization for the operation, planning, and programming of US intelligence analysis and collection.

(NSC/DC) National Security Council Deputies Committee The senior sub-Cabinet interagency forum for consideration of policy issues affecting national security. The NSC/DC prescribes and reviews work for the NSC interagency groups discussed in a directive. The NSC/DC helps to ensure issues brought before the NSC/PC or the NSC have been properly analyzed and prepared for decision. The regular members of the NSC/DC consist of the Deputy Secretary of State or Under Secretary of the Treasury or Under Secretary of the Treasury for International Affairs, the Deputy Secretary of Defense or Under Secretary of Defense for Policy, the Deputy Attorney General, the Deputy Director of the Office of Management and Budget, the Deputy Director of Central Intelligence, the Vice Chairman of the Joint Chiefs of Staff, the Deputy Chiefs of Staff to the President for Policy, the Chief of Staff and National Security Advisor to the Vice President, the Deputy Assistant to the President for International Economic Affairs, and the Assistant to the President and Deputy National Security Advisor (who shall serve as chair).

(NSC/PC) National Security Council Principals Committee The senior interagency forum for consideration of policy affecting national security. The regular members of the NSC/PC consist of the Secretary of State, the Secretary of the Treasury, the Secretary of Defense, the Chief of Staff to the President, and the Assistant to the President for National Security Affairs, who serves and chair.

(NSL) National Security Letter A letter from a United States government agency demanding information related to national security. It is independent of legal courts and therefore is different from a subpoena. It is used mainly by the FBI when investigating matters related to national security. It is issued to a particular entity or organization to turn over records and data pertaining to individuals. By law, NSLs can request only non-content information, such as transactional records, phone numbers dialed, or sender or recipient of the letter from disclosing that the letter was ever issued.

NSS National Security Staff

NIST National Institute of Standards and Technology

Non-Disclosure Agreement (commonly referred to as "Gag Orders") Contracts intended to protect information considered to be proprietary or confidential. Parties involved in executing a NDA promise not to divulge secret or protected information.

NRC National Research Council

NRO National Reconnaissance Office

NSA National Security Agency

NSD/DoJ National Security Division of the Department of Justice

O
ODNI Office of the Director of National Intelligence

ODOC NSA's Office of the Director of Compliance

OIA/DoJ Office of International Affairs of the Department of Justice

OMB Office of Management and Budget

OSD Office of the Secretary of Defense

OTA Office of Technology Assessment

P

PATRIOT Act An Act of Congress that was signed into law by President George W. Bush on October 26, 2001. The title of the act is a ten-letter acronym (USA PATRIOT) that stands for Uniting (and) Strengthening America (by) Providing Appropriate Tools Required (to) Intercept (and) Obstruct Terrorism Act of 2001.

PCLOB Privacy and Civil Liberties Oversight Board

Pen Register A device that decodes or records electronic impulses, allowing outgoing numbers from a telephone to be identified.

PII Personally identifiable information

PIBD Public Interest Declassification Board

R

(RAS) Reasonable Articulable Suspicion/Reasonable Grounds to Believe (as applied to Section 215) A legal standard of proof in United States law that is less than probable cause, the legal standard for arrests and warrants, but more than an "inchoate and unparticularized suspicion or 'hunch'"; it must be based on "specific and articulable facts", "taken together with rational inferences from those facts."

Rockefeller Commission Headed by Vice-President Nelson Rockefeller, the commission issued a single report in 1975, which delineated CIA abuses including mail openings and surveillance of domestic dissident groups.

RSA Algorithm (Rivest-Shamir-Adleman) An Internet encryption and authentication system that uses an algorithm developed in 1977 by Ron Rivest, Adi Shamir, and Leonard Adleman. The RSA algorithm is the most commonly used encryption and authentication algorithm and is included as part of the Web browsers from Microsoft and Netscape and many other products.

S

Section 215 Statutory provision of FISA that permits the government access to business records for foreign intelligence and international terrorism investigations. The governing federal officials are permitted the ability to acquire business and other 'tangible records' which include: business records, phone provider records, apartment rental records, driver's license, library records, book sales records, gun sales records, tax return records, educational records, and medical records. Under this provision, federal investigators can compel third-party record holders, such as telecom firms, banks or others, to disclose these documents. In order to use this provision, the US government must show that there are reasonable grounds to believe that the records are relevant to an international terrorism or counterintelligence investigation.

Section 702 Statutory provision for the targeting of individuals reasonably believed to be non-U.S persons located outside the United States.

(SSL) Secure Sockets Layer A commonly used protocol for managing the security of a message transmission on the internet.

(SIGINT) Signals Intelligence Intelligence derived from electronic signals and systems used by foreign targets, such as communications systems, and radar communications system.

Social Networking A dedicated website or other application that enables users to communicate with each other by posting information, comments, messages, images, etc.

Splinternet Also referred to as "cyberbalkanization" or "Internet Balkanization", it is the segregation of the Internet into smaller groups with similar interests, to a degree that they show a narrow-minded approach to outsiders or those with contradictory views.

T

Third Party Doctrine Provides that information "knowingly exposed" to a third party is not subject to Fourth Amendment protection because one "assumes the risk" that the third party will disclose that information. The doctrine holds that the information that individual disclosed to businesses credit card transactions, phone records, etc. doesn't carry with it a "reasonable expectation of privacy" under the Fourth Amendment, as one has "assumed the risk" that this information might at some point be disclosed.

TIP Transatlantic Trade and Investment Partnership

Trap-and-Trace A device or process that captures the incoming electronic or other impulses which identify the originating number or other dialing, routing, addressing, and signaling information reasonably likely to identify the source of a wire or electronic communication, provided, however, that such information shall not include the contents of any communication.

Tutelage The codename of a classified NSA technology used to monitor communications used on military networks.

W

Warfighter Military personnel with a combat or combat related mission. Whistle-Blower A person who tells someone in authority about something they believe to be illegal that is happening, especially in a government department or a company.

Wiretap To place a device on (someone's phone) in order to secretly listen to telephone calls.

Z

Zero Day Exploitation Taking advantage of security vulnerability on the same day that the vulnerability becomes generally known. There are zero days between the time the vulnerability is discovered and the first attack. It is an exploit of vulnerability in software, which is being utilized for the first time and which, therefore, is unknown to defensive software.

From LIBERTY AND SECURITY IN A CHANGING WORLD Report and Recommendations of The President's Review Group on Intelligence and Communications Technology, December 12, 2013.

Historical Snapshots

1890–1891

- Massive immigration that was transforming the nation left the rural South largely unaffected
- Two-thirds of the nation's 62.9 million people still lived in rural areas; 32.7 percent were immigrants or the children of at least one immigrant parent
- New Irish women immigrants to America, in demand as servants, outnumbered the men in 1890
- The census showed that 53.5 percent of the farms in the US were fewer than 100 acres
- The first commercial dry cell battery was invented
- Three percent of Americans, age 18 to 21, attended college
- *Literary Digest* began publication
- Population of Los Angeles reached 50,000, up 40,000 in 10 years
- Restrictive anti-black "Jim Crow" laws were enacted throughout the South
- The first full-service advertising agency was established in New York City
- Thousands of Kansas farmers were bankrupted by the tight money conditions
- The $3 million Tampa Bay Hotel was completed in Florida
- American Express Traveler's Cheque was copyrighted
- Ceresota flour was introduced by the Northwest Consolidated Milling Company
- George A. Hormel & Co. introduced the packaged food Spam
- Painter Paul Gauguin arrived in Papeete, Tahiti
- The penalty kick was introduced into soccer
- The International Brotherhood of Electrical Workers was organized

- New Scotland Yard became the headquarters of the London Metropolitan Police
- Eugène Dubois discovered *Homo erectus* fossils in the Dutch colony of Java
- Bicycle designer Charles Duryea, 29, and his toolmaker brother James designed a gasoline engine capable of powering a road vehicle
- Edouard Michelin obtained a patent for a "removable" bicycle tire that could be repaired quickly in the event of puncture
- The Jarvis winch, patented by Glasgow-born Scottish shipmaster John C. B. Jarvis, enabled ships to be manned by fewer men and helped develop the windjammer
- Rice University and Stanford were chartered
- John T. Smith patented corkboard using a process of heat and pressure to combine waste cork together for insulation
- American Express issued the first traveler's checks
- Commercial bromine was produced electrolytically by Herbert H. Dow's Midland Chemical Company in Michigan
- Bacteriologist Anna Williams obtained her M.D. from the Women's Medical College of New York and worked in the diagnostic laboratory of the city's Health Department, the first such lab in America
- Chicago's Provident Hospital became the first interracial hospital in America
- The lapidary encyclical "Of New Things" by Pope Leo XIII declared that employers have the moral duty as members of the possessing class to improve the "terrible conditions of the new and often violent process of industrialization"
- Educator William Rainey Harper became president of the new University of Chicago with funding from merchant Marshall Field and oilman John D. Rockefeller
- Irene Coit became the first woman admitted to Yale University
- The electric self-starter for automobiles was patented

- The Automatic Electric Company was founded to promote a dial telephone patented by Kansas City undertaker Almon B. Strowger, who suspected that "central" was diverting his incoming calls to a rival embalmer
- Important books included *Tess of the d'Urbervilles* by Thomas Hardy; *The Light That Failed* by Rudyard Kipling; *The Picture of Dorian Gray* by Oscar Wilde, and *Tales of Soldiers and Civilians* by Ambrose Bierce

1892–1893

- American industry was benefiting from the 1890 decision by Congress to increase tariffs on foreign goods from 38 to 50 percent, making U.S. manufactured items less expensive
- New York City boss Richard Croker's fortune was estimated to be $8 million, not including his own railway car and a $2.5 million stud farm
- An improved carburetor for automobiles was invented
- The first successful gasoline tractor was produced by a farmer in Waterloo, Iowa
- Chicago's first elevated railway went into operation, forming the famous Loop
- The $1 Ingersoll pocket watch was introduced, bringing affordable timepieces to the masses
- The General Electric Company was created through a merger
- Violence erupted at the steelworkers' strike of the Carnegie-Phipps Mill at Homestead, Pennsylvania
- President Benjamin Harrison extended for 10 years the Chinese Exclusion Act, which suspended Chinese immigration to the United States
- The United States population included 4,000 millionaires
- The name Sears, Roebuck & Company came into use
- Pineapples were canned for the first time
- Diesel patented his internal combustion engine
- The Census Bureau announced that a frontier line was no longer

discernible; all unsettled areas had been invaded
- The first automatic telephone switchboard was activated
- Cream of Wheat was introduced by Diamond Mill of Grand Forks, North Dakota
- New York's 13-story Waldorf Hotel was opened
- The first Ford motorcar was road tested
- The Philadelphia and Reading Railroad went into receivership
- Wrigley's Spearmint and Juicy Fruit chewing gum were introduced by William Wrigley, Jr.

1894

- Approximately 12,000 New York City tailors struck to protest sweatshops
- The first Sunday newspaper color comic section was published in the *New York World*
- Antique-collecting became popular, supported by numerous genealogy-minded societies
- A well-meaning group of anglophiles called the America Acclimatization Society began importing English birds mentioned in Shakespeare, including nightingales, thrushes and starlings, for release in America
- Overproduction forced farm prices to fall; wheat dropped from $1.05 a bushel in 1870 to $0.49 a bushel
- The first Greek newspaper in America was published as the *New York Atlantis*
- New York Governor Roswell P. Flower signed the nation's first dog-licensing law, with a $2.00 license fee
- Hockey's first Stanley Cup championship game was played between the Montreal Amateur Athletic Association and the Ottawa Capitals
- Thomas Edison publicly demonstrated the kinetoscope, a peephole viewer in which developed film moved continuously under a magnifying glass
- Workers at the Pullman Palace Car Company in Illinois went on strike

to protest a wage reduction; President Cleveland ordered federal troops onto the trains to insure mail delivery

- Labor Day was established as a holiday for federal employees
- Congress established the Bureau of Immigration
- Congress passed a bill imposing a 2 percent tax on incomes over $4,000, which was ruled unconstitutional by the U.S. Supreme Court
- The United States Government began keeping records on the weather
- Astronomer Percival Lowell built a private observatory in Flagstaff, Arizona, and began his observations of Mars
- The Regents of the University of Michigan declared that "Henceforth in the selection of professors and instructors and other assistants in instruction in the University, no discrimination will be made in selection between men and women"
- French Baron Pierre de Coubertin proposed an international Olympics competition to be held every four years in a different nation to encourage international peace and cooperation
- The *Edison Kinetoscopic Record of a Sneeze* was released in movie theaters

1895

- Mintonette, later known as volleyball, was created by William G. Morgan in Holyoke, Massachusetts
- Oscar Wilde's last play, *The Importance of Being Earnest*, was first shown at St. James's Theatre in London
- The Treaty of Shimonoseki was signed between China and Japan, marking the end of the first Sino-Japanese War
- The U.S. Supreme Court ruled that the federal government had the right to regulate interstate commerce, legalizing the military suppression of the Pullman Strike
- The first professional American football game was played in Latrobe, Pennsylvania, between the Latrobe YMCA and the Jeannette Athletic Club

- Rudyard Kipling published the story "Mowgli Leaves the Jungle Forever" in *Cosmopolitan* illustrated magazine
- George B. Selden was granted the first U.S. patent for an automobile
- Wilhelm Röntgen discovered a type of radiation later known as x-rays
- Oscar Hammerstein opened the Olympia Theatre, the first to be built in New York City's Times Square district
- Alfred Nobel signed his last will and testament, setting aside his estate to establish the Nobel Prize after his death
- Two hundred African-Americans left from Savannah, Georgia, headed for Liberia
- George Brownell patented a machine to make paper twine
- The Anti-Saloon League of America was formed in Washington D.C.
- Frederick Blaisdell patented the pencil
- George Washington Vanderbilt II officially opened his "Biltmore House" on Christmas in Asheville, North Carolina
- Auguste and Louis Lumière displayed their first moving picture film in Paris
- The London School of Economics and Political Science was founded in England
- W. E. B. Du Bois became the first African-American to receive a Ph.D. from Harvard University
- The gold reserve of the U.S. Treasury was saved when J. P. Morgan and the Rothschilds loaned $65 million worth of gold to the U.S. Government

1896–1897

- The bicycle industry reported sales of $60 million; the average bike sold for $100
- The earliest trading stamps, issued by S&H Green Stamps, were distributed
- Michelob beer was introduced
- The Klondike gold rush in Bonanza Creek, Canada, began

- The *Boston Cooking School Cook Book* was published, advocating the use of precise measurements to produce identical results
- Radioactivity was discovered in uranium
- William Ramsay discovered helium
- Five annual Nobel Prizes were established in the fields of physics, physiology and medicine, chemistry, literature, and peace
- Bituminous coal miners staged a 12-week walkout
- Continental Casualty Company was founded
- Dow Chemical Company was incorporated
- Radio transmission over long distances was achieved by Gugielmo Marconi
- Winton Motor Carriage Company was organized
- The NYC Health Board began enforcing a law regulating women in mercantile establishments
- Mail Pouch tobacco was introduced
- Ronald Ross discovered the malaria bacillus
- Wheat prices rose to $1.09 per bushel
- Jell-O was introduced by Pearl B. Wait
- Boston's H.P. Hill used glass bottles to distribute milk

1897

- Thorstein Veblen developed the concepts for his book, *Theory of the Leisure Class*, which stated, "conspicuous consumption of valuable goods is a means of reputability to the gentlemen of leisure"
- Continental Casualty Company was founded
- Radical Emma Goldman, advocate of free love, birth control, homosexual rights and "freedom for both sexes," was arrested
- The Royal Automobile Club was founded in London
- John Davison Rockefeller, worth nearly $200 million, stopped going to his office at Standard Oil and began playing golf and giving away his wealth
- The Presbyterian Assembly condemned the growing bicycling fad for

enticing parishioners away from church
- Motorcar production reached nearly 1,000 vehicles
- Nearly 150 Yiddish periodicals were being published, many of which advocated radical labor reform, Zionism, and even anarchism, to obtain reform
- Republican William McKinley was sworn into office as America's 25th president, helped by $7 million raised by manager businessman Mark Hanna, compared with $300,000 raised by opponent William Jennings Bryan
- Prospectors streamed to the Klondike in search of gold
- The Winton Motor Carriage Company was organized

1898
- "Happy Birthday to You," composed by sisters Mildred and Patty Hill in 1893 as "Good Morning to All," was becoming popular
- The "grandfather clause" marched across the South, ushering in widespread use of Jim Crow laws and restricting most blacks from voting
- Pepsi-Cola was introduced in North Carolina, by pharmacist Caleb Bradham
- J.P. Stevens & Company was founded in New York
- Toothpaste in collapsible metal tubes was available due to the work of Connecticut dentist Lucius Sheffield
- The trolley replaced horsedrawn cars in Boston
- Wesson Oil was introduced
- The boll weevil began spreading across cotton-growing areas of the South
- *The New York Times* dropped its price from $0.03 to $0.01, tripling circulation
- The Union Carbide Company was formed
- Uneeda Biscuit was created
- Bricklayers made $3.41 per day and worked a 48-hour week, while

marble cutters made $4.22 per day
- America boasted more than 300 bicycle manufacturing companies
- Cellophane was invented by Charles F. Cross and Edward J. Bevan

1900
- President William McKinley used the telephone as part of his re-election campaign; he was the last Union soldier to be elected president
- Nationwide, 13,824 motorcars were on the road
- Hamburgers were introduced by Louis Lassen in New Haven, Connecticut
- The number of advertising agencies in New York City increased from 44 in 1870 to more than 400
- Firestone Tire and Rubber Company was founded based on a patent for attaching tires to rims
- John Davison Rockefeller's wealth was estimated to be $200 million
- A dinner party in New York attracted publicity when cigarettes rolled in $100 bills were given to guests before dinner
- The cost of telephone service fell dramatically as more companies offered a 10-party line, allowing that many customers to share one line
- The U.S. led the world in productivity, based on gross national product, producing $116 billion compared with $62.2 billion in Great Britain, $42.8 billion in France and $42 billion in Germany
- 30,000 trolley cars operated on 15,000 miles of track across America
- Cities like New York and San Francisco had one saloon for every 200 people
- Louis Comfort Tiffany opened his first glass studio in New York
- America's economic boom entered its fourth year with 0.1 percent inflation
- Cigarette smoking was extremely popular and widely advertised, particularly by American Tobacco
- Excavation had begun on the New York subway system
- U.S. railroads were charging an average of $0.75 per ton-mile, down from $1.22 in 1883

- Automobile manufacturer Ransom Olds sold 425 cars during the year
- The U.S. College Entrance Examination Board was formed to screen college applicants using a Scholastic Aptitude Test
- The Junior League of the New York Settlement House attracted young débutantes to serve the less fortunate
- Puerto Rico, obtained in the Spanish-American War in 1898, was declared a U.S. territory
- A tidal wave in Galveston, Texas, killed 4,000 people
- The U.S. Navy bought its first submarine

1901

- Major movies included *The Philippines and Our New Possessions, The Conquest of the Air, Drama at the Bottom of the Sea* and *Execution of Czolgosz,* the man who shot President William McKinley
- Pogroms in Russia forced many Jews to America
- The U.S. constructed a 16-inch, 130-pound breech-loading rifle that was the most powerful in the world
- Popular songs included "Ain't Dat a Shame?," "The Night We Did Not Care," "When You Loved Me in the Sweet Old Days" and "Maiden with the Dreamy Eyes"
- The first U.S. Open golf tournament under USGA rules was held at the Myopia Hunt Club in Hamilton, Massachusetts
- The U.S. granted citizenship to the five civilized tribes: the Cherokee, Creek, Choctaw, Chicasaw and Seminole
- West Point officially abolished the practice of hazing cadets
- The Boston Museum of Fine Arts was given funds to purchase Velásquez's portrait, *Don Baltazar and His Dwarf*
- Books included *Up from Slavery* by Booker T. Washington, *To a Person Sitting in Darkness* by Mark Twain, *The Psychopathology of Everyday Life* by Sigmund Freud, *The Octopus* by Frank Norris and *Springtime and Harvest* by Upton Sinclair
- North Carolina proposed a literacy amendment for voting

- *The Settlement Cookbook,* published by a Milwaukee settlement worker to help immigrant women, carried the phrase, "The way to a man's heart is through his stomach"
- Peter Cooper Hewitt created the first mercury-vapor electric lamp
- Four widows of Revolutionary War soldiers remained on pensions; one veteran of the war of 1812 still lived
- Researchers discovered a connection between obesity and heart disease
- Of the 120,000 U.S. military troops on active duty, 70,000 were stationed in the Philippines fighting the insurgency
- South Dakota passed legislation making school attendance mandatory for children eight to 14 years of age
- The first vacuum cleaner was invented to compete with the Bissell Carpet Sweeper
- The military began placing greater emphasis on the science of nutrition after England had to reject three out of five men in its recruiting for the Boer War in 1899
- Vice President Teddy Roosevelt was made an honorary member of the Hebrew Veterans of the War with Spain; many of its members had fought as Roosevelt's Rough Riders during the Spanish-American War
- Christy Mathewson of New York pitched professional baseball's first no-hitter, defeating St. Louis 5-0
- The length of time required to cross the Atlantic Ocean was one week, compared to one month in 1800
- The median age of men for their first marriage was 25.9 years, and 21.9 for women

1902–1903

- The Brownie Box camera was introduced by Eastman Kodak Company, costing $1.00
- Firestone Tire and Rubber Company began operations based on a patent for attaching tires to rims
- The first modern submarine, the *Holland,* was purchased by the navy

- Uneeda Biscuits achieved sales of more than 10 million packages per month
- Life expectancy nationwide in 1900 was estimated to be 47 years
- The U.S. census reported the U.S. population at 76 million and projected that it would grow to 106 million over the next 20 years, pushed by a steady influx of immigrants
- Membership in the American Federation of Labor reached the million-person mark
- The National Association of Manufacturers launched an anti-union campaign that promoted the right of Americans to work when and where they pleased, depicting labor organizers as agitators and socialists
- The price of coal in New York went from $5.00 to $30.00 a ton during a five-month strike of anthracite coal workers
- Rayon was patented by U.S. Chemist A. D. Little
- Russian American Morris Michtom and his wife introduced the teddy bear with movable arms, legs, and head
- Philip Morris Corporation was founded
- Charles Lewis Tiffany, founder of Tiffany and Co., died, leaving an estate of $35 million
- The automat restaurant was opened by Horn & Hardart Baking company in Philadelphia
- The Wright Brothers made the first sustained manned flights in a controlled gasoline-powered aircraft
- The 24-horsepower Chadwick motorcar cost $4,000, capable of going 60 mph
- Massachusetts created the first automobile license plate
- Bottle-blowing machines cut the cost of manufacturing electric light bulbs
- The Harley-Davidson motorcycle was introduced
- An automatic machine to clean a salmon and remove its head and tail was devised by A.K. Smith, speeding processing and cutting costs

- Sanka Coffee was introduced by German coffee importer Ludwig Roselius

1904

- Marie Louise Van Vorst infiltrated factories to expose the problems of child labor
- Post Toasties were introduced by the Postum Company
- The St. Louis Fair spawned iced tea and the ice cream cone
- *Ladies' Home Journal* published an exposé of the U.S. patent medicine business
- Montgomery Ward mailed three million free catalogues, while Sears, Roebuck distributed a million copies of its spring catalogue
- Typhoid fever in NYC was traced to "Typhoid Mary" Mallon, a carrier of the disease who took jobs handling food, often under an assumed name
- The National Women's Trade Union League was formed by middle-class and working women to foster women's education and help women organize unions
- The New York Society for the Suppression of Vice targeted playing cards, roulette, lotto, watches with obscene pictures, and articles of rubber for immoral use
- Florida gained the title to the Everglades swamp and immediately made plans for drainage
- Louis Sherry's on NYC's 5th Avenue opened the New York Riding Club, where members could eat in the saddle
- A Packard Model F went from San Francisco to New York City in 51 days, the first authenticated transcontinental auto trip
- Women's groups led by the wealthy, who were fighting for better conditions for working women, were branded "the mink brigade"
- Horace Fletcher's book *ABC of Nutrition* advocated chewing your food 32 times a bite, sparking a special trend for mastication
- Malaria and yellow fever disappeared from the Panama Canal after

army surgeons discovered the link to mosquitoes and developed successful disease control

- The sixth moon of Jupiter was sighted
- Marie Curie discovered two new radioactive elements in uranium ore—radium and polonium
- *The Shame of the Cities* by Lincoln Steffens, *History of the Standard Oil Company* by Ida Tarbell, and *In Reckless Ecstasy* by Carl Sandburg were published
- Laura Ziegler held a grand opening for her brothel in Fort Smith, Arkansas, hosted by the mayor and other dignitaries; her cost of $3 was higher than the $1 charged at most establishments
- President Teddy Roosevelt ruled that Civil War veterans over 62 years were eligible to receive a pension
- Central heating, the ultraviolet lamp, Dr. Scholl arch supports, E. F. Hutton, the Caterpillar Tractor Company and offset printing all made their first appearance
- Thorstein Veblen coined the phrase "conspicuous consumption" to describe the useless spending habits of the rich in his book, *Theory of Business Enterprise*
- The counterweight elevator was designed by the Otis Company, replacing the hydraulic elevator and allowing buildings to rise more than 20 stories
- The U.S. paid $40 million to purchase French property in the Panama Canal region
- The New York subway opened, with more than 100,000 people riding on the first day
- Popular songs included "Give My Regards to Broadway," "Meet Me in St. Louis, Louis" and "Come Take a Trip in My Air-Ship"
- A massive fire in Baltimore destroyed 26,000 buildings
- The Olympics were held in St. Louis as part of the St. Louis Exposition, and basketball was presented as a demonstration sport

- Novocain, the crash helmet, snow chains and the vacuum tube were invented

1905–1906

- Industrial Workers of the World (IWW) attacked the American Federation of Labor for accepting the capitalist system
- A New York law limiting hours of work in the baking industry to 60 per week was ruled unconstitutional by the Supreme Court
- U.S. auto production reached 15,000 cars per year, up from 2,500 in 1899
- William Randolph Hearst acquired *Cosmopolitan* magazine for $400,000
- Royal Typewriter Company was founded by New York financier Thomas Fortune Ryan
- Sales of Jell-O reached $1 million
- Oklahoma was admitted to the Union
- Planters Nut and Chocolate Company was created
- A-1 Sauce was introduced in the U.S. by Hartford's G.F. Heublein & Brothers
- Samuel Hopkins Adams' *The Great American Fraud* exposed the fraudulent claims of many patent medicines
- Anti-liquor campaigners received powerful support from the Woman's Christian Temperance Union, lead by Frances E. Willard, who often fell to her knees and prayed on saloon floors
- Former President Grover Cleveland wrote in *The Ladies' Home Journal* that women of sense did not wish to vote: "The relative positions to be assumed by men and women in the working out of our civilizations were assigned long ago by a higher intelligence than ours."
- President Theodore Roosevelt admonished well-born white women who were using birth control for participating in willful sterilization, a practice known as racial suicide

1907–1908

- *The New York Times* inaugurated the custom of dropping an illuminated ball to greet the new year in what everyone now calls Times Square
- Cadillac was advertised at $800.00, a Ford Model K at $2,800.00
- Horses were sold for $150.00 to $300.00
- The first self-contained electric clothes washer was developed in Chicago
- The American Society for Keeping Woman in Her Proper Sphere was formed
- The first Christmas "stamps" were sold to raise money for tuberculosis research
- Mother's Day is celebrated, unofficially, in Philadelphia, Pennsylvania
- New York City passed the Sullivan Ordinance prohibiting women from smoking in public places
- Publication of the *Christian Science Monitor* began
- Wealthy American Reformer Maud Younger founded the Waitresses' Union in San Francisco after waitressing herself in order to learn about the life of working women
- The first canned tuna fish was packed in California
- Westinghouse Electric went bankrupt
- Two subway tunnels were opened to traffic in New York City
- The "Rich Man's Panic" resulted in financial reforms that increased the flexibility of the money supply and eventually led to the Federal Reserve Act of 1913
- The U.S. Supreme Court issued a unanimous ruling holding that laws limiting the maximum number of hours that women can work to 10 hours a day are constitutional
- Many U.S. banks closed as economic depression deepened
- President Theodore Roosevelt called a White House Conference on conservation

- Cornelius Vanderbilt's yacht, the *North Star,* was reported to cost $250,000 with a yearly maintenance bill of $20,000
- The 47-story Singer Building in New York became the world's tallest skyscraper
- Both the Muir Woods in California and the Grand Canyon were named national monuments worthy of preservation
- The first transatlantic wireless telegraph stations connected Canada to Ireland, and messages could be sent for $0.15 a word
- The AC spark plug, Luger pistol, and oscillating fan all came on the market
- Alpha Kappa Alpha, the first sorority for black women, was founded in Washington, D.C.
- Nancy Hale became the *New York Times'* first female reporter
- The U.S. Army bought its first aircraft, a dirigible, but because no one could fly it except its owner, it was never used
- The Olympic Games were played in London with the U.S. the unofficial winner with 23 gold medals
- Thomas Edison's Amberol cylinders, with more grooves per inch, extended the length of time a single recording would play from two to four minute
- More than 80 percent of all immigrants since 1900 came from Central Europe, Italy, and Russia

1909

- D.W. Griffith featured 16-year-old Mary Pickford in his films and she made $40.00 a week starring in silent movies
- 20,000 members of Ladies Waist Maker's Union staged a three-month strike and won most of their demands
- A tobacconist convention protested the automobile, concerned that it would lure people away from homes and clubs and smoking would be diminished
- The Sixteenth Amendment to the Constitution, authorizing income

taxes, was passed by Congress

- More than 25 miners were killed in an explosion at the Saint Paul Mine in Cherry, Illinois
- Chicago's Jane Addams, founder of Hull House, ended her term as appointed member of the Chicago Board of Education, where she had lobbied for compulsory education and laws to end child labor
- Milton Hershey, the father of the modern candy industry, had sales of $5 million a year making almond bars, kisses, and chocolate cigars
- The National Association for the Advancement of Colored People was founded by W.E.B. DuBois, Chicago reformer Jane Addams, Mary W. Ovington, and others
- The International Ladies' Garment Worker's Union called a strike to protest poor working conditions and low wages
- The Kansas attorney general ruled that women may wear trousers
- Western women began to wear V-neck shirts, which some condemned as immoral
- The U.S. Congress passed the Mann White Slave Traffic Act to prohibit interstate and foreign transport of females for immoral purposes
- The U.S. Senate heard a resolution to abolish sex discrimination in the Constitution

1910–1911

- Nationwide only 43 percent of 16-year-olds were still in school
- Western Union abolished the $0.40 to $0.50 charge for placing telegraph messages by telephone
- *Women's Wear Daily* began publication in New York
- U.S. cigarette sales reached 8.6 billion cigarettes, with 62 percent controlled by the American Tobacco Trust
- Florida orange shipments rebounded to their 1894 level
- 70 percent of bread was baked at home, down from 80 percent in 1890
- *The Flexner Report* showed most North American medical schools were inferior to those in Europe

- Halley's Comet stirred fear and excitement, as many hid in shelters or took 'comet' pills for protection
- The average man made $15.00 for a 58-hour work week and 42 percent was spent on food
- A movement began to restrict the sale of morphine except by prescription
- More than 10,000 nickelodeons were now operating nationwide
- Father's Day and the Boy Scouts of America made their first appearances
- The concept of the "weekend" as a time of rest gained popularity
- New York's Ellis Island had a record one-day influx of 11,745 immigrants in 1911
- 2,200 communities nationwide had between 2,500 and 50,000 people; in 1860 the number was 400 communities
- Actress Blanche Sweet was one of D.W. Griffith's regulars in the one- and two-reelers that dominated the movie industry
- David Horsley moved his study from Bayonne, New Jersey, to the Los Angeles suburb of Hollywood to establish a movie studio on Sunset Boulevard
- The Underwood Company attempted to create a noiseless typewriter
- The Triangle Shirtwaist factory fire in New York City aroused nationwide demands for better work conditions, a fire made deadly because the single exit door was locked to prevent the workers from stealing thread
- A record 12,000 European immigrants arrived at Ellis Island on a single day
- During a discussion concerning trade with Canada, a congressional group proposed to annex the neighboring country
- The Self-Mastery Colony in New Jersey and Parting of the Ways home in Chicago were created to help the deserving poor
- California women gained suffrage by constitutional amendment

- F.W. Woolworth was incorporated
- The electric self-starter for the motorcar was perfected and adopted by Cadillac
- Marmon Wasp won the first Indianapolis 500-mile race, averaging 75 miles per hour
- Direct telephone links were opened between New York and Denver
- The use of fingerprinting in crime detection became widespread
- On the fiftieth anniversary of the Battle of Bull Run, Civil War veterans from both the North and South mingled at the battlefield site
- Marie Curie won an unprecedented second Nobel Prize, but was refused admission to the French Academy of Science
- 60,000 Bibles were placed in hotel bedrooms by the Gideon Organization of Christian Commercial Travelers
- The socialist-backed magazine, *The Masses,* was founded in Greenwich Village, printing articles concerning "what is too naked for the money-making press."
- A climbing divorce rate of one in 12 marriages, from one in 85 in 1905, caused concerns

1912–1913
- Congress extended the eight-hour day to all federal employees
- Women composed a quarter of all workers employed in nonagricultural jobs
- L.L. Bean was founded by merchant Leon Leonwood Bean
- Medical schools opened their doors to women in the 1890s, but admission was restricted to five percent of the class
- One-third of American households employed servants, who worked 11 to 12 hours a day
- Domestic service was the largest single category of female employment nationwide, often filled by immigrants
- Nationwide approximately 57 percent of 16- and 17-year-olds no longer attended school

- Ford produced more than 22 percent of all U.S. motorcars
- Oreo biscuits were introduced by National Biscuit Company to compete with biscuit bon-bons
- A merger of U.S. film producers created Universal Pictures Corporation
- A&P began rapid expansion featuring stores that operated on a cash-and-carry basis
- Brillo Manufacturing Corporation was founded
- Congress strengthened the Pure Food and Drug Law of 1906
- The 60-story Woolworth building opened in New York
- Peppermint Life Savers were introduced as a summer seller when chocolate sales traditionally declined
- 5,000 suffragists marched down Pennsylvania Avenue in Washington, D.C., where they were heckled and slapped
- Congress strengthened the Pure Food and Drug Law of 1906
- The "Armory Show" introduced Post-Impressionism and Cubism to New York
- Vitamin A was isolated at Yale University
- Zippers, in use since 1891, became popular
- Grand Central Station in New York City was completed
- Henry Ford pioneered new assembly-line techniques in his car factory
- A Chicago company produced the first refrigerator for domestic use
- The first jury of women was drawn in California
- The first federal income tax was imposed on incomes over $3,000, affecting 62,000
- U.S. industrial output rose to 40 percent of the world's total production, up from 20 percent in 1860
- Camel, the first modern, blended cigarette, was produced, with a package design inspired by "Old Joe," a dromedary in the Barnum & Bailey circus
- A sheriff in Spartanburg, South Carolina, was tried for preventing a lynching, then acquitted

- Teacher Bridget Peixico was fired after 19 years by the New York Board of Education when she became a mother, but reinstated by the courts, which ruled that "illness…caused by maternity (cannot be) construed as neglect of duty."
- The Schaeffer pen, Quaker Puffed Rice, Chesterfield cigarettes, a dental hygienist's course, and the erector set were all introduced for the first time

1914

- The Federal League, baseball's third major league after the American and National Leagues, expanded to eight teams
- Rookie baseball pitcher George "Babe" Ruth debuted with the Boston Red Sox
- Movie premieres included *The Perils of Pauline, The Exploits of Elaine, Home Sweet Home,* and *Kid Auto Races at Venice*
- Theodore W. Richards won the Nobel Prize in chemistry for his work in the determination of atomic weights
- Thyroxin, the major thyroid hormone, was isolated by Edward Kendall at the Mayo Clinic
- Yale University opened its Coliseum-sized "Bowl" large enough to seat 60,000
- *The New Republic* magazine, passport photo requirements, non-skid tires, international figure skating tournaments, Kelvinator and The American Society of Composers, Authors and Publishers (ASCAP) all made their first appearance
- Pope Pius X condemned the tango as "new paganism"
- Former President Theodore Roosevelt returned from South America with 1,500 bird and 500 mammal specimens and a claim that he had discovered a new river
- The writings of Margaret Sanger sparked renewed controversy about birth control and contraception
- Chicago established the Censorship Board to remove movie scenes

depicting beatings or dead bodies

- Tuition, room and board at Harvard University cost $700 per year
- Ford Motor Company produced 240,700 cars, nearly as many as all other companies combined
- The outbreak of war in Europe spurred U.S. production of pasta, which had previously been imported
- Popular songs included "St. Louis Blues," "The Missouri Waltz," "Play a Simple Melody," "Fido Is a Hot Dog Now," and "If You Don't Want My Peaches, You'd Better Stop Shaking My Tree"
- In college football, five first team All Americans were from Harvard
- New York was the nation's largest city with population of 5.3 million, Chicago boasted 2.4 million, Philadelphia 1.7 million and Los Angeles 500,000 President Woodrow Wilson declared Mother's Day an official holiday

1915–1916

- The United States population passed 100 million
- Boston had constructed 26 playgrounds in the city
- An attempt by Congress to exclude illiterates from immigrating, a bill promoted by the unions to protect jobs, was vetoed by President Howard Taft in 1913, reasoning that illiteracy, which was often due to lack of opportunity, was no test of character
- U.S. Pullman-car porters pay reached $27.50 per month, prompting U.S. Commission on Industrial Relations to ask if wages were too high
- Kraft processed cheese was introduced by Chicago-based J.L. Kraft and Brothers
- Pyrex glass was developed by Corning Glass researchers
- IWW organizer Joe Hill was executed by firing squad
- The Woman's Peace Party was founded with social worker Jane Addams, the founder of Hull House in Chicago, as its first president
- The Victor Talking Machine Company introduced a phonograph called the Victrola

- An easy divorce law requiring only six months of residence was passed in Nevada
- D.W. Griffith's controversial three-hour film epic, *The Birth of a Nation,* opened in New York, with a ticket cost of an astronomical $2.00
- A Chicago law restricted liquor sales on Sunday
- American Tobacco Company selected salesmen by psychological tests
- After Mexico requested that the United States remove its troops during the Mexican Civil War, 17 Americans and 38 Mexicans died in a clash
- The U.S. bought the Virgin Islands from Denmark for $25 million
- Railway workers gained the right to an eight-hour day, preventing a nationwide strike
- Ring Lardner published *You Know Me Al: A Busher's Letters*, John Dewey wrote *Democracy and Education* and Carl Sandburg's *Chicago Poems* was released
- The Federal Land Bank System was created to aid farmers in acquiring loans
- Popular songs included "Ireland Must Be Heaven for My Mother Came from There" and "There's a Little Bit of Bad in Every Good Little Girl"
- Orange Crush, Nathan's hotdogs, Lincoln Logs and mechanical windshield wipers all made their first appearance
- Margaret Sanger opened the first birth control clinic in the country, distributing information in English, Italian and Yiddish
- The Mercury dime and Liberty fifty-cent piece went into circulation
- High school dropout Norman Rockwell published his first illustration in *The Saturday Evening Post*
- Actor Charlie Chaplin signed with Mutual for a record $675,000 salary
- Multimillionaire businessman Rodman Wanamaker organized the Professional Golfers Association of America
- South Carolina raised the minimum working age of children from 12 to 14
- Lucky Strike Cigarettes were introduced, costing $0.10 for a pack of 20

- Stanford Terman introduced the first test for measuring intelligence, coining the term "IQ" for intelligence quotient

1917

- Oregon defeated the University of Pennsylvania 14–0 in college football's 3rd Annual Rose Bowl
- German saboteurs set off the Kingsland Explosion at Kingsland, New Jersey, leading to U.S. involvement in World War I
- President Woodrow Wilson called for "peace without victory" in Europe before America entered World War I
- An anti-prostitution rally in San Francisco attracted 27,000 people after which 200 houses of prostitution were closed
- WW I Allies intercepted the Zimmermann Telegram, in which Germany offered to give the American Southwest back to Mexico if Mexico declared war on the United States; America responded by declaring war on Germany
- The Original Dixieland Jazz Band recorded their first commercial record, which included the "Dixie Jazz Band One Step"
- The Jones Act granted Puerto Ricans United States citizenship
- The first Pulitzer Prizes were awarded to: Laura E. Richards, Maud Howe Elliott, and Florence Hall for their biography, *Julia Ward Howe;* Jean Jules Jusserand for *With Americans of Past and Present Days*; and Herbert Bayard Swope for *New York World*
- The Silent Protest was organized by the NAACP in New York to protest the East St. Louis Riot as well as lynchings in Texas and Tennessee
- An uprising by several hundred farmers against the newly created WWI draft erupted in central Oklahoma and came to be known as the Green Corn Rebellion
- Dutch dancer Mata Hari was falsely accused by the French of spying for Germany and executed by firing squad
- President Woodrow Wilson used the Federal Possession and Control Act to place most U.S. railroads under the United States Railroad

Administration, hoping to more efficiently transport troops and materiel for the war effort

1918

- As an energy-saving measure, the nation adopted daylight saving time during the war, 150 years after it was first recommended by Benjamin Franklin
- Girls Scouts collected peach stones which, when heated, turned into charcoal for use in gas mask filters
- Women assembled bombs in defense plants, learned to repair cars, carried the mail, directed traffic and worked as trolley car conductors
- The Committee on Public Information turned out patriotic press releases and pamphlets by the millions and drew upon a roster of 75,000 speakers to provide speeches for every occasion
- Civilians abstained from wheat on Mondays and Wednesdays, meat on Tuesdays, and pork on Thursdays and Saturdays
- Some Americans swore off any beer that had a German name, sauerkraut became "liberty cabbage," hamburger was "Salisbury steak," and dachshunds were called "liberty pups"
- Labor unrest was at its most turbulent since 1890, as inflation triggered 2,665 strikes involving over four million workers
- Inflation reached 8.9 percent, dramatically increasing prices
- *The Economic Consequences of the Peace* by J. M. Keynes, *Ten Days That Shook the World* by John Reed and *Winesburg, Ohio* by Sherwood Anderson were all published
- Seventy lynchings occurred in the South as membership in the Ku Klux Klan increased to 100,000 across 27 states
- Herbert Hoover was named director of a relief organization for liberated countries, both neutral and enemy
- Peter Paul's Konobar, the Drake Hotel in Chicago and a state gas tax (in Oregon) all made their first appearance
- Hockey's Stanley Cup was cancelled after one player died and many

others were stricken with the deadly flu

1919–1920

- Boston police struck against pay scales of $0.21 to $0.23 per hour for 83- to 98-hour weeks.
- The cost of living in New York City was up 79 percent from 1914
- The dial telephone was introduced in Norfolk, Virginia
- Wheat prices soared to $3.50 per bushel as famine swept Europe
- Kellogg's All-Bran was introduced by the Battle Creek Toasted Corn Flakes Company
- U.S. ice cream sales reached 150 million gallons, up from 30 million in 1909
- *The New York Daily News* became the first tabloid (small picture-oriented) newspaper
- Boston Red Sox pitcher and outfielder Babe Ruth hit 29 home runs for the year and the New York Yankees purchased his contract for $125,000
- More than four million American workers struck for the right to belong to unions
- The Bureau of Labor Statistics reported that 1.4 million women had joined the American work force since 1911
- Following the 1918 strike by the Union Streetcar Conductors protesting the employment of female conductors, the War Labor Board ruled in favor of the continued employment of women
- Southern leaders of the National Association of Colored Women protested the conditions of domestic service workers, including the expectation of white male employers of the right to take sexual liberties with their servants

1921

- The first religious radio broadcast was heard over station KDKA AM in Pittsburgh, Pennsylvania

- Henry E. Huntington bought Gainsborough's *The Blue Boy* and Reynolds' *Portrait of Mrs. Siddons* for $1 million
- Books included John Dos Passos' *Three Soldiers*; *Symptoms of Being Thirty-Five* by Ring Lardner; *The Outline of History* by H.G. Wells, and *Dream Psychology* by Sigmund Freud
- The DeYoung Museum opened in Golden Gate Park, San Francisco
- The Mounds candy bar, Eskimo Pie, Betty Crocker, Wise potato chips, Band-Aids, table tennis, and Drano all made their first appearance
- The Allies of World War I Reparations Commission decided that Germany was obligated to pay 132 billion gold marks ($33 trillion) in annual installments of 2.5 billion
- The Emergency Quota Act was passed by Congress, establishing national quotas on immigration
- Cigarette consumption rose to 43 billion annually despite its illegality in 14 states
- The first vaccination against tuberculosis was administered
- Researchers at the University of Toronto led by biochemist Frederick Banting announced the discovery of the hormone insulin
- Adolf Hitler became Führer of the Nazi Party
- Harold Arlin announced the Pirates-Phillies game from Forbes Field over Westinghouse KDKA in Pittsburgh in the first radio broadcast of a baseball game
- Sixteen-year-old Margaret Gorman won the Atlantic City Pageant's Golden Mermaid trophy to become the first Miss America
- Literature dealing with contraception was banned and a New York physician was convicted of selling *Married Love*
- Centre College's football team, led by quarterback Bo McMillin, defeated Harvard University 6-0 to break Harvard's five-year winning streak
- Albert Einstein was awarded the Nobel Prize in Physics for his work with the photoelectric effect

- During an Armistice Day ceremony at Arlington National Cemetery, the Tomb of the Unknowns was dedicated by President Warren G. Harding
- Hyperinflation was rampant in Germany after the Great War, where 263 marks were needed to buy a single American dollar

1922

- Seventeen-year-old Clara Bow won a magazine contest for "The Most Beautiful Girl in the World," while Charles Atlas won for "World's Most Perfectly Developed Man"
- During his third trial, movie star Roscoe "Fatty" Arbuckle was exonerated of starlet Virginia Rappe's murder, but not before a highly publicized sex trial
- The self-winding wristwatch, Checker Cab, Canada Dry ginger ale, and State Farm Mutual auto insurance all made their first appearance
- California became a year-round source of oranges
- Automobile magnate Henry Ford, who earned $264,000 a day, was declared a "billionaire" by the Associated Press
- Radio station WEAF objected to airing a toothpaste commercial, deciding that care of the teeth was too delicate a subject for broadcast
- The first commercially prepared baby food was marketed
- The U.S. Post Office burned 500 copies of James Joyce's *Ulysses*
- The mah-jongg craze swept the nation, outselling radios
- Protestant Episcopal bishops voted to erase the word obey from the marriage ceremony
- Thom McAn introduced mass-produced shoes through chain stores for $3.99 a pair
- Hollywood's black list of "unsafe" persons stood at 117
- Radio became a national obsession, listened to for concerts, sermons and sports
- Syracuse University banned dancing
- A cargo ship was converted into the first U.S. aircraft carrier

- Publications for the year included T.S. Eliot's *The Waste Land*, F. Scott Fitzgerald's *The Beautiful and the Damned* and H.G. Wells's *The Outline of History*; Willa Cather won the Pulitzer Prize for *One of Ours*
- The tomb of King Tutankhamen, in the Valley of the Kings, Egypt, was discovered
- New York's Delmonico's Restaurant closed
- The first mechanical telephone switchboard was installed in New York
- Broadway producer Florenz Ziegfeld forbade his stars to perform on radio because it "cheapens them"
- *Vanity Fair* reported that the flapper "will never . . . knit you a necktie, but she'll go skiing with you. . . . She may quote poetry to you, not Indian love lyrics but something about the peace conference or theology"

1923–1924

- The Popsicle was patented under the name Epsicle
- Butterfinger candy was marketed by dropping parachuted bars from an airplane
- Commercially canned tomato juice was marketed by Libby McNeill & Libby
- The electric shaver was patented by Schick
- A.C. Nielson Company was founded
- Zenith Radio Corporation was founded
- 10 auto makers accounted for 90 percent of sales; a total of 108 different companies were now producing cars
- Hertz Drive Ur Self System was founded, creating the world's first auto rental concern
- 30 percent of all bread was baked in the home, down from 70 in 1910
- The first effective chemical pesticides were introduced
- *American Mercury* magazine began publication
- Radio set ownership reached three million
- Ford produced two million Model T motorcars, with the price of the

touring car falling to $290.00
- Dean Witter and Company was founded
- Microbiologists isolated the cause of scarlet fever
- Emily Post published *Etiquette,* which made her the arbiter of American manners

1925-1926

- James Buchanan "Buck" Duke donated $47 million to Trinity College at Durham, North Carolina and the college changed its name to Duke
- College football surpassed boxing as a national pastime, largely because of the popularity of "Galloping Ghost" Red Grange
- With prohibition the law of the land, party-goers hid liquor in shoe heels, flasks form-fitted to women's thighs, and perfume bottles
- The Charleston, a dance that originated in Charleston, South Carolina, was carried north and incorporated into the all-black show *Shuffle Along*; white dancers immediately adopted the lively dance
- The U.S. Supreme Court declared unconstitutional an Oregon law that required all grammar school-aged children to attend school
- When Henry Ford paid $2.4 million in income tax, 500,000 people wrote to him begging for money
- The Methodist Episcopal General Conference lifted its ban on theatre attendance and dancing
- Walt Disney began creating cartoons, featuring "Alice's Wonderland"
- Currently, 56 different companies were selling home refrigerators, with an average price of $450
- The permanent wave, contact lenses, IBM, deadbolt locks, and the college-bound notebook all made their first appearance
- Florida land prices collapsed as investors learned that their purchased lots were under water
- The $10 million Boca Raton Hotel in Florida was completed
- Al Capone took control of Chicago bootlegging
- Chesterfield cigarettes were marketed to women for the first time

- Aunt Jemima Mills was acquired by Quaker Oats Company for $4 million
- Machine-made ice production topped 56 million pounds, up 1.5 million from 1894
- The first ham in a can was introduced by Hormel
- The first blue jeans with slide fasteners were introduced by J.D. Lee Company
- Synthetic rubber was pioneered by B.F. Goodrich Rubber Company chemist Waldo Lonsburg Serman
- Cars appeared for the first time in such colors as "Florentine Cream" and "Versailles Violet"
- 40 percent of Americans earned at least $2,000 a year
- "Yellow-Drive-It-Yourself-Systems" became popular, costing $0.12 a mile for a Ford and $0.22 a mile for a 6-cylinder car
- Earl Wise's potato chips were so successful he moved his business from a remodeled garage to a concrete plant
- Wesson Oil, National Spelling Bees, and the *New Yorker* magazine all made their first appearances
- Congress reduced the taxes on incomes of more than $1 million, from 66 to 20 percent
- The Book-of-the-Month Club was founded
- To fight the depression in the automobile industry, Henry Ford introduced the eight-hour day and five-day work week
- With prohibition under way, the Supreme Court upheld a law limiting the medical prescription of whiskey to one pint every 10 days
- 2,000 people died of poisoned liquor
- *The illegal liquor trade netted $3.5 billion a year, with bootleg Scotch at $48 a case
- The movies became America's favorite entertainment, with more than 14,500 movie houses showing 400 movies a year
- The United States sesquicentennial was celebrated

- *True Story Magazine* reached a circulation of two million with stories such as "The Diamond Bracelet She Thought Her Husband Didn't Know About"
- Flues with slide fasteners were introduced by H.D. Lee Company
- Philadelphia's Warwick Hotel and the Hotel Carlyle in New York were opened
- 40 percent of all first-generation immigrants owned their own homes, while 29 percent of all second-generation immigrants were homeowners
- Kodak introduced 16 mm film
- Sinclair Lewis refused to accept the Pulitzer Prize because it "makes the writer safe, polite, obedient, and sterile"
- Martha Graham debuted in New York as a choreographer and dancer in *Three Gopi Maidens*
- *The Jazz Singer,* the first talking film, made its debut
- Women's skirts, the shortest of the decade, now stopped just below the knee with flounces, pleats, and circular gores that extended from the hip
- Ethel Lackie of the Illinois Athletic Club broke the world's record for the 40-yard freestyle swim with a time of 21.4 seconds

1927–1928

- 20 million cars were on the road, up from 13,824 in 1900
- Transatlantic telephone service between London and New York began at a cost of $75.00 for three minutes
- J.C. Penney opened its 500th store, and sold stock to the public
- Wonder Bread was introduced
- Broccoli became more widely marketed in the United States
- Rice Krispies were introduced by W.K. Kellogg
- Peanut butter cracker sandwiches, sold under the name NAB, which stands for National Biscuit Company, were sold for $0.05 each
- U.S. per capita consumption of crude oil reached 7.62 barrels
- Presidential candidate Herbert Hoover called for "a chicken in every

pot and two cars in every garage"
- The Ford Model A appeared in four colors including "Arabian Sand"
- The Hayes list of dos and don'ts for Hollywood films included licentious or suggestive nudity, ridicule of clergy, and inference of sexual perversion
- The Al Capone gang netted $100 million in the illegal liquor trade as Prohibition continued
- President Calvin Coolidge urged the nation to pray more
- The post-war education obsession included a variety of "how-to" courses and books
- A phonograph with an automatic record changer was introduced
- Volvo, Lender Bagels, and Movietone News all made their first appearances
- The German dirigible *Graf Zeppelin* landed in Lakehurst, New Jersey, on its first commercial flight across the Atlantic
- Future President Herbert Hoover promoted the concept of the "American system of rugged individualism" in a speech at New York's Madison Square Garden
- Three car mergers took place: Chrysler and Dodge; Studebaker and Pierce-Arrow; and Chandler and Cleveland
- The Boston Garden officially opened
- The first successful sound-synchronized animated cartoon, Walt Disney's *Steamboat Willie* starring Mickey Mouse, premiered
- The first issue of *Time* magazine was published, featuring Japanese Emperor Hirohito on its cover
- North Carolina Governor O. Max Gardner blamed women's diet fads for the drop in farm prices
- *Bolero* by Maurice Ravel made its debut in Paris
- George Gershwin's musical *An American in Paris* premiered at Carnegie Hall in NYC
- The clip-on tie was created

- Real wages, adjusted for inflation, had increased 33 percent since 1914
- Nationalist Chiang Kai-shek captured Peking, China, from the communists and gained U.S. recognition
- Aviator Amelia Earhart became the first woman to fly across the Atlantic Ocean from Newfoundland to Wales in about 21 hours
- The first all-talking movie feature, *The Lights of New York,* was released
- Fifteen nations signed the Kellogg-Briand Peace Pact, developed by French Foreign Minister Aristide Briand and U.S. Secretary of State Frank Kellogg
- Actress Katharine Hepburn made her stage debut in *The Czarina*
- Scottish bacteriologist Alexander Fleming discovered curative properties of penicillin
- *My Weekly Reader* magazine made its debut
- Ruth Snyder became the first woman to die in the electric chair
- Bell Labs created a way to end the fluttering of the television image
- President Calvin Coolidge gave the Congressional Medal of Honor to aviator Charles Lindbergh

1929

- A Baltimore survey discovered rickets in 30 percent of the children
- The U.S. Presidential inauguration was carried worldwide by radio
- German Kurt Barthel set up the first American nudist colony in New Jersey, which began with three married couples
- Of the 20,500 movie theaters nationwide, 9,000 installed sound during the year to adapt to "talkies"
- Calvin Coolidge was elected director of the New York Life Insurance Company
- The "Age of the Car" was apparent everywhere, as one-way streets, traffic lights, stop signs, and parking regulations were hot topics
- At least 32,000 speakeasies thrived in NYC, while the Midwest called similar institutions "beer flats," "Blind Pigs," and "shock houses"

- On September 3, the stock market peaked and on November 13, it reached bottom, with U.S. securities losing $26 billion in value
- Within a few weeks of the stock market crash (Black Tuesday), unemployment rose from 700,000 to 3.1 million nationwide
- Following the stock market crash, New York Mayor Jimmy Walker urged movie houses to show cheerful movies
- Coast-to-coast commercial travel required 48 hours using both airplanes and overnight trains
- Lt. James Doolight piloted an airplane using instruments alone
- Commander Richard E. Byrd planted a U.S. flag on the South Pole
- W.A. Morrison introduced quartz-crystal clocks for precise timekeeping
- Ford introduced a station wagon with boxed wood panels
- Radio program *Amos 'n' Andy* was so popular that Atlantic City resorts broadcast the show over loudspeakers
- Admission to New York theaters ranged from $0.35 to $2.50
- On St. Valentine's Day, six notorious Chicago gangsters were machine-gunned to death by a rival gang
- American manufacturers began to make aluminum furniture, especially chairs
- The cartoon *Popeye*, the Oscar Meyer wiener trademark, 7-Up, front-wheel-drive cars, and *Business Week* magazine all made their first appearances

1930–1931

- Unemployment passed four million
- More than 1,352 banks closed in 1930, and 2,294 closed in 1931
- The first analog computer was placed in operation by Vannevar Bush
- The U.S. car boom collapsed in the wake of the Depression and one million auto workers were laid off
- Gasoline consumption rose to nearly 16 billion gallons
- Trousers became acceptable attire for women who played golf and rode horses

- Radio set sales increased to 13.5 million
- Advertisers spent $60 million on radio commercials
- Boeing hired eight nurses to act as flight attendants
- *Fortune Magazine* was launched by Henry R. Luce at $1.00 per issue
- The University of Southern California polo team refused to play against the University of California at Los Angeles until its one female member was replaced by a male
- Laurette Schimmoler of Ohio became the first woman airport manager, earning a salary of $510 a year
- The fledgling movie industry now employed 100,000 people
- Alka-Seltzer was introduced by Miles Laboratories
- Clairol hair products were introduced by U.S. chemists
- Bird's Eye Frosted Foods were sold nationally for the first time
- Unemployment reached eight million, or 15.9 percent, inflation was at -4.4 percent, and the gross national product at -16 percent
- For the first time, emigration exceeded immigration
- As the sale of glass jars for canning increased, sales of canned goods declined
- Admissions to state mental hospitals tripled in 1930-1931 over the previous eight years
- More than 75 percent of all cities banned the employment of wives
- The National Forty-Hour Work Week League formed, calling for an eight-hour workday in an effort to produce more jobs
- Major James Doolittle flew from Ottawa to Mexico City in a record 11 hours and 45 minutes
- Pope Pius XI posed for the first telephoto picture to be transmitted from the Vatican, a picture that took 10 minutes to transmit
- To generate income, Nevada legalized both gambling and the six-month divorce
- Nearly 6,000 cases of infantile paralysis struck New York and many cities experienced partial quarantines

- Farmers attempted to stop an invasion of grasshoppers with electrified fences; 160,000 miles of America's finest farmlands were destroyed by the insect
- Alka-Seltzer was introduced by Miles Laboratories
- Chicago gangster Al Capone was convicted of evading $231,000 in federal taxes
- New York's Waldorf-Astoria Hotel was opened
- Silent film extra Clark Gable appeared in the movie *A Free Soul*, gaining instant stardom, while Universal studios recruited Bette Davis

1932

- *Forbes* magazine predicted that the number of television sets would reach 100,000, up from 15,000 in 1931
- As the depression worsened, wages dropped 60 percent in only three years
- Wages for picking figs were $0.10 per 50-pound box, $1.50 a day for 15 boxes; for picking peas the pay was $0.14 cents a pound
- New York's Radio City Music Hall, with 6,200 seats, opened as the world's largest movie theater
- The Winter Olympics in Lake Placid, New York created an interest in snow skiing
- The Zippo lighter, Mounds candy bar, Fritos corn chips, Johnson Glo-Coat wax, and tax on gasoline all made their first appearance
- Reacting to the depression, President Herbert Hoover reduced his own salary by 20 percent
- The FBI created a list of "public enemies"
- *Light in August* by William Faulkner, *The Good Earth* by Pearl S. Buck, *Death in the Afternoon* by Ernest Hemingway and *Sweeney Agonistes* by T. S. Eliot were all published
- James Chadwick discovered the neutron
- Radio premieres included "The George Burns and Gracie Allen Show," "National Barn Dance," "The Jack Benny Program" and "Tom Mix"

- Unemployment was officially recorded at 23.6 percent
- Across America, 31 percent of homes had telephones
- Amelia Earhart became the first woman to make a solo transatlantic flight
- Movie openings included *Mata Hari, Scarface, Dr. Jekyll and Mr. Hyde* and *Tarzan, the Ape Man*
- President Hoover declared: "Grass will grow in the streets of 100 cities" if Franklin Roosevelt was elected
- The "Great I Am" Movement, promising wealth to its followers, gained popularity
- The Federal Reserve Board's index of production was down 55 percent from 1929
- Baseball cards began to appear in packages of bubble gum, accompanied by tips on how to improve one's game

1933

- Construction of the Golden Gate Bridge began in San Francisco Bay
- Congress voted for independence for the Philippines, against President Hoover
- The Twentieth Amendment to the United States Constitution was ratified, changing Inauguration Day from March 4 to January 20, starting in 1937
- *The Lone Ranger* debuted on the radio
- The New York City-based Postal Telegraph Company introduced the singing telegram
- In Miami, Florida, Giuseppe Zangara attempted to assassinate President-elect Franklin D. Roosevelt
- *Newsweek* was published for the first time
- *King Kong*, starring Fay Wray, premiered at Radio City Music Hall in NYC
- Mount Rushmore National Memorial was dedicated
- President Franklin Roosevelt proclaimed, "The only thing we have to

fear, is fear itself."

- Frances Perkins became U.S. Secretary of Labor and the first female Cabinet member
- Dachau, the first Nazi concentration camp, was opened
- The Civilian Conservation Corps was established to relieve unemployment
- Karl Jansky detected radio waves from the Milky Way Galaxy, leading to radio astronomy
- The Tennessee Valley Authority was created
- The Century of Progress World's Fair opened in Chicago
- Walt Disney's *Silly Symphony* cartoon *The Three Little Pigs* was released
- The first drive-in theater opened in Camden, New Jersey
- The electronic pari-mutuel betting machine was unveiled at the Arlington Park race track near Chicago
- The first Major League Baseball All-Star Game was played at Comiskey Park in Chicago
- Army Barracks on Alcatraz was acquired by the Department of Justice for a federal penitentiary
- Albert Einstein arrived in the United States as a refugee from Nazi Germany
- The Dust Bowl in South Dakota stripped topsoil from desiccated farmlands
- The Twenty-first Amendment officially went into effect, legalizing alcohol in the U.S.
- The first Krispy Kreme doughnut shop opened in Nashville, Tennessee

1934

- Leni Riefenstahl directed *Triumph of the Will*, documenting the rise of the Third Reich in Germany
- Donald Duck, Walgreen's drugstores, Flash Gordon, Seagram's Seven Royal Crown and the term "hi-fi" all made their first appearance

- Ernest and Julio Gallo invested $5,900 in a wine company
- The birth of the Dionne quintuplets in Ontario stirred international interest
- The ongoing drought reduced the national corn crop by nearly one billion bushels
- Edna St. Vincent Millay published *Wine from These Grapes*; F. Scott Fitzgerald completed *Tender Is the Night*
- Dicumarol, an anticoagulant, was developed from clover
- "Tumbling Tumbleweeds," "I Only Have Eyes for You" and "Honeysuckle Rose" were all popular songs
- The Securities and Exchange Commission was created
- *It Happened One Night* won Best Picture, Best Director (Frank Capra), Best Actress (Claudette Colbert) and Best Actor (Clark Gable)
- The U.S. Gold Reserve Act authorized the president to devalue the dollar
- Enrico Fermi suggested that neutrons and protons were the same fundamental particles in two different quantum states
- The FBI shot John Dillinger, Public Enemy No. I, generating a hail of publicity
- Greyhound bus lines cut its business fares in half to $8 between New York and Chicago to encourage more traffic

1935–1936

- The Social Security Act passed Congress
- The Emergency Relief Appropriation Act gave $5 billion to create jobs
- Fort Knox became the United States Repository of gold bullion
- One-tenth of one percent of U.S. corporations made 50 percent of earnings
- Sulfa-drug chemotherapy was introduced to relieve veneral disease sufferers
- Nylon was developed by Du Pont
- Beer cans were introduced

- One-third of farmers received U.S. treasury allotment checks for not growing crops
- New York State law allowed women to serve as jurors
- Polystyrene became commercially available in the United States for use in products such as kitchen utensils and toys
- An eight-hour work day became law in Illinois
- Margaret Mitchell's *Gone with the Wind* sold a record one million copies in six months
- A *Fortune* poll indicated that 67 percent favored birth control
- Trailer sales peaked; tourist camps for vacationing motorists gained popularity
- Approximately 38 percent of American families had an annual income of less than $1,000
- Ford unveiled the V-8 engine
- Recent advances in photography, including the 35 mm camera and easy-to-use exposure meters, fueled a photography boom
- The population of America reached 127 million
- *Life* magazine began publication, with an early claim that one in 10 Americans had a tattoo
- New York's Triborough Bridge opened, with a toll of $0.25
- The National Park Service created numerous federal parks and fish and game preserves, adding a total of 600,000 additional acres to state preserves
- Mercedes-Benz created the first diesel-fueled passenger car
- The WPA Federal Art Project employed 3,500 artists who produced 4,500 murals, 189,000 sculptures and 450,000 paintings
- Dust storms destroyed large portions of farmland in Kansas, Oklahoma, Colorado, Nebraska and the Dakotas
- A sleeper berth from Newark to Los Angeles cost $150
- New York's Fifth Avenue double-decker bus fare was between $0.05 and $0.10
- Margaret Mitchell's book, *Gone with the Wind*, sold a record one million

copies in six months

- The photo-finish camera, bicycle traffic court, screw-cap bottle with pour lip, the Presbyterian Church of America and Tampax all made their first appearance
- Congress passed the Neutrality Acts designed to keep America out of foreign wars
- A revolt against progressive education was led by Robert M. Hutchins, president of the University of Chicago
- Molly Dewson of the National Consumers' League led a fight to gain the appointment of more female postmasters
- The first successful helicopter flight was made
- The "Chase and Sanborn Hour," with Edgar Bergen and Charlie McCarthy, and "The Shadow," starring Robert Hardy Andrews, both premiered on radio

1937–1938

- The United Automobile Workers were recognized by General Motors as sole bargaining agent for employees
- Minimum wage policy for women was upheld by the Supreme Court
- Packard Motor Car Company sold a record 109,000 cars
- General Motors introduced automatic transmission
- Icemen made regular deliveries to more than 50 percent of middle class households
- Spam was introduced by George A. Hormel & Company
- *Popular Photography* magazine began publication
- Congress's wage-and-hour law limited the work week to 44 hours
- Recovery stumbled, *Wall Street's Dow Jones Industrial Average* fell
- Eastern Airlines was created
- Owens-Corning Fiberglass Corporation was incorporated to produce products utilizing newly developed fiberglass
- High-definition color television was demonstrated
- The ballpoint pen was patented

- Consumption of beef and dairy products increased by three percent
- Nylon stockings went on sale
- From September 1, 1936, to June 1, 1937, 484,711 workers were involved in sit down strikes
- A study showed that people spent 4.5 hours daily listening to the radio
- Spinach growers erected a statue to cartoon character Popeye in Wisconsin
- Seeing-eye dogs came into use for aiding the blind
- The Fair Labor Standards Act established the Minimum Hourly Rate at 25 cents
- The Federal National Mortgage Association known as Fannie Mae was established
- Aviator Howard Hughes set a new record, flying around the world in three days, 19 hours
- The March of Dimes' Polio Foundation was created by Franklin Roosevelt
- A Gallup poll indicated that 58 percent of Americans believed that the U.S would be drawn into war, and 65 percent favored boycotting German goods
- Race horse *Seabiscuit* defeated *War Admiral*, earning the title best horse in America
- Action comics issued the *Superman* comic
- New York staged a World's Fair called "The World of Tomorrow" which was visited by 25 million people
- Fifty percent of Americans polled selected radio as the most reliable news medium, while 17 percent chose newspapers
- Orson Welles's radio adaptation of *The War of the Worlds* was broadcast, causing mass panic by listeners who thought that his story of aliens landing in the eastern U.S. was real
- Adolf Hitler was named *Time* magazine's "Man of the Year"
- Kate Smith sang Irvin Berlin's "God Bless America" on an Armistice

Day radio broadcast
- Disney Studios released *Snow White and the Seven Dwarfs*
- Thornton Wilder's play *Our Town* was performed
- A toothbrush became the first commercial product made with nylon yarn as the bristles
- Oil was discovered in Saudi Arabia
- Heavyweight boxing champion Joe Louis knocked out Max Schmeling in round one of their rematch at Yankee Stadium in New York City
- In the prior five years, 60,000 German immigrants had arrived in America
- Movie box office receipts reached an all-time high and averaged an annual $25 per family

1939

- World War II began in Europe with the Germans invading Poland in September and the Russians invading Finland in November
- The Birth Control Federation of America began its "Negro Project" designed to control the population of people it deemed less fit to rear children
- The Social Security Act was amended, allowing extended benefits to seniors, widows, minors, and parents of a deceased person
- After the Daughters of the American Revolution (DAR) denied her the chance to sing at Constitution Hall because of her race, Marian Anderson sang at the Lincoln Memorial in Washington, D.C., before a crowd of 75,000
- *Reader's Digest* reached a circulation of eight million, up from 250,000 10 years earlier
- Despite the depression, the sale of radios continued to rise so that 27.5 million families owned 45 million radio sets
- The Federal Theatre Project was disbanded after accusations of communist influence
- Hollywood production code restrictions were lifted, allowing Clark

Gable in *Gone with the Wind* to say, "Frankly, my dear, I don't give a damn."

- Enrico Fermi and John R. Dunning of Columbia University used the cyclotron to split uranium and obtain a massive energy release, suggesting a "chain reaction"
- Paul Miller developed the insecticide DDT
- Due to the war, Finland stopped shipping cheese to the U.S., and Swiss production took its place
- Gangster Louis Lepke surrendered to popular newspaper and radio columnist Walter Winchell, who handed him over to J. Edgar Hoover
- The U.S. Supreme Court ruled that sit-down strikes were illegal
- The first baseball game was televised
- General Motors controlled 42 percent of the U.S. market in cars and trucks, and the company's 220,000 employees made an average of $1,500 annually
- Transatlantic airmail service, the marketing of nylon stockings, the use of fluorescent lighting, and Packard's air-conditioned automobile were all introduced
- The Sears, Roebuck catalogue still featured horse-drawn farm wagons, washing machines run by gasoline, and refrigerators designed to cool with a block of ice
- Zippers on men's trousers became standard equipment

1940

- RKO released Walt Disney's second full-length animated film, *Pinocchio,* and Tom and Jerry make their debut in *Puss Gets the Boot*
- Martin Kamen and Sam Ruben discovered Carbon-14, the basis of the radiocarbon dating method used to determine the age of archaeological and geological finds
- *Truth or Consequences* debuted on NBC Radio
- Booker T. Washington became the first African-American to be depicted on a U.S. postage stamp

- Following the resignation of Neville Chamberlain, Winston Churchill became prime minister of the Great Britain
- McDonald's restaurant opened in San Bernardino, California
- In WWII action, the Dutch and Norway armies surrendered to German forces as France fell
- President Franklin D. Roosevelt asked Congress for approximately $900 million to construct 50,000 airplanes per year
- The Auschwitz-Birkenau concentration and death camp opened in Poland
- WW I General John J. Pershing, in a nationwide radio broadcast, urged all-out aid to Britain in order to defend America, while national hero Charles Lindbergh led an isolationist rally at Soldier Field in Chicago
- The U.S. transferred 50 U.S. destroyers to Great Britain in return for 99-year leases on British bases in the North Atlantic, West Indies, and Bermuda
- Nazi Germany rained bombs on London for 57 consecutive nights
- In Lascaux, France, 17,000-year-old cave paintings were discovered by a group of young Frenchmen hiking through Southern France
- The Selective Training and Service Act of 1940 created the first peacetime draft in U.S. history
- The U.S. imposed a total embargo on all scrap metal shipments to Japan
- Franklin D. Roosevelt defeated Republican challenger Wendell Willkie to become the first and only third-term president
- Agatha Christie's mystery novel *And Then There Were None* was published

1942–1943
- Unemployment nationwide fell to 4.7 percent from its 1933 high of 25.2 percent
- Office of Price Administration was formed to control prices
- A tire-rationing plan and gas rationing began

- Paine, Webber, Jackson, & Curtis was created
- Zinc-coated pennies were issued by the U.S. Mint
- Florida surpassed California as the leading U.S. producer of oranges
- Kellogg introduced Raisin Bran cereal
- Sunbeam bread was introduced
- Maxwell House instant coffee was included in military K rations
- Dannon yogurt was introduced
- U.S. automobile production was halted until 1945
- Congress approved income-tax withholding from paychecks
- Zenith Radio Corporation introduced a $40.00 hearing aid
- Shoes were rationed to three pairs per year, per person
- The sale of sliced bread was banned
- Sale of Bibles increased 25 percent as religious books grew in popularity
- Women's trousers sold 10 times more than the previous year
- Vegetables consumed in the U.S. came from victory gardens (40 percent) and gardens developed by Japanese-Americans detained in camps
- The motion picture industry produced 80 war movies
- Enrico Fermi secretly accomplished a controlled nuclear fission reaction at the University of Chicago; he sent a coded message to President Franklin D. Roosevelt: "The Italian navigator has entered the new world."
- Reports of the deportation of Jews from Occupied Western Europe reached the U.S.

1944

- President Roosevelt's $109 billion federal budget earmarked $100 billion for the war effort
- Rent controls were imposed nationwide
- American Broadcasting Company (ABC) was created by Lifesavers millionaire Edward Noble

- Russell Marker pioneered the oral contraceptive, Syntex S.A.
- An automatic, general purpose digital computer was completed at Harvard University
- The Federal Highway Act established the interstate highway system
- War was costing the U.S. $250 million per day
- The GI Bill of Rights was enacted to finance college education for veterans
- U.S. soybean production rose as new uses were found for beans
- U.S. grocers tested self-service meat markets
- Gasoline averaged $0.21 per gallon
- American Jewish Congress reported that over three million Jews were killed by the Nazis
- Paper shortages limited Christmas cards, causing recycling of brown grocery bags and publishers to experiment with soft-cover books
- *Amos 'n' Andy* was canceled after 15 years and 4,000 consecutive radio shows
- Uncle Ben's converted rice appeared
- On D-Day (June 6) the Normandy invasion was mounted by 6,939 naval vessels, 15,040 aircraft, and 156,000 troops; 16,434 were killed, 76,535 were wounded, and 19,704 went missing
- Nearly half the steel, tin, and paper needed for the war was provided by salvaged goods
- Jell-O became a popular dessert substitute for canned fruit, and baking powder sales fell as women continued to join the work force
- Horse racing was banned because of the war
- A New York judge found the book *Lady Chatterley's Lover* obscene and ordered publisher Dial Press to trial
- Bill Mauldin's cartoon *Willie & Joe,* originally in *Yank* and *Stars and Stripes,* was picked up by the domestic press and achieved great acclaim
- More than 81,000 GIs were killed, wounded, or captured in the Battle

of the Bulge, Germany's last big offensive of the war
- Because of a shortage of cheese and tomato sauce, the sale of pasta fell dramatically
- Gen. Douglas MacArthur returned to the Philippines; his American army annihilated the troops commanded by Gen. Tomoyuki Yamashita, the Tiger of Malaya; 50,000 Japanese were killed, and fewer than 400 were captured
- Nationwide, 372,000 German POWs were being held in the United States
- The Dow Jones reached a high of 152, a low of 135, and unemployment was 1.2 percent
- Victory bonds became an obsession, with actress Hedy Lamarr offering to kiss any man who bought $25,000 worth; Jack Benny auctioned his $75 violin—*Old Love in Bloom*— for a million dollars' worth of bonds
- "Kilroy was here" became the graffiti symbol of valor for GIs everywhere
- Herr Adolf Hitler was among the citizens of enemy nations whose assets were frozen during the war; $22,666 from the sale of *Mein Kampf* was later used to pay Americans' claims against enemy nationals
- Chiquita brand bananas were introduced
- $80 million was spent on spectator sports in the U.S. who had 409 golf courses
- Seven laboratories refined and improved DDT, of which 350,000 pounds monthly was used by the military to spray in an effort to reduce typhus and malaria

1945
- President Franklin Delano Roosevelt died in office and Harry Truman became president
- WW II ended
- Penicillin was introduced commercially

- Approximately 98 million Americans went to the movies each week
- The Beechcraft Bonanza two-engine private plane was introduced
- The U.S. Gross National Product was $211 billion, double the GNP of 1928
- Ballpoint pens, costing $12.50 each, went on sale
- About one million Americans suffered from malaria
- Tupperware Corporation was formed
- Strikes idled 4.6 million workers, the worst stoppage since 1919
- The Dow Jones Industrial Average peaked at a post-1929 high of 212.50
- Wage and price controls ended in all areas except rents, sugar, and rice
- U.S. college enrollments reached an all-time high of more than 2 million
- Ektachrome color film was introduced by Kodak Company
- Tide Detergent was introduced
- Timex watches were introduced with at starting price of $6.95
- Hunt Foods established "price at time of shipment" contracts with customers
- The U.S. birth rate soared to 3.4 million, up from 2.9 million in the previous year
- Super glue and coats for lapdogs were introduced
- New York State forbade discrimination by employers, employment agencies and labor unions on the basis of race, the first time in American history a legislative body enacted a bill outlawing discrimination based on race, creed, or color
- The Boy Scouts collected 10 million pounds of rubber and more than 370 million pounds of scrap metal during the war, while Chicago children collected 18,000 tons of newspapers in just five months
- Ernie Pyle's *Brave Men,* a celebration of military heroism, sold more than a million copies; Richard Wright's *Black Boy,* a memoir of black life, sold 540,000 copies
- An RCA 10-inch television set sold for $374.00

1946

- United Airlines announced it had ordered jet planes for commercial purposes
- Dr. Benjamin Spock's *The Common Sense Book of Baby and Child Care* was published, written while he was in the Navy Medical Corps in charge of severe disciplinary cases
- FDR's stamp collection brought $211,000 at auction
- Automobile innovation included wide windows on the Studebaker and combined the wood station wagon and passenger car with the Chrysler Town and Country
- With more men returning from war, the birth rate increased 20 percent over 1945
- Albert Einstein and other distinguished nuclear scientists from the Emergency Committee of Atomic Science promoted the peaceful use of atomic energy
- A year after the end of WW II, the military went from 11 million to one million soldiers
- As wages and prices increased, the cost of living went up 33 percent over 1941
- With sugar rationing over, ice cream consumption soared
- The National Broadcasting Company and Philco Corporation established a two-way television relay service between New York and Philadelphia
- Blacks voted for the first time in the Mississippi Democratic primary
- Oklahoma City offered the first rapid public treatment of venereal diseases
- Former Secretary of State Henry Wallace became editor of the *New Republic*
- *The New Yorker* published John Hersey's *Hiroshima*
- John D. Rockefeller, Jr., donated $8.5 million for the construction of the United Nations building along the East River in New York City
- *Family Circle, Scientific American,* and *Holiday* all began publication

1947

- A Gallup poll reported that 94 percent of Americans believed in God
- Gerber Products Company sold two million jars of baby food weekly
- *A Streetcar Named Desire* by Tennessee Williams opened on Broadway
- The Freedom Train, with 100 of America's greatest documents, toured the United States
- The American Meat Institute reported that Americans abandoned wartime casseroles for meat five nights a week
- Seventy-five percent of all corn production was now hybrid
- *Esquire* magazine promoted the "bold look" for the man of "self-confidence and good taste," featuring wide tie clasps, heavy gold key chains, bold striped ties, big buttons and coordinating hair color and clothing
- Bikini bathing suits arrived on American beaches
- The American Friends Service Committee won the Nobel Peace Prize
- One million homes had television sets
- Gillette and Ford paid $65,000 to sponsor the first televised baseball World Series, during which an estimated 3.7 million people watched the Brooklyn Dodgers fall to the New York Yankees
- New York began a fluoridation program for 50,000 children
- Drive-up windows at banks were gaining popularity
- House prices doubled, and the price of clothing increased 93 percent from 1939
- Minute Maid Corp., Ajax, Everglades National Park, the Cannes Film Festival and the Tony Awards all made their first appearance
- American Association of Scientific Workers urged the U.S. to study bacteriological warfare

1948

- Nationwide, 50 cities banned comic books dealing with crime or sex, as psychiatrist Fredric Wertham charged that heavy comic-book reading

contributed to juvenile delinquency
- President Harry Truman ordered racial equality in the armed forces
- Jack Benny sold his NBC radio program to CBS for $2 to $3 million, and the IRS took 75 percent for personal income taxes
- A transistor developed by Bell Telephone Laboratories permitted miniaturization of electronic devices such as computers, radios and television
- Gerber Products Company sold two million cans and jars of baby food weekly
- Dial soap was introduced as the first deodorant soap
- Garbage disposals, heat-conducting windshields, Nestlé's Quick, Michelin radial tires and Scrabble all made their first appearance
- The Nikon camera was introduced to compete with the Leica
- 360,000 soft-coal workers went on strike, demanding $100 per month in retirement benefits at age 62
- Dwight D. Eisenhower requested that the Democratic Party draft him as a candidate for president of the United States
- Peter Goldmark of CBS invented a high-fidelity, long-playing record containing up to 45 minutes of music
- Ben Hogan won the U.S. Open and was the top PGA money winner with $36,000
- A new liquid hydrogen fuel was created that was touted as having the potential to send men to the moon
- The Dow-Jones Industrial Average hit a high of 193
- The United Nations passed the Palestine Partition Plan, creating the State of Israel
- Mahatma Gandhi was assassinated by a Hindu extremist

1949

- Visas were no longer necessary for travel to many countries outside the Iron Curtain
- The FCC ended an eight-year ban on radio editorializing, and stations

were warned to present all sides of controversial questions

- Harry Truman, surprising the pollsters, won a second term, inviting blacks, for the first time, to the Presidential Inaugural, which was telecast
- The postwar baby boom leveled off with 3.58 million live births
- The minimum wage rose from $0.40 to $0.75 an hour
- Congress increased the president's salary to $100,000 per year, with an additional $50,000 for expenses
- The Polaroid Land camera, which produced a picture in 60 seconds, sold for $89.75
- Following the communist takeover of China, and Russia's development of the A-bomb, many feared an impending war with Russia
- The United Nations Headquarters in New York was dedicated
- Despite inflation fears, prices began to fall
- The Dow Jones hit a high of 200, while unemployment averaged 5.9 percent
- More than 500,000 steelworkers went on strike, which ended when companies agreed to workers' pension demands
- Hank Williams joined the country music program, the *Grand Ole Opry*.
- *Life* magazine asked, "Jackson Pollock: Is He the Greatest Living Painter in the U.S.?"
- The Hollywood Ten were fired for refusing to tell the House Un-American Activities Committee if they were communists, filed suit against Hollywood producers
- A poll indicated that women believed three children constituted the ideal family and wanted no babies until the second year of marriage, while 70 percent of families believed in spanking, and less than 30 percent said grace at meals
- Baby-boom children reached kindergarten age and educators estimated that school enrollment would increase 39 percent the following year
- Postwar demand for automobiles fueled a record-breaking buying spree

- Gov. James E. Folsom of Alabama signed a bill forbidding the wearing of masks, attempting to stop raids by hooded men who whipped people, particularly minorities
- 90 percent of boys and 74 percent of girls questioned in a national poll of HS students believed it was "all right for young people to pet or 'neck' when they were out on dates"
- Lawyer Frieda Hennock was the first woman member of the Federal Communications Commission

1950–1951

- The Korean War began
- Congress increased personal and corporate income taxes
- Auto registrations showed one car for every 3.7 Americans
- Blue Cross insurance programs covered 3.7 million Americans
- Five million homes had television sets, compared to 45 million with radios
- President Harry Truman ordered the Atomic Energy Committee to develop the hydrogen bomb
- Boston Red Sox Ted Williams became baseball's highest paid player with a $125,000 contract
- Senator Joseph McCarthy announced that he had the names of 205 known Communists working in the State Department
- Otis Elevator installed the first passenger elevator with self-opening doors
- Coca-Cola's share of the U.S. cola market was 69 percent compared to Pepsi-Cola's share at 15 percent
- The FBI issued its first list of the Ten Most Wanted Criminals
- The first kidney transplant was performed on a 49-year old woman at a Chicago hospital
- Charles M. Schultz's comic strip, *Peanuts,* debuted in eight newspapers
- Smokey the Bear, an orphaned cub found after a forest fire in New Mexico, became the living symbol of the U.S. Forestry Service

- *Betty Crocker's Picture Cookbook* was published
- Miss Clairol hair coloring and Minute Rice was marketed
- M&M candy, created in 1940, was now stamped with an "M" to assure customers they were getting the real thing
- The first Xerox copy machine was introduced
- The average cost of a four-year college was $1,800, up 400 percent since 1900
- The 22nd Amendment to the Constitution, limiting the term of the president to two terms, was adopted
- Univak, the first general-purpose electronic computer, was dedicated in Philadelphia
- CBS introduced color television in a program hosted by Ed Sullivan and Arthur Godfrey
- Lacoste tennis shirts with an alligator symbol were introduced in the U.S. by French manufacturer Izod
- Earl Tupper created the home sale party to market his plastic storage containers directly to householders
- *Jet* news magazine was launched
- Chrysler Corporation introduced power steering in cars
- More than 75 percent of all U.S. farms were now electrified
- Harvard Law School admitted women
- Nationwide 3.8 million people played golf on approximately 5,000 courses, comprising 1.5 million acres of land
- North Korean forces crossed the thirty-eighth parallel, took Seoul, and rejected American truce offers
- H&R Block, formed in 1946 in Kansas City, began offering tax preparation services when the IRS stopped preparing people's taxes
- Margaret Sanger urged the development of an oral contraceptive
- The Metropolitan Life Insurance Company reported a link between 15 pounds of excess weight and dying younger than the average life span
- Massive flooding covered more than a million acres of land in

Oklahoma, Kansas, Missouri and Illinois

- The latest census reported that eight percent of the population was more than 65 years old, up from four percent in 1900
- For the first time in history, women outnumbered men in the U.S.
- Julius and Ethel Rosenberg were sentenced to death for espionage against the U.S.
- President Truman dispatched an air force plane when Sioux City Memorial Park in Iowa refused to bury John Rice, a Native American who had died in combat; his remains were interred in Arlington National Cemetery
- Sugarless chewing gum, dacron suits, pushbutton-controlled garage doors, telephone company answering service, college credit courses on TV, and power steering all made their first appearance
- Charles F. Blair flew solo over the North Pole
- Entertainer Milton Berle signed a 30-year, million-dollar-plus contract with NBC
- New York and other major cities increased the cost of a phone call from $0.05 to $0.10

1952

- The Federal Reserve Board voted to dissolve the A.P. Giannini banking empire, headed by Transamerica Corporation, which controlled the nation's largest bank, Bank of America
- Popular movies included *High Noon, The Greatest Show on Earth,* and *The African Queen*
- The Metropolitan Opera in New York charged $8.00 for an evening performance and $30 per seat on opening night
- Books published included *Invisible Man, East of Eden, The Natural, The Old Man and the Sea,* and *Charlotte's Web*
- Vice presidential candidate Richard M. Nixon declared he was not a quitter in his famous "Checkers" speech
- Jonah Salk at the University of Pennsylvania began testing a vaccine

against polio
- W. F. Libby of the University of Chicago dated Stonehenge in England to 1842 BC
- Reports circulated that the U.S. had exploded a hydrogen bomb
- Sony introduced the transistor radio
- Songs included "Walking My Baby Back Home," "Wheel of Fortune," and "Glow Worm"
- Nationwide, 55,000 people were stricken with polio, an all-time high
- The New Revised Standard Version of the Holy Bible was published
- The U.S. Air Force reported 60 UFO sightings in two weeks
- President Harry Truman ordered seizure of the nation's $7 billion steel industry to prevent a walkout of 650,000 workers, but the Supreme Court ruled the move unconstitutional
- *The Today Show* premiered on NBC-TV
- Edward Mills Purcell and Felix Bloch won the Nobel Prize in physics for work in the measurement of magnetic fields in atomic nuclei
- *Mad Magazine* was introduced, with a circulation of 195,000; 55 percent of college students and 43 percent of high school students voted it their favorite periodical
- Products making their first appearance included the 16 mm home movie projector, two-way car radios, adjustable showerheads, bowling alleys with automatic pin boys and Kellogg's Sugar Frosted Flakes
- Fifty-two million automobiles were on the highways, up from 25 million in 1945
- Thirty-seven-year-old Jersey Joe Walcott knocked out Ezzard Charles to become the oldest heavyweight boxing champion at 37
- An all-white jury in North Carolina convicted a black man for leering at a white woman 75 feet away, deemed assualt

1953
- The Screen Actors Guild adopted by-laws banning communists from membership

- A link was made between coronary heart disease and diets high in animal fats
- New York subway fares rose from $0.05 to $0.15
- Nationwide, 30 million attended performances of classical music, 15 million attended major league baseball, and 7.2 million children took music lessons
- The Dow Jones Industrial Average showed a high of 293 and a low of 255
- Per capita state taxes averaged $68.04
- An airmail stamp cost $0.07 per ounce and a postcard stamp cost $0.02
- All-black military units had largely disappeared, with 90 percent integrated into white military units
- Leland Kirdel wrote in *Coronet* magazine, "The smart woman will keep herself desirable. It is her duty to be feminine and desirable at all times in the eyes of the opposite sex."
- In the McCarthyism age, libraries were ordered to remove books by "communists, fellow travelers, and the like"
- Lucille Ball and Desi Arnaz signed an $8 million contract to continue "I Love Lucy" for 30 months
- Optimistic about peace with Korea, president Dwight D. Eisenhower restored the traditional Easter egg roll for children on the White House lawn
- *TV Guide* and *Playboy* both began publication
- The number of comic books exploded, comprising 650 titles
- Nationwide, 25 percent of young Americans were now attending college, thanks to the GI Bill—an increase of 65 percent from before the Second World War
- President Eisenhower pledged rigid economy in government, a lifting of controls, and an effort toward a more balanced budget
- During his inaugural address, Eisenhower called on Americans to make whatever sacrifices necessary to meet the threat of Soviet aggression,

defining the contest as a matter of freedom against slavery
- Charlie Chaplin said it was "virtually impossible" to continue work in the United States because of "vicious propaganda" by powerful reactionary groups
- General Motors introduced the Chevrolet Corvette, the first plastic-laminated, fiberglass sports car, at a cost of $3,250
- Elvis Presley paid $4.00 to cut "My Happiness" in Memphis for his mother's birthday
- Russia's Joseph Stalin died in May and the coronation of England's Queen Elizabeth occurred in June
- New York's Seeman Brothers introduced the instant ice tea
- Nearly half of U.S. farms now had tractors
- 17 million homes had television sets
- Four out of five men's shirts sold in America were white
- The DC-7 propeller plane, Sugar Smacks, 3-D cartoons and movies, and Irish Coffee all made their first appearance

1954–1955
- The Supreme Court declared racial segregation in public schools illegal
- The first nuclear-powered submarine, *Nautilus,* was launched
- Gasoline averaged $0.29 per gallon
- Texas Instruments introduced the first practical silicon transistor
- Taxpayers with incomes of more than $100,000 paid more than $67,000 each in taxes
- Sales of Viceroy cigarettes leaped as smokers shifted to filter-tipped cigarettes
- Open-heart surgery was introduced by Minneapolis physician C. Walton Lillehe
- RCA introduced the first color television set
- The $13 million, 900-room Fontainebleau Hotel opened at Miami Beach
- *Sports Illustrated Magazine* was introduced
- Swanson & Sons introduced frozen TV dinners

- Dr. Jonas E. Salk, U.S. developer of anti-polio serum, started inoculating school children in Pittsburgh, Pennsylvania
- The U.S. boasted 1,768 million newspapers, publishing 59 million copies daily
- The U.S. population contained six percent of the world's population, 60 percent of all cars, 58 percent of all telephones, 45 percent of all radio sets, and 34 percent of all railroads
- Marian Anderson, the first black soloist of the Metropolitan Opera, appeared as Ulrica in *Un Ballo* in Maschera
- Blacks in Montgomery, Alabama, boycotted segregated city bus lines, and Rosa Parks was arrested for refusing to give up the only seat available, which was in the front of the bus
- The first Chevrolet V-8 engine motorcar was introduced
- The federal minimum wage rose from $0.75 to $1.00 per hour
- Whirlpool Corporation was created by the merger of three companies
- *National Review* and *Village Voice* began publication
- Crest was introduced by Proctor and Gamble
- Special K breakfast food was introduced by Kellogg Company
- The nation now had 1,800 suburban shopping centers
- The number of millionaires in the United States was reported to be 154
- New television shows introduced that year included *The Adventures of Rin Tin Tin, Father Knows Best, Lassie,* and *Tonight* with Steve Allen.
- HEW Secretary Oveta Culp Hobby opposed the free distribution of the Salk vaccine to poor children as "socialized medicine by the back door"
- Disneyland in Anaheim, California, opened
- The first television press conference featured President Dwight Eisenhower
- Smog and poisoned air became a public concern
- *Confidential Magazine* had a circulation of 4.5 million readers
- President Eisenhower suffered a heart attack, and the stock market plunged $14 billion

- The population explosion created a shortage of 120,000 teachers and 300,000 schoolrooms
- Weekly church attendance comprised 49 million adults—half the total adult population
- Jacqueline Cochran became the first woman to fly faster than the speed of sound
- Nationwide, the U.S. had 214,000 physicians, 95,000 dentists, and 1,604,000 hospital beds
- The Chase Manhattan Bank, Sperry Rand, H&R Block, and the Dreyfus Fund all made their first appearance
- Racial segregation on interstate buses and trains was ordered to end
- President Eisenhower submitted a 10-year, $101 billion highway construction program to Congress
- The AFL and CIO merged, with George Meany as president
- The Dow Jones Industrial Average hit a high of 488, and a low of 391
- The Ford Foundation gave $500 million to colleges and universities nationwide
- Whirlpool Corporation merged with Seeger Refrigerator Company and began producing refrigerators, air conditioners, and cooking ranges

1956

- The nation boasted 7,000 drive-in theaters
- The DNA molecule was photographed for the first time
- Teen fashions for boys included crew cut haircuts known as "flattops"
- Procter and Gamble created disposable diapers called Pampers
- Ford Motor Company went public and issued over 10 million shares which were sold to 250,000 investors
- A survey showed 77 percent of college-educated women were married, 41 percent worked part-time, and 17 percent worked full-time
- Boston religious leaders urged the banning of rock 'n' roll
- Eleven percent of all cars sold were station wagons
- Airlines carried as many passengers as trains

- Broadway openings included *Waiting for Godot, Long Day's Journey into Night, My Fair Lady, Bells Are Ringing and Separate Tables*
- After vowing never to allow Elvis Presley's vulgarity on his TV show, Ed Sullivan paid Presley $50,000 for three appearances
- Midas Muffler Shops, Comet, Raid, Salem cigarettes, La Leche League, Imperial margarine and women ordained as ministers in the Presbyterian Church all made their first appearance
- Don Larsen of the New York Yankees pitched the first perfect game in the World Series
- John F. Kennedy won the Pulitzer Prize for *Profiles in Courage* and *Russia Leaves the War* by George F. Kennan won in the U.S. History category
- An art canvas purchased in Chicago for $450 was discovered to be a Leonardo valued at $1 million
- Television premieres included *As the World Turns, The Edge of Night, The Huntley-Brinkley Report, The Price Is Right* and *The Steve Allen Show*
- Soviet Premier Nikita Khrushchev assailed past President Joseph Stalin as a terrorist, egotist and murderer
- American colleges began actively recruiting students from the middle classes
- Martin Luther King, Jr. said, "Nonviolence is the most potent technique for oppressed people. Unearned suffering is redemptive."
- Hit songs included "Blue Suede Shoes," "Hound Dog," "Mack the Knife," "The Party's Over" and "Friendly Persuasion"
- European autos gained in popularity, including Volkswagens, Jaguars, Ferraris, Saabs and Fiats
- Ngo Diem was elected president of South Vietnam

1957–1958

- President Eisenhower sent paratroopers to Little Rock, Arkansas, to protect nine black students seeking to attend all-white Central High

School
- "Beat" and "beatnik" took hold as words to describe the "Beat Generation"
- Unemployment in the U.S. reached 5.2 million, a post-war high
- Martin Luther King, Jr., helped organize the Southern Christian Leadership Conference (SCLC) and became its first president
- Evangelist Billy Graham held a five-month-long revival at Madison Square Garden in New York that attracted more than 500,000 people
- After 38 years, *Collier's Magazine* published its final issue
- Tennis player Althea Gibson became the first black athlete to win at Wimbledon
- *Sputnik I,* the first manmade satellite, was sent into orbit around the earth by the Soviets
- Painkiller Darvon was introduced by Eli Lilly
- A University of Wisconsin study showed that 20 percent of Americans lived in poverty
- New York's first trolley car was retired
- Frisbee was introduced by Wham-O Manufacturing
- Per capita margarine consumption exceeded butter
- A record 4.3 million babies were born
- The cost of 100,000 computerized multiplication computations fell from $1.26 in 1952 to $0.26.
- Volkswagen sold 200,000 Beetles and Ford introduced the Edsel
- An intensive study of birth control with pills was begun in Puerto Rico
- *Fortune* named Paul Getty America's richest man, with his wealth estimated at $1 billion
- Average wages for a factory production worker were $2.08 an hour, or $82.00 a week
- BankAmericard credit card was introduced
- First-class postal rates climbed to $0.04 per ounce
- The VD rate increased from 122,000 cases to 126,000, the first increase since 1948

- Sweet'n' Low sugarless sweetener was introduced
- The Everly Brothers' song "Wake Up Little Susie" was banned in Boston
- One in three women went regularly to the beauty shop, many for apricot or silver-colored hair

1958

- *Life Magazine*'s series, "Crisis in Education," focused on major U.S. educational problems, including poor curricula, overcrowding, and poorly paid teachers
- The Pizza Hut chain began in Kansas City
- Paul Robeson, denied a passport for eight years because of his Leftist comments, was allowed to tour overseas
- The cost of college doubled from 1940 to 1958 to $1,300 a year
- The construction of a nuclear power plant at Bodega Head, California, was stopped by a court action of environmental groups
- Gasoline cost 30.4 cents per gallon
- Paperback edition of *Lolita* sold a million copies
- Elvis Presley was inducted into the army as No. 53310761
- Eleanor Roosevelt was first on the "Most Admired Women" list for the 11th time, and Queen Elizabeth was second
- SANE (Scientists Against Nuclear Energy) was formed with 25,000 members
- Several television quiz shows were exposed for providing contestants with answers beforehand
- Ford Motor Company introduced the Edsel
- Unemployment reached a postwar high of 6.8 percent
- The United States' standing army included 2.6 million men and women
- Kansas and Colorado were invaded by grasshoppers
- John Kenneth Galbraith's book *The Affluent Society* contended that materialism and conformity characterized the U.S. and argued for redistribution of income to end poverty

- The sale of television sets topped 41 million
- First-class postal rates climbed to $0.04 per ounce
- Sixty-four percent of American households now had incomes above $4,000 a year
- More than 250,000 people attended the Jehovah's Witness Convention at Yankee Stadium
- The Grammy award, John Birch Society, Chevrolet Impala, Sweet 'n' Low, Cocoa Krispies, American Express, and Green Giant canned beans all made their first appearance

1959

- To offset the rising cost of tinplate, Coors beer started using an aluminum can
- Movie premieres included *Ben-Hur* starring Charlton Heston; *Some Like It Hot* with Tony Curtis, Marilyn Monroe and Jack Lemmon; and *Pillow Talk* featuring Doris Day, Rock Hudson and Tony Randall
- Mary Leakey discovered the skull of the 1.78 million-year-old *Australopithecus* in the Olduvai Gorge, Tanganyika
- Television's top-10 shows were *Gunsmoke*; *Wagon Train*; *Have Gun, Will Travel*; *The Danny Thomas Show*; *The Red Skelton Show*; *Father Knows Best*; *77 Sunset Strip*; *The Price Is Right*; *Wanted: Dead or Alive* and *Perry Mason*
- The Soviet *Lunik II* became the first manmade object to strike the moon
- Rock 'n' roll stars Buddy Holly, Ritchie Valens and the Big Bopper were killed in an airplane crash
- Modern art was declared duty-free
- The U.S. Navy successfully orbited a Vanguard satellite, the forerunner of the first weather station in space
- "A Raisin in the Sun," "The Miracle Worker," "The Tenth Man," "Five Finger Exercise," "Sweet Bird of Youth" and "Mark Twain Tonight" all premiered on Broadway

- Fiction bestsellers included *Exodus* by Leon Uris, *Doctor Zhivago* by Boris Pasternak, *Hawaii* by James Michener, *Lady Chatterley's Lover* by D. H. Lawrence, *The Ugly American* by William J. Lederer and Eugene L. Burdick, *Poor No More* by Robert Ruark and *Dear and Glorious Physician* by Taylor Caldwell
- NASA selected the *Mercury* Seven astronauts: John Glenn, Scott Carpenter, Virgil Grissom, Gordon Cooper, Walter Schirra, Donald Slayton and Alan Shepard
- Perry Como signed a $25 million contract with Kraft Foods

1960

- The National Association of Broadcasters reacted to a payola scandal by threatening fines for any disc jockeys who accepted money for playing particular records
- Four students from North Carolina Agricultural and Technical State University in Greensboro, North Carolina, began a sit-in at a segregated Woolworth's lunch counter, which triggered similar nonviolent protests throughout the southern U.S.
- Joanne Woodward received the first star on the Hollywood Walk of Fame
- Adolph Coors III, chairman of the board of the Coors Brewing Company, was kidnapped for $500,000 and later found dead
- The U.S. announced that 3,500 American soldiers would be sent to Vietnam
- Arthur Leonard Schawlow and Charles Hard Townes received the first patent for a laser
- The U.S. launched the first weather satellite, TIROS-1
- *Ben Hur* won the Oscar for Best Picture
- A Soviet missile shot down an American spy plane; pilot Francis Gary Powers was captured, tried, and released 21 months later in a spy swap with the U.S.
- President Dwight D. Eisenhower signed the Civil Rights Act of 1960 into law

- The U.S. FDA approved birth control as an additional indication for the drug Searle's Enovid, making it the world's first approved oral contraceptive pill
- Nuclear submarine *USS Triton* completed the underwater circumnavigation of Earth
- The Soviet Union beat Yugoslavia 2-1 to win the first European Football Championship
- Harper Lee released her critically acclaimed novel *To Kill a Mockingbird*
- Presidential candidates Richard M. Nixon and John F. Kennedy participated in the first televised presidential debate
- Nikita Khrushchev pounded his shoe on a table at a United Nations General Assembly meeting to protest the discussion of Soviet Union policy toward Eastern Europe
- Black entertainer Sammy Davis, Jr. married Swedish actress May Britt, causing a stir
- Basketball player Wilt Chamberlain grabbed 55 rebounds in a single game
- Production of the DeSoto automobile brand ceased
- President Eisenhower authorized the use of $1 million toward the resettlement of Cuban refugees, who were arriving in Florida at the rate of 1,000 a week
- The U.S. Supreme Court declared in *Boynton v. Virginia* that segregation on public transit was illegal
- The U.S. Census listed all people from Latin America as white, including blacks from the Dominican Republic, European whites from Argentina, and Mexicans who resembled Native Americans
- The world population was 3,021,475,000

1961–1962
- President Kennedy established the Peace Corps two months after his inauguration

- DNA genetic code was broken
- New York's First National Bank offered fixed-term certificates of deposit
- IBM's Selectric typewriter was introduced
- Harper and Row was created through a merger
- Right wing activities of the John Birch Society stirred concerns in Congress
- Black and white "Freedom Riders" tested integration in the South, and were attacked and beaten in Alabama
- Cigarette makers spent $115 million on television advertising
- R.J. Reynolds acquired Pacific Hawaiian Products Company in an attempt to diversify away from tobacco products
- Sprite was introduced by Coca-Cola Company
- A Gallup poll recorded that 74 percent of teens interviewed believed in God, 58 percent planned to go to college, most of the 16- to 21-year-old girls interviewed expected to be married by age 22, and most wanted four children
- 4,000 servicemen were sent to Vietnam as advisers
- Minimum wage rose from $1.00 to $1.25 per hour
- Canned pet foods were among the top three selling categories in grocery stores
- The Cuban missile crisis pitted the United States against the Soviet Union
- President Kennedy reduced tariff duties to stimulate foreign trade
- Electronic Data Systems was founded by H. Ross Perot
- 90 percent of American households had at least one television set
- The American Broadcasting Company (ABC) began color telecasts 3.5 hours per week
- Diet-Rite Cola was introduced as the first sugar-free soft drink
- Tab-opening aluminum drink cans were introduced
- In May, 1962, the stock market plunged 34.95 points, the sharpest drop since the 1929 crash

- Late-night television show, *The Tonight Show*, with Johnny Carson, began
- Demonstrations against school segregation occurred throughout the South
- President John F. Kennedy contributed his salary to charity
- The Dow Jones Industrial Average reached a high of 767
- Movie premieres included *To Kill a Mockingbird*, *Long Day's Journey into Night*, *The Manchurian Candidate*, *The Longest Day* and *Lawrence of Arabia*
- The Students' Nonviolent Coordinating Committee (SNCC) organized the freedom ballot in the South, aggressively registering blacks to vote in Mississippi, Alabama and Georgia
- Astronaut John Glenn orbited the earth three times, saying, "It was quite a day. I don't know what you can say about a day when you see four beautiful sunsets."
- Popular songs included "Go Away, Little Girl," "What Kind of Fool Am I?," "I Left My Heart in San Francisco" and "The Sweetest Sounds"
- Nine New York daily newspaper unions staged a strike that lasted five months
- Walter Cronkite replaced Douglas Edwards on the *CBS Evening News*
- Jackie Robinson was inducted as the first African-American into the Baseball Hall of Fame
- *One Flew over the Cuckoo's Nest* by Ken Kesey, *Happiness Is a Warm Puppy* by Charles M. Schulz, *Sex and the Single Girl* by Helen Gurley Brown, and *Pigeon Feathers* by John Updike were all published
- *Mariner II* became the first successful interplanetary probe, confirming that the high temperatures of Venus were inhospitable to life
- Rachel Carson's book *Silent Spring* stated that more than 500 new chemicals were entering our bodies because of widespread insecticide use
- *Who's Afraid of Virginia Woolf?* opened on Broadway

- Inflation was at 0.4 percent, unemployment at 5.5 percent
- Eighty percent of households had a telephone

1964

- The first meeting between leaders of the Roman Catholic and Orthodox churches since the fifteenth century took place between Pope Paul VI and Patriarch Athenagoras I in Jerusalem
- In his first State of the Union Address, President Lyndon Johnson declared a "War on Poverty"
- Surgeon General Luther Leonidas Terry reported that smoking may be hazardous to one's health (the first such statement from the U.S. Government)
- Thirteen years after its proposal and nearly two years after its passage by the Senate, the 24th Amendment, prohibiting the use of poll taxes in national elections, was ratified
- General Motors introduced the Oldsmobile Vista Cruiser and the Buick Sport Wagon
- The Beatles vaulted to the #1 spot on the U.S. singles charts with "I Want to Hold Your Hand," and launched the "British Invasion" with an appearance on *The Ed Sullivan Show*
- The Supreme Court ruled that congressional districts must be approximately equal in population
- Muhammad Ali beat Sonny Liston in Miami Beach, Florida, and was crowned the Heavyweight Champion of the World
- Teamsters President Jimmy Hoffa was convicted by a federal jury of tampering with a federal jury in 1962
- In *New York Times Co. v Sullivan*, the Supreme Court ruled that, under the First Amendment, speech criticizing political figures cannot be censored
- The first Ford Mustang rolled off the assembly line at Ford Motor Company
- A Dallas, Texas, jury found Jack Ruby guilty of killing John F. Kennedy

assassin Lee Harvey Oswald
- Merv Griffin's game show *Jeopardy!* debuted on NBC
- The Beatles dominated the top five positions in the Billboard Top 40 singles in America: "Can't Buy Me Love," "Twist and Shout," "She Loves You," "I Want to Hold Your Hand," and "Please Please Me"
- Three high school friends in Hoboken, NJ, opened the first BLIMPIE restaurant
- The Rolling Stones released their debut album, *The Rolling Stones*
- The New York World's Fair opened to celebrate the 300th anniversary of New Amsterdam being taken over by British forces and renamed New York in 1664
- John George Kemeny and Thomas Eugene Kurtz ran the first computer program written in BASIC (Beginners' All-purpose Symbolic Instruction Code), an easy-to-learn, high-level programming language
- College students marched through Times Square and San Francisco in the first major student demonstration against the Vietnam War
- Three civil rights workers were murdered near Philadelphia, Mississippi, by local Klansmen, cops, and a sheriff
- President Johnson signed the Civil Rights Act of 1964 into law, legally abolishing racial segregation in the United States
- At the Republican National Convention in San Francisco, presidential nominee Barry Goldwater declared that "extremism in the defense of liberty is no vice," and "moderation in the pursuit of justice is no virtue"
- The Supreme Court ruled that, in accordance with the Civil Rights Act of 1964, establishments providing public accommodations must refrain from racial discrimination
- Cosmic microwave background radiation was discovered
- Dr. Farrington Daniels's book, *Direct Use of the Sun's Energy*, was published by Yale University Press
- The first Moog synthesizer was designed by Robert Moog

1965

- Americans purchased $60 million worth of prescription weight-loss drugs, twice the dollar amount spent just five years earlier
- "Flower Power" was coined by Allen Ginsburg at a Berkeley antiwar rally
- Unemployment, at 4.2 percent, was at its lowest point in eight years
- The 1,250-room Washington Hilton opened in Washington, DC
- The U.S. Immigration Bill abolished national origin quotas
- Avis Rent-A-Car was acquired by International Telephone and Telegraph
- The Voting Rights Act, which eliminated literacy tests and provided federal oversight in elections, stimulated a dramatic increase in voting by African-Americans
- America's place in harvesting seafood fell from first in 1945 to fifth as the country became a major fish importer
- The U.S. Supreme Court struck down a Connecticut statute forbidding the use of contraceptives and eliminated state and local film censorship
- Pope Paul VI visited the United Nations headquarters and delivered a message of peace
- After extended hearings on cigarette smoking, Congress required that cigarette packages warn: "Caution: Cigarette smoking may be hazardous to your health"
- Americans paid $7.5 million more than in 1940 for prepackaged food
- The birth rate fell to 19 per 1,000 people, the lowest since 1940
- Cereal packaged with fruits preserved through freeze-drying was introduced
- Miniskirts, Cranapple, Diet Pepsi, the Sony home videotape recorder and all-news radio stations made their first appearance
- A 150-mile commuter rail system in San Francisco and Oakland began construction
- Kraft foods sponsored the first commercial television program

transmitted between the U.S. and Switzerland via the *Early Bird* communications satellite

- Production of soft-top convertible automobiles reached a record 507,000
- For the first time since 1962, the administration did not ask Congress for a fallout shelter construction program
- The U.S. Public Health Service announced an ambitious program to eradicate syphilis in the U.S. by 1972

1966–1967

- Student protests against the Vietnam War began
- Student deferments from the draft were abolished, and draft calls reached 50,000 young men a month
- The National Organization for Women (NOW) was founded
- The largest year-to-year rise in the cost of living since 1958 was announced—2.8 percent
- The term "Black Power" was introduced into the Civil Rights movement, signifying the rift between the pacifist followers of Martin Luther King, Jr.'s SCLC and the militants following Stokely Carmichael, SNCC and CORE
- Taster's Choice freeze-dried instant coffee was introduced
- 41 percent of non-white families made less than $3,000 annually
- *New York World Journal & Tribute* closed; *Rolling Stone* magazine was founded
- 2.7 million Americans received food stamp assistance
- Nearly 10,000 farmers received more than $20,000 each in subsidies
- Annual per capita beef consumption reached 105.6 pounds
- Burger King Corporation was acquired by Pillsbury Corporation
- New style dance halls, like the Fillmore in San Francisco, introduced strobe lights, liquid color blobs, glow paint, and psychedelic posters
- The Clean Waters Restoration Act allocated funds for preventing river and air pollution
- The National Association of Broadcasters instructed all disc jockeys to

screen all records for hidden references to drugs or obscene meanings

- The U.S. population passed 200 million
- The Rare and Endangered Species list was introduced by the Department of the Interior
- The phrase "Third World" for underdeveloped countries gained currency of usage
- Connection between a low-cholesterol diet and a reduced incidence of heart disease was shown in a five-year study
- Both CBS and NBC televised the Super Bowl
- The first rock festival was held at Monterey, California, featuring the Grateful Dead and Big Brother and the Holding Company starring Janis Joplin
- Heavyweight boxer Muhammad Ali was denied conscientious objector status after refusing induction in the Army
- The United States revealed that it had developed an anti-ballistic missile defense plan against Chinese attack
- Hit songs included *Natural Woman, Soul Man, I Never Loved a Man, Penny Lane, By The Time I Get to Phoenix,* and *Can't Take My Eyes Off You*
- Army physician Captain Harold Levy refused to train Green Berets heading to Vietnam in the treatment of skin disease, and was court-martialed and sent to prison
- Coed dorms opened at numerous colleges across the country
- *Sgt Pepper's Lonely Hearts Club Band* by the Beatles won a Grammy for best album
- Jogging, Mickey Mouse watches, protest buttons and psychedelic art were popular fads
- U.S. troop levels in Vietnam reached 225,000 and the U.S. death toll reached 15,997
- Thurgood Marshall became the first African American appointed to the U.S. Supreme Court

- Television premieres included *The Flying Nun, The Carol Burnett Show, Ironsides* and *The Phil Donahue Show*
- Annual beef consumption, per capita, reached 105.6 pounds, up from 99 pounds in 1960
- Black leader Rap Brown said of the ghetto riots, "Violence is as American as apple pie"

1968–1969

- The U.S. gross national product reached $861 billion
- Vietnam War protests intensified across the nation
- Richard Nixon was elected president
- BankAmericard holders numbered 14 million, up 12 million in two years
- Civil Rights leader Rev. Martin Luther King, Jr., was assassinated in Memphis, Tennessee and riots occurred in over 199 cities nationwide
- Senator Robert F. Kennedy was assassinated in Los Angeles shortly after winning the California Democratic primary
- Responding to the King and Kennedy assassinations, Sears & Roebuck removed toy guns from its Christmas catalog
- Automobile production reached 8.8 million
- Volkswagen captured 57 percent of the U.S. automobile import market
- Television advertising revenues hit $2 billion, twice that of radio
- First-class postage climbed to $0.06
- Yale College admitted women
- Uniform Monday Holiday Law was enacted by Congress, creating 3-day holiday weekends
- Nationwide 78 million television sets existed
- Neil Armstrong walked on the moon
- Pantyhose production reached 624 million pairs in 1969, up from 200 million in 1968
- The average U.S. farm produced enough food for 47 people, and the average farm government subsidy was $1,000

- Blue Cross health insurance covered 68 million Americans
- *Penthouse* magazine began publication, and *Saturday Evening Post* folded
- The National Association of Broadcasters began phasing out cigarette advertising
- The U.S. began the first troop withdrawals from Vietnam, and Vietnam casualties exceeded the total for the Korean War
- Richard Nixon's 43.3 percent victory was the lowest presidential margin since 1912
- Pope Paul VI's ban on contraception was challenged by 800 U.S. theologians
- 20,000 people were added monthly to NYC's welfare rolls, as one-fourth of the city's budget went to welfare
- The Vietnam War became the longest war in U.S. history and approximately 484,000 U.S. soldiers were fighting in it
- President Nixon announced the withdrawal of 25,000 U.S. troops from South Vietnam
- Music concerts drew millions as artists such as the Rolling Stones, the Who, Joan Baez, Jimi Hendrix and the Jefferson Airplane launched tours
- A copy of the first printing of the Declaration of Independence sold for $404,000
- "The Johnny Cash Show," "Hee Haw," and "The Bill Cosby Show" all premiered
- Following student protests, universities nationwide either made ROTC voluntary or abolished the program
- After weeks of debate, U.S. and Vietnam delegates agreed only on the shape of the table used when South Vietnam and the National Liberation Front joined the talks
- Black militant defendant Bobby Seale was ordered bound and gagged by Judge Julius Hoffmann when Seale repeatedly disrupted the

Chicago Eight trial

- The popularity of paperback novels detailing life in "today's easy-living, easy-loving playground called suburbia" skyrocketed
- Actor Richard Burton bought Elizabeth Taylor a 69.42-carat diamond from Cartier
- John Lennon and Yoko Ono married
- 448 universities experienced strikes or were forced to close as student demands included revisions of admissions policies and the reorganization of academic programs
- *Penthouse* magazine, vasectomy outpatient service and automated teller machines all made their first appearance
- The underdog New York Jets, led by quarterback Joe Namath, upset the Baltimore Colts to become the first AFL Super Bowl winner
- Robert Lehman bequeathed 3,000 works valued at more than $100 million to the Metropolitan Museum of Art
- Bestsellers included Philip Roth's *Portnoy's Complaint*, Jacqueline Susann's *The Love Machine*, Mario Puzo's *The Godfather*, and Penelope Ashe's *Naked Came the Stranger*
- To protest the Miss America contest, feminists dropped girdles and bras in the trash
- Hippie cult leader Charles Manson was charged with the Hollywood murders of pregnant Sharon Tate and three others
- The first draft lottery was held

1970

- Pan American Airways offered the first commercially scheduled 747 service from John F. Kennedy International Airport to London's Heathrow Airport
- Black Sabbath's debut album, regarded as the first heavy metal album, was released
- The Chicago Seven defendants were found not guilty of conspiring to incite a riot, in charges stemming from violence at the 1968 Democratic

National Convention, while five were found guilty on the lesser charge of crossing state lines to incite a riot

- The Nuclear Non-Proliferation Treaty went into effect, after ratification by 56 nations
- The United States Army charged 14 officers with suppressing information related to the My Lai massacre in Vietnam
- Postal workers in a dozen cities went on strike for two weeks and President Nixon assigned military units to New York City post offices
- Earth Day was proclaimed by San Francisco Mayor Joseph Alioto
- Paul McCartney announced the disbanding of the Beatles, as their twelfth album, *Let It Be*, was released
- An oxygen tank in the *Apollo 13* spacecraft exploded, forcing the crew to abort the mission and return in four days
- Four students at Kent State University in Ohio were killed and nine wounded by Ohio National Guardsmen during a protest against the U.S. incursion into Cambodia
- The U.S. promoted its first female generals: Anna Mae Hays and Elizabeth P. Hoisington
- *Venera 7* was launched and became the first spacecraft to successfully transmit data from the surface of another planet
- The Women's Strike for Equality took place down Fifth Avenue in New York City
- Elvis Presley began his first concert tour since 1958 at the Veterans Memorial Coliseum in Phoenix, Arizona
- The first New York City Marathon took place
- Guitarist Jimi Hendrix died in London of drug-related complications
- *Monday Night Football* debuted on ABC
- In Paris, a Communist delegation rejected President Nixon's October 7 peace proposal for the Vietnam War as "a maneuver to deceive world opinion"
- Garry Trudeau's comic strip *Doonesbury* debuted in dozens of U.S. newspapers

- Southern Airlines Flight 932 crashed, killing all 75 on board, including 37 players and five coaches from the Marshall University football team
- The Soviet Union landed *Lunokhod 1* on the moon—the first roving remote-controlled robot to land on a natural satellite
- The North Tower of the World Trade Center was the tallest building in the world at 1,368 feet
- Alvin Toffler published his book *Future Shock*

1971

- President Richard Nixon ordered a 90-day freeze on wages and prices
- First-class postal rates rose to $0.08 per ounce
- *New York Times* published the first installment of the "Pentagon Papers," a classified history of American involvement in the Vietnam War, and 75 percent of those polled opposed publication of the secret papers
- Tennis player Billie Jean King became the first woman athlete to earn $100,000 in one year
- The Supreme Court mandated busing as a means of achieving school desegregation
- A poll showed that 34 percent of Americans found marriage obsolete, up from 24 percent in 1969
- *Look* magazine ceased publication
- Beef consumption per capita rose from 113 pounds to 128.5 pounds
- Cigarette advertising was banned by Congress from television
- Three fourths of all moviegoers were under age 30
- *Gourmet* magazine circulation doubled to 550,000 in just four years as the fancy food industry continued to grow
- Phrases "think tank," "body language," "gross out," and "workaholic" all entered the language
- The National Cancer Act was passed, providing $1.5 billion a year for research, as the president urged an all-out attempt to find a cure
- The Supreme Court ruled that qualification for conscientious-objector

status necessitated opposing all wars, not just the Vietnam War
- The Metropolitan Museum of Art paid a record $5.5 million for a Velásquez portrait
- The diamond-bladed scalpel was developed for eye microsurgery
- Young women were appointed U.S. Senate pages for the first time
- The U.S. Supreme Court ruled that companies may not refuse to hire women with small children if the same policy is not applied to men
- The United States Public Health Service no longer advised children to be vaccinated against smallpox
- Direct dialing began between New York and London
- Snowmobiles, dune buggies, auto trains, and a law banning sex discrimination all made their first appearance

1972–1973

- Nearly 30 percent of U.S. petroleum was imported
- Dow Jones closed at 1,003.15 on November 14, above 1,000 for the first time
- San Francisco Bay Area Rapid Transit System opened
- *Ms. Magazine* began publication and *Life* magazine suspended publication
- The Polaroid SX-70 system produced color prints
- NYC's 110-story World Trade Center opened
- America's birth rate fell to 15.8 per 1,000, the lowest since 1917
- The average farmer produced enough food for 50 people and farm labor represented five percent of the work force
- The median sales price of an existing single-family house reached $28,900
- Vodka outsold whiskey for the first time
- The Law Enforcement Assistance Administration's budget rose to $700 million
- By a five-to-four vote, the Supreme Court ruled that capital punishment was "cruel and unusual punishment" pending further

legislation from the states

- The number of fast-food establishments increased to 6,784, up from 1,120 in 1958
- The Massachusetts Supreme Court ruled unconstitutional a law prohibiting the sale of contraceptives to single persons
- Congress passed Title IX, which entitled women to participate equally in all sports
- The Nobel Peace Prize was awarded to Henry Kissinger and North Vietnamese Le Duc Tho, who refused the honor
- Television premieres included *Barnaby Jones*, *Police Story*, *The Young and the Restless* and *The Six-Million-Dollar Man*
- Space-exploring *Pioneer X* produced significant detail of Jupiter and its great red spot
- *The Sting* with Paul Newman and Robert Redford captured the Academy Award for Best Picture
- Popular movies included *The Paper Chase*, *Scenes from a Marriage*, *The Last Detail*, *The Exorcist* and *American Graffiti*
- A computerized brain scanner known as CAT was marketed
- Hit songs for the year were "Tie a Yellow Ribbon," "Delta Dawn," "Let's Get It On," "Me and Mrs. Jones," "Rocky Mountain High," "Could It Be I'm Falling in Love?" and Roberta Flack earned the Best Record Grammy for "Killing Me Softly with His Song"
- Richard Nixon resigned the presidency of the United States and vice president Gerald Ford became president
- The OPEC oil embargo raised the price of crude oil by 300 percent, causing shortages and long lines at the nation's gasoline pumps
- Bestsellers included *Jonathan Livingston Seagull* by Richard Bach, *Once Is Not Enough* by Jacqueline Susann, *Breakfast of Champions* by Kurt Vonnegut, Jr. and *I'm O.K., You're O.K.* by Thomas Harris
- Words and phrases entering popular usage were Skylab, juggernaut, biofeedback, ego trip, let it all hang out, and nouvelle cuisine

- The "pet rock" fad captured the imagination of America

1974–1975

- The pocket calculator was marketed
- 110,000 clothing workers staged a nationwide strike
- Unemployment reached 6.5 percent, the highest since 1961
- The universal product code was designed for the supermarket industry
- Year-long daylight savings time was adopted to save fuel
- 3M developed Post-it stock to stick paper to paper
- ITT's Harold Green was the nation's highest paid executive at $791,000 per year
- Time, Inc., issued *People Magazine* devoted to celebrity journalism
- Walgreen's drug chain exceeded $1 billion in sales for the first time
- The first desktop microcomputer became available
- The Equal Opportunity Act forbade discrimination based on sex or marital status
- Minnesota became the first state to require businesses, restaurants, and institutions to establish no-smoking areas
- New York City averted bankruptcy with a $2.3 billion federal loan
- The biggest money-making films of the year were *Towering Inferno, Earthquake,* and *The Exorcist*
- Beef consumption fell nine percent, while chicken consumption rose nearly 35 percent
- Car sales fell 35 percent from 1973, and home construction was down 40 percent
- McDonald's opened its first drive-through restaurants
- AT&T, the world's largest private employer, banned discrimination against homosexuals
- Time-sharing of vacation real estate was introduced in the United States
- A record 120,000 Americans declared personal bankruptcy
- The "typical" nuclear family—working father, housewife, and two

children—represented only seven percent of the population; average family size was 3.4, down from 4.3 in 1920

- Harvard changed its five-to-two male to female admissions policy to equal admissions
- Unemployment reached 9.2 percent
- The Atomic Energy Commission was dissolved
- The Supreme Court ruled that the mentally ill cannot be hospitalized against their will unless they are dangerous to themselves or to others
- Chrysler, and other auto companies, offered rebates to counter record low sales
- The Brewers' Society reported that Americans consumed an average of 151 pints of beer per year, 11.5 pints of wine, and 9.1 pints of spirits
- *Penthouse* sales surpassed those of *Playboy*
- The Rolling Stones tour grossed $13 million, and singer Stevie Wonder signed a record contract for $13 million
- A Massachusetts physician was convicted of manslaughter by a Boston jury for aborting a fetus and was sentenced to a year's probation
- Rape laws were changed in nine states, lessening the amount of corroborative evidence necessary for conviction and restricting trial questions regarding the victim's past sex life
- An endangered whooping crane was born in captivity
- TV advertisements for tampons appeared for the first time

1976–1977

- The Dow Jones Industrial Average peaked at 1,004, inflation hit 8.7 percent, and unemployment hit 8.3 percent
- Jimmy Carter was elected president
- Bicentennial festivities swept the nation, highlighted by 'Operation Sail' in NYC in which 16 of the world's tallest and oldest windjammers along with thousands of other ships began a tour of the world's major ports
- Congress passed a law to admit women to military academies

- The Supreme Court ruled that employers were not required to give paid maternity leave
- Renowned lawyer F. Lee Bailey defended Patty Hearst, daughter of publisher William Randolph Hearst, against changes of bank robbery claiming she was 'brainwashed'
- President Gerald Ford ordered a major inoculation campaign against a projected swine flu epidemic
- The repeal of the Fair Trade law prevented manufacturers from fixing retail prices
- Colossus Cave, the first computer game, was designed at Princeton
- The arrest rate for women since 1964 rose three times faster than the rate for men
- Sales of bran cereals and high fiber bread increased dramatically, as consumers responded to widely published medical reports of health benefits of high-fiber diets
- California legalized the concept of "living wills," giving the terminally ill the right to decree their own deaths
- The Apple computer was developed in a California garage
- Average SAT scores dipped to 472 (math) and 435 (English) from 501 and 480 in 1968
- One of five children lived in a one-parent home, as three out of five marriages ended in divorce
- ABC offered the industry's first $1 million per year contract to Barbara Walters of NBC
- Clothier Abercrombie & Fitch declared bankruptcy
- Mobil Petroleum bought Montgomery Ward for $1 billion
- Balloon angioplasty was developed for reopening diseased arteries of the heart
- 20,000 shopping malls generated 50 percent of total retail sales nationwide
- American Express became the first service company to top $1 billion in sales

- *Li'l Abner* cartoon ceased publication
- Three major networks controlled 91 percent of prime-time audiences
- Cheryl Tiegs, the world's highest-paid model, earned $1,000 a day
- 1.9 million women operated businesses
- The U.S. and Canada signed a pact to build a gas pipeline from Alaska to the Midwest
- Consumers boycotted coffee due to soaring prices
- Sales of imported cars broke all records, passing 1.5 million
- The Supreme Court reversed a New York law that prohibited the distribution of contraceptives to minors
- The FDA banned the use of the additive Red Dye # 2 in foods, drugs, and cosmetics
- Widespread looting occurred during a blackout in NYC and Westchester county that affected nine million people
- Pepsi topped Coca-Cola in sales for the first time
- 45 million people watched the highest-rated TV interview in history, featuring former President Richard Nixon on the *David Frost* program, for which he was paid $600,000, plus 10 percent of the show's profits
- The Supreme Court ruled that the spanking of schoolchildren by teachers was constitutional
- CBS anchor Walter Cronkite helped arrange a meeting in Israel between Egyptian president Anwar Sadat and Israeli Prime Minister Menachem Begin
- Elvis Presley died, and within a day of his death, two million of his records sold
- Men's fashion became more conservative, marked by narrow, small-patterned silk ties and Oxford and broadcloth shirts
- More than 400,000 teenage abortions were performed, a third of the U.S. total
- The CB radio fad resulted in record sales
- Generic products, pocket TVs, and public automatic blood pressure

machines all made their first appearance

1978

- Television's late-night host, Johnny Carson, made $4 million, while *Happy Days'* star Henry Winkler made $990,000
- Alex Haley's book *Roots* sparked an interest in genealogy, particularly among African- Americans
- Fifty percent of all shoe sales were sneakers, topping 200 million pairs
- Airline deregulation eliminated federal controls on fares and routes, as eight airlines controlled 81 percent of the domestic market
- Legal retirement age was raised to 70
- Gold sold for $245 per ounce
- California voters adopted Proposition 13 to control property taxes
- The tax code permitted 401(k) savings plans for the first time
- Legalized gambling in Atlantic City, NJ; microchip technology in washing machines; *Garfield* cartoons; pocket math calculators; and 45-rpm picture disc records all made their first appearance
- Morris the Cat, the advertising symbol for Nine Lives cat food, died at the age of 17
- The number of unmarried couples living together more than doubled from 523,000 in 1970 to 1,137,000
- Attracted by jobs and housing, more than 1,000 families were moving to Dallas, Texas, each month
- Pepsico acquired Mexican fast-food chain, Taco Bell
- The cost of a first-class postage stamp rose to $0.15 per ounce
- The USDA warned of the dangers of nitrites in processed and cured meat products, reporting that sodium nitrite may cause cancer
- Edith Bunker, a character on the television show *All in the Family*, said, "With credit, you can buy everything you can't afford"
- The King Tutankhamen show touring America produced $5 million for the Cairo Museum
- Attendance for the North American Soccer League rose 50 percent to

5.3 million fans

- *If Life Is a Bowl of Cherries—What Am I Doing in the Pits?* by Erma Bombeck, *The World According to Garp* by John Irving and *The Complete Book of Running* by James Fixx were all on the bestseller list

1979

- The divorce rate increased 68 percent since 1968 and the median duration of marriage was 6.6 years
- The Sony Walkman, a portable cassette player with headphones, was introduced
- U.S. Trust reported that 520,000 Americans—one in every 424—were millionaires
- Sales of health foods zoomed from $140 million in 1940 to $1.6 billion
- Jiffy Lube fast oil-change automotive service center opened
- Inflation was at its worst in 33 years, and prices increased more than 13.3 percent
- The Supreme Court ruled that "husbands only" alimony laws were unconstitutional
- Ford Motor Company acquired 25 percent of Japan's Mazda Motor Company
- The near-meltdown of a nuclear power plant at Three Mile Island ignited anti-nuclear fears nationwide
- California became the first state to initiate gas rationing, creating alternate-day purchasing
- Avon Products acquired Tiffany and Company
- The prime lending rate at banks hit 14.5 percent
- Massachusetts became the seventh state to increase the legal drinking age from 18 to 20
- Jane Fonda and Tom Hayden toured 50 cities to speak out against nuclear power
- Electronic blackboards, nitrite-free hot dogs, Cracker Jack ice cream bars and the video digital sound disc all made their first appearance

- The play *Grease* passed *Fiddler on the Roof* as the longest-running Broadway show
- More than 315,000 microcomputers were sold

1980

- Yellow ribbons became a symbol of American concern for the hostages in Iran
- The divorce rate had grown from one in three marriages in 1970 to one in two
- The World Health Organization announced that smallpox had been eradicated
- A 10-year study correlated fatal heart disease to the saturated-unsaturated fat ratio in the diet
- The combination of First Lady Nancy Reagan's elegance and the wedding of Lady Diana to Prince Charles stimulated a return to opulent styles
- Cordless telephones, front-wheel-drive subcompact cars, 24-hour-a-day news coverage and *Discover* magazine made their first appearance
- The prime rate hit 21 percent, and gold was $880 per ounce
- Supply-side economics proposed that government increase incentives, such as tax reform, to stimulate production
- The 1980 U.S. Census reported the smallest population growth since the Great Depression
- *Dallas, M*A*S*H, The Dukes of Hazzard, 60 Minutes, Three's Company, Private Benjamin, Diff'rent Strokes, House Calls, The Jeffersons* and *Too Close for Comfort* were top-rated television shows
- An eight-year Veteran's Administration study showed Vietnam vets suffered more emotional, social, educational and job-related problems than did veterans of other wars
- Top albums of the year included Pink Floyd's *The Wall,* Blondie's *Eat to the Beat, Off the Wall* by Michael Jackson and *Glass Houses* by Billy Joel

- Researchers at the University of California, San Diego, reported that "passive smoking" can lead to lung cancer
- The "Stop Handguns Before They Stop You" Committee ran an advertisement reading, "Last year handguns killed 48 people in Japan, 8 in Great Britain, 34 in Switzerland, 52 in Canada, 58 in Israel, 21 in Sweden, 42 in West Germany, 10,720 in U.S. God Bless America"

1981–1982

- The IBM Personal Computer was marketed for the first time
- 12,000 striking air-traffic controllers were fired by President Ronald Reagan
- Public debt hit $1 trillion
- New York and Miami increased transit fares from $0.60 to $0.75 per ride
- Kellogg's introduced Nutri-Grain wheat cereal
- U.S. first-class postal rates went to $0.18, then $0.20
- Sears & Roebuck bought real estate broker Coldwell Banker & Co., and a securities concern, Dean Witter Reynolds
- The U.S. population hit 228 million
- National unemployment rose to eight percent, including 16.8 percent for blacks and 40 percent for black teenagers
- A court order broke up the A&T U.S. monopoly into AT&T long-distance and regional telephone companies
- The Japanese marketed a wristwatch-sized television with a 1.2-inch screen
- *USA Today,* the first national general interest daily newspaper, was introduced
- 2.9 million women operated businesses
- Braniff International Airline declared bankruptcy
- United Auto Workers agreed to wage concessions with Ford Motor Company
- U.S. Steel acquired Marathon Oil

- The computer "mouse" was introduced by Apple
- The first successful embryo transfer was performed
- NutraSweet was introduced as a synthetic sugar substitute
- 35.3 million lived below the poverty line
- Cellular telephones ("carphones") became available to motorists, costing $3,000 plus $150.00 per month for service
- VCR sales increased 72 percent from the previous year; the U.S. now boasted 3.4 million units in use
- The Rubik's Cube tested the patience of Americans
- Dr. Ruth began her radio talk show, emphasizing sexual issues

1983

- Prices for computers plummeted—Timex sold a personal computer for $99.95, while the Commodore VIC 20 sold for $199—and they were used in 1.5 million homes—five times the number in 1980
- The first artificial heart transplant recipient was Barney Clark, age 61
- The Vietnam Veterans' Memorial, inscribed with the 57,939 names of American soldiers killed or missing in Vietnam, was dedicated in Washington, DC
- Dun and Bradstreet reported a total of 20,365 bankruptcies by October, the highest figure since the Great Depression
- The United Auto Workers agreed to wage concessions with Ford Motor Company
- Efforts at library censorship tripled, and books under fire included *The Adventures of Huckleberry Finn*, *The Grapes of Wrath*, and *The Catcher in the Rye*
- The computer "mouse" was introduced by Apple
- The first successful embryo transfer was performed
- Columbia, the last all-male college in the Ivy League, began accepting women
- President Ronald Reagan proclaimed May 6 "National Day of Prayer" and endorsed a constitutional amendment to permit school prayer,

which was defeated

- A professional football strike cut the regular season to nine games
- The proposed equal rights amendment (ERA) ran out of time for passage, receiving 35 of the 38 state ratifications required
- Ocean Spray was introduced in paper bottles
- The compact disk, polyurethane car bumpers, the Honda Accord, and the NCAA major college basketball championship for women all made their first appearances
- Ameritech received the FCC's first cellular phone license
- Bestselling books included *In Search of Excellence* by Thomas J. Peters and Robert H. Waterman, *Megatrends* by John Naisbitt, *Jane Fonda's Workout Book* by Jane Fonda and *On the Wings of Eagles* by Ken Follet
- Over-the-counter drug packaging became more "tamper-proof" in response to the 1982 cyanide tampering of Tylenol bottles in Chicago
- Hit songs featured "Billie Jean," "Every Breath You Take," "Maniac," "Total Eclipse of the Heart," "Say, Say, Say," and "Islands in the Stream"
- Average tuition for four-year private colleges was $7,475, while Harvard cost $8,195
- Martin Luther King, Jr. became the first person since Abraham Lincoln whose birthday was declared a national holiday
- Worldwide AIDS cases totaled 2,678, with 1,102 deaths since it appeared in 1978
- MTV was received in 17.5 million homes
- *A Chorus Line* became the longest-running show in Broadway history
- Following the terrorist truck bombing in Beirut that killed 239 Marines, South Carolina Senator Ernest Hollings said, "If they've been put there to fight, then there are far too few. If they've been put there to be killed, there are far too many."
- The per-capita personal income in New York was $12,314; in Alaska, $16,257; and in Mississippi, $7,778

- Magazines with the highest circulation were *Reader's Digest, TV Guide, National Geographic, Modern Maturity, Better Homes and Gardens,* and *AARP News Bulletin*

1984

- Dow and six other chemical companies settled with Agent Orange victims for $180 million
- The California Wilderness Act passed, designating 23 new areas in 20 states
- The Supreme Court modified the Miranda ruling to say that illegally obtained evidence was admissible in court if otherwise obtainable
- Vanessa Williams, the first black Miss America, resigned after sexually explicit photographs of her surfaced in a national magazine
- Major movie openings included *Amadeus, The Killing Fields, Places in the Heart, Beverly Hills Cop, Ghostbusters, The Gods Must Be Crazy, The Karate Kid* and *Terminator*
- The American Cancer Society made specific dietary food recommendations endorsing whole grains and fruits and vegetables high in vitamin A and C
- Bruce Merrifield won the Nobel Prize in chemistry for developing an automated method to make proteins
- *The Bill Cosby Show* premiered on television featuring for the first time a professional upper middle class black family
- The Olympics produced a record $150 million surplus after being run as a private enterprise for the first time
- After four-year closure and a cost of $55 million, the Museum of Modern Art in NYC reopened at twice its original size
- Androgynous rock singers such as Michael Jackson, Boy George, Prince, Duran Duran and Grace Jones captured national attention
- President Reagan proclaimed in his State of the Union speech, "America is back standing tall, looking to the eighties with courage, confidence and hope"

- The unemployment rate reached 7.5 percent, and stock market reached a high of 1,287
- Television premieres included *Miami Vice, The Bill Cosby Show, Murder, She Wrote,* and *Highway to Heaven*
- Ages of the U.S. Supreme Court justices became an issue in the national election with five of the nine justices over the age of 75
- Sheep cloning, a woman walking in space, the Apple Macintosh, required seatbelts use, male bunnies at the Playboy Club and PG-13 ratings all made their first appearance
- The Reagan administration threatened to withdraw aid from nations that advocated abortion

1985

- The AMA reported that medical malpractice suits had tripled since 1975, and the average award increased from $95,000 to $333,000
- The U.S. Army ruled that male officers were forbidden to carry umbrellas
- Videocassette movie-rental income equaled movie theater receipts
- "Live Aid" concerts in Philadelphia and London were viewed on television by 1.6 billion people and grossed $70 million for famine-stricken Africa
- Highly addictive, inexpensive cocaine derivative "crack" became popular, selling for $5 to $10 per vial
- Parents and school boards fought over keeping AIDS-afflicted children in public schools
- General Westmoreland dropped his $120 million 1982 libel suit against CBS for its documentary alleging that he deceived the public concerning Vietcong strength
- A single optic fiber carried 300,000 simultaneous phone calls in Bell Laboratory tests
- Capital Cities Communications bought television network ABC for $3.5 billion

- The Nobel Peace Prize went to the International Physicians for the Prevention of Nuclear War, founded by two cardiologists, one at Harvard, the other in Moscow
- The Supreme Court upheld affirmative-action hiring quotas
- World oil prices collapsed, bottoming out at $7.20 per barrel
- The U.S. national debt topped $1.8 trillion
- NYC transit fares rose from $0.75 to $1.00
- Coca-Cola introduced new-formula Coke but public outcry forced Coke to bring back the "Classic Coke" one year later
- Rock Hudson became one of the first public figures to acknowledge his battle with AIDS, raising public awareness of the disease
- The words golden parachute, leveraged buyout, and poison pill all entered the corporate language

1986–1987

- U.S. Protestants numbered 53 million in more than 23,000 churches
- The Supreme Court upheld Affirmative Action hiring quotas
- The U.S. national debt topped $2 billion
- The Dow Jones Industrial Average hit 1,955 and the prime rate dropped to seven percent
- Retailer Sears & Robuck celebrated its 100th anniversary
- Office Depot, one of the first office supply warehouse-type stores, opened in Lauderdale Lakes, Florida
- A supercomputer capable of 1,720 billion computations per second went online
- The first bio-insecticides, designed to eliminate insects without harming the environment, were announced
- Elementary and secondary schoolteachers earned an average salary of $26,700
- Approximately 35 percent of high school graduates entered college
- The Hands Across America chain, stretching from New York City to Long Beach, California, raised $100 million for the poor and homeless

- Eight airlines controlled 90 percent of the domestic market
- The Clean Water Bill passed to address pollution of estuaries and rainwater
- A New York Stock Exchange seat sold for $1.5 million
- The trade deficit hit a record $16.5 billion
- Harvard University celebrated its 350th birthday
- Fitness foods (high in fiber and low in sodium, fat, cholesterol, calories, caffeine) accounted for 10 percent of the $300 billion retail food market
- The first open-air use of a genetically engineered bacteria, a frost retardant, was attempted on strawberry plants
- Under a new law, three Americans became the first foreign lawyers permitted to practice in Japan
- The stock market peaked at 2,722 in August, then fell a record 508 points in a single day in October
- When sports coverage of the U.S. Tennis Open intruded into traditional news time, journalist Dan Rather stormed off the set and TV screens were blank for six minutes
- The federal budget exceeded $1 trillion for the first time
- *The Last Emperor*, *Fatal Attraction*, *Three Men and a Baby* and *Radio Days* all held their movie premieres
- Fifty thousand people gathered at Graceland in Memphis, Tennessee, on the tenth anniversary of Elvis Presley's death
- Sixty percent of American kitchens had microwave ovens
- Forty states restricted smoking in public buildings, restaurants and schools, following the Surgeon General's warnings on the negative impact of secondhand smoke
- Toni Morrison's *Beloved* won the Pulitzer Prize for fiction; David Herbert Donald won the biography prize for *Look Homeward: The Life of Thomas Wolfe*
- The last known dusky seaside sparrow died of old age, marking the extinction of the species

- Congress overrode the president's veto of the $20 billion Clean Water Bill
- The phrase "couch potato" came into popular usage
- Allan Bloom's book, *The Closing of the American Mind*, criticized the U.S. educational system and called for a return to "great books" in its attack on cultural relativism
- Fifty-eight-year-old artist Andy Warhol died of a heart attack after routine gallbladder surgery
- Ansell America became the first condom manufacturer to advertise on television
- Professional baseball player Mark McGwire set a rookie home run record at 49
- The Supreme Court ruled that states may require all-male private clubs to admit women

1988

- Black teenager Tawana Brawley gained national publicity when she claimed she was raped by a group of white men; a grand jury found no evidence of the charges and called her advisors, including Al Sharpton, "unethical"
- Ninety percent of major corporations reported sexual harassment complaints
- Former chief aid Donald Regan claimed that Nancy Reagan used astrology to plan her husband's activities
- Women accounted for nearly half of all graduating accountants, one third of MBAs and one quarter of lawyers
- American lawyers' salary averaged $914 a week, nurses $516, and secretaries $299
- Robots were used for picking fruit
- Fundamentalists picketed *The Last Temptation of Christ*, but the film was an unexpected financial success
- Professional heavyweight boxer Mike Tyson's fight with Michael Spinks

produced a $40 million gate, and Spinks was knocked out in one round
- U.S. auto makers produced 13 million cars and trucks
- Harvard scientists obtained the first animal patent for a genetically engineered mouse with immune properties
- *The Eight-Week Cholesterol Cure*, *The Bonfire of the Vanities*, *Trump: The Art of the Deal* and *Swim with the Sharks without Being Eaten Alive* were all bestsellers
- Philip Morris bought Kraft for $12.9 billion
- Scientific experiments on the Shroud of Turin indicated that it dated from the Middle Ages, not from the time of Christ's death
- Pulitzer Prize for history was awarded to Taylor Branch's *Parting the Waters: America in the King Years 1954-1963*

1989
- Television's top programs included *Roseanne*, *The Cosby Show*, *Cheers*, *A Different World*, *Dear John*, *The Wonder Years* and *Golden Girls*
- Congress passed $166 billion legislation to bail out the savings and loan industry
- Cocaine and crack cocaine use was up 35 percent over 1985
- Sony of Japan purchased Columbia Pictures, sparking comments of Japan invading Hollywood
- Demonstrators at Tiananmen Square carried a Styrofoam Statue of Liberty as part of the protest against the Chinese government
- Scientists speculated that the New World Peruvian architecture could be as old as the Egyptian pyramids
- The movie *Batman* grossed $250 million, the fifth-highest in movie history
- *Field of Dreams*; *When Harry Met Sally*; *Glory*; *Driving Miss Daisy*; *Sex, Lies and Videotape*; and *Roger and Me* premiered at movie theaters
- Calvin Klein's lean and refined look, with soft fabrics and little or no jewelry predominated women's fashion

- *The Heidi Chronicles* by Wendy Wasserstein won both the Tony Award and the Pulitzer Prize
- Baseball Commissioner Bart Giamatti banned ballplayer Pete Rose from playing baseball for life for allegedly betting on games
- *The Joy Luck Club* by Amy Tan, *The Satanic Verses* by Salman Rushdie, *The Temple of My Familiar* by Alice Walker, *The Oldest Living Confederate Widow Tells All* by Allan Gurganus and *A Brief History of Time* by Stephen Hawking were bestsellers
- In Chicago, U.S. veterans protested at the Art Institute where the American flag was draped on the floor
- "Wind Beneath My Wings" by Bette Midler won a Grammy Award for best song
- Top singles for the year included "Every Rose Has Its Thorn" by Poison, "Miss You Much" by Janet Jackson, "Girl, You Know Its True" by Milli Vanilli and "Love Shack" by the B-52's

1990

- The Food and Drug Administration approved a low-calorie fat substitute
- Gross national product fell after eight years of growth, while housing values plummeted and consumer confidence shrank
- The *Hubble* space telescope was launched into orbit
- First appearances included McDonald's in Moscow; car models Infiniti, Saturn, and Lexus; gender-specific disposable diapers; caller ID systems; and the contraceptive implant Norplant
- Census data showed that 25 percent of the population were members of a minority group, with Asians and Pacific Islanders the fastest-growing minorities
- Dieting became a $33 billion industry
- John J. Audubon's book, *Birds of America,* sold for $3.96 million at auction
- Television premieres included *The Simpsons, Law and Order, Twin*

Peaks and *Seinfeld*

- Women constituted 11 percent of U.S. military troops, up from three percent in 1973
- An EPA report claimed that 3,800 people died annually from second-hand smoke
- The timber industry of the Pacific Northwest was outraged when the northwest spotted owl was declared an endangered species
- *Dances with Wolves* was named the Academy Awards' best picture; *Pretty Woman, Total Recall, Goodfellas* and *Home Alone* were also released
- The stock market hit a high of 2,999.75, inflation was at 5.4 percent and unemployment at 6.1 percent
- Both President Bush and Premier Gorbachev called for Iraqi withdrawal following its invasion of Kuwait

1991

- Allied forces attacked Iraq with 2,232 tons of explosives the first day, the largest strike in history, at the beginning of the Gulf War
- The economy officially went into a recession for the first time since 1982
- A record 23,300 homicides were reported nationwide
- Arlette Schweitzer, 42, acted as surrogate mother for her daughter who was born without a uterus, giving birth to her own grandchildren—twins
- Single parents rose 41 percent from 1980, while the number of unmarried couples living together was up 80 percent
- One quarter of all newborns were born to single women
- Michael Jackson signed a $1.1 billion multi-year contract with Sony
- First-class postage increased from $0.25 to $0.29
- The U.S. trade deficit hit an eight-year low
- First marriage median age was 26.3 years for men and 24.1 years for women

- Cartoon character Blondie, wife of Dagwood Bumstead, announced her need for a career
- The U.S. Supreme Court ended forced busing, originally ordered to end racial segregation
- Congress approved family leave, allowing up to 12 weeks for family emergencies
- Airlines Eastern and Pan Am went into bankruptcy, with Delta taking over most Pan Am routes and becomming the leading carrier
- The Federal Reserve slashed interest rates to spur the economy
- A single sheet of the first printing of the Declaration of Independence, bought at a flea market in the backing of a $4.00 painting, was sold for $2,420,000
- School violence escalated, and 25 percent of whites and 20 percent of blacks said they feared being attacked in school
- Walter H. Annenberg bequeathed his $1 billion art collection to the Metropolitan Museum of Art
- *Scarlett*, Alexandra Ripley's sequel to *Gone with the Wind*, sold a record 250,000 copies in one day
- Simon LeVay's study showed anatomical hypothalamic differences in gay and heterosexual men, lending credibility to the biological origin of sexual orientation
- General Motors announced plans to close more than 20 plants over several years, eliminating more than 70,000 jobs
- Motorola introduced the 7.7-ounce cellular telephone

1992

- Unemployment topped 7.1 percent, the highest in five years
- U.S. bombed Iraq for its failure to comply with United Nations-sponsored inspections
- The 10 most popular television shows were *60 Minutes*; *Roseanne*; *Murphy Brown*; *Cheers*; *Home Improvement*; *Designing Women*; *Coach*; *Full House*; *Murder, She Wrote*; and *Unsolved Mysteries*

- David Letterman was paid $16 million to move to CBS, opposite late-night host Jay Leno; Johnny Carson's last night as host of *The Tonight Show* drew a record 55 million viewers
- Bestsellers included Rush Limbaugh's *The Way Things Ought to Be*, H. Norman Schwarzkopf's *It Doesn't Take a Hero,* John Grisham's *The Pelican Brief* and Anne Rice's *The Tale of the Body Thief*
- The Supreme Court ruled that cross-burning is protected under the First Amendment, and that prayer at public school graduations is unconstitutional
- Royalties for Barbara and George Bush's dog's autobiography, *Millie's Book*, earned them $890,000
- In Kenya, Meave Leakey discovered the oldest hominid fossil to date, estimated to be 25 million years old and believed to be from the period of the ape-human divergence
- Movie openings included *Unforgiven, The Crying Game, Scent of a Woman, Malcolm X, Aladdin, Sister Act, Basic Instinct, The Last of the Mohicans, A River Runs Through It* and *White Men Can't Jump*
- Rudolph Marcus won the Nobel Prize in chemistry for his theory of electron-transfer reactions
- Eric Clapton won a Grammy award for his record "Tears in Heaven" and his album, "Unplugged"
- Poverty rose to 14.2 percent, the highest level since 1983
- At the Olympic Summer Games in Barcelona, the U.S. basketball team included Larry Bird, Magic Johnson and Michael Jordan
- More than 20,000 people in California bought guns after the Los Angeles riots, which erupted when the men accused of beating Rodney King were acquitted
- In Washington, DC, more than 500,000 people marched for abortion rights
- New-age clear beverages, mega CD video games, The Mall of America and the Intel 486 chip made their first appearance

- Research indicated that the level of HDL, or good cholesterol, may be more important than the overall blood cholesterol score
- The FDA restricted the use of silicone-gel breast implants for reconstructive purposes

1993

- A bomb blast injured hundreds in the World Trade Center bombing in New York City, and Mohammed A. Salameh was arrested for the bombing when he attempted to reclaim his $400 car rental deposit
- Major League baseball owners announced new initiatives on minority hiring
- Law enforcement agents raided a religious cult in Waco, Texas, igniting a storm of protests
- U.S. pledged $1.6 billion in aid to assist in Russian reforms
- An Oregon law permitted physician-assisted suicide
- Michigan's Dr. Jack Kevorkian was jailed twice for assisting patients' suicides
- President Bill Clinton promised "universal health coverage" comparable to that of *Fortune 500* companies, designed to help the 64 million who lacked adequate coverage
- Women received combat roles in aerial and naval warfare
- Civil rights advocate Ruth Bader Ginsburg was named to the U.S. Supreme Court
- *Jurassic Park* became the highest-grossing movie of all time
- IBM announced an $8.9 billion restructuring, and eliminated 60,000 jobs
- President Clinton supported easing a ban on homosexuals in the military
- Statistics showed that one of three American workers were in their job less than a year, and almost two out of three less than five years
- The brown Brownie uniform changed after 66 years to include pastel tops, culotte jumpers, and floral print vests

- The inflation rate remained at 2.7 percent, the lowest in seven years
- The U.S. began testing of the French abortion pill RU-486
- Cosmologists discovered that stars and other observable matter occupied less than 10 percent of the universe
- Sears & Robuck ended its mail-order catalog business
- Thirty-year mortgages dropped to 6.7 percent, the lowest in 25 years
- The Ford Taurus topped the Honda Accord in total car sales
- The Pentium processor, one-pound personal digital assistant, and Mighty Max Toby Terrier all made their first appearances

1994

- The North American Free Trade Agreement (NAFTA) was established
- Olympic skater Nancy Kerrigan was clubbed on the right leg by an assailant, under orders from figure skating rival Tonya Harding's ex-husband
- The Superhighway Summit was held at UCLA, the first conference to discuss the growing information superhighway
- President Bill Clinton and Russian President Boris Yeltsin signed the Kremlin Accords, stopping preprogrammed aiming of nuclear missiles toward each country's targets, and also provided for the dismantling of the nuclear arsenal in Ukraine
- In South Carolina, Shannon Faulkner became the first female cadet to attend The Citadel, although soon dropped out
- Byron De La Beckwith was convicted of the 1963 murder of Civil Rights leader Medgar Evers
- Edvard Munch's painting *The Scream* was stolen in Oslo
- Aldrich Ames and his wife were charged with spying for the Soviet Union by the U.S. Department of Justice
- In *Campbell v. Acuff-Rose Music, Inc.*, the Supreme Court ruled that parodies of an original work are generally covered by the doctrine of fair use
- *Schindler's List* won seven Oscars including Best Picture and Best

Director at the 66th Academy Awards, hosted by Whoopi Goldberg

- The journal *Nature* reported the finding in Ethiopia of the first complete *Australopithecus afarensis* skull
- Kurt Cobain, songwriter and front man for the band Nirvana, was found dead, apparently of a single, self-inflicted gunshot wound
- The Red Cross estimated that hundreds of thousands of Tutsis had been killed in the Rwanda massacre
- Nelson Mandela was inaugurated as South Africa's first black president
- Nicole Brown Simpson and Ronald Goldman were murdered outside the Simpson home in Los Angeles, California and football great O.J. Simpson was charged in the killings
- President Clinton signed the Assault Weapons Ban, which banned the manufacture of new weapons with certain features for a period of 10 years
- The first version of Web browser Netscape Navigator was released

1995–1996

- The Supreme Court ruled that only a constitutional amendment can enforce term limits on Congress
- 25 percent of Americans continued to smoke cigarettes despite health warnings
- The Dow Jones Industrial Average peaked at 5,216 and unemployment was at 5.6 percent
- Casual Fridays were introduced at the workplace
- After 130 years, Mississippi lawmakers ratified the 13th Amendment abolishing slavery
- The FBI reported another sharp decline in crime rates
- President Bill Clinton's approval rating surpassed 50 percent for the first time
- About 55 percent of women provided half or more of household income
- The Centers for Disease Control reported a leveling-off of teen sexual activity, and that 52.8 percent used condoms

- New York became the 38th state to reinstate capital punishment
- Ford sold more trucks than cars, as demand for light trucks, minivans and sports utility vehicles, increased in urban and rural areas
- Mars released a blue M&M candy for the first time
- The 25th anniversary of Earth Day was celebrated
- Dow Corning declared bankruptcy after failure of its silicone breast device
- The U.S. banned the manufacture of freon because of its effect on the ozone layer
- Iraqi leader Saddam Hussein decreed economic austerity measures to cope with soaring inflation and widespread shortages caused by U.N. sanctions
- President Bill Clinton and Monica Lewinsky, a White House intern, engaged in sexual encounters at the White House
- The U.S. Army disclosed that it had 30,000 tons of chemical weapons stored in Utah, Alabama, Maryland, Kentucky, Indiana, Arkansas, Colorado and Oregon
- Sheik Omar Abdel-Rahman and nine followers were handed long prison sentences for plotting to blow up New York-area landmarks
- France detonated its sixth and most powerful nuclear bomb
- New protease-blocking drugs were shown to be effective in combating AIDS
- Congress voted overwhelmingly to rewrite the 61-year-old Communications Act, freeing the television, telephone and home computer industries to jump into each other's fields
- World chess champion Garry Kasparov beat IBM supercomputer "Deep Blue," winning a six-game match in Philadelphia
- The Space Telescope Science Institute announced that photographs from the *Hubble Space Telescope* confirmed the existence of a "black hole" equal to the mass of two billion suns
- Alanis Morissette's *Jagged Little Pill* won best rock album and album

of the year at the Grammy Awards
- Dr. Jack Kevorkian was acquitted of assisted suicide for helping two suffering patients kill themselves
- Liggett became the first tobacco company to acknowledge that cigarettes are addictive and cause cancer
- The first of the Nixon White House tapes concerning Watergate were released
- Nevada's governor designated a 98-mile stretch of Route 375 the Extraterrestrial Highway
- The Senate passed an immigration bill to tighten border controls, make it tougher for illegal immigrants to get U.S. jobs, and curtail legal immigrants' access to social services
- Guatemala's leftist guerrillas and the government signed an accord to end 35 years of civil war
- The federal government set aside 3.9 million acres in California, Oregon and Washington state for the endangered marbled murrelet

1997

- Despite a one-day plunge of 554 points, the stock market soared, up 20 percent for the third straight year, and job creation continued
- Princess Diana's death generated more press coverage than any event in the century as millions watched her televised funeral
- Controversy erupted over allegations that large contributors were invited by President Bill Clinton to stay overnight in the White House Lincoln Bedroom
- Oprah Winfrey launched a highly successful book club on her television program to encourage reading
- The price of personal computers (Compaq, Hewlett Packard, IBM) fell below $1,000
- Jerry Seinfeld announced the last season for his television show, *Seinfeld*, despite a $5 million-per-episode offer to continue
- Violent crime in NYC dropped by 38 percent; the 981 homicides was

the lowest since 1968

- Microsoft came under antitrust scrutiny for insisting that its Internet browser was intrinsic to its Windows 95 product
- The newest Barbie doll featured a larger waistline, smaller breasts, more modest clothing, and a friend in a wheelchair
- The leading tobacco companies made a $368 billion settlement with the states to settle smoking death claims
- Scottish researchers announced the cloning of an adult mammal, a sheep named Dolly
- Severe asthma, common in poor urban areas, was linked to cockroaches
- President Clinton gained line-item veto power for the first time
- Affirmative Action programs, designed to aid minorities, came under attack
- Digital cameras, DVD players, voice recognition software, and prosthetic knee joints all made their first appearances

1998

- The Dow Jones reached 9,374, and inflation was at 1.6 percent
- The undergraduate tuition at Harvard reached $22,802
- President Bill Clinton was impeached
- *Gotham: A History of New York to 1898* by Edwin G. Burrows won the Pulitzer Prize for U.S. History
- Welfare recipients dropped below four percent, the lowest in 25 years, and unemployment, interest rates, murders, juvenile arrests, births to unwed mothers, infant mortality, and gas prices also fell to 25 to 35 year lows
- Government-measured rates of obesity targeted 50 percent of the population
- Biotechnological stocks showed long anticipated potential, increasing 44 percent
- Major efforts were begun to avert the potential catastrophic "Y2K" blackout when computers may misread the year 2000 as 1900

- The South Carolina legislature approved a constitutional amendment to remove 103-year-old language that made marriages between blacks and whites illegal
- The IRS Reform Bill shifted the burden of proof from the taxpayer to the IRS
- 17 major newspapers called for President Bill Clinton's resignation after he admitted a sexual relationship with a White House intern
- *Titanic* was the highest grossing film in history at $850 million
- Tobacco companies made a $260 billion settlement with states for smoking-related illnesses

1999

- The U.S. claimed 274 of the world's 590 billionaires worldwide
- Of the original 30 companies in the 1896 Dow Jones Industrial Index, only General Electric survived the Great Depression, two world wars and the terms of 20 U.S. presidents
- *Worth* magazine declared Jupiter Island, Florida, the most expensive town in the country, whose median home price was $3.9 million
- The average American woman was 5'4", weighed 142 pounds and was a size 12
- The top one percent of earners in America had an average net worth of $5.5 million
- The annual reunion of Thomas Jefferson's descendents included the descendents of those who claimed their parents were Jefferson and his slave Sally Hemings
- NATO's mistaken bombing of the Chinese embassy in Belgrade caused further deterioration of U.S. and Chinese relations
- A series of fatal shootings at high schools across the country revived the gun-control debate and prompted many to call for mandatory background checks for gun purchases
- AIDS-related deaths fell nearly 50 percent
- The Modern Library's "100 Best Novels of the Century" list included

Ulysses, The Great Gatsby, A Portrait of the Artist as a Young Man, Lolita, Brave New World, The Sound and the Fury and *Catch-22*

- Viagra, for male erectile dysfunction, sold at a record rate of $10 a pill
- China announced that it had developed on its own the ability to make neutron bombs and miniature atomic weapons

2000

- Millennium celebrations were held throughout the world despite fears of major computer failures from the "Y2K" bug, fears that proved largely unwarranted
- America Online was bought out by Time Warner for $162 billion in the largest-ever corporate merger
- Charles Schulz, creator of the comic strip *Peanuts*, died at the age of 77
- President Bill Clinton proposed a $2 billion program to bring Internet access to low-income houses
- The Russian submarine K-141 Kursk sank in the Barents Sea, killing the 118 sailors on board
- The U.S. Supreme Court gave police broad authority to stop and question people who run from a police officer
- The International Whaling Commission turned down requests from Japan and Norway to allow expanded whaling
- The Millennium Summit among world leaders was held at the United Nations
- President Bill Clinton created the Giant Sequoia National Monument to protect 328,000 California acres of trees from timber harvesting
- Judge Thomas Penfield Jackson ruled that Microsoft violated the Sherman Antitrust Act by tying its Internet browser to its operating system
- George W. Bush was declared the winner of the presidential race in a highly controversial election against Al Gore
- The female-oriented television cable channel Oxygen made its debut
- Carlos Santana won eight Grammy awards, including Album of the

Year for *Supernatural*

2001

- U.S. golf courses increased from 13,353 in 1986 to 17,701
- Unmarried couples heading U.S. households increased from 3.2 million in 1990 to 5.5 million in 2000
- Typical set of childhood vaccinations cost $385, up from $10 in 1971
- Education reform was approved, requiring annual standardized tests in grades three through eight by 2005-6
- Former President Jimmy Carter was honored with the Nobel Peace Prize
- The War Against Terrorism legislation, authorizing the president to use force against those who perpetrated or assisted in the September 11 attacks, passed the House and Senate without objection
- A letter containing the dangerous infection anthrax was mailed to Senator Tom Daschle's office, after which the Senate Office Building was closed for three months
- Unemployment stood at nearly six percent, up from 3.9 percent a year earlier
- The USA PATRIOT Act expanded the powers of the police to wiretap telephones, monitor Internet and e-mail use, and search the homes of suspected terrorists
- President George W. Bush said during his 2002 State of the Union address: "States like those (Iraq, Iran and North Korea) and their terrorist allies, constitute an axis of evil, aiming to threaten the peace of the world"
- Enron, a $50 billion energy-trading company, became the largest U.S. company to file for bankruptcy
- The Dow-Jones Industrial Average reached a high of 11,337, and a low of 8,235
- The much-anticipated movie version of the book *Harry Potter and the Sorcerer's Stone* grossed $150 million in five days

- China was formally granted permanent normal trade status, reversing a 20-year policy of requiring an annual review for the country to expand its human rights activities
- U.S. forces continued to search for terrorist mastermind Osama bin Laden
- The United States withdrew from the 1972 Antiballistic Missile Treaty, thereby allowing the military to test and deploy missile-defense systems without restraints

2003
- Surveys indicated that 80 percent of Americans were unwilling to sacrifice taste for more healthy foods
- Iraq's oil ministry, which produced 3.5 million barrels of oil a day only five years ago, produced only five percent of that number
- School districts dominated by blacks and Hispanics spent $902 less per student on average than mostly white school districts
- *Harry Potter and the Order of the Phoenix* sold 5 million copies in the first week of publication
- Surveys showed that 40 percent of all U.S. e-mail was spam
- Thanks in part to file swapping, the sale of CDs was down 20 percent from the year 2000
- Surveys indicated that 83 percent of children believed they would go to college, 68 percent thought they would get married, and 12 percent thought they would join the armed forces
- Space Shuttle *Columbia* disintegrated during re-entry over Texas, killing all seven astronauts on board
- More than 10 million people in over 600 cities worldwide protested the planned invasion of Iraq by the United States
- An American businessman was admitted to the Vietnam France Hospital in Hanoi, Vietnam, with the first identified case of the SARS epidemic, and both patient and doctor died of the disease
- The journal *Nature* reported that 350,000-year-old upright-walking

human footprints had been found in Italy

- The Iraq War began with the invasion of Iraq by the U.S. and U.S. forces quickly seized control of Baghdad, ending the regime of Saddam Hussein
- Syracuse (New York) won the college basketball National Championship
- The Human Genome Project was completed, with 99 percent of the human genome sequenced to 99.99 percent accuracy
- Pen Hadow became the first person to walk alone, without outside help, from Canada to the North Pole
- Eric Rudolph, the suspect in the Centennial Olympic Park bombing in 1996, was captured in Murphy, North Carolina
- Martha Stewart and her broker were indicted for using privileged investment information and then obstructing a federal investigation, causing Stewart to resign as chairperson and chief executive officer of Martha Stewart Living
- The Spirit of Butts Farm completed the first flight across the Atlantic by a computer-controlled model aircraft; the flight set two world records for a model aircraft-for duration (38 hours, 53 minutes) and for non-stop distance (1,883 statute miles)
- The Concorde made its last scheduled commercial flight
- The U.S. Supreme Court upheld Affirmative Action in university admissions and declared sodomy laws unconstitutional
- Cherokee Nation of Oklahoma approved a new constitution re-designating the tribe "Cherokee Nation" without "of Oklahoma" and specifically disenfranchising the Cherokee Freedmen
- The Florida Marlins defeated the New York Yankees to win their second World Series title

2004

- Pakistani scientists admitted giving Libya, Iran and North Korea the technology to build nuclear weapons

- The U.S. required international travelers to be fingerprinted and photographed before entering the country
- President George W. Bush proposed a plan the would allow illegal immigrants working in the United States to apply for temporary guest worker status and increase the number of green cards granted each year
- Paul O'Neill, former treasury secretary, told TV news program *60 Minutes* that the Bush administration had been planning an attack against Iraq since the first days of Bush's presidency
- Two NASA Rovers landed on Mars and sent back spectacular images of the planet
- The Salvation Army reported that Joan Kroc, heir to the McDonald's fortune, had left the nonprofit entity $1.5 billion
- A computer worm, called MyDoom or Novarg, spread through Internet servers, infecting one in 12 e-mail messages
- Terrorists exploded at least 10 bombs on four commuter trains in Madrid, Spain, during rush hour, killing 202 people and wounding 1,400
- The California Supreme Court ordered San Francisco to stop issuing marriage licenses to same-sex couples
- NASA reported the discovery of a distant object in our solar system that closely resembled a planet
- The Bush administration admitted that it failed to give the commission investigating the September 11, 2001 terrorist attacks thousands of pages of national security papers
- President Bush said in a national broadcast that to abandon Iraq would fuel anti-American sentiment around the world
- Several hundred thousand demonstrators gathered in Washington, DC, to protest the Bush administration's policy on reproductive rights
- The popular search engine Google went public
- A federal judge in San Francisco said the Partial Birth Abortion Ban Act was unconstitutional because it lacked a medical exception to save

a woman's life, and placed an unnecessary burden on women who sought abortions

- United Nations Secretary General Kofi Annan said the war in Iraq was illegal and violated the U.N. charter
- The International Committee of the Red Cross found that military personnel used physical and psychological abuse at the Guantanamo prison in Cuba that was "tantamount to torture"

2005

- *Deep Impact* was launched from Cape Canaveral by a Delta 2 rocket
- The *Huygens* probe landed on Titan, the largest moon of Saturn
- George W. Bush was inaugurated in Washington, DC, for his second term as the forty-third president of the United States
- The Kyoto Protocol went into effect, without the support of the U.S. and Australia
- The People's Republic of China ratified an anti-secession law, aimed at preventing Taiwan from declaring independence
- Pope John Paul II died, prompting over four million mourners to travel to the Vatican
- The first thirteenth root calculation of a 200-digit number was computed mentally by Frenchman Alexis Lemaire
- Demonstrators marched through Baghdad denouncing the U.S. occupation of Iraq, two years after the fall of Saddam Hussein, and rallied in the square where his statue had been toppled in 2003
- Pope Benedict XVI succeeded Pope John Paul II, becoming the 265th pope
- The Superjumbo jet aircraft Airbus A380 made its first flight from Toulouse
- The Provisional IRA issued a statement formally ordering an end to the armed campaign it had pursued since 1969, and ordering all its units to dump their arms
- The largest UN World Summit in history was held in New York City

- Cartoons that included depictions of Muhammad printed in the Danish newspaper Jyllands-Posten triggered Islamic protests and death threats
- The second Chinese spacecraft, *Shenzhou 6,* was launched, carrying Fei Junlong and Nie Haisheng for five days in orbit
- Scientists announced that they had created mice with small amounts of human brain cells in an effort to make realistic models of neurological disorders
- Another second was added, 23:59:60, called a leap second, to end the year 2005; the last time this occurred was on June 30, 1998

2006-2007

- NASA's Stardust mission successfully returned dust from a comet
- United Airlines emerged from bankruptcy after 4 years, the longest such filing in history
- In Super Bowl XL, the Pittsburgh Steelers defeated the Seattle Seahawks 21-10
- The Blu-ray Disc format was released in the United States
- Massive antiwar demonstrations, including a march down NYC's Broadway marked the third year of war in Iraq
- Warren Buffett donated more than $30 billion to the Bill & Melinda Gates Foundation
- The Military Commissions Act of 2006 was passed, suspending habeas corpus for "enemy combatants"
- A Pew Research Center survey revealed that 81 percent of Americans believed it was "common behavior" for lobbyists to bribe members of Congress
- More than a million immigrants, primarily Hispanic, staged marches in over 100 cities, calling for immigration reform
- Liquids and gels were banned from checked and carry-on airplane baggage after London Police made 21 arrests in connection with an apparent terrorist plot to blow up planes traveling from the United

Kingdom to the United States
- The International Astronomical Union defined "planet," demoting Pluto to the status of "dwarf planet" more than 70 years after its discovery
- Two stolen Edvard Munch paintings, *The Scream* and *Madonna*, were recovered in a police raid in Oslo, Norway
- President George W. Bush used the fifth anniversary of the September 11, 2001, attacks to emphasize the link between Iraq and winning the broader war on terrorism, asserting that "if we give up the fight in the streets of Baghdad, we will face the terrorists in the streets of our own cities"
- Google bought YouTube for $1.65 billion
- *Pirates of the Caribbean: Dead Man's Chest* became the fastest film in Hollywood history to reach the billion-dollar mark worldwide in box office receipts
- Former Iraqi leader Saddam Hussein was sentenced to death by hanging after an Iraqi
- court found him guilty of crimes against humanity
- Massachusetts enacted Universal Health Coverage, requiring all residents to have either public or private insurance
- PlayStation 3 and Wii were released in North America
- •Smoking was banned in all Ohio bars, restaurants, workplaces and other public places
- The Ronettes, Patti Smith, and Van Halen were all inducted into Rock and Roll Hall of Fame
- Elton John played Madison Square Garden for the sixtieth time to celebrate his sixtieth birthday, joined by Whoopi Goldberg, Robin Williams, and former President Bill Clinton
- Live Earth, a worldwide series of concerts to initiate action against global warming, took place
- Led Zeppelin reunited for their first show in 25 years
- Celine Dion made the final performance of her five-year engagement at

Caesars Palace in Las Vegas
- The International Red Cross and Red Crescent Movement adopted the Red Crystal as a non-religious emblem for use in its overseas operations
- A 2,100-year-old melon was discovered by archaeologists in western Japan
- The final book of the Harry Potter series, *Harry Potter and the Deathly Hallows*, was released and sold over 11 million copies in the first 24 hours, becoming the fastest-selling book in history
- Track and field star Marion Jones surrendered the five Olympic medals she won in the 2000 Sydney Games after admitting to doping
- Beyoncé launched The Beyoncé Experience in Tokyo, Japan
- Russian President Vladimir Putin was named *Time* magazine's 2007 Person of the Year
- The Picasso painting *Portrait of Suzanne Bloch,* and *Candido Portinari's O Lavrador de Café* were stolen from the São Paulo Museum of Art

2008

- Americans elected Barack Obama as the first African American U.S. President
- An economic recession —known as the Great Recession—began that rivaled the Great Depression of the 1930s, caused in large part by banks pushing securities backed by high-interest loans to homebuyers
- President George W. Bush signed a $700 billion bill on October 3 to bail out banks and stem the financial crisis
- Television shows winning an Emmy award included NBC's *30 Rock, Comedy Central's The Daily Show with Jon Stewart,* and the first season of AMC's drama, *Mad Men*
- Seth MacFarlane signed a $100 million deal with the Fox television network to keep *Family Guy* and *American Dad* on the air until 2012, making MacFarlane the world's highest paid television writer

- *Good Masters! Sweet Ladies! Voices from a Medieval Village* won the 2008 Newbery Medal for children's literature
- Bernard Madoff was arrested and charged with securities fraud in a $50 billion Ponzi scheme
- California became the second state to legalize same-sex marriage after the state's own Supreme Court ruled a previous ban unconstitutional; the first state was Massachusetts, in 2004
- *Slumdog Millionaire*, a movie about a young man from the slums of Mumbai, India, won the Academy Award for best film, and a total of eight Oscars
- Australian actor and director Heath Ledger died from an accidental overdose at age 28, a few months after finishing filming for *The Dark Knight* for which he was posthumously awarded the Oscar for Best Supporting Actor
- The British alternative rock band *Coldplay* won the Grammy award for Song of the Year for "Viva la Vida," Spanish for either "long live life" or "live the life"
- Pope Benedict XVI visited the United States
- Bill Gates stepped down as chairman of Microsoft Corporation to work full-time for the nonprofit Bill & Melinda Gates Foundation
- Toshiba recalled its HD DVD video formatting, ending its format war with Sony's Blu-Ray Disc
- Gold prices on the New York Mercantile Exchange hit $1,000 an ounce
- Greg Maddux pitched his 5,000th career inning against the San Francisco Giants on September 19
- The New York Yankees played their final home game at Yankee Stadium against the Baltimore Orioles; they started the next season in a new stadium built across the street
- The Detroit Lions finished the football season 0-16, the first time in National Football League history that a team went winless in a 16-game season

2009

- Barack Obama was inaugurated as the 44th president of the United States in front of a crowd of over one million
- Michael Jackson died of a physician administered drug overdose, which brought a worldwide outpouring of grief
- US Airways Flight 1549 lost power in both engines shortly after takeoff from La Guardia, forcing the pilot to land in New York's Hudson River; all 155 passengers and crew were rescued with no casualties
- President Obama signed executive orders to close the Guantanamo Bay detention camp within one year and to prohibit torture in terrorism interrogations
- President Obama ordered the deployment of 17,000 additional US troops to Afghanistan
- When insurance giant AIG reported nearly $62 billion in losses during the fourth quarter, the government gave it $30 billion more in aid; AIG later announced $450 million in executive bonuses, despite its central role in the global financial meltdown and receiving billions in government bailouts
- NASA launched *Kepler Mission*, a space photometer which searches for planets in the MilkyWay that could be similar to Earth and habitable by humans
- President Obama overturned a Bush-era policy that limited federal funding for embryonic stem cell research
- Governor John Lynch signed a bill allowing same-sex marriage in New Hampshire, the sixth state in the union to do so
- President Obama announced vehicle emissions and mileage requirements under which vehicles would use 30 percent less fuel and emit one-third less carbon dioxide by 2016
- The Senate passed a bill to impose new regulations on the credit card industry, curbing fees and interest hikes and requiring more transparent disclosure of account terms

- Physician George Tiller, known for giving late-term abortions, was murdered during a Sunday service at his church in Wichita, Kansas
- The Great Recession officially ended
- Analog television broadcasts ended in the United States as the Federal Communications Commission required all full-power stations to send their signals digitally
- After an eight-month recount battle, former comedian Al Franken was sworn in as the junior senator of Minnesota, giving Democrats a majority of 60 seats
- Microsoft released Windows 7
- North Korean leader Kim Jong-il pardoned two American journalists, who were imprisoned for illegal entry, after former President Clinton met with Kim in North Korea
- Sonia Sotomayor became the third woman and the first Latina to serve on the U.S. Supreme Court
- The Justice Department announced the largest health care fraud settlement in history, $2.3 billion, involving Pfizer
- An 8.3-magnitude earthquake triggered a tsunami near the Samoan Islands, destroying many communities and harbors in Samoa and American Samoa, and killing at least 189
- President Obama won the Nobel Peace Prize
- President Obama signed the Matthew Shepard and James Byrd Jr. Hate Crimes Prevention Act, extending federal hate crime law to include crimes motivated by a victim's gender, sexual orientation, gender identity, or disability
- The New York Yankees defeated the Philadelphia Phillies to win their 27th World Championship

2010

- The Eureka earthquake shook the north coast of California, causing $43 million in losses and 35 injuries
- Google announced it was the target of a cyberattack from China

- A special election was held in Massachusetts in which Republican Scott Brown replaced the late US Senator Ted Kennedy
- The Air Force Academy in Colorado Springs opened a worshiping site for earth-centered religions on its campus promoting religious tolerance
- The Tea Party movement hosted its first convention in Nashville, Tennessee
- In Super Bowl XLIV the New Orleans Saints beat the Indianapolis Colts 31-17
- President Obama established the National Commission on Fiscal Responsibility and Reform
- The US Navy officially announced that it would end its ban on women in submarines
- A SeaWorld employee in Orlando, Florida, was killed by a killer whale during a live performance
- The District of Columbia's same-sex marriage law went into effect
- At the 82nd Academy Awards, *The Hurt Locker* won six Oscars including the first Best Director award for a woman, Kathryn Bigelow
- NASA announced that 2010 would likely become the warmest year on record due to global warming
- President Obama signed the Patient Protection and Affordable Care Act into law aiming to insure 95 percent of Americans
- An explosion at the Deepwater Horizon oil rig killed 11 workers and sank the rig, initiating a massive offshore oil spill in the Gulf of Mexico, considered the largest environmental disaster in US history
- The Dodd-Frank Wall Street Reform and Consumer Protection Act was signed into law by President Obama
- Former US Solicitor General Elena Kagan was sworn in as Justice of the Supreme Court
- The last US combat troops left Iraq
- President Obama confirmed that two packages sent to the U.S. from Yemen were filled with explosives

- The San Francisco Giants defeated the Texas Rangers to win their first World Series in 56 years
- The Federal Reserve announced it would buy $600 billion in bonds to encourage economic growth
- The San Francisco Board of Supervisors banned McDonald's Happy Meal toys, citing obesity concerns
- WikiLeaks founder Julian Assange began releasing confidential U.S. diplomatic documents
- General Motors introduced the first Chevrolet Volt plug-in hybrid electric vehicle
- President Obama signed the Don't Ask, Don't Tell repeal into law
- The Federal Communications Commission passed new net neutrality laws

2011

- Southern Sudan held a referendum on independence, paving the way for the creation of the new state
- An estimated two billion people watched the wedding of Prince William, Duke of Cambridge, and Catherine Middleton at Westminster Abbey in London
- Osama bin Laden, the founder and leader of the militant group Al-Qaeda, was killed during an American military operation in Pakistan
- The Green Bay Packers' 31-25 defeat of the Pittsburgh Steelers in Super Bowl XLV attracted 111 million viewers, making the Fox broadcast the most watched program in American TV history
- Sony, IMAX, and Discovery Communications launched 3net, a new 3D TV channel
- The world's first artificial organ transplant was completed, using an artificial windpipe coated with stem cells
- Space Shuttle *Atlantis* landed successfully at Kennedy Space Center, concluding NASA's space shuttle program
- NASA announced that its Mars Reconnaissance Orbiter captured

photographic evidence of possible liquid water on Mars during warm seasons

- *Pirates of the Caribbean: On Stranger Tides* grossed $1,043,871,802 to become the eighth film to have surpassed the billion dollar mark
- ABC cancelled of two of its long-running daytime dramas—*All My Children*, after 41 years, and *One Life to Live*, after 43 years
- Cellular phone company Verizon Wireless announced it would phase out its famous "Can You Hear Me Now?" campaign, which began in 2002
- The global population reached seven billion people

2012

- Utah banned discounts/specials on alcoholic drinks, essentially outlawing Happy Hour
- San Francisco raised the minimum wage to over $10 per hour, making it the highest in the country
- Photography pioneer Kodak filed for bankruptcy protection, no longer able to compete in the digital age
- Approximately 111.3 million viewers (one-third of the U.S. population) watched the Super Bowl
- The Kellogg Company purchased snack maker Pringles from Procter & Gamble for $2 .7 billion
- The 84th Academy Awards saw *The Artist* win Best Picture—the first silent film to win that award since *Wings* in 1927
- The shooting of Trayvon Martin, an unarmed, black 17-yearold, by George Zimmerman in Florida, ignited nationwide discussion of the role of race in America.
- *Encyclopædia Britannica* announced the end of its print editions, continuing online only
- The United States, Japan, and the European Union filed a case against China at the WTO regarding export restrictions on rare earth metals
- American golfer Bubba Watson won the U.S. Masters, defeating Louis

Oosthuizen of South Africa in a playoff
- The Guggenheim Partners purchased the Los Angeles Dodgers for $2.1 billion, the most ever paid for a professional sports franchise
- Licenses for autonomous cars in the U.S. were granted in Nevada to Google
- Goldman Sachs director Rajat Gupta was convicted of three counts of securities fraud and one count of conspiracy related to insider trading in 2011
- Connecticut repealed the death penalty
- Moody's downgraded the credit rating of 15 major world banks
- NBCUniversal bought full control of the U.S. news website MSNBC.com and rebranded it as NBCNews.com
- U.S. swimmer Michael Phelps won his 19th career Olympic gold metal, with a win in the 4 x 200-meter freestyle relay
- American scientists Robert Lefkowitz and Brian Kobilka won the Nobel Prize in Chemistry for their discoveries of the inner workings of G protein-coupled receptors
- Felix Baumgartner broke the world human ascent by balloon record, AIG announced it would pay $450 million in bonuses to top executives, despite its central role in the global financial meltdown and receiving a $173 billion government bailout; a massive public outcry followed before space diving out of the Red Bull Stratos helium-filled balloon over Roswell, New Mexico
- The Walt Disney Company purchased Lucasfilm Ltd. from George Lucas for $4.05 billion, a deal that included rights to the Star Wars and Indiana Jones franchises
- Washington became the first state to legalize marijuana
- Hostess, which includes such brands as Twinkies, announced it would file for bankruptcy, liquidate its assets, and lay off 18,500 workers

2014
- The Ebola virus epidemic in West Africa infected over 21,000 people

and killed at least 8,000

- Malaysia Airlines Flight 370 disappeared over the Gulf of Thailand with 239 people on board, presumably crashing into the Indian Ocean
- Malala Yousafzai, a 17-year-old Muslim from Pakistan, became the youngest person to win the Nobel Peace Prize, sharing the prize with Kailash Satyarthi, a Hindu from India, for their struggle against the repression of girls and women
- The Disney movie soundtrack *Frozen* was the most popular U.S. album for 13 weeks
- Colorado allowed the sale of recreational marijuana from legally licensed businesses.
- *12 Years a Slave* won the Oscar for Best Picture, grossing just under $188 million
- *Transformers: Age of Extinction* was the top grossing movie, drawing more than $1 billion in box office receipts
- The XXII Olympic Winter Games were held in Sochi, Russia
- Belgium became the first country in the world to make euthanasia legal for terminally ill patients of any age
- Russia annexed the Ukrainian territory of Crimea and began a covert military offensive against the Ukraine
- American science educator "Bill Nye, the Science Guy" defended evolution in the classroom in a debate with creationist Ken Ham
- "Happy" by Pharrell Williams was the No. 1 song on the pop charts for 10 consecutive weeks
- President Obama announced the resumption of normal relations between the United States and Cuba
- "Black Jeopardy!" became one of *Saturday Night Live's* most popular skits with cast member Kenan Thompson as game show host "Alex Treblack"
- Sony Pictures canceled its planned release of *The Interview* after threats from North Korea against the Seth Rogen-Evan Goldberg

comedy that depicts the assassination of North Korea's dictator; criticism against Sony led the studio to release the film on video on demand

2015

- The Federal Communications Commission published its rule on net neutrality regulations
- NASA's *Messenger* spacecraft concluded its four-year orbital mission over Mercury
- Maryland Governor Larry Hogan declared a state of emergency in Baltimore when protests against the death of Freddie Gray in police custody turned violent
- Dzhokhar Tsarnaev was sentenced to death for the 2013 Boston Marathon bombing
- Cuba was officially removed from the US State Sponsors of Terrorism list
- Former Olympian Bruce Jenner became the first transgender person to appear on the cover of *Vanity Fair* magazine
- Rachel Dolezal resigned as president of the NAACP Spokane, Washington amid allegations that she claimed to be black but was actually white
- In a 6-3 decision, the Supreme Court upheld subsidies for the Patient Protection and Affordable Care Act (also known as Obamacare) nationwide
- The Supreme Court ruled that the Constitution guarantees a right to same-sex marriage
- BP (British Petroleum) agreed to pay the Department of Justice an $18.7 billion settlement in reparation for the 2010 oil spill that dumped over 125 million gallons of oil into the Gulf of Mexico
- The South Carolina State House removed the Confederate battle flag from its grounds after weeks of protest, and placed it in a museum
- *Birdman* won four Oscars including Best Picture and Best Director

- Iran and a coalition including the U.S. came to an agreement in which UN sanctions against Iran would be lifted in exchange for reduction of Iran's stockpile of enriched uranium
- President Obama announced the Clean Power Plan which included the first-ever Environmental Protection Agency standards on carbon pollution from U.S. power plants
- Kim Davis, a clerk for Rowan County, Kentucky, was found in contempt of court and jailed for five days for refusing to issue marriage licenses to same-sex couples
- NASA announced strong evidence that liquid water flows on Mars during the summer months, increasing the chance of sustainable life on the planet
- President Obama ordered up to 50 U.S. special operations ground troops to be deployed in Syria to fight Islamic State militants
- Defense Secretary Ashton Carter announced that all combat roles in the military must be opened to women
- An arrest warrant was issued for comedian Bill Cosby for the alleged drugging and sexual assault of an employee at Temple University in 2004, following dozens of similar allegations

2017

- Donald J. Trump became the 45th president of the United States
- The Women's March in Washington DC comprised nearly three million, in response to the inauguration of Donald Trump, making it the biggest protest in U.S. history
- President Trump signed an executive order withdrawing the US from the controversial trade pact, the Trans-Pacific Partnership (TPP)
- The Trump administration froze all new research grants and contracts for the Environmental Protection Agency and temporarily barred its employees from posting press releases or updates to the agency's social media accounts
- The Dow Jones Industrial Average reached an all-time high of 20,000

points
- President Trump signed an executive order banning the entry of refugees of the Syrian civil war into the United States indefinitely, and all nationals of Iran, Iraq, Syria, Libya, Somalia, Sudan, and Yemen to the US for 90 days
- Neil Gorsuch filled the vacant seat on the Supreme Court left by the sudden death of Antonin Scalia
- President Trump signed an executive order to review and eventually scale back the Dodd-Frank Wall Street Reform and Consumer Protection Act put in place after the Great Recession
- In Super Bowl LI, the New England Patriots defeated the Atlanta Falcons 34-28
- Police forcibly evicted all remaining Dakota Access Pipeline protesters, arresting 33
- *Moonlight* won Best Picture at the 89th Academy Awards
- Rock and roll pioneer Chuck Berry died at the age of 90
- President Trump signed the Energy Independence Executive Order, intended to boost coal and other fossil fuel production
- The U.S. Justice Department named former FBI chief Robert Mueller as special counsel to investigate alleged Russian interference in the 2016 U.S. election and possible collusion between President Trump's campaign and Moscow
- The first gene editing of human embryos in the U.S. took place using CRISPR
- A third attempt to repeal Obamacare failed after it was voted down by 51 votes to 49
- Violent clashes broke out at a Unite the Right rally, where 32-year-old Heather Heyer was killed and many others injured when a neo-Nazi intentionally ploughed his car into a group of people
- The first total solar eclipse of the 21st century took place in the U.S.
- Hurricane Harvey, a category 4 tropical cyclone, made landfall in Texas

- A directive was signed by President Trump banning transgender military recruits
- North Korea fired a ballistic missile over northern Japan
- The Trump administration announced that the Deferred Action for Childhood Arrivals (DACA) immigration policy, set by the Obama administration, would end
- Millions of homes were left without power as the center of Hurricane Irma hit mainland Florida
- Hurricane Maria struck the U.S. territory of Puerto Rico, leaving the island devastated

Bibliography

Abelson, Harold, et al. "Keys Under Doormats: Mandating Insecurity by Requiring Government Access to All Data and Communications." *MIT.* Computer Science and Artificial Intelligence Laboratory Technical Report. July 6, 2015. Web. 29 Oct. 2017.

Ackerman, Spencer. "Fears NSA will seek to undermine surveillance reform." *The Guardian.* Guardian News and Media. June 1, 2015. Web. 30 Oct. 2017.

Ackerman, Spencer, Thielman, Sam, and Danny Yadron. "Apple case: judge rejects FBI request for access to drug dealer's iPhone." *The Guardian.* Guardian News and Media. Feb. 29, 2016. Web. 4 Nov. 2017.

Ball, James, Borger, Julian, and Glenn Greenwald. "Revealed: how US and UK spy agencies defeat internet privacy and security." *The Guardian.* Guardian News and Media. Sept. 6, 2013. Web. 29 Oct. 2017.

Ball, James. "NSA monitored calls of 35 world leaders after US official handed over contacts." *The Guardian.* Guardian News and Media. Oct. 25, 2015. Web. 27 Oct. 2017.

Barr, Bob. "The Opposition's closing statement." *The Economist.* Feb. 13, 2008. Web. 26 Oct. 2017.

Barrett, Brian. "The Encryption Debate Should End Right Now." *Wired.* Conde Nast. June 30, 2017. Web. 29 Oct. 2017.

Belknap, Michal R. *The Supreme Court under Earl Warren, 1953–1969.* Columbia, SC: U of South Carolina P, 2005.

Berger, James. "This is the media's real bias—pro-business, pro-corporate, pro-CEO." *Salon.* Salon Media Inc. Oct. 30, 2015. Web. 3 Nov. 2017.

Best, Samuel J., and Monika L. McDermott. "Measuring Opinions vs. Non-Opinions—The Case of the USA PATRIOT Act." *The Forum*. Vol. 5 (2007), No. 2, Article 7. Web. 26 Oct. 2017.

Bever, Lindsey. "Top 10 commentaries on the NSA leaks and whistleblower Edward Snowden." *The Guardian*. Guardian News and Media. June 13, 2013. Web. 3 Nov. 2017.

"Beyond Distrust: How Americans View Their Government." *Pew Research*. Pew Research Center. Nov. 23, 2015. Web. 24 Oct. 2017.

Bloustein, Edward J. "Privacy as an Aspect of Human Dignity: An Answer to Dean Prosser." *New York University Law Review*. 1964. Web. 4 Nov. 2017.

Bloustein, Edward J. "Privacy as an Aspect of Human Dignity: An Answer to Dean Prosser." *NYUL Review*. New York University Law Review. 1964. Web. 31 Oct. 2017.

Bradner, Eric. "Conway: Trump White House offered 'alternative facts' on crowd size." *CNN Politics*. CNN. Jan. 23, 2017. Web. 26 Oct. 2017.

"*Brandenburg v. Ohio*." *Cornell Law School*. Supreme Court. June 9, 1969. Web. 31 Oct. 2017.

Brandom, Russell. "Someone (probably the NSA) has been hiding viruses in hard drive firmware." *The Verge*. Vox Media. Feb. 16, 2015. Web. 3 Nov. 2017.

Brinkley, Douglas, and Luke A. Nichter. "Great mystery of the 1970s: Nixon, Watergate and the Huston Plan." *CNN*. CNN. June 17, 2015. Web. 25 Oct. 2017.

"Bush and Public Opinion." *Pew Research*. Pew Research Center. Dec. 18, 2008. Web. 7 Nov. 2017.

"Bush defends NSA spying program." *CNN*. CNN, Inc. Jan. 1, 2006. Web. 27 Oct. 2017.

Calamur, Krishnadev. "Public Opinion Supports Apple Over the FBI— or Does it?" *The Atlantic*. Atlantic Monthly Group. Feb. 24, 2016.

Web. 4 Nov. 2017.

"Civil Liberties." *Gallup*. Gallup, Inc. 2016. Web. 26 Oct. 2017.

Cohen, Adam. "Edward Snowden: A Modern-Day Daniel Ellsberg, Except for One Key Difference." *Time*. Time Inc. June 10, 2013. Web. 3 Nov. 2017.

Communications: Telephone and Telegraph Systems (Series R 1-92). *Census*. United States Census Bureau. Pdf. 26 Oct. 2017.

"'Communists in Government Service,' McCarthy Says." *United States Senate*. Senate Information Office. 2017. Web. 24 Oct. 2017.

Cooper, Michael, and Sam Roberts. "After 40 Years, the Complete Pentagon Papers." *New York Times*. New York Times Co. June 7, 2011. Web. 25 Oct. 2017.

"A Declaration of Conscience." *United States Senate*. Senate Information Office. 2017. Web. 24 Oct. 2017.

DeSilver, Drew. "Most young Americans say Snowden has served the public interest." *Pew Research Center*. Jan. 22, 2014. Web. 27 Oct. 2017.

"Electronic Communications Privacy Act of 1986 (ECPA)." *Justice Information Sharing*. U.S. Department of Justice, Office of Justice Programs. July 20, 2013. Web. 26 Oct. 2017.

Emmons, Alex. "Obama Opens NSA's Vast Trove of Warrantless Data to Entire Intelligence Community, Just in Time for Trump." *The Intercept*. First Look Media. Jan. 13, 2017. Web. 1 Nov. 2017.

Fahrenthold, David A. "With NSA revelations, Sen. Ron Wyden's vague privacy warnings finally become clear." *Washington Post*. Washington Post Company. July 28, 2013. Web. 29 Oct. 2017.

Flock, Elizabeth. "George Orwell's '1984' is a best-seller again. Here's why it resonates now." *PBS News Hour*. News Hour Productions LLC. Jan. 25, 2017. Web. 26 Oct. 2017.

"Foreign Intelligence Surveillance Act of 1978." *U.S. Senate*. Subcommittee on Intelligence and the Rights of Americans. 1978.

Web. 31 Oct. 2017.

Freeland, Amy. "Data Privacy Protection Discrepancies Could Hamper U.S. Cloud Provider Growth in Europe." *NTTCOM*. NTT Communications. Jan. 30, 2012. Web. 27 Oct. 2017.

Friedersdorf, Conor. "Choose One: Secrecy and Democracy Are Incompatible." *The Atlantic*. Atlantic Monthly Group. June 12, 2013. Web. 3 Nov. 2017.

Gabbatt, Adam. "US senators press officials on NSA surveillance programs—live." *The Guardian*. Guardian News and Media. July 31, 2013. Web. 27 Oct. 2017.

Gao, George. "What Americans think about NSA surveillance, national security and privacy." *Pew Research*. Pew Research Center. Factank. May 29, 2015. Web. 29 Oct. 2017.

Gavison, Ruth. "Privacy and the Limits of Law." *Yale Law Journal*. Vol. 89, No. 3. (Jan. 1980). 421–71.

Goitein, Elizabeth, and Faiza Patel. "What Went Wrong with the FISA Court." *Brennan Center*. Brennan Center for Justice. New York University School of Law. 2015. Web. 31 Oct. 2017.

Gore, Al. "Freedom and Security." *Alternet*. Nov. 9, 2003. Web. 26 Oct. 2017.

Gorman, Siobhan. "Satellite-Surveillance Program to Begin Despite Privacy Concerns." *Wall Street Journal*. Oct. 1, 2008. Web. 27 Oct. 2017.

Gray, David. *The Fourth Amendment in an Age of Surveillance*. New York: Cambridge UP, 2017.

Greenwald, Glenn. "NSA collecting phone records of millions of Verizon customers daily." *The Guardian*. Guardian News and Media. June 6, 2013. Web. 27 Oct. 2017.

Greenwald, Glenn. "On PATRIOT Act Renewal and USA Freedom Act: Glenn Greenwald Talks With ACLU's Jameel Jaffer. *The Intercept*. First Look Media. May 27, 2015. Web. 29 Oct. 2017.

"*Griswold v. Connecticut* (1965)." *PBS*. Landmark Cases. 2007. Web. 24 Oct. 2017.

Hardwick, Daniel W. "Defining Privacy." *Notre Dame Journal of Law, Ethics & Public Policy*. Vol. 14, Iss 2. Jan. 1, 2012.

Harris, Shane. "Giving in to the Surveillance State." *New York Times*. New York Times, Co. Aug. 22, 2012. Web. 1 Nov. 2017.

Helft, Miguel, and Claire Cain Miller. "1986 Privacy Law Is Outrun by the Web." *New York Times*. New York Times Co. Jan. 9, 2011. Web. 26 Oct. 2017.

Herman, Arthur. *Joseph McCarthy: Reexamining the Life and Legacy of America's Most Hated Senator.* New York: The Free Press, 2000.

Hersh, Seymour M. "Huge C.I.A. Operation Reported in U.S. Against Antiwar Forces, Other Dissidents in Nixon Years." *New York Times*. New York Times Company. Dec. 22, 1974. Web. 25 Oct. 2017.

"History of Encryption." *SANS Institute*. Information Security Reading Room. 2001. Pdf. 28 Oct. 2017.

Howell, Bill. *Alaska Beer: Liquid Gold in the Land of the Midnight Sun*. Charleston, SC: American Palate, 2015.

"How the USA PATRIOT Act Redefines 'Domestic Terrorism.'" *ACLU*. American Civil Liberties Union. Dec. 6, 2002. Web. 26 Oct. 2017.

Hsu, Spencer S. "Administration Set to Use New Spy Program in U.S." *Washington Post*. The Washington Post Company. Apr. 12, 2008. Web. 27 Oct. 2017.

Iannacci, Nicandro. "*Katz v. United States*: The Fourth Amendment adapts to new technology." *Constitution Center*. Constitution Daily. National Constitution Center. Dec. 18, 2015. Web. 25 Oct. 2017.

Inness, Julie C. *Privacy, Intimacy, and Isolation*. New York: Oxford UP, 1996. Web. 4 Nov. 2017.

"Inside the NSA's War on Internet Security." *Der Spiegel*. Spiegel Online. Dec. 28, 2014. Web. 4 Nov. 2017.

"In Speech, Wyden Says Official Interpretations of PATRIOT Act Must be Made Public." *Ron Wyden*. Ron Wyden Senator for Oregon. May 26, 2011. Web. 29 Oct. 2017.

"J.C.R. Licklider." *Internet Hall of Fame*. Internet Society. 2016. Web. 27 Oct. 2017.

"Joseph R. McCarthy (1908–1957)." *George Washington University*. The Eleanor Roosevelt Papers. 2006. Web. 31 Oct. 2017.

Kahn, Jonathan. "Privacy as a Legal Principle of Identity Maintenance." *Seton Hall Law Review*. Vol. 33. 2003. Web 4 Nov. 2017.

Kessler, Matt. "The Logo That Took Down a DARPA Surveillance Project." *Atlantic*. Atlantic Monthly Group. Dec. 22, 2015. Web. 1 Nov. 2017.

Kingsbury, Alex. "Declassified Documents Reveal KGB Spies in the U.S." *US News*. U.S. News and World Report. July 17, 2009. Web. 5 Nov. 2017.

Kohut, Andrew. "How the Watergate crisis eroded public support for Richard Nixon." *Pew Research*. Pew Research Center. Aug. 8, 2014. Web. 1 Nov. 2017.

Larson, Jeff. "Revealed: The NSA's Secret Campaign to Crack, Undermine Internet Security." *ProPublica*. ProPublica, Inc. Sept. 5, 2013. Web. 29 Oct. 2017.

Lazarus, David. "Europe and U.S. have different approaches to protecting privacy of personal data." *Los Angeles Times*. Dec. 22, 2015. Web. 2 Nov. 2017.

Lee, Micah. "No Really, the NSA Can't Brute Force Your Crypto." *Micahflee.com*. Micah Lee's Blog.

Lewis, Paul, and Dan Roberts. "NSA reform bill to trim back US surveillance unveiled in Congress." *The Guardian*. Guardian News and Media. Sept. 25, 2013. Web. 30 Oct. 2017.

Liptak, Kevin. "Senators should have known about snooping, says McCain." *CNN*. CNN Politics. June 9, 2013. Web. 2 Nov. 2017.

Livingstone, Neil C. "The Proposition's closing statement." *The Economist*. The Economist Newspaper Limited. Feb. 13, 2008. Web. 28 Oct. 2017.

Madden, Mary, and Lee Rainie. "Americans' Attitudes About Privacy, Security and Surveillance." *Pew Research*. Pew Research Center. Internet and Technology. May 20, 2015. Web. 3 Nov. 2017.

Mahtesian, Charles. "Privacy in Retreat, A Timeline." *NPR*. National Public Radio. Law. June 11, 2013. Web. 1 Nov. 2017.

"Margaret Chase Smith—Declaration of Conscience." *United States Senate*. June 1, 1950. Web. 1 Nov. 2017.

Matishak, Martin. "Trump's rhetoric hampers his aides' surveillance push." *Politico*. Politico LLC. Oct. 8, 2017. Web. 4 Nov. 2017.

McCullagh, Declan. "Former FBI chief takes on encryption." *CNET*. CBS Interactive. Oct. 15, 2002. Web. 28 Oct. 2017.

Mears, Bill, and Andrea Koppel. "NSA eavesdropping program ruled unconstitutional." *CNN*. CNN, Inc. Aug. 17, 2006. Web. 27 Oct. 2017.

Menn, Joseph. "Distrustful U.S. allies force spy agency to back down in encryption fight." *Reuters*. Thomson Reuters. Sept. 21, 2017. Web. 3 Nov. 2017.

Meserve, Jeanne, and Phil Hirschkorn. "ACLU Sues U.S. over 'No-Fly' List." *CNN*. CNN. Apr. 6, 2004. Web. 26 Oct. 2017.

"A Message to Our Customers." *Apple*. Apple, Inc. Feb. 16, 2016. Web. 31 Oct. 2017.

Metcalfe, Philip. *Whispering Wires: The Tragic Tale of an American Bootlegger*. Portland, OR: Inkwater Press, 2007.

Meyer, David. "Google should have been fined $1B over privacy policy, says EU justice chief." *Gigaom*. Knowingly, Inc. Jan. 21, 2014. Web. 2 Nov. 2017.

———. "Here Come the World's Toughest Privacy Laws." *Fortune*. Fortune Inc. Apr. 14, 2016. Web. 2 Nov. 2017.

Meyer, Josh. "Homeland Security said to kill spy satellite plan." *Los Angeles Times*. Los Angeles Times. June 23, 2009. Web. 28 Oct. 2017.

Mohamed, Arif. "A history of cloud computing." *Computer Weekly*. TechTarget. March 2009. Web. 27 Oct. 2017.

Moore, Adam D. "Defining Privacy." *Journal of Social Philosophy*. Vol. 39, No. 3. 2008. Web. 4 Nov. 2017.

Moore, David W. "Public Little Concerned About PATRIOT Act." *Gallup*. Gallup News. Sept. 9, 2003. Web. 1 Nov. 2017.

Musil, Steven. "Apple has support of independent voters in FBI iPhone battle." *CNET*. Mar. 8, 2016. Web. 4 Nov. 2017.

Nakashima, Ellen, and Karoun Demirjian. "Divided Senate intelligence panel advances spy-bill renewal without major changes." *Washington Post*. Washington Post Company. Oct. 25, 2017. Web. 1 Nov. 2017.

Nardone v. United States (1937). *Findlaw*. Thomson Reuters. 2017. Web. 27 Oct. 2017.

National Research Council. *Protecting Individual Privacy in the Struggle Against Terrorists*. Washington D.C.: The National Academies Press, 2008.

Newport, Frank. "Gallup Review: U.S. Public Opinion on Terrorism." *Gallup*. Gallup LLC. Nov. 17, 2004. Web. 26 Oct. 2017.

"*New York Times v. United States* (1971)." *Bill of Rights Institute*. Bill of Rights Institute. 2017. Web. 25 Oct. 2017.

"The 9/11 Commission Report." *9/11 Commission*. National Commission on Terrorist Attacks. 2004. Web. 2 Nov. 2017.

"NSA Inspector Generals Letter to Senator Charles Grassley." *NSA*. National Security Administration. Sept. 11, 2013. Pdf. 31 Oct. 2017.

"NSA slides explain the PRISM data-collection program." *Washington Post*. Washington Post Company, LLC. June 6, 2013. Web. 27 Oct. 2017.

"NSA Spying: How it Works." *EFF*. Electronic Frontier Foundation. 2013. Web. 26 Oct. 2017.

Olmstead, Kenneth, and Aaron Smith. "Americans and Cybersecurity." *Pew Research*. Pew Research Center: Internet and Technology. Jan. 26, 2017. Web. 31 Oct. 2017.

Olmstead, Kenneth. "Most Americans think the government could be monitoring their phone calls and emails." *Pew Research*. Pew Research Center. Sept. 27, 2017. Web. 5 Nov. 2017.

"*Olmstead v. United States* 277 U.S. 438 (1928)." *Justia*. Justia. 2017. Web. 31 Oct. 2017.

"The Passing of a Pioneer." *Purdue University*. Center for Education and Research in Information Assurance and Security. Nov. 26, 2013. Web. 25 Oct. 2017.

Perlroth, Nicole, Larson, Jeff, and Scott Shane. "N.S.A. Able to Foil Basic Safeguards of Privacy on Web." *New York Times*. New York Times Company. Sept. 5, 2013. Web. 29 Oct. 2017.

"President's Radio Address." *The White House*. Dec. 17, 2005. Web. 2 Nov. 2017.

"Privacy Act of 1974." *Department of Justice*. U.S. Department of Justice Office of Privacy and Civil Liberties. 2017. Web. 25 Oct. 2017.

"Prof. Ruth Gavison." *HUJI*. Hebrew University of Jerusalem. The Faculty of Law. 2017. Web. 31 Oct. 2017.

Prosser, William L. "Privacy." *California Law Review*. Vol. 48, Iss 3, Article 1. August 1960. Web. 6 Nov. 2017.

"Public Approval of Major Court Decisions." *New York Times*. New York Times Co. 2012. Web. 31 Oct. 2017.

"Public Attitudes about Birth Control." *Roper Center*. Roper Center for Public Opinion Research. Cornell University. 2017. Web. 10 Nov. 2017.

"Public Law 96-100-Nov. 2., 1979." *U.S. Senate*. United States Senate

Intelligence Committee. 1979. Pdf. 26 Oct. 2017.

"Public Remains Divided Over the PATRIOT Act." *Pew Research*. Pew Research Center. Feb. 15, 2011. Web. 26 Oct. 2017.

Rayner, Gordon, Samuel, Henry, and Martin Evans. "Charlie Hebdo attack: France's worst terrorist attack in a generation leaves 12 d-ead." *The Telegraph*. Telegraph UK. Jan. 7, 2015. Web. 30 Oct. 2017.

"A Review of the FBI's Use of Section 215 Orders: Assessment of Progress in Implementing Recommendations and Examination of Use in 2007 through 2009." *Office of the Inspector General*. Department of Justice. May 2015. Pdf. 30 Oct. 2017.

Richards, Neil, and Woodrow Hartzog. "*Apple v. the FBI*: why the 1789 All Writs Act is the wrong tool." *The Guardian*. Guardian News and Media. Feb. 24, 2016. Web. 30 Oct. 2017.

Risen, James, and Lichtblau, Eric. "Bush Lets U.S. Spy on Callers Without Courts." *New York Times*. Dec. 16, 2005. Web. 26 Oct. 2017.

Roberts, Dan. "PATRIOT Act author prepares bill to put NSA bulk collection 'out of business.'" *The Guardian*. Guardian News and Media. Oct. 10, 2013. Web. 30 Oct. 2017.

Robinson, John P. "Public Opinion During the Watergate Crisis." *Communications Research*. Vol. 1, No. 4. Oct. 1974. Web. 9 Nov. 2017.

Saad, Lydia. "Americans Generally Comfortable with PATRIOT Act." *Gallup*. Gallup News. Mar. 2, 2004. Web. 1 Nov. 2017.

Sanchez, Julian. What the Ashcroft "Hospital Showdown on NSA spying was all about." *Ars Technica*. Conde Nast. July 29, 2013. Web. 26 Oct. 2017.

Sarno, David. "Consumer Reports, Times polls find broad data privacy concerns." *LATimes. Los Angeles Times*. Apr. 3, 2012. Web. 27 Oct. 2017.

Savage, Charlie. "Classification Guide for FISA, the Protect America

Act and the FISA Amendments Act." *New York Times*. New York Times, Co. Mar. 11, 2014. Web. 25 Oct. 2017.

———. "Declassified Report Shows Doubts About Value of N.S.A.'s Warrantless Spying." *New York Times*. New York Times Company. Apr. 24, 2015. Web. 30 Oct. 2017.

Schwarz, Benjamin. "America's Think Tank." *CJR*. Columbia Journalism Review. June 2008. Web. 25 Oct. 2017.

Schwarz, Hunter. "Sales are spiking for '1984,' but it has a long history in politics." *CNN*. CNN. Jan. 26, 2017. Web. 26 Oct. 2017.

"Senator J. William Fulbright, remarks in the Senate." *Congressional Record*. U.S. Congress. Feb. 2, 1954. Web. 31 Oct. 2017.

Shapiro, Fred, and Pearse, Michelle. "The Most-Cited Law Review Articles of All Time." *Michigan Law Review*. Vol. 110, Iss 8. 2012.

Sheehan, Neil. "Vietnam Archive: Pentagon Study Traces 3 Decades of Growing U.S. Involvement." *New York Times*. New York Times Co. June 13, 1971. Web. 25 Oct. 2017.

Singer, Natasha. "Why a Push for Online Privacy Is Bogged Down in Washington." *New York Times*. New York Times, Co. Feb. 28, 2016. Web. 27 Oct. 2017.

Smith, Tom W. "The Polls: American Attitudes Toward the Soviet Union and Communism." *Public Opinion Quarterly*. Vol. 47. No. 2. 1983. Web. 6 Nov. 2017.

Solove, Daniel. "Conceptualizing Privacy." *California Law Review*. Vol. 90, Iss 4. July 2002.

Solove, Daniel J. "Conceptualizing Privacy." *California Law Review*. Vol. 90, Iss 4, Article 2. July 2002. Web. 4 Nov. 2017.

Solove, Daniel J., Rotenberg, Marc, and Paul M. Schwartz. *Privacy, Information, and Technology*. New York: Aspen Publishers, 2006.

Sorkin, Amy Davidson. "The Dangerous All Writs Act Precedent in the Apple Encryption Case." *The New Yorker*. Conde Nast. Feb. 19, 2016. Web. 31 Oct. 2017.

"SPJ Code of Ethics." *SPJ*. Society of Professional Journalists. Sept. 6, 2014. Web. 26 Oct. 2017.

"State Department Dispels Cloud Myths with Facts about US Privacy Protections." *BSA*. Software Alliance. Dec. 4, 2012. Web. 27 Oct. 2017.

Stephens, Otis H. and Richard A. Glen. *Unreasonable Searches and Seizures: Rights and Liberties Under the Law*. Santa Barbara: ABC-CLIO, 2006.

Stolberg, Sheryl Gay. "Once-Lone Foe of PATRIOT Act Has Company." *New York Times*. New York Times Co. Dec. 19, 2005. Web. 1 Nov. 2017.

Tien, Lee. "Update: Polls Continue to Show Majority of Americans Against NSA Spying." *EFF*. Electronic Frontier Foundation. Jan. 22, 2014. Web. 29 Oct. 2017.

Traynor, Ian, and Paul Lewis. "Merkel compared NSA to Stasi in heated encounter with Obama." *The Guardian*. Guardian News and Media. Dec. 17, 2013. Web. 2 Nov. 2017.

"Turning Spy Satellites on the Homeland: The Privacy and Civil Liberties Implications of the National Applications Office." *FAS*. Federation of American Scientists. Sept. 6, 2007. Web. 27 Oct. 2017.

Turn, R., and W. H. Ware. "Privacy and Security in Computer Systems." RAND. RAND Corporation. Jan. 1975. Pdf. 25 Oct. 2017.

"Unclassified Report on the President's Surveillance Program." Offices of Inspectors General. July 10, 2009. Web. 26 Oct. 2017.

Victor, Daniel. "Clinton and Trump Revealed: Our Best Investigative Reporting on the 2016 Campaign." *New York Times*. New York Times Co. Nov. 4, 2016. Web. 26 Oct. 2017.

Waddell, Kaveh. "The Long and Winding History of Encryption." *The Atlantic*. Atlantic Monthly Group. Jan. 13, 2016. Web. 28 Oct. 2017.

Wall, Wendy. "Anti-Communism in the 1950s." *Gilder Lehrman*. The Gilder Lehrman Institute of American History. 2007. Web. 24 Oct.

2017.

Ware, Willis H. "Security and Privacy in Computer Systems." *RAND*. RAND Corporation. Apr. 1967. Pdf. 31 Oct. 2017.

Warren, Samuel, and Louis Brandeis. "The Right to Privacy." *Harvard Law Review*. Vol. IV, No. 5. Dec. 15, 1890. Web. 31 Oct. 2017.

Warrick, Joby. "Domestic Use of Spy Satellites to Widen." *Washington Post*. The Washington Post Company. Aug. 16, 2007. Web. 27 Oct. 2017.

"The Watergate Story." *Washington Post*. Washington Post LLC. 2017. Web. 25 Oct. 2017.

"What is 'Islamic State'?" *BBC News*. BBC. Dec. 2, 2015. Web. 30 Oct. 2017.

Whittaker, Zack. "Microsoft admits PATRIOT Act can access EU–based cloud data." *ZDNet*. CBS Interactive. June 28, 2011. Web. 27 Oct. 2017.

"Why Islam prohibits images of Muhammad." *The Economist*. The Economist Newspaper Limited. Jan. 19, 2015. Web. 31 Oct. 2017.

Wittes, Benjamin. "William Galston on the NSA Controversies." *Lawfare*. The Lawfare Institute. June 12, 2013. Web. 3 Nov. 2017.

Zegart, Amy. "The Security Debate We Need to Have." *Lawfare*. Lawfare Institute. Feb. 23, 2016. Web. 3 Nov. 2017.

Zetter, Kim. "Magistrate Orders Apple to Help FBI Hack San Bernardino Shooter's Phone." *Wired*. Conde Nast. Feb. 16, 2016. Web. 31 Oct. 2017.

———. "PATRIOT Act Gets a Hearing." *Wired*. Conde Nast. Apr. 6, 2005. Web. 26 Oct. 2017.

Index

Z